Public Relations

Principles and Practices

IQBAL S. SACHDEVA

OXFORD

UNIVERSITY PRESS

OXFORD
UNIVERSITY PRESS

YMCA Library Building, Jai Singh Road, New Delhi 110001

Oxford University Press is a department of the University of Oxford.
It furthers the University's objective of excellence in research, scholarship,
and education by publishing worldwide in

Oxford New York
Auckland Cape Town Dar es Salaam Hong Kong Karachi
Kuala Lumpur Madrid Melbourne Mexico City Nairobi
New Delhi Shanghai Taipei Toronto

With offices in
Argentina Austria Brazil Chile Czech Republic France Greece
Guatemala Hungary Italy Japan Poland Portugal Singapore
South Korea Switzerland Thailand Turkey Ukraine Vietnam

Oxford is a registered trade mark of Oxford University Press
in the UK and in certain other countries.

Published in India
by Oxford University Press

ISBN-13: 978-0-19-569918-0
ISBN-10: 0-19-569918-1

Typeset in Book Antiqua
by Spectrum Media
Printed in India by Ram Book Binding House, New Delhi 110020
and published by Oxford University Press
YMCA Library Building, Jai Singh Road, New Delhi 110001

Dedicated to
Tavleen
Hemal
Gobind Vir

Preface

Public relations or PR is the systematic effort to create and maintain goodwill of an organization's various publics (customers, investors, dealers, vendors, employees, media, etc.), usually through publicity and other non-paid forms of communication. These efforts may also include support of arts, charitable causes, education, sporting events, and so on.

Never before in the corporate world has the term PR acquired so much importance. Rightly so, as the profession addresses some of the serious and vital aspects of a business organization. The roles and goals of PR focus on generating a positive relationship with the publics on whose response depends the success of an organization. PR thus makes conscious, careful, and creative efforts to establish relationship with the publics, based on continual flow of communications and their responses, so that the management can make viable adjustments in their policies and practices.

The PR profession was probably first heard of in India only in the later half of the twentieth century. The profession, per se, raised many questions with confusing answers, the reason being the business environment at that time not caring much about it. The protectionist policies of the government, non-existence of competition from global companies, and the resultant lukewarm market made life rather comfortable for several businessmen. Complacence, naturally, does not generate innovations. It was as if the Indian consumer, though keen to buy quality products, had resigned to the fate of buying whatever was being offered. It was a sellers' market with its obvious ramifications.

As the government clamped nationalization of banks and barred foreign companies under FERA laws, quite a few multinational corporations (MNCs) packed their bags and left. In the absence of competition or the need for it, PR naturally did not have a significant role to play.

With India adopting policies of liberalization and free market, and the resultant opening of the Indian economy, several global companies have been encouraged to arrive here, which has heated up the Indian market. The new economic order and environment has now sensitized the publics towards business organizations and the obligations the companies have towards the publics.

The MNCs from the free world, having for long experienced the benefits, role, and relevance of the profession of PR, have now been making demands on the Indian manpower resource to produce PR professionals who can take charge of this important aspect of business activity.

Consequently, India, in the past decade, has witnessed considerable growth of media schools, who are involved in training young men and women in a variety of subjects such as mass communication and corporate communication, which are all aspects of the larger discipline of PR. The media explosion in the country has further augmented the potential in this field. For instance, in Delhi alone, there are more than 20 media schools training aspiring PR professionals.

PR is now also being taught by some leading universities, colleges, and business schools. The general awareness and description of the PR functions are now perceived well in the industry circle. Today, it is difficult to imagine an organization worth its name without a PR practitioner. We can thus say that PR in India is an upcoming profession with sizable opportunities for employment in the industry as well as in government organizations, with prospects of good career advancement.

About the Book

PR is a vast subject and embraces several aspects of an organization. *Public Relations: Principles and Practices* has been conceived keeping in mind the demand and desire for a comprehensive book on the subject. An effort has been made to cover a wide variety of subjects—from basic definitions to the execution of PR programmes; relations with several publics such as customers, dealers, vendors, media; and new topics such as lobbying, negotiation skills, etc.

With business booming in India and the publics becoming more sensitive to the relevance of business companies in their lives, perceptions about the PR profession have tremendously changed amongst the publics, particularly in the mind of business leaders.

The book has been designed specially keeping in mind the needs and expectations of students pursuing courses in mass communication, corporate communication, etc. and aspiring PR professionals. The book will also serve as an add-on to aspiring management professionals from business schools and will also serve as a handy tool for the practicing corporate managers.

Pedagogical Features

Each chapter of the book begins with a chapter outline and contains illustrations, examples, and exhibits to explain the various concepts. An effort has been made to keep recent examples, so that their relevance may be comprehensible to the reader. End chapter exercises include concept review questions that test the reader's understanding of the concepts discussed in the chapter, and project work that aims to help students develop further interest and knowledge. In addition to these, a list of key PR terms is also provided in each chapter. Some chapters have case studies followed by discussion questions to illustrate the concepts discussed in the chapter.

Coverage and Structure

The book is divided into five parts—Fundamentals and Emergence; Process and Practice; Skills; Applications; and Support Service.

The first part—*Fundamentals and Emergence*—gives an overview of PR fundamentals and the emergence of PR across the world and in India. Chapter 1 is devoted to basic fundamentals of the profession, the definitions and explanations, the functions of PR, and the working profile of a PR person. Chapter 2 covers the emergence of the PR profession, its beginning, the second world war, the changing scenario, the present and the future, the communication explosion today, and the challenges that professionals face due to advancement of information technology. Chapter 3 paints the Indian scenario in the pre-independence and post independence era as far as PR and other related developments are concerned.

The second part—*Process and Practice*—consists of four chapters. Chapters 4–7 discuss in detail the PR window for developing a PR programme, which includes scanning the environment, creating a communication plan/strategy, implementing the plan, and measuring its impact.

The third part—*Skills*—focuses on key communication and negotiation skills, which are essential for PR professionals. Chapter 8 discusses at length the area of communication as a responsibility of PR. Chapter 9 delves into the art and techniques of negotiations in the corporate world in view of takeovers becoming a trend.

The fourth part—*Applications*—discusses PR relations with several publics and other key topics. Chapter 10 discusses PR support to marketing in terms of integrated marketing communications and its ramifications. Chapters 11–13 address various aspects of PR relations with customers, dealers, and vendors. Chapter 14 covers the important function of communicating to employees for solving problems, increasing productivity, and generating employee loyalty to the organization. Chapter 15 deals with PR in the financial area of a company with special reference to building relations with the investor publics. Chapter 16 discusses the nuances of dealing with the media, which is considered a major responsibility of PR professionals and revolves around the objectives and strategies of media relations. Chapter 17 deals with corporate social responsibility, with special reference to community relations. Chapters 18 and 19 are dedicated to the core subjects of corporate image and corporate identity, the relationship between the two, and the steps and actions involved in building image and identity. Chapter 20 covers the newly emerging strategy of PR, that is, event management. Chapter 21 concentrates on crisis management, which is considered to be the acid test of a PR professional. Chapter 22 is devoted to the area of government PR. Chapter 23 discusses the involvement of PR in the art of lobbying. Chapter 24 concentrates on corporate advertising as a means of boosting corporate image. Chapter 25 discusses the systems and techniques of publishing a house journal, which works as a mirror and mouth piece of a corporation. Chapter 26 details the ethics of PR.

The final part—*Support Service*—discusses PR agencies. Chapter 27 elaborates on the roles and goals of a PR agency, and how to select and evaluate PR agencies.

Acknowledgements

Writing this book has been a long cherished dream inspired by friends, colleagues, and bosses, who have been very liberally sharing with me their ideas and experiences. I have been fortunate to have bosses of several nationalities, mainly from America, where the PR profession has already attained maturity and has earned its rightful position in the board rooms of several worldwide corporations.

My thoughts go back about three decades when I enjoyed the benefit of the wisdom of a veteran tyre industry captain, Mr R.E.O. Carey of Goodyear, who was a thorough PR person. I would be failing in my duty, if I do not pay my tribute to Mr Moe. F. Reilly, the world-renowned PR professional and PR director of Goodyear International Corporation. I also recall my association, though brief, with Mr Sanat Lahiri of Dunlop, who rose to the position of president of the International Public Relations Association (IPRA). I am also proud of my association with the former heads of Goodyear India, Dr Roop Singh Bhakuni and Mr Neville P. Moos.

My associations with personalities such as George P. Burrill, R.E. Fricke, Bruce Erwin, Austin Evans, Donald McDonald, and Morsou Miota, have not only left with me great memories of the trials and tribulations of the management game, but also lessons which can be shared with the future generation of PR professionals.

Several friends involved in the profession in India have not only inspired me but unknowingly have made contributions to my effort of writing this book. Personalities such as Ms Chandni Luthra of ITDC; Dr Jaishri Jethwaney of IIMC; Mr Subash Chopra, veteran journalist from *London Times*; Dev Sagar Singh, former deputy editor of *The Indian Express* and current Ji Ji press of Japan; Chetan Chaddha, the then consulting editor, *Observer of Business and Politics*; Major General Sitanshu Kar, director of Defence Public Relations; and Mr Vijay Joshi from Defence Public Relations extended tremendous moral support in my endeavours.

I owe special thanks to my family members—my wife Mohana, a teacher, who partnered me in my agony and ecstasy alike, and two beautiful daughters Sona and Roopa, who with their learned disposition, provided the necessary moral support and encouragement. Thanks also to two friendly young men, Mr Manvinder Singh and Lt Col. Harmeek Singh, the husbands of my daughters, who often share a lot of ideas with me on a variety of subjects. The rare love and affection shared with me by my three grandchildren Tavleen, Hemal, and Gobind, is a silent but salient contribution to my mindset.

My special thanks go to several students from Delhi University, YMCA, Vidya Bhavan, IIMC, MERI, etc., the constant interactions with whom made me realize the need for this book, to bridge an important academic and professional gap.

Last but not the least, the book would not have been possible without the liberal support and guidance of the Oxford University Press team members.

It will give me immense pleasure to receive suggestions, comments, and contributions at my e-mail id: iqbalsachdeva@yahoo.com.

IQBAL SACHDEVA

Contents

PART II: PROCESS AND PRACTICE

PART III: SKILLS

PART IV: APPLICATIONS

PART I

FUNDAMENTALS AND EMERGENCE

1 Public Relations Fundamentals

THE INTER-DEPENDENT WORLD

Famous philosopher, Aristotle, said, 'Man is a social animal'. Gone are the days, when people could be self-reliant and self-sufficient in meeting their needs of survival. Today, the society has come to acquire a paradigm of 'inter-dependence' so that every person is dependent on another for the satisfaction of their needs. This has culminated into a situation where corporations and the public relate to each other.

There is hardly an individual or an organization, which is able to accomplish their goals without the help from public. Business people depend on customers for sales and profits; organizations depend on employees for productivity and quality of their products; industry relies on several engineers and skilled men and women to produce products that satisfy human needs, like food, clothing, cars, and homes; society depends on the government to provide utilities, and law and order; the younger generation depends on schools and colleges for education and career advancement; and men and women of all ages depend on religious institutions for spiritual and moral guidance. All these have culminated into a great need for relationships and communications among all people at all levels.

The birth of democracies worldwide and the concept of 'power to the people' have generated the importance of people's opinions on various issues concerning the human race. Today, matters are not resolved by the use of force or wars, but by the exchange of ideas and opinions, popularly called 'public opinion'. As such, our society can be said to have been arranged into opinion groups sharing various values and ideas among the group members. Never before in history has the opinion of an individual or groups of people or 'public' been more vital to the success of business, social, religious, and political institutions than at present times.

The inter-dependence of people, businesses, governments, and social and religious organizations, has given birth to a new philosophy and a function of management, which has come to be known as 'public relations'.

DEFINITIONS OF PUBLIC RELATIONS

Unlike several seasoned professions or disciplines, there is no single definition, which can be considered competent and comprehensive enough to define public relations. As such, there are about 500 definitions on the subject, for the simple reason that any one who experienced and practised public relations, coined their own definition from their own experiences.

However, some of the definitions given in Exhibit 1.1 make interesting reading and are relevant. These are some of the leading definitions that several professionals have attempted to write to streamline the profession.

But Dr Rex F. Harlow, a well known American professional, undertook the task of collecting such definitions published since the turn of the century, breaking them into major elements, and classifying the basic, central ideas that these definitions included. From his analysis of 472 definitions, he produced a working definition that is both conceptual and operational:

Public relations is a distinctive management function which helps establish and maintain mutual lines of communication, understanding, acceptance and cooperation between organization and its publics; involves the management of problems or issues; helps management to keep informed on and responsive to public opinion; defines and emphasizes the responsibility of management to serve the public interest; helps management keep abreast of and effectively utilize change; serving as an early warning system to help anticipate trends; and uses research and sound and ethical communication as its principal tools.

However, the 35th National Conference of the Public Relations Society of America, in November 1982, presented a more competent and comprehensive definition (See Exhibit 1.2), highlighting the roles and goals of public relations

---

EXHIBIT 1.1   Definitions of public relations

'Relations with the general public, as through publicity; specifically, those functions of a corporation, organization, etc, concerned with attempting to create favourable public opinion for itself.'
– *Webster's New Word Dictionary*

'Public Relations is the management function which evaluates public attitudes, identifies the policies and procedures of an individual or an organization with the public interest, and executes a programme of action to earn public understanding and acceptance.'
– *Public Relations News*, USA

'The purpose of Public Relations practice is to establish a two way communication to resolve conflicts of interest, and to establish understanding based on truth, knowledge and full information.'
– Sam Black–a British PR practitioner

Public Relations is 'The management function which gives the same organized and careful attention to the asset of Goodwill as is given to any other major asset of business.'
– John W. Hill

'Public Relations is a combination of Philosophy, Sociology, Economics, Language, Psychology, Journalism, Communication, and other knowledges of a system of human understanding.'
– Herbert M. Bans

'Public Relations is the attempt by information, persuasion and adjustment to engineer public support for an activity, cause, movement or institution.'
– Edward L. Bernays

'Public Relations is 'the communication and interpretation and communication of ideas from an institution to the publics and the communication of information, ideas and opinions from those publics to the institution, in a sincere effort to establish a maturity of interest and thus achieve the harmonious adjustment of an institution to its community.'
– Scott M. Cutlip and Allen H. Center

'Good performance, publicly appreciated because adequately communicated.'
– *Fortune* magazine

---

in the total structure of today's complex, pluralist, and inter-dependent society. The definition brought out the importance of activities, their results as well as the knowledge needs of a professional.

A study of the foregoing definitions, leads us to conclude with an ethical statement.

Public relations is ninety per cent doing good and ten per cent communicating about it. Public relations cannot and should not gloss over the bad deeds of an organization to make them look good, but can and should professionally help to get credit for a job well done by the organization.

PUBLIC RELATIONS PRACTICE

The several definitions and their understanding helps us to draw an outline of the functions of public relations practice in an organization, as the following:

1. Public relations is a top management function and deserves as much attention as given to the other assets as manpower, money, material, machinery, etc.
2. Public relations has the responsibility of establishing relationship between an organization and its various constituent public groups like employees,

EXHIBIT 1.2   Public Relation Society of America's official statement on public relations

Public relations helps our complex, pluralistic society to reach decisions and function more effectively by contributing to mutual understanding among groups and institutions. It serves to bring public and public policies into harmony.

Public relations serves a wide variety of institutions in society such as businesses, trade unions, government agencies, voluntary associations, foundations, hospitals, and educational and religious institutions. To achieve their goals, these institutions must develop effective relationships with many different audience or publics such as employees, members, customers, local communities, shareholders and other institutions, and with society at large.

The managements of institutions need to understand the attitudes and values of their policies in order to achieve institutional goals. The goals themselves are shaped by the external environment. The public relations practitioner acts as a counsellor to management, and as a mediator, helping to translate private aims into reasonable, publicly acceptable policy and action.

As a management function, public relations encompasses the following:

- Anticipating, analysing, and interpreting public opinion, attitudes, and issues which might impact, for good or ill, the operations and plans of the organization.
- Counselling management at all levels in the organization with regard to policy decisions, courses of action and communication, taking into account their public ramifications and the organization's social or citizenship responsibilities.
- Researching, conducting, and evaluating, on a continuing basis, programmes of action and communication to achieve informed public understanding necessary to the success of an organization's aims. These may include marketing, financial fund raising, employee, community, or government relations and other programmes.
- Planning and implementing the organization's efforts to influence or change public policy.
- Setting objectives, planning, budgeting, recruiting and training staff, developing facilities, in short, managing the resources needed to perform all of the above.

Examples of the knowledge that may be required in the professional practice of public relations include communication arts, psychology, social psychology, sociology, political science, economics, and the principles of management and ethics. Technical knowledge and skills are required for opinion research, public issues analysis, media relations, direct mail, institutional advertising, publications, film/video productions, special events, speeches and presentations.

In helping to define and implement policy, the public relations practitioner utilizes a variety of professional communication skills and plays an integrative role both within the organization and between the organization and the external environment.

Formally adopted by PRSA Assembly, 6 November 1982.

customers, dealers, vendors, shareholders, media, community, government, parliamentarians, etc.

3. Public relations is considered to be the eyes and ears of a company, as it monitors the awareness levels, opinions, attitudes, behaviours, and responses of various publics.

4. As public relations is considered to be the catalyst of change, it is entrusted with the duty of engineering changes in the awareness, opinions, attitudes, and behaviours of the publics.

5. Public relations is also expected to evaluate and measure the impact of organizational policies, procedures, and actions on various publics.

6. Public relations also plays an advisory role of counselling the management

to modify and adjust those policies, procedures, and actions conflicting with public interest in the interest of smooth functioning of the organization.

7. Public relations is the watch dog of corporate interests and public expectations and as such counsels the management for the formation of new policies, procedures, and actions, which are mutually beneficial to organization and publics.

8. Since the public relations professional is expected to be communications specialist, the job entails the focused responsibility to maintain a two-way communication between publics and the organization.

9. Public relations monitors the winds of change, has anticipation of the crisis and works as an early warning system, for gearing up the management grapple with the eventualities.

Sam Black, in his book *Practical Public Relations*, sums up the functions of public relations discipline, to avoid confusion or misunderstanding of certain organizational actions and behaviours (Black 1996).

Public relations practice includes:

1. Everything that is calculated to improve mutual understanding between an organization and all with whom it comes in contact, both within and outside the organization.

2. Advice on the presentation of the 'public image' of an organization.

3. Action to discover and eliminate sources of misunderstanding.

4. Action to broaden the sphere of influence of an organization by appropriate publicity, advertising, exhibitions, films, etc.

5. Everything directed towards improving communication between people or organization.

Public relations is not:

1. A barrier between the truth and the people.

2. Propaganda to impose a point of view regardless of truth, ethics, and the public good.

3. Publicity aimed directly at achieving sales, although public relations activities can be very helpful to sales and marketing efforts.

4. Composed of stunts or gimmicks. These may be useful at times to put across ideas, but fail completely if used often or in isolation.

5. Unpaid advertising.

6. Merely media relations, although media work is a very important part of most public relations programmes.

7. Political in central and local government. It is to promote democracy through full information and not to advance the policy of any political party.

To cap all the foregoing definitions, public relations is a two-way communication between an organization and target groups for the following three benefits:

1. It resolves conflicts of interest.
2. It seeks common ground/areas of mutual interest.
3. It establishes understanding based on truth, knowledge, and complete information.

This is the process, purpose, and practice of public relations.

In other words, public relations practice is not a strategic exercise to manipulate people for the benefits of the organization, but has a mediator role to establish a win-win situation between the organization and the publics, for a lasting relationship. Refer to Exhibit 1.3 for definition of public relations.

STRENGTHS OF A PUBLIC RELATIONS PROFESSIONAL

Specific personality traits, skills, and talents are the prerequisites for those who seek public relations (PR) as a career (See Exhibit 1.4). Landing in PR by chance and not by choice is fraught with pitfalls and can be a threat to success. The strengths, can undoubtedly be cultivated, through training and education in the discipline.

Has Excellent Communication Skills

Ability to communicate is the specialization area for a PR professional. Their major job responsibility in an organization is to solve the communication problems of the company. This ability makes them a distinct person in the organization as compared to hundreds of other people working in a company. They should have a natural flair for verbal and written language.

Has Good Knowledge of Media

Media relations in many organizations is a major part of the job responsibility of a PR person. It is but natural that they should have a thorough knowledge of the working of media, print, electronics, or Internet media. Their ability to get along well with the media professional, can be an asset to the organization, which helps the company to generate lot of favourable media coverage and resultant good corporate image.

Understands the Management Process

Since public relations is a top management function, the PR person should thoroughly understand the functioning of the management. Their knowledge of management science and particularly organizational behaviour helps them to have a sense of direction in carrying out their public relations role.

EXHIBIT 1.3   The Definition of PR—a middle published in *The Observer of Business and Politics*

The definition of PR

ONE day, at the Bangalore Press Club, I bumped into a Kannada intellectual, Gavacha, with a bushy salt-pepper beard. He was already in high spirits when I introduced myself to him as a PR man.

'Oh, PR?' he said. 'Wining, dining and mutual appreciation is, perhaps, the most appropriate description of the profession.

Embarrassed a bit, I said, 'not really. PR is a demure profession of building bridges of understanding amongst people.'

'I think, you PR guys are known as the 'Gin brigade' of a company: said Gavacha in a lighter vein.

'When a company starts making profits, enough profits, it thinks of looking for the most charming lady in town to make her the PRO: he said.

'Public Relations is an important management function. It starts the day a business is set up, and ends, perhaps, a day after a business is wound up,' I asserted in an effort to defend the profession.

'No,' said Gavacha, 'when a company is in trouble, the chips are down and profits shrink, the first causality is the charming lady. After all, what has she been doing there, except smiling, shaking hands and doling out goodies.

'That is the fallacy of the Indian business who thinks that the charming lady is the last to be hired and the first to be fired.

Smiles and shakehands is just about 10 per cent of the job. In fact, PR is 90 per cent doing good job and 10 per cent talking about it. More than the beauty, it is the brains that count here.'

'You don't need a lot of brains for the job. I have seen PR guys handling a rare Scotch for the boss, manage a tough plane or train ticket for him, fix a bureaucrat or a politician or even broken hearts....Looks do count here,' said Gavacha with conviction.

'Agreed that looks count everywhere. But the PR is now an organised profession. So much so that more than 20 national conferences have been held in India.'

'Yea! the fun-loving and self-seeking men and women invented 20 glamourous opportunities to have a good time at corporate expense,' he retorted.

'But some serious-minded delegates produced papers to bring out professionalism,' I exerted.

'But only to eulogise their buddies. The PR profession is still struggling for recognition and you have miles to go. I understand that some self-styled pseudo-PRs have hijacked the movement,' he said.

'Yes! but it's everywhere that some unethical self-seekers creep into institutions and try to take the movement after their molds and motives. But the movement lives,' I consoled Gavacha, putting my hand on his shoulder.

'Yes! but the time is now that you PR guys should get serious, get organised and get the profession a rightful place as a management discipline'; preached Gavacha.

Our talk was broken with the arrival of Sivan on the scene, with his usual broad face and pipe tucked in between his large moustache, another PR man.

Sivan worked for an industrialist-turned-politician and was a high-flying executive who could pull wires in Delhi sitting right in Bangalore.

'You are getting serious on a beautiful evening like this,' he interjected. 'Let's enjoy our drink.' Asking us to lift our glasses and say 'Cheers: Sivan said, 'I will give you the real definition of PR. It means '*Pee Yaar*!'

And we all clicked our glasses with a loud laughter.

Source: The Observer, 4 October 2000.

EXHIBIT 1.4 Strengths of a PR professional

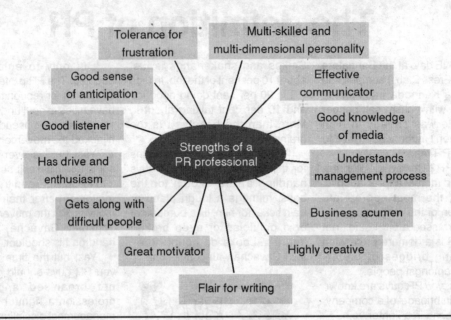

Tolerance for frustration

Multi-skilled and multi-dimensional personality

Good sense of anticipation

Effective communicator

Good listener

Good knowledge of media

Strengths of a PR professional

Has drive and enthusiasm

Understands management process

Gets along with difficult people

Business acumen

Great motivator

Highly creative

Flair for writing

Should have Business Acumen

The main business of any organization is to generate and expand a profitable venture. A PR person should have the necessary business sense and actively contribute to the bottom lines in the balance sheet of the company. Well exposed as they are expected to be, they can be a contributor of great business ideas and opportunities for the growth of the organization. Sure enough they should not be a cosmetic attachment to the organization, but an active player in the process of its progress.

Is Highly Creative

Creativity makes for a creative organization, which stands out distinctly in the business world. PR professional should be competent and courageous enough to have 'out of the box thinking' to inspire the organization and its members to adopt new and unusual ideas essential for its growth and prosperity. Being a communications specialist, they should have the imagination and style to communicate creatively to the publics relevant to the organization's business.

Has Flair for Writing

More often than not, a public relations person is a resource person for media. One of their major obligation is to feed the media with news, stories, and articles of journalists' interest, which may highlight the contributions of the organization towards national growth and prosperity. Information about launch of new products, new achievements, new innovations and other human interest items that deserve highlighting, have to be presented to the media in an accurate and ready to publish form. No surprise, sometimes a business newspaper carries about fifty per cent of the editorial material contributed by public relations. Therefore, the flair to write like a journalist is not only desirable but essential.

Should be a Great Motivator

The leadership qualities in the professional should come to their help to motivate people to perform at their optimum level. Their verbal and written communication skills will stand in good stead for them to trigger enthusiasm amongst people in the organization.

Gets along with most Difficult People

Getting along with people is an art. The world is a difficult place and people's behaviour is difficult to predict. The challenge of getting along with people, particularly more difficult people, calls for a cool mind and pleasant peaceful disposition which the professionals must master.

Has Drive and Enthusiasm

Enthusiasm is contagious. There may be frustrations, personal or professional, but a PR person should never let them out, instead demonstrate ample enthusiasm and drive to do their job of enthusing others to keep the organizational morale high for success.

Is a Good Listener

Listening is one sure way of learning and gathering feedback for making the necessary changes and adjustments for a PR practitioner. Listening is an art which calls for keeping one's own ego and emotions under control. The sensitive feedback if gathered properly through attentive listening, can provide a sense of direction for professional plans and strategies.

Has Good Sense of Anticipation

A PR person should have a radar like-sense of anticipation about the shape of things to come. They are the one who are responsible for ringing the early warning bell about the crisis which may be brewing or the new opportunities knocking at the door.

Has Tolerance for Frustration

Every new idea or value system will meet opposition and has to be advocated in the mutual interest of the publics and the organization. The initial opposition will cause sizable frustration. But determined professionals, who have made up their mind about the cause or issue, will not flinch in their efforts. However, the public relations person should put up a brave front, absorb frustration, and emerge victorious.

DUTIES AND RESPONSIBILITIES OF A PUBLIC RELATIONS MANAGER

The public relations manager will report directly to the managing director and will be responsible for all public relations operations for the company. These include publicity, employee communications, internal and external publications, community relations, public relations support to marketing, manufacturing, personnel and finance divisions, etc.

Employee Communications

The public relations manager will work closely with personnel department in establishing first class communications between management and employees. These will be established by weekly news sheets, employee publications, support of sports activities, special events and other means of keeping employees informed in terms of promoting productivity, efficiency, discipline, regular attendance, safety and quality, etc.

Internal and External Publications

The public relations manager will be responsible for editing, publishing, and production of all PR publications issued by the company. These can include a weekly news sheet, a monthly or bi-monthly employees' newspaper, and a dealer's publication and other outside publications for spreading goodwill amongst various company related publics.

Community Relations

Under the direction of managing director, the public relations manager will establish and maintain a good relationship with the community adjacent to the plant as well as with the national community. This will involve planned tours; representation of company at local functions; cooperation with local officials, schools and charities; liaison with local government officials, etc.

Media Relations

The public relations manager will be responsible for all relations with the local and national, both print and electronic media for transmission of company information for publicity. They will be responsible for acting as spokespersons for the company and will be responsible for answering all questions from the representatives of the media during press meets. They will also maintain a record of press coverage obtained for the company, for submission to management on monthly basis.

PR Support to Marketing

The public relations manager will maintain constant liaison with the sales and marketing divisions and will provide all possible public relations and publicity support to marketing division. Such support will include product and institutional publicity, assistance in launching new products, development of market related publicity material, counsel and guidance on the public relations aspects of marketing, publication of the dealer magazine and assistance in dealer relations.

PR Budgeting

With inputs and approval from the managing director and other directors of the company, the public relations manager will prepare the annual public relations budget and will maintain control of public relations expenditures so that budget levels do not exceed.

PR Support to Financial Operations

The public relations manager will coordinate his/her activities with the finance director for the publication of annual financial report to share holders, handle release of information to the press, and organize the logistics for the annual general meeting of the company share holders.

PR Agency Coordination

The public relations manager will be responsible for selection and liaisoning with the designated public relations consultancy for briefing, planning, finalizing, and executing the public relations plans and programmes, as finally approved by the managing director. They will also be responsible for managing the financial aspect of this company–agency relationship.

Website Management

The public relations manager, in consultation with the managing director, sales and marketing director and in coordination with the public relations agency, will keep updating the company website for proper projection of company image. They will also keep a track of the visitors to the site and keep the scores for reporting in their monthly activity report.

EXHIBIT 1.5   Ten commandments for a PR professional

1. Be frank, fearless but polite, polished, and positive. Smile.
2. Develop trust with management—be a guide, friend, and counsellor.
3. Be genuinely interested in people, and problems. Listen and empathize.
4. Make creativity your forte. Conceptualize ideas into words and visuals.
5. Communicate. Communicate. Communicate—Up, down, sideways.
6. Build a sound media network and be responsive to mediamen.
7. Don't white wash or glorify lies or half truths to mislead people.
8. Endeavour constant intellectual updates and be a culture vulture.
9. Organize your life—Plan your work and work your plan.
10. Generate organizational excitement to build a 'win-win' environment.

Monthly Reports

The public relations managers will submit a report of their activities each month to the managing director in accordance with the management's monthly report guidelines.

Exhibit 1.5 highlights the ten commandments for a PR professional and Exhibit 1.6 details the PR objectives of a company.

In conclusion, let us look at an outline of the system of writing a monthly PR report to the management for a multi-national company (See Exhibit 1.7).

EXHIBIT 1.6   Public relations objectives of a company

1. Stronger contribution to employee relations, with the purpose of helping to increase individual productivity, reduce absenteeism, and build stronger 'family feeling' amongst all employees.
2. More scientifically-directed effort to help build stature, identity, and acceptance of the company as a progressive, contributing corporate citizen of the national and plant area communities.
3. Specific public relations programmes co-ordinated with sales and marketing, to help build the quality reputation for all company products.
4. Closer co-ordination with sales and marketing in supporting specific marketing operations, introducing new products, dealer relations, and sales training.
5. Better advance planning, in cooperation with management, to optimize the contributions of public relations to achievement of corporate objectives and solution of major corporate problems.
6. More planning and review, on an annual, quarterly and monthly basis, to ensure that the public relations programme is being directed specifically to the advancement of the company's most important goals.
7. More 'imagineering' in the creation and operation of purposeful public relations projects and in institutional and product publicity.
8. Planned contribution to better communications throughout the company among all its elements.
9. The continued upgrading of all public relations personnel.

EXHIBIT 1.7   Guidelines to PR managers for writing a monthly PR report

Timing

Monthly report to the director of public relations are due at the headquarters by the 10th of each month. Plan to mail them as soon as possible after the first.

Reporting by Category

The report should be concise, clearly written, and fully explain the role played by public affairs.

Follow this outline:

Major and noteworthy activity

List here in some details what you consider to be your most important activities of the month. Items listed here need not be repeated elsewhere.

Community relations   Mention all projects planned or completed that involve public affairs working directly with various segments of the community or supporting company projects. Subjects will range from civic betterment projects and company facilities available for community use to helping solve environmental problems and keeping the public informed about plant situations.

Sales and marketing support   Describe support to sales campaigns, introduction of products and dealer grand openings through press kits, releases, and special events. Also cover publicity and displays provided in conjunction with fairs and vehicle shows and demonstrations.

Programmes and projects   List here press conferences in support of sales, support for corporate and local company programmes and events, employee communication projects, hosting of office/plant visitors, special assignments from management, etc.

Racing   Cover advance and follow-up publicity on local events, special media programmes, operation of hospitality centres, hosting of dealers and other VIPs, develop-ment of special exhibits.

Media results   Briefly describe significant newspaper, magazine, TV, and radio coverage of company news.

Also list local stories prepared, adapted and distributed, and releases for local use. Report the total number of press clippings generated on a monthly and yearly basis.

Publications   Mention new publications; special publications; changes in format, frequency or distri-

bution; and special editions. Call attention to special stories and unusual efforts by editors and writers.

Also list the current production status of all publications.

People   Report any change in public relations staffing, honours won by the members of the department and any other significant personal news dealing with outside activities, illness or family status changes.

If a news item about you or your activities doesnot fit under any other category, list it separately at the end.

Avoid attaching a large number of clips, but do include any major story you've collected during a month.

General comments   Your monthly reports serve several purposes:

1. Informing him about your activities and showing your effectiveness
2. Generating story and picture leads and ideas for the editors of company publications
3. Providing material for use in the house journal
4. Updating various divisions at headquarters on country developments

It is important, therefore, that the public relations manager in each country files a report each month. A brief report that hits only the highlights is acceptable occasionally if there is no time for the longer form.

Press Release Suggestions

For best results, plan the content of your press releases before you begin to write. According to John Stahr in *Write to the Point, the Byoir Style Book*, most experienced writers follow these guidelines:

Analyse   Take an objective look at the whole subject about which you are writing. Decide what is good about it, what is bad about it; what is interesting about it; what is dull about it; what the central fact is; what its tributary facts are; what you want the reader to decide from what you say about it.

Organize   Make a few notes. Think for a time. Make an outline, if it is a long piece. Decide what you are going to say first, then how the second and third and subsequent things attach.

Think about your audience   Do your best to think like them. What would catch your attention? What would keep your attention? What would make the kind of permanent impression that you want to make?

One thing that often comes up in any discussion of style is the matter of length of sentences. Short sentences and paragraphs undoubtedly are desirable. They are easy to understand. They can be useful as a mental punctuation tactic in a text that otherwise, of necessity, is running to fairly long ones.

But the short sentences are not necessarily better than long ones in every context. Perhaps the best formula, Stahr says, is: 'Just tell the story'.

Policies on Publications

General publications   To assure accuracy and uniformity, copy for anniversary, recruiting, plant tour or similar brochures produced by international subsidiary companies that describe the company policies and operations worldwide should be submitted to corporate public affairs at headquarters for approval before being sent to the printer.

Publications with strictly local content, such as those of plant employees, dealers, and sales personnel, are exempted from the approval process, however.

Employee and consumer publications   Every issue of your publications must carry the name and address of the publisher and the name of the editor, as required by law in most countries. Some countries require even more information, such as the name of the printer.

Inclusion of the editor's name gives readers and potential contributors an identity to whom they can address requests, complaints, story leads, pictures, and other communications.

Use of the Corporate Name

Use the correct form of the corporate name in all correspondence with third parties, and in all documents. Publications stories and press releases should also conform when referring to the present company in headquarters.

Release of Company Information

Release of technical information   Written approval is needed for the release of any company technical information. Fax/e-mail requests to corporate public affairs at headquarters for clearance with the patent and trademark department, and, depending on the subject matter, to the vice president of engineering, research and development and technical services.

In each case, your written request for approval must specify the exact purpose of the release and the same release may not be made for another purpose without your submitting another request in writing.

'Technical information' is information of any kind which can be used, or adapted for use, in the design, production, manufacture, utilization, or reconstruction of articles or materials. The information may be in the form of a model, prototype, blueprint, photo, motion picture, slide, or operating manual or even a technical service.

Release of non-technical information   You are your company's contact with newspapers, magazines, and television and radio stations for publicity or news. Employees other than company officers who want or need to communicate with the media directly must obtain your permission to do so.

Any lecture, talk, and address concerning the organization to be delivered outside the company also needs your advance approval.

Release of information on capital programmes   You need permission to release public media information on any major capital investment project, for a new plant, and expansion or modernisation. Fax/e-mail your request to corporate public affairs at headquarters for clearance with the worldwide president, and/or appropriate region vice president. The managements of international subsidiary companies do not have the authority to approve releases of capital information.

In addition, the timing and manner in which approved investment information is to be released must be coordinated by public affairs.

Organization's employee, dealer and sales publication are considered to be 'public media' because they are seen beyond the company circle and, therefore, should also follow the approval procedure on stories dealing with capital projects.

Communications with Shareholders

All formal communications with your company's shareholders through annual reports, quarterly reports or other messages addressed to all shareholders as a whole need the approval of the director of public relations at headquarters.

Approval is not required for responses to letters from individual shareholders, however.

Policies Covering Company Trademarks

Trademarks appearing on merchandise   With the growing practice of putting corporate trademarks on toys, model kits, racing jackets and caps and other merchandise, you expect to receive requests for approval of such usage from other firms, organization or individuals. Authorization to use company trademarks frequently is granted because of anticipated publicity value to the company but only by written licence.

Fax/e-mail complete information on each request, including the name and address of the proposed user and how the trademark would be used, to the director of public relations at headquarters.

Following approval, a written license will be executed by the patent and trademark department to the party intending to use the trademarks.

Officers of the international subsidiary companies may not grant trademark authority.

Publicity or sales use of trademarks Requests for the third-party use of company trademarks in a sales promotional or publicity manner also require the drafting of a written licensee. Fax/e-mail full details to the director of public relations at headquarters.

The PR manager should always be alert for unauthorised use of company trademarks by third parties. Report such usage to the patent and trademark department at headquarters.

Trademarks used in advertising Requests by persons or companies outside the organization for the use of company references in their advertising should be faxed/e-mailed to the director of advertising at headquarters for approval in conjunction with the law and patent and trademark departments and the appropriate product division vice president.

This approval process covers use of the company's name, logotype, product names, and trademarks plus photographs or descriptions of company facilities, equipment, or manufacturing processes.

Summary

In conclusion, the corporations world over have adopted, practised, and implemented their well thought out and planned programmes, in a perennial manner, and have benefitted tremendously from the public relations effort.

In the inter-dependent world of today, it is important for an organization to establish harmonious relations with several publics, employees, customers, dealers, vendors, government, media and community, etc. to generate understanding and suitable response to companies policies, procedures and actions.

Organizations no longer can adopt a fixed or tough stance on issues, but must adjust to the changing social, economic, and political environment.

Public relations has roles and goals of monitoring and advising the organizations in the mutual interest of the organization and publics, about the policies, procedures, and actions. It also has the responsibility of engineering changes conducive to business.

Last but not the least, public relations professionals are expected to be communication specialists and have responsibility to keep the flow of two-way communication between the organization and publics, but they definitely are not propagandists, which has negative connotations.

Key Terms

Conflict of interest A situation that can arise if a person or firm acts in two or more separate capacities and the objectives in these capacities are not identical

Goodwill The value of a business over and above its tangible assets

Pluralistic society The existence or toleration of a diversity of ethnic groups or different cultures and views within a society

Propaganda In general, a message designed to persuade its intended audience to think and behave in a certain manner

Public opinion The general attitude or feeling of the public concerning an issue; the voice of the people

Publicity Type of promotion that relies on public relations effect of a news story usually carried free by mass media. The main objective of publicity is not sales promotion, but creation of an image through editorial or 'independent source' commentary

Publics Communities of people at large (whether or not organized as groups) that have a direct or indirect association with an organization: Customers, dealers, vendors, employees, investors, media, community, government, students, etc.

Concept Review Questions

1. Select any four definitions of public relations and explain why they are the most appropriate for describing the profession.
2. What is public relations and what is not? Why? Describe and explain in detail.
3. What are the strengths that a public relations person must possess to be a successful professional?
4. What are the duties and responsibilities of a public relations manager in an organization? Explain.
5. Discuss the policies pertaining to a company's trademarks.

Project Work

1. Develop a hypothetical list of public relations objectives of a computer manufacturing company.
2. Write a monthly activity report for the information of the managing director of your company where you are working as public relations manager.
3. Develop an imaginary advertisement for inserting in *The Economic Times* on the occasion of Silver Jubilee of your company.

References

Bahl, Sushil (1991), *Public Relations Manual*, Advertising Agencies Association of India, Bombay, India, pp. 5–6.

Black, Sam (1996), *Practical Public Relations*, Universal Book Stall, New Delhi, pp. 16–17.

Cutlip, Scott. M., Allen H. Centre, and Glen M. Broom (1985), *Effective Public Relations*, 6th edition, Prentice-Hall of India Private Limited, New Delhi, India, pp. 3–4.

Harlow, Rex F. (1976), 'Building a Public Relations Definition', Public Relations Review USA (Winter 1976 issue), p. 36.

Moore, H. Frazier and Frank B. Kalupa (2005), *Public Relations, Principles, Cases and Problems*, 9th edition, Richard D. Irwin Inc., USA, reprinted in India by Surjeet Publications, New Delhi, p. 8.

The Observer, vol. X, no. 236, 4 October 2000.

2 Emergence of Public Relations

ANCIENT TIMES

From ancient times to the modern day, public relations, like other disciplines of human activity, has come a long way to attain professional maturity. The origin of public relations, however, can be traced back to the dawn of civilization (See Exhibit 2.1). It perhaps started with the realization of ancient humans that it is not possible to survive alone. The ancient man felt the need for relationship and therefore of communication with members of their communities. This was the start of the inter-dependence by humans. The man came to be known as 'social animal'. The phenomena like informing, persuading, and uniting people, though appear elements of the modern society, yet they have been there since the early civilization.

Goals, techniques, tools, and ethical standards change with the passage of time. Primitive leaders, for example, were concerned with maintaining control over their followers through the use of force, intimidation, or persuasion. If these failed, magic—totem, taboo, or supernaturalism—was invoked.

With the development of a script for writing messages, method of communicating and selling ideas to each other experienced a significant change. The Olympic games and other events in the history provided a platform for the interchange of opinions and the emergence of a national spirit. The Greek city states reflected public opinion more and more. Leaders became increasingly aware of their public relationships.

Then the Romans adopted the concept of public opinion—the oratory of Cicero; the historical writings of Julius Caesar; the temples, statues, paintings, and pamphlets of the era, all were media of public opinion. The Roman adage *Vox populi, vox dei* (The voice of the people is the voice of God) represents the beginning of the public relations discipline.

The foundations of the present-day public relations function are seen in the American Revolution, which was not a popular, spontaneous uprising, but rather a carefully planned and executed movement (Moore and Kalupa 2005).

The evidence of public relations can also be found in the ancient history of India where the writings of the earliest times mention about the kings and their spies, whose function was to provide sensitive feedback on public opinions to the king, eulogize the king amongst people or spread grapevines that favour the kingdom. History reveals the stories of the kings themselves going to the streets, in the guise of a common man, to collect information about the joys and sorrows of the people they ruled.

Thirteen centuries passed between the fall of the Roman Empire in AD 475 and the *Enlightenment* of the 18th century. During the Dark Ages, public opinion played little part. With the *Renaissance*, which was characterized by a secular movement stressing the rights of reason to investigate nature and society, the basis of the modern world was laid, with its emphasis on the individual and the society. The *Reformation*, a religious movement, stressed the rights of the individual conscience. In the *medieval* world, church and the state had been one. The church moulded public opinion, and its power and effectiveness depended upon its public relations activities. The rise of medieval guilds introduced a new factor that developed opinion outside the church and led to the development, first, of small business, then, of larger, more extensive enterprises. In England the struggle between the nobility and the crown resulted in the *Magna Carta* (1215), which became the basis of the Bill of Rights (Moore and Kalupa 2005).

Public relations was used many centuries ago in England, where the kings maintained Lords Chancellor as *Keepers of the King's Conscience*. The kings recognized the need for a third party to facilitate communication and adjustment between the government and the people. So was born the word *propaganda* in the seventeenth century, when the catholic church set up its *Congregatio de propaganda,* congregation for propagating Christianity (Cutlip et al. 1985).

THE 20th CENTURY

Public relations has been there, in some form or the other, since time immemorial, though not in the form as practised today. The discipline had its beginnings in the last quarter of the 19th century, with the advent of utilities like rail roads and other industries which expanded across America. This new economic development necessitated the need for public relations to play its role in terms of communicating to the people, who were directly or indirectly affected by the developments and consequential changes in life styles. As such, public relations witnessed some initial existence and meaningful growth.

The dawn of the 20th century, with its changing economic and social scenario posed many new challenges for the society. The American history has recorded that it was Samuel Adams and his fellow revolutionaries who planned and utilized the public relations means and methods to succeed in the American War of Independence. Significantly, revolutionaries such as Samuel Adams and his associate, Thomas Paine used pamphlets and public events to raise public support for the American Revolution. Soon after the Civil War, Alexander Hamilton and James Madison used the power of communication to develop and establish the American Constitution.

Once the Civil War was over, American life experienced many important changes. Peace prevailed, which consequently resulted in development and rise of large-scale business and industry.

Some of the enlightened and enterprising American businessmen, in the early decades of the 20th century, felt the need to favourably project the meaning and relevance of their business to the society, and, therefore, resorted to meaningful public relations efforts. This led to the establishment of public relations and publicity counselling firms who would work as advisory or consulting outfits for the industry. Some of the business houses even established public relations departments in their firms. From this phenomenon onwards, the practice of public relations appear to have moved ahead significantly.

FAMOUS PERSONALITIES

The famous personalities who contributed significantly for the growth and development of public relations are Leone Baxter, Edward L. Bernays, George Creel, Paul Garrett, Denny Griswold, Rex F. Harlow, John W. Hill, Ivy Lee, Earl Newsom, and Arthur W. Page.

The contribution of these American personalities in the field of public relations is admired and appreciated all over the world. So dedicated they were to the new discipline that many of them had to sacrifice their family life and corporate career—a price that they had to pay for their courage and conviction for the cause of public relations.

EXHIBIT 2.1   Public relations profession—a chronology

Ancient Times

1800 BC   Earliest example of educational materials, a farm bulletin produced in ancient Iraq telling farmers how to grow crops.

1st century BC   Romans coined the phrase *Vox populi, vox dei* (The voice of the people is the voice of the God). Underscored the emerging importance of public opinion.

Middle Ages

15th century AD   A variety of handbills and broad sides were used to promote various causes in the decades following the invention of movable type of Johann Gutenberg in 1946.

1623   Pope Gregory XV created College for Propagating the Faith, the first large scale use of public relations, created by the Roman Catholic church to retain followers and solicit converts in the aftermath of the Reformation. Origin of the modern term propaganda.

Colonial Times

1641   Harvard College launched first systematic fund raising in the United States.

1748   King's College (now Columbia University) used first news release to solicit press coverage.

1773   Colonists staged Boston Tea Party, a pseudo-event that helped crystalize public opinion.

1787   The Federalist Papers, a series of eighty five pamphlets that were also reprinted as articles in newspapers, were produced to generate support for the formal creation of the United States and passage of its Constitution.

19th Century

1820s   Amos Kendall, a member of Andrew Jackson's kitchen cabinet, served as the first US presidential Press Secretary.

1840s   P.T. Barnum pioneered press agentry by promoting local appearance by his touring circus.

1850s   American railroads used publicity, advertising, and printed materials to attract tourists and settlers to the American West.

1889   First corporate public relations department established by Westinghouse, a year after Mutual Life Insurance Company created a 'species of literary bureau' to coordinate advertising and publicity. Westinghouse ultimately prevailed in the ensuing 'battle of the current' to promote the benefits of alternating current (AC) versus the direct current (DC) invented earlier by Thomas Edison and the General Electric Company.

1896   The use of modern publicity in political campaigns began with the presidential election contest between William McKinley and William Jennings Bryan.

1897   General Electric creates a Publicity Department.

Dawn of the 20th Century

1900s   Corporations started to use a variety of techniques to promote positive relationships with customer. For example, Ford pioneered press product previews (1895) as well as auto racing (1903) as a means to promote its products. Chicago Edison was the first to use an external magazine (1903), films (1909), and stuffers inserted in customer bills (1912).

The Publicity Bureau was organized in Boston as the nation's first publicity firm and forerunner of today's public relations agency.

1906   Ivy Lee was hired to represent the industry in the anthracite coal strike. Lee issued his 'Declaration of Principles', considered the birth of modern public relations counselling. Lee later represented J.D. Rockefeller's interests in the Colorado Fuel strike in 1914, also known as the bloody 'Ludlow Massacre'.

1916   The Committee on Public Information, headed by George Creel, promoted public support of American involvement in the World War I.

1923   Edward L. Bernays published *Crystallizing Public Opinion* popularized the term 'public relations counsel'. He also taught the first public relations course at the New York University.

Depression/New Deal Era

1927   Arthur W. Page was named Vice President–Public Relations at AT&T, accepting the job only if he were allowed to be involved in policy making. Page would distinguish himself as the leading corporate practitioner of the century by emphasizing the importance of co-operation with the public and the disclosure about corporate activities.

1929 'The Golden Jubilee of Light' celebrated the 50th anniversary of the invention of the electric light bulb—probably the greatest worldwide public relations event of the century, orchestrated by Edward L. Bernays.

1933 The first political campaign firm was established by husband and wife team of Clem Whitaker and Leone Baxter, who pioneered modern electioneering with several famous campaigns in California.

1934 Franklin Delano Roosevelt used his famous 'Fireside Chats' to instill confidence in the American people.

1934 Edward Bernays develops successful 'Green Ball' campaign for Lucky Strike cigarettes.

1936 First widespread use of public opinion polling.

World War II

1942 Office of War Information, headed by Elmer Davis, promoted public support and involvement in the World War II.

1945 The Advertising Council (formerly the War Advertising Council) was recognized to create information campaigns on behalf of various social causes.

1945 US Government announces, in a carefully crafted press release, that an American plane dropped an atomic bomb on Hiroshima.

1946 First widespread use of television publicity.

1948 The Public Relations Society of America is founded.

Baby Boom

1953 The United States Information Agency (USIA) was created to disseminate news and cultural information abroad.

1960 Edward Bernays leads an effort to inform the public about dangers of smoking through a massive campaign.

1982 Six people in a Chicago suburb who took Tylenol capsules die of cyanide poisoning, causing a PR nightmare for McNeil Labs and Johnson & Johnson.

1989 Tanker Exxon Valdez runs aground in Prince William Sound in what becomes the largest oil spill in the US history.

1993 A report breaks that a syringe is discovered in a can of Pepsi: Pepsi responds by calling for direct and immediate action.

1999 Anheuser–Busch launches public-service-campaign against driving under the influence of alcohol.

2000 World celebrates the completion of millennium and arrival of millennium baby. BBC carries TV series of the great personalities who shaped this world in the last century.

2001 Terror strikes the American World Trade Tower killing thousands of Americans. George Bush addresses world nations through global TV networks to solicit public opinion against terrorism.

2005 Start of the Iraq war to annihilate terrorism and weapons of mass destruction with CNN mounting high powered telecasts to keep the world citizens informed.

The term 'public relations', as known today, was first used in 1882 by Dorman Eaton, a lawyer, while addressing the Yale Law School. But it was not until 1916, that the term 'public relations' was put into practice professionally and the American who is considered as the initiator of this move was Ivy Lee.

After an initial stint as an investigative journalist, Ivy Lee turned into a public relations consultant and opened an agency *Lee, Harris & Lee*. In direct contrast to the 'public be damned' attitude of many business and financial leaders of the day, Lee counselled his clients with open and honest communication. In his famous *Declaration of Principles* to newspaper city editors, Lee pledged to supply the press and the public with prompt and accurate information on behalf of his business clients.

The document—*Declaration of Principles*—drew a clear distinction between the role of his *Press Bureau* (as the term 'public relations' was not yet in common use) in supplying news and information and the role of advertising agencies of the day, whose main job was to push sales of their clients. Lee was perhaps the first official public relations practitioner in the world whose clients included some leading businesses like rail road, oil, coal companies, and also some mine owners.

Another legendry figure in public relations was Edward L. Bernays, often called the 'Father of public relations', who adopted public relations as a professional activity, which had a much more crucial role to play than merely dealing with the media. In 1923, he wrote his book *Crystallizing Public Opinion*, which was an immediate success and gave him an opportunity to deliver a series of lectures on the new discipline of 'public relations'. Thus the first text book and first series of university lectures on public relations both happened in 1923, which is an important landmark in the history of the profession.

Late in 1955, he wrote his famous book *The Engineering of Consent* which delved into the concept of public relations as a systematic way of generating persuasive publicity. The concept continues to hold good with even the modern day public relations practitioners.

THE FIRST WORLD WAR

Public relations, though not recognised as such, has always existed as a discipline that dealt with the system of communication. With the outbreak of the First World War arose a global need and effort to influence the public opinion. When on 6 April 1917 the United States of America entered the First World War, almost immediately, a committee on public information was set up to direct the flow of information to the people. The committee at that time followed the concept of 'one way persuasive communication'. Headed by George Creel, the committee was responsible for consolidating public opinion in support of the war effort through a well-orchestrated and nation-wide propaganda campaign.

Twelve years after the war, yet another historical development that had a far-reaching impact on the public relations profession was the stock market crash of 1929, which plunged the American economy into a well known 'Great Depression'. Rampant unemployment, and resultant public frustration and anguish erupted in widespread criticism of the business enterprises.

CORPORATE INTEREST IN PUBLIC RELATIONS

The business barons became a whipping target of criticism for the leaders of the 'New Deal', while they made efforts to bring the American nation back from the brink of economic collapse. Unprecedented business controls and regulations were enacted and imposed at the federal level. Against the barrage of criticism from the politicians and the media and gripped by an acute inferiority complex and business setbacks, it was the time for the businessmen to rise to the occasion and adopt a 'high profile'.

Finding the publicity drives by business enterprises, to retrieve lost reputation, the need to develop an organized form of public relations was felt more than ever before. Business magnates realized the need to regain the public confidence lost during the depression, by establishing public relations departments and employing public relations managers to improve the public image of their businesses.

EARLY PUBLIC RELATIONS MANAGERS AND AGENCIES

Paul Garrett was one such manager, whom the General Motors (GM) Corporation employed in 1931. At GM Garrett built an innovative corporate programme, which was popularly adopted by other corporations.

Denny Griswold and her husband Glen published the public relations newsletter the *Public Relations News* in 1944, which made invaluable contribution to the profession for more than four decades.

Dr Rex F. Harlow, a professional of repute, who started his public relations career in 1912, continued up to 1983 as educator, editor, publisher, and consultant. He was the first editor of the *Public Relations Journal of America* and one of the founding fathers of the Public Relations Society of America. Harlow also took up the onerous task of collecting some 500 definitions of public relations and consolidated them into one single and comprehensive definition.

Earl Newsom established his public relations consultancy firm in 1935 and remained consultant to some large corporations like Standard Oil Company, Ford Motor Company, General Motors Corporation, etc.

The other notable public relations pioneers of this time included Benjamin Sonnenberg, John W. Hill, Carl Byoir, and Henry Rogors. John W. Hill founded *Hill & Knowlton* in the US state of Ohio in 1933. Hill built the world's first broad service public relations counselling firm, adding such services as public affairs and financial relations and also established branches in Europe and Asia. *The Making of a Public Relations Man* is his autobiography, which is his contribution to the profession as it describes the evolution of the role of public relations in modern business management. The book also dealt with the challenges and opportunities in the profession which was fairly new at that time.

In 1930, Carl Byoir founded his public relations firm in Cuba, before moving it to New York City. At mid-century *Carl Byoir Association* and *Hill & Knowlton* were the two leading public relations agencies retained by some major US corporations.

In the beginning of the fifties, a few companies had established public relations departments with major responsibility to cultivate relations with federal government and the political people in power. During this time, Henry C. Rogers and his partner, Warren Crown formed an agency named *Rogers & Crown* in California, which became the largest and the most successful public relations firm on the West Coast.

Rogers, in his autobiography *Walking the Tightrope,* presented a candid account of challenges of performing a balancing act between a high powered client and the formidable media.

THE SECOND WORLD WAR

The post-World War II period saw an increase in the number of corporate public relations departments and the rapid growth of newly formed public relations firms, many of them started by returning war veterans.

The name of Arthur Page will remain in history as a single individual who made sizable contributions to the practice of public relations. He remained the head of public relations for the American Telephone and Telegraph Company from 1927 to 1947 and did much to establish public relations as a management function. He counselled managements that gaining public approval should be based on performance in the public interest. His philosophy is enshrined in the statement—'All business in a democratic country begins with public permission and exists by public approval. If that be true, it follows that business should be cheerfully willing to tell the public what its policies are, what it is doing, and what it hopes to do. This seems practically a duty.'

During the fifties, many of the largest advertising agencies operated public relations units under the agencies' name. Most of these agency wings did not last long as big advertising clients expected the agencies to provide public relations service at low or no cost. With profits eroding, the agencies had no choice but to close down their public relations wings. This made them deficient to compete with independent public relations firms whom the clients regarded as hard core public relations professionals who deserved a suitable consultation fees.

The role of business in society has been under constant attack since the unrest of late sixties. Therefore, a traumatized business community undertook new philanthropic and community initiatives, and made it a part of the public relations officer's job responsibility. Thus, perhaps, was born the new concept of obligation of business towards society, now known as corporate social responsibility.

MODERN TIMES

In the seventies, the advertising agencies, including those that had earlier abandoned their own public relations units, recognized that public relations was an important component of a 'full service' agency. They also saw public relations as a contributer to profits and a strategic means to gain access to client's top management.

The first major public relations firm to be bought by an advertising agency was *Carl Byoir & Association,* acquired by *Foote, Cone & Belding* in 1978; it was subsequently sold in 1989 to *Hill & Knowlton.* Other major acquisitions included *Burson Marsteller* by *Young & Rubicam* and *Hill & Knowlton* by *J. Walter Thompson.*

Over the last part of the 20th century, public relations emerged as a major and vital discipline in business and industry. Several multi-national and global corporations took it very seriously as a top management function and have also cashed upon its potential in establishing and furthering their interest in the world markets and communities.

Impressed by the role of public relations, governments and bureaucrats worldwide, irrespective of time, place, and culture, have been its votaries. It is very difficult to think of a king, president, or a government official who was not a successful public relations practitioner. So, today, there is not an aspect of human life, whether it is politics, religion, health, or education where public relations does not have a role to play.

The crumbling of mighty Soviet Union, the emergence of Israel, the Oil Cartels, the 9/11 Disaster, and Bush–Blair unity to contain Iraq and emergence of United Europe, are all the areas, where the hopes and aspirations of the people are being constantly addressed by all those involved in the discipline of public relations, where exchange and acceptance of viewpoints is a major question of our modern times.

After the US, the next most widely developed territories for public relations are Canada and the UK followed by countries of Western Europe and Asia. Asia, with its great variety of religions, cultures, and growing businesses has tremendous potential for public relations profession and its practitioners. With its surging population of young people taking to professions and resultant disposable incomes, Asia is a vast market for products and services, marketed both by local as well as global companies. A host of multinational companies setting up operations in Asian countries is a common sight. This market development naturally brings several related challenges and opportunities which public relations profession will have to address.

PUBLIC RELATIONS—CHANGING ROLE

Public relations, today, is an essential management function in government, corporations, and non-profit organizations throughout the world—so much so that it is being termed as one of the most important professions in the world.

Philip Kotler (2000), the marketing guru of the 20th century, wrote, 'Public Relations can account for its growth by its great versatility, its aptitude for drama, and its capacity to break through the information clutter and capture attention and interest.'

He also commented, 'Of the five major communication tools—advertising, personal selling, promotion, direct marketing and public relations—it is the last two that are receiving the most attention and recording the most growth.'

Big Budget Game

In year 2000, public relations was estimated to be $3.4 billion industry in the US and $4.6 billion worldwide, according to the Council of Public Relations firms, based in New York City. Although, there is no comprehensive industry-wide accounting of public relations budgets, yet 2001 *Thomas L. Harris/Impulse Research Public Relations Client Survey*—the largest annual survey in the field—revealed that the average public relations budget of 1500 major US corporations, with average revenue of $3.5 billion, who participated in the survey, was almost $1 million. The same companies, each spent $1.3 million in public relations fees with their public relations consultancy firms.

Professional Metamorphosis

Public relations, as a profession and discipline, is going through a metamorphosis of changing from being a fire-fighting device to a long-term and planned activity in an organization. It is no longer a cosmetic attachment to the organization, but a strategic top management function.

Like in other professions such as marketing, law, or medicine, public relations involves itself with feedback, evaluation, and accountability of its functions and activities. It relates itself to communications, education and understanding amongst employees, the media, opinion leaders, and other target audiences with whom the organization is deeply involved for its corporate success. Public relations is intimately sensitive to the acceptance of corporate ideas by the audiences and their consequent actions.

Public relations practitioners today are far more professional in their education, attitudes, and actions. They are no more a decorative outfit of the organization, but are deeply involved in the process of management. They act as advisers, counsellors, and even the conscious keepers. Being serious-minded visionaries, they are paid well, at par with some of the senior professionals in marketing, manufacturing, and finance, etc. No surprise, that quite a few public relations professionals have carved a position for themselves in the board rooms of several companies.

Media and Public Relations

The days of PR men working as errand boys between the organization and media are over. Public relations then, had one connotation of being someone, who handled press releases to generate free publicity. But the last part of the 20th century has witnessed a media explosion, like never before in human history. The multiplicity of TV channels, the mind boggling number of newspapers, particularly the emergence of financial journalism, the multiplying of glossy specialist magazines, the mobile telephony, and the internet noise, all have made the public relations job more challenging like never before.

Realizing the exigencies of the changed scenario, the corporate world, today, is in dire need of hardcore professionals who understand the intricacies of complex business. Backed with their profound knowledge of the functioning of media and its potential to generate particular kind of public responses, every industry is keen to honourably hire real professionals.

Media is also faced with new kind of challenges. Media, today, suffers from the problem of plenty. Information for them is a saleable commodity which their customers, readers, and viewers, look for, to take some serious business decisions. Today, media has to own what they write or show because a slip here or there, can cause serious damage to some businesses and even their own. Therefore, media looks to the public relations people as serious-minded resource persons, who bring some hardboiled and serious news for transmission. The media–PR relationship has thickened, with equal responsibility on both to keep this interaction dependable, credible, and long lasting.

PR—Marketing the Organization

There is a complete paradigm shift in the profession. Today public relations is no longer just information dissemination, but in innumerable ways, a 'discipline' to market the organization as a strong, healthy, and professionally run organization. In the competitive world today, it has become an utmost necessity to ensure a positive perception or good image in the minds of several publics, upon whose positive response depends the success of an organization.

This very need has lead to the need of a scientific approach to developing a corporate identity in the world, the reflection of which identity actually means image. Over a period of time, the professionals have acquired the necessary skills and techniques to manage the corporate identity, around which revolves the existence and growth of a corporation.

The profession, as such, is faced with the challenge of building relationships with several kinds of publics or target groups, from employees to customers, dealers to shareholders, community to parliamentarians, government to media, so that they all perceive the organization positively and extend the kind of responses the organization expects from them.

PR Support to Marketing

The focus in marketing of products and services is shifting from being 'transactional' to 'relationship' marketing. Whereas the transactional marketing is geared to successful completion of a one-time transaction, the relationship marketing is all about building an ongoing relationship with customers.

In collaboration with the marketing setup of several organizations, public relations plays a vital role in conceptualizing and executing the system of 'Integrated Marketing Communications' (IMC). The concept involves harnessing the power of various tools of marketing communications like public relations, advertising, sales promotion, publicity, direct marketing, and personal selling and canalize them into one single thematic direction. The effort when directed professionally, creates synergy in the market, thus making it possible for the organization to achieve its sales and communication goals.

Community Relations Effort

Today, the business of the business is not only doing the business, but also to make the lives of the people more enjoyable and worth living. This is called the 'social responsibility of business' in management terms. Most of the leading business organizations take keen interest in the neighbouring communities around their plants and offices, not just because the community provides the valuable human resource to the industry, but also that the community's opinions and perception about the organization has a powerful ripple effect amongst various publics.

This social obligation is also being termed as the need of projecting the organization as a good 'corporate citizen', which, not only means abiding by the laws of the land but also participating in community's efforts in improving the quality of life and living standards.

An industry's safeguards against the spread of pollution through discharge of industrial effluence is being seen as one vital part of the community public relations.

Employee Public Relations

Like charity, good public relations also begins from home. Worldwide, the industry has experienced and learnt that satisfied employees are more loyal and productive for the organization; and what ensures that satisfaction and high performance is information shared with the workforce through effective communications. Many modern and professional managements have assigned this responsibility to public relations, in league with personnel or HRD managers.

With the surge of trade unions and their loud mouthed and even militant methods to contest for better rights for the workers, in terms of wages and better working conditions, managements are faced with the necessity to maintain the adversary relationship with the unions. The only lubricant that can oil the creaking wheels of industry is free flow of communications, which is the direct responsibility and area of specialization of public relations practitioners.

With growing industrialization the challenges will get hard to harder, and the public relations professionals in the employee relations will have to rise to the occasion to hone their communication skills, and, perhaps, feel proud in calling themselves as blue-collared PR professionals.

Public Affairs

With the progressive emergence of democratic forms of governments all over the world and also with the maturing of some of the democracies like American, European, Canadian, and Indian, the need for public relations professionals to understand the intricacies of the political and social environment has become essential. No business can survive and function in isolation from the political and social environment.

The situation has brought in its wake several challenges for the public relations persons to deal with the exigencies as they influence the corporate business and thus, provide the expertise to the managements to grapple with various short-term and long-term problems. The function has now acquired the new nomenclature called 'public affairs'.

Lobbying in parliament and the government, and convincingly advocating the corporate view points is the name of the game. This job assignment generally goes to very senior and experienced professionals with a vision, either with aptitude and taste for law or to personnel with legal education and backgrounds.

The professionals play several roles like a watch dog of the industry interests, counsellor to the management and sometimes work as 'Ombudsman' between the organization and its publics.

Terrorism—Violent and Economic

Amongst the leading challenges for the public relations professionals is the burning issue of terrorism and violence. Never before in the history of mankind has such a serious threat been posed to the people and especially those who run governments the world over. The catastrophe of 9/11 terror attack on the twin towers in New York to merciless, brutal insurgence on a Russian school in Chechnya, and 26/11 attack on Mumbai hotels, all call for public concern in general and public relations in particular. Instances like the 1984 anti-Sikh riots in Delhi, storming of Indian parliament, communal violence in Maharashtra, Gujarat, and Orissa, bomb blasts all over the country leave behind a trauma which will take a long time to heal.

Besides the blood spilling and spine chilling violence, some more damaging design of terrorism is being seen perpetrated by some nations. Economic and intellectual terrorism in the garb of WTO, eco-terrorism, racial and religious maligning, language and ethnic based biases converted into ideological warfare coupled with sinister biological and technological designs, are some of the threats to humanity.

Public relations profession has now to move from simple to hi-tech and inventive and the creative ways and means of communication, to educate and transform the public opinion against these issues that threaten the very existence of the human race. Widening professional vision, wisdom, and technological update, is the need of the hour for public relations to rise to the occasion and grapple with evil designs of the vested interests.

Summary

From ancient times to the modern, the discipline of public relations has come a long way to establish itself as a profession. Over the last one century, public relations witnessed several changes and developments that shaped its future.

Several personalities, who recognized the importance of public opinion, advocated the cause of two-way communication with the publics. The First and the Second World War necessitated the setting up of committees and information systems, for mustering support for the war effort.

The American Civil war, the Great Depression, and conflict between people and businesses generated the need for public relations to express and impress the need for co-existence of conflicting groups for progress and growth. The leading corporate houses developed their own public relations departments headed by people with vision and far sight.

The last quarter of the 20th century, with multi-nationalism and globalization of business and the advent of media explosion and computers, have brought about several challenges of greater specialization for the public relations profession.

The sinister developments like terrorism—both violent and economic, poverty, and diseases, have brought about several challenges for the professionals to the rise to the occasion and foster new and rational mind sets amongst publics, for harmony to prevail.

Public relations is now no more a cosmetic attachment to the organizations but an important management function. The fast changing environment and the resultant challenges are an invitation to all the professionals with maturity, vision, and wisdom.

Key Terms

Blog Any kind of diary published on the Internet, usually written by an individual but at times also by corporate bodies

Editorial An article in a newspaper or magazine that expresses the opinion of its editor or publisher on a current issue

Full service agency An advertising agency that provides a comprehensive professional service to its clients

Professional metamorphosis Transformation of profession from traditional to modern

Public affairs Public relations efforts of a firm that are associated with government agencies, mass media, public interest, and pressure groups

Search engine Computer programme that searches databases and Internet sites for documents containing keywords specified by a user

Vox populi, vox dei Greek adage to denote that 'voice of the people is the voice of God'

Concept Review Questions

1. Write a comprehensive note on the history of public relations with special reference to the American scene.
2. Write biographical note on some of the personalities who were responsible for shaping up the development of public relations as practised today. ·
3. Sketch a short chronology of major events in the history of public relations.
4. What are the challenges and opportunities that the profession of public relations faces in the 21st century? List them and discuss in detail.

References

Cutlip, Scott M., Allen H. Center, and Glen M. Broom (1985), *Effective Public Relations*, 6th edition, Prentice-Hall of India Private Limited, New Delhi and Prentice-Hall, Inc., New Jersey USA, p. 23.

Kotler, Philip (2000), *Marketing Management, Millennium Edition*, Prentice-Hall of India Private Limited, New Delhi, p. 550.

Moore, H. Frazier, and Frank B. Kalupa (2005), *Public Relations, Principles, Cases and Problems*, Richard D. Irwin, Inc., USA and printed in India by Surjeet Publications, Delhi, pp. 23–24.

3

Public Relations in India

PUBLIC RELATIONS—A HISTORICAL PERSPECTIVE

'And yet, as a professional one constantly feels the need for reappraisal, analysis, and self-searching. We are still a Cinderella amongst the professions. The image of public relations man is still confused. Even now, the role of PR is nebulous one, in the minds of more men than we dare to admit,' Dr Pramod Vyas, the then president of the Public Relations Society of India, at the 3rd All India Conference in 1972 opined. Fortunately for public relations practitioners in India, the scenario has since changed for better but not that bright.

Unlike the United States of America, where public relations has matured into a highly accepted management discipline, the profession, though grew in India, but at a very slow pace.

In a historical perspective, the presence of public relations is witnessed in Indian walks of life, but in different forms known as *Dharma* or *Vichar* and *Achar*. The *Panchtantra Tales* of ancient times, are full of stories of kings and queens initiating a two-way dialogue with the subjects to ensure peace and harmony in their kingdoms. They invented various ways and means to communicate to the people and also gather feedback about their reactions and responses to various state policies and programmes. The kings, courtiers, and their spies kept their eyes and ears open to the public opinion. They really cared much about it and would rarely go against the public opinion. Not too much concerned about the morality of the issue, Lord Rama's banishing his wife Sita to forests on the maligning comment by a menial washerman, is one glaring example of the issue. The Indian history is fraught with similar instances.

However, the history of public relations discipline in India can be traced to two phases, one pre-independence era and the other post independence era (See Exhibit 3.1).

EXHIBIT 3.1   The history of public relations discipline in India

PRE-INDEPENDENCE PERIOD

1776 William Bolt announced the **publication of a newspaper** for keeping Englishmen informed about happenings in England.

1780 James Augustus Hicky started **Bengal Gazette,** also called *Hicky's Gazette*—advocated freedom of expression.

1781 Six newspapers started from Bengal by Englishmen including **Madras Courier** and **Bombay Herald** (*Madras Courier* later merged with *Bombay Herald*).

1799 Government issued **Press Regulations**—rules making it necessary to publish the names of the editor, printer, and publishers.

1800 Serampore missionaries published **Samachar Darpan** and **Miratool Akhbaar** to propagate social reforms.

1822 **Bombay Samachar,** a Gujarati newspaper started about business and politics.

1830 **Mombai Vartaman**, a vernacular paper started publication.

1831 **Jan-e-Jamshed,** a vernacular paper started.

1839 **Bengali press** published nine newspapers with circulation of 200 copies each. British themselves had 26 newpapers (six of them dailies).

1850 **Bombay Darpan** began publication.

1857 British 'Crown' took over India from East India

Company and imposed the **Gagging Act** to restrict press freedom.

1876 Gujarati press of Bombay excelled in defence of Indian way of life.
Vernacular Press Act promulgated.

1885 The inaugural meeting of the **Indian National Congress** held in Bombay and ignored by British run press, but *Kesari* founded by Lokmanya Tilak gave wide coverage.

1892 In two decades appeared **famous newspapers** like *The Times of India*, the *Pioneer*, the *Madras Mail*, and the *Amrita Bazar Patrika*.

1900 'Indian Review' started by G.A. Natesan

1909 With the progress of literacy in the ranks, '**Fauji Akhbaar',** a weekly journal containing news and views on military matters started by the Indian Army to reach out to its personnel (See Exhibit 3.2). The journal was initially published in Urdu from Allahabad although its office functioned from Simla. It was also an attempt to insulate the Army from the political movement gathering momentum in the country.

1910 **Indian Press Act** promulgated and champions of freedom of press like Aurobindo Ghosh of *Bande Mataram*, B.B. Upadhayaya of *Sandhya*, and B.N. Dutt of *Jugantar* prosecuted.

1911–14 The British government banned 50 works in English, 114 in Marathi, 52 in Urdu, and 51 in Bengali.

1911 Delhi Durbar—India's capital transferred from Culcutta to Delhi (Public information floated about new capital).

1913 'Bombay Chronicle' Bombay established. (Mouth piece of freedom struggle).

1911–12 Philanthropic Age and Community Relations. The house of TATAs endowment to provide higher education abroad for Indian graduates of merit and construction of model industrial township. The policy found its most striking expression with the establishment of the TATA Iron and Steel Company which went into production in 1912.

1914–18 The First World War Publicity Boards were set up for war related publicity and to maintain relations with the press.

1915 Mahatma Gandhi returns to India from South Africa.

1918 The Central Publicity Bureau established at Simla. Indian Press delegation visits theatres of war.

1919 The Central Bureau of Information established (presently, Press Information Bureau). Headed by B.G. Horniman, editor, *Bombay Chronicle* later deported to England.

The **Swaraj Party** let by C.R. Das, Vallabhbhai Patel, and Motilal Nehru, launched its own publications, the *Banglar Katha* in Calcutta, the *Swadesh Mithram* in the South and *Hindustan Times, Pratap,* and *Basumati* in the North.

1923 The English edition of **Fauji Akhbaar** made its appearance.

1930 The Railways Commercial Publicity Bureau started. The GIP railways carried on a publicity campaign in England utilizing the mass media to attract tourists to India. The Publicity Bureau of the Railways also introduced a travelling cinema within India.

1935 The Government of India Act passed. Mahatma Gandhi launches Civil Disobedience Movement. Indian Press Ordinance promulgated.

1936 Bureau of Public Information (Government of India) established. The word 'Public' has significance. Central Bureau of Public Information with Principal Information Officer as the head.

1939–45 The Second World War.

1939 Creation of a **Directorate of Information and Broadcasting** (Government of India). Bureau of Public Information and All India Radio were placed under the Directorate.

1940 Public Relations Directorate, India Command, came into being with the appointment of Brigadier I.S. Jehu as the director. The creation of the post marked a sort of revolution in defence services which had been a closed book to the public in India. The objective was to build a bridge between the armed forces, the Indian media, and the public.

1941 Full fledged **Department of Information and Broadcasting** (Government of India) created. The Viceroy's Executive Council was expanded with the addition of an Information Member, and a Department of Information and Broadcasting created with a Secretary as overall incharge. It extended its activities to the National War Front, *Counter Propaganda Directorate–Advertising Consultant, the war purpose Exhibition and Films Division.*

Creation of Directorate of Inter-Service Public Relations for Defence publicity.

Appointment of a PRO to the Agent General for India in Washington (promotion of trade). The concept of public relations recognized.

1942 Quit India Movement Strengthening of communication system by Mahatma Gandhi for mass enlightenment against British.

Simultaneous efforts by the government information machinery to contain freedom movement and promote the efforts.

1942 Directorate of Public Relations was transferred from the Defence Department or War Department as it had become a part of Government headquarters. DPR was made directly responsible for publicity to troops and for military press censorship, uptill then carried out by the Director of Military Intelligence. It was now called Inter Services Public Relations Directorate and became a joint medium of publicity for all the three services—army, air force, and navy.

1945 End of Second World War Continuance of official publicity machinery even after the end of World War II. From war information to 'public welfare' information.

The strength of the Inter-Services PR Directorate was progressively reduced on the termination of the war, when its overseas commitments came to an end. Only a skeleton staff was left at the time of partition of the Indian subcontinent in 1947.

The end of World War II witnessed a little indefiniteness and uncertainty for the Defence Public Relations Directorate as its mandate pertained to the war. Doubts were dispelled soon and the directorate was called upon to publicize the efforts of the armed forces in the evacuation of the refugees from Pakistan. Later it had to carry out its responsibilities during the 1947–48 Kashmir and Hyderabad operations.

House of TATAs Public Relations Division The house of TATAs established a public relations division at their Bombay office, the first PR Division in private sector.

1946 Interim Government with Jawaharlal Nehru as Prime Minister called for generation of publicity.

POST INDEPENDENCE PERIOD

1947 **Independent India—The Age of Public Relations** Creation of Ministry of Information and Broadcasting, Government of India with Sardar Vallabhbhai Patel, Deputy Prime Minister as minister incharge.

A sustained attempt was made to inform and educate the public and to create better relations for the government and other organizations.

The union government established new media units and expanded the existing one.

After 15 August 1947, with the appointment of separate chiefs for the three services, the Public Relations Directorate was placed directly under the Ministry of Defence. In September 1947, it was decided that the Ministry of Information and Broadcasting which was responsible for all government publicity, should also be responsible for publicity regarding the defence services to project a holistic and coherent view of the government. Accordingly, the post of Joint Principal Information Officer was created by the I & B Ministry. The First AFIO assumed charge on 15 November 1947.

1948 **Lok Sampark** First book in Hindi on Public relations authored by Mr Rajindra, M.A., the then Director of Public Relations, Punjab.

1950 **New Constitution of India** comes into force (Fundamental Rights) with government reaching out to the people with new democracy.

1951–56 **First Five Year Plan** Plan publicity campaigns undertaken.

1953 Fauji Akhbaar rechristened **Sainik Samachar.**

1956 **Nationalization of General Insurance Companies** (Public Sector PR).

1958 **Public Relations Society of India (PRSI)** founded as a national body for promotion of public relations profession.

1960 **Growth of Public Sector Public Relations** and multi-national public relations. Public relations efforts started in the Indian business houses.

1962 **Chinese Invasion of India** Defence publicity undertaken to gather public support in the aftermath of setback.

1965 First Indo-Pak war. Launch of the **Jai Jawan, Jai Kisan** by Prime Minister Lal Bahadur Shastri. The Armed Forces Information Office was re-designated as Directorate of Public Relations, Ministry of Defence.

1966 **Public Relations Society of India** registered under the Indian Societies Act XXVI of 1961 with headquarters in Bombay and Mr Kali H. Mody as founder president.

1968 **First All India Public Relations Conference in New Delhi** Theme was 'Professional Approach'.

1969 **Banks Nationalization** Public sector public relations gains momentum

1970s Public relations active in private sector due to Licence Raj. **Public sector public relations platform** under 'SCOPE'.

1975 **Internal Emergency proclaimed** Publicity through government media stepped up to justify the actions. Media revolted in so many ways against strangulation of freedom of the press.

1975 First nuclear test conducted by India, campaign to justify the test launched.

1980 **Proliferation of Economic Media**, financial public relations emerges.

1982 **World Public Relations Congress in Mumbai**, with the theme 'The Inter-dependent World'.

Second Indian Press Commission Report released.

1987 **April 21** First National Public Relations Day observed.

1989 Appointment of **First UGC National Professor in Public Relations**.

1991 **New Industrial Policy: Emergence of Public Relations agencies;** affiliation with international PR firms. Expansion of PR both in Indian and foreign companies to meet competitive environment.

1992 **Launching of the Bachelor of Public Relations Degree** in Dr B.R. Ambedkar Open University, Hyderabad.

1993 **The first UGC National Seminar on Public Relations Education and Training** in India at Osmania University.

1997 **Launching of** *Public Relations Voice* the first professional journal in Hyderabad.

1998 **The first Asia Pacific PR Meet and 20ᵗʰ All India PR Conference** in Kolkata, theme: 'The Brave New World of Public Relations'.

2000 **Heralding the millennium** celebrated world over and India. Arrival of the Millennium child to highlight India's exploding population.

Indian Airlines plane hi-jacked to Kandahar. India tries to solve the crisis through information and public relations route. Success controversial.

2001   India's **second nuclear test** conducted. World anguished. India launches an information campaign to justify and assure that energy to be used for peaceful purposes.

Kargil war and the post publicity to garner public support.

Terrorist attack on Parliament of India and the aftermath public relations efforts to generate global public support.

2002   **Tehelka** sting operations against corruption in politics and defence deals. Parties and the government's efforts to sober the efforts and maintain image.

BJP India Shining Campaign punctured in the general elections.

2007   The Directorate of Public Relations, Ministry of Defence, mounted the biggest PR effort in its history, possibly second only to the one during World War II, to provide the best ever publicity to the **Military World Games,** the fourth edition of which was held in Hyderabad and Mumbai. The occasion also marked the **transition of the Photo Division from analogue to digital format.** Over 750 media persons from home and abroad covered the event.

2008   **Indo-American nuclear deal controversy** and the information efforts by parties for and against the deal.

India launches 'Chandrayan' – an unmanned mission to the moon to boost national image.

Terrorist attack of 26 November on Mumbai hotels threw new challanges to the PR profession to maintain public morale.

PRE-INDEPENDENCE ERA

Though a tradition is evident that Indian businessmen have been large heartedly contributing to public welfare in terms of setting up night halt *sarais* for travellers and building temples, etc., the 'philanthropic' activity of industrial houses can be said to have started in right earnest in 1892 when the House of Tatas founded the J.N. Tata endowment to provide higher education abroad for outstanding Indian graduates. The public welfare policy found its most striking expression when the Tata Iron and Steel Company Limited went into production (1911–12). The founders of TISCO, with their far sight and humanitarian bent of mind, planned community relations in India, which reflected in their building Sakchi (known as Jamshedpur or Tatanagar) as India's first model industrial township, to provide an all round way of life to the employees, on the lines done by many such industrial enterprises in the developed world.

One of the earliest examples of public relations in India, dictated by commercial needs, is provided by the Indian Railways. In their effort to promote passenger traffic, the (GIP) railways, for example, carried on a publicity and public relations campaign in England, utilizing the mass media and pamphlets to attract tourists to India. Inside the country, the publicity bureau of this railway introduced a travelling cinema which held open-air shows of films at fairs, festivals and other places. Subsequently, these PR measures were also adopted by other railways. The Railway Board set up publicity bureaus in London and New York, which undertook extensive advertising in newspapers and journals. These bureaus also participated in exhibitions abroad to popularize the Indian Railways and promote tourist traffic.

EXHIBIT 3.2   Fauji Akhbaar—The Army Newspaper

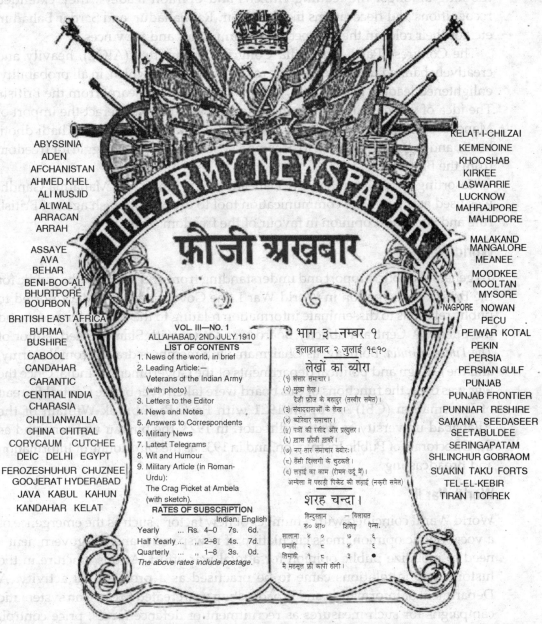

THE ARMY NEWSPAPER

फ़ौजी अख़बार

ABYSSINIA
ADEN
AFCHANISTAN
AHMED KHEL
ALI MUSJID
ALIWAL
ARRACAN
ARRAH

ASSAYE
AVA
BEHAR
BENI-BOO-ALI
BHURTPORE
BOURBON
BRITISH EAST AFRICA
BURMA
BUSHIRE
CABOOL
CANDAHAR
CARANTIC
CENTRAL INDIA
CHARASIA
CHILLIANWALLA
CHINA CHITRAL
CORYCAUM CUTCHEE
DEIC DELHI EGYPT
FEROZESHUHUR CHUZNEE
GOOJERAT HYDERABAD
JAVA KABUL KAHUN
KANDAHAR KELAT

KELAT-I-CHILZAI
KEMENOINE
KHOOSHAB
KIRKEE
LASWARRIE
LUCKNOW
MAHRAJPORE
MAHIDPORE

MALAKAND
MANGALORE
MEANEE
MOODKEE
MOOLTAN
MYSORE
NAGPORE NOWAN
PECU
PEIWAR KOTAL
PEKIN
PERSIA
PERSIAN GULF
PUNJAB
PUNJAB FRONTIER
PUNNIAR RESHIRE
SAMANA SEEDASEER
SEETABULDEE
SERINGAPATAM
SHLINCHUR GOBRAOM
SUAKIN TAKU FORTS
TEL-EL-KEBIR
TIRAN TOFREK

VOL. III—NO. 1
ALLAHABAD, 2ND JULY 1910
LIST OF CONTENTS
1. News of the world, in brief
2. Leading Article:—
   Veterans of the Indian Army
   (with photo)
3. Letters to the Editor
4. News and Notes
5. Answers to Correspondents
6. Military News
7. Latest Telegrams
8. Wit and Humour
9. Military Article (in Roman-
   Urdu):
   The Crag Picket at Ambela
   (with sketch).
RATES OF SUBSCRIPTION
                         Indian. English
Yearly   ... Rs. 4–0   7s.   6d.
Half Yearly ... „ 2–8   4s.   7d.
Quarterly   ... „ 1–8   3s.   0d.
The above rates include postage.

भाग ३—नम्बर १
इलाहाबाद २ जुलाई १९१०
लेखों का ब्यौरा
(१) संसार समाचार।
(२) मुख्य लेख।
   देशी फ़ौज के बहादुर (तस्वीर समेत)।
(३) संवाददाताओं के लेख।
(४) ब्योरवार समाचार।
(५) पत्रों की रसीद और प्रत्युत्तर।
(६) ख़ास फ़ौजी ख़बरें।
(७) नए तार समाचार ब्यौरा।
(८) हँसी दिल्लगी के चुटकले।
(९) लड़ाई का काम (रोमन उर्दू में)।
   अम्बेला में पहाड़ी पिकेट की लड़ाई (नक़री समेत)

शरह चन्दा।

हिन्दुस्तान		विलायत	
रु० आ०		शिलिंग पेन्स०	
सालाना	४ ०	७	६
छमाही	२ ८	४	६
तिमाही	१ ८	३	•

मैं महसूल फ़्री कापी होगी।

Printed and published at the Pioneer Press, Allahabad. Sold also at Messrs. Wheeler & Co.'s Railway Bookstalls, and at the Pioneer

The British government used public relations techniques for the acceptance and furtherance of British rule in India. To garner support and foster loyalty to the king amongst the leading citizens and opinion leaders, they extended recognitions and decorations like Lord, Sir, Rai Bahadur, and Sardar Bahadur, etc. for their roles in their respective communities and provinces.

The Congress Party, All India Congress Committee (AICC), heavily and creatively banked upon their public relations prowess, which, in all probability, enlightened leaders like Gandhi, Nehru, and Patel, had learnt from the British. The idea of wheel spinning was used to symbolically counteract the import of Manchester made cloth to India. The adoption of dress code like Khadi dhoti, kurta, and topi, was adopted to become a symbol of India's struggle for freedom from the British rule.

Resorting to fasting in jail by Shaheed Bhagat Singh and Mahatma Gandhi was used as a powerful communication tool to express anguish against British rule and stir world opinion in favour of the freedom struggle.

World War I

To generate public support and understanding from and amongst the public for the British participation in World War I, the Government of India resorted to public relations to disseminate information relating to the war, to the press, and the public. A Central Publicity Board was set up with Stanley Reed, editor of *The Times of India*, Bombay, as Chairman, with members drawn from the army, and the foreign and political departments of the Government of India. Once the war was over, the functions of this board were taken over by the Central Bureau of Information (CBI) set up in 1921 with Prof. Rushbrook William of the Allahabad university as its first director. In 1923, the bureau was renamed as the Directorate of Public Instruction, and in 1931 as the Directorate of Information and Broadcasting.

World War II

World War II coincided with a number of new factors, such as the emergence of a vocal public opinion, mass circulation of newspapers, and the government's need to mobilize public opinion for a total war effort. At this juncture in the history, public relations came to be practised as a professional activity. A Department of Information and Broadcasting was created to carry on systematic campaigns for such measures as recruitment of defence forces, price control, and rationing of food grains. The department comprised a number of units, such as the war purposes exhibition unit, the films division, and the central bureau of public information.

Commercial Interest

Simultaneously, certain commercial organizations, which had already been practising in an unconscious manner, began organizing their PR activity in a conscious way. The house of Tata formed a public relations division at its head office in Bombay in 1945. Subsequently, several other organizations, during this period, carried out public relations programmes in the form of institutional advertising campaigns in the press to win public understanding for their business ventures.

POST INDEPENDENCE ERA

The Independence of India in 1947, the partition of India, the formation of Pakistan, and the migration of millions of people in Punjab and Bengal brought in a completely new environment and the consequent challenges. The resettlement of migrants and the restoration of confidence in the riot-torn country was a major challenge. India adopted a socialistic democratic pattern of government and the new political institutions like the Parliament and the State Legislatures, were elected for the first time, on the basis of adult franchise. Measures like the Industrial Policy Resolution and the Industrial Development Regulations Act were brought into action. This necessitated for both government and the business organizations to adopt a conscious and deliberate policy of public relations. Thus the PR profession took roots in India in the right perspective.

Some of the multi-national companies, drawing upon their own expertise in public relations, began to make use of these techniques to survive and grow in independent India. In the 50s and early 60s, companies such as Burma-Shell, Dunlop India, Goodyear, Hindustan Lever, Indian Oxygen, Esso, Caltex, IBM, Union Carbide, Philips, and ITC set up departments to execute programmes of public relations in a systematic manner. Indian companies also began to set up their own public relations units to carry on organized public relations activity.

EMERGENCE OF PROFESSIONALISM

A national association of public relations practitioners was established in 1958 to promote the recognition of public relations as a profession and to formulate and interpret to the public the objectives and potentialities of public relations as a strategic management function.

The society functioned as an informal body till 1966 and was registered under the Indian Societies Act XXVI of 1961, with headquarters in Mumbai (then Bombay). The father figure of professional public relations practitioners in India,

Mr Kali H. Mody, was the founder President of Public Relations Society of India (PRSI) from 1966 to 1969.

April 21 is a red letter day in the history of Indian public relations. It is because the *National PR Day* is celebrated on this day all over the country since 1968 as the 1st All India Conference was organized in Delhi on 21 April 1968. It was at this very conference that a code of ethics was adopted and the parameters of the profession were defined.

PRSI, who have chapters and members in almost all the states of India, have so far organized 30 All India Public Relations Conferences on a variety of themes and issues concerning the profession (See Exhibit 3.3).

EXHIBIT 3.3   All India Public Relations Conferences

No.	Venue	Year	Theme
1st	New Delhi	1968	PR: A professional approach
2nd	Madras	1970	Role of PR in management
3rd	Calcutta	1972	PR and changing social environment
4th	Bombay	1974	Towards more responsible citizenship
5th	New Delhi	1976	Towards greater professionalism
6th	Cochin	1978	Public relations in the eighties
7th	Calcutta	1980	New dimensions in public relations
8th	Bombay	1982	The interdependent world (merged with 9th PR World Congress)
9th	Bangalore	1984	Dynamics of developmental communication: PR perspectives
10th	New Delhi	1986	Changing Indian scene: PR challenges
11th	Hyderabad	1988	One country: One people
12th	Calcutta	1989	Public relations: The state-of-the-art
13th	Bangalore	1990	Change: A challenge for future
14th	Cochin	1991	IT: A challenge to communicators
15th	New Delhi	1992	India in the new world order
16th	Madras	1993	Ushering in a new era: PR issues
17th	Bombay	1994	Wings of change: PR challenges
18th	Jaipur	1995	PR: The decade ahead
19th	Ooty	1997	Image management: A password for the 21st century
20th	Calcutta	1998	The brave new world of PR (Calvision'98) (1st Asia/Pacific PR meet)
21st	Chandigarh	1999	Image India public relations strategy
22nd	Hyderabad	2000	PR challenges: 2000 and beyond
23rd	New Delhi	2001	Exploring opportunities
24th	Guwahati	2002	Transcending new frontiers
25th	Bangalore	2003	Communication for global peace
26th	Kolkata	2004	Re-inventing PR roadmap to success
27th	New Delhi	2005	Quest for leadership role in public relations
28th	Lucknow	2006	Governance with human face—Emerging trends and role of PR
29th	Chennai	2007	PR and infrastructure development in India
30th	Guwahati	2008	PR in nation building

OPENING OF INDIAN ECONOMY

The recognition of the evolution in India's economic and political scenario is extremely relevant to understanding the way in which public relations profession has changed in India. In the sellers market, with limited products and consumer choices, there was a limited need for information.

But with the free market economy, competition in the market, and wider consumer choices, public relations is faced with the challenge to rise to the occasion in the area of information management. The advent of Maruti car revolution is one such example. India, a country, where at one point of time a car and a telephone connection would be available after a long wait, can now be purchased by a customer almost instantaneously. To add to the revolution, Tata has now announced the 'one lakh Nano' car soon to be visible on the urban and rural roads of India (See Case Study).

LIBERALIZATION AND CORPORATE INTEREST

The economic liberalization after 1991 has brought myriad choices for the consumer, with increase in the forces of competition within the Indian industry. The corporate sector realized that they were no longer interacting, only with the press, but also with an extended public consisting of customers, shareholders, suppliers, dealers, banks, financial institutions, overseas buyers, employees, local authorities, and the members of the community. For a strategic and focused communication with these varied publics, companies began to rely heavily on public relations.

Thus, so far the corporate houses, which had long remained untouched by competition, realized that the perception of people about their business had suddenly become crucial. This opened new opportunity for PR profession. Several companies opened PR departments and even contracted PR consultancies.

Significantly enough, the 26th Conference of the PRSI, deliberated hard to draw up an agenda for the public relations profession to steer the profession into greater involvment in the corporate activities and professional excellence. It also laid lot of emphasis on education and the need to get connected with the international community of public relations professionals. The adoption of a ten point programme was a step in this very direction (See Exhibit 3.4).

TOWARDS PROFESSIONAL RECOGNITION

To continue to promote and encourage excellence and healthy competition amongst the professionals, PRSI at the 29th Conference at Chennai also announced

---

EXHIBIT 3.4   Ten point public relations roadmap

1. Recognition of public relations education as an independent academic discipline.
2. Promotion and induction of in-service PR training by the Indian Institute of Mass Communication (IIMC), New Delhi, Public Relations Society of India and state governments as continuing professional development programme.
3. Research and evaluation as an integral part of the public relations practice and teaching.
4. Adoption of e-public relations with new media tactics for speedy communications.
5. Media strategy in combination with interpersonal, traditional media, mass media and IT new media and in tune with the Indian environment.
6. New deal for rural India: A strategy for grass root public relations.
7. Making public relations a multi-disciplinary function to support human relations, finance, and marketing as integrated public relations communication management approach.
8. Indian public relations to be made internationally competitive in liaison with global alliance for public relations and communication management.
9. Making public relations indispensable to CEO.
10. Elevation of public relations to the top management level with access to board room.

Adopted at 26th All India Public Relation Conference 2004.

---

that the outstanding exhibition of talent and creativity would be recognized. It invited public relations practitioners across the country to present their best works in bringing out house journals, bulletins, brochures, annual reports, and corporate films, to compete in the public relations national awards. Corporates, public relations agencies, public relations consultancies, and advertising agencies were entitled to compete for the efforts made by them during April 2006 to March 2007.

The categories of works considered for competition are given in Exhibit 3.5.

EXHIBIT 3.5   Public relations excellence awards

Award	Eligible participant
• House Journal (English)	Editor
• House Journal (Hindi)	Editor
• Bulletin (English)	Editor
• Bulletin (Hindi)	Editor
• Mass Awareness Campaign	Organization
• E-newsletter	Editor
• Corporate Website	Website manager
• Corporate Film (Hindi)	Producer
• Public Relations in Action	PR consultants and agencies
• Event Management	Event manager and agencies

MEDIA SCENE

Unlike the West, in India, all media—print, radio, television, cinema, and Internet have been growing simultaneously and are expected to grow in the foreseeable future.

The approach paper in the Eleventh Five Year Plan that started on 1 April 2007 pointed out that 'one of the sectors which has consistently outperformed' the rate of growth of gross domestic product in India, is the 'entertainment and media services sector'.

TV Comes to the Scene

The television boom changed the mass media scenario drastically with the people's access to information. Information was no longer limited to only the rich and the educated. The common man began to see the elite lifestyles of the advanced and affluent world. People's hopes and aspirations experienced an awakening and strong desire to translate pictures into reality. The turbulent changes in the governments in each election in the last two decades, brought in by people through their ballot power, are significant. The increasing expectations and demands now being made by well-informed people through mass media, are getting due attention by government agencies for corrective actions. Public relations definitely has a role of its own, when it uses mass media as its tool of communication.

India is the only country in the world with over three dozen 24-hour television channels that broadcast a variety of entertainment content, debates, quiz events, news, and views on current affairs taking places in the country. The quality of such telecast is often a debatable point. To keep the channels going on 24 × 7 basis with an eye on advertising revenue, the channels have often been blamed for sensationalizing the trivialities. A TV channels' top priority is now to clock better TRP ratings for the sake of higher advertising earnings, rather than the viewer's interest.

The Internet Revolution

The revolutionary breakthrough brought about the worldover by Internet seems to have knocked down the territorial walls between various countries and have integrated the world into one world popularly called 'Global Village'. Naturally, India could not have remained untouched by this communication explosion. The Internet coverage, though slow, has steadily covered a large chunk of Indian population and the number of 'net surfers' is ever on the increase.

Whereas access to information of all kinds—social, cultural, political, economic etc. has come easy, it has opened new vistas for the public relations profession. For instance, the social, corporate, and commercial information logged on to the websites in the form of advertising has reported encouraging results.

According to a 2008 PricewaterhouseCooper's report, web advertising in India should have been to the tune of Rs 4.5 billion by the end of 2008. It has grown 69 per cent in 2007, 60 per cent in 2006, and 69 per cent in 2005. Total average growth for Internet advertising is 65 per cent against 19 per cent for the entire entertainment and media industry. Globally, the total advertising revenues for the Internet are pegged at $44 billion.

Even if this creates nervousness in other media, there is no real cause for worry yet. Volumes of online advertisement remain very low. Notably, the websites for print media, which are now looked at as mere extensions of newspapers, are already becoming a point of key interaction between web users and the mainstream media world over and India is not far behind. Even though Internet companies are borderless, thanks to their reach, they may have to resort to localization of content in each country or region. This should change soon if Indian websites are to keep pace with the global growth trend (*The Times of India*, 22 April 2008).

Rural Public Relations: A Challenge

The fact remains that 70 per cent of India's population lives in villages with a mindset of their own. Linking the rural and the urban is a challenge for those connected with rural uplift and the overall economic prosperity.

India's six lakh villages compared to 3000 cities and towns, represents a picture of rural and urban imbalance. Also the major metros are the epicentre of all media activities, though perhaps lot of news would also emanate from the rural sector. As almost all the corporates have their headquarters in major metros of India, the focus naturally is on the urban sector. Experts think that each village serves as a mini-democracy from where the public opinions originate and travel to the top. Concerned as a profession with public opinion, public relations can hardly afford to ignore the rural sector.

Realizing the importance of Prime Minister Dr Manmohan Singh's announcement of a 'New Deal for Rural India', and the surge of rural markets, corporates like TATAs, Birlas, ITC, etc. are venturing into rural businesses like never before. The introduction of e-chaupal network by ITC has roughly covered about 30,000 villages in the past half decade. The loan waiver of Rs 70,000 crore for the farmers in the 2007–08 union budget loudly announces the future hot spot of Indian economy.

With Internet stations established by ITC right in their village, farmers are now logging on to Indian language websites to get local weather forecasts, modern farming practices, and even to know more remunerative prices for their crops, etc. This makes the institution like a *gram panchayat*, to serve an important forum for Indian public relations to communicate more effectively to the rural public.

The Mass Media

Like in the developed world, the mass media in India today virtually influences the society and intrudes into the lives of almost every citizen. Mass media is playing an increasingly important role in shaping not only the way people dress and speak but also the way they think and act. In other words, it is an important factor in moulding public opinions and shaping the life styles of the publics.

The qualitative changes in the field of journalism during the past two decades have brought in new challenges for the PR professionals. Also since the media men are no longer satisfied with one sided stories or the handout variety of journalism, they are making more demands on the public relations practitioners. The growth of pink press and the demand for economic and commercial news, has brought this need to the fore front. A public relations professional is now expected to be a resource person, who should collect and distribute in-depth, true, and comprehensive information and make it available to the media, when the demands are put before him. No surprise, a major portion of an economic newspaper is, as if, written, by public relations people.

Also due to fast changing market scenario and high media exposures, the consumers are a lot better informed and react faster to any adverse news about a company's management or its products. Hence, an organization functioning in competitive environment needs the support of public relations to counter any adverse publicity, and even neutralize the damaging impact of any competitive campaign which are out to destroy the organization. The Cola wars in India during the last decade is a case in focus.

Addressing the 26th All India Public Relations Conference in 2007, Mr N. Ram, Editor-in-Chief of the *Hindu*, Chennai, had said that 'the media scene in India is better than that in the US and UK … The daily press reached some 18 crore Indians and the TV some 40 crore viewers, radio 45 crore listeners, the internet 70 lakh people.' According to him, the media has to perform the following five-fold functions:

1. Providing credible information
2. Doing critical investigation
3. Educating the public
4. Agenda setting
5. Propaganda function dictated by commercial values.

Surge of Film Industry

The onslaught of the new media of entertainment like audio and video once almost threatened the existence of an old trusted friend of the audiences—the cinema. The memorable serpentine queues at the box office for Raj Kapoor films, who made epoch making hits on the silver screens, was, as if, going to fade out. But the film industry came alive like a phoenix out of extinction.

Thanks to the recognition of film production as an industry and the resultant benefits, Bollywood has boomed to a whopping Rs 5600 crore industry with almost four billion tickets sold every year. Once a legendary film like *Satyam Shivam Sundram* was made by Raj Kapoor for a mere Rs 85,000, which is perhaps less than what the producers spend on a song today.

Bollywood has never been bigger and more focused. More than Rs 3000 crore in public and private money is being spent over a year on a variety of films. The new concept of multiplexes has helped to multiply the screens and the producers are talking in terms of a 2000-screen releases (The number of screens to serve as a measure of success for a film). As such the records are being broken. Thanks to the hundreds of nameless public relations professionals who have contributed their professional skills in planning, promotion, and communicating all about Bollywood to the target publics.

Needless to say, cinema has come to stay as a tool not only for mere entertainment but as a powerful medium of social change, commercial promotions, and an agent of change in public parlance (*India Today*, 14 April 2008).

CRISIS MANAGEMENT NEEDS

A free market economy like the one adopted by India, is fraught with complexities. Constant changes like social, cultural, financial, or in government policies, tend to create crisis situations, big and small, which call for a professional crisis management effort. When a crisis threatens the very survival of a corporation, a public relations exercise may become indispensable. For instance, the largest private sector steel company TATA undertook an extensive public relations exercise to avoid being nationalized. Similarly, Union Carbide, after the Bhopal gas tragedy, sought help and guidance from top notch public relations professionals. Escorts, when threatened by a hostile take over by Lord Swaraj Paul, resorted to a well integrated public relation programme to save itself. Umpteen number of industrial unrest cases, at local and national level, resort to public relations to get public support for the issues through public relations crisis management strategies.

PR AGENCIES—GROWTH AND CHALLENGES

With a view to match up with the growing needs of the corporate sector, both private and public, several advertising agencies have opened up their public relations arms, either to take care of their existing advertising clients or to rope in new ones.

Several seasoned advertising professionals have diversified into public relations and quite a few have started their own breakaway agencies or consultancies, which is a very healthy trend for the growth of public relations profession.

Several multi-national companies with global operations have now arrived in India. They have started making demands on the local agencies to be compatible with their worldwide operations. To rise to the occasion and cash on the business opportunities, quite a few Indian PR agencies have sought intellectual and financial tie ups with some of the well known international agencies.

For instance, IPAN, a division of J. Walter Thompson (India) has tied up with Hill & Knowlton. Famous Burston Marsteller has an Indian partner, an ex-advertising professional, who runs his public relations consultancy. There are a number of other smaller outfits that have collaborated with some well known European and American public relations firms.

The PR agency business has come of age. The agencies (See Exhibit 3.6) have attained professional maturity to meet the challenges, the major one being to establish their credibility with clients. Many agencies, accordingly, have refurbished their shops by acquiring or hiring the necessary talents from areas like advertising, direct marketing, research, and media relations management. To cope up with the hyper activity in the financial markets and client needs, the agencies have retained in their wings the professionals like chartered accountants, financial experts and even some economic writers.

The continual turbulence in the stock market and several companies clamouring to attract public funds, the public relations agencies are in demand to provide the necessary expertise to such enterprises to create a hype in the financial market. Despite volatile markets and active 'bulls and bears' the promoters' and investors' interest has a booming effect on the growth of advertising industry. So when the 'sensex' becomes the pulse of the nation's

---

EXHIBIT 3.6   Some leading PR agencies and clients

Agency	Leading clients
20:20 Media	Abode, Canon, Google, Capgermini, Oracle
Adfactors	ABN-AMBRO, Alembic, Barclays, DLF, IL&FS Inv.
Integral PR	Audi, Coca Cola, Wockhardt, Bicardi, Emirates
IPAN	Berger Paints, Castrol, Hitachi, Ford, Nokia
Lexicon	Air Canada, BMW, Cadbury, Goodyear, Kodak
Positive Communications	Maruti, Grasim, ICI Paints, Mitsubishi, Blackberrys
Sampark	ITC, American Express, Exide, Airtel, Bajaj
The Practice	Lakshmi Machines, Infocom, Radio City, ING Vysya
Core PR	HFCL, Infotel, Swaraj Mazda, Ranbaxy, Glaxo
Mudra	Reliance

economy, it has also become the heartthrob of public relations agencies. As India surges on the path of economic growth, the future holds a promise for the professional agencies.

Public Relations—a Top Management Function

More often than not, and rightly so, public relations is defined as the top management function. Needless to say that all activities of the organization which directly or indirectly affect its image and public perception are the top priority of any chairman and managing director. The public relations professional, who logically should report directly to CMD, as the practitioner then is in a vantage position to coordinate such functions and activities. In fact, more of the public relations professionals in United States of America report to the top man and even are members of the board. It should also make sense in India in the context of the changing business scenario.

Unfortunately, public relations is considered and practised, at top management level only by some professionally managed multinationals now doing business in India, who have brought along the legacy of the seriousness attached to this sensitive profession. The fact remains that several Indian practitioners do not occupy or enjoy the coveted position in the management hierarchy. But the credit goes to some dedicated and competent men and women, who started their public relations career at very low levels, and have made long strides to some very senior positions in some of the Indian organizations.

PUBLIC RELATIONS EDUCATION IN INDIA

'One of the prerequisites of any profession that wishes to be taken seriously, is the existence of recognized body of knowledge and the professional standards that bind its members and governs their conduct' was a comment by a panel of speakers on the subject of PR education at the 29th Public Relations Conference in Kolkata.

Thanks to the spread of PR education by some public relations and other media training schools (See Exhibit 3.7), it is roughly estimated that India's public relations agencies employ more than 2000 PR professionals at the middle level management every year. At the same time there should be a couple of lakh of men and women, who have gone through education and picked up jobs in the corporate sector.

Emphasizing the importance of education, the panel chaired by Subir Ghosh, the former national president of PRSI, noted some pertinent points, which are as follows:

- Education gave us a sense of personality in society, thus its importance.

EXHIBIT 3.7   A few renowned public relations institutes of India

1. Amity School of Communication, Noida, UP
2. Apeejay Institute of Mass Communication, New Delhi
3. Bhartiya Vidya Bhavan, New Delhi
4. Indian Institute of Mass Communication, New Delhi
5. Indian School of Communication, Pune
6. Mudra Media Institute, Ahmedabad
7. Narsee Monjee Institute of Management, Mumbai
8. Pioneer Media School, Delhi
9. School of Communication and Management, Kochi
10. School of Convergence, Noida
11. Sophia B.K. Somani Polytechnic, Mumbai
12. Sri Aurobindo Institute of Mass Communication, Delhi
13. Times School of Marketing, Delhi
14. Wigan and Leigh College, New Delhi
15. Xavier Institute of Mass Communication, Mumbai
16. YMCA Institute of Media Studies & Information Technology, New Delhi

---

- PR education developed in India in 1970 as vocational study at the under graduate level.
- Bhartiya Vidya Bhavan and New Delhi YMCA started PR education in 1970 and 1980.
- India needs a well thought out strategy for PR education, training, and research.
- PR profession and training effort has not been aggressive enough to take up strategic challenges.
- Educators in public relations must standardize the curriculum and define the gamut of public relations functions.

Notably several practicing public relations professionals and former public relations managers from some multinationals are rendering a yeoman's service to the profession by working as guest faculty to some of the renowned media and public relations institutes. This is helping raise a band of trained public relations practitioners of the future.

TOWARDS PROFESSIONAL MATURITY

In today's public relations profession, there appears to be no room for smart talkers and operators. Public relations is a knowledge-based intellectual profession. The entire gamut of public relations, which was earlier restricted to handling media and occasionally bringing out a house journal, is no more relevant. The new breed of professionals, who are serious minded people, are virtually indispensable to modern business.

The role description for PR profession given by late Prime Minister of India, Mrs Indira Gandhi is quite relevant: 'Economic operations are becoming increasingly specialized and contemporary living with the decline of the hold of religion, of family ties and civic obligations, is compelling people to be "lonely crowds". At the same time, the mass media are creating mass societies emphasizing stereotyped images, urges and aspirations. In such a situation, public relations can play a mediator role between the individuals and the group. At one level, they deal in stereotypes but at more imaginative level, they humanize the institutions.'

While addressing a symposium organized by the World Economic Forum at Davos, Switzerland, in 1992, the then Prime Minister of India, Mr P.V. Narasimha Rao, rightly emphasized the crucial importance of public opinion, 'This is no time to rule India by sheer majority. One can get a law passed or can get a vote, but if you can't win the hearts and minds of people, it is not worthwhile. ...There are so many shades of grey. One must have consensus to get the willing cooperation of people...'

In other words, public relations profession in India has come to attain maturity, so much so, that the interest now percolates down to grassroots levels from the people in top notch positions in business and politics. In conclusion, the profession and professionals have a bright future, provided they enter the vocation by choice and not by chance.

Summary

Public relations profession, though existed in India in the history, was not practised consciously and under the nomenclature.

The professionals organized themselves into a society called Public Relations Society of India and organized the first conference in 1972, where the profession was termed as the 'Cinderella of Management'.

The history of the development of the profession can be divided into two parts—pre-independence era and the post independence time.

The outbreak of the First and Second World Wars brought about drastic changes in the attitude and strategies of the government as they realized the importance of creating a public opinion in support of the war through organized information channels. This led to the formation of Information Committee and ultimately the Ministry of Information and Broadcasting.

The commercial interest in the profession developed when the house of TATA started the philanthropic activities and setting up industrial township of Jamshedpur and also sponsoring bright graduates for studying abroad on their scholarship scheme.

The Indian Railways undertook public relations efforts in England to attract English tourists to India and resorted to sharing of relevant information with tourists for their comfort and satisfaction.

The growth of public sector undertakings and their need to create and generate public support for their businesses gave impetus to the profession of public relations.

The policy of economic liberalization attracted many multinationals to open their business in India who brought along the legacy of fully developed professional knowledge and skills in public relations. Today, almost all the companies worth their name have public relations departments.

The Public Relations Society of India has so far held 30 All India Conferences including one international conference, which speaks of the maturity and recognition for the profession.

Media, which once had their own bias towards the public relations practitioners and the profession as such, have changed their responses, so much so, that public relations is now considered as a major resource for several corporate stories. The surge of the pink press in India is a notable development.

The public relations education has spread, though at a slower pace, yet India can boast of more than 20 media schools offering post graduate level programmes with consequent remunerative jobs for the people in industry.

With continued policy of liberalization and encouragement for the foreign direct investment in India by world class multinationals and the surge of the Indian business towards growth, the prospects for the growth and maturity of public relations look bright.

Key Terms

Communication explosion   Multiplicity of media outlets, like newspapers, magazines, TV, radio, cinema, Internet, etc.

Dissemination   Broadcast of an idea or message on a large scale to make it reach a wide audience

Endowment   Gift of money or income producing property to a public organization (such as a hospital or university) for a specific purpose (such as research or scholarships)

Handout   An announcement distributed to members of the press in order to supplement or replace an oral presentation

Institutional advertising   Promotional message aimed at creating an image, enhancing reputation, building goodwill, or advocating an idea or the philosophy of an organization

Mass media   Non-personal channels of broadcasting a message to the general public, principally the national newspapers, radio, and television

Television rating point (TRP)   Audience measurement measuring how many people are in an audience, usually in relation to radio listenership and television viewership

Concept Review Questions

1. Trace the history of public relations profession in India in two phases—the pre-independence era and the post independence years.
2. Briefly draw up an outline of the chronology of events in India that have direct and indirect relationship with the practice of public relations.
3. Write a detailed note about the Public Relations Society of India and its activities for the promotion and recognition of the profession.

4. Paint a profile of the public relations education in India and the advent of public relations and communication institutes, as far as their contribution to the maturity of profession is concerned. What additions and modifications would you suggest to make this training more comprehensive and relative to the job responsibilities of a public relations practitioner?
5. What are developments and changes in the economic scenario in India, which you think, brighten up of the chances of growth of the public relations profession?

Case Study

Ratan's Revolution*

Tata 'Nano' is most likely to stand as a testimony to India's engineering, designing, and manufacturing skills. Priced at Rs 1 lakh, it holds promises to usher in the second road revolution since the launch of the Maruti 800 in the 1980s.

Tata's Nano car, priced at $2,500 or Rs 1 lakh, would be the cheapest four-wheeler in the world, next to the cheapest car the Chinese QQ3, which costs $5,000 (Rs 2 lakh). Indexed for consumer price inflation, the Nano is less than half the price of the 1983 Maruti 800, which was Rs 48,000. Consider the arithmetic of the proposition, the EMI or equated monthly installment for the Nano could range between Rs 2,200 per month for a five-year loan. At over 20 km per litre of petrol, the car would have an operating cost of Rs 2.5 per km, which is well worth the safety of travelling on four wheels and the pride of personal mobility.

The launch of the Nano is timed to perfection. Consider the synchronization with the emergence of India as a manufacturing centre that helped them cut costs, along with high-growth market with a scaleable potential. Currently, 80 lakh two-wheelers, 13 lakh cars, and 6 lakh three-wheelers are sold in India every year. Add 5 lakh used car sales. Hypothetically, each of these buyers is a potential customer. At the price Nano is being offered, there could be a new set of users—a fittest replacement for fuel-guzzling old taxis or unstable three-wheeled rickshaws.

But it wasn't just the arithmetic of this proposition that prompted Tata to think about a people's car. Typically, the trigger was a social concern. On a wet August night in 2003 Mumbai, when Tata was driving back home from his office Bombay House in Flora Fountain, he saw a young couple travelling with their two children on a two-wheeler and was struck by the enormous risks of riding on a wet road.

Tata set up a core team of 500 (including those in charge of setting up the plant) and worked on the concept for four years. Tata's brief was that: It would seat four, have a low operating cost and meet all safety and emission standards. The team dumped the nascent design and focused on the process of building what a car would be differently.

All along, the competition, including Japanese and Korean giants, ostensibly masters of efficient design and innovative pricing, scoffed at the very proposition of a car that cost a lakh

*Source: Adapted from *India Today*, 21 January 2008 and the *Tata website*—www.tata.com, 4 April 2008.

of rupees. 'Can't be done', they said. Osama Suzuki, president, Suzuki Motors, jokingly speculated that 'it would be a three-wheeler or a stepney'. Tata, who wears his Indian identity as proudly and prominently as the Titan watch on his wrist, was confident that his team could make it possible. 'Barriers to innovation,' he said, 'were usually in the mind.' He believed that there was room at the base price and with the skills of Indians, known for engineering cost-effective solutions, it could be done.

The car, as seen in the Auto Expo, is not revolutionary in its looks or in the material used. As far as the looks are concerned, it leans towards the Benz's Smart. But the similarity ends there. The Nano is very, very Indian. What is revolutionary is the thinking, the philosophy behind the design. It has all been done before, but the elegance of the packaging makes such a big draw. The architecture, for instance, the placement of the engine below the rear seat, delivers cost and operational efficiency.

As Tata points out, 'The rear passenger seat is on the engine, so you have space; the engine is driving the wheels directly so you save engineering for the drive; you save the space in the bonnet and construction helps keep the cost down yet meets safety standards.' The result is dramatic in terms of utility and costs; the location of the engine also enabled the designers to give the car a rakish face that is bound to attract the youth as much as the running cost will.

Indeed the Nano—which means small in Parsi–Gujarati—turns out to be a font of innovation, generating as many as 40 new patents for Tata Motors. It wasn't all smooth-sailing; there were hiccups. Tata also wanted to deploy a home-grown engine, but dropped the idea when it didn't meet the core team's benchmark. The car now uses a 624cc, two-cylinder engine tuned by Fiat and powered by Bosch electronics. It also plans to deliver the car with a 700cc diesel engine, which is still being tweaked, that can deliver 30 km per litre.

As the Tatas worked on the Nano, word got around that they had probably cracked the formula. The competition had employed every trick, including fielding photographers to get a view of the car, but failed, even though the car was tested around Pune and elsewhere in the country.

Other worries include the battle of perception being waged by environmentalists and competitors. Of course, the rant about congestion is arithmetically flawed because it would take years for Tata Motors to manufacture millions of cars to jam the roads. As of now, the best they can do at full capacity is 2.5 lakh cars, and that is less than half of the total planned capacity expansion in other car plants.

Due to the political opposition in the name of farmers losing farmlands, Tata has been now forced to move the plant from West Bengal to Gujarat and you could argue that the car is 'late' yet the metro consumers' target are a different segment of youth, women, and second car aspirants who would wait for Nano. The relocation, most hopefully will help the arrival of the car in the Indian market, but with some delay, which the economy car seekers may have to bear.

Notably, Tata Motors said to have put together a financing scheme and designed a new distribution system for rural and semi-urban markets. It is this potential that makes the Nano Ratan's road revolution. The car, when rolls out of the plants in Gujarat is most likely to serve as a symbol of good public relations for the house of Tatas.

Discussion questions

1. What has been the source of inspiration behind the start of the second road revolution by Mr Ratan Tata in conceiving the design and development of Rs 1,00,000 car called Nano? What organizational actions did he take to make it happen?
2. The launch of Nano at the Auto Expo 2008 can be termed as major public relations exercise undertaken by Tata. Do you agree? Please write a lucid report on the launch programme.

References

India Today, 21 January 2008, vol. XXXIII, no. 15, New Delhi, pp. 32–35.

India Today, 14 April 2008, vol. XXXIII, no. 15, New Delhi, p. 1.

Lahiri, Sanat, 'Public Relations in India', a monograph by Sanat Lahiri, published by PR Society of India, Kolkata Chapter, 26 January 1994.

Narasimha Reddi, C.V. (1998), *Public Relations Voice*, 'The State of Public Relations Profession', vol. 2, no.1, October–December 1998, pp. 5–7.

Rao, Narasimha (1992), 'India: A Powerful Engine for Growth of Asian and Global Economy', a handout by the Directorate of Advertising and Visual Publicity, Ministry of Information and Broadcasting, Government of India, New Delhi, No.1/28/91 PPIII, February 1992, pp. 1–2.

The Times of India, 'Adding Net Worth—Web Advertising is Growing but Volumes Remain Low', 22 April 2008, p. 20.

Vyas, Promod (1972), Introductory address at the 3rd All India Public Relations Conference, Kolkata, 1972—A record of proceedings published by Public Relations Society of India, p. 1.

PART II

PROCESS AND PRACTICE

4 PR Plan Phase I: Scan the Environment

PUBLIC RELATIONS—INCREASING RECOGNITION

Every management has a duty and responsibility to manage the organization through its functions of planning, organizing, leading, and controlling. Public relations, which is considered a management discipline, comes under the purview of top management.

The profession has now attained such levels of maturity that no organization worth its name can afford to ignore the practice of public relations. Naturally, the demure position brings along the professional responsibility to come up to the hopes, expectations, and aspirations of the management.

The organizations in world's free markets have already experienced the usage of public relations profession, as a powerful management tool. India, despite half century of so called PR movement, has yet a long way to go. Some still consider it to be a dreamy, glamorous, and light hearted profession practised by some high profile, well connected manipulators.

But to the hard core professionals, it is the intellectual side of organizational process. It is the art and science of communicating to 'engineer the consent' of publics either to accept an idea or concept or to reject it. It is science, as it follows a logical and well-structured approach and an art as it is a thought provoking programme with creative ramifications.

Propaganda? No

Lest we misunderstand, it is not sheer propaganda to brainwash or cloud people's minds, in favour or against a value system or issue, but public relations has to play the role of a facilitator to help people to see a perspective and make their own decisions. Public relations, therefore, work as an agent or a catalyst of change. Though change is a constant factor, yet it does not always come about the way it is desired. The change has to be engineered or managed through planning. That is why, planning and planning alone should make the public relations discipline work. Unlike propaganda, the effort is based on dissemination of knowledge and full information truthfully, so that the publics can themselves decide to adopt a change. There is no scope for or imposing ideas on people, neither people let you do that, but an effort can be made to facilitate the change.

On the contrary, according to Dr Joseph Goebbels, the notorious propaganda minister of Hitler, 'Propaganda has only one object ... to conquer the masses. Every means that furthers this aim is good; every means that hinders it, is bad'. 'Our propaganda is primitive,' he admitted, 'because the people think primitively. We speak the language the people understand...Only in the hands of political artists do the masses become a people and the people a nation. ...The task of propaganda, given the suitable avenues, is to blanket every area of human activity so that the environment of the individual is changed to absorb the (Nazi) movement's world view'(Lochner 1948).

PUBLIC RELATIONS WINDOW

The public relations window (See Exhibit 4.1), outlines a four step system of running public relations and communications programme/campaign for seeking change in the mindset of the target publics and create and generate the desired responses towards an organization, institution, or a cause.

The window scientifically and graphically explains the practical approach to the practice of public relations, particularly in the area of corporate communications. It can also be applied to communications in the marketing and employee relations, or for that matter, any area where change management endeavours are to be made.

EXHIBIT 4.1　The public relations window

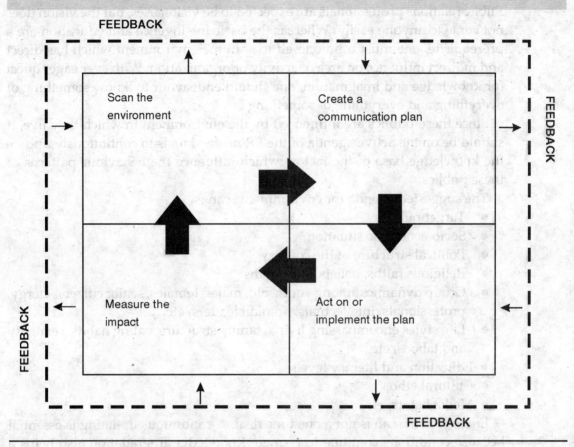

The window has been divided into four boxes, with each box representing one step in the direction of developing a public relations programme, namely:

1. Scanning of the environment
2. Creation of a communication plan/strategy
3. Action or implementation of the plan
4. Measurement of the impact

The outer dotted lines with inward and outward arrows represent the constant feedback in and out, to relate and adjust the campaign programme to the changing environment. The in-box arrows guide the stepwise, development and direction of the programme.

Whereas this chapter addresses the phase one, i.e., 'Scan the environment,' the next three boxes will be dealt within chapters that follow, i.e., chapters 5, 6, and 7.

SCAN THE ENVIRONMENT

Public relations professionals are expected to be visionaries, but the vision does not come to anyone easily. Whereas the basic intelligence and education are a prerequisite, one must train oneself to scan the environment which has direct and indirect influence on area of activity or organization. With ever eager quest for knowledge and imagination, one should endeavour to 'know something of everything and everything of something'.

Since these publics are influenced by the environment in which they live, it should be on the active agenda of the PR professionals to continuously update the knowledge base of the factors which influence the behaviour patterns of these publics.

The suggested agenda for environment scan is:
- Target publics
- Socio-economic situation
- Political structure of the country
- Religious faiths, beliefs, and myths
- Group dynamics among youth, old, males, females, senior citizens, clergy, professionals, intellectuals, opinion leaders, etc.
- Life styles encompassing living, family structure, eating habits, sexuality and taboos, etc.
- Education and literacy levels
- Cultural ethos
- Media habits, etc.

Environment scan is not a one time deal. A continuous updating is essential because conditions continue to change. Knowledge upgradation also helps a professional to avoid some dangerous and costly mistakes.

For instance, it is highly inappropriate to tell the 'Green Peace' crusaders to ignore some pollutants. It might be dangerous to advocate the nutritious value of beef sausages to the orthodox Hindu vegetarians in India.

Also, the most creatively created communication campaign to control population in the rural segment, if communicated in the urbanized vocabulary, will cut no ice. Imposing Hindi or English on audiences, who are not well versed in the language, is meaningless. The main objective of public relations is to communicate messages that reach directly to the publics, rather than showing off creativity or proficiency in a language.

In the absence of knowledge update, or sheer ignorance, a PR professional might unknowingly take an anti-constitutional stance, unmindful of the constitutional guarantees and liberties enshrined in the constitution of a country.

The first step in the right direction, would be to understand fully the expectations of various publics of the organization. Therefore, it would be appropriate, to list the publics and their hopes and expectations. This eventually, will help to adopt and execute certain policies and actions the way publics expect these to be.

TARGET PUBLICS

The top priority on the scan list should be to know fully well the psychographics of the target publics, which may include employees, customers, shareholders, dealers, vendors, government, media, legislators, and community, whose mindset change is sought. The public relations person should then plan and strategize communications to generate the desired response.

The target public can be divided into two kinds, internal and external. Employees of an organization represent the internal public, as they are considered insiders and as such a part of the corporate family. They are also called 'captive audience', not that they are in the captivity of the organization, but because they are available for communication at the known addresses and at the time of choice by the organization. Chapter 14 deals with the subject in detail.

External publics are the target audiences, scattered and far flung, and are generally difficult to communicate with as their whereabouts are not readily available. Mass media play a vital role to reach these publics. They are customers, shareholders, dealers, vendors, media, government, legislators, and community, (See Exhibit 4.2). Relations with these audiences have been dealt with separately in the respective chapters, devoted to each public.

Needless to say, it will be appropriate to develop a profile of each public so as to attain a clear perception about their behaviour patterns, expectations, hopes

EXHIBIT 4.2   Two kinds of publics

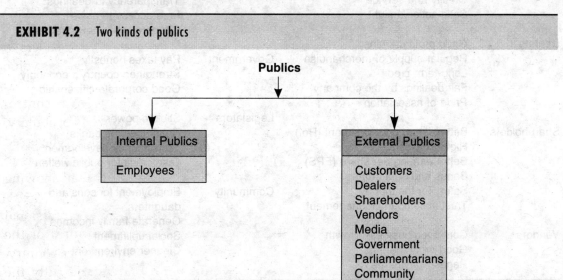

and aspirations, so that this information can be related to the organizations' business objectives, vision, and mission.

EXPECTATIONS OF PUBLICS

The business world is full of conflicts of interest and all humans are busy pursuing their own interest in conflict with others. Therefore, all relationships are dependent on understanding the needs and expectations of each party involved. If an organization has some expectations from various publics, then such publics also expect matching responses from the organization. This reciprocity generates understanding, goodwill, and harmonious relations with publics. Therefore, it should be appropriate to look at the mutual expectations of each public (Exhibit 4.3).

Employees

Whereas every company expects loyalty and optimum levels of performance from their employees, these 'associates' also have some expectations which are often pronounced loudly by the employees and their unions. Some commonly known expectations are better wages, profit bonus, and incentives to perform at

EXHIBIT 4.3	**Public expectations**			

Publics	Expectations	Publics	Expectations
Customers	Value for money Quality and service Satisfaction/delight	Media	Pride of association Transparency in dealings Free access to news Cooperation in news gathering
Dealers	Good profit margins Regular supply of merchandise Long-term credit Fair dealings by the company Pride of association	Government	Pay taxes honestly Strengthen country's economy Good corporate citizenship
		Legislators	Stick to power
Shareholders	Better return on investment (RoI) Higher dividends Better earning per share (EPS) Bonus and right shares		Reinforce vote banks Constituency development Take credit for public welfare
	Safety for the money Trust in company management	Community	Employment for sons and daughters Generate family incomes
Vendors	Continued business growth Good profit margins Regular payments		Social upliftment Cleaner environment

higher levels of efficiency, safety from work related injuries, or avoidance of industrial accidents.

The employees also have a strong desire for job security as it is directly related to the subsistence and betterment of their families. Employees, like all humans have some social needs for career growth and designations that will earn for them status in their society (See Exhibit 14.1 in Chapter 14).

Last but not the least, people who have worked for long years in a company, desire to be consulted in the process of management and growth plans. On the other hand, the managements would also like to gain benefit from employees' long work experience and talents. (Also see chapter 14; Exhibits 14.2 and 14.3).

Customers

No business organization can afford to ignore the expectations of their customers. Several professionally managed companies have adopted customer-focus policies, as they understand that the *mantra* for success is to 'make the customer win, to make the company win'. Today, the 'customer relations management' has acquired the proportions of a full-fledged subject in the management education system.

Customers want value and returns for their hard earned money in terms of better quality of products and services. Customer satisfaction is the very basis of their purchase action. No dissatisfied customer ever returns to a company to buy one more time. Several global companies have now adopted the philosophy of 'customer delight' so that the customer remains loyal. A new concept of 'relationship marketing' has received lot of attention of the marketing professionals, who believe that once a customer gets related to the company, the relationship should be kept alive for a very long time, through servicing the customer in many ways, and the one generally known way is 'after-sale-service' (See chapter 11).

Dealers

Dealers are up front ambassadors of a company, who directly interface with the customers on behalf of the company. They represent the company and whatever relationship they start with the customers, goes a long way to earn the goodwill of the customers for themselves and a lot for the company they represent. Rightly so, the marketing professionals consider dealers as partners in business.

Since the business interactions always have the undertones of a conflict of interest, the company–dealer relationship is often termed as 'love–hate' relationship.

All said and done, making profit is the top priority that dealers have as an expectation of their principals. Dealers expect regular supply of products, so that they can sell regularly to promote their business, per se, serve the customers.

Like all businessmen they want long credit terms, and fair dealings in terms of the company keeping their commitments about the commissions and incentives. That is why this relationship is very sensitive.

Though some lesser known companies will offer high commissions and incentives, they will yet find it hard to find franchisees. On the contrary, some established companies, with powerful brands, will offer low commissions, yet for reasons of pride of association, many dealers would like to be the franchise holders of such companies. Who would not like to be a petrol pump dealer for an oil company? These associations enhance dealers' social status and add prestige to them in their communities (See chapter 12).

Shareholders

Literally, shareholders or the stakeholders are part owners of a public limited company. Collectively, they are a powerful public who have invested their hard earned money in shares and debentures of the company. Theirs is investment in the organization with hopes of sharing the profits of the company. Naturally, they have an expectation of better returns on investment in terms of good dividends and higher earnings per share in the stock market. They also hope that the company may float some bonus shares in ratios like, one-for-one, or two-for-one and if the additional capital is to be raised, the shares, enjoying high quotations, will be allotted to them on right basis. Last but not the least, they have trust in the company and expect that their investment will remain safe and protected and yield good rewards (See chapter 15).

Vendors

Besides the pride of association, which naturally enhances a vendor's social status and business prospects, the vendors who are like subsidiaries of a company, want to grow along with the growth of their principal buyer organization.

Vendors are an important support system in industry, who keep the manufacturing and marketing lines moving by keeping up the regular supply of parts, components, and services. They themselves are small businesses, whose growth depends on the growth of their principals. Therefore, they have an expectation of regular flow of business as important partners of the enterprise. They wish to have reasonably good margins of profit and payment cycle to match with supply cycle mutually agreed upon. No other business is so inter-dependent as the vendor–buyer relationship. Both parties have an expectation to keep up the mutual commitments. Vendors, if angered, for one reason or the other, can jam the production lines by choking supplies (See chapter 13).

Media

In today's competitive world and the corporations becoming an important subject of discussion in board rooms and drawing rooms, media plays an important role is carrying all the pertinent information to all the interested publics. Needless to say that with the growth of 'pink press', the mushrooming of newspapers and quite a few TV channels exclusively focusing on corporate business, media has an expectation of free flow of news and transparency in the business organizations. Media hate to be manipulated or to face any hurdle in the way of news collection. Therefore, sharing news with media for ultimate spread of the information about the company is a very desirable exercise. 'Since bad news is a good news for media,' transparency helps to keep the corporate perspective objectively portrayed in front of the various publics, through media channels, print and electronics (See chapter 16).

Government

No business can exist, grow, and thrive without the favourable policies and actions of a country's government. Whereas an enterprise tries to advocate the interests of the industry to the government, for formation of policies and tax structure conducive to growth, the government expects the organization to pay taxes honestly. It also expects certain actions and plans of the industry which go a long way to strengthen the economy of the country in terms of industrialization, self sufficiency in food and agriculture, employment and certain other related matters, which directly or indirectly affect and contribute to the country's prosperity. The ultimate agenda of every government is to follow policies which will improve the standards of living of the population.

The organization should act and project as a 'good corporate citizen' and fulfil its obligations towards the corporate social responsibility, which means improving the quality of life for the people (See chapter 22).

Legislators

In a democratic country like India, where the legislators represent people from their constituencies and vote banks, they expect sizable cooperation from industry. No doubt, the legislators have one prime priority, i.e., to somehow stick to the power. In the process they need the vote and support of their voters, who also have expectations of improving their standards of living.

In a bid to come up to the expectations of their voters, the legislators look towards the industrial houses to come to their help in starting certain projects in their constituencies which will generate employment and propel commercial activities. Industries, run as enterprises, would naturally venture into areas which are viable for their growth and expansion and look forward to a congenial social and political environment. If provided by the legislators through business friendly policies, this complimentary role can go a long way. The relationship, however, has to be mutually beneficial (Also see chapter 23).

As the Indian democracy matures, the legislators have to put on a different attitude towards business organizations, and shed that old malice towards business. Some of the organizations sometimes take initiatives to educate and update this public about their policies and programmes, to get a favourable support in the parliament in the formation of pro-business legislations. Lobbying is now an in-thing in India (See chapters 22 and 23).

Community

Communities living around the plant towns and at a national scale look towards the corporations to come forward and fulfil their obligations to the society. The plant towns expect gainful employment for their sons and daughters to add to the family incomes, and thereby improve their style and quality of life. At the same time, the community expects that the industry will not pollute the air and water with discharge of industrial affluence. The community does not want that on one hand, the industry should give jobs to their wards and on the other, take away their health through water and air pollution.

On a national scale, people want organizations to demonstrate that the only business of the business is not only to make profit but also contribute to the quality of life by contributing some share of their earnings towards improvement of public health and education.

Tata's Cancer Research Institute, Birla Institute of Engineering, Escorts Heart Hospital, Fortis Chain of Hospitals by Ranbaxy, etc. are some of the examples of corporate world doing their bit for public health and education.

Confederation of Indian Industry (CII) have taken a lead role to sensitize Indian business houses to this social obligation. The term 'corporate social responsibility' is being taken as an important area of business world (See chapter 17).

SOCIO-ECONOMIC SITUATION

Experts believe that the root cause of all the social problems in the world is the economic situation in a particular country. The world history stands witness that poorer the country, more complicated is the society. The situation leads to economic instability and many residual problems. A rough and ready agenda based on economic indicators should serve as a basis of the programmes that public relations want to undertake. A good look at these indicators should help to keep the plan on track. The agenda is:
• Micro and macro indicators
• Population and manpower
• Literacy levels
• Poverty alleviation
• Wages and unions
• Agriculture and food situation

Micro and Macro Indicators

Besides the major macro economic indicators like GDP, fiscal deficit, rupee vs dollar, inflation and sensex, micro indicators like per capita income, wages, etc. that affect the quality of life, should also be tracked for a feel of the pulse of the publics. The macro economic indicators that influence the behaviour patterns of the public are agriculture, forestry and fishing, manufacturing, electricity, gas and water supply, construction, mining and quarrying, trade, hotels, transport and communications, financing, insurance, real estate and business services, community, social and personal services.

Today, when media is playing the role of dissemination of a variety of information to people, such indicators are often published at intervals for newspapers and periodicals and particularly the pink press gives this information in details. One such insertion in *The Mint* serves as an example (See Exhibits 4.4 and 4.5).

EXHIBIT 4.4   Economic indicators

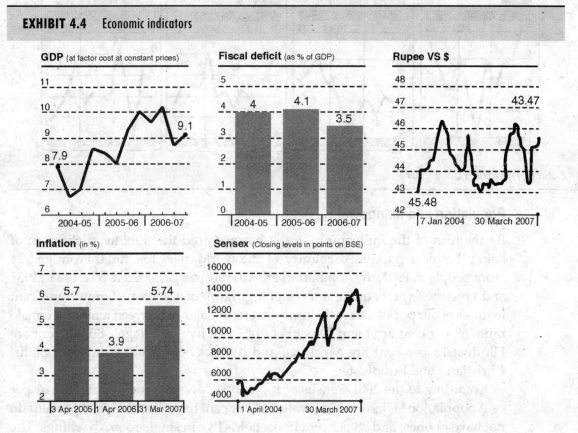

Source: The Mint,. 1 June 2007.

EXHIBIT 4.5   Economic trends in diverse sectors

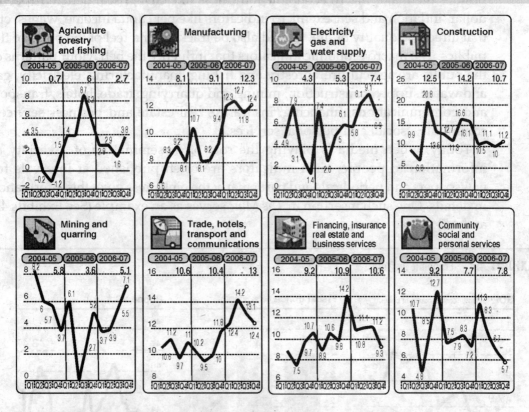

Source: *The Mint*, 1 June 2007.

Population and Manpower

By the turn of the millennium, India has acquired the dubious distinction of being the most populated country of the world, next to China. From just 24 crore people in 1901, the population growth rate has galloped to 35 crore in 1951 and now the experts quote a threatening figure of 110 crore. Some significant features of our populace are the conspicuous imbalance between male and female ratio; 52 per cent are men; 70 per cent of India live in villages; 80 per cent are Hindus; 15 per cent are Muslims; and balance 5 per cent comprises Sikhs, Christians, and Buddhists.

According to the 2001 Census of India, it is very pathetic to note that 61 per cent population lacks drinking water; 44 per cent have electricity; 90 per cent do not have phones; and 38 per cent households live in single room dwellings. The per capita income rounds to about US$ 886 compared to Japan $34,000 and US$30,000. The minimum monthly wages legally stands at Rs 2,250 (*Hindustan Times* 2003).

Literacy Levels

The levels of literacy in the country should be of a great concern to the public relations practitioners, as higher the literacy level, easier it becomes to communicate to the people. Until the full coverage of rural population by TV, reaching the rural masses has been a riddle. India's failure on population front is sometimes attributed to this bottleneck. With the awakening of people towards education, the literacy is said to be at 60 per cent level with the states of Kerala and Mizoram topping the list with almost 91 per cent literacy, according to the National Family Health Survey (NFHS), 2007. Bihar, is perhaps, the least literate state.

Poverty Alleviation

According to a report in *The Times of India*, New Delhi (23 February 2001), the National Sample Survey Organization (NSSO) and the Planning Commission has recorded that the percentage of people living below the poverty line has come down to 26 per cent in 1999–2000 from 36 per cent as compared to 1992–93. The government has undertaken many plans and programmes to alleviate poverty by public distribution system of food grains and other essential items to the poor. The society has been classified into various sections and subsidies are granted to these sections to facilitate their upliftment. Sections like scheduled castes and scheduled tribes and some backward classes are granted such assistance by giving them preferential reservations in employment and education, etc.

After success with the public sector organizations, the crusaders for the 'equal opportunity' regime are so enthusiastic that they have now been advocating for preferential reservations of jobs in the private sector companies, which has been received by industry captains with some mixed feelings.

Unions and Wages

The labour movement in India was started by Indian National Congress under the banner of Indian National Trade Union Congress (INTUC) in 1920, followed by communist led union called All India Trade Union Congress (AITUC) . Almost all the leading political parties have their trade union wings. Some of the famous ones are Centre of Indian Tade Unions (CITU) led by Marxist communists and Hind Mazdoor Sangh (HMS), sponsored by Bharatiya Janata Party. Unfortunately the trade unions are active only in the organized sector, but there is floating of mass of labour force which works in the unorganized sector with no voice or representation in industry. Millions of daily rated agricultural workers have no unions whatsoever to raise any voice for their rights.

The Indian government has enacted a Minimum Wages Act in 1948, under which the minimum wage made mandatory for industry is Rs 2250, which is in sharp contrast to poverty line that ends at Rs 5000 per month.

Agriculture and Food Situation

Agriculture is the dominant sector of Indian economy, which determines growth and sustainability. About 65 per cent of the population still relies on agriculture for employment and livelihood.

Indian agriculture, however, has made milestones. The green revolution transformed India from a food deficient stage to a surplus food market. In a span of three decades, India has become a net exporter of food grains. Despite these major structural transformations, the agriculture sector continues to accommodate the major share of the workforce.

India is yet to emerge as a significant trade partner in the world agriculture market. India holds around 1 per cent of the global trade in agricultural commodities. With the ongoing trade negotiations under the World Trade Organisation (WTO), Indian agriculture is witnessing a phase of diversification. Attention has been shifting to high-value crops from traditional crops.

WTO has put India in the driving seat for agriculture trade. The drive will be a successful ride only if we identify the opportunities and challenges, which are:

- Substantial liberalization of trade
- More market access opportunities
- More transparency and stability of global market.

Thus it is essential to reorient the agricultural system towards enhanced competitiveness and make it more market driven.

On the food front, the food processing industry is of enormous significance for India's development because of the vital linkages and synergies it promotes between the two pillars of our economy, industry and agriculture. The sector, however, has to go a long way.

During the last one decade, India moved from a position of scarcity to surplus in food. Given the trade in production of food commodities the food processing industry in India is on an assured track of growth and profitability. It is expected to attract phenomenal investment in capital, human, technological, and financial areas.

The total food production of India is estimated to double in the next ten years. Hence there is an opportunity for large investments in food and food processing technologies, skills, and equipment.

As per a study conducted by McKinsey and Confederation of Indian Industry (CII), the turnover of the total food market is approximately Rs 2,50,000 crore (US$69.4 billion). Besides, the government has also approved proposals for joint ventures, foreign collaborations, industrial licenses and 100 per cent export oriented units envisaging sizable foreign investments (*The Times of India* 2001).

POLITICAL ENVIRONMENT

The political system of India can be best described as laid out in the Preamble to the Constitution of India, which reads:

> *We, the people of India, having solemnly resolved to constitute India into a sovereign socialist secular democratic republic and to secure to all its citizens: Justice, Social, Economic & Political; Liberty of Thought, Expression, Belief, Faith & Worship, Equality of Status & Opportunity, Fraternity assuring the dignity of the individual and Unity & Integrity of the Nation: In our Constituent Assembly this 26th day of November, 1949, do hereby adopt, enact and give to ourselves this Constitution.'*
>
> (CII website 2007)

As such it is pertinent for a public relations professional to know that the political system and Constitution of India grants some fundamental rights to the people, namely, the right to equality, right to freedom, right to stand against exploitation, freedom to practise any religion. The citizens also have right to adopt any culture and may attain education to the levels they desire. The system also grants the citizens of India to seek certain constitutional remedies for or against certain causes or issues.

Every citizen of India, irrespective of caste, creed, and colour, enjoys certain freedoms, freedom of speech and expression, freedom to assemble peacefully, freedom to form unions and associations, freedom to move freely anywhere in India, freedom to live in any part of the country, and practise any profession or occupation of their choice.

All this basic knowledge helps a professional to avoid any mistake in the process of developing communications for the target publics and not to fall in any trap ultra vires of the Constitution.

RIGHT TO INFORMATION

Public relations practitioners, in all probability, should be happy to see the Right to Information Act coming into force. As champions of transparency and deeply interested in the dissemination of full and truthful information to the publics, the public relations professionals may gather all the strength from the right of people to know. The act serves the cause of safeguarding the ethics of public relations discipline and strengthen practitioners' position to stand against any unethical pressure brought on them to manipulate information.

The Right to Information Act 2005 (Act No. 22/2005) is a law enacted by the Parliament of India giving citizens of India access to central government records. The Act applies to all states and union territories of India, except the state of Jammu and Kashmir which is covered under a state-level law. Under the provisions of the Act, any citizen (including the citizens within J&K) may request information from a 'public authority' (a body of government or 'instrumentality of State'), which is required to reply expeditiously or within thirty days. The Act also requires every public authority to computerise their records for wide dissemination and to proactively publish certain categories of information so that the citizens need minimum recourse to request for information formally.

This law was passed by the Parliament on 15 June 2005 and came into force on 13 October 2005. Information disclosure in India was hitherto restricted by the Official Secrets Act 1923 and various other special laws, which the new RTI Act now relaxes.

The Act specifies that citizens have a right to:
- Request any information (as defined)
- Take copies of documents
- Inspect documents, works, and records
- Take certified samples of materials of work
- Obtain information in form of printouts, diskettes, floppies, tapes, video cassettes or in any other electronic mode or through printouts (The Constitution of India).

SOCIETY, RELIGIONS, AND CULTURE

India is a spirit soaked in the spirit of religion. People are guided and directed by the tenets of their religion, which comes to them by their birth. There are rare instances in which someone converts into a religion different than that of his birth. Although some religious enthusiasts have been making ardent efforts to aggressively and seriously market their faiths and values to convert people or at least have a revered view of their faith.

Manu, in his code of conduct book called *Manusmriti*, classified India's population into four main classifications, which were not based on the basis of birth but by the profession people practised to make a living. Brahmins, the learned class, whose job was to learn and spread education in the society; Kshatriya, the ruling class, entrusted with the responsibility to protect the society and their civil liberties against outside aggressors; Vaishyas, the traders, involved in trade and commerce; and Shudras, the menial workers, who had the duty to clean and maintain hygiene.

The main religions practised in India are Hinduism, Islam, Sikhism, Christianity, Jainism, Buddhism, and Parsi faith. Each religion has a code of

EXHIBIT 4.6   Religions of India at a glance

Religion	Holy book	Prophet
Hinduism	Vedas, Gita Ramayana	Sri Krishna Sri Rama
Islam	Holy Quran	Prophet Mohammed
Sikhism	Holy Granth Sahib	Adi Granth and ten Gurus
Christianity	Holy Bible	Lord Jesus Christ
Buddhism	Tripitaka	Lord Buddha
Jainism	Jinvaani	Lord Mahavira
Parsi	Zendavista	Fire God

conduct and a holy book to be worshiped. Each faith has its own religious places of worship for people to congregate to pray. Exhibit 4.6 gives a clear view of the simplistic version of India's complex web of religions.

A society is known by the culture it practises. Anthropologists and sociologists define culture as the 'way of living' built by a group of human beings, which are transmitted from generation to generation. The various aspects of culture reflect in the formation of social institutions including family, educational, religious, governmental. Culture includes both conscious and unconscious values, ideas, attitudes, and symbols that shape the patterns of human behaviour, that are passed from one generation to another. These distinct patterns of their social conduct distinguish one cultural group from the other.

India is a complex web of cultures which is sometimes a mind boggling situation. Yet it is very interesting and educative to understand the culture and prevent the public relations people from making some basic mistakes while addressing several social and cultural ethos areas for generating modification in the behaviour patterns, so necessary for cultural change for the sake of progress.

A rough and ready collection of various traditions and behaviour patterns of the members of a society, in certain situations and events in life, as listed in the well known 'Murdock's Culture' model (See Exhibit 4.7) should help the public relations practitioners to understand the cultural traits of a society. While studying the cultural ethos of target publics, it should be pertinent enough to gather the sensitive information to avoid any pitfall in addressing issues concerning that particular public. For example, the sentiments of a predominantly

---

EXHIBIT 4.7 Murdock's culture model

Murdock's universal aspects of culture

Age-grading	Etiquette	Inheritance rules	Pregnancy usages
Athletic sports	Faith healing	Joking	Property rights
Bodily adornment	Family	Kin-groups	Propitiation of
Calendar law	Feasting	Kinship nomenclature	supernatural beings
Cleanliness training	Fire making	Marriage	Puberty customs
Cooking	Folklore	Mealtimes	Religious ritual
Co-operative labour	Food taboos	Medicine	Residence rules
Cosmology	Funeral rites	Modesty concerning	Sexual restrictions
Courtship	Games	natural functions	Soul concepts
Dancing	Gestures	Mourning	Status differentiation
Decorative art	Gift giving	Music	Surgery
Divination	Government	Mythology	Tool making
Division of labour	Greetings	Numerals	Trade
Dream Interpretation	Hair styles	Obstetrics	Visiting
Education	Hospitality	Penal sanctions	Weaning
Eschatology	Housing	Personal names	Weather control
Ethics	Hygiene	Population policy	
Ethnobotany	Incest taboos	Postnatal care	

Source: Moran and Stripp (1997).

---

vegetarian public may be badly hurt, if unknowingly, a company like Wenky's or Al Kabir communicate to them the merits of meat eating. In the Indian context, there are several issues like child marriage, dowry, or *sati pratha*, where the best public relations campaigns seem to have little effect. Until the cultural roots of a problem or behaviour patterns of the target publics are fully understood, it may not be possible to strike at the very root of a problem.

CHANGING PSYCHOGRAPHICS

Change is known to be a constant factor. After World War II, the world has changed a lot. The political, economic, religious, and cultural changes have swept Europe and the rest of the world.

India is no exception. The pre-independence society was more traditional and conservative. People followed the norms, rituals, and value system handed down from generation to generation. But the information explosion, the changing economic order, and the integration of world as one 'global village' has also changed the Indian society to a large extent.

From life styles to vocabulary, from behaviour patterns to dress codes, from family values to individualistic priorities, the social psychographics have tremendously changed and will further adopt the new life styles, as they come about due to high worldwide exposures and increasing economic pressures.

EXHIBIT 4.8   A society in transition

The aspirations of the Indian middle class are beginning to show. Though still conservative in consumption, expenditure, and savings, they are increasingly aspiring to a modern lifestyle. Research by CLSA and Mindscape, covering 1,616 households' in 16 state capitals, found that children's education and careers continue to be the main focus, but expenditure on homes, entertainment, and gadgets are rising.

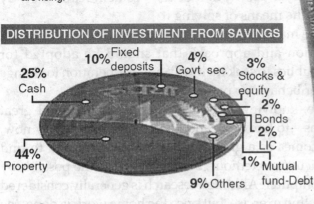

DISTRIBUTION OF INVESTMENT FROM SAVINGS

25% Cash
10% Fixed deposits
4% Govt. sec.
3% Stocks & equity
2% Bonds
2% LIC
1% Mutual fund-Debt
9% Others
44% Property

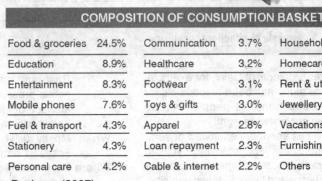

COMPOSITION OF CONSUMPTION BASKET					
Food & groceries	24.5%	Communication	3.7%	Household help	2.2%
Education	8.9%	Healthcare	3.2%	Homecare	1.5%
Entertainment	8.3%	Footwear	3.1%	Rent & utilities	1.3%
Mobile phones	7.6%	Toys & gifts	3.0%	Jewellery	1.3%
Fuel & transport	4.3%	Apparel	2.8%	Vacations	0.7%
Stationery	4.3%	Loan repayment	2.3%	Furnishing	0.6%
Personal care	4.2%	Cable & internet	2.2%	Others	10.0%

Source: The Hindustan Times Business (2007).

Exhibit 4.8 should serve as an indicator of the changing Indian society in terms of their life styles. Public relations practitioners should keep in mind the changing scenario and psychographics while on the job, in the process of adjusting the traditional with modern.

SITUATIONAL ANALYSIS—FORMAL AND INFORMAL RESEARCH

It is but logical that before we start working on a public relations programme on an issue or an organization, we should be very sure to understand the present state of affairs, the correct definition of the problem that we have at hand, and other related contributory factors to the situation that exists today.

Like a seasoned journalist depends on his age-old system of getting answers to the five Ws and one H (Who, What, When, Where, Why, and How) to get the full story or situation, the same system should be applied to get at the genesis of the problem or issue. Once ascertained, the situation should help a public relations person to move forward with appropriate strategies and actions (See Exhibit 4.9).

In other words, the problem should be fully researched to arrive at correct definition of the problem. Generally, it is believed that if we know the problem, we know the solution. The correct description of the problem leads the way towards the solution and also the means of solving it.

Since communications is the main responsibility of public relations, this will also guide the course of action and approach that should be adopted for communicating to the target publics to seek their help and cooperation to change and adopt the desired ways or behaviour patterns.

In today's information age, knowing facts and figures has assumed great importance for the professions—to know all, and know well. Fortunately now, the information technology comes as a great help to conduct research to find facts. Once that was very difficult and tedious, but has now become possible by clicking a few fingers on the computer. Although research is generally considered to be a very dull and uninteresting exercise, but once the home work is done, the

---

EXHIBIT 4.9   An example of situational analysis

Let us take the traffic problems of Delhi, for example, where a bus service alone has been responsible for killing more than one hundred people in road accidents. Let's get our answers right:

Who   Blueline bus service, self styled drivers, crazy motor cyclists, wayward cyclists, cycle rickshaws, three-wheeled auto rickshaws, horse and bullock drawn vehicles, etc.

What   More than 100 people killed by Blue Line buses alone and many injured not reported even.

Why   Poor road sense amongst Delhiites
Our vehicle population, 40 lakhs, 1000 added up everyday
Insufficient and inefficient police
Young first generation drivers, keen to show off speed and cars
Rash and negligent driving due to economic pressures (to increase revenue).
Menace of jumping red lights.
Irate pedestrians and jay walking habits.

When   Mostly rush hours of morning and evening
Festivals and political rallies.

Where   Busy business districts, industrial areas, and slum clusters skirting main roads and ring road.

How   High influx of rural population lacking urban discipline.
One formal research, as a sample, can be conducted by taking a count of red light violations, on a designated busy crossing at the peak hour, 8 am to 10 am without a policeman on duty.
The count can be quantified into percentage of violations at this time span to show the gravity of the problem.

pains will give lot of pleasure to a professional, as it will provide a sense of direction to keep the programme on track.

An early researcher, who helped build automotive industry, C.F. Kettering, once described this attitude towards research in these words:

> *Research is a high hat word that scares a lot of people. It needn't. It is rather simple. Essentially, it is nothing but a state of mind—a friendly welcoming attitude toward change. Going out to look for change, instead of waiting for it to come. Research...is an effort to do things better and not be caught asleep at the switch. The research state of mind can apply to anything. Personal affairs or any kind of business, big or little. It is the problem solving mind as contrasted with the let-well-enough-alone mind. It is the composer mind, instead of the fiddler mind; it is the 'tomorrow' mind instead of the 'yesterday' mind.*

The research attitude calls for the fact-finding, listening, and systematic problem definition to help bridge gaps between organizations and their publics. As other divisions of company such as, marketing, finance or personnel, etc. have adopted research-based approach to address their problems, so should the public relations, to play its effective role in the total organization.

For the purpose of public relations practice, two kinds of research can be conducted—formal and informal.

Formal Research

Although the purpose of all research is to get actual and factual data, yet the formal research focuses itself directly to the objective of the research. Thus, the formal research methods are so designed as to get more objective and systematic data, which has to be carefully and logically applied on some of the objects and subjects, that represent the problem or an issue.

Obviously, organizing such research on one's own may not be cost effective to the company. Fortunately today, there are many sources that are available and can be taken advantage of at low or no cost. Many universities, colleges, media training institutes, newspapers, periodicals, and TV channels conduct frequent opinion polls on several issues concerning the nation and communities of readers and viewers.

Questionnaires and interviews

Formal personal interviews on a pre-set list of questions is conducted to read the mind scape of the publics. Such reports are then collated to arrive at a consensus of public opinion on an issue or a problem. The advantage of such interviews is that the respondents' response can be either candid or genuine and help to arrive at a realistic conclusion.

More often than not respondents are asked through mail or Internet to fill their response in the questionnaire and mail back. Such responses, because of the absence of personal touch, may let the respondent go ahead with full freedom and express his heartfelt and honest opinions. Sometimes, the researchers promise to donate a token sum to a charity for every questionnaire filled and responded or even promise a supply of free sample of their product. Recently, Colgate asked netizens to fill up a questionnaire and promised a free sample of toothpaste to be mailed to their home address. The quantum of such responses depends on the kind presentation and the human interest involved..

McDonald's have been doing this frequently, prompting their customers to fill up a questionnaire to ascertain the expectations of customers and the quality of food and housekeeping of their restaurants (See Exhibit 4.10).

India, on this front, is quite organized and some of the readily available sources of gathering information are Tata Consultancy Service's annual book of statistics, government's Central Statistical Organization. Doordarshan and All India Radio also regularly gather trends about their viewership and listenership, where information and data can serve as barometer of the media habits of India's diversified publics.

Informal Research

Informal research, which means getting closer to the people, knowing them, reading their mindsets, or probing their mind scape, is a valuable tool that public relations professionals use. In fact, there is always an organizational need for the personnel with an inclination and interest in getting closer to the people and collecting sensitive feedback. It is not easy. This kind of attitude and behaviour calls for some personal sacrifice, lowering your ego, to stepping down to the level of people's intellect and reading their inner most thoughts. Many professionals will be termed as extroverts, with a natural flair for milling around the people. Excessive handshakes and broad smiles are often taken for a superficial personality, but deep inside, the public relations persons are very articulate and thoughtful about what they do.

But the danger is that extroverts meet extroverts. The opinions of the loud majority may not be the representative opinion. Depending entirely on this feedback may backfire and the public relations programme may lose direction and objective.

Networking

Networking is the lifeline of every managerial job, and public relations is no exception. Since gathering the sensitive feedback from the 'grapevine' is the professional necessity of the job, to develop a network of 'friends' inside and outside the organization, should serve as eyes and ears of the management vis-

EXHIBIT 4.10 McDonald's restaurant review

We request you to spare a few minutes of your precious time to review our restaurant. And tell us how we measure up on the following areas. Once you have completed this form, please place it in the suggestion box. Thanks for helping us to serve you better.

	Excellent	Good	OK	Bad
SERVICE				
Courtesy	⊖	⊖	⊖	⊖
Speed	⊖	⊖	⊖	⊖
FOOD				
Appearance	⊖	⊖	⊖	⊖
Taste	⊖	⊖	⊖	⊖
CLEANLINESS				
Outside	⊖	⊖	⊖	⊖
Dining area	⊖	⊖	⊖	⊖
Toilets	⊖	⊖	⊖	⊖
VALUE FOR MONEY	⊖	⊖	⊖	⊖
OVERALL EXPERIENCE	⊖	⊖	⊖	⊖

DATE OF VISIT _____ TIME OF VISIT _____

OUTLET VISITED _____

How often do you visit our restaurant(s)?	Please tick	Name _____
	Male ☐	
Daily ☐	Female ☐	Date of birth _____
		Date of anniversary _____
Weekly ☐	Age Group	_____
	1–7 ☐	
Monthly ☐	8–12 ☐	Address _____
	12–15 ☐	
Occasionally ☐	16–24 ☐	
	25–34 ☐	
	35–44 ☐	
	44+ ☐	

Please contact the duty manager with any questions, complaints or suggestions to allow us to deal with them now, if possible.

Source: Adapted from www.slideshare.net/guest47c65d/mcdonalds.

à-vis public relations. It is a hard reality of life that people inside and outside the organization are playing conflicting roles. As such one should be very sensitive enough to know the friends and foes alike. The objective is to gather sensitive information, rather than taking sides with one group or the other. It is just appropriate to show detachment than alignments.

Memberships

Professional organizations always encourage their public relations people to take membership of several social and professional organizations, like rotary clubs, lion clubs, management associations, industries, manufacturers association, etc. These groups are generally a forum for voicing out problems and solutions, that plague these groups and the role, if any, a corporation is expected to play.

On community front, from where a company draws a major portion of its workforce, it serves as a good sounding box for the variety of opinions expressed by community leaders about the actions and policies of an organization, which reflect on corporate obligations towards the community.

This forum is the fountain head of all the sensitive information that a company needs to remain in tune with the ever-changing environment.

Toll free phone calls

Several companies with worldwide operations and a global consumer base have adopted the toll free phone call system where the customers can call the company, from anywhere in the world, to voice out their complaints, suggestions, or grievances. These calls serve as a very sensitive feedback about an organization's policies, products, and actions.

An analysis of such calls can provide considerably authentic information that should be taken into account for formulation or adjustment of organizational public focus policies.

The Indian Railways have been using this system at their central reservation offices in New Delhi, where the travellers can record their opinions into the fixed line phone. Dell Computers uses this system for marketing as well as customer care network.

Consumer forums

With the growing awareness of the relationship between corporations and consumers, the consumer activists have organized themselves to protect the consumer interests. The consumer-focus forums monitor prices, quality, weights, and even go to the extent of contesting in courts, the exaggerated claims that a company may make for their products.

The new Indian law has instituted consumer courts for the redressal of consumer complaints and grievances. If proved wrong, the corporations are liable to pay the damages to the consumers that may have been caused to them for non-compliance of the commitments or claims made in a company's advertisements.

Ombudsman

The term *Ombudsman* originated when the position was first established in the Swedish government in 1713. It means an official who investigates reported complaints, reports findings, and helps to achieve equitable settlements. Growing dissatisfaction with ever-longer lines of communication to increasingly isolated managers and bureaucrats has brought about widespread adoption of this informal information gathering method.

In countless non-government organizations in the developed world, the concept of ombudsman has proved useful in providing feedback and ideas for solving problems while they are still manageable. An ombudsman generally investigates and recommends solutions to the problems. In certain cases they have the authority to take action on the complaints. As such the role and scope of authority varies widely.

The Times of India was, perhaps, the first organization in India to institute the office of an ombudsman, but with no notable role or success. The concept of *Lokpal* has often been discussed in the parliament but the law still awaits approval.

If they like to take the initiative, they can assume the role of ombudsman, without getting the public relations professionals themselves designated as such. The benefit of this initiative would be direct two-way communication with publics and collection of information sensitive to the organization.

If sincerely used and competently staffed, the ombudsman position can be an important means of obtaining organizational feedback. As this method relies on people seeking out the opportunity to make their feelings and complaints known, care should be taken not to interpret information by this method as representative of the many less-assertive members of an organization's publics (Moran and Stripp 1997).

Media tracking

Tracking the media content is one objective way of determining as to what is being reported in the media. Press clippings and broadcast monitor reports, generally available from some clipping service agencies, have been used as the basis for tracking and analysing the media content. But the media content indicates only what is being printed or broadcast, and not what is read or heard. Also it does not indicate, whether or not the readers, listeners, or viewers learned or believed the message content.

Analysing the editorials and letters to the editor may yield little more than the views of editor and publisher. One can plot on a graph, the news content on a quarterly, half-yearly, or annual basis, in the categories like favourable, unfavourable, or neutral, to track public opinion.

Today, the umpteen number of blog spots are flashing a variety of spots contributed by a cross section of the society to express their divergent views. Follow up of a couple of leading blog spot sites on the net can lead to gathering informations pertinent to the issues or organizations.

Salesmen's daily call reports

Every professionally managed sales and marketing organization makes it mandatory for its field sales force to file a 'daily call report' at the end of each day. Besides listing the names of the customers called upon, there is also a slot reserved for pointedly writing the salient feedback of the happenings in the market concerning competition, major customers and also some environmental briefs that directly or indirectly affect the company's business.

Often the information is collated at the corporate office to watch the changing business environment. Public relations persons can scan these reports and sift the information pertinent to the area of interest.

Besides, the branch managers also write a monthly report to the top management, which serves as a good and dependable feedback to the corporate management vis-à-vis public relations.

Summary

Public relations is a knowledge-based profession. This chapter discussed at length, the first step in the direction of environment scan as represented by the first square of the public relations window.

To establish relationship and under-standing and also to generate desired responses, the corporate concerns itself with the mindsets of the various publics. Publics, internal and external, also have certain expectations from a corporation, and matching promises with performance forms the basis of this relationship. As such the expectations of the employees, customers, dealers, vendors, shareholders, media, community, etc. have been discussed threadbare.

The chapter also deals with laying the ground work for planning a public relations programme. The environment—political, social, cultural, economic—both at micro and macro level, has strong bearing on the behaviour patterns of the publics.

To keep the public relations programme on track, it is also necessary to have the situational analysis in clear focus, which calls for research, both formal and informal.

The systems and channels of gathering feedback has been discussed at good length. No doubt, homework is always a boring aspect of learning, yet when done thoroughly has its own rewards.

Key Terms

Corporate social responsibility (CSR)   A firm's sense of responsibility towards the community and environment (both ecological and social) in which it operates, and draws resources and sustenance from

Customer delight   Moving beyond customer satisfaction to discover and fill each customer's unseen yet essential needs, virtually eliminate the negative, and drive customers to new levels of repeat purchasing, loyalty, and sheer delight, by exceeding their expectations

Debenture   A bond backed by the general credit of the issuer rather than a specific lien on particular assets

Earnings per share (EPS)   Net income of a firm divided by the number of its outstanding shares, the shares held by the stockholders

Free markets   Where buyers and sellers can make the deals they wish to make without any interference, except by the forces of demand and supply

Group dynamics   Interaction of complex intra and inter-personal forces operating in a group which determine its character, development, and long-term survival

Ombudsman   A person with high social acceptance appointed to receive and redress public grievances for an organization

PR window   Graphic showing four step public relations system

Relationships   A marketing system to establish long-term customer relations

Shares   Certificates or book entries representing ownership in a corporation or similar entity

Concept Review Questions

1. As planning is very basic to any public relations programme, draw and discuss the public relations window concept for your understanding the system.
2. Draw up an agenda for environment scan in an effort to update your knowledge base, and briefly explain the social, political, economic aspects of this effort.
3. What are the kinds of publics that an organization should establish relationship and understanding with? Briefly explain their expectations from a corporation.
4. Situational analysis is crucial to understanding an issue or a problem. As a correct description of the problem helps to put the public relations programme on the right track, what is the formal and informal research system that should be followed? Explain.
5. Explain the terms 'demographics' and 'psychographics'. How are they relevant to determining the mind scape of the target publics?

Project Work

1. Draw up a demographic and psychographic profile of India's population and relate it to some of the social problems like bride burning for dowry, female foeticide, and male/female imbalance.
2. Develop the profile of a middle class customer, below 25 years, working,

male and female, and give conclusions as to how he/she would respond to the newly launched Reliance Fresh store in their locality.

3. Visit one Ford and Maruti dealer each and draw up a comparison of their hopes, aspirations, and expectations from their principal companies. How do both dealerships lead us to some conclusions, which will be helpful in planning our public relations programme?

References

Lochner, Louis P., *The Goebbels Diaries,* Fireside Press, Inc , USA, 1948, p. 22.

Moran, Robert T. and William G. Stripp (1997), *Dynamics of Successful International Business Negotiations,* Jaico Publishing House, Bombay, India in arrangement with Gulf Publishing company, Houston, Taxas, USA, p. 45.

Scott, Cutlip M., Allen H. Center, and Glen M. Broom (1985), Prentice-Hall International, Inc, USA, p. 202.

Hindustan Times, New Delhi, India, 'India Unlimited Population', 11 July 2003.

The Hindustan Times Business, 'A Society in Transition', New Delhi, India, 1 November 2007, p. 26.

Mint, 'The Economic Indicators', HT Media Limited, New Delhi and Mumbai, India, 1 June 2007.

The Times of India, New Delhi, reporting findings of National Sample Survey Organization and the Planning Commission, 23 Feblruary 2001.

CII website, Google search engine, logged on 31 October 2007, Agriculture & Food Processing section.

5 PR Plan Phase II: Develop a Communication Plan

COMMUNICATION—A VITAL LINK

'Communication', as per the Oxford dictionary, 'is the activity or process of expressing ideas and feelings or of giving people information.' By communication we mean the interpretation and reception of ideas or information, i.e., a transaction of ideas. It would be difficult to think of anything that takes place, or makes a sound or a gesture, or does not some way communicate.

Communication is, perhaps, the only link that has kept alive the human race. Right from time immemorial, humans have had an urge and need to communicate with each other to get the necessary responses. It, perhaps, started with the time Eve asked Adam in the Garden of Eden to pluck for her that beautiful looking forbidden red apple, and the world was plunged into a need to communicate their emotions to each other.

The world has come a long way since the biblical story. Humans, all along in the history, have been experimenting with the idea of speeding up communications. This very urge pushed the system to smoke signals to pigeon mail to telegraphic Morse code. The inventions of telephone, wireless television, and now mobile telephone to Internet, are all but reflections of the human urge to communicate, and communicate speedily and meaningfully.

From simple one-to-one communication to group communications, time has changed with the emergence of the new phenomenon called mass communication, which uses modern media tools to communicate sensitive messages to masses. The media explosion in the last part of the 20th century and the dramatic surge forward in the beginning of the 21st century has sensitized masses so much towards information that people act and react according to the messages that they receive, almost constantly twenty four hours of the day.

Communication — the vital link — has the following characteristics:

- Communication is a means of purposeful dialogue.
- Communication is vital to human existence.
- Communication is like breathing. Just as we cannot stop breathing without fatal risk, we cannot stop communicating without the risk of a disaster.
- Effective communication is the lifeblood of an organization.
- Communication lubricates the difficult process of commercial and industrial life.
- Progressive organizations and professional managers invest substantial resources and valuable time to develop people's communication skills to improve their productivity and the corporate growth.
- Marketers powerfully communicate to generate the desired responses from customers in terms of sales and profits.
- Public relations professionals creatively communicate to publics to facilitate logical responses to actions and policies of the organization.
- Personally and professionally, humans are entirely dependent on effective communications.

Denis McQuail (1975) sums up, 'We buy certain goods and services because of advertisements in the media, go to a film praised in the newspapers.' And 'Our minds are full of media-derived information and impressions. We live in the world saturated by media sounds and images, where politics, government, and business operate on the assumption that we know what is going on in the wider world' (Cutlip et al. 1985).

A professionally managed company systematically runs its communication system to attain its corporate objectives and goals. It is a well thought out plan, according to which an organization has to run the communication programme, that too not by fits and starts, but continuously. Experts agree that free flow of communication, downward, upward, and horizontally, is a continuous exercise which yields good dividends for the company.

All said and done, communication is the lifeline of an organization. But the public relations professional uses the power of communication to create synergy between the organization and the publics, for reasons of creating goodwill and under-standing.

CREATE A COMMUNICATION PLAN

Specialization in the communication discipline is the forte of a public relations professional. Whereas other management systems function smoothly or otherwise, public relations fills in the gap by creating organizational excitement and commitment through a creative and professionally designed communication programme.

Keeping in view the public relations objectives of an organization and the need to meet them, it is but essential that a well structured communication plan should be developed to meet these corporate objectives.

A rough and ready agenda for developing such a plan should work as a framework for this effort, which is to

- Develop a mission statement.
- Develop a punch line for the programme.
- Finalize a thematic logo for the communication programme.
- Consider use of a mnemonic device to add power to the programme.
- Design and develop communication material like handout, brochures, and other literature.
- Write newsletters, press releases, backgrounders, speeches, presentations, etc. in advance.
- Design visual communications like billboards, posters, banners, streamers, festoons, etc.
- Plan orders on designers and printers well ahead of time to economize and ensure quality production.
- Create an activity calendar.
- Develop budget and get management approval.

It will be appropriate to study the senstivities and delicacies of some of the important elements involved in the development of a communication plan.

Develop a Mission Statement

Developing a mission statement is like stating the objective of the public relations programme in a most succinct way. It is like the most condensed version of the objective that the public relations programme seeks to achieve. Rather than making a long winded statement of what the programme is aiming at, it is pin pointing very specifically at the job to be done and the responses that the organization stipulates from various publics to make the programme a success.

Let's be clear in our mind that the mission statement is the demonstration of creative skill of stating voluminous information into a condensed form. Brevity and creativity, should go hand in hand, in stating the mission. Once conceptualized well, the mission statement is bound to generate public cooperation and support for a particular cause or an issue.

A mission statement should be a precise and concise version of the philosophy behind the programme being run by the company to achieve a specific goal. There is no room for showing off great copy writing skills but a conscious effort to simply state the mission in unambiguous terms to reach the target publics straight and get registered with the perceived intent and content.

The mission statement should spell out the roles and goals of both the parties involved, i.e., organization and publics. Before we set out to develop the statement, it is necessary to determine the focus area for action, whether the focus is more on the work culture to which the employees are used to, or the focus is pointing towards some management actions and policies, which call for a change or modification.

Such statements can be developed for a short-term communication programme or for a value system that the organization would like to adopt as a new management philosophy to rejuvinate the firm or to bring about a change in the corporate culture. Whatever the focus, the mission statement should be specific, objective oriented, action oriented, or culture oriented. Besides the public relations manager working on it, it is highly rewarding to involve people from the management. If appropriate and relevant, even the employees can be involved in hammering out a statement acceptable to all.

When a multinational company adopted the total quality management system, it formed a group to specifically work on the mission of inculcating the TQM at all levels of the organization. The mission statement given in Exhibit 5.1 is one representative example of the mission statement developed by this group.

In brief, the mission statement should include characteristics like:

- Should be crisp
- Easy to understand
- Tightly written and focused
- More colloquial than intellectual
- Easy to convert into a graphic, etc.
- Should include the public relations programme logo
- Should philosophize the mission
- Should be inspiring

EXHIBIT 5.1   Sample mission statement

OUR COMPANY WILL ENDEAVOUR FOR CONSTANT IMPROVEMENT IN THE QUALITY OF PRODUCTS AND SERVICES TO MEET OUR CUSTOMERS' NEEDS. THIS IS THE ONLY MEANS TO SUCCESS AND PROSPERITY FOR THE COMPANY, OUR EMPLOYEES, AND INVESTORS

MANAGING DIRECTOR

- Should preferably be signed by the head of the firm to lend seriousness to the mission
- Once frozen, it should be treated with reverence
- Mission statement is sanctimonious and serious
- May eventually become an icon for the organization

Voltas, with all its past reputation and image, realized that the public perception of the company was, as if, of a traditional and systems ridden company. There was perhaps an impression in public mind that it is an old-fashioned company and is not moving ahead to grow and modernize.

Rightly so, the company adopted a public-relations programme to transform the company into a more vibrant and modern company. The management decided to project that the company should be perceived as an organization out to acquire a new and modern outlook and ready to rise and shine in the corporate world.

As such the company developed a very powerful 'Mission & Vision 2001' statement which states the organization's overall mission and also some specific steps and actions that it stipulates to transform itself into an entirely new and dynamic company (See Exhibit 5.2).

Develop a Punch Line

A punch line is a powerful instrument of communication, of driving a message home in the shortest possible time. A punch line is the condensation of the total message zeroed on in the fewest words. It is direct, hard hitting, crisp, humourous sometimes, meaningful, in the shortest version. Some communication specialists

---

EXHIBIT 5.2   Voltas mission and vision

Voltas vision 2001

*VIGOUR * VISION * VALUES
THE NEW GENERATION VOLTAS

We will be among the 10 most admired corporations in the country with leadership focus on:
- Delivery of products and services, which are globally competitive
- Continuous improvement of our products, process, and people
- A learning organization of committed and contributing employees who share the competitive agenda
- Continuing satisfaction of our customers and all our stock holders
- Sensitive concern for society, environment and our values of justice, fair play, and integrity
- Expansion in our areas of core competence and development of competencies for new product-market-growth opportunities.

Source: Voltas House Journal.

---

think it is a message that 'punches the nose' of the target publics for instantaneous registration.

Any communication or public relations programme has a meagre chance to take off without a punch line. Therefore, more often than not, the programme is conceptualized with the birth of a punch line.

A punch line is a concept that represents the entire message of the public relations programme; becomes integral part of the plan; and if missing, the plan may look headless or devoid of action.

A punch line cuts through the maze of information and brings out the order out of several main and peripheral messages which could be confusing, vague or ambiguous. But the punch line is forthright and straightforward.

To have impact and high degree of memorability, a punch line can be born out of the common parlance or *lingua franca* of the publics. There is hardly any scope of any copywriter or concept creator to show off their great vocabulary by using words that do not travel straight to head and heart. That is why the punch line should be down to earth and even colloquial.

Lucky for the public relations professionals that the world has become multi-lingual and multi-cultural. This greatly widens the scope of developing punch lines which are interesting, tongue twisting, and even musical. Such short messages have high speed memorability and amusement value, and naturally good for professionals.

More than half century ago, Unilever introduced a cigarette in Punjab (when Punjab meant Punjab, Haryana, Himachal, and even Pakistan) called 'Lamp'. It was, no doubt, a down market cigarette and needed to be popularized well. The creative team noticed that Punjab water, which is generally very sweet, was now being drawn out by newly introduced hand pumps as against old style of water wells.

So the agency painted the towns red with the punch line *Pani pump da, cigarette Lamp da*. The punch line was an instant hit and even today, people remember the line and buy the cigarette branded Lamp. It created niche in the market that Lamp means a cigarette. Smokers were often heard demanding the fag at cigarette vends as *'Ah do lamp day day!'* (Give me two lamps, i.e., cigarettes).

The power of a punch line cannot be exaggerated or undermined. The line is a vital link in the communication programme and once registered may stay in the minds of publics for long and may generate the desired responses (See Exhibit 5.3).

Develop a Communication Theme Logo

A logo design is generally developed in terms of a graphic illustration which revolves around the theme of the total message. The message converted into a graphic centres around the philosophy, culture, desired actions, and many more

EXHIBIT 5.3   Some famous punch lines

Organizaton	Punch line
Unilever	*Pani pump da, cigarette Lamp da!*
BMW	The ultimate driving machine
Goodyear	Protect Our Good Name
Philips	Sense and Simplicity
Congress party	*Congress ka Haath, Aam Aadmi ke Saath!*
Louis Philippe	The upper crest
Deutsche Bank	A Passion to Perform
Bosch	Invented for Life
NECC	*Sunday ho ya Monday, roze khanyen ande!*
Malaysia	Malaysia! Truly Asia

aspects of the public relations programmes. As pictures speak louder than words and generate the desired response spontaneously, logo becomes an instrument of powerful communication.

Once frozen, a logo is intended to stay for a very long time, in all its glory, form, colours, type fonts, etc. It assumes the overtones of a sanctimonious symbol expected to be treated with reverence. In fact, the organizations love their logos and very fanatically guard them from misrepresentation, twisting, or mishandling. Organizations understand that even a slightest change or twisting or distortion can go a long way in disturbing the positive public perception that has been formed over decades or more.

Even a slightly tampered logo, in terms of colours or pictorial design, etc. makes the loyal publics doubt the very genuineness of the organization. They suspect that some other company may be masquerading it to promote their self interests.

Many companies carry on their corporate logo for more than a century and safeguard it very meticulously. The changes or modifications, if any, carried out by the company, are well advertised in the media to keep the public perception intact. Several multinationals have developed their corporate identity programme manuals, which must be followed religiously in their subsidiaries all over the world. IBM, Bata, Revlon, Philips, Goodyear, Sony, etc. make sure all over the globe that their logos appear in the same shape, size, colour, and style for the global recognition.

Similarly, any public relations communications programme should pay sufficient attention to the development of a logo design and pursue it with zeal to maintain the uniformity and sanctity. This is one way of registering messages in the right perspective in the minds of the target publics.

Adopt a Mnemonic Device

A mnemonic device or a graphic is generally a moving representation of the public relations programme. It is often used in communication and advertising system to gain audience's prompt attention. A mnemonic device is an improvised object that speaks volumes about an idea, theme, issue, situation, value system, supplemented with words or a voice over.

Just as the rising sun from behind the hills, or a cock on a dung hill heralding the morning with his 'cock-a-doodle-do' represent the start of a new day, it also has the connotation of optimism, comfort or a good night sleep, or an austere life style.

Depending on the public relations programme, the organization, the audience perception, the value system, culture, history, symbols, a mnemonic device when used will facilitate quick recall of the idea being communicated.

Selection of a device has to be very smart and considered decision, because different graphics in the world carry different connotations, biases, and prejudice and may produce feelings of love, hatred, violence, or compassion amongst various publics.

The idiom 'One man's meat is other man's poison' holds good in such situations. Since public relations undertakes to facilitate the mind set change, the selection of device calls for a very high degree of creativity for demure considerations.

Communication Tools and Actions

No public relations programme can take off until the communication tools are exploited fully. Tools are like vehicles of communication which have to be utilized with the receivers of the messages kept clearly in mind.

There are umpteen number of tools that are available. But the use of such tools call for some homework. Before the message is loaded on to these communication tools, the message has to go through a process of maturity. Once the message is ready for transmission, tools can be innovated to be compatible with the message, so as to carry the message and deliver it to the target publics for necessary results. Before a message is loaded up, the message has to go through a process to emerge as a competent and mature piece of communication. The stages of this process can be:

Concept stage

The conceptualization of an idea is valuable because it is the stage of the birth of an idea. Conceptualizing is considered as an exercise to sift the main focus of the message out of a mass of available information. Once the idea is seen in clear focus as a cutting edge of a communication tool, the time is right for going ahead.

Writing stage

Once the concept is frozen, it is time to dress up the idea with a smart copy. The verbal part of the communication calls for flair for writing, power to express the idea to drive it home. A public relations professional himself may have sufficient skills to write or it is advisable to tap the public relations agency's resources. A well thought out agency brief can be transmitted to the agency which is expected to be professionally competent to translate the concept into a powerful copy.

Design stage

Many public relations persons are good in developing pencil roughs of the communication messages, which with the help of the commercial artists or the agency's creative department can be transformed into a powerful visual design. To effectively marry the visuals with the copy, a public relations agency, either uses its own in-house art studios and copy writers or sometimes outsource the skills for developing such visual communications.

Print paint stage

Once the concept, copy, and design are finalized, it is time to go for mass production. Whereas the outdoor display materials like banners, billboards, streamers, festooners, etc. will need execution by painters, all other materials may have to printed in quantities, deemed sufficient for spreading the message evenly.

It is only advisable that the material should be ordered well ahead of time in the interest of economy and quality of production of the materials. The jobs which are rushed cost more and adversely affect the quality of production. Therefore, 'planning ahead' is a good strategy.

With the advancement of technology coupled with computer innovations, the tools of communication have multiplied. Blinking neon signs, moving electronics signs, sky writing, blimps, and flashing information are a common sight. Exhibit 5.4 showing the stages of development of various communication tools should serve as a good source of information.

In today's world of aggressive marketing and sales promotions, the agencies are experimenting with new ideas to execute nationwide sales promotion programmes, in terms of developing new tools. Escorts, a tractor manufacturing company, used a talking poster in one farm fair to reach out to farmers. As a farmer stands in front of the poster, it addresses the viewer with a pre-recorded message, with some movement of hands and eyes to generate response.

Create an Activity Calendar

As public relations is a planned and sustained communication effort to facilitate a change in the mindset of publics, planning an activity calendar or a schedule

EXHIBIT 5.4   Communication tools—development stages

Tools	Concept	Design	Write	Action
Handouts	pencil rough	develop	copy	print
Brochures	pencil rough	develop	copy	print
Literature	pencil rough	develop	copy	print
Newsletters	pencil rough	develop	copy	print
Press releases	get news	develop	copy	print
Backgrounders	get data	develop	copy	print
Speeches	list points	develop	copy	print
Presentations	rough sketch	finalize	develop	record
Billboards	pencil rough	develop	slogans	paint
Posters	pencil rough	develop	slogans	print
Banners	pencil rough	develop	slogans	paint
Streamers	pencil rough	develop	slogans	paint
Festoons	pencil rough	develop	slogans	paint

of actions or events should be drawn out in a very thoughtful manner. Planning such a calendar is like developing a roadmap for the programme, which will keep the efforts on track. Whatever is not planned becomes haphazard and leads to confusion and chaos. No management will like such confusion or disorder.

Depending upon the duration for which the communication programme will be run, a month wise 'plan-at-a-glance' should be developed for a follow up (See Exhibit 5.5).

Starting with the inauguration of the programme to events like meetings with publics, media coverage, inward communication with employees, special TV appearances, events and ceremonies, should be included in plan.

Once the schedule is presented to the management and approvals obtained, it will put the programme on rails and keep moving. A word of caution would be that, as far as possible, no deviations or fluctuations in the programme should be allowed. The postponements may send a wrong signal to the publics and would be dangerous, as it may hurt the credibility of the plan.

Working in teams is viewed as a good management system. Therefore, to involve and solicit the support from several managers of various departments, it is but essential to share the calendar with them. It will help the managers to block the dates and timings on which their presence and participation will be necessary. Such appointments should be kept under track to avoid fizzling out.

Once the public relations person does his homework well, and makes the plan ready, this puts him in the driver's seat to drive the programme to success.

EXHIBIT 5.5   Activity calender

Monday	Tuesday	Wednesday	Thursday	Friday	Saturday	Sunday
1	2 11 a.m. inauguration	3	4 Press kit distribution	5 Community leaders meet	6	7 Address rotary club
8	9 Press conference	10	11	12 Chairman TV appearance	13	14
15 Show T.V. report to employees and distribute handouts	16	17	18 Put up publicity posters	19	20 Dealers cocktail	21
22	23 Journalists plant visit	24	25 PR ads in HT, TOI, Hindu, Deccan Herald, Statesman, and Telegraph	26	27	28 Family Day in plant
29	30 Customers club visit	31				

COMMUNICATION MEDIA STRATEGIES

Scott, Cutlip, and Broom (1985) opine, 'Lack of strategic thinking and planning can lead to communications programmes that reinforce controversy rather than resolve them; waste money on audiences that are not there; or add confusion, instead of clarification, to misunderstanding. In this process an organisation is, in effect, making tomorrow's decisions today. Many of the difficult public relations problems currently being dealt with were born of yesterday's spur-of-the-moment decisions' (Cutlip et al. 1985).

As part of the homework, which is generally a dirty word for all managers including public relations, certain critical aspects of the communication system should be considered.

Target Publics

As all communication messages are not meant for all the publics, it is of utmost importance that we should determine the target public and profile them well. Amongst all the publics—customers, employees, dealers, vendors, shareholders, media, and community, etc.—it is relevant to look at the psychographics and demographics of each public.

Taking a cue from the marketing people, who have developed a social pyramid to identify their target audience, the public relations professionals can also carefully study this pyramid, and cut out communications according to the mental, social, and economic level of each public. (See Exhibit 5.6). The audiences have been classified in the social pyramid as A1 and A2, B1 and B2, C, D, and E according to their educational qualification, social status, professions, and income levels. Just as the advertising professionals are making use of this, it should come handy for making communication decisions in the public relations area as well.

Category A1 and A2 is considered to be the upper upper class or the creamy layer of the society; B1 and B2 is upper middle and upper classes; and C, D, and E are lower middle, lower, and lower lower classes, respectively.

This leads us to the conclusion that our approach, communication, and level of vocabulary will have to be adjusted according to the parlance of each section of the society. Otherwise we run risk of getting misunderstood and creating ill will rather than goodwill. Needless to say, each section of the society has its own parlance, grievances, cultural taboos, and dos and don'ts and public relations persons should be well exposed to then, as public relations is the business of people.

Communication Adoption Process

The well known and traditional advertising model called AIDAS can be adopted in understandng the system of communication adoption. Humans never immediately accept an idea or proposal and habitually resist any suggestion for change. The adoption of an idea has to go through a process. AIDAS when spelled out simply stands as:

A – AWARENESS is created about an idea or system
I – INTEREST is generated in the idea
D – DESIRE is kindled to try out the idea
A – ACTION is taken to adopt the idea
S – SATISFACTION is enjoyed when the idea is found useful

Naturally, the media and social environment play a vital role in learning about the ideas and system. Some ideas get well accepted very fast due to peer pressure whereas some take time. Besides the media exposures, public tends to learn and

EXHIBIT 5.6 Socio-economic classification

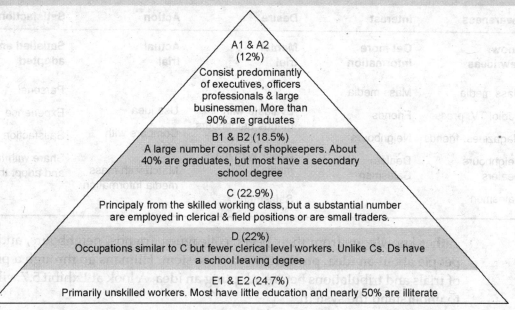

A1 & A2 (12%)
Consist predominantly of executives, officers professionals & large businessmen. More than 90% are graduates

B1 & B2 (18.5%)
A large number consist of shopkeepers. About 40% are graduates, but most have a secondary school degree

C (22.9%)
Principaly from the skilled working class, but a substantial number are employed in clerical & field positions or are small traders.

D (22%)
Occupations similar to C but fewer clerical level workers. Unlike Cs. Ds have a school leaving degree

E1 & E2 (24.7%)
Primarily unskilled workers. Most have little education and nearly 50% are illiterate

- The Market Research Society of India categorizes socio-economic groups based on both occupation and education of the chief wage earner of the household.
- These eight classes are A1, A2, B1, B2, C, D, E1, and E2. A1 is the uppermost socio-economic class and E2, the lowest.
- Sections A and B refer to high-class—Constitutes 21 per cent a quarter of urban population.
- Section C refers to middle-class—Constitutes 21 per cent urban population.
- Sections D and E refer to low-class—Constitutes over half the urban population.

Occupation	Education						
	Illiterate	Less than4 yrs in school	5-9 yrs of school	School certificate	Some college	Graduate	Post-graduate
Skilled	E2	E1	D	C	C	B2	B2
Unskilled	E2	E2	E1	D	D	D	D
Shop owner	D	D	C	B2	B2	A2	A2
Petty trader	E2	D	D	C	C	B2	B2
Employer of-							
Above 10 persons	B1	B1	A2	A2	A1	A1	A1
Below 10 persons	C	B2	B2	B1	A2	A1	A1
None	D	C	B2	B1	A2	A1	A1
Clerk	D	D	D	C	B2	B1	B1
Supervisor	D	D	C	C	B2	B1	A2
Professional	D	D	D	B2	B1	A2	A1
Senior executive	B1	B1	B1	B1	A2	A1	A1
Junior executive	C	C	C	B2	B1	A2	A2

Source: http://www.timm.indiatimes.com/examples/timm/ecoclass.jsp; http://www.naukarihub.com/india/fmcg/consumencloss/socio-economic.

EXHIBIT 5.7 Process of adoption of AIDAS

Awareness	Interest	Desire	Action	Satisfaction
Know new ideas	Get more information	Mental trial	Actual trial	Satisfied and adopted
Mass media	Mass media			Personal
Radio, TV, press	Friends	Evaluate with friends neighbours	Use idea	Experience
Magazines, friends	Neighbours		Compare with friends	Satisfaction
Neighbours Dealers	Dealers Salesmen	Check with mass media	Match with mass media information	Share with friends and adopt the idea
Salesmen		Salesmen		

gather knowledge from their peers, colleagues, friends, neighbours, and sales people about an idea, product, or value system. Humans go through a process of trials and tribulations before adopting an idea. A look at Exhibit 5.7 will help to understand the system.

COMMUNICATION MESSAGE STRATEGIES

Registration and reception of right responses depend on the appropriateness of a communication message. A well thought out message, keeping in view the public's level of understanding can do miracles, but a careless or a poor quality message can spell disaster. A look at various aspects of message management should help.

Forum

Developing and focusing on a platform from which a message should be addressed to the public, is of great significance. Forum or platform means a stance or stand which should form the central theme of the message. The forum can be wrapped up in a slogan or brief explanation of the theme of the programme. The slogan, as such, should have all the qualities in it for inducing quick registration. For instance, most of the cosmetic companies address the women publics from beauty forum; men's soap address men from health forum; life insurance companies address the public from social security forum; Congress party addresses electorate from *Garibi Hatao* forum; and BJP from the *Hindutva* forum.

Vocabulary

Besides communicating with the publics in the language that they speak, read, or write, it is essential that vocabulary should be adjusted as per the intellect or education levels or even the social parlance of the publics. The messages meant for high profile audience A1 and A2 are always different from the ones used by E audience. Therefore, the message should be in line with the social placement of a public on the social pyramid. To highlight the importance of vocabulary, we know that the parlance of a taxi driver and a Mercedes car owner is bound to be different. So should differ the vocabulary levels.

Celebrity Involvement

Credibility of a communication message, to a large extent, depends on the personality of a person who speaks these words. Many mundane messages go unnoticed, but when the same message is relayed by a person of substance, they carry lot of weight and become quotable quotes.

When a celebrity like Amitabh Bachchan speaks the message of polio eradication, it is noticed, understood, and acted upon more often than not. When a star like Aishwarya Rai appeals for eye donation, it stirs humanitarian feelings in the heads and hearts of the publics. Therefore, it is a good tactic to rope in a celebrity to speak out a message. No surprise that to lend seriousness to the matter of road safety, the Chief Minister of Delhi, Mrs Shiela Dixit herself speaks every now and then on the radio and TV channels, appealing for safe driving on Delhi roads. It is not different than the great advertising companies adopting a brand ambassador for their company products.

The selection of a celebrity for transmitting the message should be guided by the topic of the message and the personality traits or position of such dignitary. Since such famous personalities do not come for free, the budget considerations should also be a factor. But for several humanitarian causes, many famous people come forward on a voluntary basis to do the role gratis. All factors taken into account, mixing and matching the message and the personality will call for judgmental decisions.

MESSAGE TRANSMISSION STRATEGIES

The selection of right media for transmission of messages to the right publics assumes great importance. The most brilliant message when loaded on to a medium that does not reach the audience is simply a waste of time and money. Obviously, it is necessary to determine the media habits of the publics for whom the communication is intended. Writing an article on the maintenance of a tractor in a women's magazine will be a waste of time, as hardly any woman will be interested in reading that. So the right message in the right medium for the right public is the answer.

Since media greatly influence the behaviour patterns of the publics, working with the media helps to create a hype and contributes to the chances of rejection or acceptance of an idea, issue, or a value system. Generally, there are two routes to creating a hype—first, media relations, which when handled well will generate plenty of favourable publicity; and second, the paid advertising for a cause or an organization to generate awareness for the purpose of popularising an idea or a brand or to build or correct the image of an institution. We should look at both aspects of media management.

Media Relations and Publicity

One of the major skills in which the public relations professionals specialize is the deft handling of media relations. The main objective of generating media responses is to get publicity for the organization, which is virtually free. Generating publicity is considered by some companies as one of the major responsibility of a public relations person.

According to Dr Jaishri Jethwaney (2007), 'Public Relations is used for "monitoring" journalists through proactive interaction with them on a continuous basis to keep up flow of "soft" and "hard" stories about the brands and the company, to counter negative publicity, to handle crisis situations, and to control damage as far as possible' (Jethwaney and Jain 2007).

H. Frazier Moore and Frank B. Kalupa (2005) opine, 'The news media constitute a major factor in public relations, controlling the flow of publicity through the most important channels of public communication. Good working relationships with editors, reporters, editorial writers, cameramen, columnists, and broadcasters and understanding of their editorial needs is essential in securing good publicity coverage' (Moore and Kalupa 2005).

Therefore, to generate publicity, working with the media or maintaining media relations, is best done when it is based on a strategy and follows a systematic process. A good strategy seeks opportunities to match goals and objectives of the organization with the interest of journalist. As in any good communication strategy, understanding the needs of the audience, in this case media men, is important in communicating with them effectively. Also see chapter 16 on media relations. The 'Population Reports' published by USAID outlines some of the roles that public relations professionals can play to facilitate publicity (See Exhibit 5.8).

Publicity is Free

Publicity has been defined as that activity which generates non-personal stimulation of a thought process or a demand for a product, service, or business unit by planting commercially significant news about it in a published medium or obtaining favourable presentation of it on radio, television, stage, or print media, that is not paid for by the sponsor. Publicity is free.

EXHIBIT 5.8   Public relations support to media

United Nations Media Relations

A training bulletin of the United Nations about disseminating family planning messages to the masses through media relations, outlines the obligations that a UN representative has towards media. Most organisations that work well with the news media rely on proven techniques, methods and materials, which include:

- Providing accurate, timely, and interesting information
- Collecting and analysing information about the news media's interests and needs
- Producing news releases, feature stories, opinion pieces, newsletters and other readily usable material
- Preparing press kits, fact sheets, expert lists, and other aids for journalists
- Presenting story ideas to journalists, and responding to their request for information and assistance
- Arranging and assisting with news conferences, site visits and other events that interest the news media
- Helping journalists to make contact with programme staff, including arranging interviews
- Dealing with opposition and public controversies when they arise, and countering false rumours

Source: USAID Population Reports (1995).

Publicity means all those activities where public relations persons make deliberate, imaginative, and creative attempts to prepare company or product slanted news stories and features and make endeavours to interest the media in using such news stories.

Many professionalized companies have realised that managing publicity efforts require special skills in writing good publicity stories which should interest the media and for this very professional requirement, this job function is assigned to public relations professionals.

A company and its products come to the attention of the public through being newsworthy. Here a marketing company pays nothing for the media coverage it receives. The results of such free publicity can be spectacular.

Many companies do take good advantage of the selling potential of good publicity, and several marketing organizations gear themselves up to make deliberate efforts to generate publicity, considered 'free advertising'.

One vital question arises—Why publicity is so much more powerful than advertising or sales promotion? First, publicity is highly credible. Unlike advertising and sales promotion, publicity is not usually perceived as being sponsored by the company. So consumers perceive this information as more objective and place more confidence in it. Publicity information may be perceived as endorsed by the medium in which it appears.

The bottom line is that publicity is *news,* and people like to pass on information that has news value. Publicity thus results in significant amount of free, credible, word of mouth information regarding the firm and its products (Belch and Belch 1975).

Advertising

While defining advertising, Philip Kotler (2000) said, 'Advertising is any paid form of nonpersonal presentation and promotion of ideas, goods, or services by an identified sponsor.'

'Advertisers include not only business firms but also museums, charitable organizations, and government agencies that direct messages to target publics. Advertisements are a cost effective way to disseminate messages, whether to build brand preference for Coca Cola or to educate people to avoid hard drugs.'

Though marketing firms undertake advertising purely for brand building and product promotion, public relations may use advertising as a tool of communication to the target publics. Since this is a paid form, all steps that marketing professionals take to run their advertising programmes, should be adopted by public relations practitioners.

It will not be out of place to take care of the well known five Ms of advertising:

Mission: What are communication objectives? What mindset change do we want to bring about?

Money: How much is it worth to reach our objectives? How much can be spent?

Message: What message should be sent? Is the message clear and easily understood?

Media: What media vehicles are available? What media vehicles should be used?

Measurement: How should the results be measured? How should the results be evaluated and followed up?

The public relations professionals resort to paid advertising to achieve some specific communication objectives and use advertising as a tool to manage certain organizational objectives, which can be company perception, institutional projections, corporate identity and image building, reinforcing consumers' confidence, crisis management, etc. Some generally known forms of advertising are:

Perception oriented advertising

Publics perceive organizations on the basis of experience that they have with a company, hearsay or what they see or hear in the environment. If left to shape up itself, it may turn out to be what a firm does not want it to be and may harm a company's chances for success or growth. Therefore, well thought out messages are transmitted to the publics through media channels, to keep the public perception in line with the company's objective plan.

Institutional advertising

An advertising programme highlights the history, achievements, and major milestones of the organization to build confidence amongst publics about the professional management. The exercise helps boost levels of trust and credibility in the organization's success story and generate desired responses (Also see chapter 15).

Corporate image and identity advertising

Every firm, small or big, is known by the corporate logo, which it develops to communicate its core competencies and distinct strengths to eventually gain recognition for the corporate symbol or identity in the corporate and commercial world. The logo, as such, becomes a symbol of corporate culture, technology, leadership, customer satisfaction, and trust amongst publics. To reinforce its symbol of identity and culture, an organization advertises to bolster public confidence.

Consumer confidence reinforcement advertising

Several customer driven and successful companies have embraced the relationship marketing philosophy. As they thrive on customer confidence in the company's offerings, the firms communicate from time to time to the customers to reinforce their trust and confidence. Customer service linked events are advertised to attract their attention and involve them so that the relationship between the firm and consumers continues to grow and thrive in mutual interest (See chapter 11).

Advertising in a crisis situation

From a storm in a cup of tea to a tempest in the ocean, every firm, one time or the other confronts a crisis situation. From destruction by acts of God to man made crisis, handling crisis is the top management responsibility and public relations is pushed into the forefront of a crisis situation. More often than not, the crisis deepens when the communications break down and the challenge becomes more severe. Hence public relations resorts to advertising to clear the mist (See chapter 21).

BUDGETING AND APPROVALS

Managements always carefully look at the bottom lines of all the activities and actions of their organization. Therefore, whatever plans are worked out and finalised should be converted into cold statistics in terms of rupees. When convinced that the plans and programmes are in order and workable, the obvious question that is raised, invariably, is—'How much is this going to cost the company and what are the benefits that will accrue out of this public relations exercise?' Therefore, detailed budget should be presented to the management and explicit approval taken in advance. In fact, no programme can start, until the financial approval is obtained.

Professionally managed companies have formats lined up for presenting such budgets and obtaining top management approvals. So it may be appropriate to go along the established practice to avoid controversies and unnecessary discussions. When the budget is cast in the format provided by the firm, the details and figures get comprehended easily and fast enough to facilitate approvals.

Summary

Developing a communication programme to execute a public relations campaign programme is essential. Based on the environmental scan (chapter 4) information, the plan should be drawn out to cover all the essentials of a communication programme.

Mission statement should capture the philosophy and objective of the public relations programme. It should be short, crisp, and clearly spell out the spirit and objective of the programme. It should even spell out the roles and goals of the internal and external publics.

Programme should adopt a thematic logo, which should represent the core message graphically or pictorially, with enough power for prompt registration on the mind screen of publics.

Punch line, a condensation of the message with fewest words and high memorability works wonders to get quicker registration. It is not sheer rhyming or poetical singsong but the programme philosophy captured in least words, easy to remember and easy to speak, to become a part of corporate parlance.

Mnemonic device is used to provide movement to the message that facilitates to draw publics' necessary attention for the success of any communication programme.

Media management includes deciding forum for addressing the publics, media tactics like media relations or media advertising, celebrity involvement, so essential to reach the message to target publics.

Last but not the least, budgeting for financial approvals of management is but essential to kick off the programme.

Key Terms

Backgrounder   A document that explains the history of a company or product

Banner   A long strip of material displaying a slogan, advertisement, etc.

Billboard   A large sign installed on a vantage point of high visibility, used for displaying advertisements

Five Ms of advertising   Mission, money, message, media, measurement

Forum   Communication plank or platform to address the target publics

Group communication   Three or more persons in a group meeting

Logo   Recognizable and distinctive graphic design, stylized name, unique symbol, or other device for identifying an organization

Mission statement   Written declaration of a firm's core purpose and focus which normally remain unchanged

Mnemonic device   A device, such as a formula or rhyme, used as an aid in remembering

One-to-one communication   Dialogue between two persons

Poster   A sign posted in a public place as an advertisement

Press release   An official statement or account of a news story that is specially prepared and issued to newspapers and other news media for them to make known to the public

Publicity   Free mentions in media generated through media relations

Punch/catch line   Simple and catchy phrase accompanying a logo or brand, that encapsulates a product's appeal or the mission of a firm and makes it more memorable

Concept Review Questions

1. Define and describe communication. What are the kinds of communications that an organization practises to run the management business?
2. What is a mission statement? Explain how and why a statement should be developed? What factors and characteristics should be taken into consideration while making one ready?
3. Punch line is the most focal part of the public relations communication programme. Explain the statement.
4. Carrying the right message to the right public is of utmost importance to the success of a communication plan. Explain it with special reference to the social pyramid.
5. Advertising is a tool of public relations, but PR is not a tool of advertising. Please explain and justifiy the statement.

Project Work

1. Keeping in view the chaotic traffic situation and some fatal accidents in your city, say Delhi, please develop a public relations communications plan for solving the problem through change in the mindset of the citizens.

References

Belch, George E. and Michael A. Belch (1975), *Introduction to Advertising and Promotion*, 3rd edition, Irwin McGraw-Hill, USA, pp. 533–534.

Cutlip, Scott M., Allen H. Center, and Glen M. Broom (1985), *Effective Public Relations*, 6th edition, Printice Hall International Editions, USA, pp. 221–260.

Jethwaney, Jaishri and Shruti Jain (2007), *Advertising Management*, Oxford University Press, New Delhi, India, p. 564.

McQuail, Denis (1975), *Towards Sociology of Communication*, Collier-MacMillan, London.

Moore, H. Frazier and Frank B. Kalupa (2005), *Public Relations, Principles, Cases and Problems*, Richard D. Irwin Inc. USA, Surjit Publications, New Delhi, p. 175.

'Population Reports' (1995), Population Information Programme Centre for Communications Programmes, The John Hopkins School of Hygiene and Public Health, USA with USAID support, p. 2.

6 PR Plan Phase III: Implementation of Communication Plan

IMPLEMENTATION OF PR PLAN—A TOUGH TASK

Now the public relations programme enters the third square in the public relations window (See chapter 4 Exhibit 4.1), which denotes taking action or the implementation of the communication plan prepared as phase II (Chapter 5).

A professionally prepared plan can be successful only if implemented seriously and meticulously. An excellent plan may not work if not put into action with single minded dedication. The management professionals opine that action is a magic word and possibly even a mediocre plan, when implemented vigorously, can produce outstanding results. So a good plan, when implemented with professional seriousness, will surely make the programme a grand success.

Since public relations is termed as the process of facilitating a change in the mindset of the publics, the action strategies are fraught with several hurdles, road blocks, and speed breakers. One of the major problems with humans is the strong tendency to resist change. Therefore, an attempt to break the ice is the first and foremost challenge of this process.

RESISTANCE TO CHANGE

Resistance to change is a universal tendency of human nature. It has been observed by behavioural scientists that even if people like to change, they still show their habitual ritual to reject suggestions for change. Fear of failure, risk of loss, or physical or mental discomfort pose serious problems. Although change is the constant factor in our social, political, economic, or cultural set up, it should be interesting and rewarding to observe and study publics' various reasons for resistance to change.

Social Conformity

Social conformity is a dominant factor in all societies. Humans generally conform to the behaviour patterns of their peer groups. 'While in Rome, do as the Romans do' is an age-old idiom but continues to be as good as it has been since time immemorial. We all copy our neighbours yet the fact of the matter is that people conform to the social norms and succumb to the social pressures.

Clifford T. Morgan and Richard A. King with his associates (1986) opine, '.... Each one of us spends considerable time with other people, in formal and informal groups, we are frequently exposed to conformity pressures with which we comply. Many of the things that we do in groups like the clothes we wear, the opinions we express, the choices we endorse are the results of conformity pressures. Acting in concert with others is such an integral part of social life that it is of little interest to ask whether or not conformity occurs.'

All this means that humans live by social conformity or social control, which is considered a risk to challenge the socially accepted norms. This generates a serious threat to public relations professionals when they plan to advocate an idea or value system which challenges the social conformity.

Philip Kotler (2000), well known marketing guru, on the inside front cover page of the millennium edition of his book *Marketing Management* highlights that 'Companies should think about the millennium as a golden opportunity to gain mindshare and heartshare' of the publics. It is very meaningful because public relations addresses this very thrust area of social activity intimately related to marketing and other human disciplines.

Reasons for Resistance to Change

Bringing about a change is not a haphazard effort based on guesses or gut feelings of public relations professional, but a well planned exercise. The logical way to go about is to know the reasons for resistance to change and work out plans and strategies to soften the resistance for ultimate acceptance of the changed value system. Individuals or organizations do not respond until they see some benefits of embracing the change. Most people hate change until they see something there in it for themselves, particularly the jingles it may send into their pockets. Exhibit 6.1 interestingly shows the sources of resistance to change by individuals and the organizations.

Once the plan is ready, it should give the courage of conviction to the public relations professionals and also inspire them to enthusiastically launch upon the programme of action.

The action or implementation warrants all the enthusiasm and seriousness. Many experienced professionals know and tell that this stage of activity is a tough test and calls for tons of energy, perseverance, and untiring persistence.

More often, it is frustrating than inspiring to see people exhibiting complacency in registering the communication messages, due to the human tendency to resist change.

People suffer from a habitual ritual of opposing, resisting, criticizing, and even throwing away the new messages. But the professionals know that for ultimate success, they should courageously go through this transition time and put up a brave front to all types of pin pricks and criticism.

EXHIBIT 6.1 Sources of resistance to change

Individual sources

Habit To cope with life's complexities, we rely on habits or programmed responses. But when confronted with change, this tendency to respond in our accustomed ways becomes a source of resistance.

Security People with high need for security are likely to resist change because it threatens their feeling of safety.

Economic factors Changes in job tasks or established work routines can arouse economic fears if people are concerned that they won't be able to perform the new tasks or routines to their previous standards, especially when pay is closely tied to productivity.

Fear of the unknown selective information processing Change substitutes ambiguity and uncertainty for the known. Individuals are guilty of selectively processing information in order to keep their perceptions intact. They hear what they want to hear and they ignore information that challenges the world they have created.

Organizational sources

Structural inertia Organizations have built in mecha-

nisms like their selection processes and formalized regulations to produce stability. When an organization is confronted with change, this structural inertia acts as a counterbalance to sustain stability.

Limited focus of change Organizations are made of a number of interdependent subsystems. One can't be changed without affecting the others. So limited changes in subsystems tend to be nullified by the larger system.

Group inertia Even if individuals want to change their behaviour, group norms may act as a constraint.

Threat to expertise Changes in organizational patterns may threaten the expertise of specialized groups.

Threats to established power relationships Any redistribution of decisionmaking authority can threaten long established power relationships within the organization.

Threat to established resource allocations Groups in the organization that control sizable resources often see change as a threat. They tend to be content with the way things are.

Source: Robbins, Stephen P. (2005).

MESSAGE MANAGEMENT

One major challenge that public relations confronts, starts with the development of the messages and then to the delivery and the feedback about the registration of the messages. Until a message is developed competently and creatively, delivered to the target public through right medium, and ascertained that the message is registered the way it was intended, there is a sizable risk of the system going a flop. That is why message management is the most focused responsibility of a public relations professional. One of the several reasons, and an important one, for hiring a public relations person is that he is expected to be a communications specialist.

Creativity—A Challenge

Often lot of tribute is paid to creativity in the matter of developing exciting, educating, directing, and entertaining messages. But the vital question is—creativity for what purpose? Creativity is not practised for the sake of creativity, but creativity has to be subjugated to the objective of solving the communication problems of the organization.

Despite several books and theses eulogizing the importance of effective communication, and the writing mechanism devised by experts, it is an individual's personal and intellectual prowess that lends a particular flavour to the messages. Copywriters—good copywriters—are a rare species to come across. However, it is of vital importance for a public relations person to be well versed in the techniques and mechanisms of writing proficiently.

Murphy et al. (1997) say, 'To compose effective written and oral messages, you must apply certain communication principles. These principles provide guidelines for choice of content and style of presentation, adapted to the purpose and receiver of your message. Called the "seven Cs" they are *completeness, conciseness, consideration, concreteness, clarity, courtesy, and correctness...*'. (See chapter 8 Exhibit 8.2).

Though the basic knowledge about writing is an important factor, yet the level of personal intellect, reasonably good vocabulary, the ability to conceptualize ideas, and dress them up creatively, is a vital forte for a public relations professional. Right concept, right words, right message for the right public, is the simple and significant description of this skill set.

For a message to achieve successful and clear registration with the public, the intent and content of the message should have some important characteristics:

1. The message should be so designed and delivered so as to gain favourable attention of the publics for whom the communication has been designed.
2. The language of the message should be generated out of the common parlance of the target public. Until it identifies itself with the vocabulary of the people it may not generate the necessary interest and response.

3. The piece of information so transmitted must kindle some personality needs and should also suggest ways and means to satisfy those needs or solve some of the problems confronted by the publics. Needless to say, also known as secondary needs, the personality needs are the ones which individuals make efforts to satisfy. These needs are social relations, esteem in society, and to be in peace with one's inner soul.
4. The communication should not only address the individual needs, but also those needs of the publics to which they belong. The suggestions to meet the needs should be in line with the group dynamics and norms, which every society has, as part of the social control.

MASS COMMUNICATION

With the media explosion having taken place in the world with the advent of TV, cable network, Internet, mobile telephony and other virtual reality mediums, reaching publics has become more complex.

Today, mass media is a power to reckon with. The power of mass media can hardly be exaggerated, as it exerts a tremendous influence on the society as far as the value system of the individuals and the groups, is concerned. Public relations has to wield this weapon with full knowledge of the working of the mass media, as a vital and powerful tool for bringing about a change in the mindset of the people.

The power of mass communication vis-à-vis mass media has been eulogized by many communication specialists. Daniel Lerner terms them as 'mobility multipliers' and Wilbur Schramm considers them to be 'magic multipliers'. When handled deftly, mass media can do miracles for an organization, and can spell disasters if mishandled or used without fundamental understanding and imagination.

India, where 50 per cent of the population is below the age of 30 years, and eager to experiment with professions and gain success in society, the young people are highly influenced by their high exposures to mass media. Thanks to the growth and development of several new channels of communication, the last half century has witnessed a sea change in the mindsets, vocabulary, and value systems of the people.

Public relations, as such, has to keep abreast with the changes that are taking place, and accordingly develop and deliver messages that go well with thought process of the publics. More often than not, the ideas when communicated from the listeners' or viewers' point of view, have greater chance of getting accepted. Therefore, it is very relevant for professionals to acquaint and update themselves with the changing value systems of our times.

Persuasive Power of Mass Communication

The tremendous influence and persuasive power that mass communication messages have on the publics, reflect in many ways in our society.

1. Mass communication with its great persuasive power almost takes over the function of communicating on behalf of the society. The messages are, as if, born out of the common parlance of the society and smack of public likes, dislikes, taboos, etc.
2. The converting power of mass communication reflects into public psyche, as over a period of time, eventually the society itself becomes a vehicle of communication for or against social issues or a value system. Coming across approvals or disapprovals of certain events or developments is almost a daily affair. Media channels like newspapers and TV stations carrying out opinion polls on certain public affairs is a familiar sight.
3. Mass communication messages seem to empower publics with making certain decisions through mass approval or disapprovals. The society works as a early warning system for certain events or a nation's policies which are expected to come about. Several government policies finding public favour or opposition has become essence of a democratic system.
4. The downward messages to publics by organizations, public and private, are evaluated by the publics, who generate suggestions, solutions to problems, changes, and modification and help to design the kind of society they like to live in and enjoy life.

How Mass Communication Works

Simply stated, mass communication is the process of mass persuasion by spreading a message to the desired public. The efficacy of a message is generally measured by the number of people reached and the number of times the message has been repeatedly exposed to them. How public extend their response to messages is a measure for the assessment of the effectiveness of an idea. With the advent of several communication channels and the resultant cultural complexities and growth of human mind, the process has become more complicated.

According to Philip Lesley (1992), 'There is a very wide range of mental capacities, even within any specified group or classification of people. For simplification, however, we may generalize that most people tend to have either "abstract" or "concrete" minds. The abstract thinker is the writer, the artist, the idea person, who lives with intangibles, is excited by unseen prospects, and seeks the unknown and the new. The concrete thinker is the production man, the accountant, the lawyer—the practical person who generally must feel or see something before he recognizes its existence; who is trained to resist as untrustworthy anything that cannot be measured.'

'Both of these types are essential to the proper working of the society and indeed to the success of any substantial organization. ….When any idea, concept, product, or service is exposed to a group made up of both types, the range of acceptance by the individuals can vary from complete to entirely negative.'

As a generalization of the above concept, we can say that the society is a combination of two kinds of people, the class and the mass. The mass communication process addresses itself to masses for the acceptance or rejection of a value system. As such a lot of publicity and communication material witnessed by us, day in and day out, is targeted at the masses. But if studied deeply, most of these messages seem to generate only an awareness amongst publics about the existence of such an idea. Superficially, it may attain a mere threshold level of registration, when the acceptance of the message may still remain a distant reality.

Time and again, it has been observed that when messages are solely directed at the masses, they do not make any dent until there is participation of the elite class of people. The failure of the family planning programme of the Government of India, which is considered a major public relations failure by many, is attributed to this very reason. It has been observed that most of the communication campaigns were directed at the masses in isolation of the upper class people.

Almost every mass society, everywhere, considers the class members as their role models and hence opinion leaders. Once such opinion leaders, political and social, professionals like doctors, lawyers, journalists, writers and intellectuals, poets and painters, etc., accept an idea, there are greater chances of its acceptance by masses too. The clergy or the spiritual leaders, who are a conduit of messages to the masses, particularly play a vital role. Once a message or value system is accepted and adopted by these opinion leaders, the message percolates to the masses for a willing acceptance, as masses aspire to shape their lives as per the behaviour pattern of the creamy classes of society.

In other words, the route to reach the masses and attain acceptance is through the opinion leaders or the upper classes. Exhibit 6.2 further illustrates the point. Once the opinion leaders, the role models for masses, approve and adopt an idea, it trickles down to the masses for acceptance in expectation of the benefits that classes are already getting out of it.

The Ripple Effect

The mass of humanity is often compared to a stagnant pool of water. A pebble when thrown into the silent pool, sends a series of concentric circles in the water, thus disturbing the pool's tranquility. These circles keep constantly spreading and receding at the pool end. Similarly, when a message is flashed into the tranquil pool of humanity, it sends ripples of ideas amongst the publics.

EXHIBIT 6.2   Mass communication system

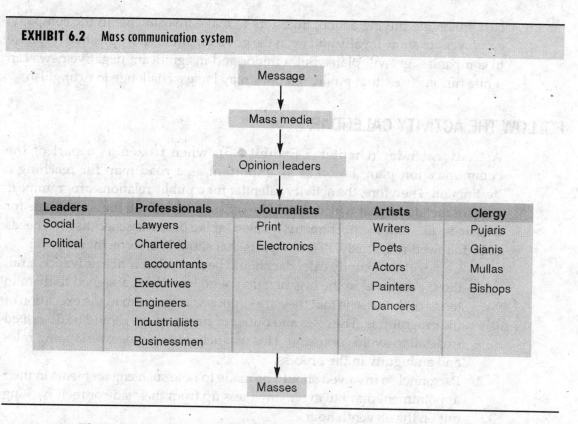

Leaders	Professionals	Journalists	Artists	Clergy
Social	Lawyers	Print	Writers	Pujaris
Political	Chartered	Electronics	Poets	Gianis
	accountants		Actors	Mullas
	Executives		Painters	Bishops
	Engineers		Dancers	
	Industrialists			
	Businessmen			

The 'ripple effect' technique is used by many political parties to build or demolish a public opinion on certain issues and causes with the objective to garner support from their vote banks. Popularly known as the 'word of mouth publicity', it is resorted by the parties with a pre-meditated brief, with considerable success. Instead of using media—print and electronics—the parties use their workers as communication vehicles for spreading the parties' programme agenda. Enough care is taken to develop the brief for a suitable public consumption, starting with party cadres to supporters and on to the voters. The ideas, thus, multiply and spread fast enough to achieve 'ripple effect'.

Public relations professionals also use the technique carefully and creatively to spread the message as a vehicle of mass communication. But the great pitfall in this process is the dangerous tendency of negative messages spreading faster than the positive ones. Positive messages though move slow, yet would eventually have positive effect on the minds of the publics. The 'rumour mill' always works overtime to spread baseless and mischievous messages which can be so damaging that repairing them becomes an uphill and expensive task for public relations.

In the business and corporate world, the benefits of ripple effect are tremendous. The positive results that the word of mouth may create are—inspire customers into buying action, investors to make investments in the company, employees to show loyalty and even the government to show positive response to companies' growth plans. But a minor and insignificant negative news can ignite furious fires, that public relations may have a challenge to extinguish.

FOLLOW THE ACTIVITY CALENDAR

Activity calendar (chapter 5 Exhibit 5.5), when frozen as a part of the communication plan, becomes as important as a road map for reaching a destination. Therefore, the activity calendar for a public relations programme is a sacrosanct document which should be considered with all the seriousness for a business like follow up. The activity calendar is a date wise checklist that needs to be followed religiously. A few aspects that should be borne in mind are:

1. Copies of the activity calendar should be circulated well in advance, to all those personnel in the organization, who have roles assigned to them in terms of the actions that they are supposed to perform in the execution of the programme. The roles and duties of such persons should be described in detail to avoid confusion. This will help in avoiding overlapping roles and ambiguity in the process.

2. Personnel so involved should be made to note such engagements in their appointment diary to avoid any mess up from their side or their backing out on the eleventh hour.

3. It is also a good idea to keep such personnel informed about the progress made. Circulating a periodic status report on the activities listed on the calendar can generate appreciation. People should be mentioned by names instead of positions, every now and then to provide the necessary motivation which all humans need.

4. Public relations person should work more as a coordinator than performing the assingnments himself. He should work like a smart moderator who plays the role of inspiring people to do their bit for the organization's public relations effort. Particularly, when personnel from other departments like finance, manufacturing, and marketing are involved, enough excitement should be created to get their full support.

5. Public relations professional must follow up the activity calendar religiously like a fanatic and demonstrate utmost dedication to the effort. As far as possible, no compromise should be done on changing dates or postponements of the activities, as this will send wrong signals about the public relations person acting superficially. This may even convey an impression of the lack of dedication for the cause and hurt their credibility. One may even run the risk of the programme going flop at the start itself.

6. Ample enthusiasm and interest should be demonstrated in the activity calendar. Enthusiasm being contagious by nature, peers and associates and even the target publics will feel enthused and excited, which are essential for the success of a programme. Frustrations, which are bound to be there in execution process, should not show up, but be absorbed supportingly. The spirits should be kept high, as any inkling of public relations buckling under pressure may lead to low morale, which is again dangerous for the success.

7. The agenda is bound to be heavy. So in addition to the help and co-operation of peers in the organization, it is only advisable to rope in the public relations agency for the necessary professional support in the execution of certain activities that need infra structural help.

8. Once the campaign programme is successfully accomplished and objectives met, public relations deserves credit and kudos, but thanking all for the generous support that the associates extended in the process should also be taken care of. A letter of thanks or symbolic mementos to all will make everyone proud of the contribution that public relations thrived on.

To sum up, the activity calendar should be treated with respect to earn professional respect and excellence.

CONSTANT MONITORING AND MID COURSE CORRECTIONS

During the course of action, the public relations person has to be very vigilant to watch and monitor if all actions are in keeping with the plan. They should be like persons sitting on a radar screen watching the actions and reactions of the target publics.

It is very relevant to look at the dotted line all around the Public Relations Window (chapter 4, Exhibit 4.1) and the arrows directing in and out. They represent the constant effort of collecting feedback from the publics and relating the same to the campaign programme. If the feedback and the responses are positive as stipulated, there is something to feel happy about that the communication process is running as per planned. But if it is otherwise, public relations should gear up to do the fire fighting and plan mid course correction. Whatever elements need modifications and adjustments, these should be carried out fast enough. In this situation there is no room for complacency. Some elements of the communication system that should get public relations attention are:

Forum

If the communication 'forum' from which the audience is being addressed, is not finding favour with the public, it should be modified. The well known congress party election campaign with *Garibi Hatao* was being interpreted by people as *Garib Hatao*. The party, for reasons of their own, did not move in the matter, prompt enough, to change the slogan well in time. Observers opine that it was too late and congress lost election.

Signs and Symbols

Similarly if the signs and symbols or the graphics representing the theme of the programme are generating some animosity or confusion or opposition, public relations should be prompt enough to change or modify them. For whatever reason, the congress party shed the 'plough hitched by a pair of bullocks' symbol to adopt a 'human hand' to appeal to all sections of the electorate rather than only farmers. The hand carries the connotation of support and social security for all sections of the population. The BJP lotus flower symbol born out of Hindu mythology and representing the cultural and economic ethos of India, continues to thrive.

The corporate world zealously guard their brand logos and corporate identity signs and do lot of loud drumming whenever such logos undergo a change or modification, just to maintain the mental perception amongst their publics.

Colours

Colours communicate tremendous connotations (See Exhibit 6.3). Use of colours should be decided carefully. Various colours in various geographical locations in the world generate different emotions amongst publics. Certain colours are associated with certain religions. Light blue represents peace and white the purity and sobriety of human character. Black is considered inauspicious by many. So making a right choice is essential.

Type Face and Size

Use of particular type face and size for a particular message has lot of connotative meanings. Type fonts used for business communications are generally different than the ones used for social purposes to communicate happy and sad occasions alike. Therefore, the messages need to be dressed up in the right type family to generate right response of gaiety or sobriety. Times Roman is generally used for business message, but type fonts like Arial or Script represent different moods. Similarly the small size type, say 14 points represent sobriety of a message while the sizes above 24 points shout for attention and smack of urgency. Also care has to be taken about the type being light face or dark face, as both have connotations of their own.

Public relations does not have to be rigid in approach but should take full advantage of the public mood, through constant monitoring and feedback and be ready to modify or carry out mid course corrections in the campaign

Red: Red colour represents heat and fire. It also has the connotation of exuberance, enthusiasm, excitement, passion, bravery, and chivalry. Blood red stands for a sanguine warfare and victory. It also has come to stay as a symbol of communist struggle against social inequality and injustice. *Lal jhanda* (red flag) is symbolic of a revolt or agitation world over, for economic rights of the working classes.

Brown: Brown to many may represent masculinity or sophistication, but being 'brown' carries a negative connotation of being black or brown Asian aping the white west. However, Cadbury's chocolate brown and Coke's dark brown have come to stay as colours of fun and enjoyment.

Yellow: Yellow, when used in combination with black and red, has the great potential of attracting public attention. It is a pleasant colour and is used by communicators to represent harvesting season and prosperity. Yet the word 'yellow' is often used by educated sections of the society, as something cheap and sensational and not sober, such as yellow journalism. The colour does not stand out alone and needs a combination with other dark colours to create contrast and win attention. Yet the Liptons Yellow Label tea acclaims the high quality and the elite style of tea drinkers.

Green: Green has some good and some not so good connotations. Besides 'going green with envy' it is perceived by many as orthodox. Green also represents agricultural prosperity and abundance. It also stands for freshness and enjoyment. Environmentalist organization such as Green Span uses the colour to campaign for environment protection.

Blue: Different shades of blue connote different meanings. Sky blue speaks of world peace or the United Nations. Dark blue stands for naval outfits and denim blue represents working classes. Some companies, such as the Standard Chartered Bank and Goodyear use various shades of blue as their house colours.

Black: Black though considered inauspicious colour by some, yet is the most frequently used colour for all communications. When used in combination with yellow and red in designing visuals, it lends power of attraction and seriousness to the message.

Orange: Orange with its version of saffron enjoys the connotation of freshness and bravery, patriotism, and sacrifice. Its combination with other colours is often exploited by graphic artists to convey powerful concepts. Soft drink companies such as Mirinda and Fanta use orange to connote a pleasant feeling of freshness.

programme. So the communication messages should be so generated that they meet public approval. Imposing ideas on the people is dangerous, as eventually the public rejection may result in disasters.

Summary

Public relations is often complimented as the harbinger of change. All communications floated with this objective more often than not face public resistance. The social conformity factor is too difficult to shed. Publics are under peer pressure and shy away from change for several reasons. The corporations are no exception.

Creatively harnessing the power of communication is a challenge. Messages, verbal or non-verbal, need to be designed to meet the level of understanding of the publics. There is hardly any scope for a show off of hyperbolic vocabulary. The messages should be generated out of the general parlance of people. The seven Cs of a message should help to manage the message design, development, and delivery. Public relations persons are often advised 'not to impress, but only express'.

Mass communication is a magic multiplier of messages for the consumption of the masses, but the route to reach them is through the opinion leaders whom the society generally considers as their role model. To get an idea accepted or rejected, it is appropriate to sell it first to the opinion leaders for percolation and acceptance by the masses.

Once the activity calendar has been developed and frozen, public relations should follow it up for implementation action seriously and religiously. Any deviation and postponement may take the fizz out of the show.

Public relations is not a one time deal but needs constant monitoring. Any unpalatable message should be considered for modifications. The programme should be flexible enough to incorporate midcourse corrections for success.

Key Terms

Corporate identity   Combination of colour schemes, designs, words, etc., that a firm employs to make a visual statement about itself and to communicate its business philosophy

Group inertia   Reluctance to oppose group norms

Mind share   A consumer's awareness of a particular brand or product compared to that of its rivals

Peer group   A social group consisting of people who are equal in such respects as age, education, or social class

Social conformity   Behavioural or attitudinal compliance with recognized social patterns or standards

Structural inertia   Lack of will to change management structure of an organization

Yellow journalism   A style of journalism that makes unscrupulous use of scandalous, lurid, or sensationalized stories to attract readers

Concept Review Questions

1. What is social 'conformity' and how does it pose hurdles in the way of acceptance of a change? What are the reasons for an individual and a corporation to resist change?
2. Creativity in the area of communication is the forte of a public relations professional. What are the seven rules for developing a good communication message? Explain.
3. Explain the persuasive power of mass communication. How do the messages percolate to masses? What is a ripple effect? Explain.
4. What is the concept called 'forum'? How colours, type faces, and font sizes carry particular connotations in communications? Explain.
5. Although public relations should be rigid enough to adhere to the plan laid out in the 'activity calendar' yet, in response to public reactions, it should be sensitive enough to carry out some mid course corrections. Explain.

References

Kotler, Philip (2000), *Marketing Management, Millennium Edition*, Prentice Hall of India Private Limited, New Delhi.

Kumar, Keval J. (2001), *Mass Communication in India,* Jaico Publishing House, Mumbai, India, p. 15.

Lesly, Philip (1992), *Handbook of Public Relations and Communications,* 4th edition, Probus Publishing Company, 1925, USA and printed in India by Jaico Publishing House, Bombay, p. 43.

Morgan, Clifford T., Richard A. King, John R. Weisz, and John Schopler (1986), *Introduction to Psychology*, McGraw-Hill International Editions, 7th edition, Singapore, p. 356.

Murphy, Herta A., Herbert W. Hildedrandt, and Jane P. Thomas (1997), *Effective Business Communications,* International Edition, The McGraw-Hill Companies Inc. USA, pp. 31–32.

Robbins , Stephen P. (2005), *Organizational Behavior*, Prentice Hall of India Private Limited, New Delhi, p. 553.

7 PR Plan Phase IV: Evaluation of Impact

ORGANIZATION'S CONCERN—IMPACT OF PR PLAN

The public relations window (See chapter, 4 Exhibit 4.1) which conceptualizes the system of running a public relations programme, now reaches the fourth and the final square or stage. With budgeted money spent on the execution of the programme, with the objective to bring about a change in public mindset, it should now be evaluated, whether or not the public relations exercise paid for and the impact that the communication plan stipulated has been achieved.

More than the creativity and power of communication tools that have been used in the process, what concerns an organization is the impact, if created. Lest, all the time and efforts to showcase the communication content and visuals, are lost, it is of vital meaning to a company to know whether the total public relations exercise did, what it was supposed to do, and if the stipulated change has been brought about and the problems solved.

Many public relations practitioners seem to put a lot of focus on the activities that they carry out to implement the public relations plan but often lose sight of the fact that managements are more interested in results. Organizations are more interested in the ends rather than the means used for achieving the ends. However, if the professionals would like to make their managements proud and earn the credit for a job well done, then there is no escape from researching the impact and demonstrating to all concerned as to how well the programme was planned and professionally executed and objectives achieved.

EVALUATION RESEARCH PROCESS

In the words of Scott M. Cutlip et al. (1985), 'Impetus for increased emphasis on the evaluation step also results from management's insistence on accountability for the increasing sums being spent on public relations. Increasingly practitioners are being asked to document that the programmes produce measurable results and that the return is commensurate with the cost. Public relations, like other line and staff functions, is being evaluated by how much it contributes to the advancement of the organization's mission. Executives in all types of organizations, from the largest corporations to the smallest non-profit groups, ask for evidence of programme impact particularly when budgets are being reviewed and new budgets set.'

Public relations effort of the firms is obviously not merely aimed at a show off or boasting and bragging about their greatness. The business world always have a well placed focus on bottom lines. Managements are keen to assess the quantum of contributions that public relations is directly or indirectly making to profits or the financial health of the company. Many enlightened and serious minded executives accept that public relations is not just a cosmetic attachment to the organization, but an important functionary to carry out specific operations. Therefore, no practitioner should shy away from the uncomfortable word 'research', but take the bull by the horns.

Researching impact will not only help the PR professionals to demonstrate the success of the plan but also enhance their respect as professionals. However, research has some dreadful connotations. Many organizations either carry out a superficial and face saving exercise or avoid research for cost saving reasons. Sometimes the research may be a politically motivated exercise by one element of the management to embarrass their rival peer groups. However, the research is definitely a valuable system to measure the impact.

The enlightened and seasoned practitioners would be more than willing to undertake the research to determine the *impetus* achieved by the public relations programme, so that the challenge and benefits are in clear focus. Naturally, proving that the exercise has been worth the time, money, and human energy spent, will not only highlight the relevance of the effort, but also establish the credibility of the public relations discipline. Research helps to separate the facts from fiction and bring a clear vision to the company about the shape of things to come and the challenges that await the organization.

H. Frazier Moore and Frank B. Kalupa (2005) opine, 'Basic studies in public relations and communication, including the concept of influence, social behaviour, social groups, opinion formation, attitude change, persuasion, the role of the opinion leader, criticism, and other aspects of human relationships, are important areas of public relations research which have so far been largely neglected by business and left to the social scientists.'

In view of the above, the public relations job may not only be confined to planning and execution of a communication programme, but the fourth step, i.e., 'measuring the impact', should be a crucial, hence essential part of the exercise. Some practitioners, due to fear of failure and the resultant criticism, may prefer to stay away from research. Whereas the success may overwhelm them with pride, the failure may depress or frustrate them beyond measure. So professionals should be aware that more often than not, the credit for success may go to someone favourite of the big bosses and the blame for failure to the public relations. Therefore, the measurement of programme impact is professionally justified and essential. The nature of the research effort is generally confined to two areas—communication effect research and impact research.

COMMUNICATION EFFECT RESEARCH

The communication effect research, as described by the advertising professionals, is an effort to determine how effectively a message communicates an idea to the target publics. The efficacy of a message depends on the quality of a message, delivery through right media and to the right publics. The communication should have the basic qualities as outlined in chapter 5.

This aspect of research should address two issues; first, the qualitative and second, the quantitative. Whereas the qualitative aspect of the communication research should be probed for its efficacy in developing and delivering the messages to the target public for registration and the quantitative aspect should assess the volume of communication tools generated in the process.

Qualitative Assessment

Philip Kotler (2000), while dealing with advertising communications, opines that an advertising message for that matter any message, should be rated on five counts: 1. Attention gaining power; 2. Read through facility; 3. Cognitive qualities; 4. Affectiveness of appeal; and 5. Behaviour action. He suggests a rating sheet for evaluation of any message from poor to great. Exhibit 7.1 should explain this.

Since public relations uses advertising as a tool of communication, advertising evaluation standards should be, by and large, relevant. As advertising is a tool of public relations, but public relations is not a tool of advertising, the success of a tool is the success of its creator, i.e., public relations.

EXHIBIT 7.1 Communication rating sheet

Criteria	Score	Out of
(Attention) How well does the ad catch the reader?	—	20
(Read through) How well does the ad lead the reader to read further?	—	20
(Cognitive) How clear is the central message or benefit?	—	20
(Affective) How effective is the particular appeal?	—	20
(Behaviour) How well does the ad suggest follow-through action?	—	20
Total	—	100

The scale on the basis of which the score is evaluated is the following:

```
0          20         40         60         80        100
   Poor ad    Mediocre ad   Average ad    Good ad    Great ad
```

Source: Kotler (2000).

As a public relations practitioner is expected to be a creative communicator, his natural ability to write creatively is his essential qualification. He enjoys a natural flair for writing, complimented by his free flowing vocabulary. But this sensitive area has its own pitfalls as all messages and relevant vocabulary or compositions, are not good for all publics. One piece of writing that looks very competent and interesting for one group of people, may not find favour with the other section, as they may consider it difficult to understand or even offending. So matching the levels of communication with the mental or educational levels of the audience poses a major challenge. For reasons of bench marking, a number of systems have been suggested and the Gunning Fog Index as a fairly comprehensive one.

The Gunning Fog Index

In linguistics, the Gunning Fog Index is a test designed to measure the readability of a sample of English writing. The resulting number is an indication of the number of years of formal education that a person requires in order to easily understand the text on the first reading. The Gunning Fog Index can work as a handy tool for public relations specialists to test the effectiveness of a communication message for a particular public, as far as its readability and comprehensive qualities are concerned.

The Gunning Fog Index, as outlined by Lesikar and Pettit Jr (1996), can be used with the review of some simple steps. Its ease of interpretation is enhanced by the fact that the index computed from these steps is in grade level of education. For example, an index of 7 means that the material tested is easy reading for someone at the seventh grade level; an index of 12 indicates high school graduate level of readability; and an index of 16 indicates college graduate level.

Four steps have been advised to calculate the Fog score:

1. **Select a sample:** For long pieces of writing, use at least 100 words. As in all sampling procedures, the larger the sample, the more reliable the results are. Thus, in measuring readability for a long manuscript you would be wise to select a number of samples at random throughout the work.

2. **Determine the average number of words per sentence:** First count words. Then count sentences, treating as sentences all independent clauses. Divide the total number of words by the total number of sentences.

3. **Determine the percentage of hard words per sentence:** Words of three or more syllables are considered hard words. But do not count as hard words (a) words that are capitalized, (b) combinations of short, easy words (grasshopper, dishwasher, bookkeeper), or (c) verb forms made into three-syllable words by adding *ed* or *es* (repeated, caresses).

4. **Add the two factors computed above, and multiply by 0.4:** The product is the minimum grade level at which the writing is easily read.

Application of the Gunning Fog Index is illustrated with the following paragraph:

'In general, construction of pictograms follows the general procedure used in constructing bar charts. But two special rules should be followed, first, all of the picture units used must be of equal size. The comparisons must be made wholly on the basis of the number of illustrations used and never by varying the areas of the individual pictures used. The reason for this rule is obvious: The human eye is grossly inadequate in comparing areas of geometric designs. Second, the picture or symbols used must appropriately depict the *quantity* to be illustrated. A comparison of the navies of the world, for example, might make use of miniature ship drawings. Cotton production might be shown by bales of cotton. Obviously, the drawings used must be immediately interpreted by the reader.'

Inspection of the paragraph reveals these facts. It has 10 sentences and 129 words for an average sentence length of 13. Of the total 129 words, 26 are considered hard words. Thus, the percentage of hard words is 20. From this data, the Gunning Fog Index is computed as follows:

Average sentence length	13
Percentage of hard words	20
Total	33
Multiply by	0.4
Grade level of readership	13.2

This exercise amongst others is recommended by the communication experts to assist the public relations professionals to ensure that the effect of the communication works out as per the stipulated communication objectives.

Pre-starting stage and post release stage

To assess suitability of a message for a particular kind of publics, the mechanism can be applied at *pre-starting* and the *post release stages*.

At the *pre-starting stage*, the practitioners may do some informal random sampling of a piece of communication by testing them with the representatives of the intended public, to gauge their reaction and responses. If found compatible, it should serve as an assurance that the message will find its suitable registration with the intended public.

At the *post release stage*, the practitioners formally try to get the feedback and sift the findings out of the mass of information collected through surveys or questionnaires, and draw conclusions. If the messages are in line with the objectives of the programme, it is well and good, otherwise the need for strategic adjustments or modifications in the communication platform or vocabulary is to be determined.

Several companies conduct some formal research, either through well designed sample surveys with questionnaires directed at the target audience, to feel the pulse of the public and to determine if the programme has been on track. For cost saving reasons, the companies either use the staff resources or college interns to conduct such surveys. Depending on the size and seriousness of the issue, organizations also use either the research departments of their public relations agencies or commission external opinion poll research agencies. Obviously, the fees involved for such assignments generally match with the reputation and stature of the professional companies. All such compatibility search is supplemented by another mechanism called public relations audit.

PUBLIC RELATIONS AUDIT

To determine the effectiveness of public relations endeavours, the companies are interested in assessing the returns that they expect or anticipate from the investments made in public relations efforts. The quality of the public relations projects and the impact it leaves on publics, are of considerable concern to the managements. Therefore, the public relations audit, namely the communication audit is not in vogue as a fashion, but as a business necessity.

H. Frazier Moore and Frank B. Kalupa (2005) are of the opinion, 'Intelligent, responsible public relations, which implies a willingness to state one's case candidly and listen respectfully to the publics one serves, can play an important role in helping a company capitalize on its strengths. Just as importantly, it can help to discover the direction by which a company may strive to overcome its weakness. The public relations audit can provide a valuable management tool to accomplish these purposes and its increasing use is one of the most promising signs of maturity in the modern practice of public relations.'

The public relations audit should cover four steps:
1. **Determine management perception:** Do a SWOT (Strengths, Weakness, Opportunity, and Threats) analysis of the company. Also identify the target publics and research target publics' views on issues and problems with well designed questionnaires.
2. **Determine public perception:** Start a dialogue with target publics to ascertain whether the company and public perceptions match.
3. **Determine the perception gap:** Discover and define the gaps revealed by SWOT and relate to the present scenario.
4. **Develop a plan to bridge the gap:** Develop a strategic and comprehensive communication plan to be proposed to the management.

Once the public relations audit is complete and the diagnosis reveals some facts that need to be taken care of, the public relations specialist can take certain actions, to attain the desired impact, as per the project objectives.

Quantitative Assessment

Whereas the assessment of the impetus created by the intrinsic qualities of the communication aspect of public relations project is of prime importance, doing a quantitative audit of the various communication tools used is desirable and the necessary. This will give the practitioner two advantages; one, the framework (See Exhibit 7.2) developed for monitoring the efforts will keep the plan on track; two, readily showcase the volume of activities generated throughout the campaign period.

Programme tracking matrix

Many a specialist, who have been doing a splendid job in the organizations, miss out on this aspect of keeping their company managements informed about the volume of work involved in carrying out the public relations responsibilities. The spread of activities, as such being outstanding and voluminous, may be proclaimed impressive. But beware that the transparent nature of this exhibit may facilitate practitioner's peers to take credit for something they have never done or had some peripheral involvement. The public relations may be used as a whipping boy for organizational failures and deprived of the credit and appreciation that it deserves.

Exhibit 7.2, when created at the beginning of the year and followed through, month by month, also works as a road map to keep public relations programme on rails and assure and reassure the specialist that the project is progressing as per planned.

Explicitly speaking, the matrix when created by the practitioners will reduce the total plan into a tabulated single sheet road map with major efforts and events planted monthwise for a follow up action. This serves as a ready

EXHIBIT 7.2   Quantitative assessment

Quantitative communication audit

Communications	Jan	Feb	Mar	Aprl	May	Jun	Jul	Aug	Sept	Oct	Nov	Dec	Week Month
Customer bulletin–W	///	//	//	//	//	//	//	//	//	///	///	///	5000
Employees newsletter–W	////	////	////	////	////	////	////	/////	/////	////	////	/////	3000
Dealer newsletter–F	//	//	//	/	//	/	//	//	/	//	///	///	500
House journal–M	/	/	/		/	/	/	/	/	/	/	/	5000
Direct mailer–Q				/			/		/			/	10000
Posters				/				/	/	/		//	20000
Banners	/			/				/		/		//	700
Corporate ads						/					/	/	1000
Stickers	/		/				/					//	10000
POP material			/			/						//	5000
House flags	/								/			/	500
Annual report												/	25000
Chairman speech												/	2000
Retiree magazine–Q			/			/			/			/	500
Open house–A									/				500

W = weekly   F = fortnightly   M = monthly   Q = quarterly   A = annual

reckoner to track the progress being made at various stages of the programme execution.

The matrix also serves as a constant evaluator of the programme, as the plan progresses through the timetable. The deviations or failure to take an action on the scheduled dates send warning signals to the professional that the project may suffer due to lack of interest or dwindling enthusiasm and commitment.

Come December or the close of the scheduled timetable, it becomes clearly evident that the project progressed as per plan. The implementation, for the time being will mirror the impact that has been created amongst the publics, leave alone the formal research that may be conducted later to translate facts and figures to ascertain the impact.

Converting the success into cold statistics that remains to be done, can either be conducted through an in-house research effort or by commissioning an outside agency, depending on the size and proportions of the project.

With all the publications, newsletters, posters, stickers, and reports created and a well documented photo or video coverage, it can be a grand occasion for the practitioner to organize a presentation to the management to showcase the enormous operation as well as the impact it created. Naturally, it is time for the public relations division to take credit for what it did, and if not, why?

Media tracking

Amongst the several responsibilities of public relations, media relations is one major assignment. Many organizations keep a good track of the amount of press clippings collected every month. Some even would count the amount of column centimeters earned every month and finally have a yearly assessment.

The reasons for this quantification are meaningful, as the coverage generated in the media is absolutely free and very rewarding in terms of the role the media focus plays in getting free publicity for the organization. Many shrewd businessmen think, though not logical, that more the column centimeters generated, more is the saving on direct advertising expenses. Although in principle, this public relations effort to generate free publicity, theoretically and fundamentally, should not be considered a replacement for the advertising programme, yet the amount of space earned free, is perceived as clear savings.

Also, the power of media coverage compared to the one paid for advertising is much more in terms of the credibility that media reports enjoy, in sharp contrast to advertising. After all, the credibility of an advertisement is always doubted, as the audiences understand it as a sponsored insertion with a tinge of exaggeration. As such an advertisement is rarely rated 100 per cent true. Some ad watchers call advertising a bunch of 'true lies'. But the editorial material, both in print and electronics media, enjoy a high degree of public trust.

Therefore, it is advisable that public relations should take the opportunity to demonstrate to the management the column centimeters earned vis-à-vis the amount of money saved for the organization. The fact remains that business organizations are a money game and the money saved is the money earned, and for that matter a direct contribution to the bottom line called profit.

As demonstrated in Exhibit 7.3, the savings may be presented to express and impress the management with the contributions made by public relations. This may also puncture the management myth that public relations handles only the spending side of business. But it is also a direct contributor to the financial strength of the company.

Through the above media relations efforts, 511 column centimeters of space worth Rs 7,99,824 has been earned free, which is definitely an outstanding achievement. Managements generally are not well exposed to the system of advertising. Therefore, it may be appropriate to multiply the space earned free in each publication with its col/cm. rate to arrive at the value of the space. When the value of the total space thus earned free in each publication, added up, the figure should look grand and impressive.

Now had the organization bought that much space in media, it will directly put burden on the public relations budget. Either the budget may have to be stretched or the company may have to forego certain communication programme, in favour of media relations efforts by public relations.

EXHIBIT 7.3   Public relations contribution

Quantification of press media coverage

Newspaper	Space earned col/cm	Rate @ Rs col/cm	Free space worth Rs	Circulation copies
Hindustan Times	15 × 3 = 45	3000	135,000	10,50,000
Times of India	20 × 3 = 60	3400	204,000	11,50,000
Indian Express	25 × 3 = 75	300	22,500	1,50,000
Statesman	17 × 3 = 51	400	20,400	2,00,000
Telegraph	12 × 3 = 36	2400	86,400	4,50,000
Hindu	21 × 3 = 63	2550	160,650	3,15,000
Financial Express	25 × 2 = 50	800	40000	1,50,000
Economic Times	20 × 3 = 60	1400	84,000	1,95,000
Mint	13 × 2 = 26	625	16,500	4,00,000
Hindu Business Line	15 × 3 = 45	675	30,374	1,52,000
Total	511		799,824	4,060,000

Note: All figures are hypothetical for demonstrating the concept.

INTERPRETING THE IMPACT

Cee B.M. van Riel (1995) while commenting on the importance of evaluation of any public relations programme, expressed, 'It is often difficult to quantify the contribution that communication makes towards realizing the objectives of an organization. One important reason for this is the lack of a standard procedure for automatic measurement. This does not mean that it would be a simple matter to determine whether the objectives have been met, although it is by no means impossible.'

Riel adds, 'A process evaluation is the evaluation, by means of a theoretically derived standard protocols, of internal processes during the preparation and implementation phases. A production evaluation is aimed at determining whether the communication objectives vis-à-vis the target groups have been met. This may be analysed in terms of changes in knowledge, attitude and behavioural intentions.'

Cutlip, Center, and Broom (1985) opined, 'Specific criteria for evaluating programme effects should be clearly stated in the objectives that guided programme preparation and implementation. Those criteria will centre on changes or maintenance of knowledge, predispositions, and behaviours of internal and external publics, and the consequences theoretically associated with these cognitive, attitudinal and behavioural outcomes' (See Exhibit 7.4).

EXHIBIT 7.4	Levels and criteria for evaluating public relations programmes
Impact	Social and cultural change
	Objective met—problem solved
	Number who repeat behaviour
	Number who behave in desired manner
	Number who change attitudes
	Number who change opinions
	Number who learn and absorb
	Message awareness
Implementation	Readership, viewership, listenership, attendance
	Reach of the message
	Media coverage
Plan	Distribution of messages—number
	Message style—logo, punchline
	Message management—forums
	Information—adequate through research/intelligence

Source: Cutlip et al. (1985).

Some of the criteria listed by them are as follows:

The number of people who learn message content

As already discussed in this chapter, it is very vital that the communication messages should be exposed to the publics to move them from the unawareness level to the awareness levels. It is like transferring the information and updating the skills of the people to make them comprehend the merits or demerits of an issue or an idea. Many customer driven companies make deliberate efforts to educate customers in the proper installation and usage of the equipments they sell. Microsoft and HCL make user friendly computers which guide the buyers about the proper operation so that they get the best out of their gadgets. They have realized that computer literacy pays dividends. The effort contributes to the lifestyle changes which generate greater demand. Tyre companies promote pleasure motoring to impact greater tyre usage and brand loyalty.

The number of people who change their opinions

Inculcating a change in public opinion is an uphill task and fraught with circumstances that make many a public relations programme inconsequential. With ever increasing vehicle population in Delhi, the police, over and above several administrative measures, have launched a high profile communication campaign to impact sane driving in the interest of road safety. Umpteen newspaper advertisements and mass distribution of educational literature to the motorists, seems to yield negligible results. One of the reasons, perhaps, is the young inexperienced drivers with poor driving reflexes. The influx to Delhi, by unurbanized population, in search of job opportunities, erode the impact. So the measurement of change in opinion poses problems.

The number of people who change their attitudes

A person's high or low social status or his conservative or liberal pre-disposition may have little to do with his attitude. Reams have been written about having a positive attitude. Education and knowledge are expected to change the attitude of the publics, but not really. A highly educated person may be highly conservative in his attitude. The male dominated Indian society still longs for the birth of a son compared to the gloom that spreads in a family on the arrival of a daughter. Even the affluence may be counter productive. Punjab and Haryana, despite being the most affluent states of India with good literacy levels, their imbalance of male-female ratio is a matter of national concern. Some prominent social and religious organizations like the Shiromani Gurudwara Prabandhak Committee (SGPC) in Punjab, have taken up a public relations programme to prevent female foeticide, so rampant in the state.

The number of people who act in the desired fashion—behavioural change

The difference between promise and performance, more often than not, shows a wide gap. Hearing people loudly talking for or against an issue may make one believe that people have changed their behaviours. Unfortunately, people talk something and do something else. The evils like bride burning and dowry demands are often condemned in public. Conduct a survey, and you may find none may be able to truthfully tick 'No' on the question: 'Did you accept dowry from girl's parents?' Who will admit that he cheated on Income Tax payment? Ask a young man, 'Will you marry an out-of-caste girl against the wishes of his parents?', and the answers will be deceptive. Until the power of a public relations programme can engineer a genuine behavioural change, it cannot be termed successful.

The number of people who repeat or sustain the desired behaviour

One major objective of any public relations project is to maximize the number of people, who change their behaviour and sustain the pattern over a longer period of time. Temporary changes cannot be counted as success. The celebration of Safety Week might reduce the number of traffic violations or accidents during that week, but if the figures zoom back to usual or beyond, the police may not be entitled to take credit for this public relations effort. One major public relations failure of India on the family planning front can, perhaps, be attributed to the half-hearted approach, with population zooming past one billion. Only a long-term sustainable behavioural change brought about by public relations, can be entitled to success.

Programme goal achieved or problem solved

Contrary to the belief that several people hold, particularly the bureaucrats, that no problem can be solved without the imposition of strict rule of law, public relations has to address many sensitive problems. Where the law fails, public relations as the process of persuasion has a chance to succeed. Many social marketing campaigns like child marriage, child labour, aids awareness, blood donations by Red Cross, eye donations appeals, etc. may have a better chance to succeed. The philanthropic issues, when touched by public relations on an emotional plank, may succeed. You may ban smoking in public areas by law and impose severe penalties for the offenders, but people still do not stop smoking. The traffic policemen, hiding behind bushes, to penalize offenders, may feel proud of the number of drivers caught, yet the roles will be more meaningful if they fit into the public relations efforts of the authorities to instill better road sense amongst the citizens.

Contribution to positive social and cultural change

Public relations is considered to be the facilitator of change. The bottom line of any programme should be to see a change taking place in the social and cultural environment. Though change is a constant factor in societies, yet it takes a considerably long time for a change to come about. The communications trickle into the thought process of the publics drop by drop and one day, perhaps in a few years, publics do realize that they have changed. In India, a look half century backwards, will help us to visualize the change that has taken place in the cultural ethos. From a conservative and spirituality soaked society, the publics have emerged more pragmatic and businesslike. The history, perhaps, is a better witness to such changes.

In the words of Cutlip, Center, and Broom (1985), 'Those in the calling derive their professional motivation and fulfil their social responsibilities by concerning themselves with impact at the level of social and cultural change. They will be judged by future generations accordingly.'

Summary

The measurement of impact, as a fourth and final phase of any public relations programme, is the final verdict on the success. To determine success, and its quantum, a public relations specialist needs to research the impact.

Although, to some specialists, research is a dreadful word, yet it is a must, not only to assess their own professional position, but also to demonstrate to their managements that the returns more than justify the budgets expended on the public relations.

Two kinds of research have to be taken up. First, the communication effect research to determine the efficacy of the communication, as far as its reach and level is concerned, to match the intellect level of publics. This calls for a challenge of creativity in writing messages compatible with the educational and mental levels of the publics. The messages can be tested with application of certain testing models.

Second is the quantification of the volume of communications transmitted to the publics through various tools of communication like newsletters, journals, posters, events, etc. The quantification of media relations exercise, which involves generation of free publicity for the cause or the organization, may be projec-ted by putting a currency tag to the effort. The volume of free space in print media and time slots in the electronic media, when converted into rupees, will make a business sense to the managements.

The impact created by a public relations programme should necessarily be further quantified as far as the economic, social, and attitudinal or behavioural changes it helps to engineer.

Key Terms

Cognitive quality   The ease or speed with which a message is understood

Gunning Fog Index   A test designed to measure the readability of a sample of English writing

Programme tracking matrix   A format to assess the success of a public relations programme

Public relations audit   A research tool that examines and assesses all aspects of an organization's activities to diagnose the extent to which each public is receiving and responding to the messages targeted towards them

Social behaviour   Any behaviour caused by or affecting another individual, usually of the same species

Social groups   Two or more humans who interact with one another, accept expectations and obligations as members of the group, and share a common identity

Concept Review Questions

1   It has been reported in the media that last year more than 100 persons have been killed by blue line buses in Delhi, and in accidents due to factors like poor road sense and violation of traffic rules. Please develop a public relations programme to generate awareness and mindset change amongst citizens to save precious lives. Please support your answer with words and visuals.

2.   What is qualitative research carried out by public relations practitioners to assess the registration power of communications for a certain level of public?

3.   What are the various yardsticks that should be applied to evaluate the impact that a particular public relations campaign has achieved after the completion of a public relations exercise? Explain.

4.   What is public relations audit? Explain the nuances and steps involved in conducting such an audit?

References

Cutlip, Scott M., Allen H. Center, and Glen M. Broom (1985), Prentice Hall International editions, Prentice Hall Inc, USA, pp. 290, 296, 303–307.

Kotler, Philip (2000), *Marketing Management, Millennium Edition*, Prentice Hall of India Private Limited, New Delhi, pp. 594, 304.

Lesikar, Raymond, V. and John D. Pettit Jr (1996), *Business Communication, Theory and Application*, Richard D. Irwin, Inc, Illinois, p. 748.

Moore, H. Frazier and Frank B. Kalupa (2005), *Public Relations, Principles, Cases and Problems,* 9th edition, Richard D. Irwin, Inc., USA, printed in India by Surjeet Publications, Delhi, pp. 108 and 116.

Riel, Cees B.M. van (1995), *Principles of Corporate Communication*, Prentice Hall, Hertfordshire, p. 130.

PART III

SKILLS

8

Communication and Public Relations

COMMUNICATION AND PUBLIC RELATIONS

Public relations and communication are two inseparable parts of one discipline. Whereas communication is regarded by experts as a dynamic process of exchange of information between two persons during which a relationship develops between them, public relations is the system of making the process more effective and successful. Communication has been described as a transactional process of exchange of messages, to negotiate on certain topics and issues, to establish a mature relationship based on understanding. Public relations practitioners have a focused responsibility of managing the communications system, which is driven by them for the same objective of generating relationships based on understanding and goodwill. As such communication plays a subordinate role to the functioning of public relations discipline.

Communication is synonymous with the practice of public relations. The objective being the same, that is, to establish understanding with the publics, communication is a unique tool that public relations wields to make it happen. If public relations succeeds in informing, persuading, and influencing the public attitudes for or against a value system, or bring about a change in public responses, the credit for making this happen goes to public relations practitioners for creatively designing and delivering the messages, and thereby ensure the efficacy of communications.

Communication is the lifeline of human existence. Communication is a continuous process like breathing, which is so essential to a living being that the stoppage of it can be fatal. Similarly, the process of communication, if breaks down, may mean a disaster. Hundreds of tragedies and wars can be attributed to the breakdown of communication.

Communication is perhaps the most important activity that all humans indulge in. We spend a large part of the day in communicating than doing anything else. Perhaps, a larger share of time goes to talking and listening. When people are not talking or listening, they still seem to be communicating in so many other ways like reading, writing, gesturing, drawing, etc. or use their body to communicate ideas or moods to others. Gesturing like smelling, frowning, or smiling, are all forms of communication, which humans adopt to carry themselves well in this world.

Communication has helped the present society to develop the way it is and will further play its catalytic role for the future generations.

The power of communication has further helped the civilization to organize themselves into a system of working together as groups or teams in inter-dependent roles. The formation of gigantic global organizations and their smooth functioning depends on the way they effectively run their communication system.

Thanks to the urge of humans to communicate, and communicate frequently and instantaneously, the communication and information explosion has become a reality in the last part of the 20th century. It is a miracle to see a piece of science fiction turning into a reality. The fairy tales of telepathy or communicating through sub-conscious mind have come alive with the invention of Internet and mobile telephony.

THE COMMUNICATION PROCESS

Wilbur Schramm, Director of the Institute of Communication Research, USA (1955) wrote, 'Communication comes from the Latin *communis*, common. When we communicate we are trying to establish a "commonness" with someone. That is, we are trying to share information, an idea, or an attitude. At this moment I am trying to communicate to you the idea that the essence of communication is getting the receiver and the sender "tuned" together for a particular message. At this same moment, someone somewhere is excitedly phoning the fire department that the house is on fire. Somewhere else a young man in a parked automobile is trying to convey the feeling that he is moon-eyed because he loves the young lady. Somewhere else a newspaper is trying to persuade its readers to believe as it does about the republican party. All these are forms of communication, and the process in each case is essentialy the same.'

Communication, effective or otherwise, seems to be happening as a natural human phenomenon, but experts have developed a logical process, for a proper understanding of the system. Communication, when has an objective, has to be delivered as a message. This means the transfer of a message and its meaning from the sender to the receiver. Thus the elements involved in the process are *the sender, encoding, the message, the channel, decoding, the receiver, noise,* and *feedback* (See Exhibit 8.1).

The *sender* initiates a message by encoding a thought. The *message* is the actual physical product from the sender's *encoding*. When we speak or write, we gesture, move arms and hands, and the expression on our faces are all messages.

The *channel* is the medium through which the message travels. It is selected by the sender, who uses the formal or informal channels. Formal channels are as per the official practice adopted by a company, whereas the informal channels are used for sending social or personal messages.

The *receiver* is the objective to whom the message is directed. For success, it is essential that a commonality of language, both verbal and non-verbal, should exist. This will facilitate the process of *decoding* the message for proper understanding by the receiver.

Noise represents communication barriers that distort the clarity of the message. The possible noise sources could be garbled information, cultural differences, or perception problems.

Feedback, the final link in the communication process, is the check on the success of the messages transmitted, as far as the originality of the message from the sender to the receiver is concerned.

Despite understanding the fundamentals of this process, it is generally believed that communication is never perfect. In fact that lacuna is the main

EXHIBIT 8.1 The communication process

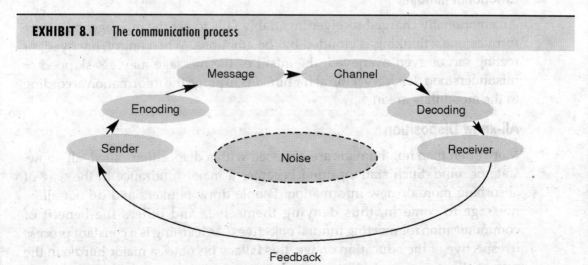

problem of this simple system. The barriers in the way of communication, if understood well, can be borne in mind to avoid communication foul ups.

BARRIERS IN COMMUNICATION

The process of communication is fraught with barriers, which are either born out of the human need to mould messages to be favourable to their own interest, or certain emotional and environmental influences that deeply affect the process of communication. When the parties involved in the process consciously safeguard against such factors, the chances of success of the communication improve considerably.

Manipulation

Since people listen what they like to listen and see what they like to see, the sender purposely manipulates the information such that it finds favour with the receiver. The element of truthfulness is either negated or distorted to suit one's objectives like a subordinate twisting the details to make it favourable to the boss. Higher the number of layers of authority in a management, greater is the possibility of manipulation of information.

Problem of Plenty

If the information received by the receiver is more than one can handle or absorb, the communication clarity will suffer. More the information, more the distortions. The receivers have the tendency to skip or ignore the information they cannot absorb, which may result in miscommunication.

Emotional Mindset

An emotionally charged receiver invariably fails to get the message in its pure form as one's thinking is clouded by the emotions. When angry, annoyed, or feeling sad or even overjoyed, the intent of the message may get skipped or misunderstood. It is very natural for humans to judge the information according to the mood they are in.

All-know Disposition

More often than not, humans are obsessed with a disposition called 'all know' state of mind. Such state of mind becomes a major hindrance in the way of absorbing more or new information. People draw blinkers and do not allow message to come in, thus denying themselves and others the benefit of communication for meeting mutual objectives. As learning is a constant process irrespective of the education or age, this fallacy becomes a major hurdle in the way of effective communication.

Frozen Evaluations

Several receivers freeze their ideas and impressions about certain value systems and personalities and are not willing to change their mind. There are many obscure and illogical or fixed ideas that people have, which prevent them from looking at the message objectively. Rightly so they stand in the receiver's way to understand the message in the right perspective. The pre-conceived notions are dangerous to the free flow of communication.

Sender's Credibility

The sanctity and purity of a message, to some extent, does not depend on the message itself but, more often than not, it rests on the sender's credibility. It depends on who is saying what. There is often a question mark put on the message—who said it? When a credible personality is quoted then it becomes believable. This is one of the reasons that most of the communication programmes for the organizations, public and private, are associated with certain celebrities. Aishwarya Rai advocating the cause of eye donation or Amitabh Bacchan supporting the 'polio eradication' campaign makes a credible sense to the public. ·

Word Meanings

The real meanings of the words do not exist in the dictionaries but they are in the heads and hearts of the people. Depending on the level of education, age, or their cultural backgrounds, different words have different connotations to different people. Each profession has its own vocabulary and when used in the same professional circle poses no problems, but when related to other professional groups, may be grossly misunderstood. Due to the diversity of workforce, the global companies tend to adopt a parlance which is commonly used and understood by all the employees without much problem.

The words would generally convey three kinds of meanings, *denotations*, *connotations*, and *euphemisms*.

Denotations

The denotative meaning of a word is the most direct or specific meaning. A word means the same to everyone. There is no ambiguity of any kind or colouring in the meanings. For instance, there are no two meanings of the words like boy, girl, table, chair, or water, etc.

Connotations

Connotation is an idea or feeling invoked by a word in addition to its primary or literal meaning. The world may have different connotations for different words. The meanings of the words are perceived in correlation to the pre-fixed values or ideologies formed by receivers over a period of time, based on their backgrounds or experiences that they had in life. Influences like media reports or statements by public or business leaders may lead to certain connotations. Same words carry negative or positive connotations for different people. For instance the word 'unions' may have a negative connotation for a manager but a positive one for the trade union leader. Similarly, the word 'fat' when used as 'fat girl' may have negative connotations but 'fat cheque' connotatively makes a positive sense.

Euphemisms

Euphemism is a mild or less direct word substituted for one that is harsh or blunt when referring to something unpleasant or embarrassing. It is the art of making the unpleasant pieces of communication pleasant, the unbelievable believable, or sugar coating the bitter pill. The more command senders have on their language, the more proficient they are in coining out messages which, though hard, may sound digestible to the receiver.

Public relations professionals, expected as they are to be good communicators and masters of the language, use euphemisms to hard sell certain hard facts concerning an issue. Advertising copy writers particularly specialize in playing up some mundane facts about a product to a romantic fringe. Political leaders' speeches are often fraught with euphemisms as they indulge in lot of rhetoric to play to the voter's galleries.

EFFECTIVE COMMUNICATION CHARACTERISTICS

To ensure effectiveness of communication, written or oral, due care has to be taken that the message does not get distorted in the process of transmission. To attain clarity in the interest of all concerned, sender and receiver, individuals or organizations, it is important to observe some basic well established thumb rules well known as 7 Cs of communication—*completeness, conciseness, consideration, concreteness, clarity, courtesy, and correctness* (See Exhibit 8.2).

Reams have been written about these principles, but the above ready reckoner should serve all public relations practitioners in good stead to hone their writings or oral messages into more effective and purposeful ones.

In today's complex world inundated with 'plenty of information', the communication science, as a system, has matured into a very specialized area of activity. The discipline has branched out to some special kinds of communication practised by individuals and corporations, which are:

1. *Intrapersonal communication*
2. *Interpersonal communication*
3. *Group communication*
4. *Organizational communication*
5. *Mass communication*
6. *Non-verbal communication*

EXHIBIT 8.2   The seven Cs of effective communication

1. **Completeness**
   a. Provide all necessary information
   b. Answer all questions asked
   c. Give something extra, when desirable

2. **Conciseness**
   a. Eliminate wordy expressions
   b. Include only relevant material
   c. Avoid unnecessary repetition

3. **Consideration**
   a. Focus on 'You' instead of 'I' or 'We'
   b. Show audience benefit or interest in the receiver
   c. Emphasize positive, pleasant facts

4. **Concreteness**
   a. Use specific facts and figures

   b. Put action in your verbs
   c. Choose vivid, image-building words

5. **Clarity**
   a. Choose precise, concrete, and familiar words
   b. Construct effective sentences and paragraphs

6. **Courtesy**
   a. Be sincerely tactful, thoughtful, and appreciative
   b. Use expressions that show respect
   c. Choose non-discriminatory expressions

7. **Correctness**
   a. Use the right level of language
   b. Check accuracy of figures, facts, and words
   c. Maintain acceptable writing mechanics

Source: Murphy et al. (1997).

Intrapersonal Communication

Intrapersonal communication is like conversing with the self and the divine. In India, a country which is soaked in the spirit of spirituality, the religious teachers often put a lot of emphasis on '*Know thy self, before you know God*'. This form of communication is construed as meditation and soul searching to arrive at the truth. This form of communication, makes humans to be in tune with themselves.

Meditation, which as per Swami Mukunda Goswami of Iskon (2002) means concentrating on oneness of all the things called *Brahman*, or meditation on anything in general or nothing or even meditation on meditation. This covers whole range of processes, from intellectualization to trance, contemplation, yoga, devotion, *tapasya*, focusing, self hypnosis, deliberation, consideration, study, speculation, reflection, rumination, religious ecstasy, adoration, and glorification. Whatever, we think, feel, say, or do can be part of the meditation, as semi-conscious states and dreams, known as pre-cognitive thinking, also affect our behaviour.

The Indian spiritual thought is full of nuances and delicacies of this metaphysical side of life.

Interpersonal Communication

Interpersonal is generally a one-to-one dialogue between two persons. This is a direct face-to-face interaction with the help of language and paralanguage or body language, common to both the persons. This commonality of understanding is essential for successful interpersonal communication. This mutual interaction when conducted well with positive mindset creates good understanding and goodwill between the two humans. When mishandled due to circumstances like linguistic or cultural differences, it may lead to misunderstanding, confusion or even a conflict. The interpersonal communication tends to be successful and fruitful among the two persons, who have trust in each other, otherwise, one of them will raise barriers and the conversation may break down.

Also persons from similar backgrounds, education, professions, and experience communicate well with each other. A doctor understands the vocabulary of a doctor and a legal professional finds it very comfortable to talk to his co-professionals. People from diverse backgrounds and professions may often have problems of understanding each other.

Humans, animals, and even birds maintain some kind of personal private territories and guard such privacy with lot of obsession. Leave aside humans, even dogs and birds violently bark and chirp, respectively, in protest, when their territorial privacy is invaded. Directly invading into someone's private territory is often considered ill manners and lack of cultural polish. The inter-personal communication or interaction would generally pass through three stages before climaxing into a successful relationship. The three stages are as follows.

The exploration stage

The human dialogue customarily starts with greetings, as prevalent in a particular cultural set. The smile, nodding the head, or a shake hand can start the conver-sation. Starting with weather and politics, the talk progresses into professional or cultural areas.

Experienced salesmen, including public relations practitioners, learn the art of 'ice breaking' by friendly greetings and move ahead with a positive compliment about customers' smart dress, learned disposition, or certain achievements by them or their family. Sizing up the response, a smart salesperson, starts entering into the territories so far prohibited by their target customers.

Probing stage

Sensing that humans are willing to sacrifice some privacy by sharing certain personal information about their business, social attributes, or health situations, the conversation progresses ahead. That is why the marketing and sales persons are trained in questioning techniques to determine the mindset or the priorities of customer's needs, so that they can offer a product, service, or solution or even suggestions on an issue or a problem. Most of the professional and business discussions will conclude here, and rightly so. This interaction is limited to a formal relationship.

Relationship stage

Depending on the degree of relationship or liking for each other, humans allow each other to enter the closely guarded private and personal territories. It is like inviting some friends and relatives to the inner chambers of your house. The barriers are lifted up and a relationship of understanding and closeness is formed. The inter-personal communication reaches its highest stage or climax of the mutual dialogue.

Volumes have been written about this important human interaction, as this is the very basis of progress, profits, happiness, and relationships in this world fraught with social, cultural, political, and commercial complexities.

Group Communication

Two is company and three a crowd, the old saying is still relevant. Contrary to the one-to-one conversation, the group communication involves the participation of three or more people. Peculiarly, the larger the group, more difficult it becomes to communicate amongst the members of a group. When one member speaks and others listen, it is more of a monologue rather than a dialogue. However, the public speaking skills of participants help them to get noticed and emerge as leaders. The effectiveness of communication also depends on the size of the group. Larger groups pose more communication problems. The homogeneous groups, where members already know each other, may be less problematic than the groups whose members are strangers and are meeting for the first time.

In groups, the feedback or knowing the reactions and responses of the participants is not direct or spontaneous and many times the genuineness of the ideas put forth by the people may be difficult to detect.

The formation of groups is easy when people from the same profession, ideology, or religion meet and deliberate their ideas. Groups like rotary and lion clubs, media persons, or public relations professionals meeting often to exchange ideas, is a common sight.

However, before a group emerges homogeneous, the group members have to go through five stages: *formation, conflicts, normalization, performance,* and finally, *disbanding* (See Exhibit 8.3).

Formation

This is the induction and orientation stage when the group members assemble and start interaction. Participants try to 'break ice' and strike initial introductions. Each member tries to project himself the best way, to look good in the estimation of the other member.

Conflicts

As the members assemble they start demonstrating their 'holier than thou' attitude. They loudly put forth their opinions and ideologies backed by their

---

EXHIBIT 8.3 Emergence of a group

Forming	The first stage in group development, characterized by much uncertainty
Storming	The second stage in group development, characterized by intra-group development
Norming	The third stage in group development, characterized by close relationships and cohesiveness
Performing	The fourth stage in group development, when the group is fully functional
Adjourning	The final stage in group development for temporary groups characterized by concern with wrapping up activities rather than task performance

Source: Robbins (2005).

---

experiences, etc. They argue on issues and values and authenticate them with their knowledge and experience. Soon they mellow down and start understanding and accommodating each other.

Normalization

The participants start buying each other's ideas. However, after the initial hard and soft selling of their ideas and positions when everything has sobered down, a consensus prevails and things start getting normal. They now seem to form team and show willingness to work together.

Performance

Now a positive attitude of understanding and co-operation emerges and members get down to complete the task for which they have met. They start reaching agreements on the solutions devised by the group. The group becomes cohesive and homogeneous.

Disbanding

At this final stage the group prepares to disband as the task assigned to it has been accomplished. This is true of the task force groups, formed for a specific purpose. Peculiarly, some members may feel elated about their performance during the meetings and others may feel depressed due to the non-acceptance of the values they hold dear to their heart. The loss of fellow feeling developing during the proceedings may also have a dampening effect on some.

Group communications, today, have become an integral part of the management process. From the stage of recruiting people for various organizational jobs to managing the day-to-day functions, group communication works as a vital link amongst managers to communicate with each other and co-operate on several projects undertaken by the organization.

Group communication is often used as a medium of brain storming by the employees to explore ways and means to solve problems and achieve success. As members bring along their diversified talents to such group meetings, the

EXHIBIT 8.4 Merits and demerits of group communication	
Merits	**Demerits**
Collective wisdom	Long-winded discussions waste time
Diversity of views brings new dimensions	None responsible for failures
Helps creative solutions	Domination by bosses/loud speakers
Decisions acceptable to all	Groups lobby for vested interests
Democratic in nature	Majority vote can sometimes make wrong decisions
Experts share skills with generalists	Costly—time, money, and energy spent
Ensures employee participation	Irrelevant rhetoric lead nowhere

organization can take full advantage of the collective wisdom of the people. However, the group communication is not devoid of certain demerits of its own (See Exhibit 8.4).

Needless to say, public relations practitioners often use the group communication techniques in their job performance to increase an awareness or build consensus on certain issues concerning the organizational growth.

Organizational Communications

Business organizations of today have become enormous and complex organisms. Unlike a smaller sole ownership company, where the words of the owner is law or policy, the large conglomerates are now termed as 'industrial democracies'. With several layers of authority distributed to managers with responsibilities to run their departments or divisions, the only common link which keeps the people connected to each other and keeps the organization unified, is the effective and efficient management of communication system.

Functions of communication

Within and outside an organization, big or small, communication plays a vital role in keeping the company going. Amongst the several functions performed through the use of communication, four functions are notable *control, motivation, emotional expression,* and *information.*

Control   The management function of controlling is administered through communications. Monitoring policies and procedures and also making people to follow the system, communication plays a vital role. Handling customer complaints, or employees' grievances, etc. is carried out in accordance with the pre-determined system.

Motivation   Inspiring people or motivating them to perform at their optimum levels of efficiency or persuading customers to buy company products or prompting shareholders to invest in the company, to a major extent, depends on the efficacy of the communication system developed and adopted by the organization.

Emotional expression Professional organizations consciously try to build a fellow feeling amongst members of the workforce or those associated with it. People get emotionally attached to the companies and often exchange their emotions with each other as if they are the members of one family. They think it to be a right forum to share their joys and sorrows with each other. Thus, this 360 degree communication becomes a medium of expression for people's emotional feelings and serves as a valuable feedback for the management.

Information Transmission and availability of information, more often than not, forms the basis of decision making by managers. Therefore, communication is a vital link in the management chain. Communication, correct and timely, facilitates the individuals and groups to take right decisions so essential to keep the organization on the growth track.

Furthermore, the communication, in an organizational set up, can flow *vertically* and *horizontally*.

Vertical communication

The vertical dimension can be further classified into *upward* and *downward* directions.

Downward communication Every organization has to perform the management functions of planning, directing, leading, and executing its corporate programmes, for which publics' understanding and cooperation is but an utmost necessity. Therefore, an organization sends downward messages of a variety of nature, to the employees, customers, dealers, vendors, etc. as part of its well thought-out and planned effort. Obviously, such communications are designed and consigned to generate a particular response from the publics. This 'downward' communication is an effective tool that organizations use to achieve the management objectives with the help and cooperation of several publics.

Upward communication Just sending downward communication is not enough. When a message reaches the publics, it is natural that the messages will be interpreted, evaluated, and will generate several reactions like objections, problems, solutions, suggestions, contributions, acceptance or may be rejections and protests.

As a two-way communication system is the name of the game called public relations, organizations have to keep their ears to the ground, to gauge reactions to its messages. Commonly known as 'feedback', or upward communication, it is an integral part of the process. If the message is liked and accepted by the publics, the upward feedback affirms it, that the nature of such messages should continue to be sent downwards. But if the publics have reservations, then it is only advisable that the message should be recycled, modified, or adjusted to fit into the framework of public mind.

Grapevine Besides the formal networks that organizations use to collect feedback, the informal system called *grapevine* is well known. The grapevine concept is mainly used in the area of employee communication. The peculiar characteristics of the grapevine are that, first, it is not controlled or run by the management, second, the employees trust the grapevine information/news more than the management communiqués, and third, it is used by self-styled leaders and vested interests (See chapter 14).

Public relations profession does not seek to force or impose values on people, but facilitates the process of acceptance or rejection of an idea or action. Therefore, the organizational communication guide the management to make desirable adjustments.

Horizontal communication

When managers of all levels in an organization communicate laterally, the system is termed as horizontal communication. Needless to say, no organization can function smoothly and succeed in meeting its goals, until managers communicate and co-operate to work together as teams, to carry out operations and projects. A well-oiled horizontal communication system denotes a well-knit, co-ordinated, and proficient organization.

Computer-aided communication

With the advancement of information technology, organizations today use computer-aided communication systems, namely, *e-mail, instant messaging, intranet* and *extranet links, videoconferencing*, etc.

E-mail Electronic mail or e-mail sent and received through Internet with computer generated messages, has taken the world by storm. It has several benefits. It is economical, can be quickly written, edited, and stored, and can be distributed from one person to hundreds, with the click of a button. The world is talking about paperless organizations. But the drawback is that there is no face-to-face communication and it lacks the personal touch in the messages.

Instant messaging Instant messaging is real-time e-mail and they pop up on receivers, computer screens, for immediate attention. It is a very fast and in-expensive way of remaining in touch with all those concerned with the company's business.

Intranet and extranet links Intranets are privately owned, organization-wide information networks that look and act like a website to which the people connected with the company have access. In addition, companies are now creating extranet links that connect internal employees with selected suppliers, customers, and strategic partners.

Videoconferencing Videoconferencing is an extension of intranet or extranet systems. It permits the company personnel to have a meeting with people at different locations worldwide. Live audio and video images of the members allow them to see, hear, and talk. Thus, one can have interactive meetings without physically travelling to be together at the same location.

Mass Communication

Never before in the history of mankind, the power of mass communication has seen itself at the height of its glory. The power of mass communication has been eulogized by many experts. Daniel Lerner describes the mass messages as 'mobility multipliers' and Wilbur Schramm termed them as 'magic multipliers'.

The definition

Wilbur Schramm (1955) opines that the process of communication is basically the same, but the elements change in case of mass communication. He says, 'The chief source of mass communication, is a communication organization or an institutionalized person. By a communication organization we mean a newspaper, a broadcasting network or station, a film studio, a book or magazine publishing house. By institutionalized person we mean such a person as the editor of a newspaper, who speaks in his editorial columns through the facilities of the institution and with more voice and prestige than he would have if he were speaking without the institution.'

Mass communication organization

In principle, the mass communication organizations work the way an individual does. Such outfits operate as decoder, interpreter, and encoder. A TV news channel editor, for instance, decodes the news stories received by him, he checks them, edits them or redo them, and telecast them. The inputs are evaluated, interpreted, reworked, and telecast through the medium of television.

Receiving clusters

The receivers or the destination of such messages are the individuals at the end of media channels. The individuals are diversified and scattered mentally and geographically, yet they form themselves into invisible groups or clusters. The viewership of a TV channel may contain several kinds of receivers and that too for various kinds of programmes, telecast during day and night, to young people, young ladies, new mothers, middle-aged housewives, professionals, senior citizens, etc. They can even be classified as clusters watching particular programmes, like the group that watched 'KBC' (*Kaun Banega Crorepati*) or housewives watching *sas bahu* serials.

Audience research

Compared to face-to-face communication, the feedback in mass communication is a difficult situation. Since the sender and the receiver are not face-to-face, there is no or little feedback from the receiver to the sender. However, the feedback comes from the inferential expressions like the TRP rating dropping or increasing for a particular programme. However, to bridge this gap the mass communication organizations conduct exhaustive audience research.

Mass communication and society

The power of mass media has a pervasive effect on the society. In fact, experts think that the mass communication takes over the function of *society communicating*. The society starts functioning as decoder, interpreter, and encoder. The society decodes the environment for its members, watches the imminence of dangers or a promise of high entertainment. Thus the society itself becomes a vehicle or channel of communication of several crucial messages to the society, which has a very powerful influence on the social mindset for or against an issue or system. It generates patterns of mass behaviour. Today it has become the very basis of a democratic society.

Gaining attention

With explosion of mass media and with so many media competing with each other, getting attention of the target audience has become a major challenge of the mass communication. Which medium can fight the clutter of TV channels, newspapers, magazines, FM radios, mobile phones, Internet, etc. is a major challenge for all those directly or indirectly involved in the mass communication area. Some programmes or news stories or e-mails are so emotive and intrusive in nature, that some lesser compelling ones have to wait for audience attention.

Conditions for success

Wilbur Schramm (1955) outlines four conditions for the success of individual or mass communication:

1. The message must be so designed and delivered as to gain the attention of the intended destination.
2. The message must employ signs which refer to experience common to source and destination, so as to 'get the meaning across'.
3. The message arouses personality needs in the destination and suggests some ways to meet those needs.
4. The message must suggest a way to meet those needs which are appropriate to the group situation in which the receiver is placed. The group norms desire comformity to its code of conduct and the violation is generally resented by the group members.

The four elements, message, situation, personality, and group, play a vital role in the successful impact of a communication. More than half century of the communists' experience in mastering the mass communication, they think that until they can control three of the four elements, the results cannot be predicted. Notorious propagandists like Joseph Geobbels of Hitler fame, perhaps, mastered the subject, but with unfortunate sinister designs.

In conclusion, the public relations practitioners, have lot of lessons to learn from the history of the last century and the current events, to sharpen their mass communication skills.

Functions of mass communication

Mass communication is, perhaps, one single factor which deeply influences our lives in all areas of activity—social, economic, political, cultural, and even spiritual. It serves not only as a means of information and education, but also as a great source of entertainment.

Inform   Information is a valuable commodity. The strength of an individual and organization can very well be judged by its information base. One great source of information for the society and the business community is mass communication vis-à-vis the mass media. Media takes on itself the responsibility of scanning the environment, social, cultural, political, economic, etc. and makes its business spread to the various publics. In fact, mass media is a miracle of the century.

News   No news is any more the good news. Imagine this world without news. Fortunately, the system of mass communication, constantly, flashes the news every minute, every hour of the day and night. News brought to us right into our homes is not only a necessity of modern man but also our lifeline. The news has also attained the proportions of an entertainment.

Sell   Mass communication in the form of advertising, sales promotion, publicity, and public relations, work like fuel that rev up the marketing engine. Companies, private and public, have colossal advertising budget running into crores of rupees to market and sell their products and services to the customers. The rising standards of living of the people in India and elsewhere can be attributed to the power of advertising and mass communication, which educate the customers about the products they needed but did not know where to buy them. Advertising serves as a bridge between the company and the customers.

Educate   Watching or reading the mass media tools like TV, newspapers, and magazines is an education itself. Mass communication has come to stay as a medium of knowledge management system. The 'how to' kind of information appearing in the mass media, makes lot of sense to the publics who are keen to know as to how to split the facts from fiction.

Advice   Mass communication plays a useful advisory role in the society. Advising young students about the educational facilities, job opportunities, young mothers on fending for their babies, middle aged to keep good health, seniors to ensure financial stability and self dependence, are all the roles mass communication is usefully doing at almost negligible price. Imagine a 50 page newspaper costs rupees two and a fifty paise only.

Direct   A useful role of directing people on certain dos and don'ts, or following a new tax law, or obeying traffic rules, of even alerting people about the outbreak of certain deadly diseases, earthquake, floods, or terrorism are all being brought to the public by the mass communication system. The familiar Delhi Police advertisements is one good example of the government directing people through mass media.

Entertain India's multi-billion rupee entertainment industry, through mass communication, quenches the people's thirst for entertainment. Films, telefilms, soap opera, photo features, tourism sites, romance, crime, music and dance, painting and singing, are all heavily dependent on mass communication to reach the audiences to satisfy their entertainment urges.

Develop Developmental journalism is a new branch of the discipline which specializes in reporting stories on social, agricultural, technological, and business development. The advent and maturity of pink press and exclusive business TV channels are all part of the mass communication, which make tremendous contribution to publics' urge to improve their prospects in social and business life. The success stories serve as a source of inspiration for many aspiring and enterprising people to emulate the success.

Non-verbal Communications

Humans through their existence in the world have developed the languages and the dictionaries, where the word meanings are written. People interact in the world with the help of these words and their meanings. But humans are also endowed with a paralanguage, which supplements his verbal communications. This is also known as non-verbal communication or body language. Verbal communications until supported by the non-verbal postures and gestures, do not seem to make sense, as far the sincerity or honesty of a message is concerned. The messages can be dressed up strategically, but fortunately, the non-verbal version has no room for manipulation. It is mostly true, real, and genuine.

Non-verbal communications can be divided into three broad categories, *appearance, body language*, and *silence, time*, and *sound.*

Appearance

Appearance of a person, message, written and oral, and surroundings, all convey meanings. A person's *dress* conveys the background, profession, state of mind, age, nationality, religion, and even intentions. The saying 'God made men, and tailors made gentlemen' is not only amusing but also meaningful. Also the dress generates the desired responses in the people. The wardrobe management is an important part of professionals paraphernalia. The appearance of envelope in your mailbox amply conveys the nature of the message, urgent, intimate, official, or junk mail. Surroundings in which a manager works conveys his status and authority. The ambience of a well furnished carpeted, and air conditioned office, convey a manager's senior position in the organization.

Body language

Body language or paralanguage is honest communication and is not manipulative. *Facial expressions, gestures and postures, smell and touch* all convey meanings. The eye contact or avoidance or drooping eyes indicate honesty, modesty, or dishonesty. Actions speak louder than words. The hand shake styles convey warmth, indifference, or hatred whereas sitting postures communicate relaxed disposition or otherwise. Showing watch to someone conveys that discussion should end, though discourteous. *Smells* indicate fire or imminent danger. Soft *touch* means show of good feelings and hard shows animosity. A kiss on cheek or friendly pat on shoulder communicate some special emotions. Harsh voice means command and soft show polite request.

Silence, time, and sound

Silence, longer than desirable conveys serious hard feelings. Silence also sometimes indicates your willingness for a relationship. *Time* is the essence of action just like justice delayed is justice denied. Different *sounds* denote different messages. Loud laugh may mean ridiculing, grinding throat an insult or challenge. Temple bells, train whistles, steam leaks or roar of a car engine communicate various messages.

Whereas a good communicator needs a good understanding of the language, they also need a good understanding of the non-verbal side of the human behaviour. Paralanguage of non-verbal communications sincerely supports the verbal messages and most often indicate the truthfulness or otherwise of the message. Public relations practitioners need a good understanding of both the languages for success.

Summary

This chapter explores the nuances and the variety of communication per se and the sensitivities of the process. It also runs a brief but lucid commentary on the various kinds of communication used by humans and organizations.

The process of communication outlines the system developed by experts and the involvement of eight elements involved in the process of communication namely sender, encoding, message, channel, decoding, receiver, noise, and feedback. The barriers in the way of effective communcation have been outlined for understanding. Communication system is fraught with difficulties such as distortions in the way of transmission and solution, which to some extent lies in following the 7 Cs of communication.

Communication is practised by professionals and organizations in various ways. Understanding the self is known as the intrapersonal communication that is conversation with self and the eternal powers.

The interpersonal communication, that is, face-to-face interaction, is the very basis of human exchange of ideas and business propositions. The interaction matures through three stages of interpersonal communications, exploration, probing, and the relationship.

Group communication is the norm for working in organizations as teams. The transition process of a group becoming homogeneous has been highlighted. The merits and demerits of group communication have also been exhibited.

Organizational communication being the lifeline of a company, enough informations have been included to understand the process and system from downward, upward, horizontal to computer generated communications.

The intricacies of the 'look simple' mass communications have been discussed compactly along with the functions and roles played by it in today's media dominated world.

Last but not the least, the non-verbal communications, though a big subject in itself, has been touched upon for the basic understanding of the system.

Key Terms

Catalytic role   A role that facilitates change

Cohesive group   Well knit and compatible group

Communis   Greek word for 'common' or making information common

Consensus   Middle ground in decision making, between total assent and total disagreement. It implies that everyone accepts and supports the decision, and understands the reasons for making it

Euphemism   Sugar coated harsh messages or sheer rhetoric

Frozen evaluation   A person acquiring fixed ideas

Grapevine   Feedback circulating amongst employees

Information explosion   The rapidly increasing amount of published information and the effects of this abundance of data

Layers of authority   Hierarchy in an organization

Magic multipliers   Messages that get multiplied with magical speech

Parlance   The style of speech or writing used by people in a particular context or profession

Pink press   Economic newspapers generally printed on pink paper

Ready reckoner   A chart to find ready answers/information

Rhetoric   The ability to use language effectively, especially to persuade or influence people

Concept Review Questions

1. Establish your understanding about communication, its importance, process, and functions in industrial and commercial life.
2. What are the barriers in the way of effective communication? Explain. What steps and actions should be borne in mind to ensure clarity in the messages?
3. Explain the difference between intra- and interpersonal communication. What stages a face-to-face interaction has to pass to mature into a mutually beneficial relationship?

4. Group communication has become a norm in todays' industrial and commercial organizations, why? What are the stages that a group has to pass through to become integrated and successful?
5. Explain the merits and demerits of group communication.
6. What is organizational communication? What are its kinds, roles, and goals?
7. Explain the concept of mass communication. What are the roles of mass communication? What are the four conditions that every mass communication message should fulfil to be successful?
8. What is paralanguage? Can body language be manipulated? What are the kinds of non-verbal communications that communicate more strongly and sincerely than verbal communication.

References

Goswami, Mukunda (2002), 'Be One with Yourself, and Eternally Different', 6 August 2002, *Hindustan Times*, New Delhi, p. 13.

Murphy, Herta A., Herbert W. Hildebrandt, and Jane P. Thomas (1997), *Effective Business Communications*, 7th edition, The McGraw-Hill Companies, Inc USA pp. 32–57, 471.

Robbins, Stephen P. (2005), *Organizational Behavior*, 11th edition, Prentice Hall of India Private Limited, New Delhi, India, pp. 240–241.

Schramm, Wilbur (1955), *Advertising Management Selected Readings*, Richard D. Irwin Inc, Illinois, USA, reprinted in India by D.B. Taraporevala Sons and Co. Private Ltd, Bombay, pp. 77, 86, 91–99.

9

Negotiating Skills and Public Relations

Chapter Outline
- Negotiations and public relations
- Negotiations and conflict
- Negotiation process

NEGOTIATIONS AND PUBLIC RELATIONS

'All human beings are walking, talking libraries of diverse experiences. In our conversations with these human libraries and in our observations of their negotiations, we have witnessed the Hegelian dialectic of thesis versus antithesis and the resulting synthesis. What else can one expect when the human libraries' philosophy sections put Karl Marx in touch with Adam Smith, when the religion sections place the holy Koran next to the Upanishads, ...or when the pure science sections merge nuclear fission with acupuncture. It is like listening to tribes of birds singing back and forth to each other. Sometimes the birdsong amounts to a sweet warbling, at others a horrendous squawking' (Moran and Stripp 1997).

In other words, man is the most complex animal ever created by God and everybody is somebody here in this world and carries certain values, beliefs, and priorities and objectives to be met in life. But the reality of life is that in this inter-dependent world, harnessing and managing this human diversity is one primary and the biggest challenge for humans. Public relations practitioners cannot remain unaffected or distanced by this need of human interaction or negotiations, to get the necessary co-operation from people to attain individual and corporate objectives. This inherent diversity points the arrow towards the management of conflict, where the art and science of negotiations is the name of the game.

Going by most of the definitions, public relations is the art and science of a two-way communication to resolve conflicts of interest, to engineer people's consent, make adjustments, and establish an understanding between individuals and the organizations. Therefore, public relations professionals by virtue of their job, inherit negotiation function as a crucial part of their job profile.

NEGOTIATIONS AND CONFLICT

'We each must deal with conflict in our personal and organizational activities. Conflict involves a disagreement about the allocation of scarce resources or a clash of goals, statuses, values, perceptions, or personalities. Much of the conflict we experience arises from our communication of our wants, needs, and values to others. Sometime, we communicate clearly, but others have differing needs. Sometime, we communicate poorly, and conflict emerges because others misunderstand us. Managers can, of course, use dominance and suppression in handling conflicts with employees. But negotiations can help us manage conflicts of all types in a more effective and mutually satisfying way. Negotiation is a process by which two parties interact, through various communication channels, to resolve a conflict jointly' (Stoner, Freeman, and Gilbert, Jr 2002).

In this world full of conflicts of interest between managements and unions, customers and marketing organizations, investors and promoters, suppliers and buyers, governments and corporates, communities and manufacturing facilities, public relations has an important role to play. The business, local and global, becoming competitive, where big fish wants to eat the small fish, and the presence of hostile takeovers, and guerilla marketing tactics, the activities, most often, climax into negotiated settlements. Although public relations wields the sharp edged weapons of communication, to condemn and contradict many sinister and malicious rumours and proddings, yet when it comes to the negotiation table, this very communication art and science takes another form called 'bargaining through communications'. The conflicting roles have to be managed and harmonized for corporate tranquility. The top managements, with public relations as part of their portfolios, heavily depend on the strategies and tactics that can be devised to win.

'Negotiation permeates the interactions of almost every one in groups and organizations. There is the obvious: labour bargains with management. There is the not so obvious: managers negotiate with employees, peers, and bosses; sales people negotiate with customers; purchasing agents negotiate with suppliers. And there is the subtle: a worker agrees to answer a colleague's phone for a few minutes in exchange for some past or future benefit. In today's team-based organizations, in which members are increasingly finding themselves having to work with colleagues over whom they have no direct authority and with whom they may not even share a common boss, negotiation skills become critical' (Robbins 2005). He defines negotiation as a process in which two or more parties exchange goods or services and attempt to agree on the exchange rate for them.

NEGOTIATION PROCESS

Although in our day-to-day life, negotiation process seems to get routinized and does not need creativity because what gets absorbed into our reflexes tends to become blunt and corroded. Therefore, it is important to remain conscious about the process and continually keep sharpening our negotiation tools to be more effective to acquire a winning edge.

Experts suggest that all negotiators need to keep sharpening their skills for high performance. Obviously, it is relevant to look at the process of negotiations and prepare for every negotiating event coming up in our personal and business life. The process involves five steps: 1. *Planning*; 2. *Dialogue*; 3. *Deliberation*; 4. *Closing*; and 5. *The aftermath* (See Exhibit 9.1).

Planning

Planning ahead or doing the necessary homework before going to a negotiation meeting is an essential part of the preparation. Planning means collecting all the information and data about the subject of the meeting. It means evaluating all aspects of the agenda and working out strategies to make the outcome of the negotiations, a success. Some of the steps that can be taken as a part of the planning process are the environment scan, the present situation, information gathering, other's experience, negotiators' team building, protocol, issues involved, perception—theirs versus ours, etc. (See Exhibit 9.2).

The planning effort should address some important aspects like the following:

Time table

A well thought out time table for the planning effort should help the negotiators equip themselves for the challenge. How much time is spent on planning efforts is less important than the strategic usage of time. Negotiation process is generally faced with time bound slots in the working schedule of the busy executives, who are generally hard pressed for time. So the right scheduling helps.

EXHIBIT 9.1 Negotiation process

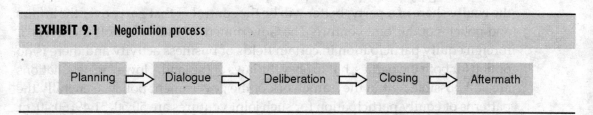

EXHIBIT 9.2 Ten commandments for negotiators

1. Determine if the subject is negotiable. Get facts to ensure what winning means to you.
2. Make up your mind whether the agreement is going to be strategic or cooperative—'win-lose' or 'win-win'.
3. Form a team comprising specialists to support you. Observe protocol.
4. Do not disclose your timetable and keep the schedule tight.
5. Make a powerful opening to carry everyone along with smooth communications. Ensure a comfortable venue to set the tone.
6. Mind your language. Measure information before release to keep control of the proceedings.
7. Be persuasive but diplomatic. Avoid rhetoric. Keep ears to the ground to know what is cooking in the other party's camp.
8. Don't get bogged down in a poor deal. Have a leeway to walk out.
9. Get the agreement signed with mutual consent and don't leave without it. Be a gracious winner.
10. Strike a relationship in case a dispute arises later. Litigation is expensive and should be avoided.

Exploring options

One should be prepared to consider a wide range of options for proposals, one may like to put forth or which are likely to be put forth by the other negotiating group. It is, perhaps, a good idea to list the proposals and their ramifications, and conduct an in-house evaluation to arrive at a decision, so as to find out which option is the best. However, one should be flexible and open to the proposals offered by the other party. Although it is very difficult to have a standard list of options, yet some of the sensitive areas in which proposals and counter proposals may be presented by the negotiating parties can be: *price, partnership, sharing positions, profit sharing, technology transfer, royalty payments, duration of contract, disputes and damages, etc.*

Price   The most sensitive issue during the negotiations is the price on which the parties bargain hard because price determines the gains and losses to each party. Besides other gains that may accrue out of the deal, the financial side is clearly visible to both parties. What is the best price for one party may be least attractive to the other. However, a compromised price can be worked out in terms of profit and loss or the break-even level.

Partnership   For negotiations concerning the setting up of joint ventures, the subject of equity participation figures prominently during the parleys. Higher the equity share of a party, better will be the control of that party over the affairs and policies of the joint venture. The Government of India controls the levels of foreign equity participation in certain fields of business activity and there is no option for both the parties, but to obey the laws of the land. However, negotiations are still possible within the framework of the government policy. Generally the patterns of equity participation for such joint ventures are 50:50, 51:49, 60:40, or

70:30, etc. Though India is receptive to foreign direct investment (FDI), yet certain fields like insurance and media, etc. have certain restrictions to follow.

Sharing positions   Sharing management positions in the organization is another area which calls for negotiations. The question as to whose nominee will be the chairman and managing director becomes a debatable point. Besides incumbents for certain other key positions becomes a debatable point. Positions like finance, manufacturing technology are often a bone of contention between the parties. Before the Maruti Udyog was fully taken over by the Japanese Suzuki Motors, a big controversy raged between the government and Suzuki, as to whose representative will be the chairman and managing director, which was finally settled through negotiations.

Profit sharing   The ratio proportion of profit sharing is another burning issue, particularly in joint ventures with overseas partners. As a rule, the profit sharing should be in accordance with the level of equity participation, yet there are certain inbuilt issues that need to be settled. The quantum of profit to be retained and re-invested in the company's growth, could be one issue which needs negotiations in all its ramifications. Multinational companies need to negotiate with their local partners the pattern of profit sharing, as far as the repatriation of profits to their home countries is concerned. The government does have some guidelines in this regard, yet the legal interpretations call for a negotiated settlement.

Technology transfer   The technology perfected by one organization is a valuable intellectual property and the transfer for such technologies most often goes through the process of negotiations. Terms such as safe guarding the confidentiality and exclusivity of a technology, and licensing the local partners to manufacture hi-tech products under their close technical supervision, call for understanding. Certain multinational companies would depute their technical managers to control and monitor the confidentiality. Until Bosch entered the Indian market themselves, they had such an arrangement with Motor Industries Company Ltd (MICO), which manufactured spark plugs and fuel injection system used in diesel vehicles under their technical supervision. The products carried the mark 'MICO licence Bosch'.

Royalty payments   The technology transfer, naturally, is not free. An arrangement has to be arrived at whether the technology is to be bought outright for a price or it is licensed for a period, on payment of a royalty. There are quite a few technical collaborations, which are signed amongst the parties to produce products under a renewable agreement after certain number of years. The negotiations at the initial stages and at the renewal stages assume significant importance. The main issue is the payment of royalty or a licensing fee to the principals, for usage of their technology, which needs to be settled. The well known Apollo Tyres started manufacturing tyres in India in technical collaboration with Continental tyres of Germany, through obvious negotiations.

Duration of contract   Though considered a low priority, it is a factor of some magnitude to both the parties. Negotiations many times focus on this aspect with a far sight and anticipation of the environmental and business changes that might take place rendering the contract redundant or highly valuable. Generally, such negotiated contracts are signed between the parties for three to five years. The trade agreements between nations, bonds signed between the employees and the employers or companies and dealers, etc. are a few examples.

Disputes and damages   Since the underlying idea of all negotiations is to, ultimately, have smooth trouble-free relationship, yet there can be a difference of opinion or clash of interests. Most of the agreements carry a tail piece covering the legal side of the redressal system with a provision for payment of damages caused or compensation for violations resulting in loss of reputations and money. Also some arbitration clauses are put in with mutual consent. However, this is the legal side of the negotiation system, where legal professionals will have their opinions exchanged and settled.

Information gathering

It is only advisable that the negotiator should conduct the initial research through relevant literature available on the subject, exchange ideas with people who had experience of negotiations with a particular group or their organizational culture. Websites of the other party involved in the process should help. Libraries are a treasure for scanning and developing a wider perspective.

Once the information is gathered, there is a need to develop a strategy. As a part of the strategy, it is essential to determine the 'best alternative to a negotiated agreement' (BATNA) for both the sides. BATNA determines the lowest value acceptable to the negotiator and whatever is higher than one's BATNA should be acceptable. Similarly, any offer to the other side which is more attractive than their BATNA should be acceptable. Knowing the BATNA of the counterpart paves way for success. Even if they don't accept it, the negotiator might be able to make them change theirs, and have an agreement (Stoner, Freeman, and Gilbert Jr 2002).

Consider implications

It is often said that one should take a longer start to make a longer jump. Evaluating the short- and long-term implications of the proposals should help to take appropriate decisions. Strategically, many business people would be willing to make some short-term concessions to win a deal which should be more profitable in the long run. This may call for calculations by an accountant if the negotiations are of financial nature. The strategy could be 'lose now, win later'.

Building a team

One has to learn from the Japanese, who are considered to be tough negotiators. The unique characteristic of the Japanese is to work in teams, so much so, that sometimes it is difficult to know who is the leader. The Japanese form teams based on the area of specialization of each member whose opinion is held in esteem, while taking some crucial decisions. In other words, even if one is the leader of the negotiating team, it is advisable to carry along a team of experts on different aspects of the proposal under negotiation. As a strategy, a team of experts is kept as standby, in the next room or kept alive on a hot line, for consultations at various stages of the parleys between the two parties.

Dialogue

Dialogue, as the word denotes, is the time for information exchange during which the negotiators make proposals and counter proposals. This process of exchange is a continual flow of ideas, acts, words, and gestures that are aimed at selling a proposal to the counterparts. This exchange allows an opportunity to both the parties to understand mutual expectations. This face-to-face behaviour may sound like war of wits with moods swinging up and down, left and right, and to certain extremes of a stalemate. Some of these familiar behaviours are:

Irritants

Certain words and phrases sound vague and spell out no definite value or volume of benefits for the counterpart. Words such as 'fair', 'generous offer', or 'reasonable', etc. carry no conviction, hence are not persuasive. These kinds of expressions may irritate the other party and switch them on to a negative frame of mind.

Counter proposals

The proposals floated by the other party should not be responded with a counter-proposal because it may enlarge the dimension of the dialogue or may make the interaction go off track. A counter proposal may (a) introduce an additional option which may complicate or cloud the clarity, (b) may not generate any interest, as the counterpart is concerned more about their own proposal, (c) may be perceived as a blockade or disagreement.

Defensive and offensive attacks

As far as possible, negotiators should avoid defending or attacking the counterpart because the atmosphere once charged with animosity, bringing it back to normalcy, can be difficult. This is no area for playing the blame game but an opportunity to generate an atmosphere of cordiality and cooperation to come to an agreement. For instance, avoid using sentences such as 'It is entirely your fault' or 'Do not blame me for that', because such expressions can trigger intensity.

Behaviour pattern

Demonstration of a positive and constructive behaviour pattern helps to set the tone of the negotiation in the right direction. Courtesy and polishness when demonstrated in the right earnest, should help to carry the negotiations smoothly to a happy conclusion. Expressions like 'May I make a suggestion' or 'May I ask a question?' or 'May I draw everybody's attention to …..?' can set the friendly tone. This kind of behaviour pattern helps (a) to generate a positive attention and response, (b) allow the negotiator and his counterpart time to gather thoughts for clearer understanding, (c) induce formality and decency, and (d) reduce ambiguity and lead to clarity of communication. However, as a word of caution, the 'disagreement' to a proposal should not be demonstrated right at the start, but should be logically and neutrally put forth to modulate acceptance. This also can work as face saving for the counterpart.

Test, understand, and summarize

To test ideas put forth so far and to ensure their understanding by the other side, it is a good strategy to summarize the discussion at intervals of the discussion. This helps to keep the negotiations on track. Summarizing is a compact restatement of points so far discussed. This ensures proper understanding and also cuts out misconceptions, that can, possibly, crop up.

Asking questions

Questioning at intervals is like taking the temperature of the meeting. Questioning is important to negotiation process as they (a) provide data about the counterpart's thinking and position, (b) gain control over the discussion, (c) provide alternatives to some of the direct disagreements, (d) keep the other party representatives active and reduce their thinking time, and (e) give negotiator party breathing time to monitor their own thought process.

Express feelings

It is natural that one party would be keen to know the other party's feelings about the proposals put forth by them. Giving expression to such feelings is quite appropriate, but not in a manner of refuting, but with diplomatic modulations. It is very democratic to disagree, but the expression of disagreement needs to be peddled with the poise of a diplomat. Hearing a comment from the counterpart which is not true may call for a expression such as 'I am not sure how to react. If the information given to me is true then I would accept it yet I feel some doubts in my mind about its accuracy. So part of me feels happy and part of me feels rather suspicious. Can you help me to resolve this'. There is a small risk of hurting the trust, but then it gets fortified with right answer.

Dilute arguments

Giving too many reasons in support of the main arguments may arm the other party with a point to contest and dispute. Sticking to the main two or three arguments supported by well-focused reasons will help. But if found that the main arguments are able to hold water, it is quite advisable to move to some subsidiary reasons to dilute the arguments without losing focus.

Deliberation

Deliberation is the process by which the negotiators evaluate the interaction, adjust their understanding of the counterpart's requirements, and reformulate expectations, preferences, and proposals, in an effort to resolve conflicting interests.

The deliberation aspect encompasses three major aspects of the negotiation process, *trust levels*, *risk-taking capacity*, and *decision-making systems*.

Trust levels

Mutual trust or mistrust is the underlying idea of every negotiation process. More often than not, the negotiators have to infer the counterpart's true interests, intentions, and preferences. If a good level of mutual trust exists, well and good, otherwise the negotiators should precisely spell out for themselves the real motives of the other party.

Broadly speaking, trust implies an expectation of a persistent faith in the moral social order and in the process of negotiation, trust means reliance on the accuracy of the counterpart's information and the confidence, that the joint decisions would lead to a desired agreement between the two parties.

Trust is influenced by two factors, the law of the land and the moral code of conduct. Breaches or violations, if any, can either be resolved by legal system or by a social pressure to refrain from trespassing the moral code. Going by the reputation of the negotiating parties for honouring their word, several agreements thrive on the friendly, harmonious, and trusting nature of the parties.

Risk-taking capacity

Negotiations always have an under current of risk involved in terms of loss. Such losses can be 'loss of image', 'loss of respect', or even 'financial loss'. Taking a calculated risk is considered a good business strategy, but as far possible, negotiators would like to be sure of the risk involved.

Avoiding ambiguity in the agreements can avoid uncertainty or risk. Negotiators are classified into two categories, *cautious* and *adventurous*. The cautious ones want to ensure coverage of all loose ends but the adventurous ones gamble their stakes in the hope of winning. Accordingly, a decision has to be made.

Decision-making system

In most of the professionally managed companies, the decisions during the course of negotiations are based on the company's past experience and practices, the management structure of the company, their communication system, and the personalities involved.

There are two types of decision-making processes adopted by the organizations—*autocratic* and *democratic*. In the autocratic system, the power to take decisions rests with top executives or business leaders. The authority is not delegated to the negotiator or the negotiating team, but the final say rests in the hands of top management.

In the democratic system, as the word denotes, the decision making is based on participative system, in which each team member is consulted and their consent is taken. The negotiating committee works on behalf of the organization, and may recommend its decision to the management for a final approval.

In one view, the pluralistic make up of the negotiating team, for reasons good or otherwise, may prolong the decision-making process.

Sometimes, some major decisions may also be influenced by some outside forces like government policies, shareholders or unions' opinions, etc. For instance, India's Essar Steel Holding Limited offer for US based steel maker Esmark Inc. ran into roadblock with the United Steel Workers (USW), a representative union of steel workers in the US and Canada, vowing to block the deal. The USW union demanded the Esmark to scrap its agreement with Essar, claiming that the deal violates the union's contract with Esmark. The Esmark representative commented that USW is a strong labour union and Essar would definitely have to negotiate with them before finalizing the deal.

The legal hurdles can be another reason for delay or stalemate. The merger talks between top managers of India's biggest mobile phone services firm Bharti Airtel Limited and MTN Group Limited, Africa's largest phone firm, assisted by investment bankers and lawyers, continued to grapple with various regulatory hurdles in the way of final agreement. The US Office of Foreign Assets Control (OFAC) do not allow a US citizen or agency to deal with any person or agency blacklisted in the past. MTN has operations in the countries covered by OFAC (Iran, Syria and Liberia, Iraq, Myanmar, Sudan, North Korea, etc.), which may pose as a roadblock (*The Mint*, 2008).

Closing

All negotiations, after going through the pains and gains of the process, finally have to come to a close in the shape of an agreement. An agreement document outlines the details about the exchange of conditional promises, which both the parties undertake that they will act in certain ways based on the mutual reciprocity.

As the promises are a reflection of intentions to act or refrain from acting contrary to the agreed norms, in certain situations, cultures, and individual mindsets, their breaking may be tolerated or expected.

To avoid expensive misunderstanding or resultant expensive litigation, it is desirable that the negotiator must set up a system of two-way communication, understandable to the parties, that will lead to a mutually acceptable agreement, with an effective mechanism to enforce promises.

Kinds of agreements

Broadly speaking, there are two forms of agreements—first, *specific* and second, *implied*. The specific ones stipulate a detailed written agreement covering all contingencies, requiring minimum cooperation and both the parties are bound by a mechanism like the legal system. The implicit ones are generally oral and relationship based, leaving enough room for the parties to cooperate with each other in solving problems or contingencies. However, classifying them into watertight categories is never possible; every agreement is based on relationships, from start to finish.

The Aftermath—An Opportunity

As soon as a negotiated agreement has been signed between the two parties, this may be the end of the story for the negotiators, but the beginning for a public relations opportunity. It is, perhaps, the time for the negotiating team to sit back and relax, but the public relations practitioner's role begins where the others' have ended.

May be it is time for celebrations and to let the rest of the world know that it has happened. Some of the actions that public relations can contemplate can be:

Spread the news

Depending on the national or international importance of the agreement, it becomes a business necessity to let the rest of world know about it. For instance, if it is a merger or a take over, it is a crucial public relations opportunity to communicate to all the concerned publics, so that they absorb, understand, and develop their own responses to the new development. Positive news generates positive responses and otherwise.

Business stakes

People have business stakes in every business. And also as no business can flourish in isolation, the publics such as customers, dealers, suppliers, share-holders, etc. all need to be communicated with about the organization's new business partners or owners. As such, the effort calls for professional indulgence in spreading a positive perception to enlist public cooperation and support.

Employees' anxiety

Employees, more than any other public, become anxious to know about the new management, its policies, and their future prospects, new challenges, and job security. New managements introduce new teams, arrange chess boards in their own style which can mean some organizational turbulence. To allay their fears and to restore their comfort and confidence levels, employees should be informed about the shape of things to come.

Media handling

Business today is under media scanner. Before the pink press comes with lights flashing, public relations will put into action their plans to handle the news hungry media. Calling a press conference to break the news in the right perspective, introducing the new top management leaders, their profiles and future policy and growth plans, are all a part of the game plan. Needless to say, a pre-planned press release when distributed in a timely manner, should put all speculations to rest.

New corporate identity

Possibly, in the event of a merger or take over, company may acquire a new name and thus need a new identity to be developed and projected. Public relations professional have the role and responsibility to redesign and project the new company identity in the market. To mention the familiar advertisement 'Naya naam, wahi kaam' should make sense in the corporate world. This may involve reworking the total identity programme from the new company logo, a fresh look for the stationary and all other props.

Summary

The world is full of conflicts. Everybody is somebody here. All carry their own values, needs, wants, and priority in life. Organizations and the managers cannot remain aloof from this conflict. Resolving conflicts of interest through the process of negotiations is one of the challenges in every organization. Negotiation is a system of arriving at a consensus through a process of give-and-take. Since the area directly concerns itself with the efficacy of communication, public relations professionals have a definitive role.

The process of negotiation generally passes through five stages—planning, dialogue, deliberation, closing, and the aftermath. Each of these stages calls for certain preparations and cautions to be taken care of by the negotiators to win. Planning to gather all information, objectives, and time tabling, etc. has to be taken care of before jumping into the foray.

The dialogue calls for the right language for the right set of circumstances. Speaking cautiously and thoughtfully in measured terms should help to keep the focus on the main issues involved in the negotiations.

Deliberation part is introspection by negotiators about the perception they carry about the other party and what the opposite party carries about them. Team building is an important step in the right direction. Anticipating and ensuring the desired outcome of the negotiations is of vital importance. The negotiators have also to be guided by the decision-making system in their organizations, whether it is autocratic or democratic.

Closing negotiations should culminate into a written or verbal agreement. If the objective of the deal is specific in nature, and is devoid of any relationship base, then it is generally expected to be a written agreement duly signed by both the parties. Where the basis of agreement is mutual trust and reputation and also the past relationship experienced by the parties, even a verbal agreement is desirable.

The aftermath stage calls for main concentration by the public relations people. The outcome needs to be communicated well to all the concerned publics for generating the necessary positive responses. The developments like change in management teams, the decision to rename the company, may call for redesigning and developing a new corporate identity programme, to project the new business philosophy and image of the changed organization.

The chapter also outlines some exhibits showing the process, mutual perception of the parties, and the commandments for successful negotiations.

Key Terms

Antithesis A proposition that is the opposite of another already proposed thesis

Behaviour pattern A recurrent way of acting by an individual or group towards a given object or in a given situation

Conflict management The process of resolving a dispute or a conflict permanently, by providing each side's needs, and adequately addressing their interests so that they are satisfied with the outcome

Hegel German philosopher whose three stage process of dialectical reasoning was adopted by Karl Marx

Perception An attitude or understanding based on what is observed or thought

Protocol The rules of correct or appropriate behaviour of a group, organization, or profession

Stalemate A situation in which further progress by opposing parties seems impossible

Synthesis In Hegelian philosophy, the new idea that resolves the conflict between the initial proposition thesis and its negation antithesis

Concept Review Questions

1. Establish your understanding of the process of negotiations. What steps and actions you should bear in mind if you have been assigned the role of negotiator on behalf of the organization you work for?
2. Discuss the ten commandments for a negotiator to demonstrate your basic knowledge of negotiating traits.
3. What steps and actions you will take, if your company is threatened with a hostile take over, to negotiate an amicable settlement. What kind of agreement does this situation call for—specific or implied, and why?

4. The aftermath of a settlement calls for certain efforts for a public relations professional to generate public recognition and responses to the new arrangement. Draw up an action plan to achieve the objective.

Case Study

Microsoft–Yahoo Marriage

For the last two years the proposed marriage between world's two major conglomerates, Microsoft and Yahoo, still seems to be hanging in balance. The negotiations started in late 2006, are still wading through troubled waters. The proposals and counter proposals have remained inconclusive, much to the amusement of the third party Google.

In late 2006, both the parties discussed various options from a partnership to a merger, making no headway. Three months later, in 2007, Yahoo told Microsoft that the time was not opportune in view of the brighter prospects Yahoo management saw due to the new technology in advertising system becoming a reality.

As if desperate to acquire the Yahoo's Internet capabilities and potential, the Microsoft CEO Steve Ballmer made a lucrative offer of $44.6 billion and a $31 per- share cash-and-stock takeover, at the beginning of 2008. Subsequently, Microsoft made this offer public as a result of which their own share price fell down 6.6 per cent and the Yahoo share got a boost to clock 48 per cent increase and attained $28.38 per share. Naturally, Yahoo rejected the Microsoft effort as too low.

Come April 2008, Microsoft set a three week timeframe for Yahoo either to negotiate or face a proxy showdown and even a cut in the offer price. Yahoo again rejected the offer claiming that they expected a higher bid.

Both parties came to the negotiating table where Yahoo asked for details of the Microsoft integration plans and also raised some non-financial but critical issues that would have a bearing on the deal. Soon after a few weeks, Microsoft raised its offer to $33 per share, or $47.5 billion, that is more than $ 5 billion over the previous offer. Now Yahoo demanded $37 per share or about $5 billion more. Consequently Microsoft called off negotiations.

Hardly two weeks had passed, when Microsoft pronounced that it still needed to create an Internet powerhouse that could be a rival to Google. Therefore, Microsoft was still interested in Yahoo.

Perhaps, afraid of the power of US search engine Google, Microsoft has now hastily revived efforts to reach some kind of a deal with Yahoo, as this software giant seems to have doubts whether it can achieve those goals on its own. Microsoft's off and on interest in Yahoo has generated a lot of speculation amongst financial analysts, investors, customers, and employees about the shape of things to come.

According to newspaper reports and the people who know say that there are some confidential discussions going on between the two giants, with obvious concern to not get beaten by Google.

The history will tell the future developments and the details of the negotiations whenever these witness a finale.

Discussion questions

1. Discuss the Microsoft and Yahoo negotiations with special reference to the role played by public relations vis-à-vis the media.
2. Hoping that this marriage of two giants will become a reality, what role do you see for yourself during and aftermath of this agreement. Develop a hypothetical plan.

References

Moran, Robert T. and William G. Stripp (1997), *Dynamics of Successful International Business Negotiations*, Gulf Publishing Company, Texas, USA and published in India by Jaico Publishing House, Mumbai, p. 9.

Robbins, Stephen P. (2005), *Organisational Behavior*, 11th edition, Prentice Hall of India Private Limited, New Delhi, pp. 434 and 437.

Stoner, James A.F., R. Edward Freeman, and Daniel R. Gilbert, Jr (2002), *Management*, 6th edition, Prentice Hall of India Private Limited, New Delhi, p. 539.

The Mint, New Delhi, vol 2, no. 119, 19 May 2008, pp. 15 and 24.

PART IV

APPLICATIONS

Marketing PR and Integrated Marketing Communications

PUBLIC RELATIONS SUPPORT TO MARKETING

'Public relations has often been treated as a marketing stepchild, an afterthought to more serious promotion planning. But the wise company takes concrete steps to manage successful relations with its key publics. Most companies operate a public relations (PR) department. The PR department monitors the attitudes of the organization's publics and distributes information and communications to build goodwill. When negative publicity happens, the PR department acts as a troubleshooter. The best PR departments spend time counselling top management to adopt positive programmes and to eliminate questionable practices so that negative publicity does not arise in the first place,' wrote Philip Kotler, the marketing guru in 2000.

There have been times in the history of public relations when marketing and the PR professionals did not share a common vocabulary. Marketing people always have one focus and that is to contribute to the bottom line profits of the company. They, perhaps, do not worry themselves as to how and what factors contribute to the attainment of profit goals. Many enlightened marketing professionals think today, and rightly so, that marketing is all about communicating the right messages to the right people. That is the area of concern and specialization for the PR professionals.

With the passage of time and attainment of professional maturity, both marketing and public relations have developed a relationship of kissing cousins, so much so, that a new term called marketing public relations (MPR) has emerged. This denotes the seriousness that both professions now attach to this relationship with the sole objective of winning the marketing game, both in short and long runs. Rightly so, the modern marketing system now proclaims public relations as the 5th P of marketing, the first four being the product, place, price, and promotion.

Hitherto, public relations was expected by the marketing people as an add-on tool to their marketing technology in terms of generating some free publicity in the media or create a media hype that make the products and the company to ride the popularity current. Today the story does not end here but begins. All the marketing activities of a company are being supplemented by public relations. Public relations is a vital support system for the marketing people for the total gambit of marketing activities, starting with launching a new product to projecting, protecting, positioning, reinventing, and promoting the product. In addition, the public relations' efforts to build and maintain corporate image provides the necessary strength to the marketing efforts.

A look at the definitions of marketing and public relations should help us to understand the intimate connection between the two streams of business management.

The American Marketing Association (AMA) defines the term 'marketing' as:

'The process of planning and executing the conception, pricing, promotion, and distribution of ideas, goods and services to create exchanges that satisfy individual and organizational objectives.'

The AMA definition recognizes that exchange is a central concept in marketing. For exchange to occur, there must be two or more parties with something of value to all, a desire and ability to give up that something to the other party, and a way to communicate with each other.

A step ahead, marketing facilitates the exchange process by carefully examining the needs and wants of consumers, developing a product or service that satisfies these needs, offering it at a certain price, making it available through a particular place or channel of distribution, and developing a programme of promotion or communication to create awareness and interest.

On the other hand, public relations is in action 'when an organization systematically plans and distributes information in an attempt to control and manage the nature of publicity it receives and its image, is really engaging in a function known as public relations'. Experts think that public relations is 'the management function which evaluates public attitudes, identifies the policies and procedures of an individual or an organization with the public interest, and executes a programme of action to earn public understanding, and acceptance'.

Marketing is the management of four Ps—product, price, place, and promotion—the elements of marketing mix. But the communication function called public relations equipped with training and techniques to communicate as its forte is termed as MPR.

MPR is an extension of public relations. Thomas L. Harris describes MPR as the

'process of planning, executing and evaluating programmes that encourage purchases and consumer satisfaction through credible communication of information and impressions that identify companies and their products with the needs, wants, concerns and interests of consumers' (Harris 1993).

In other words, MPR is market driven, whereas the total public relations embraces the various aspects of a company's relationship with other publics like employees, shareholders, media, government, community, etc.

MPR Goals

So that the marketing and public relations partnership in achieving the organizational goals grows and flourishes, most of the marketing and public relations people should agree that it is always advisable to set certain MPR goals. The goals can be to: *enlarge awareness base, develop a loyal consumer base, build credibility, adopt relationship marketing, earn consumer testimonials to inspire new customers, build market excitement at pre- and post-advertising launch stages, inspire sales force and dealers, keep promotional costs under tab, influence the opinion leaders.*

Enlarge awareness base

MPR skillfully and creatively distributes publicity stories to the media to highlight the company, products, business leaders, new service policies. The column centimetres thus generated free in the media help the company to gain focus in the minds of the consumers. Once registered, the messages trigger the recall rating of the organization resulting in desired responses, much longed for by the marketers.

Incidentally, higher the awareness base of a company, lesser is the need to advertise at higher frequency, other factors remaining under control. In other words, lesser quantum of advertising means lesser advertising expenditure. The money saved is money gained.

Develop a loyal customer base

Creating customers and retaining customers is the name of the game called marketing. It may be easy to create customers who can be made to buy company products once. But it is more an uphill task to make customers come back and keep coming back time and again. In other words, the challenge is to create a bank of loyal customers. Loyal customers are profit because selling becomes routinized for the salesmen, as they don't have to make a sales pitch again and again. This saves a company's valuable selling time.

Loyal customers often give valuable suggestions for product improvement and greater customer satisfaction. They also inspire new customers to buy with confidence and help in meeting MPR objectives. Bata's Ambassador brand shoe enjoyed the loyalty of elite customers who always insisted on buying their favourite shoe, over and over again, for almost over fifty years, until Bata launched and promoted their premium brand shoe Hush Puppy.

Build credibility

Even the most creative and powerful advertising suffers from a credibility problem. Customers always perceive the message as an exaggeration. But when MPR places a piece in the editorial content of a newspaper or telecasting media, it enjoys a high degree of credibility. Undoubtedly customers trust in the company as a valuable asset on which the marketers can thrive for a long time.

Adopt relationship marketing

Gone are the days of 'Sell and Forget'. In today's competitive world, where companies are vying with each other to cultivate and satisfy customers, building bridges of understanding with the customers has been adopted as a marketing technique called relationship marketing. Marketers keep telling customers 'Madam! After you have bought our washing machine, we are still around to see that the machine works fine and you should have no problem. We are only a phone call away and that too a toll free one'. Toll free telephones, SMS messages, and Internet websites are now used to build and maintain a relationship with customers. MPR knows well that a customer's word-of-mouth publicity creates a strong ripple effect, positive though slow, but the negative spreads like wildfire and needs to be kept under control.

Earn customer testimonials to inspire new customers

A database of satisfied customers is like a treasure for MPR. Customers, when pleased, turn spokespersons for the company. For instance, the testimonials or letters of appreciation, obtained from customers, testifying high product performance, are used by marketers as well as sales people, as a tool to assure and reassure the new customers that the company is a reliable business outfit, worth a trust and response. MRF tyres have been using such testimonials as part of their advertising programme to boost customer confidence.

Build market excitement at pre- and post-advertising launch stages

MPR is an exciting game. There is no place for dull headed and slow moving people. When innovative and exciting messages about the new products, usages, customer benefits, etc. are flashed, they trigger excitement in the market and prompt people to try new ideas. Strategic opportunities for dramatizing the company products and obtaining publicity, pay dividends in terms of triggering faster sales.

Inspire sales force and dealers

Keeping the morale high of the sales force and the dealers and retailers is a vital function of marketing. A frustrated sales force or tired and bored dealers, can never sell and succeed. Stories about the new technological changes in the product quality and increased customer benefits, human interest stories, and the news about high corporate achievements, generate enthusiasm amongst sales personnel and retailers, to sell with confidence. Hero Honda announcing the rolling out of the millionth motor cycle from their plants, became the talk of the town amongst upwardly mobile young generation and gave a great boost to the total marketing network.

Keep promotional cost under tab

MPR certainly costs less than the promotional efforts undertaken in terms of direct mails, freebies, discounts, dealers' window dressing, media advertising, etc. Public relations always has an edge over the paid attempts of the company to grab a better share of the consumer's mind or share of voice in the market. The launch of pleasure drug, Viagra, did not see any significant advertising, but took the market by storm, largely due to the efforts put in by MPR.

Influence the opinion leaders

It is a well established fact that what the leaders do, people follow. Several behaviour patterns visible in our society are a bye-product of the 'follow-the-leader' system. Successful businessmen, professors, actors, teachers, legal professionals, journalists, and artists are role models in the society. Masses follow their life styles, dress, hair styles, vocabulary, and the use of products, which is so important for the MPR effort. So the communication attempts to convince and impress the leaders about the products, values, and styles pay high dividends.

MPR Roles

After the goals have been set, MPR's role to make goals a reality should be looked at. Some of the MPR roles are: *build and maintain corporate image, support to new product launches, assist products to attain maturity, recycle and reposition the products, boost public interest in certain product categories, target specific groups, manage controversies and crisis situations.*

Build and maintain corporate image

Many a time, more than the superior quality of a product, what helps it to be accepted by consumers is the good corporate image. Public relations carries a specific responsibility of building as well as maintaining a positive perception about the company in the minds of the people. A good positive mindshare

EXHIBIT 10.1   Philip's image boosting advertisement—Champion of champions

Champion of champions
Philips CFL rated "Best Buy" by Consumer Voice. Philips is the true champion according to the Consumer Voice* CFL Comparative Test', setting the gold standard when tested against 13 major brands.
With its long life and excellent energy efficiency, you're able to enjoy better light for longer. For ultimate performance, only one brand stands out from the field.

*Consumer Voice is a government recognized, independent consumer research and testing organization.
'Test Conducted in 2006.

PHILIPS
sense and simplicity

Source: The Mint (2008).

inspires consumer confidence in the company's products, and hence, success for the marketing effort. London's famous and expensive store, Harrods, sells even its carry bags at £15 a piece, and consumers buy the bags just to show off, even if they could not afford to buy anything at all from this expensive store. Philip's advertisement titled 'Champion of Champions' boasting about their winning the 'Consumer Voice Award' is meant for image boosting for the company as well as their products (See Exhibit 10.1).

Support to new product launches

Much before the actual new product launch event, public relations swings into action and starts circulating media stories about the new products about to be launched. Enough ground and awareness get created and consumers start eagerly awaiting the products. The competition in the car market has become cut throat. It is quite common to read stories about the new car launches. The great success story of Maruti 800 followed by half a dozen other models can be attributed to the media hype created by public relations effort. The latest Nano car story from the house of Tata's had taken the country by storm much before the car was actually launched.

Assist products to attain maturity

Taking products from the launch stage over to the maturity stage, also called hump, is the ultimate dream of every marketer. The advertising alone may not be able to do it, until the process of communicating to the consumers by other credible means is kept up. Public relations plays a definite role in weaving success stories, and customer satisfaction episodes to gather the necessary support. Once a product reaches the hump, there comes the tough challenge of keeping it on the hump for as long as possible and prevent its decline, the start of which is a danger signal for the marketers. Reinforcing consumer faith and loyalty in the products comes naturally to the public relations professionals. The 'Rooh Afza' sharbat by Hamdard Dawakhana has stayed over the hump for the last 100 years and is considered as India's oldest brand. MPR can also take credit that there is still not born a meaningful competitor to Rooh Afza, which continues to be the uncrowned king of the sharbat market.

Recycle and reposition the products

What goes up must come down. The law of nature also applies to the products. A company's products which attain the height of glory in the market, one time or the other, have to see the slide down. Smart marketers rejuvenate and recycle the products, relaunch them and again take them up at the maturity level. Surf, a detergent from Hindustan Unilever, has witnessed several recycling exercises and continues to be recycled every now and then. MPR definitely plays its role in the process.

Repositioning the products is a well thought out game that marketers play. One of the challenges is to enhance the status of the products in the market. Many products suffer from the reputation of a down market status and clamour for enhancement or repositioning. Shifting a product from a price conscious consumer segment to a status conscious customer area is a challenge. 'Parachute', which started as an ordinary coconut hair oil, has been raised to the segment of more discerning customers wanting to make a style statement. Decidedly, MPR has an important role to play.

Boost public interest in certain product categories

Due to several social and cultural reasons, certain categories of products do not find favour with certain segments of customers. The taboos stand firmly in the way. Sometimes price or health risks come in the way. To demolish certain biases and taboos, public needs education to adopt certain products. In Gujarat, eating eggs has been a taboo in the religiously vegetarian society, despite people's poor physical standards. The poultry producers adopted the MPR strategies to promote consumption of eggs, by spelling the egg as 'vegg'. This understandably lifted the social taboo to some extent.

Target specific groups

To expand the consumer base or to venture into new customer segments, a need arises to target new segments with appropriate communications. Larger the consumer base, better are the chances of the marketing success. With increasing number of women drivers in India, Goodyear started a 'women's car rally' to target lady drivers. The public relations effort in holding such rallies in major metros of India, to some extent helped the company to enter the new segment of lady drivers. Besides targeting the younger set of people, McDonald's also targets the office goers segment, with a time and money saving quick meal packages at their fast food restaurants, during lunch breaks.

Manage controversies and crisis situations

The product content, quality, or policies can often stir the market with some turbulence. In a crisis situation, the MPR is often under test. Clearing the misunderstandings and restoring normalcy become a major challenge, that calls for public relations help. The familiar Cadbury, Coca Cola, and Pepsi controversies stirred by some consumerists are a case in focus when the company had to resort to high powered public relations campaigns to allay all fears in the minds of the consumers to restore the lost confidence in their products.

Market public relations strategies

MPR to work has to adopt the same reliable four step system—scan the environment, create a communication plan, implement the plan, and evaluate the impact (See chapters 4, 5, 6, and 7).

INTEGRATED MARKETING COMMUNICATIONS

The Concept

The American Association of Advertising Agencies defines integrated marketing communications as:

'Integrated Marketing Communications is a concept of marketing communications planning that recognizes the added value of a comprehensive plan that evaluates the strategic roles of a variety of communication disciplines for example, general advertising, direct response, sales promotion, and public relations and combines these disciplines to provide clarity, consistency and maximum communications impact through the seamless integration of discrete messages.'

'Integrated marketing communications calls for a "big picture" approach to plan marketing and promotion programmes and coordinating the various communication functions. It requires firms to develop a total marketing communication strategy that recognizes how all of a firm's marketing activities, not just promotion, communicate with its customers. Customer's perceptions of a company and/or its various brands are a synthesis of the bundle of messages they receive (such as media advertisements, price, direct marketing efforts, publicity, sales promotion, and type of store where a product is sold)' (Belch and Belch 1995).

Hitherto, the marketer practised and used the various tools of communication like advertising, sales promotion, direct marketing, and public relations and publicity, in isolation of each other. Each tool is made to yield its own communication strategies and budgets. Each discipline had its own course charted separately and implemented in the best interest of the attainment of corporate marketing objectives. Some large companies with a wide range of products would have an independent manager assigned to manage each tool, almost in isolation of others.

Realizing the impact of singing the same message in a concert, which calls for perfect coordination and harmony to produce good music, the marketers developed the concept of integrated marketing communication. Rather than displaying five works of art in a picture gallery, they thought of painting all the five themes on a larger screen to create harmony and cohesion of one thought and objective that is meeting the marketing goals of the company. The idea worked.

Having benefited from the strategy called integrated marketing communications, more and more organizations have embraced the new concept. Thus, the concept advocates harmonized marriage of five tools of communication to produce messages that impact the consumers to generate the necessary responses. The marketing communication tools are: *advertising, promotion, direct marketing, personal selling,* and *public relations and publicity,* called the 'five finger story'. When each tool of communication is represented by a finger, unite into a fist, it creates synergy of a punch, that can impact the market and the customers (See Exhibit 10.2). It is but necessary here to define and describe each tool and then bring out a synthesis of them all, to have a fairly good idea about this 'five finger story'.

Advertising

As defined by the marketing guru Philip Kotler, the definition reads:

EXHIBIT 10.2 Integrated marketing communication (IMC)—the five finger story

'Advertising is any paid form of non-personal presentation and promotion of ideas, goods or services by an identified sponsor.'

Some of the characteristics of advertising are noteworthy. Some key words have a fundamental connotation and should be seen in that perspective.

The word *paid* reflects that almost always it costs an organization to advertise. There is nothing free in advertising. The advertiser has to buy the space in the print media and time slots in the electronic media. Advertising costs start right from the time an agency starts working on the concept, prepares layouts, makes final artworks, and then loads on to the media vehicles. There could be some exceptions, where a voluntary organization gets a sponsor to pay their advertising like the ads put up by Red Cross for voluntary blood donations, or fundraising advertisements by the Blind Relief Association.

The *non-personal* element signifies the loading of advertising messages on to the mass media vehicles to a faceless audience. The television, Internet, newspapers, magazines, etc. carry the messages to the people, who are never specifically known to the advertiser. The advertiser does not get the immediate feedback as to how the message was received by the target audience and how they reacted, until a research is conducted to know the public response. Unlike personal selling where a sales person gets spontaneous reactions and responses from a customer, the advertising, as if, sells the products to the customers in the absence of the sales person. That is why, some experts define advertising as salesmanship in print.

The identified sponsor component stands for the advertiser, the name of the company, its address, phone numbers, website, where the consumers can make a direct contact to buy, sell, or get the products serviced. The marketers even give the names of their dealers and distributors to facilitate contact between consumers and the company, for mutually beneficial relationship.

As an extension or an explanation of the above definition, Dorothy Cohen (1988) suggested another definition, which is as follows:

'Advertising is a business activity, employing creative techniques to design persuasive communication in mass media that promote ideas, goods, and services in a manner consistent with the achievement of the advertiser's objectives, the delivery of consumer satisfaction and the development of social and economic welfare.'

In today's cut throat competition, the power of advertising can hardly be exaggerated. Advertising has a great influence on the people and many hold the opinion that advertising is the force that constantly triggers changes in the society. The way society walk, talk, dress up, and behave is all, perhaps, under the influence of advertising. However, it will be interesting to know as to how advertising works.

Functions of advertising

In the modern scenario of free market economies of the world, advertising is a force to reckon with. No business can flourish without advertising and no society can develop and improve its life styles without the active role played by advertising. Paying his tribute to the discipline of advertising, US President, Franklin D. Roosevelt, had said:

'If I were starting life over again, I am inclined to think that I would go into advertising business in preference to almost any other. This is because advertising has come over to cover the whole range of human needs and also because it combines real imagination with a deep study of human psychology. Because advertising brings to the greatest number of people actual knowledge concerning useful things, it is essentially a form of education. It has risen with ever growing rapidity to the dignity of an art. It is constantly paving new paths. The general rising of standards of modern civilization among all groups of people during the past half century would have been impossible without the spreading of knowledge of higher standards by means of advertising.'

According to the Advertising Agencies Association of America and other professional associations, advertising is a force that fuels the engine of economy. With advertising budgets running into billions of dollars, advertising generates gainful employment for millions of people all over the world. That is why, advertising is a force that energizes the economic system.

Though advertising is put to use by all and sundry for various kinds of objectives and functions, the few generally known functions are: *familiarization, reminder value, news value, shake off market inertia,* and *value addition to products.*

Familiarization   Advertising performs a vital function of making the entry into the minds of the consumers, who, hitherto, had never heard of the product or service. Advertising generates awareness about the availability of a product which the consumers can buy, use, and enjoy the benefits. As such, advertising is an education in itself.

Reminder value   Humans suffer from a serious problem of memory lapse. Everyday consumers see scores of advertisements in the media; it is almost impossible to retain and remember every one. However, when reminded by advertising a couple of times, consumers recollect and make up their mind to take a buying action.

News value   Advertising works as a powerful vehicle of carrying the news to the people, not only the news that we see in the newspapers or TV news channels, but the news about new innovations. Thanks to advertising, news like advent of transistor radio, mobile phones, television and now Internet, etc. spread quite fast. New detergents, I-pods, walkman, music systems, new drugs, etc. have become common knowledge. The Maruti revolution, Delhi–New York non-stop flights, life saving drugs, contraceptive pills, etc. have become a part of our vocabulary, thanks to advertising.

Shake off market inertia   Procrastination is the worst enemy of progress. Unless someone urges one to act, there is no progress. Advertising exerts a social and economic pressure on people to act. Winston Churchill, the war time prime minister of England, had said that advertising attracted an individual with a promise to work a little harder so that he could buy a few things more to make life liveable and comfortable. Advertising is a powerful incentive to set the chain reaction of economic factors into motion and raise individual productivity.

Value addition to products   Consumers will not buy unless they see value for their hard earned money. Value addition is a process of communicating the benefits that a consumer will enjoy by buying a product. Many mundane products owe their acceptance to advertising. Luxor pen advertises the smooth writing of their pens by advertising *'Siyahi ya malai!'* (While you write, you feel moving a pen with a creamlike smoothness, so it's no ink, it's cream).

Promotion

Promotion has been defined as the coordination of all seller-initiated efforts to set up channels of information and persuasion to sell goods and services or promote an idea. Promotion has also been described as those activities that provide extra value or incentives to the sales force, distributors, or the ultimate consumer and can stimulate immediate sales.

Compared to advertising, which builds a powerful base of loyal customers but at a very slow pace, sales promotion is like a bubble burst, which creates a temporary excitement in the market and triggers increased sales. Measuring the impact of advertising is often a question mark in the minds of marketers, as the objectives of advertising are long-term and broad based like greater market penetration through greater awareness, brand building, increase in mind share, and ultimately the market share. Sales promotion on the contrary, stimulates immediate responses through promising extra benefits to the price conscious customers, who are always willing to switch brand loyalties.

As the marketing has become tougher and competition stiffer, more and more organizations have been shifting major chunks of their advertising budgets to sales promotion for quicker results. The parity between sales promotion and advertising in some companies may touch 70:30. The factors that influence such decisions are, dealers' greater role in the market, shifting brand loyalties and preference for cheaper substitutes, consumers becoming more price conscious, brands clutter, new retail malls providing shopping pleasure and convenience, online and telemarketing facilities, etc.

Popularly known to marketers as sales promotion it comprises two categories: (1) *Consumer targeted promotions;* (2) *Trade targeted promotions.*

Consumer targeted promotions

The consumer targeted promotions are mainly directed at the end users of the products or services, which promise some immediate benefits to them in terms of savings, better health, more quantity for same price, attractive discounts till stocks last or contests and discount coupons, etc. The sole idea behind such promotions is to excite consumers to take action now, before it becomes late. The objective is to register immediate sale and meet the sales and marketing targets (See Exhibit 10.3).

Trade targeted promotions

Such sales promotion campaigns are directed at channels of distribution such as dealers, retailers, and wholesale distributors. Incentives like higher trade discounts, turnover discounts, free samples, all expense paid trips for high performers, store decorations, supply of free promotional materials, training programmes, co-operative advertising, are extended to motivate and inspire

---

EXHIBIT 10.3   Discount sales—Om Books

Source: Hindustan Times (2008).

such people to promote company products and boost the corporate image.

Both types of promotions use certain tools and techniques to trigger enthusiasm and excitement in the market, to achieve marketing objectives (See Exhibit 10.4).

Direct Marketing

Direct market is an effort by an organization to cut through the cordons of various channels of distribution and reach the consumers directly. The marketing organization communicates directly with the pre-selected target consumers to induce their interest into company's products and clinch deals. Direct marketing is an effort to seek out customers, shake them out of their inertia and show them the benefits they would derive out of the proposals.

Direct marketing is step ahead of direct mail advertising or providing product catalogues to the customers to facilitate their choosing and ordering products through mail orders. Today it involves a number of marketing techniques like telemarketing, online ordering, or through direct-response advertisements. Several companies such as Dell Computers, Tupperware, Encyclopedia Britannica have adopted this marketing system.

In his *Dictionary of Marketing Terms*, Peter Bennett (1988) defines direct marketing as :

> *The total of activities by which the seller, in effecting the exchange of goods and services with the buyer, directs efforts to a target audience using one or more media (direct selling, direct mail, telemarketing, direct action advertising, catalogue selling, cable TV selling, etc.) for the purpose of soliciting a response by phone, mail, or personal visit from a prospect or customer.*

The direct marketing system caught up in America in a big way because of the frequent changes in the life styles of American society. The prosperous

---

EXHIBIT 10.4   Promotools—consumers and trade

Consumer targets	Trade targets
Contests	Store decorations and POP (Point of Purchase) material
Games	Exhibitions
Lotteries	Events and shows
Sweepstakes	Promotional allowances
Demonstrations	Consumer contact programme
Coupons	Compensate for coupons
Rebate and freebies	Co-operative advertising
Interest free loans	Training programmes
Entertainment	Trade-in allowance
Lucky draw–big prize	Holidays for high sales
Free samples	Dealer club awards
Tie-ins	Turn over commission

American generation seemed to have enough money but not enough time. Therefore, direct marketing very appropriately filled up the gap.

India, with the opening up of economy and the arrival of several multinational corporations with world known brands, the direct marketing communication tool has also entered the Indian life to a considerable extent. With explosion of the mobile telephony, the telemarketers are mushrooming from selling insurance, cars, bank loans, to health foods, garments on phone. The Internet marketing companies such as e-bay, etc. have added lot of power to the direct marketing techniques. Some of the Indian media houses like *The Times of India* and the *Hindustan Times* have set up their own direct marketing wings and also started publishing special business to business pages for bringing the buyer and seller closer to each other. The surge of cable TV everyday flashes dozens of messages, enticing prospects to phone order, many fancy merchandise from beauty aids to kitchen items, from weight loss gadgets to potency pills. The SMS service fills up the gaps, if any, in the process.

Media for direct marketing

A marketing organization utilizes various media for reaching the consumers directly. The main characteristic of such media is that it has to have a direct reach to the target customers. Some of the media utilized are as follows:

Direct mail   The mailers addressed to the customers by name are delivered through post in their mail boxes. Though a powerful medium it does not enjoy any prestige. Popularly known as 'junk mail', many receivers are averse to even opening such mailers. Media follows a data base of mailing list. According to one observation, an American receives about four mailers every week on an average and the nation is bombarded with 40 billion mailers. With the advent of e-mail, there is a separate 'junk mail' folder which does not receive much attention.

Catalogues   Companies like Sears chain store of America produces an illustrated catalogue for consumers to place mail orders. Now such catalogues can be browsed on their websites. Burlington started this effort in India with very little success. Yellow pages publication did meet some success. Tabloids like 'Free Ads' could not sustain for a long time.

Broadcast media   Marketing outfits use TV, radio, or telephone calls to invite customers to buy. The mobile telephony in India has now revolutionized this marketing technique of calling customers or sending them SMS to generate response. The arrival of FM radio has gained some pulling power to excite and incite customers to a buying action.

Infomercials   This media technique is used to enliven some thoughts lying dormant in the minds of customers and prompt them to act through the dissemination of information related to health, earning money, losing weight, dieting, etc. *Kamasutra* condoms used this strategy through Internet to reach some serious minded married males to seek bliss without risk.

Print media   Newspapers and magazines are utilized to put some direct response advertisements to generate responses. The media suffers from the notorious clutter problem that hinders the reach of messages to the intended target audience.

Telemarketing   The introduction of toll free telephone numbers prompt the customers to directly call the companies for placing orders. Dell Computers have used this strategic medium as their major marketing system.

Cybershopping   The surge of Internet has made it possible for customers to shop on the net, right in the comfort of their homes. The faceless marketing has been quite a success. e-Bay is one of the forerunner in the utilization of this media.

It is also relevant to look at the *merits* and *demerits* of direct marketing. Depending on the needs and techniques used, small and big companies can plan usage of direct marketing with rewarding results (See Exhibit 10.5).

Personal Selling

Another element of the IMC or the communication mix is personal selling. It is a form of face-to-face communication with a customer when a sales person tries to persuade a customer to purchase a company's products or services. This interpersonal interaction involves a direct contact between the seller and the buyer.

This direct and interpersonal communication lets the sender immediately receive and evaluate feedback from the receiver. Known as dyadic communication, it allows for more specific modification of the message and more personalized communication between the parties. The seller seeks to motivate the prospective customer to behave favourably towards the seller. Unlike other

EXHIBIT 10.5   *Direct marketing—merits and demerits*

Merits	Demerits
Selective reach—low wastage	Lacks prestige in selling
Segmentation capabilities	Mailing lists get outdated
Frequency control	Respondents' mood matters
Flexibility	
Time scheduling possible	
Personalization	
Economical	
Measurement is faster	

elements of the communication mix, personal selling is an upfront contact with the customers with no intermediary factors.

Amongst the theories of selling, the most acceptable and workable theory is known as 'AIDAS Theory of Selling'. Based on the initials of five words used in the abbreviation AIDAS, each word stands for a stage in the selling process. Thus the five stages are: (1) *Attention,* (2) *Interest,* (3) *Desire,* (4) *Action,* and (5) *Satisfaction* Professional sales professionals think that during a successful sales transaction, a customer's mind passes through these five mental states, and the sequence when followed, can result in sale (See Exhibit 10.6). A brief review of each of these stages should be appropriate in the context of integrated marketing communications system.

AIDAS is an old established theory based on the experiential knowledge of selling professionals and should be, perhaps, a century old. Incidentally, this very theory is also followed by advertising professionals in the formation of message and advertising designs. The fundamental system is as good today, as it was long ago.

Attention   In personal selling situation it is very important to be able to gain favourable attention of the customer. Sales personnel master the art of using some 'ice breakers' to make a good impression, and follow it through with good conversational skills and likeable personal appearance. This is the entry point. Once the entry is gained, there is good possibility of smooth sailing.

Interest   Skilled sales personnel start creating interest in their product or proposition through personal enthusiasm, product literature, or presentations. Since it is important to know the needs of the customers, salesmen master the art of questioning customers to read their mind.

Desire   Generation of a desire, which may be lying dormant in the mind of the customer, is very crucial to this stage of personal selling. Keeping sales story on track and handling objections and obstacles is part of the process to kindle the desire.

Action   This stage, also known as closing the sale, is the climaxing time for the dialogue, when the customer should be willing to take the buying action. Sales persons are most afraid of this situation. Lest the customer backs out at the end

---

EXHIBIT 10.6   AIDAS theory of personal selling

A – **Attention**	Gaining favourable attention
I – **Interest**	Creating interest
D – **Desire**	Kindling desire
A – **Action**	Inducing action
S – **Satisfaction**	Build satisfaction

---

moment, they understand and use their well perfected closing techniques to gclinch the sale.

Satisfaction   Assuring and reassuring the customer that his decision was wise and he is bound to enjoy the due benefits out of the product, is the last part of the personal selling situation. Selling professionals take leave of the customer with an eye on future relationships and more orders.

Relationship marketing

The personal selling process now has attained a reasonable maturity. Contrary to the belief that the customer–seller dyad is a one time deal, the process has graduated to a long-term relationship between the company and the customers, with sales people being a common link. Once you sell, you don't forget your customers but keep in touch with them to provide after sales service and even explore possibility of repeat sales to them. Wider the network of customers a salesperson has, better are his chances, nay his company's chances, for success. Therefore the term relationship marketing is a favourite of marketers.

As mentioned above, the seller–buyer dyad has culminated into a kind of relationship. Rather than focusing on some short-term goals of meeting sales targets, the concept stipulates a kind of partnership for mutual benefits. The seller company benefits in terms of sales and profits and the customer enjoys the long-term satisfaction of benefits and a continued support system. This is truer in the area of consumer durables like white goods, cars, motor cycles, computers, and heavy engineering equipment marketing.

Public Relations and Publicity

'Because consumers are exposed to so much advertising these days, they often try hard to avoid it—and are very skeptical of it when they do get exposed to it. To reach these hard-to-reach consumers and to convey messages to them in a manner that is more credible partly because it is more subtly delivered, more and more companies are today devoting a portion of their communication budget to the use of PR for marketing purposes. Some of the different ways in which this is done ... most of them have in common, is the delivery of message about the brand not through paid, explicit advertising, but rather through an implied or explicit endorsement of a credible third-party media source, such as the editorial content of newspaper or magazine, or by associating themselves with a sports or cultural event, or a charitable organization' (Batra et al. 1998).

In other words, PR has an edge over advertising as far as the credibility of the messages is concerned. Comparing the editorial and advertising content of a media, say newspaper, editorial mentions are looked at and believed in by the consumers, and advertising always suffers from a credibility gap. However, public relations uses advertising as a tool of communication, but with a natural and creative presentation.

At this point of time, it is also appropriate to distinguish between publicity and public relations. Publicity in a limited sense is creating media hype through distribution of news stories to the media, whereas PR is a larger function to communicate, build public understanding and acceptance, which uses publicity as its tool of communication through editorial content. If PR covers a whole gambit of activities, publicity is just one part of it.

PR is a very demure function of a management to establish a two-way communication between an organization and its publics, namely, customers, dealers, suppliers, shareholders, media, government, legislatures, community, etc. to establish mutual understanding and to resolve conflicts of interest.

PR uses many other tools like special publications, community welfare activities, charity and fund raising, sponsorships of some special events, institutional advertising, celebrity endorsements or testimonials, media relations, lobbying, etc. to project and maintain the image perception of an organization.

However, in the marketing context, all that PR undertakes cumulatively contribute to the image of an organization, which in itself is a prime mover that triggers many buying actions in the market place. The actions and activities help the organization to market their products and services with prestige and confidence. For definitions and explanations, see Chapter 3 on Public Relations in India.

Publicity

Publicity is the name of the game indulged in by the PR professionals and marketers to soft pedal news stories, articles, feature articles, photographs in the form of press releases, video clips, backgrounders and photo features, and graphics, etc. which are of readers' and viewers' interest. Organizing a press conference to break a news like new product launches, new service policies, etc. is another way of generating publicity. Media is naturally interested in what their audiences are interested. Therefore, they pick up the material and publish or telecast free of charge. Publicity, therefore is free. Publicity means free of charge coverage of the company activities and information in the media.

Contrary to advertising, which is always generated by an identified sponsor, publicity need not have an identified sponsor. Public relations serves as an important information or news source, identifying what may not be necessary. With the advent of financial press and business TV channels, a very high content of such media is generated by resource persons called public relations practitioners. For more information on the subject, also see Chapter 16 on Media Relations.

Organizing publicity It is mostly handled by the public relations practi-tioners, who skillfully generate materials of media interest to get the coverage. Smarter and creative a PR person is, bigger can be their harvest of clippings and media mentions. Although it is not possible to arrive at a list of activities that can generate publicity, yet going by the experience and success in certain aspects of publicity, few areas offer readymade opportunities like: *new stories and editorial mentions, sports and event sponsorships, social marketing, product/service oriented placements, contests and lucky draws,* etc.

News stories and editorial mentions: Invention of a new drug to cure cancer or Aids, Pakistani girl undergoing an operation in an Indian hospital, a hole in the heart, a honeymoon on the moon, and similar kind of human interest stories, catch the attention of the media vis-à-vis the readers and get favourable coverage. The medical miracle of All India Institute of Medical Sciences operating on conjoined twins, or producing a test tube baby, got good publicity for the institute. A negative publicity is also not ruled out. Cadbury, Pepsi, and Coca Cola getting noticed for some health hazardous material in their products, generated lot of adverse publicity.

Sports and events sponsorships: Sponsorship of sporting events by the companies offer major publicity opportunities. The DLF IPL floating 20:20 cricket matches amongst the state teams sponsored by big names such as Vijay Mallya, Shahrukh Khan, and Preity Zinta have become an obsession for the nation and the media. No TV channel, newspaper, or magazine can afford to ignore these events.

Sponsored programmes like Hero Honda *Sare Ga Ma Pa, Grammy Awards Night, Indian Idol, Star Parivar Awards Night,* get tremendous media attention. Whereas the viewers get hooked on to the programmes for entertainment, media benefits in terms of increased advertising revenues and the sponsors generate robust publicity for their organizations.

Social marketing: Communications highlighting the corporate social responsibility efforts or other social issues are the main focus of such publicity efforts. Aids, road safety, populations control, female foeticide, dowry deaths, etc. are amongst the several issues that get due media publicity to help these social causes.

Product/service oriented placements: Many fashion designers like Ritu Beri and Rohit Bal get promotions for their talents and business by getting credit for specially designing costumes for movie stars. Car and motor cycle makers place their products in some exciting movie scenes to highlight them. Travel and tourism companies offer their premises and sites for shooting of films to promote their hotels and resorts for tourists and honeymooners. The famous Ray-Ban sunglasses were publicized by providing them to Tom Cruise in the movie *Top Gun.*

Contests and lucky draws: Contests and lucky draws are organized by the companies to heighten the consumer interest in their products. Introduction of entry forms, or nominating best performer of the show named after their product, are general rules. The famous 'I am a Complan boy!' and 'I am a Complan girl' can be examples of identifying a healthy boy and girl with a health drink. The *Hindustan Times* organized a media jamboree to attract readers' attention by asking them to fill up their participation coupon to entitle themselves for a grand lucky prize of a premium brand car.

Knowing the value and interests of the readers in the products, media highlights the new arrivals in their special columns. For instance, a newspaper on a Sunday pullout highlighted a diamond studded watch that is priced one crore rupees. Supplements like Top Gear, What's Hot (*The Times of India*), and Splurge (*Hindustan Times*), discuss features and benefits of several products, from cars to cosmetics, from health to homemaking, etc.

IMC IN A CONCERT

Having gone through the nuances of all the five tools of communication, it is time to conclude. The concept of integrated marketing communications (IMC) means harnessing the power of all the tools—advertising, promotion, direct marketing, personal selling, and public relations and publicity—into a unifying force to target the messages to the consumers in one voice (See Exhibit 10.7). It is like orchestrating one and the same tune in a concert that produces harmonious music that sounds sonorous to the listeners. When all the five fingers of the five fingers concept, which stands for each finger representing one tool of communication, join together in a fist, they should have all the force of unity of message like the power of a punch. The common focus of this unified communication punch, though not literally, is to impact the customer.

EXHIBIT 10.7 Communications concert to impact the customer

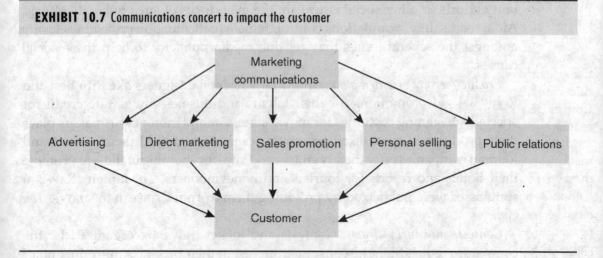

The IMC concept also stipulates that consumers are addressed by the same marketing organization in a variety of ways like image-building advertising, public relations, direct marketing, sales promotions, point-of-purchase materials, media news mentions, and the sales force calls. These different communications would emanate from a single source with one vision behind all the messages. Consumer, as such, should be hearing the messages, so seamlessly designed and delivered, that they reach the consumer in one voice.

All this effort implies that different marketing communication elements need to be created in a well-coordinated manner by all the departments of the company and the PR and advertising agencies specializing in the management of each communication tool. Seamless coordination and synergizing all the communication tools together can make the integrated marketing communications work well for the success of a marketing programme.

Summary

The relationship between marketing and public relations (PR) has been discussed at length. Having seen the power of PR and the communications generated by it, a new term called marketing public relations (MPR) has been coined to cover the whole gambit of activities jointly undertaken by PR and marketing.

MPR plays several important roles in support of marketing for organizational success. MPR contributes to the marketing effort in many ways such as enlarging the awareness base for the company, develop customer loyalty, build credibility, promote relationship marketing, make satisfied customers, testify to new customers, help in advertising campaign launches, launch new products and recycle old products, product positioning, build corporate image, and even manage controversies and crisis situations.

MPR now graduates to the new concept of marketing communications called integrated marketing communications (IMC), which encompasses five tools of communications, that is, advertising, promotions, direct marketing, personal selling, and public relations and publicity, and generates an integrated programme to transmit messages to the consumers in a concert. Called the five finger story, where each finger represents one communication tool when closed like a fist, it becomes an impactful message to the customers in the market.

Each tool has its own characteristics and functions in its own way. Advertising contributes to the marketing efforts generating familiarization with the company, has reminder and news value, shakes off market inertia, and adds value to the products. The way advertising works is also included.

Promotions which stimulate the market and the customers into a buying action by promising additional benefits in the same cost, has its own kinds—the customer targeted promotions and trade targeted promotions.

Direct marketing concept has been discussed with its tools like direct mailing, catalogues, broadcast media, infomercials, telemarketing, cybershopping, etc. There is also a one shot glimpse at the merits and demerits of direct marketing.

Personal selling, which is a very wide subject and an area of specialization in itself, has been discussed with its popular selling technique called AIDAS. It also dovetails a brief on the relationship marketing.

PR and publicity has been briefly described, as there is enough to study in the other chapters of this book. However, the distinction between PR and publicity has been highlighted.

In conclusion, the integrated marketing communication is a system of seamless co-ordination amongst the above communication tools, which vitally contribute to the marketing communication effort by merging their characteristics and peculiarities together, targeting to meet the marketing goals of a company.

Key Terms

Celebrity testimonial   Recommendation from a celebrity affirming the performance, quality, and/or value of a product or service

Communication mix   The range of approaches and expressions of a marketing idea developed with the hope that it be effective in conveying the ideas to the diverse population of people who receive it

Institutional advertising   Promotional message aimed at creating an image, enhancing reputation, building goodwill, or advocating an idea or the philosophy of an organization, instead of sales promotion

Promotools   Tools used in the promotional process

Recycling products   Reinventing the old products

Relationship marketing   Maintaining a long-term relationship with customers to retain them for repeat purchases and brand loyalty

Relaunch products   Launch old product in a new package, etc.

Social marketing   Application of commercial marketing concepts, knowledge, and techniques to non-commercial ends (such as campaigns against smoking and drunken driving) for the society's welfare

Concept Review Questions

1. Establish your understanding of the concept of Marketing Public Relations (MPR)? What are the functions that MPR performs to extend the necessary support to the marketing efforts of a company? Write a lucid note on the subject.
2. What are the reasons for the integrated marketing communications concept gaining popularity amongst marketers and public relations practitioners? Do you think the concept is workable and has a future? Discuss.
3. How do you differentiate between public relations and publicity? What roles and goals each has? Are they complementary or independent of each other? Clarify your basic understanding.
4. Advertising, direct marketing, and personal selling have supportive roles. Do you agree? Elaborate the characteristics and functions of each of these marketing tools.

References

Batra, Rajeev, John G. Myers, and David A. Aaker (1998), *Advertising Management,* 5th edition, Prentice Hall of India Private Limited, New Delhi, p. 96.

Belch, George E. and Michael A. Belch (1995), *Introduction to Advertising and Promotion—An Integrated Marketing Communication Perspective,* Irwin McGraw-Hill, USA, pp. 6 and 454.

Bennett, Peter D. (1988), *Directory of Marketing Terms,* American Marketing Association, Chicago, USA, p. 58.

Cohen, Dorothy (1988), *Advertising,* Scott Foresman and Co. USA, p. 5.

Harris, Thomas L. (1993), *The Marketer's Guide to Public Relations,* Wiley, New York, p. 12.

Hindustan Times–HT City, 24 May 2008, p. 3.

Kotler, Philip (2000), *Marketing Management, Millennium Edition,* Prentice-Hall of India Private Limited, New Delhi, p. 605.

Moore, H. Frazier and Frank B. Kalupa, (2005), *Public Relations, Principles, Cases and Problems,* 9th edition, reprinted in India by Surjeet Publications, New Delhi, p. 5.

The Mint, 28 May 2008, vol. 2, no. 127, p. 3.

11

Customer Relations

INDIA—CUSTOMERS GALORE

India, with her surging middle class with growing disposable incomes and a large consumer base, is the current story. The Indian consumer story is one that has caught the attention of the rest of the world. The salient features of the growing Indian economy, like 50 per cent population below 30 years of age and that too with good purchasing power, enhanced availability of products and services coupled with easy credit, have all attracted the attention of several multinationals, who are eyeing for growth and expansion of their markets. No surprise that several global companies have entered the Indian market and now there is not a brand which is not available to Indian consumers for the asking.

While consumerism has seen a gradual build-up, what is certain today is that there has been a sizable uptake in consumption. Whether it is mobile phones, credit cards, garments or fast moving consumer goods (FMCG) items, people clearly seem to be spending more, particularly on discretionary items. And the consumers are seen everywhere, be it the large metros, the emerging new cities, the small towns or even in rural India. What is more, these new consumer segments are quite diverse, be it the technology savvy children, the independent youth, the empowered urban woman, or the first time rural customer.

With the turn of the 21st century, the market scenario has tremendously changed and is fast changing towards the customers becoming tougher and tougher. It is rather a complex game to be in the area of selling and satisfying customers. Once the Indian market was a protected market with no competition, whatsoever, at least from the overseas companies. The market was safe from the foreign invaders. But the Indian market has now become a major hunting ground for several multinationals who either have already entered or are planning to enter the scene to take advantage of the large customer base that India offers.

THE MIDDLE CLASS MINDSET

While the scenario has changed from the seller's market to the buyer's market, naturally now the consumers are out to call the shots. Particularly the middle class, which is a major segment of the market, is aspiring to enjoy better standards of living.

When asked, now that the arrival of Nano car is around the corner, what are their plans to further fortify their position in the market, Mr Ravi Kant, Managing Director, Tata Motors (2008), highlighted their company's focus on servicing the customers to their entire satisfaction. He thinks that the market scenario in India is fast changing and so are changing the various consumer segments and their mindsets.

He said, 'There are lot of factors. Number one is the urbanization of minds. The communication revolution is making quick change in consumer's minds. The quick change is that urbanization of mindset is happening even with a person who is living in the rural area. ... I think this is a revolutionary change that is happening in the country. The second thing is that there are more younger people in India, which means there is a greater desire. A younger person wants to do (things) faster than the older generation.

The third is that discretionary income is going dramatically up. It is that portion of a person's income that is available for saving or spending on non essentials. It is what remains after expenses for basic needs (such as food, clothing, shelter, utilities) and prior commitments (such as school fees and loans) are deducted from the disposable income, whatever extra income remains becomes discretionary. Finally, the fourth part is road network and, more importantly, the rural network which is coming up'…which makes many think that 'I am young, I am 23 years old. So I want to make it happen fast …And finally, the road is connected… so I can go to a new movie theatre there. I can take my family. I will marry and take my wife for a dinner outside. So it is the basic things that a human being desires. I can send my children to a better school 50 km away.'

The one lakh Tata Nano car eventually emerges as a symbol of the change in the consumer mindset, an answer to their long pending needs to conquer distances within their means and improve their life styles. The emphasis, obviously is on customer satisfaction. Nano now represents the hopes and aspirations of the middle class customers. Media has already started pronouncing it as a genuine public relations attempt by the house of Tatas.

THE NEW SHOPPING PATTERNS

Notably the Indian customers are also changing their ways in their desire to emulate their richer cousins in the world's developed economies. With the surge of large shopping malls with everything available under one roof, the trend of teleshopping and online shopping, the purchasing habits have drastically changed. Indian consumers today, can buy an insurance or carry on their banking and stock transaction on computer or phone. Opening of chain stores such as Reliance Fresh, Big Apple, Birla More for You, or 6 TEN, in almost all localities of major metros, have added to the shopping convenience and pleasure of the customers. Housewives these days do not need to visit stores and are being serviced by these neighbourhood stores, even by home delivery of groceries. Consumers do not even need to buy newspapers to get their news and get an e-paper version of the *Hindustan Times*, every morning, by browsing page by page.

In this context it is interesting to note that where there are opportunities to appease the customers, there are also some threats to the economic structures. Philip Kotler (2000) wrote, 'These new shopping capabilities signify a brand new world of proliferating opportunities and proliferating threats. Silicon Valley is only one symbol of a brave new world characterized by digitalization, robotization, telecommuting, artificial intelligence, virtual reality, and other technological advances. At the same time, what is magnificent opportunity for millions of consumers and businesses is a major and sometimes deadly threat to others. Banks will have to close branches; travel agencies and brokerage firms will need to reduce staffs; automobile manufacturers will reduce the number of auto dealerships; and many bookstores, music stores, and video stores will close their doors. Technological advances are a double-edged sword—they create opportunities and they destroy opportunities.'

In other words, the focus has been shifting from the sellers to the buyers, from manufacturers and marketers to the customers. In this world flooded with information, though customers often face a problem of plenty, yet they are able to acquire information as per their needs for products, their competing brands, prices, delivery system, and even the sellers' arrangement for providing after-sale service. Therefore, the companies which are conscious and alive to the philosophy of returning value for money to the customers, have to continually research customers needs and wants, and provide products, that will meet their needs, and at a price they are willing to pay. This is simple marketing fundamental called 'customer satisfaction'. The saying that 'customer is the king' nay 'customers are queens', must be borne in mind. Perhaps, it is tougher to please a queen, than the king.

TOTAL CUSTOMER SATISFACTION

Hundreds of books have been written on the subject of customer satisfaction. Thousands of anecdotes and quotations eulogize the business philosophy of satisfying the customers. There are definitions galore on the subject. But the basic description of the subject is that when a customer's expectations are met fully as per promises made by a product or its seller, customer satisfaction becomes a reality. Once again the basic public relations philosophy holds good, that to make people see the truth in whatever is said, the gap between the promise and performance should be minimum.

Kotler (2000) writes, *'Satisfaction is a person's feelings of pleasure or disappointment resulting from comparing a product's perceived performance (or outcome) in relation to his or her expectation.'*

Put differently, satisfaction is a phenomenon of matching the perceived performance of a product, as per the expectations of a buyer. Naturally, if the performance falls short of the promise, the customer feels dissatisfied, and if it meets or exceeds the promise, the customer is satisfied nay delighted. Knowing well the expectations of the customers to get value for their hard-earned money, several companies propagate to their people to raise the levels of their own dissatisfaction with the products they make, so that they meet the customer expectations. A well-known multinational tyre company uses the punch line 'The best is yet to come!' to communicate to the customers that though they make best tyres, yet are not satisfied, and are making efforts to make something better than the best. This is the customer satisfaction philosophy.

Higher the customer satisfaction, higher the customer loyalty. Enlightened marketing organizations know that the purpose of their business is not just to create customers but also to retain customers. Yet it is hard reality of life that customers do switch loyalties. The day they find that there is a better product available, they will switch over. So the challenge of retaining customers is a serious one.

Several marketing organizations strive hard to ensure customer satisfaction, yet doing that much is not enough. The customers who are just 'only satisfied' may shift to other products when they come across better ones. Therefore, the new buzz word is 'customer delight' rather than just satisfaction. Delight generates a sense of relationship with the company, not based on reasoning but on emotions, and the customers remain loyal for long. Thus, creating emotional bond with the customers is the new philosophy called 'total customer satisfaction'.

PUBLIC RELATIONS AND CUSTOMER SATISFACTION

More than 1100 million men, women, and children, who make up the Indian consumer market determine the success or failure of every industrial or commercial enterprise in the nation. There are no two opinions that every business organization cannot succeed without a clear focus on the consumer. Consumer concern is of paramount importance to the growth and progress of any organization.

Obviously, developing a relationship with this massive consumer public is an affair of high magnitude even for the largest companies. Customers are the life blood of every business and are a special public, who deserve a high priority attention. Some of the leading manufacturing and marketing corporations of the world have established special sections in their PR divisions, dedicated entirely to the customer relations. Such sections are staffed with specialist in several areas of consumer activity like publicity, product testing, home making, fashion, public speaking, lady customers' psyche, publication of information, and even correspondence with the consumers.

In the opinion of H. Frazier Moore and Frank B. Kalupa (2005), 'Good consumer relationships depend heavily upon the value of the products and services provided by a producer to consumers and the social responsibility and integrity the producer demonstrates in its role as a corporate citizen. No PR communications can change consumer attitude towards a company that produces inferior merchandise, sells it at an excessive price, fails to give good service, or offends the public by questionable or irresponsible acts.'

The PR professionals hold the opinion that the public relations practice is founded on the principle that to enjoy good reputation and image, a company must deserve it before it desires. Corporate reputation is closely linked to the product value. The image perception of a company in the minds of the consumers is a direct reflection of quality and image of the products it markets. Consumers measure the product value by the features and benefits they get out of the product, its good design or style, sound performance, and easy availability in a number of models, sizes, colours, types, and fair prices.

The satisfaction is realized by the customers almost immediately from the FMCG products, but in the case of consumer durables, the products must be backed by a sound guarantee, comprehensive service policy, trained service personnel, regular maintenance, and easy availability of spare parts. The service aspect of such products creates customer satisfaction and form an integral part of the effective customer relations programme of reputable companies.

In other words, PR efforts of a company cannot make the product and the company look good in the eyes of the customer if they are not genuinely good. Public relations is considered as a 90:10 story, that is, 90 per cent produce best quality products backed by service and satisfaction and 10 per cent communicating about it to get the necessary credit to the company for the job well done. It cannot be and should not be perceived in the reverse order. So 'do good and look good' is the mantra in the area of consumer relations. A sincere concern for the consumer indicates the right direction for any business.

THE CONSUMER MOVEMENT

'Consumerism, a word not even in dictionaries until just a few years ago, is one of those words, a word that is not only a symbol of our times but a symptom, both a causative and a cause. Many in business still consider consumerism a scary word because it grew out of protest, conflict, and crisis. It was a catalyst for change that quickly swept away many attitudes and opinions most Americans grew up believing. But as with other changes consumerism is no longer so frightening now that we have learned to live with it. ...Now it has matured from the conflict and crisis of yesterday into the concern and commitment of business and other organizations today. Just as consumerism has changed, so have the public relations strategies needed to deal with it,' wrote John W. Felton (1992).

With the growth of free economies in the world and the competition forcing the breakdown of monopolies, the consumer movement in the world is a new and powerful phenomenon. So as to counteract the vested company interests with greed to maximize profits at the cost of consumers, there is born a consumer movement in the world. Consumer movement started in US when the Americans organized themselves into groups to protect and fight for the consumer rights. Consumer crusaders have served as a pressure point for the business to contain them from exploiting the consumers. In US, there emerged a clamouring for consumer rights in every part of business relations be it product safety, truth in advertising, sufficient labeling, and full warranties. The government came up with full support of the consumer movement and helped it to grow and flourish. It is relevant to acquaint ourselves with some of the consumerist organizations.

Consumerist Organizations—USA

Ralph Nader's network

Ralph Nader is often named as the pioneer of consumer movement in America, who started the movement in a small way. His ideas and ideology, which came to protect the consumers against exploitation by unethical business, became the buzzword. The move flourished and later branched out into other walks of American life. Ralph Nader network has a huge network of lawyers, lobbyists, writers, and staffers in more than 20 organizations. His public citizen outfit is associated with six different groups, with goals and roles of their own. The groups are Health Research Group, Congress Watch, the Capitol Hill News Service, and the Public Interest Research Groups.

Consumer Federation of America

The Consumer Federation of America (CFA) has a membership of more than two hundred groups like labour unions, cooperatives, National Farmers Union and other social service organizations like National Board of the YMCA.

Consumer action for improved food and drugs

With a variety of food and drugs flooding the marketing, monitoring their quality, efficacy, or price have been a problem. The consumer action group was formed to support the legal and legislative goals for the improvement of food and drugs.

National consumer information centre

The National Consumer Informtion Centre (NCIC) was mainly formed to safeguard the interests of the minorities in the consumer movement. The organization keeps up its voice by organizing national conferences and also works as a clearinghouse of information to several consumer rights groups across America.

Consumer Movement—India

The consumer movement in India is a misnomer. There are hardly any organization which can be named to have voluntary associations to fight for the rights of the consumers. Since India went through bouts of shortages and consumers had no choice but to buy whatever was available at whatever price they could, the Indian consumer, as if, was voiceless and not conscious about their rights and responsibilities.

However, the Government of India formed a Ministry of Consumer Affairs and decided to observe 24 December every year as National Consumer Rights Day. To ensure fair trade practices and prevent consumers from the unscrupulous traders, the government started a public awareness communication campaign titled *jago grahak jago*' and continues to run series of advertisements in the print as well as in the electronic media. Perhaps, there is no research conducted about the objectives achieved by this campaign. However, the authorities have outlined certain rights, duties, and responsibilities of the consumers, which enjoy some legal support.

Consumer rights

- *Right to safety*   To be protected against the sale of goods and services, which are spurious/hazardous to life
- *Right to information*   To know the quality, quantity, weight, and the price of goods/services being paid for, so that you are not cheated by unfair trade practices
- *Right to choose*   To be assured, wherever possible, access to a variety of goods and services at a competitive price
- *Right to be heard*   To be heard and be assured that your interest will receive due consideration at appropriate forum
- *Right to seek redressal*   To seek legal redressal against unfair or restrictive trade practices or exploitation
- *Right to consumer education*   To have access to consumer education

Consumer responsibilities

- Obtain full information regarding quality and price before making any purchases.
- Be careful about false and/or misleading advertisements.
- Purchase goods having quality marks like ISI/Agmark etc., as and where available, for safety and quality.
- Obtain proper receipt/cash memo for purchases made and guarantee/warranty card duly stamped and signed by the seller, wherever applicable.
- Approach consumer forum for redressal of consumer grievance against sale of defective goods or deficient services or adoption of unfair or restrictive trade practices.
- Bargain on MRP (Maximum Recommended Price).

The government has also set up Consumer Courts at the centre and state levels to facilitate the redressal of consumer grievances with some success. It might make some segments of Indian customers happy to note that such consumer courts have started making some crucial customer friendly judgments. For instance, the national consumer disputes commission has directed the New India Insurance Corporation Limited to pay Rs 2.5 crore to the owner while coming down heavily on the insurance company for denying the ceramic factory owner's claim, which had caught fire a few years ago. Jaipur Ceramic had taken an insurance policy from the company for Rs 8 crore. The claim was denied to the client on the ground that the damages were of lesser amount. However, Justice M.B. Shah pronounced that the insurance company is directed to pay the amount within six months.

Good news for the consumerists, if any in India, that such judgments should go to assure consumer protection against certain malpractices.

WHO IS A CUSTOMER?

Earl Nightingale (1990), the renowned US trainer said very aptly, 'There never has been ...there is not now ...and there never will be any boss but the customer. He is the one boss you must please. Everything you own... he has paid for. He buys your home, your car, your clothes. He pays for your vacation and puts your children through school. He will give you every promotion you will ever obtain during your lifetime ...and he will discharge you if you displease him.'

Therefore satisfying this customer is of prime importance. The popular anecdote in the selling circles goes around that one satisfied customer in ten years will bring you 100 more. One dissatisfied customer in ten years will prevent 1000 prospects coming to you. Taking this saying seriously, L.L. Bean Inc company developed a mission statement for their employees to care for the customers (See Exhibit 11.1).

Furthermore, L.L. Bean gained recognition for its belief in the philosophy of customer satisfaction. The company deals in mail-order business in clothing and equipment for rugged living and have unified their internal and external marketing public relations programmes.

EXHIBIT 11.1 Who is a customer?

- A customer is the most important person ever in this office ...in person or by mail.
- A customer is not dependent on us ....we are dependent on him.
- A customer is not an interruption in our work ... he is the purpose of it. We are not doing a favour by serving him ... he is doing us a favour by giving us the opportunity to do so.
- A customer is not someone to argue or match wits with. Nobody ever won an argument with a customer.
- A customer is a person who brings us his wants. It is our job to handle these profitably to him and to ourselves.

Source: L.L. Bean Inc.

McDonald's Marketing Philosophy

Marketing organizations are facing tough competition today. Marketing and sales people are preached by the bosses to develop a 'killer instinct' towards competition. Many companies are still obsessed with the feeling that bringing in customers is the major responsibility of marketing people and if they cannot, they are not held in good estimation of the management of that company. But the fact remains that the marketing professional can be effective only if the company with the cooperation of its employees have developed a value based delivery system for the customers. The company has to ensure that the employees are motivated enough to carry out the system with enough enthusiasm and dedication. For example, take the case of McDonald's who have made the marketing of a burger a great success story. Their philosophy, as reported in the *USA Today* (1998), is as follows:

'Everyday an average of 38 million people visit its 23,500 restaurants in 109 countries. People do not swarm to McDonald's outlets solely because they love the hamburger. Some other restaurants make better-tasting hamburgers. People are flocking to a system, not a hamburger. Throughout the world, this fine-tuned system delivers a high standard of what McDonald's calls QSCV—quality, service, cleanliness, and value. McDonald's is effective to the extent that it works with its supplier, franchise owner, employees, and others to deliver exceptionally high value to its customers.'

In other words, the customers do not hang around McDonald's due to any kind of addiction to their burgers but to a promise of value satisfaction. It is not true just about one restaurant but is a phenomenon all over the world. The numbers given above are a decade old and have multiplied ever since. The uniformity of quality, service, taste, presentation, price, courtesy by employees, ambiance, and a promise of value makes people walk into their worldwide outlets with confidence and comfort. Several restaurants have cropped up now in once forbidden domains of the world like China and Russia. The value has also brought about a universality of world tastes among people of several nationalities be it USA, Russia, India, Singapore, or South Africa.

Life Insurance Corporation of India

Life Insurance Corporation (LIC) of India, which is the largest life insurance company in the country, has been concentrating in reaching out to all the insurable persons in the country. Their recent advertisement on the 'Health Protection Plus' plan demonstrates their concern for their customers by showing a mother and a child. The punch line reads—When it comes to health insurance, I trust only LIC...because things could go wrong anytime, anywhere (See Exhibit 11.2).

EXHIBIT 11.2   LIC's health insurance plan

"When it comes to health insurance, I trust only LIC...

...because things could go wrong anytime, anywhere."

Presenting

LIC's Health Protection Plus.
A Unique Health Insurance Plan
from India's largest insurance provider.

* Hospital cash benefit
* Major surgical benefit
* Domiciliary treatment benefit
* Income tax benefits U/S 80D

LIC's HEALTH PROTECTION PLUS
UNIT LINKED HEALTH INSURANCE PLAN
(UIN: 512L253V01)

LIC
भारतीय जीवन बीमा निगम
LIFE INSURANCE CORPORATION OF INDIA

www.licindia.in

• The premiums paid in Unit Linked Life Insurance Policies are subject to investment risks associated with capital markets and the NAV of the units may go up or down based on the performance of the fund and factors influencing the capital market an the insured is responsible for his/her decision. • The Life Insurance Corporation of India is only the name of the insurance company and Health Protection Plus is only the name of the unit linked life insurance contract and does not in any way idicate the quality of the contract, its future propect or returns • Past performance may not be an indicator of the future performance • Insurance is the subject matter of solicitation • Tax benefits are subject to changes in tax laws • For more details on risk factors, terms and conditions please read sales brochure carefully before concluding a sale.

LIC/09/09-10/ENG

Source: The Economic Times, 30 April 2009.

LG Electronics—India

The Korean giant, LG Electronics, who entered the Indian market as a small player in the white goods market, hope to touch a turnover of Rs 10,000 by the end of the decade. LG gained a high penetration in the Indian market mainly because they amply demonstrate their faith in the customer service.

Their latest advertisement reads 'No waiting—Introducing 2.1.1 prompt response after sales service—call back to customer within 2 hours. Service engineer visit within 1 day. In a promised 1-hour time slot' (See Exhibit 11.3).

EXHIBIT 11.3   No waiting—prompt response 2.1.1 by LG

No waiting
Introducing 2.1.1 Prompt Response After Sales Service

Introducing LG 2.1.1, India's first Prompt Response Service. A quick after-sales service specially appointed to nurture your relationship with LG and ensure the sound functioning of all your LG products. Give us a call, send an SMS or simply a mail to get Instant registration. After which, we call you back within just two hours to fix an appointment at your convenience. Our expert LG Engineer will be at your service within a day within the promised one hour time slot. No waiting at all!

—— One Wise Decision Complete Happiness. ——

ONE CALL DOES IT ALL
1800-180-9999
(MTNL/BSNL Toll Free) or
39-01-0909
(Prefix STD Code)
SMS No. 5757554

ONE CLICK DOES IT ALL
lgservice@lgindia.com
www.lgindia.com

'Source: ORG-gfk, retail audit Jan - Dec 2007. LG 2.1.1 Service available on select products in select products in select cities in select areas. Please check out from the customer care executive on toll-free number to know your product and area coverage. This is not claim to repair the unit on the same day but only to attend the complaint call after registration of the complaint. "Visit within 1 day" shall

Regd. Office: LG Electronics India Pvt. Ltd., Plot No. 51, Udyog Vihar, Surajpur - Kasna Road, Greater Noida-201 306, U.P., Tel: 0120-2560900. **Customer Helpline:** Happycalls@lgindia.com; **Branch Office Delhi:** LGEIL, A-27, Mohan Co-oprative, Industrial Estate, New delhi.

Source: Hindustan Times, 30 May 2008.

CUSTOMER RELATIONS PROGRAMME

Jim Fox (1975), Chairman, James F. Fox Inc., in an address before the consumer conference, in Washington DC, had said: 'I am a little chagrined when I realize that consumer affairs is not given high priority in the corporate agenda, nor ranked highly in the corporate hierarchy. Consumer affairs cannot be used as a cosmetic. It is not just public relations, it is not government relations, nor is it quality assurance. It is all of these, and more. Like public relations, it had better stem from the top person and it had better pervade the entire organization. It has to begin with product design and plant design.'

Arvind Sahay (2008) in an article in *Outlook Business*, titled 'Hospital, Heal Thyself' wrote, 'Customer service (or the lack of it) has been identified as one of the leading causes for customer defections. In one instance, 150,000 customers wrote back in response to an advertisement that asked readers if they felt they were the worst treated car customers in the country. This gave a new firm a point of entry into the UK market, and helped it grab substantial market share on the back of better customer service. In India, private medical care has progressed rapidly in recent times. But how good is the customer service in this sector?'

Naturally, listening to the customers is an important part of the customer relations programme. Customers loyal to a company's product get emotionally and physically involved in the organization. Elizabeth M. Gillespie (2008) wrote about the famous US coffee chain and the response to their newly launched website: 'Hundreds of coffee-obsessed consumers in the US chimed in moments after Starbucks Corporation launched a website asking customers to pitch changes the company should make to revive its struggling US business. ....Before it went live, Chris Bruzzo, Starbucks' Chief Information Officer, said he was hoping a few hundred ideas would trickle in the first few days. About 300 suggestions were posted in the first hour after the shareholders meeting, which drew a crowd of 6000 and was closely watched by Wall Street analysts hungry for details on the company's turnaround plans. By the end of the week, more than 1,00,000 votes had been cast, Bruzzo said.'

Therefore, the customer PR is the top management responsibility which is entrusted with authority to act rather than be a silent spectator to the happenings in the organization. Like any good management system, it is advisable that before the PR takes on itself the task of running a consumer service and satisfaction programme, certain objectives of such a programme should clearly be stated. The objectives of the programme will, however, depend on the nature of products and services, size of the company and its resources, and its consumer service policy. The size of the consumer base should also be a determinant factor.

Obviously, it is neither possible nor feasible to work out a model customer service programme, yet some of the elements which most of the programmes can stipulate, can be the following.

Consumer Philosophy Statement

A consumer service policy statement should be drawn with the blessings of the top management and should be publicized well for the knowledge of consumers. Needless to say, it should be fair to all consumers irrespective of their status and potential.

Consumer's Opinion Feedback

A system to evaluate consumers' opinions about the policies, practices, products, or services should be in place. A feedback system helps the company to keep the ears to the ground to review and reform products and policies.

Public Perception Audit

A periodic audit system about the public perception of the organization's performance, products, or services, when in place, should help the company to monitor whether the programme is on track. If misunderstood by the consumers, it can spell disasters. The consumers' comments, serious or casual, about the quality, price, value, service, or quality of the products, which when sifted objectively, may reveal valuable information for course correction.

Monitor Customer Complaints

Monitoring customer complaints promptly ensures speedy customer satisfaction. Determining the nature and pattern of complaints is a valuable education for the consumer affairs programme. Knowing the reasons and nature of customer complaints and using the information to remove wrinkles in the policy and procedures is important to avoid repetition of such complaints. Also timely redressal makes all the difference. Reducing the customer response time sends home some satisfied customers to return again and bring more customers. Devising a well designed complaint handling procedure to document and sample customer response letters is helpful for communicating to customers.

One of the very sensitive area that concerns every customer focused company is the proper handling of complaints. Customers, when aggrieved naturally get agitated and lose temper. Knowing fully well that every complaint is an opportunity to sell more, it is vital that personnel who deal with the customers upfront should know how to handle complaints to the entire satisfaction of the customers. Certain steps and precautions, when taken with care, can go a long way to win over the customers for long (See Exhibit 11.4).

EXHIBIT 11.4   Handling customer complaints

Listen! Listen! Listen!	Listen attentively to customers. Don't interrupt, take notes, and respond positively.
Ask questions	Questions when asked properly will help arrive at the problem. Questions help customers to regain their cool and state real problems.
Look sad and glad	Look sad to show your concern and happy that problem can be solved.
Empathize	Put yourself in customer's shoes and empathize. Use body language to show your feelings that you really care.
Know customer's need	Customer may argue on principles and need nothing. Show a gesture of goodwill like a free service. etc.
Be frank	Be honest. State your limits. Pleasantly tell what you can do to help. Frankness is bitterness but ends in sweetness.
Explain alternatives	Aggrieved customer may be selfish and irrational. Give alternatives to pick and choose. This may make him happy and satisfied.
Act promptly	Take speedy action and see it through. Prompt others involved. Actions speak louder than words. So act fast.
Ensure satisfaction	See off customers with a pleasant hand shake. Ensure chances for more sales later.

Product Adjustment Committee

Forming a product adjustment committee is helpful to work within the framework of a predesigned and fair system to adjust the defective products to the entire satisfaction of the consumers.

Consumer Suggestion System

Devising a toll free telephone number to receive consumers' inquiries, information, or suggestions that can be of considerable value.

Ensure Employee Involvement

Inspire and train employees to provide prompt and courteous and friendly service to the consumers. The way salesmen, delivery men, or a receptionist responds to a customer creates a long lasting impression that the company cares about the customers. Public relations should design and develop training programmes for the employees in customer relations management.

Customer Education Programme

Educating the customer about the proper usage of products, service policies, and complaint redressal procedures, through special publications and distribution of instructional/advisory literature is helpful. A detailed communication programme to reach consumers, employees, new media, and potential customers give enough mileage to the company. To help truck fleet operators to save expenditure on tyres, a tyre company would publish a handy booklet titled 'Six ways to reduce tyre costs', which even today is well received. India's well known jeweller, Tribhovandas Bhimji Zaveri, doles out an attractive card to their customers giving tips about proper care that customers can take to protect their expensive gold ornaments (See Exhibit 11.5).

Packaging and Labelling

Ensuring proper labelling of the products clearly showing quantity, quality, price, and ingredients used in the making of the products, assures and reassures customers to buy with confidence and faith in the products/company.

EXHIBIT 11.5   A jeweller's advice to customers

Jewellery is a delicate piece to be preserved for generations to come. Intricate and delicate workmanship gives beauty to the jewellery. Therefore handle all your jewellery with extra care to avoid breakage of joints or denting on the piece. Jewellery, if worn, continuously may cause weight loss especially in rings, chains, bangles etc., and even the designs could also get worn out. So, take care while doing household chores.. Do not get your jewellery polished/cleaned from roadside polishers as they take out the gold by putting the jewellery in nitric acid.

WE ADVISE

Do clean your jewellery softly with chemois leather every week to retain the original lustre. To wash the jewellery use soap & water and clean carefully with a soft brush.

Do examine your studded jewellery periodically (say once in three months) for any wear & tear of the prongs which hold the stones; loose/broken prongs may result in stones falling off.

Do take extra care when wearing enamelled jewellery. Use them gently and avoid dropping them on hard surfaces or banging against each other while wearing. Enamel does NOT wear off when washed with soap & water however it should be handled very carefully as it may chip off due to mishandling.

Do polish silver articles with Silvo polish for the original shine. Silver utensils can be washed with soap & water.

DO NOT store silver articles in newly painted cupboard or a safe for long periods. Air them once in a while to natural environment to retain its shine.

DO NOT bring your jewellery in contact with mercury, acid, perspiration, oil, perfume etc, if by chance it happens, wash it off with soap & water with soft brush. In the event of contact with mercury or acid, bring it to us immediately for proper cleaning as the acid may still be eating away the gold.

DO NOT expose diamond jewellery to soaps, cream, powder & dirt as it will dim the brilliance of diamond.

DO NOT leave diamond jewellery in a drawer as it can scratch other jewellery and even damage itself. Store them in a box safe keeping.

DO NOT put a pearl string back into an airtight box immediately after use as perspiration and cosmetics are likely to affect the shine of pearls. Use a cloth moist with a solution of ¼ part of eau-de-cologne & ¾ part of water to wipe the pearls after use till the original shine is restored and air them for a while before storing.

DO NOT expose pearl jewellery to heat as it will turn them brown.

EVERYTHING NEEDS CARE JEWELLERY NEEDS CHILD CARE!

Source: Jeweller Tribhovandas Bhimji Zaveri's card.

Dialogue with Consumerists

It is advisable to keep the dialogue open with the consumer extremists, who actively fight for the consumer rights. Cooperating with them in their efforts to project company's constructive approach to consumer movement most often pays.

Contacts with Opinion Leaders

Opinion leaders are an important channel of communication to the society at large. Maintaining contacts with the opinion leaders, loyal customers, store managers, etc. helps to keep the company and its products in favourable focus.

MAINTAINING GOOD CUSTOMER RELATIONS

'One of the best ways to create customer satisfaction is to increase enjoyment of your product or service to make sure it is used, and to extend its uses. This can apply whether it is a sophisticated goods like a sewing machine, camera, or motor-car or something simple like flour, margarine, knitting wool, or a garden aid. This can also be applied to services such as banking, insurance, hotels and restaurants, travel agencies, and airlines. You could just manufacture, distribute, and advertise and leave it at that. But why stop there? Why not communicate with your customers by means of PR?', wrote Frank Jefkins (2006).

Obviously, communicating with customers to keep in touch with them is the magic that can continue to make customers happy and satisfied. With enough information researched about customers' understanding and attitudes, the organization can develop a communication plan to inform customers about the policies and practices of the company, as related to customers' needs and expectations.

That is why, professional marketing companies undertake periodical surveys to find out publics' approvals or rejections of their products, policies, and practices, advertising styles, sales promotion techniques, service and adjustment policies, prices, packaging, and other peripheral information about image perception of the company.

THE COMMUNICATION MEDIA

Once the strategic decision about the communication plank for distributing consumer friendly information is taken, the material written, printed, published, or created, can be selected to ensure the right information to the right people. The media vehicles for loading information has to be governed by the reading habits, viewership habits, and other factors like the sources from which the consumers gather news and information. Different segments of customer publics may have to be catered to by different media, as all media are not good for all market segments. For instance, the medium that is good for urban consumers may not cut ice in the rural market. However, a look at the media available should make sense. Some of the media vehicles can be: *verbal communications, plant visitations, open house, audiovisual communication, print material, publicity, websites, external publications, direct mail advertising, institutional advertising, special events, etc.*

Verbal Communications

The spoken word or oral communication is one of the most powerful medium that people working in the organizations use to accomplish customer relations goals. The latest advertising slogan by IBM is very significant to note—'Talking creates customers, actions retain customers'.

Whatever the employees, the insiders, speak to the external public carry a great credence. Therefore, to make this channel a powerful medium, the employees who are upfront communicating with the customers, should be given proper training or briefing about their expected interaction with the customers. Public relations has a role in developing a proper training programme to train employees in the area of customer dialogue.

It has been observed that such activities start top down. Starting with the senior managers, to supervisors, to field men, such programmes set healthy trends and traditions. With the means and tools, that fall within the functioning norms of the public relations departments, activities like group discussions, lectures, class room training through slide shows, video clips, films, etc. can be used to prepare the personnel for customer interaction.

Formal talks by the senior executives to the groups like rotary clubs, lion clubs, round tables, jaycees, ladies clubs, etc. and also informal conversations of employees with their families and friends, relatives and neighbours, serve as an effective medium for creating a general atmosphere of understanding and goodwill for the company.

Plant Visitations

Several manufacturing companies with an eye on customer clusters invite groups to conducted plant tours. Influentials in the community like municipal members, doctors, legal professionals, teachers, and preachers are invited to see the operations and talk to the company executives. Such visits are a feature of good public relations that create a favourable impression amongst these groups, who work as carriers of goodwill messages to all those who come under their influence. Such visits help in building a band of people, who talk good about the company in their day-to-day conversations.

Coca Cola, for instance, when they entered the Indian scene, took bus loads of school children to their plants. They gifted free coke to drink and return gifts of pencils, erasers, miniature coke bottles, caps, and T-shirts to the young kids. The favourable word spread very fast and created a large consumer base for the company. Companies like Goodyear, Escorts, Metal Box had fixed visitation days, generally Saturdays, when the employees have been encouraged to bring their families and friends for a plant tour. Special requests from schools and colleges for educational trips are also welcome.

Open House

As a part of the internal public relations with employees and their families and friends, who are also a large segment of customers, companies organize an annual open house show, when people are invited to see for themselves as to how the products are made under safe, healthy, and hygienic conditions. A plant visitation booklet and a small memento is presented to visitors to take home to decorate their sitting rooms. Such small objects become good starters of conversations about the company in community circles. Notably, the attitudes of those who have visited the plant and have seen the operations, generally become favouruable for the organization. In Goodyear India plants, such an event is named as 'family day' to welcome all members of the community, who form a good part of the consumer public.

Audiovisual Communication

Companies with large consumer base use television and radio, audio and video CDs as a good medium of communication. Many programmes created by the companies which have public interest and benefit, are picked up by radio and TV channels and are telecast free. For instance, the footage of Formula I races in the world distributed by some car makers and automobile accessories makers, are picked up by TV channels to cater to their viewers' taste. However, the scenes are changing and TV companies vie with each other for telecasting rights for some major events in the world like 20:20 cricket matches or World Cup football, where marketing companies also tuck in their messages, to reach customers.

Motion pictures, produced on certain themes like moon landing, star wars, royal wedding, racing or sporting heroes are wrapped around company themes to make a dent in the consumers' mind.

Video recorded lectures by business leaders on topics like management, revolutionary products, and innovations serve as a source of inspiration for many aspiring young and middle aged career seeking students and managers. Recorded lectures by Bill Gates or India's N.R. Narayana Murthy of Infosys, carry lot of audience appeal. Putting such audiovisual material on the Internet has become the latest means of reaching a larger volume of consumer public.

Publicity

Media today has become the main source of dependable information for the publics. Consumer opinions are formed by the information that public gathers through press, television, radio, Internet, etc. Public relations departments of several companies prepare press releases, articles, backgrounds, photographs, video clips and distribute them to mass media to generate publicity. The system is further revolutionized by the arrival of Internet. Google, for instance, distributes their press releases, all over the world, through e-mail to major media outlets as well as journalists. So much so, they attach the video coverage of certain events which can be downloaded for suitable use by media channels, to ultimately reach a mass of consumers world over.

Websites

Today, there is hardly any company, worth its salt, that does not have a website of its own. The websites are regularly updated for the mutual benefit of consumers and the company to create long lasting bonds between the two. Information about the company, its products, policies and practices, management leaders, you name it, is available readily for usage by consumers. This medium wields a tremendous influence on the mindset of the consumers and when managed professionally, promises rich dividends of consumer goodwill for the companies.

External Publications

To build goodwill and image amongst external publics, especially customers, large and medium sized companies bring out special publications with focus on the market. Colourfully produced publications projecting products and management leaders in full view, impact the consumer mind making a favourable opinion about the organization. Besides giving consumer friendly information like product usage, company achievements, and important milestones, the publications carry special stories on some important consumers patronizing company products to enhance their profits. Dunlop Gazette would regularly carry success stories and photographs of some leading truck and bus fleet operators. Such publications go a long way to win friends for the companies and generate favourable influence in the market.

Direct Mail Advertising

Direct mail advertising distributing useful literature, handouts, booklets, educational materials, invitations to consumer clubs, etc., is run and monitored by public relations departments of several large and mid-size companies. Companies have built strong data bases of customers which are occasionally used to post such material to the work places or homes of the consumers. One of the pitfalls of this medium is the laborious task of updating the mailing lists, that is deleting the old and adding new ones. Several professional bodies and institutions keep their membership lists confidential or make available for a price.

Institutional Advertising

Institutional advertising is a medium used by PR professionals to inform consumers about the growth and progress of an organization and activities like innovations and achievements, research and contribution to the betterment of quality of life. Some companies run some public service advertising campaigns to educate consumers on social issues like aids, drug abuse, road safety, economic progress, or environmental protection (Also see Chapter 24).

Special Events

Event management has become big business, not because of a trend but for the immediate benefits that the organizers of such events gain in terms of consumer attention and appreciation. The messages get registered fast enough to generate responses. The events are used as a strategic media by the companies to reinforce their position and credentials with the consumers. The events show consumer benefits for attending events like free service camps, heavy discounts on purchases made during the event, lucky draws or gift hampers to appease consumers and to create a relationship. Some of the visible events are Hero Honda service camp for motor cycle customers, LG service campaign, Maruti monsoon mania for motorist to check their vehicle before monsoon sets in, JK Tyre clinics, MNTL health mela, etc.

Summary

India is a surging market where streets are full of customers. With the disposable incomes of the middle class rising, there is an upswing in the consumption patterns. The middle class is aspiring to improve their life styles and the Nano car is slated to become a symbol of middle class aspirations.

With the change in marketing techniques and technological advances, the consumer behaviour is undergoing a sea change. From cars to mobile phones, credit cards to shopping malls, the buying patterns of the consumers have witnessed a drastic change.

Indian consumer today is flooded with information about new products and is overwhelmed with information overload. The concept of total customer satisfaction is taking a front seat. Marketers have a need to genuinely work for returning value for customers' money. Promises if not kept, will boomerang on the companies.

Consumer movement in India is a misnomer. However, the consumerism in the US is a major factor that determines many policies and programmes of the marketing companies. Pioneers like Ralph Nader and his network are worth a mention. To generate the necessary awareness, the Government of India have initiated a public service advertising campaign with '*Jago Grahak Jago*' theme. Also the Consumers' Rights Day is observed once a year, to keep up the public involvement. Consumer courts have also been set up at the centre and state levels, which seem to be doing some good work.

Customer satisfaction philosophy adopted by certain companies have paid good dividends. Certain companies like L.L. Beans and McDonald's take lot of pride in preaching and practising the ideology that 'customer is the real boss'.

PR has a vital role to play in developing and running of the customer relations programme for a company. The effort involves researching to determine the hopes and aspirations of the consumers, and developing a consumer relations programme focused on dissemination of consumers friendly information to generate and maintain relations with the consumer.

Consumers need to be kept informed and connected with the companies through various media of communications. Equipped as the PR practitioners are with the tools and techniques of running a communication system, creative and appropriate usage of various media help in making it happen.

Key Terms

Artificial intelligence   Software technologies that make a computer or robot perform equal to or better than normal human computational ability in accuracy, capacity, and speed

Consumer durables   Manufactured products that have a relatively long life, such as cars or televisions; also known as white goods

Consumerism   Organized efforts by individuals, groups, and governments to help protect consumers from policies and practices that infringe consumer rights to fair business practices

Customer loyalty   Measure of commitment in consumer preferences, based on degree of satisfaction

Discretionary income   Portion of an entity's income available for saving, or spending on non-essentials. It is what remains after expenses for basics and prior commitments are deducted from the disposable income

Fast moving consumer goods (FMCG)   Products sold in supermarkets that move off the shelves quickly and must constantly be replenished

Public perception audit   Periodic assessment of the nature of perception by various publics through research efforts

Silicon valley   Nickname for the region in North California that contains a huge concentration of computer and Internet companies

Telecommuting   Substitution of telecommunications for transportation in a decentralized and flexible work arrangement, which allows part or full time employees to work at home via a computer attached to the employer's data network

Virtual reality   The computer-generated simulation of a three-dimensional image or environment that can be interacted with by using special electronic equipment

Concept Review Questions

1. Define and describe the market scenario of India with special reference to the surge of middle class consumers, their mindset and changing–buying behaviours.

2. Tata's new Rupees one lakh Nano car is the symbol of middle class aspirations. How? Describe the philosophy and the customer focus strategies of Tatas for success.

3. Draw up a scenario about the American and Indian consumer movement. What are the rights and responsibilities of a customer? Discuss the 'Jago Grahak Jago' advertising campaign run by the government. Do you think it is successful?

4. Establish your understanding of the customer satisfaction philosophy. Also write a critical note on the efforts of some of the leading companies in this area.

5. Draw up an outline of customer relations programme while discussing the elements of such a plan with reference to a company of your choice.

6. Media plays an important role in developing and maintaining good customer relations. Do you agree? What media mix do you suggest for customer relations plan for a consumer durable company?

References

Felton, John W. (1992), *Lesly's Handbook of Public Relations and Communications*, 4th edition, Probus Publishing Company, Chicago, USA, published in India by Jaico Publishing House, Bombay.

Gillespie, Elizabeth M. (2008), 'Starbuck Webside Flooded with Customer Ideas', *Hindustan Times Business*, New Delhi, India, p. 1.

Hindustan Times, Delhi, 30 May 2008, p. 5.

Jefkins, Frank (2006), *Public Relations for Your Business,* Management Books 2000 Ltd, Gloucestershire, UK and published in India by Jaico Publishing House, Mumbai, p. 105.

Kant, Ravi (2008), 'Tata Motors Mulls Vehicle Financing, Hopes to Overcome Launch Delays', *The Mint,* New Delhi, India, vol 2, no. 129, p. 6.

Kotler, Philip (2000), *Marketing Management, Millennium Edition*, Prentice Hall of India Private Limited, New Delhi.

Moore, H. Frazier and Frank B. Kalupa (2005), *Public Relations, Principles, Cases and Problems,* Richard D. Irwin, Inc, USA, reprinted in India by Surjeet Publications New Delhi, India, p. 459.

Sahay, Arvind (2008), *Outlook Business,* New Delhi, India, p. 77.

Sundram, Veena (2008), *Metro Now,* New Delhi, vol. 1 no. 134, 6 June 2008, p. 13.

The Economic Times, 30 April 2009, p. 11.

USA Today (1998), 'Mac Attacks', 23 March 1998, p. 1.

12

Dealer Relations

DEALER'S VITAL ROLE

'Middlemen are parasites' and 'Eliminate the middlemen and prices will come down' are charges that have been made for centuries. 'Assume the marketing intermediaries are legally banned. You now decide that you would like to have a loaf of whole-wheat bread. Beginning with the wheat farmer, explain how the present distribution system works. In other words, how does the wheat turn into a loaf of bread and reach into your hands? If this system was eliminated, what would a consumer have to do to get a loaf of bread? How much do you think a loaf of bread would cost?'—These are some of the questions raised by Philip Kotler (2000). Obviously, it is difficult to imagine the elimination of this channel called 'dealers' in the present marketing system.

But going in for a franchise can be more expensive than starting a business 'from scratch' but the success rate of franchises is generally higher than for startups, as you are investing in a product with a proven track record and the franchiser generally provides training, marketing support, and other services to the franchisee. According to Small Business Association in the US, the franchiser starts to have a 8 per cent risk of failure as compared to 85 per cent for non-franchised start-ups. It is easy to understand why franchising is becoming a welcome business strategy for the economic growth of India. It may be interesting to look at the facts and figures of Indian franchising (See Exhibit 12.1).

To assist businessmen in identifying, evaluating, and negotiating a franchise and retail business opportunity, an event management company Franchise India Holdings Limited organizes franchise and retail opportunities shows. They have already organized more than a dozen such shows in some of the major business centres of India.

DEALER RELATIONS

Dealers or franchisees are a vital link between the manufacturer and the customers and hence, an important public for a company. Therefore, the good business relations of any company with their dealers is of prime importance. From mid-sized to large companies, all feel the need for cultivating good relations with dealers who represent the companies upfront to the customers. Many marketers are of the firm opinion that it is the dealers who can make or mar the chances of success of a brand in the market.

Highlighting the importance of company–dealer relations, D. D. Freese, formerly of Ford Motor Company's dealer policy board, commented, 'A prime factor in the success of our industry must be our dealers. It is our dealers who must meet the prospects and change them into customers. As they succeed, our production lines keep moving. We desire to maintain the closest cooperation with them. We want their operations to be profitable and to this end we want to achieve understanding with them to the highest degree.'

EXHIBIT 12.1   Franchising in India, 2008

Size of the franchise industry	Over Rs 6500 crore
Franchise companies in India	Approximately 1075
Franchisees in India	Approximately over 75,000
Rate of industry growth	25–30 per cent
Most franchised sector	Education and training followed by food and beverage
Most emerging sector	Retail

Source: The Times of India, 12 June 2008.

Howard S. Christie Jr, director of the dealer relations section of General Motors Corporation, says, 'General Motors cannot progress without a successful dealer organization. Similarly, a dealer cannot succeed unless he is selling products made by a successful manufacturer. Each must complement the other, and thus there is a strong interdependence between the two. Good, competitive products and fair, equitable distribution policies help insure General Motors dealers a proper profit opportunity.'

As such, 'Securing and maintaining harmonious working relationship with the distributive networks is as important as building and maintaining favourable reputations with final buyers. Dealer outlets are customers for the products, and collectively they bear responsibility for making the "payoff" sales to the final buyers. Unless the supply of product flows through to final buyers, marketing channels clog, and all previous personal selling and other marketing efforts are wasted,' wrote Richard R. Still, Edward W. Cundiff, and Norman A.P. Govoni (2005).

The dealer outlets are an extension of a manufacturer's sales organization, as they handle the products and assist in sale to the end users. Often a customer's only point of contact with the company is a dealer. A customer's confidence in individual outlets is frequently a crucial factor influencing the decision making process of a customer, for buying a particular company's products. Dealers are a company's on-the-spot representatives. They are a company's ambassadors in the market. Therefore, a dealer's reputation is influenced by the image of a company, the quality of products, and the style of advertising and sales promotion. Therefore, in the view of a marketing professional, the importance of establishing and maintaining good relations with the dealers network can hardly be exaggerated. Whereas dealers are concerned about their own profit, at the same time, indirectly they also contribute to the company's bottom lines.

LOVE–HATE RELATIONSHIP

All said and done, the relationship between the dealers and manufacturing companies is often said to be a 'love–hate' relationship. 'It is like an arranged marriage between the two parties. Unlike an Indian marriage, it is more often on the rocks,' said one marketing manager. Dealers love companies because they are a source of merchandise for them to sell and make profits, and they hate their principals, because they think that the companies are very unreasonable in their dealings with them.

However, good dealer relations depend on both the company and the dealers recognizing their mutual responsibility towards each other and the ultimate customer. Fulfilment of this mutual responsibility is essential to business success and it is possible if each enjoys public acceptance. Following an attitude of mutual cooperation and trust is fundamental to a fair, profitable, and friendly business association.

Both the manufacturers and the dealers understand that it is in their mutual interest to make a fair profit in performing their respective functions in supplying the customers with products, of which they both can be proud of. The fact remains that both parties take business risk by investing their money. The organization invests millions in research and development to improve their products and also execute a promotional programme to make it acceptable to the customers. On the other hand, dealers also risk their investments in stocking products in the hope to sell them at a profit.

This relationship has been described as a philosophy called 'risk sharing partnership'. As such when the manufacturers and dealers work together, sharing common problems and recognizing mutual obligations, a profitable relationship is assured. This relationship can be described as a 'troika', that is, a relationship amongst three parties, the focal point of which is the customer. Their amicable and harmonious relations will ultimately reflect on the common goal of serving the customer to his entire satisfaction (See Exhibit 12.2.).

EXHIBIT 12.2   Troika—Company, dealer, and customer

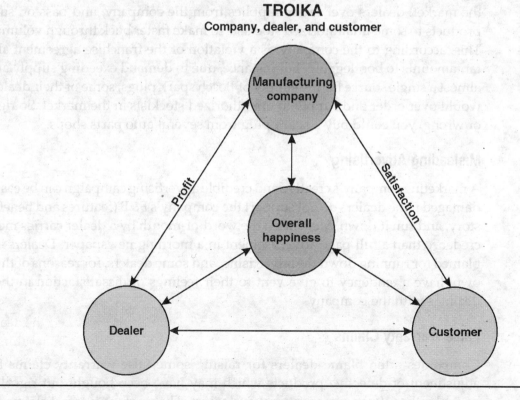

TROIKA
Company, dealer, and customer

COMPANY'S VIEWS ON DEALERS

Both the company and the dealers have certain view points and perceptions about each other which are pertinent enough to note. The conflict of interest between the company and the dealers more often than not leads to criticism for each other. Whereas the company wants to get the best side of the dealer to meet their marketing objectives, at the same time dealers, in their concern for making profits, demand better deals and facilities. The companies have some views about their dealers, which are interesting to know.

Profiteering by Overcharging

With an eye on moving their inventories faster and enhancing their margins of profit, dealers often mislead the customers. Selling products on a price higher than the one recommended by the company is a common instance in the marketplace. Due to short supply of a certain product or abundant availability of competitive products, dealers manipulate prices and even justify such actions.

Bootlegging

Companies, due to strategic distribution policies, would like to restrict supply of their products only to authorized dealers. If the product is well accepted in the market, dealers over order supplies from the company, and pass on such products to some unauthorized stockists to make faster buck through volumes. This, according to the company, is a violation of the franchise agreement and tantamounts to bootlegging. For instance, due to demand exeeding supply and almost a single source for the supply of Bosch spark plugs, some of their dealers would over order and supply to unauthorized stockists in the market. So right or wrong, you could buy a spark plug from several auto parts shops.

Misleading Advertising

A marketing company's creative and credible advertising campaign can be easily damaged if the dealers do not support the company's F&B (features and benefit) story, and run it down. Most often the word-of-mouth by a dealer carries more credence than a full page advertisement in a morning newspaper. Dealers are blamed for running down the advertising, and some dealers, for reasons of their own, have a tendency to give vent to their feelings of dissatisfaction in their dealings with the company.

False Warranty Claims

Companies often blame dealers for raising some false warranty claims for adjustment of defective products which may have been bought out right, as scrap, by them from some ignorant customers. The purpose is to get claims for such adjustments to make extra profits, one way or the other. Many dealers because of their volume of business and influence, persuade sales people to allow some sales policy adjustments and claim full price credit for the defective products.

Inventory Manipulation

Dealers are not rational when it comes to stocking the full range of products manufactured by the company. They would like to stock only the fast moving and profitable merchandise and avoid, some how, to indent slow moving and low profit items. Fast selling products naturally mean faster turnover of currency sales and higher quantum of profits. The slow moving inventories mean money blocked and increase in interest costs. Dealers manipulate by underselling the slow moving inventories in bulk and overcharge for the fast moving products, thus balance out their bottom lines.

Unfair Competition and Price Cutting

Indulging in unfair competition and price cutting is usual tendency amongst the multi-brand dealers. In a situation like this the dealers intentionally under quote or over quote the prices. The level of price quotation is taken as an indicator of brand acceptance of a product in the market. Higher the quote, the products get sold at premium and that too with prestige. This often forces the companies to show extra favours to some key dealers to encourage them to quote their prices higher than their competitors, to maintain their supremacy or leadership position in the market.

Apathy to Promotions

Companies spend millions to promote their products in terms of sales promotion programmes, consumer contacts, promotional literature, and store decorations, but until dealers see some monetary benefits, they show only superficial interest in such campaigns. It forces quite a few companies to allow some credit notes to the dealers towards promotional expenses. Many companies use dealers' show windows and dealer identification signs, at their own expense to increase their visibility in the market. Bridgestone and Ceat Tyres developed the Tyres Shoppes in their dealers premises, either entirely on their own expense or negligible cost sharing.

Callous Attitude

Dealers believe strongly in the philosophy that in business, nobody is anybody's friend. As long as dealers make profits out of a company franchise, they continue to show an empathetic attitude. The moment scenes change, they change too.

Yesterday's friends can be tomorrow's competitors. To many inspiring and motivating sales stories of a sales person seem to have only one conclusion: 'Show me the colour of money!' Stories of dealers' callous attitude abound in all markets of the world (See Exhibit 12.3).

EXHIBIT 12.3　Paid in the same coin

'If you do 110 per cent of your sales target, I will send you to Bangkok on a holiday (alone); if not, then with your wife.' Proclaimed my Italian boss, good naturedly. Perhaps, he knew I was going to meet my target anyway.

I had already done 90 per cent, and for the balance all I needed was orders for 15 truck tyres, 20 car tyres, and 5 large truck tyres.

I had banked on my one-time dealer friend, Mangat Rai, whom I had not visited since I quit my Blackstone job a year ago.

I hoped to revive my old contact with him, though on the back of my mind I was somewhat apprehensive of not being a welcome visitor to his shop. This was because no dealer can afford to annoy his supplier by hobnobbing with his competitors. And dealers, as I know them, are ruthless Shylocks, who want their pound of flesh. They want higher margins and long credits, especially from the new companies.

But I had no authority to bend my company rules.

'Good morning, Rai Sahib,' I greeted Mangat Rai, who nodded listlessly.

There he sat majestically, behind the sales counter, talking to customers with the same goldrimmed glasses resting on his fair, round, prosperous face, with pan saliva oozing out of his mouth corners, and with his gold-plated watch and a large gold ring flashing on his right hand. His face brightened as he counted wads of currency notes.

Three hours passed. Mangat Rai was still busy and spared only occasional, scornful glance for me, as if asking me to leave.

'Tea?' he asked the customers, and as he looked at me, I said: 'Yes.' The salesman in me was still hoping against hopes.

Mangat Rai was now ready to go home for lunch, leaving me in lurch. He looked at his gold watch.

As I was about to kick-start my scooter, his servant came to me and said: 'Chai ki chavanni dete jao, Seth ne bola hai (Pay your 25 paise for the tea, Seth has said).

The message was loud and clear; he never ever wanted me to visit him again.

I searched through my wallet and gave the servant the only one old George V vintage British coin, called 'Chavanni' (now no more in circulation) that I had.

I left the shop with a heavy heart, never to return.

Dealers are nobody's friends, I said to myself.

Somehow, I could still complete my 110 per cent quota to keep my job going in the new company.

Five years later, Blackstone suffered heavy losses and closed down, hitting hard people like Mangat Rai. The new Italian company that I was working with had done well and my good performance had earned me the position of a regional manager.

One day, our office boy placed a business card on my table.

Mangat Rai was waiting to see me. I remembered the ugly old story and made him wait the whole day to teach him a lesson.

As the clock struck six, it was time to close. Mangat Rai meekly entered my office.

'Good evening, Sir!' he greeted me timidly and stood waiting.

Mangat Rai was not the same. His golden watch and gold ring were missing and a cheap plastic frame had replaced his golden spectacles. He looked humble and older.

'Won't you sell my cup of tea back to me, Sir?' he pleaded with emotion choked voice, putting the same George V vintage coin in front of me. I recognized the coin that I had paid for his tea five years ago.

Mangat Rai's eyes welled with tears and mine too. I got up and gave him a bear hug and tears rolled down our cheeks.

I wrote my order book, and he signed as our new dealer in silent gratitude. We became good friends again.

Source: The Observer of Business and Politics, 22 June 2000.

DEALER'S VIEWS OF A COMPANY

Most often the dealers have a lot of caustic and critical views about the companies, policies, procedures, and behaviour of the managers. Mutual criticism is a part of the conflict of interest and each one wants to get the better side of the other for their own benefits, the common denominator of which is profit. The 'holier than thou' attitude of both the dealers and the company is, but a reality of life in the marketing game. Some areas that dealers consider sensitive are discussed here.

Franchise Agreements

Most of the dealers think that the franchise agreements that are imposed by the company on them are always one sided and, hence, very stiff. Some clauses and conditions cover only the company's interests and not the dealers'. These put the dealers at the mercy of the company, who have no choice but to play a subordinate role. Dealers have no say, whatsoever, in matters concerning the supply and commissions and handling of customers' complaints.

Overproduction and Overloading

To meet corporate profit goals, the companies often overproduce to meet or exceed their production capacities, resulting in excess supply to the dealers. Companies often overload dealers with excess inventories and then pressurize them to sell and pay company bills on time, as per the terms imposed on dealers. Dealers get stuck with a lot of unwanted supplies and are forced to somehow off-load them. This results in delayed payments from customers and in turn from dealers to the company. Dealers come under criticism for no fault of theirs. This results not only in the loss of a dealer's reputation, but also relationship with the company. Due to delayed payments, dealers lose certain prompt payment discounts and overriding commissions, which affect their bottom lines.

Bypassing Dealers

Dealers often blame their principals for bypassing them and selling directly to certain customers, particularly where bulk supplies are involved. The company deprives them of the opportunity to make lump sum profits, which the company conveniently keeps for itself. The fact remains that as a matter of marketing policy, several companies handle institutional sales themselves, where dealers have no role. Similarly, some 'rate contract' sales to the government are also taken care of by the company themselves. But the dealers have a gripe.

Compelling to Stock Full Product Line

Companies, though expect dealers to stock full range of products manufactured and marketed by them, yet it is very unreasonable to force the dealers to keep products which are either irrelevant to the market locations or move sluggishly out of their counters. As such, products get overaged or expire before they reach the customers. Therefore, the company should consider certain factors and reason them out, before forcing the dealers.

Lopsided Distribution

Dealers think that company managements move by their whims and wishes and distribute products in a haphazard manner. The company thinks that appointing five outlets for the same product in a small town, does not make sense. This deprives dealers an opportunity to do comfortable business. Dealers do think that appointing a sole distributor in each town is just the right way.

Low Margins and Commissions

Companies whose products are well accepted in the market and are backed by sufficient advertising and sales promotion, often allow meagre commissions to dealers and also dictate tight payment terms. This adversely affects dealers' margins and makes business unattractive. However, in certain cases the volumes help. Most of the petrol dealers crib for low commissions but clamour to keep dealerships as the volume of sales promise good returns.

Compel to Advertise

Dealers often accuse their principals of forcing them to advertise. Dealers are asked to participate in the co-operative advertising and share the cost up to a certain percentage. Since expenditure means a cut in the profits, dealers detest the idea.

Pay for Store Decoration

Decorating the show windows or creating a particular type of ambiance in the store is often imposed on the dealers. Since such expenditures are generally sizable, dealers do not approve these ideas. However, dealers think it is the obligation of a company to decorate dealers' stores at their own expense, as ultimately it is the company who gets the benefit of projecting the company image and brand salience.

Bossing and Threats

Dealers think they are the owners of their businesses and do not have to have a boss. Yet the marketing and sales personnel from the companies dictate them and often threaten them with cancellation of their dealership. Their playing the 'big brother' is not liked by the dealers.

OBJECTIVES OF DEALER RELATIONS

Dealer relations, as a part of the marketing public relations (MPR), are crucial. The success or failure of a marketing organization, to a large extent depends on the understanding and cooperation of the dealers. So PR has certain roles and responsibilities to make this relationship more meaningful and rewarding for both the company and the dealers. The PR objectives for cultivating and maintaining good dealer relations depends on the marketing policies of a company.

Dealer relations are generally based on the 'different folks, different strokes' policy. Depending on the products and the distribution policies, the marketing organizations go for three kinds of dealerships: (1) Exclusive dealers, (2) Selective dealers, generally multi-brand, and (3) Well spread dealerships. Nike, world's largest shoe maker, is a good example of selective distribution (See Exhibit 12.4).

'The relationship between a manufacturer and its wholesale and retail dealers is determined by the policies of the manufacturer. Obviously, relationships with exclusive dealers are necessarily close, but in the case of selective and general dealers, mutual interest and involvement is limited. Manufacturers of automobiles and petroleum products, which are sold through one dealer in a given area, usually have close relationships with their retail outlets. Producers of foods, beverages, hardware, drugs, and staple products sold by many retailers of the same type, have more limited relations with wholesalers and retailers,' says H. Frazier and Frank B. Kalupa (2005).

Accordingly, the PR objectives will have to be determined in the light of the above situations. However, we should look at the overall objectives of the dealer relations, which are: *better dealer understanding of the company policies, monitoring dealers' attitude, better product knowledge for dealers, sales training, identification*

EXHIBIT 12.4   Nike distribution pattern

Nike sells its athletic shoes and apparel through six different kinds of stores: (1) Specialized sports stores, such as golfers' pro shops, where Nike has announced plans for a new line of athletic shoes; (2) General sporting goods stores, which carry a broad range of styles; (3) Department stores, which carry only the newest styles; (4) Mass merchandise stores, which focus on discounted styles; (5) Nike retail stores, including Niketowns in major cities, which feature the complete line, with emphasis on the newest styles; and (6) Factory outlet stores, which stock mostly seconds and closeouts. Nike also limits the stores that can carry its products.

Source: Marketing Management (2000).

---

programme, advertising support, dealer's suggestions and complaints, dealership management system, generate dealer loyalty through free flowing communications.

Better Dealer Understanding of the Company Policies

There is always a need to promote a better understanding of the company policies amongst the dealers. Fault finding with the policies and practices is a common sight in the company–dealer relations, but when communicated properly, a good sense and harmony prevails. Though there is never a time when dealers will not agitate about something, yet an amiable dialogue can help diffuse the conflict or reduce its intensity.

Monitoring Dealers' Attitude

Perhaps, it is not the status of the dealers that matters, but what really matters is their attitude. A dealer's positive or constructive attitude towards the company should work as a stepping stone to greater mutually beneficial relations. Whereas it pays dealers to show a proactive stance towards the company, it also helps the company to make up its mind about the pattern of behaviour and volumes of business possibilities in the months and years to come. This paves way for greater growth and progress, for both the company and the dealer. Public relations have a role to feed dealers with information and success stories to keep dealers in the right frame of mind.

Better Product Knowledge for Dealers

One major forte of every salesperson is their product knowledge. Dealers and their sales personnel who are involved in direct selling to the customers, are no exception. This is an important objective of every MPR programme to keep updating the product knowledge of dealers through various communications like newsletters, dealer magazine, special bulletins, product literature, etc. Dealers or their representative makes a powerful impression on the customers, if their product knowledge is authentic.

Sales Training

Sales training is a powerful means to equip the dealers with the knowledge and skills that can help in increasing their sales volumes. The sales training on the tools and techniques of selling and serving the customers promotes professionalism. Tools like demonstration kits, sales presentations, assistance in selection and induction of dealers' salesman, and sales contests, all inspire dealers and their personnel.

Identification Programme

Dealer identification that is providing standard company signs outside the dealer's premises is an important part of strengthening the dealer network. Such signs establish a dealers' identity in the market and work as traffic builders to their business premises. A well designed identification programme is one of the major objectives of dealer relations. Such signs enhance dealers' prestige and reputation in the market and respect in their communities. Dealers often take lot of pride of this association with the company, which serves as a healthy indicator of good dealer relations. Bata, for instance, has a well developed identification programme. The Bata signage with uniform white logo writing on red surface provides a conspicuous identification to company owned stores and dealer outlets, all over the world. McDonald's and KFC are similar examples.

Advertising Support

MPR helps the dealers in their advertising efforts by providing them advertising plans, store and window displays, outdoor displays, signs, and direct mail advertising. Companies provide ready-made mailers with a slot provided for dealers to stamp them with their names and addresses, for mailing to their customers.

Dealer's Suggestions and Complaints

The sensitive feedback often comes in the form of complaints. PR is receptive to this feedback on matters concerning the advertising and sales promotion programmes of the company. Often the dealers feel isolated in the face of high powered advertising campaigns and long for participation. They express their feelings, which look like complaints or suggestions. This sensitive feedback is a valuable information which can set the system on track. As such the ideas, suggestions, or even complaints should be heard with focused attention as useful information for course correction.

Dealership Management System

It pays the company management in aiding the dealers and distributors in improving their management methods with better interior store arrangement and equipment; more lighting; inventory control system; improved accounting and credit control, store records and systems, delivery service, and pricing; and better store organization and personnel.

Generate Dealer Loyalty

Stimulating dealer's or distributor's interest in the process of manufacturing products inculcates a feeling of involvement and loyalty towards the company. Loyalty helps in fortifying the partnership relationship, which is so essential to all round success. One of the major means of galvanizing relations with the dealers and generating loyalty is to ensure free flow of information to the dealers, which they can understand and adopt for their own business success.

GOOD DEALER RELATIONS

According to Frank Jefkins (2006), 'One of the most important aspects of market education is winning over your distributors whether they be wholesalers, retailers, brokers, or agents. Your own sales force is important in this respect too. It is easy to assume that distributors will take stocks because of generous trade terms or the weight of advertising. Distributors are not just people who are order takers and shelf fillers, not even in supermarket chains. They have to have faith in what they are selling, and very often they have to show evidence of this in their ability to advise customers.'

Therefore, good dealer relations is not one way traffic, but thrives on a mutual trust. Good dealer–company relations depend on both the parties watching their mutual interests. Manufacturers have an obligation to further the interests of the dealers in taking care of certain aspects of franchisee's business. Since the ultimate goal of both is to serve the customers to their entire satisfaction, it is important for the manufacturer to produce best quality products at a right price and covered by a liberal warranty. The benefits of marketing efforts, advertising and promotion of products, should also percolate to the dealers, so that they can sell company products with pride and prestige. There is also a need for a fair distribution and to back up the products with prompt and comprehensive service. All these actions should naturally help the dealers to make a fair amount of profit.

Dealers too have some responsibilities as enumerated in the business ethics of the company. They have a moral obligation of dealing with the customers in a fair and courteous manner and not indulge in any unfair trade practices that brings disrepute to the company. Indulging in misleading advertising, manipulating prices or misrepresenting the company in an irresponsible manner, will lead to ill will between the company and the dealers. The sound financial position of the dealer, which should help him to honour his commitments to the company, goes a long way in creating an atmosphere of cordiality and understanding. Tata's advertisement for dealerships in different parts of Delhi and NCR shows what they look for in their dealers (Exhibit 12.5).

'Good manufacturer–distributor–dealer relations depend upon both manufacturers and dealers recognizing their responsibilities to consumers and to each other. Understanding and cooperation are essential if each is to enjoy

EXHIBIT 12.5   Tata's advertiment for dealerships

DEALERSHIPS REQUIRED

TATA MOTORS–Passenger Car Business

....at NORTH DELHI, SOUTH DELHI

and GHAZIABAD

India is on a fast growth trajectory for the car market and is expected to continue this pace through out the next decade. With a turnover of over Rs. 32,000 crores, Tata Motors is already India's largest automobile company. Tata Passenger Car brands like the Indica, Indigo, Sumo and the Safari have earned the trust of over a million customers—and the number is growing with each passing year.

Come, partner with Tata Motors as a Passenger Car Dealer. Leverage your strengths with those of Tata Motors. Maximize your opportunities even as Tata Motors constantly expands its portfolio of passenger vehicle products and services, including the recently unveiled peoples' car, the Tata Nano.

All we seek from you is a passion for cars, total commitment to customer satisfaction, strong financial background and an integrated facility.

Applications can be downloaded from www.tatamotors.com/contactus/. For any information or assistance, you can e-mail us at pcbuddnorth@ tatamotors.com or call us on 0124-2805141-14/6453450. Completed applications must reach us on the address mentioned in the application form within 10 days from the date of release of this advertisement.

TATA MOTORS

Source: The Times of India, 4 August 2008.

public acceptance. Fulfilment of these mutual responsibilities is so essential to business success that some manufacturers incorporate in their franchise agreements a statement of the specific responsibilites of the manufacturer and dealer, the performance of which is fundamental to a fair, profitable, and friendly business association,' wrote H. Frasier Moore and Frank B. Kalupa (2005).

MANUFACTURER'S SUPPORT TO DEALERS

Depending on the type of dealers, manufacturers in their mutual interest lend a suitable support to them to make them more effective in the market. The companies run a well integrated support system to keep the dealers connected with the company. This is strategically important in the competitive situation. Some companies who adopt a strategy of 'guerilla marketing' often like to hijack some good dealers. According to some industry members, on their entry into the Indian market, a well known tyre company, Bridgestone converted some old faithful dealers into their own franchisees, luring them with lucrative commissions and fully paid showroom decorations and merchandising support.

Professional marketing companies generally have some counselling services that they run to support their dealer networks. These services can be in the areas: *business management, public relations support, advertising support, mechanical service support,* and *support to selling skills.*

Business Management

Management counselling is generally extended to some large key dealers, as the company considers them the backbone of their business. Therefore, the company extends the necessary support to the dealers so that they run their business professionally, based on good management systems. A well structured training programme is developed to train them in certain areas of business activity like organizational structures, inventory control, cash flow management, advertising and sales promotion, administration, modernization of facilities, customer relations management, etc. Escorts tractors have been conducting several training programmes for their dealers, their managers, and service mechanics. Maruti Udyog also conducts certain dealer development training programmes.

Public Relations Support

None other than the dealers represent the company in their cities, towns, and communities; so it is only appropriate for a company to extend the necessary public relations support to them. Dealers are like the local spokespersons and are considered a credible source of information to people in general and customers in particular. Generally, dealers are encouraged to participate in their local community activities concerning education, health and hygiene, social welfare, and other local events. So that they can locally handle certain events like customer meets, media relations, etc., dealers are provided with some quick learning manuals to handle local public relations. Also readymade speeches and press releases are provided to take care of PR needs. To take care of media relations and public speaking, Goodyear published mini books for the guidance of dealers. Escorts in their dealer magazine 'Profitably Yours' have been updating dealers on such areas of activity.

Advertising Support

Certain large-sized exclusive key dealers are almost like subsidiaries of their parent principals. Their names written along with the company's name means a reliable extension of the company. Ford, for instance, prefixes the names of the dealers to strike clear identity and authenticity of dealers. Examples are 'Harpreet Ford', etc. The principals encourge dealers to undertake advertising activities, for which they get support in some areas as the following:

- National level advertising campaigns
- Local level advertising
- Dealer's identification to build traffic
- Free layouts, copy, mats, stereos, computer downloads, and printouts for dealer adaptations
- Direct mail pieces
- Letterheads, business cards, folders, product literature, booklets, and pullouts
- Posters, POP materials, counter cards, shelf hangers, danglers, festoons, stickers, and banners
- Film clips, video CDs, commercials, and jingles for TV, and radio advertising
- Novelties like calendars, key chains, pens, pencils, ash trays, playing cards, golf balls, rulers, etc.
- Co-operative advertising
- Dealer's advertising and merchandising training programmes

Mechanical Service Support

Consumer durables manufactured and marketed by the companies have to be backed by after-sales service as the customers who buy cars, washing machines, air conditioners, and TVs, do not merely buy machines but an assurance of a trouble-free performance with low maintenance cost and efficient running. Dealers of such products have to be equipped with means to provide service to the customers. To make it happen, manufacturers provide dealers and their mechanics, training in service management, operation, and also the necessary equipment. Some of the companies maintain training schools to conduct courses in systems of service management, maintenance mechanism, and operations. Some toll free phones are hooked on to dealers to take care of the service needs of the customers. MRF tyres converted their dealers into service outlets equipped with skills and machines to fit and balance vehicle wheels. Maruti has appointed a network of service stations in India who are authorized to render authentic service to car owners. An advertisement put by the company gives a good idea of the concept (See Exhibit 12.5).

Another example, though looks mundane, but means a lot for some of the proud owners of Mont Blanc writing instruments is that. The company advertised for a complimentary service for the ailing pens for two days. Incidentally, Mont Blanc brand pens are one of the most expensive writing instruments in the world and carry lot of prestige for those who own and consider the pens as a prized possession. The company has now expanded their product range to meet the discerning needs of high profile corporate executives. They introduced wallets, watches, cuff links, tie pins, lap top bags, etc.

Support to Selling Systems

Each company adopts its own selling style. Sales people are briefed and trained to master the selling systems and adopt a particular vocabulary for handling customers during sale. Though salespersons are often expected to have a natural flair for talking convincingly to the customers, yet there has to be a method in the talking style. Sales training is imparted to dealers and their sales personnel to conduct themselves in a manner compatible with the reputation of the company and the nature of the product being sold. Starting with product knowledge and demonstrating benefits to the customers, certain selling aids are developed and provided for use while talking to the customer. Sales kits, demonstration sets, cut models, flip charts, and power point presentations are provided to be handled by dealers and sales people. Some Japanese companies impose a dress code on the dealer personnel to improve dealer/company visibility and enhance customer confidence. Maruti has standardized on light blue shirt and dark blue trousers for sales personnel and a dark blue dungaree for mechanics, which is almost mandatory.

COMMUNICATING TO THE DEALERS

One sure way to build relations based on understanding and goodwill is to communicate sufficiently and avoid communication breakdown. Communicating to dealers for that very reason is no different. PR takes special care to keep the dealers informed so as to keep their morale high so that they can enthusiastically carry out their selling and servicing activities.

Frank Jefkins (2006), who fondly calls this effort as market education, wrote '...while marketing education of pre-selling tactics are not widely adopted by the marketing and advertising fraternity, many organizations which appreciate the role of PR do in fact prepare the ground well and seek a favourable marketing situation well in advance of a launch. They do not merely rely on advertising as a panzer assault.'

Marketing education is synonymous with marketing communication to the people operating in the marketplace, mainly dealers and field sales force. As such, a free and frequent flow of communications from the company to all those interfacing with the customers helps in boosting morale, courage, and confidence in the selling job. According to Jefkins, adopting a marketing education and communication strategy has the following four-fold effect.

1. Communications help minimize sales resistance.
2. Communications help the sales force to adequately spread the merchandize on to the dealer's counters with ease and ahead of the launch of the advertising campaign.
3. The advertising profile can be adjusted lower to save costs, by taking advantage of the awareness already created through communications.
4. Communications ensure more effectiveness to advertising as market is already sensitized about the products and services going to be launched.

COMMUNICATION MEDIA

The public relations divisions of the companies generally use media tools for communicating to the dealers to educate them and motivate them—first, oral communications and second, mass communication. Whereas the oral communication efforts constitute of interface with company's sales force who are in constant touch with dealers, either individually or through groups meetings, etc., the mass media relies upon the printed word and the electronic messaging.

Oral Communications

Organizations use the spoken word to a large extent as a medium of communicating to the dealers. The most common and perhaps the most effective way of communicating is through the sales force members. During their rounds of daily calls on the dealers they transmit lot of information which is of strategic importance to the dealers. During the sales calls on these outlets to book orders to beef up dealers' inventories, sales personnel verbally share information about product improvements, new innovations, business policy changes, modifications in the commissions and incentive systems, and also make presentations to equip dealers and their counter salesmen, in selling skills.

Sales personnel being the upfront representatives, companies entrust them with responsibility to extend vital support to dealers in terms of handling customer complaints and warranty claims, etc., to ensure customer satisfaction. In turn, the company keeps the sales personnel briefed and updated about changes in company policies, practices, and product lines. To make the oral communications work well, generally, the kinds of meetings conducted are: *one-to-one interactions, small group discussions, regional level dealer meetings*, and *countrywide dealer conferences*.

One-to-one interactions

The one-to-one interactions are generally held between the sales personnel and the dealer. Besides negotiating business and orders for the products of the company, sales people share information which is sensitive to business, product deliveries, prices, commission, and discount structures, etc. Sales representatives being professionals, they often talk to dealers' counter salesmen to share product knowledge and skills to handle customer queries. Many companies provide ready made flip charts to their sales representatives to conduct on-the-spot mini sales training programmes for dealers and their men.

Small group discussions

Certain dealership outfits, due to the nature of the products that they sell, employ a couple of dozen employees who handle sales and mechanical servicing. Depending on the needs and eventualities, small group discussions are led by the company representative along with the franchise owner, where a presentation is followed by question–answer session to clarify certain doubts about product, performance, service, operation, etc. This leaves a lasting impression in inspiring them to do their jobs professionally, with ultimate common aim to satisfy customers.

Regional level dealer meetings

When the occasion demands or an eventuality arises, dealers are invited to regional meetings by the regional managers of the company. Many companies today operate on the 'profit centre' concept, where each regional office performance is assessed on the basis of contributions made by a region to profit bottom lines of the company. Since dealers are partners in business, regional meetings are either organized sporadically or on a pre set time table, say monthly, quarterly, or half yearly. Such meetings serve a useful purpose of building a two-way communication between dealers and the company. The feedback thus collected helps the company to adjust their policies and practices to come up to the hopes and aspirations of the dealers, which goes a long way to establish cordial relations so essential for business growth and meeting corporate targets.

Countrywide dealer conferences

To several companies, holding a national level dealers' conference is a ritual. Such conferences help to inspire and motivate dealers, give them an opportunity to voice out their suggestions and problems, socialize with other dealers from distant corners of the country. The conferences, both for the managers and dealers, provide an opportunity for cross fertilization of ideas, and knit the dealers together for all round growth and profitability. Companies like Maruti, Hero Honda, Mahindra and Mahindra, and Escorts organize annual dealers' conference. Some of the items on the agenda of such conferences are the following:

- Knit dealers community together to create a fellow feeling.
- Collect sensitive feedback about market scenario, company policies, products, and services.
- Communicate to the dealers about company's growth plans, new product, innovations, research, and developments.
- Assure and reassure dealers that their association with the company is valuable. Also highlight the organization's expectations from the dealers.
- Recognize high performing dealers with awards and rewards.
- Train and develop dealers' mindset to be compatible with company's programme to maintain its leadership position in the market.
- Share strategies with dealers to combat competition.
- Announce marketing and sales targets for the next year and seek dealers' participation in meeting such objective.

Mass Communication

Mass communication uses print and electronic media as its tools. Mass communication is a vast subject which encompasses many means of communication to achieve objectives. There are quite a few media vehicles that public relations use to reach dealers and keep them connected with the company for mutual benefit of business growth. Some of the tools, which are often used are: *dealer magazine, dealer newsletters, video clips, VCDs and DVDs, booklets, folders, and product literature, annual reports, exhibitions, and displays,* and *dealer awards and rewards.*

Public relations has a vital role to play in this area to generate and distribute such information to the dealers community to keep their morale high, which is so essential for a selling job. Let us briefly look at some of these commonly used tools:

Dealer magazine

Also known as external house journal, dealer magazine exclusively focuses on dealer development and dealer activities. Such publications brought out at intervals like monthly, bi-monthly or quarterly, highlight the information that is sensitive to dealers' business. The magazine brought out by the PR division highlights some high performances by dealers, their unique ways of conducting business, customer satisfaction stories, new product introductions, and complete profiles of certain dealers. Dealers, definitely, look forward to receive such publication at regular intervals, as they feel that the publication is for them and about them.

Dealer newsletters

Published by PR in coordination with marketing division, a weekly or fortnightly newsletter, generally of one or two sheets, printed back to back, give fast breaking news about the company dealers, products, and achievements, etc. Such newsletters help to build spontaneous dealer interest. Some dealers maintain a complete file of such newsletters and use it as reference.

Video clips

On demand, companies supply video clips of the current TV commercials being used in national advertising campaigns. Some enterprising dealers use such clips on the local cable networks along with their names, which is inexpensive but promise high business mileage.

VCDs and DVDs

Recorded speeches of the business leaders or the company bosses are circulated to the dealers for them to view and get inspired. Sometimes, such CDs are played at the regional or annual dealer conferences. The idea is to enthuse dealers about the pride of association with a prestigious organization.

Booklets, folders, and product literature

Some prestigious, informational, and multi-coloured publications like booklets, folders, and product literature are provided to the dealers in sufficient quantities, with a slot to print their dealership name and address and mail them to their key customers and influential people in their communities. These promise double benefit to the dealers and to the principal company.

Annual reports

A company's annual report is a prestigious publication to showcase the power and image of a company. Generally, well produced, the report gives a comprehensive picture of the present and the future of the company. As such it is an important document which influences many decisions and builds company image. Many dealers who are shareholders, in any case get this publication, yet the annual report is mailed to several key dealers to bolster their faith in the company. The effort instills confidence and pride of association amongst the dealers.

Exhibitions and displays

Dealers are often encouraged to participate in local events like farm fairs, exhibitions, carnivals, and jamborees and create displays on the sidelines to enhance visitors' interest. This is an excellent opportunity to showcase the products as well as dealers' credentials in the local area. PR departments develop collapsible display kits which can be shipped to various locations and can be erected in almost no time. Many dealers believe this is a great opportunity for them to cash upon by displaying company products and even book on the spot orders from the visitors. As a sales promotion effort, some companies would announce special discounts for the customers during the exhibition time.

Dealer awards and rewards

To motivate dealers to perform well, marketing organizations motivate dealers to meet certain sales targets to be eligible for membership of elite clubs formed by the company. Targets are assigned to the dealers to meet and beat with a promise of handsome rewards and awards. Escorts Limited floated three clubs, Gold Club, Silver Club, and Bronze Club, with targets assigned to dealers to be eligible for such prestigious club memberships. The company rewards these achievements with an all expense paid foreign trip to Gold Club members, trip to Kathmandu for Silver Club members, and an all expense paid trip to Tirupati, etc. for the Bronze club members. This generates a very healthy competition amongst dealers and enthusiasm to meet sales targets to be eligible for higher club memberships.

Summary

Dealers are a vital link between the marketing division of the company and the customers. They are an integral and crucial part of the distribution system and, hence, an important public for the public relations. Therefore, establishing a relationship, based on goodwill and understanding, with the dealers is a crucial function. This is a tripartite relationship called 'troika' where the company, dealers, and customers are involved, with ultimate focus on customer service and satisfaction.

As India is fast moving towards free market, the role of dealers or franchisees is slated for greater and vital participation in the process of economic growth.

The business relations between the company and the dealers always have the under current of 'conflict of interest'. Generally called 'love–hate relationship', each of them have critical views about each other. However, the relationship has to continue with each side striving to get the best of the other. They have a responsibility to each other.

Public relations, with the objective of generating dealer loyalty, has certain objectives to meet in terms of monitoring their attitudes, suggestions, and complaints and at the same time assisting them with information and support so that they can conduct their business in best mutual interest. Extending public relations, advertising, and merchan-dizing support to the dealers are crucial aspects of public relations role.

Communication, a two-way free flow of information, is the foundation of good relationship. Public relations, through various channels such as oral communications through sales force and mass communication tools such as dealer magazines, newsletters, booklets and product literature, annual reports, media relations training, and awards and rewards, etc., makes continuous efforts to nurture this relationship.

Key Terms

Franchising Arrangement where one party (the franchiser) grants another party (the franchisee) the right to use its trademark or trade name as well as certain business systems and processes, to produce and market a good or service according to certain specifications

Lopsided distribution Unplanned and haphazard distribution of products in the market

Market education Communication efforts to spread education and awareness about a company's products, their usage, customer benefits, etc.

National advertising campaign Coordinated series of advertisements appearing in print and/or electronic media over a specific time period to provide country-wide coverage

Principals Manufacturing and marketing companies who appoint dealers to sell their products

Product line Group of closely related products sold by a company. Items within a product line usually share a targeted market niche, manufacturing process, and usage

Sales resistance Reasoned (objective) or emotional (subjective) opposition to a buying proposition. Skilled salespeople try to overcome sales resistance by probing and understanding the prospect's stated and hidden concerns through careful questioning and listening, and by showing how their offer fits their needs

Troika A tripartite relationship between the company, dealer, and the customer

Concept Review Questions

1. Dealers are a vital link between a company and the customers and public

relations plays a moderator's role to keep the company–dealer relations working well in the mutual interest. Explain the concept.

2. Due to a 'conflict of interest' the company and the dealers are critical of each other. What reasons each party has? How can this adversary relationship be transformed into a philosophy of 'risk sharing partnership'. Explain the MPR support system that companies adopt to make it happen.

3. Two-way communication is the basis of good dealer relations. What role does public relations play to keep up this relationship? Discuss various media tools that are used to sustain this relationship.

4. Draw up a list of public relations objectives for running a dealer relations programme. Also explain each objective in detail.

References

Jefkins, Frank (2006), *Public Relations for Your Business*, Jaico Publishing House, Mumbai, pp. 112 and 113.

Kotler, Philip (2000), *Marketing Management, Millennium Edition*, Prentice Hall of India Private Limited, New Delhi, India, pp. 497 and 514.

Moore, H. Frazier and Frank B. Kalupa (2005), *Public Relations, Principles, Cases and Problems*, Richard D. Irwin, Inc, USA, and published in India by Surjeet Publications, New Delhi, pp. 358 and 360.

Still, Richard R., Edward W. Cundiff, and Norman A.P. Govoni (2005), *Sales Management Decisions, Strategies and Cases*, Prentice-Hall of India Private Limited, New Delhi, p. 223.

Sachdeva, Iqbal, *The Observer of Business and Politics*, New Delhi, 22 June 2000, vol. X, no. 162.

The Times of India, New Delhi, Franchise India supplement, 12 June 2008, p. 15.

The Times of India, New Delhi, 4 August 2008, p. 3.

Vendor Relations

VENDOR RELATIONS

No manufacturer of any consequence can function in isolation of the several big and small vendors or suppliers. It is almost impossible for a manufacturing and marketing organization to function without the support of vendors, who supply components of the products it makes and markets. Said in most traditional terms, no manufacturer can manufacture anything, not even a pin or a large tank, without the participation of vendors in the process.

World over, be it China, India or America, the vendor–manufacturer relationship is a reality of life. The system of interdependence between the two parties makes things workable and practical. From IBM to Infosys, Reliance to Ranbaxy, Kingfisher to Kentucky Fried Chicken, and Maruti to Mahindras, the reality of interdependence is the same.

As the industry is expanding and diversifying into various businesses, manufacturers' dependence on suppliers is ever increasing, particularly for specialized materials and components needed in the production of the scientific and complex equipments. From daily usage articles to technical products, required to satisfy the growing demands of general consumers, or industrial consumers producing mother machines, the role of vendors is also multiplying.

'Suppliers provide materials and services that are worth approximately one-half of the income from sales of manufacturers. Large manufacturers, with all of their facilities, people, and know-how, could not operate without the help of the thousands of resources that supply materials, parts, and services. Competition for the products and services of reliable suppliers is going keener. Producers realize that their suppliers are a primary source of quality products, sales, and profits,' wrote H. Frazier Moore and Frank B. Kalupa (2005).

Besides manufacturers, there are hundreds and thousands of trading and marketing companies who are dependent on vendors for a variety of merchandise like drugs, medicines, food items, toiletries, cosmetics, clothing, hardware, parts, etc. for selling to the end users. Imagine the elimination of this vital link, called the vendor, between the shopping merchants and the shoppers, the total supply chain may come to a halt and even jeopardize life in towns and cities of the world.

With the growth of business in India and introduction of largely diversified range of products, the urgency of discovering vendors, who can supplement the manufacturing and marketing efforts, is becoming dire. Each industry involved in production of industrial and consumer products is looking for such vendors. For that very reason, some agencies are organizing exhibitions and trade fairs to bring buyers and vendors together, so that they can establish a relationship of interdependence. Media often carries advertisements announcing such events to draw attention of all those interested (See Exhibit 13.1).

The business world is an inter-dependent world, where one business depends on the other for support. There are vendors to the vendors. A vendor of some car parts to the car manufacturer is the primary supplier, whereas this supplier is dependent on quite a few secondary suppliers for supply of steel, oils, rubber parts, etc. to keep their commitments with the buyer organization.

The fact remains that a large percentage of such vendors are small business outfits, who depend on some bigger business organization. Perhaps, 80 per cent suppliers to the Maruti Udyog are small businesses, manufacturing parts and employing ten to a couple of hundred employees. According to some rough estimate, a car manufacturer like Maruti have some 12,000 suppliers, primary and secondary, put together. Each of these vendors specialize in manufacturing certain components of a car.

Vendors, also known as ancillary units, are not only concentrated around the manufacturing plants of large manufacturers, but are located in the far flung locations. Tata, for instance, have suppliers spread over the length and breadth of the country, who adhere to their supply schedules to keep the production lines moving in their truck and car making plants.

EXHIBIT 13.1   Inviting vendors to a trade fair

Source: Hindustan Times, 27 June 2008.

The makers of one particular line of products also have common vendors. The vehicle manufacturers, for instance will have vendors who are common to quite a few manufacturers. A vendor may be making one single component, which is interchangeable to all makes and models of a vehicle or may even be producing different components for different buyer companies according to their designs and specifications. For instance, a tyre maker caters to all the vehicle manufacturers either with one size tyre or various sizes compatible with different makes and models. But the spark plug manufacturer meets vehicle makers' demands with one universal spark plug, which fits into all vehicles, from a motor cycle to a high-powered dumper truck.

In India, the emerging large retail stores and shopping malls are largely dependent on the regular supply of a variety of items to their stores from the reliable vendors. Reliance Fresh, who are retailing hundreds of products in their stores, are dependent on hundreds of vendors for help, to keep their shelves full all the time to meet the demands of their customers. Big Apple, Birla More for You, Subhiksha, or 6 TEN are no exception. So the vendor is an important link in the supply chain and needs to be cared for running the business smoothly.

Therefore, the purchaser–vendor relations are of a great consequence for the smooth running of any business—manufacturing and trading. Since public relations is an all-embracing discipline and vendors an important public, there is a vital role that the public relations has to play to keep this strategic relationship going and growing.

VENDORS' EXPECTATONS

The buyer–vendor relation is not a one-time deal. This is a continuous relationship, and if maintained and nurtured carefully, is beneficial to both purchasers and vendors. It is not a one-way traffic but typically a two-way relationship, where inter-dependence is the name of the game. Both the purchaser and the vendors have expectations from each other, and certain obligations to each other, which should be fulfilled in the long-term mutual interest.

Whereas the purchasers, to maximize profits' have an expectation to buy material of the best quality at a fair price, at the same time vendors, in order to have a feeling of loyalty towards the company, definitely have some meaningful expectations, which are: *fair returns on investments, regular business, growth prospects, fair dealings, financing, vendor development, technology transfer, transparency,* and *pride of association.*

Fair Returns on Investments

Like any businessman, big or small, vendors expect an attractive return on the capital invested by them. Every vendor is an entrepreneur who sets up business of manufacturing of components, etc. by installing plant and machinery, buy raw material, employ labour and bear overheads to run the business. Therefore, vendors expect fair margins on their investments. Good profit margins is a reasonable expectation. Vendors vend their merchandise to the purchasers, with expectation for profit from their business enterprise.

Regular Business

One of the major attractions of getting associated with a large company for a vendor is the prospect of regular business. As a practice with most of the manufacturing companies, the orders are placed on the vendors with a yearly schedule of the supplies that the vendors are expected to supply month after month. This regularity of business provides a good advantage to the vendors in the sense that their production lines are committed for the whole year and they do not have to hunt for business every now and then. Vendors expect that the schedules will continue to be operative and there would be minimum risk of discontinuation of supply orders, which can jeopardize business.

Growth Prospects

It is but a natural expectation that once a vendor gets associated with an organization, the supplier should also grow relatively. If the buyer company expands its production capacity, the vendor should also have the benefit of this expansion in terms of a relative increase in quantum of orders on him. The growth prospects should be visible to the vendor, so that the vendor can respond accordingly to come up to the expectation of the buyer company in terms of enhancement of the vendor's production capacity.

Fair Dealings

Like all businessmen, the vendors also expect fair dealings from the buyer companies. The terms and conditions about delivery and payments, incentives for stepped up deliveries to meet manufacturer's production lines schedules, continuity of business without surprises, friendly understanding of a partnership philosophy, should all be honoured. Although this is a mutual response system, the vendors, particularly smaller ones, are always under the risk of sudden cut off or delay in payments, which can affect their cash flow and create hardships.

Financing

Depending upon the specialized skills to produce a particular component, many large buyer companies go a step ahead to finance their vendors of long standing and proven reliability. The manufacturers facilitate the vendors in their leasing of manufacturing equipment, etc. to cope with the enhanced production capacities. Manufacturers would even extend some soft loans adjustable against supplies and demonstrate their philosophy of inter-dependence. Such vendors will naturally owe their progress and growth to the manufacturers and go all the way to demonstrate their loyalty towards the buyer organizations.

Vendor Development

Amongst the hundreds of vendors, the manufacturers continuously spot the vendors with growth potential and extend all the help to such vendors to enhance their capacities. Vendors have an expectation that the companies should continue to extend them the support in terms of management techniques, labour handling, materials, quality improvement, cash flow management, and other related areas. Manufacturers are always on the look out for some potential small time vendors who can be groomed into larger and reliable source of supply of certain materials and components.

Technology Transfer

Manufacturers, through their expensive research and development efforts, acquire technologies which come to stay as the intellectual property of an organization. Such patented and registered technologies generally are closely held and confidential and not freely shared with vendors. But the vendors always have an expectation that such technologies should be transferred to them so that they can translate the know-how into better quality of components strictly as per the requisite specifications. Certain companies do share such confidential information with their vendors on the basis of trust or on certain terms and conditions on an 'oath of confidentiality'. However, in the mutual interest, sharing technology benefits both the manufacturers and the vendors.

Transparency

Many professionalized companies believe and maintain a good degree of transparency with their vendors as they consider this relationship as 'partnership in progress'. Manufacturers build a sense of mutual trust and maintain a relationship, which is transparent. Though this is a strategic relationship between the two business organizations, yet the dichotomy is minimum. Vendors do have an expectation to be considered as integral part of the manufacturer's operation.

Pride of Association

Vendors want to be proud of their association with large companies and want to be known as vendors for such reputable organizations. If the image of the buyer organization is high and positive, vendors naturally get the benefit of this association, in terms of enhancement of their prestige in their communities.

BUYER COMPANY EXPECTATIONS

Outsourcing trends in industry have triggered the emergence of an inter-dependent relationship between buyers and vendors, and more and more companies are getting into long-term partnerships with each other based on understanding, mutual confidence, and a sense of integrity. Whereas the vendors have high hopes and expectations from the buyer companies, at the same time the manufacturers and trading companies, also have certain expectation from the vendors, which are: *quality, price, delivery, service, reliability,* and *responsibility.*

Quality

One of the major considerations that the buyers have while selecting a vendor is that the vendor will strictly conform to the quality standards laid down by the buyer organization. Quality in this context also means that the components and the materials will conform to the specifications prescribed by the buyers. As the supplies made by the vendors are supposed to form part of the finished product manufactured by the buyers, it is but natural that the high standards of quality control should be maintained by vendors at their facilities, so that the buyer's products continue to enjoy the reputation in the market. Certain vendors are well known for the components that they may make and manufacturers confidently advertise to that effect. Refrigerator manufacturers often communicate to the customers that the fridge is fitted with Kirloskar compressor and is backed by replacement guarantee for five years. Diesel vehicle manufacturers take pride in the fact that their engines are fitted by Bosch fuel injection equipment.

Price

Purchasing companies want to be assured that the prices charged by the vendors are fair. Manufacturers would prefer to negotiate special prices for bulk purchases as lower the cost of components, better would be the profits. However, many buyers realize that the fair price is not always the lowest price, as the quality of materials and the process make price a secondary consideration. However, the purchasers do consider it important that the vendors must make a reasonable profit and sufficient return on their capital investments in order to maintain their production facilities and quality standards. Purchasers also wish that vendors should cooperate in working out a cost analysis to arrive at a fair price, fair to both buyers and vendors.

Delivery

To keep their assembly lines running continuously, the buyer companies have to maintain certain levels of inventories. Depending on the process of manufacturing, the nature of the product, and the supply pattern of their vendors, the manufacturers maintain certain levels of inventories in their plants. But the good business sense denotes that minimum levels of inventories of the components and parts, means savings on interest costs. Higher inventories mean more money blocked, and money costs money. One of the reasons the Japanese keep their cost low and profits high enough, is the adaptation of the concept of *Kanban* or 'Just-in-Time' inventory levels (See Exhibit 13.2).

But this involves a high dependence on vendors who should deliver components religiously as per agreed schedules. Therefore, it is but expected of the vendors that they should strictly follow delivery schedules, and neither overload or starve the buyers of the crucial components and materials. Also, for this very reason, several buyers prefer vendors located in the vicinity of their plants.

Service

Besides the efficient servicing of the manufacturers in terms of prompt responses to their needs, problems, and complaints, the vendors should be proficient enough to provide after-sale-service to the end customers of the buyers. For instance, many spare parts that run into some problem during the warranty period of a machine, are referred to the vendors for making adjustments. The engine manufacturer for a car should be responsible enough to take care of the machine in case customers complain about its malfunctioning, etc. It is only expected of the vendors to participate in manufacturers' customer service campaigns to redress and rectify product problems without much delay to safeguard mutual reputation in the market.

Reliability and Responsibility

Manufacturers want the vendors to be a reliable and responsible source of materials and components. Manufacturing and marketing is a serious business

---

EXHIBIT 13.2   *Kanban* or 'Just-in-Time' (JIT) inventory system

'Traditionally, operations managers set inventory levels by using formulae that balance the average fixed costs of "buying" raw materials with the variable cost of storing them. In the mid-1970s, though, the world took notice of the Japanese *Kanban*, or **Just-in-Time (JIT) inventory system.** *Kanban* strives toward an ideal state in which production quantities are equal to delivery quantities. This minimizes carrying costs, the expense of storing, and moving inventories from storage to the production floor. Materials are bought more frequently and in smaller amounts, "Just-in-Time" to be used, and finished goods are produced and delivered "just in time" to be sold. At one time, an automaker would order a truckload of spark plugs to be delivered within a two-or-three-day window. Now that same firm will order a one-quarter load to be delivered within a 2-to-3-hour window. The Nissan plan in Smyrna, Tennessee, allows trucks a 1-hour window for delivery. In place of a warehouse, it uses a few trailers across the street from the plant for temporary storage. Trucks are loaded in order of need, with a forklift coming directly from the assembly line to pick up the parts.'

Source: Stoner et al. (2002).

and inter-dependence is the essence of this relationship. Buyer companies rely heavily on the continuous association in the mutual interest. Whereas the buyers commit themselves to certain schedules and terms and conditions of the contract, at the same time it is expected of the vendors to be equally committed in their obligations to the buyers. Any failure on the part of a vendor can mean a disastrous and emergent situation that can create panic and crisis in the materials management divisions of the manufacturing companies. Therefore, reliability and responsibility is the basis of this relationship.

While the purpose of drawing a comparison of expectations from each other is not to arrive at any conclusion as to who has greater expectations, but to bring out one fact that the buyer–vendor relationship is that of complementing each other's efforts towards a mutual goal of making the business more profitable in the short and long run. A look at the comparative expectations should clarify the concept (See Exhibit 13.3).

VENDOR RELATIONS OBJECTIVES

Since vendors are a valuable public for an organization, certain large companies assign some of the responsibilities for supporting the vendor relations programme to the PR division. Although various levels of employees are also involved in the operation starting from the purchase manager to ordering, receiving, inspection, production, and engineering, etc., yet a specific responsibility of cultivating and monitoring good relations with the vendors is a vital area of operation for PR practitioners.

Organizations, where the purchase function is administered by the purchase committee, public relations works as a part of the committee in an advisory and executive role. As PR practitioners represent the finer side of the organization, they take on themselves the role of a moderator and monitor. In this context, PR has some objectives to keep up the vendor relations going well:

EXHIBIT 13.3 Vendor–buyer expectations

Vendors	Buyers
Fair return on investment	Quality
Regular business	Price
Growth prospects	Delivery
Fair dealings	Service
Financing	Reliability and responsibility
Vendor development	
Technology transfer	
Transparency	
Pride of association	

- Monitor vendors' opinions about the company's policies and practices.
- Project and establish the company as a vendor friendly organization, genuinely interested in the mutual understanding and cooperation to keep the supply system going harmoniously.
- Ensure a humane and friendly relationship with vendors and their representatives in terms of fair and good demeanour.
- Promote mutuality and maturity of interest between the company and the vendors.
- Communicate to the vendors to demonstrate to them the latest technical information to improve their operations, enhance quality and productivity, and improve profit.
- Transmit suggestions and techniques to the purchasing personnel about good human relations, and management practices in the operational areas like inspection, receiving, accounting, payment systems, etc.
- Generate an overall atmosphere of cordiality and integration.

PUBLIC RELATIONS FOR VENDORS

The success of any PR programme for vendors depends on the formation of a company policy, which serves as a foundation stone for the effort. A buyer company draws up a vendor's policy in clear terms for the understanding and compliance of those engaged in dealing with vendors. Good relations with vendors depend on a sound and ethical buying policy and purchasing practice. Such a policy should define the roles and responsibilities of the buyers' and suppliers' representatives.

Purchasing Policy

The purchasing policy of the company should give fair and impartial consideration to any reliable vendor, big or small, who is competent to produce the material being purchased; buy on merits without indulging in favouritism but adjudge every vendor on the basis of fair price for the material of right quality and quantity and delivery at the right time; make purchases competitively wherever and whenever possible; develop multiple sources of supply for each important component; avoid placing large orders on a single vendor and thus, not become dependent solely on one vendor; give courteous and prompt reception to sales representatives; keep quotations and other private information confidential; and never accept gifts of any value whatsoever, directly or indirectly, from suppliers.

An ethical policy once frozen by the organization should set the tone and tenor for the PR involvement in the buyer–vendor relations. Since public relations is the custodian of the good name of the organization, it can actively get involved in the formation and furtherance of the policy in the organizational interest. Once the organization is known for its ethical philosophy, the vendors will be able to repose their confidence and trust in the company and do business without any kink in their dealings with the staff involved in purchasing, receiving, inspection, accounting, payment, engineering, etc.

PUBLIC RELATIONS ROLE

PR can coordinate in the efforts of the buyer organization in fostering confidence and trust amongst the vendors in two ways. In other words, the communication process to ensure a cordial and congenial environment can be designed and executed on two fronts, internal and external.

Internal Communications

To moderate the general tendency amongst the purchase related personnel to act with arrogance towards vendors can be subdued with a well developed communication programme. The behaviour of bossing over the vendors shakes vendors' confidence and stands in their way to act as active partners in the enterprise. Therefore, to curb this tendency, communication and training of the staff can go a long way to foster a cordial, mutually profitable, and satisfactory relationship. The right attitude generates right response, so essential for the partnership relationship to grow and prosper.

PR should coordinate and assist the purchasing division in developing training modules to address areas like effective interpersonal relations with the vendors, system to collect the necessary feedback about vendor's attitudes and opinions about the company, through interview and group discussion techniques. Certain booklets, handouts about the components needed, purchase policy, etc. should be developed to enhance the comfort level of vendors.

Since most of purchasing is production related and attached to the manufacturing plants, the ambiance and house keeping of the reception areas takes a back seat, which is quite irksome for the visiting representatives of the vendors. PR should get involved in improving the ambiance to see that such areas are receptive and in keeping with the overall image of the company in terms of proper air conditioning, cleanliness, and a friendly receptionist ready to assist and extend basic courtesies to the visitors. This sets the right tone to the buyer–vendor interactions.

External Communications

External communications take place with vendors, generally in two ways: Face-to-face interactions and non-personal communications, through printed or electronic mediums.

Face-to-face interactions

The miracle of meeting people face-to-face, to resolve problems and developing a lasting understanding, can hardly be exaggerated. Despite several modern means of communicating, face-to-face communication remains most effective.

Vendors' sales calls   A face-to-face interaction with the vendors or their sales representatives, is crucial. It is an opportunity for both vendors and buyers to collect information sensitive to their business. A cordial exchange during such calls is a stepping stone to good vendor–buyer relationship.

Group meetings   Buyer companies organize periodic meetings with vendors to exchange information and ideas which are mutually beneficial. The discussions may centre around quality, new product designs, deliveries, or some education or motivation for vendors. Generally presided over by the purchase director and attended by the staff involved in purchasing process, PR forms an important part of such meetings and may often be asked to address such groups, besides providing the logistics support like setting up the venue, preparing speeches and presentations, and recording proceedings for future reference.

Plant visits   Vendors are often invited to visit the manufacturing plants to familiarize them with the processes. This is a good opportunity for vendors to see their own components being put to use and also suggest ways and means to save cost, and quality improvement of methods and materials. Such interactions generate better understanding and meaningful relationships.

Vendors conference   Several manufacturing companies organize an annual vendors conference. Such conferences are addressed by the chairman and other directors of the company to unfold progress reports, future plans, and the co-operation expected from the vendors. The question–answer sessions particularly help both parties to voice out ideas and learn from each other. Manufacturers use such occasions to gain commitment from several of the vendors about price, delivery, quality, etc. Also displayed on the sidelines are the new parts and components that the purchaser company plans to buy and also identify vendors who can make and supply such parts to the company. Vendors are treated well with warm hospitality. Eicher Tractors and Escorts have been organizing such conferences to generate goodwill and strengthen vendor relations. Public relations provides all the backup support in terms of logistics, speeches, preparation, presentation, and organize publicity for the event.

Field inspection visits Large manufacturing companies, who buy thousands of components and materials, have vendors who are located at the far-flung locations in the country. Therefore, in addition to the visits by purchase managers, field inspection officials frequently visit such vendors to follow up their production programmes and expedite timely supplies to the company's manufacturing plants. Such network plays an important role in face-to-face communications with vendors and keep them interested in business. Tata trucks follows the system of running the operation with the help of field representatives who travel to vendors' work places to prompt the flow of materials to Tata's manufacturing operations.

Non-personal communications

With the active support of PR department, buyer companies use non-personal communications to keep the vendors updated, which is of vital importance in keeping vendors' interest alive. Some such means and tools of communication include: *literature, vendors' journal, annual report, electronic media, advertising and publicity, correspondence,* and *awards and rewards.*

Literature To facilitate vendors better understanding of the company's products, policies, practices, and organizational structure, relevant literature in the form of booklets, etc. is produced and circulated to the vendors. Such literature highlights the salient features of the components, their position of fitment in the final product, precautions to be taken for avoiding problems concerning quality, etc.

Vendors' journal Companies with large networks of vendors publish journals with a special focus on vendors and business related activities. PR edits such as publications, generally at quarterly periodicity, highlighting purchase related news and views, feature stories about some outstanding vendors, new products and processes, policies and systems. Such journals are aimed at integrating the vendors with the company for a long-term and loyal relationship.

Annual report A company's annual report is once in a year effort to showcase its achievements and financial results in which vendors, like all other publics are interested. More often many vendors are also the shareholders of the company and would get a copy of the annual report in the normal course. However, it is good public relations to share the copy of the annual report with vendors to communicate the feeling of partnership with the company. Besides the financial information, the report also highlights many interesting and sensitive information of vendor's interest and help them to generate ideas that can be mutually beneficial for the company and the vendors themselves.

Electronic media A variety of electronic media like VCDs and DVDs containing information about products, manufacturing process, policy, and procedures and even filmed success stories are either circulated to the vendors or played at the various group meetings or training programmes for the vendors. Sometimes the recordings of various vendors, meetings are also circulated for vendors to see and take certain actions demonstrated in these recorded presentations. To instill pride of association, companies distribute some publicity films to reinforce vendors' faith and pride in the company.

Advertising and publicity   To provide sufficient morale boosting for the vendors and earn due publicity for the organization, manufacturers resort to advertising or distributing vendors' success stories to the media, as a vendor's success means the success of the buyer organization.

Correspondence   The powerful medium of communication to the vendors is the exchange of correspondence between the buyers and vendors. When handled thoughtfully and creatively, it goes a long way to cut through the confusions and promote understanding. PR often assists in developing certain circulars to the dealers and even special letters on certain issues concerning the company and the vendors.

Awards and rewards   To recognize the outstanding services and performance of certain vendors, an awards and rewards programme is designed by the buyers. For instance, the 'top five vendors of the month' could be one event by which vendors can be inspired to compete for. The winners' photographs, when adorn the walls of the purchase division, can work wonders in the process of morale building amongst vendors.

Summary

Vendors and buyers are an integral part of an industrial organization. All manufacturers, big and small, depend on vendors for supply of components and materials to keep their production line running. Good and effective vendors are sought after by all buying organizations.

Also the traders running retail stores and gigantic shopping malls depend on vendors for continuous supply of merchandize. Reliance Fresh, Big Apple, or Subhiksha are no exception.

Vendors, who are like ancillary units of the manufacturers, have certain expectations from the buyer companies, like reasonable return on their investment, regular business, growth prospects, fair dealings, financing, technology transfer, transparency, and pride of association.

The buyer organizations also expect from vendor's good quality components and materials, fair price, on time delivery, service, and reliability and responsibility, etc.

Vendor relations programme of an organization has certain public relations objectives like monitoring the opinions and attitudes of the vendors. Public relations efforts also aim to instill amongst vendors the pride of association and loyalty. The companies undertake training of vendors to generate mutuality of interest and create a climate of cordiality and congeniality.

Good vendor relations depend basically on the well-heeled purchasing policy and efficacy of communication system. The communication system planned and run by public relations department adopts two ways to communicate, first internal communications, that is, communicating to the staff involved in dealing with vendors, and the second system has the focus on vendors.

External communications adopt two ways of spreading the necessary information, face-to-face interactions, in the form of one-to-one meetings, group discussions, and vendor conferences. The print and electronic media are also adopted to spread the messages. The use of booklet, literature, vendor's journal, annual report, electronics tools like VCDs and DVDs, correspondence, and awards and rewards, etc., play the necessary communication role.

The very foundation of the good vendor relations is the philosophy of inter-dependence and partnership in growth, fostered by a clearly spelled out purchasing policy and free flow of two-way communication between the manufacturing company and the vendors.

Key Terms

Ancillary unit   A small scale unit supporting the major industry

Intellectual property   Documented or undocumented knowledge, creative ideas, or expressions of human mind that have commercial (monetary) value and are protectable under copyright, patent, servicemark, trademark, or trade secret laws from imitation, infringement, and dilution

Kanban   A Japanese concept of Just-in-Time inventory system to save cost of warehousing inventories of parts and components and indenting the material on 1–2 hour window span

Outsourcing   Contracting, sub-contracting, or 'externalizing' non-core activities to free up cash, personnel, time, and facilities for activities where the firm holds competitive advantage

Production capacity   Volume of products that can be generated by a production plant or enterprise in a given period by using current resources

Sales call   Usually pre-arranged and face-to-face meeting between a salesperson and a customer or prospect for the purpose of generating a sale

Soft loan   Financing that offers flexible or lenient terms for repayment, usually at lower than market interest rates

Technology transfer   The transfer of knowledge generated and developed in one place to another, where it is used to achieve some practical end

Vendor   Supplier of components or parts to another company

Concept Review Questions

1.   What is the 'partnership in progress' role relationship between vendors and the buyer organizations? In today's assembly line production system, can any manufacturer succeed in producing products without the support of vendors? Explain.

2. What are the hopes and expectations that the vendors and purchasers have from each other? Draw up a comparison of such expectations to clarify your understanding of this relationship, which both parties have obligations to fulfil.

3. Enlist and explain the objectives that public relations have to make the vendor–buyer relations successful in the mutual interest of vendors and buyers. What are the various communication systems and steps that public relations plans and executes to foster this relationship?

Project Work

1. Conduct a survey of 15 Maruti vendors of the opinions and expectations from their principals. Draw up your recommendations as to how the vendor–buyer relationship could be further improved.

2. Visit a retail store, say Reliance Fresh and identify at least 25 vendors of fast selling items. Draw up a list of estimated figures of unit and currency sales to assess the role vendors play in the success of this retail store.

3. Look at the Hero Honda motor cycle and list about dozen important components and their maker's brands. Also list the service policy of the vendors of these parts towards the end use consumers.

4. Obtain the purchase policy of the LG Electronics and write a review on it from the view point of vendors.

Case Study

Asahi India Safety Glass Limited

Maruti Udyog, on its entry into the Indian market, started identifying some reliable vendors for various components and parts to be used in their Maruti Suzuki car. Traditionally, Japanese being highly quality minded, were concerned about the availability of vendors who were equipped or competent enough to conform to their quality standards. It took the company quite some time and effort to complete the exercise.

Procurement of safety glass to be fitted on to the car was one area of concern. The management brain stormed the problem and arrived at a decision to prompt Japanese Asahi Safety Glass to form a company in India in collaboration with Indian partners. Thus was born Asahi India Safety Glass Limited, one of Maruti's principal suppliers and a product of their vendor development programme. This is a good example of a vendor with the foresight and courage to not only acquire new technology but adopt practices that their principals, Maruti Udyog, had experienced.

The Indian promoters of Asahi India are the Labroo group, an industrial family of repute. Their worldwide search for a dependable, technically advanced, and committed collaborator ended with Asahi Glass Company of Japan, which is the first and the oldest glass manufacturer in that country. It is also one of the best chemical companies in the world with diversified product fields and the largest manufacturer of glass, chemicals, and ceramics. More importantly, for the Indian entrepreneur, Asahi is also the largest manufacturer of automotive safety glass with a world market share of more than 20 per cent and a share of the Japanese market of about 60 per cent. In Asahi, the Labroo found a partner, who not only had the latest technology but was willing to offer equity as well as hands-on manufacturing and technical assistance. As such a company was formed with equity participation, as the following:

(a) Maruti Udyog Limited	12 per cent
(b) Asahi Glass Co. Ltd, Japan	12 per cent
(c) Indo Asahi Glass Co. Ltd	12 per cent
(d) Shri B M Labroo and Associates	12 per cent
(e) Public	40 per cent

Asahi Glass has provided technical know-how, documentation, technical assistance, and back-up information for commercial production and it has also deputed its technicians for installing, commissioning, and running of the plant. It has also trained Indian technicians in Japan and India. Initially, an experienced Japanese executive, Mr Motoyasu Shimanaya from Asahi Glass, was appointed as managing director.

The Maruti involvement, the tie-up with Asahi Glass, the decision to have a Japanese managing director in the initial years, all combined to start this young company with 210 employees (average age, like Maruti, below 30), a typical Japanese-style.

The overall results of the company have been encouraging. It was set up within a very brief period of twelve months after foreign collaboration was approved by the government. Within three years of commencement of production, it has already doubled its capacity. The company conducted its production programme in accordance with the Japan Automobile Standards Organization (JASO) and Japan Industrial Standards (JIS) specifications.

In the real Japanese traditions, the organization put enormous emphasis on meeting quality standards and it has successfully inculcated in the employees a very high degree of quality consciousness.

Plant and equipment and manufacturing methods have been selected as per the advice of the Japanese collaborators. Asahi experts have guided and trained workers and supervisors during the production startup phase till quality had established.

The raw material is brought in from Indonesia, conforming to Asahi specifications. Each element of the work in the factory has been planned in great detail. Every process has been designed so that the work is completed to the prescribed standards. Quality inspection procedure and equipment have been provided at various stages of the production process.

Asahi India Safety Glass today reflects the standards and quality levels of its Japanese collaborators in machinery, work practices, and product sophistication. This fact has been established by the company's being rated as the leading supplier by Maruti Udyog on quality, delivery, stocks, packing, and after-sales service. The company is now not only the sole supplier to Maruti Udyog for tempered safety glass but also supply to DCM Toyota Ltd and Swaraj Mazda for the light commercial vehicles.

Discussion questions

1. Identifying and developing efficient and reliable vendors is a very tedious effort. Do you agree? What are the factors that should be considered by a manufactuer while getting associated with a vendor?
2. Draw up a picture of the efforts Maruti Udyog made while they started the production of their first car in India, with a special reference to sourcing parts and materials from the Indian vendors?

References

Chatterjee, Bhaskar (1990), *Japanese Management, Maruti and the Indian Experience*, Sterling Publishers Private Limited, New Delhi, pp. 65–67.

Moore, H. Frazier and Frank B. Kalupa (2005), *Public Relations, Principles, Cases and Problems*, Richard D. Irwin, Inc, USA, reprinted in India by Surjeet Publications, Delhi.

Hindustan Times, New Delhi, 27 June 2008, p. 8.

Stoner, James A.F., R. Edward Freeman, and Daniel R. Gilbert, Jr (2002), *Management*, 6th edition, Prentice-Hall of India Private Limited, New Delhi, p. 600.

14 Employee Public Relations

EMPLOYEE PUBLIC RELATIONS

The success or failure of an organization largely depends on the mindset of its employees. The managements have objectives to operate with maximum efficiency, run the manufacturing plants fullest to capacity, reduce overheads, make sufficient profits, and create reserves for growth and progress. All this depends on the efficiency of all those who work in an organization, called the internal publics or the employees. The real producers of the wealth in any economy are the workers, technicians, and engineers involved in the production of a company's products.

Employees' involvement and understanding are two key factors to the achievement of corporate goals. Therefore, the challenge of public relations lies in managing the internal communications, which has three primary objectives—to inform, to motivate, and to develop a spirit of openness amongst the employees, their family members, and others associated with the organization. 'Seen in their proper roles, employees make up an organization's most important publics. Constructive, mutually beneficial relationships with these publics is the first job of the PR function,' wrote Scott M. Cutlip, Allen H. Center, and Glen M. Broom (1985).

Employees' zeal, devotion, and loyalty towards the company, can be achieved by a well planned PR effort that aims at developing a well-informed, rather, correctly informed, internal publics. Humans, men and women, are not lifeless, emotionless robots, who will work when commanded and powered, as desired and designed, but are people made of flesh and blood who carry emotions and dreams about their future and their families. Besides the wages they draw from a company, employees have certain needs and aspirations. That is why, humans have to be cared for differently.

Inspired by this very philosophy, Henry Ford, the founder of the Ford Motor Company, USA, rightly visualized ideology when he said, 'Why is it that I always get a whole person when what I really want is a pair of hands?' Better known in the world as America's pioneer car maker, Ford introduced some path breaking systems in his factory in Detroit city, which initially made him unpopular but eventually a hero.

In the teeth of opposition from the fellow industrialists of his time, Henry Ford introduced the highest wage rate, popularly known as $2.14 an hour, when the prevailing rate was less than a dollar. He announced it vehemently, when other entrepreneurs accused him of ruining them.

His thoughts about good employee relations inspired him to think beyond the production of a car in America, that changed the human relations scenario in the American industry. He introduced a few unique measures in his factory, which the whole world practices today—eight hours shift, a lunch break, and two tea breaks, with Sunday as a holiday. The news about these robust employee benefits spread like wildfire amongst the American workforce. The job seekers flocked to Detroit city to seek jobs in Ford factory. So much so that this human surge is often likened to the famous gold rush in the American history.

Public relations pioneer Frank Jefkin (2006), emphasizing the importance of human relations, wrote, 'Employee relations is a planned and sustained effort for establishing goodwill and initial understanding between an organization and its employees for the purpose of maximizing his contribution towards the health of the organization.'

This very ideology of employee relations has now been adopted by many successful corporations of the world. Roger B. Smith (1983), Chairman, General Motors, in his messages to the managers, wrote, 'The need for employee understanding, involvement, and cooperation has never been greater and a broad base of information about the business is fundamental to the achievement of all these goals. More than that, GM has an obligation to keep its employees informed about important matters that affect the business and their own livelihood.'

The founding fathers of several multi-national corporations in the world have realized that the best machinery, best material, and abundance of cash resources in the company will not matter, if the employees are not skilled enough and informed enough to make an organization a success. The fact that well informed employees perform better, is now a well accepted philosophy with many professionally managed and successful companies.

Paul Litchfield, the then CEO of Goodyear International Corporation, wrote an editorial in the inaugural issue of the company house journal, the *Wingfoot Clan* published on 1 June 1912, 'We wish to make conditions in this factory as near right as possible, to make it a desirable place to work, to make each employee feel that he can get as high or higher reward for his services here as they will get elsewhere, and we wish the cooperation of each employee to help carry out this programme.'

Now 'Employees are our best asset' is a dictum carved in golden letters and displayed right in the visitor's areas, is conspicuous of the philosophy that the century old Goodyear Corporation shows off to the visitors and particularly all those who work in the company. This one message connotes that the company values its employees, now termed as associates, as much as it values the other assets of business machinery, money, materials, and of course, manpower.

The basis of good employee relations is the free flow of communications from the management to the employees and vice versa. The relationship is a two-way traffic, which assumes a significant importance in the smooth and efficient running of an organization. Emphasizing the important role played by the employee communications, E.J. Thomas, former president of the Goodyear International Corporation commented (1921), 'If I were asked to define effective communication, I would begin by saying what it is not. It is not propaganda. It is not distorting facts to fit a company's policy. It is not an off-and-on device which is used to brainwash employees or mislead people.'

In other words, employee communication is not an off-and-on system, but a planned and sustained effort by an organization. It does not mean that a company should start communication when it needs to or when it suits, but have to plan this activity on a perennial basis. PR practitioners understand the concept of two-way communications and also understand its relevance in the area of employee relations. The employees are also termed as 'captive audience' as they are readily available for communicating and getting feedback and reactions. Unlike the customers who are scattered everywhere, PR is faced with the challenge to witness almost spontaneous actions and reactions to various communications floated by the company, as employees are concentrated at one location. Therefore, a planned and sustained communication programme run meticulously, yields high dividends.

The fruitful mutual relationship of employees and managements becomes meaningful when the expectations of both parties are well understood by the management as well as the employees. No management can afford to ignore the aspirations, aptitudes, and preferences expressed by its employees. It has much to gain from a satisfied workforce, working at jobs best suited to them. The successful managements recognize that they have some obligation to perform, some social or economic functions. The managements can respond to this challenge by establishing a harmonious climate within the company. The total PR programme should focus on the people, who work for the organizational success.

EMPLOYEE EXPECTATIONS

Knowing employee expectations by any management is basic to understanding the mindset of the employees. As humans, they have their needs, wants, hopes, and desires relating to their personal progress and family welfare. Obviously, it becomes essential for a public relations practitioner to have a good feel of the pulse, before planning and launching upon a communication programme. The expectations the employees generally have are: *better wages, bonus/incentives, safety from injury/accidents, job security, welfare of self and family, career growth, social status,* and *participation in the management process.*

Better Wages

Invariably, all employees irrespective of their position or rank would like to improve their incomes, so that they and their families can enjoy better quality of life, better standards of living and afford many things like better clothes, better homes, better education for children, etc. Although most of the jobs, in addition to wages, carry some benefits and perquisites, yet the size of the pay packet apparently has greater attraction. Many employees and unions appear to be negotiating hard with their managements for the enhancement of the pay packets. Therefore, several organizations keep their focus on protecting pay packets in terms of regular increments and incentives.

Bonus/Incentives

If a company makes profits, the employees naturally have an expectation to have their share. Profit bonus is like cream on top of the cake and everyone loves it. At the end of each year, the expectations rise high, and employees and their unions start feverishly working for maximum profit bonus. Although the Indian Bonus Act provides for a payment of minimum of 8.33 per cent of the wages to the employees as profit bonus, yet the expectations always soar high every year. More often bonus becomes a major issue that threatens the industrial peace. Employee unions love to make it an important item on their agenda for contract negotiations.

Incentives, in the shape of production bonus, have been introduced by several manufacturing companies to induce and prompt employees for higher production. The incentives are paid over and above the minimum production expected of a worker on daily basis.

Several diverse opinions have been expressed for and against the incentive system. Some take it as a legitimate way of motivating workers to produce more whereas, to some, the system suffers from the demerits of that proverbial 'carrot and stick' formula, that is, habit forming and kills the initiative amongst workers to work in the normal course of their assigned duties. Yet, the fact remains that nothing is free in this world. The American dictum that 'If you want more, pay more' should make sense.

Safety from Injury/Accidents

Manufacturing facilities world over, howsoever well designed and laid out, yet suffer from fear of employees getting hurt either due to their own negligence or because of the hazardous working conditions. But the fact remains that nobody wants to get hurt or involved in an accident. It helps none, neither the employee nor the management.

An employee when hurt, may get hospitalized or confined and loses earnings due to absence from work. The management also suffers in terms of loss of a skilled and experienced hand, which hurts productivity as well as the quality of products, as their inexperienced replacement may not be able to perform at the same level of efficiency. The company may also have to spend valuable time and money on training the replaced employee.

Unfortunately, millions of man days are lost due to industrial accidents, which sometimes result in loss of life and limbs. The Indian Workmen's Compensation Act is fine, but the loss of a human life is always irreparable. Realizing the value of human life, many multinational companies consider safety as the number one indicator to determine the smooth functioning of their organizations.

Job Security

Security of job in the Indian context is considered a valuable criterion for the workforce. The risk or uncertainty about the continuity of job is a matter of concern of many employees. As the future of their families is linked to the job, it is but their expectation that they should have a secure job. In most of the cases, the job of an employee is the only source of income and sustenance. Therefore, there is a strong desire amongst employees for job security. That is, perhaps, one reason that many prefer a government job on lower wages than the private ones, as the government jobs carry a high degree of assurance about the continuity of employment. Unlike in the US, where 'hire and fire' is an accepted norm, the Indian scene is entirely the opposite.

Welfare for Self and Family

Men do not live by bread alone. They have needs and desires beyond the two square meals a day. Employees have an expectation that the employers should adopt certain policies and practices in terms of welfare measures for the employees and their families. Rest and recreation, health care, education for children, grants and scholarships, holidays and housing, and several other benefits should be available, so that the employees can put their mind, body, and soul into their jobs. Once these measures are adopted by the organization, there is no reason for the employees not to be loyal to the company and put in their best efforts to perform at an optimum level.

Career Growth

Stagnation is the worst enemy of employee morale. No one wants to remain in the position at which they joined the organization, but make a steady progress to improve their rank. A most ordinary production worker also has dreams that with the passage of time and of gaining more job experience, they would be a supervisor and even a manager, one day. Naturally, a well planned career path, the one understood by an employee improves their motivation level to strive harder to achieve more in their career. Organizations, with well heeled personnel policies, carve a career path for each employee and extend a fair chance to them to make progress.

Social Status

'Man is known by the company he keeps,' goes the old adage. Employees, in their communities, are known by the job status they have in their respective organizations. The positions or designations that fit well into the perception of neighbours and friends, matter, as they extend their responses as per the job titles of the employees. Employees also take a lot of pride in the status they have in their company. People's social success depends on the acceptability they enjoy amongst their community members, and it strongly reflects in the relationships that they enjoy amongst people in the society. More often a poor title gets them poor relations and vice versa. In India particularly, the designations invoke good, bad, and indifferent responses. Hitherto fore, a janitor known as *Bhangi* suffered from the stigma of a menial scavenger. Rightly so, the municipalities were asked to designate them as *safai karamchari* (See an interesting story in Exhibit 14.1).

EXHIBIT 14.1 The master mechanic

CHARAN Singh (CS) was a cycle mechanic who repaired cycles and tri-cycles of the American households. He was a good mechanic and with his friendly nature could be called a great 'people's man'.

Dick, the American executive of a chemical plant, one day, offered him a mechanic's job with a good salary, which CS readily grabbed. His new job, in a well-known company, won him a place in his small community and also a wife from a good family.

CS worked hard and soon became a supervisor. Bosses, who came and went, were happy with him that won him promotions and money. On his transfer, his American boss, recommended him as his successor as the 'master mechanic'. His 23 years working in that jungle of machines, had made him touch every nut and bolt. Sitting in his swivel chair, he could now close his eyes, and devise 'fixes' for troubles and breakdowns.

On the home front, he had a happy family of two daughters and a son. Neha, his daughter passed her graduation, year before last and was looking forward to get married.

In India, marriages are not made in heaven, but in the columns of a newspaper. Besides the bride's beauty, talents and education, what also counts, is the status of the father, mother and near relatives, termed as 'family status.'

It just so happened, that a couple of proposals fell through CS's fingers, just because, the boy's parents seem to say: How can we marry our son to a mechanic's daughter?'

So now CS tried hard to persuade his boss to change his title of 'master mechanic' to chief engineer, which he virtually was. 'It does not fit into the American management system,' his boss argued,

adding, 'CS! Our top cop is called "head constable" and still remains the chief. What is the problem? I don't get it. It would make sense, if you had asked for a raise.'

CS enjoyed high respect and reputation in the corporation, world wide, as the master mechanic and even travelled abroad to attend conferences. The company did not want to lose him.

That morning, with a paper in his hand, he came to see the boss. He looked tense. 'Today I want a decision. I am chief engineer, or I quit,' he said firmly, as his boss greeted him.

John, who often consulted me on Indian affairs, came and asked me: 'Hey! what is this all about?'

'CS has a problem.' I told John. 'In India, titles count, many times, more than money. So let's make an exception.' I advised.

'But then there will be a flood of such requests, "compounder" to "chemist", "supervisor" to "engineer", "specification clerk" to "technical executive" and even a "janitor" to "sanitary officer",' said John agitatedly.

'Look, if you want to keep CS, you may have to do it,' I said soberly.

John shrugged his shoulders, dismayed, and left.

That night John called the American headquarters and argued it with his bosses.

Next day there was a letter on the plant notice board which read:

'CS is appointed chief engineer with immediate effect.' Congratulatory greetings flowed to CS's from all corners. His wish was granted.

A few months later, I received an invitation to the wedding of Neha. Neha was getting married to a boy of CS choice. Yes, the 'master mechanic' had fixed it.

Source: Adapted from Sachdeva, Iqbal, *The Observer of Business and Politics*, 21 August 2000.

Participation in Management Process

After working for a number of years in a company and on a particular job, employees become experts and specialists in that area and are often proud of their expertise. Enlightened organizations do recognize this fact. Employees with rich work experience hate to be treated as robots or mere bodies who take orders from their seniors. They want to be consulted on matters concerning production, quality, cost savings, etc. so that they can proudly contribute to the business growth of the organization. Besides money, they are inspired by certain personality needs to show that they know. Professional organizations take good advantage of this pool of talents to solve or simplify problems, save expenses and provide rich motivation of their employees. The employees' suggestion schemes run by some companies like Hero Honda, Escorts, Maruti, etc. which promise rewards, awards, and recognition for employees, have paid dividends. It may be interesting to see Exhibit 14.2., which is a suggestion scheme put forward for employees of Hero Honda.

Decidedly, encouraging employees to participate in the company's business affairs may yield some spectacular innovations that can change the face of the organization. There have been instances in the world where most ordinary employees make some suggestions, which helped the companies to grow and prosper. For instance, Cadbury's wafer chocolate was suggested by the company driver and not by any high profile research agency. But it is only appropriate that organizations should create an environment where people are encouraged to think out of the box and are allowed to 'speak out' their ideas. Conservative or traditional organizations may miss the bus. For many such innovations, contributed by employees, see Exhibit 14.3.

CHALLENGES OF EMPLOYEE COMMUNICATION

When it comes to sharing of the responsibility for employee relations or to the employee communications, both the public relations and the human resource department vie with each other in claiming it as a job function for each department. The fact of the matter is that when it is everybody's business, then it is nobody's business. Professionally, both the departments should perform

EXHIBIT 14.2   A suggestion scheme for employees of Hero Honda

सुझाव सुझाओ
नाम कमाओ, दाम कमाओ
HERO HONDA

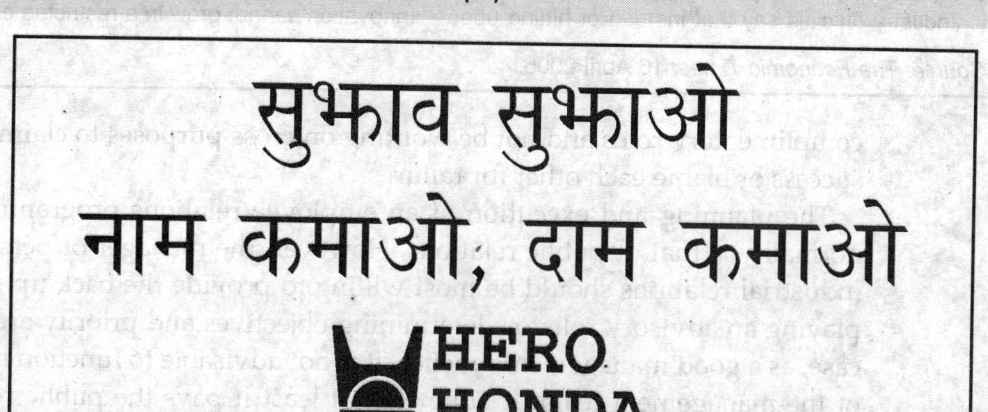

BYTES, a highly successful wafer chocolate innovation from Cadbury India, has a highly unusual origin. It was the brain child of a company driver, and not as may be supposed, the result of exhaustive customer research and development carried out by the company.

A scientist from Bangalore provided a solution to a problem facing Procter & Gamble (P&G), through Inno Centive, an online forum for a global community of 18,000 scientists. ITC's Kitchens of India was a suggestion from a master chef. The highly-successful mini-truck, Ace, from Tata Motors was designed by a team led by a younger engineer, which worked on the project and got it ready for production in just 42 months.

In a fiercely competitive marketplace, companies have begun encouraging unconventional and out-of-the-box thinking to generate innovations across products and services. Companies are not restricting innovation to R&D centres alone and are encouraging employees across functions to come up with viable plans.

'The stumbling block is what I call the not-invented-here (NIH) syndrome. If somebody comes up with a great idea but it is unacceptable because you haven't thought of it, business is bound to suffer. There is a lot of resistance to change in many companies, a mindset problem that hurts innovation. Innovation is not possible if one limits the scope of ideas to a limited few,' says ITC Foods CEO Ravi Naware.

Corporates are increasingly trying to generate innovative ideas that may not necessarily be a result of an expensive R&D process.

Industry officials say that instead of hitting upon an innovation through a strategic plan, it is often good enough to think like an ordinary consumer and come up with an equally implementable plan. Companies are setting up open forums where an employee can talk about ideas, be it a product or a cost-cutting move or any other corporate function.

Senior Cadbury India officials said that corporates would have to tap the collective innovation talent inside a company rather than isolating it to a particular department. Cadbury Bites today has even found acceptance in export markets such as Mexico and Japan.

LG India, for instance, has started a pizza lunch with MD where suggestions are taken from employees and viable ones implemented.

'Onida has always been able to come up with a product innovation different from the industry primarily because of this open innovation policy,' says Onida CMD Gulu Mirchandani. Keen to tap India's intellectual capital, technical, and scientific expertise more fully, P&G plans to collaborate with Indian individuals and companies to enhance its global R&D strength to help create and introduce new products more cost-effectively. Similarly, utility vehicle major Mahindra & Mahindra has the KC Design Mahindra contest to encourage innovation and design among students. Says Mahindra's ED Pawan Goenka, 'This contest is theme based and it gives inspiration to the company as well as the students.' Adds LG Electronics chief Y. Verma, 'As a company grows in size and complexity, it becomes essential to introduce a more formal process. At the same time, we certainly don't want to thwart free thinking and individuality of our team. Innovation cannot grow in a restricted environment.'

Source: The Economic Times, 16 April 2006.

---

complimentary roles and not be working on cross purposes to claim credit for success or blame each other for failures.

The planning and execution of an employee relations programme should normally be that of public relations. However, the manager of personnel and industrial relations should be most willing to provide the back up support in playing an advisory role for determining objectives and priority areas. In any case, as a good management practice, it is not advisable to function in isolation of the management team. If none else, at least it pays the public relations to keep in close touch with all sections of the management. Before launching upon any employees communication programme, the first and foremost step is to have a well spelled out employee relations policy, properly written and blessed by the top management. Once finalized, it is appropriate to function within the parameters of the policy, and keep the programme on track.

HR Policy Forms Basis

Moore and Kalupa (2005) wrote, 'The foundation of good employee relations is a good personnel policy that commits a corporation to providing regular work, good working conditions, fair compensation, opportunity for advancement, recognition for accomplishments, good supervision, opportunity for self expression, and desirable benefits to employees. Such a policy should express management's philosophy of providing satisfaction to employees, which induce them to give their maximum effort, skill, and loyalty to the corporation. Employees judge a company by its personnel policies and the practices of management in carrying out these policies. An employee relations programme cannot gain goodwill and understanding in a corporation that underpays, overworks, plays favourites and disregards the welfare of its employees. What is said to employees means nothing unless the words are supported by good personnel policy and management practices.'

Basic Conditions for Success

The major role of public relations function is to identify the goals of employee communication, and make endeavours to establish and maintain mutually beneficial relationships between the organization and the employees on whom depends its success.

Public relations should aim at establishing a mutual employee–employer understanding, and bear in mind some conditions that should ensure favourable reception to the employee relations programme as the following:

1. Should ensure mutual trust and confidence between the employees and the management.
2. Open and straightforward information should flow freely in all directions, upward, downward, and horizontally.
3. Communications should appeal to all ranks/positions and ensure larger participation.
4. Foster harmonious industrial relations and continuity of operations.
5. Ensure healthy and congenial environment.
6. Promote success and growth of the organization.
7. Spread good hope and optimistic feelings about the future.

What Ails the Employee Communication?

According to Harvard professor Daniel Quinn Mills (1983), there are six fundamental problems that come in the way of success of any employee communication programme. They are the following:

1. Management dictates to employees too much and listens too little.
2. Too little of what is communicated is understood.
3. Too much of the content is of concern to management, but not to workers.
4. Too much propaganda is communicated.
5. There is too little candour.
6. Communication bears too little relationship to the possibility of change.

All this boils down to one fact that most managements run the communications programmes, which are one-sided, that is, downward, from management to the employees. So naturally, the employees always seem to be asking, 'What is there in it for me?'; 'Where do I fit into the scheme of things?'; 'How can I attain my personal goals?'. If the communications can answer these kinds of questions, the messages will help reduce uncertainties, insecurity and foster job satisfaction amongst employees. The answer is the two-way communication, i.e. communicating and listening to the employee reactions (For kinds of communication, see Chapter 8).

Labour–Management Relations

Adversary relationship between the unions and the management is hard reality of industrial life. Today's corporations are industrial democracies where the employees legitimately and legally organize themselves into unions and speak about the policies and practices of the management in one voice. They would often threaten the company with a strike and bargain hard to get the best out of the managements. Though best run companies may feel proud of their deft handling of the labour relations, yet one time or the other, they may run into a situation where they are slapped with a labour strike or a lockout to face the challenge. Perhaps, only one company in India, that is, TATA, can take pride in the fact that they never faced a labour situation in the last 100 years.

However, the fact remains that it is the legitimate and legal right of the employees and their unions to raise their demands on the managements. As a part of the democratic process under India's labour laws, companies hold contract negotiations with the unions and sign agreements for three to five years to ensure industrial peace and harmony. This is a tough time for the managements. In such a situation, PR also has a role to communicate and explain issues to the employees to smoothen the way for final signing of the contract. Most often, it turns out to be a war of wits between unions and managements and the PR has to play a crucial role, through stepped up communications, in allaying fears and misgivings amongst employees, which the unions indulge in because of their typical style of functioning.

Problems Managements Face

Industry, everywhere in the world, is fraught with some common and chronic problems, which the managements spend lot of time and effort to keep under control. Perhaps there is not one single solution. It is like chronic infection in the human body which reappears after being suppressed with a course of antibiotics. However, public relations plays its own role to sensitize employees and generate responses that can reduce the intensity of the problems, which generally are, *productivity maximization, quality improvement, waste reduction, safety, banish absenteeism, loyalty, indiscipline, union pressures, etc.*

Productivity maximization

Maximizing production to meet or exceed the installed capacity of a plant is the number one priority with every manufacturing company. Despite best machinery and high technology, it is not possible until the men are inspired enough to make it happen. As higher productivity means higher sales and higher profits, motivating employees to put in their best and perform at optimum levels, is a major challenge for any industry.

Quality improvement

Higher production and poor quality is a self-defeating exercise. Prompted by a desire to earn maximum productivity incentive, employees are often tempted to devise some short cuts in the production process, hurting the quality standards. Sloppy work generates poor quality products resulting in high rejections and scrap. Sub-standard products also boomerang to the company in terms of customer complaints and higher product adjustments. All this means loss of money and market image.

Waste reduction

Some percentage of waste may normally result from the production process, but when the large quantities of material get scrapped beyond tolerance limits due to employees' apathy or carelessness, the problem takes serious proportions. The financial loss due to scrapped material contributes to the cost of manufacturing and squeeze on profit margins. If the manufacturer is forced to push up prices, it runs the risk of becoming uncompetitive in the market. Therefore, educating employees to keep waste under allowed limits is vital to cost saving.

Safety

No one wants to get hurt, as it brings pain, discomfort, and loss of wages to the employees. The companies lose skilled and experienced hands, which has a cascading effect on productivity, quality, and additional expense on training replacement employees. To avoid accidents and resultant problems, the message 'work alert, stay unhurt' needs to be inculcated amongst the employees.

Banish absenteeism

Traditionally in India, during the two harvesting seasons, the majority of labour force that hails from the neighbouring rural areas, would absent themselves from the jobs, as they have work to be done back home in their villages. This results in large scale absenteeism in industry. On certain days, the absenteeism percentage touches 35 per cent throwing operations out of gear. The industry resorts to hiring 'badli' workers to fill the gap, which means additional financial burden and sloppy work by untrained 'badli' workers. Millions of man days are lost every year in India due to this unplanned and unscheduled absence of employees resulting in a colossal loss of productivity for the nation.

Loyalty

Fostering loyalty amongst employees towards the company is a million dollar question. It is quite difficult to conclude that the best paid workers are the most loyal employees. Inculcating that sense of belonginness for the organization amongst the employees evades many employers. Loyalty is not for sale and cannot be purchased for a price. However, some successful companies can take a lot of pride in their loyal employees, because they have transformed their corporate culture in a way to generate a feeling that employees are partners or associates in their business.

Indiscipline

Several factors like lack of clear cut personnel policies, dilution of authority, discrimination, poor supervision, favouritism, and lack of information, can be root causes of indiscipline amongst employees. More the number of grievances, more intense is the problem. Lack of well planned communications and mismanagement can be major causes for indiscipline. The worst thing in the industrial scenario arises when employees behave arrogantly and indulge in disobedience and misbehaviour in general and towards their immediate supervisors, in particular. Subduing such tendencies is a serious challenge for an organization.

Union pressures

Experts have an opinion that a strong unified union is a blessing in disguise for the organization. Agreed that such unions are tough bargainers and make the management to yield to pressure, but the strong union with a good following of the employees can be a fairly good help to the organization in keeping up the agreed promises of enhanced productivity in return for higher benefits. Such a union can enforce discipline on the rank and file of the union and the employees at large. But dealing with unions is definitely something that many managers dread.

CHARACTERISTICS OF GOOD EMPLOYEE COMMUNICATION

Public relations professionals, to make a success of the employee communication, have to bear in mind some of the characteristics of good communication programme:

- Communication is a sophisticated discipline and should be handled with the same care and seriousness as the other elements of management like money, materials, machinery, and, of course, manpower.
- Management should be genuinely interested and willing to share information with the employees.
- All levels of managers should consider communications as their focused responsibility as a part of the annual appraisal system.
- Employee communication should be a continuous process rather than an off and on system.
- Enough written communication should be transmitted to take care of confusion, if any.
- Messages should be dressed up in the idiom that employees understand and should be carved out of their common parlance.
- No politics please. Communications should not be master minded to mislead employees, but should be actual and factual.
- Messages should be relayed timely as delay may cause doubts and misunderstanding amongst employees.
- To reinforce ideas, the messages should be repeated in various versions and media.
- Public relations practitioners, as specialists in communication, should play their crucial role to ensure clarity and creativity for effectiveness of the messages.

The internal PR can draw a parallel to an organization's communications to its sales force, only the players change. The main players in the production area are the supervisors of all ranks compared to members of the sales force. The purpose is to make the ideas and the company acceptable to the employees. So the PR practitioners while functioning in this area may act like communication salesmen, marketing the organization to the employees for right perception and right responses.

COMMUNICATION MEDIA

'The organization needs a framework of well planned and implemented communication programmes, using a variety of media, to meet employees' basic information needs, and to facilitate the upward flow of information and ideas,' wrote Richard Bevan and John N. Bailey (1992).

The selection of media for communicating to the employees offers a wide range from spoken word, print, visual to electronics media, etc. Factors like objectives, urgency, audience, message elements, and environment all govern the choice. PR professionals with their specialization in communication make sagacious choices to suit the objectives and timeframe for the transmission of a particular kind of information.

Amongst the several media used for communicating to the employees are: *employee publication, news bulletins, management newsletter, direct mail letters to employees homes, inserts in pay packets, booklets, posters, electronic neons, e-mails, speeches by company officials, communicating through supervisors, plant walk throughs, induction of new employees, etc.*

Employee Publication

The employee publication, also known as house journal, is one good way of reaching a large number of employees in an interesting and credible way. The contents of such a publication may differ from industry to industry, with one common objective of reaching the employees for realization of management goals. Apart from all the employee oriented success stories aimed at integrating employees into a 'family', the publication also covers topics like quality production, safety and house keeping, waste reduction, and personnel changes, etc.

House journals also run 'editorials' and signed articles on various aspects of corporate business to imbibe employees' involvement and responses. The publication also carries stories on expansion, promotions and transfers, new products, milestones in the company history, branch openings, etc. One trap that many publication editors fall in, is their enthusiasm to ensure that the managing director hog all the limelight. As the major aim of an employee publication is to foster 'family feeling' amongst employees and building employee confidence in the company, most of the news, feature stories, and pictures should project employees, achievements and keep the company activities in favourable focus within the framework of honest and accurate reporting (Also see Chapter 25).

News Bulletins

Frequently, some major developments in the company's progress take place just after the employee publication has been published. Rather than waiting for some weeks to catch up with the next issue, to tell the news quickly, accurately, and completely to the employees, the news bulletin is one logical means of doing it.

News bulletins are often used as an effective tool in the event of some unpleasant labour relations climate. Fast breaking news like an accident, fire, or a labour trouble, etc. can be very quickly explained to the employees to scotch rumours that can further aggravate the situation. It is an effective and on-the-spot means of stress communications.

A news bulletin is the quickest and least expensive means of getting the written news across to the employees. Such bulletins can be printed on quick offset system and distributed to outgoing and incoming shifts at the employee entrance. Some subjects for urgent transmission are: bonus announcement, reward for best suggestion, morale booster for higher production, editorials on slow downs, a new year message, record sales achievements, a big export order bagged by the company, visit of a VIP, introduction of a scholarship scheme, new productivity incentives, etc.

To spread the information evenly, such bulletins can also be displayed on the plant notice boards and repeated in the forthcoming issue of the employee publication.

Management Newsletters

Many company managements regularly send newsletters from top management to middle and junior managers, particularly working in the field and on the shop floor. Management newsletters are an effective mode of communicating to the supervision, which is the first level of management closely in touch with employees. So to keep them updated with necessary information about the company's progress, policy changes, expansions, installation of major new equipment, management changes, and other important subjects, newsletters can be effectively used.

If the middle management and supervisors are constantly abreast of happenings of importance throughout the company, they are well equipped to help keep the rank and file employees informed, and to offset inaccurate rumours and misunderstandings, which frequently sweep through the employees' ranks when communications are inadequate.

Direct Mail Letter to Employees' Homes

Direct mail letters to the employees' homes is a good way to relay important information or explanation of important new policies. Generally, they are excellent morale boosters because they are personal and they involve employees' families. It is advisable to restrict this medium to some very important messages such as Diwali, New Year, or company's foundation day greetings. Companies in the US use this medium to garner wives' support on difficult issues, which can benefit their families, as most of the wives play an important role in mindset formation. In India, a letter delivered to employees' homes sends wrong signals, as it may be construed as a letter of dismissal or calling employees' explanation. Therefore, only a strategic use of this medium is recommended.

Inserts in Pay Packets

This media tool should be reserved only for exceptional situations, possibly on matters relating to employees' compensation and benefits or production bonus, etc. Some employees regard their pay packets as very private and personal. Therefore, this medium should be used judiciously. However, some colourful greeting cards on occasions like Diwali or New Year, can be slipped into the packets without hesitation.

Booklets

PR practitioners make good use of booklets to translate educational messages to the employees, particularly to new employees as part of the induction programme. Other suitable subjects for such booklets can be new plant opening, new production incentives, grievances procedure, power crisis, formation of employees' cooperative society and also on problems like quality, absenteeism, safety, housekeeping, etc. For instance, several companies publish and distribute booklets on topics like energy conservation, containing illustrations showing switch-ing off electric switches when not needed, closing taps to avoid wastage of water or tips on industrial safety such as wearing hard hats and safety shoes.

Posters

Posters are low cost media but highly visual means of communication and also very effective. One of the main benefits of the posters is their reminder value. They can also be used for breaking important news to the employees. Some of the messages that can be relayed are a new product, a major company achieve-ment, a big order bagged, a production record broken, winning a safety contest, rolling out millionth product unit, upcoming events, inviting entries for contests, quality campaign, and advocate waste reduction. Message on posters have to be brief and crisp which can be grabbed by employees in one glance. With photocopy and computer printing facilities available in-house, posters can be produced at a short notice and inexpensively.

Electronic Neons

The electronic neon signs with moving messages, is the latest medium available. Such neons can be programmed every hour to make important announcements and achievements. When placed at vantage points like employees' canteens and plant entrance, they work very well as no one misses them.

E-mails

With the advancement of information technology, many organizations provide e-mail identity to their employees where they can be reached with tremendous speed. Many employees have access to computers in their homes. With cyber cafés getting spread rapidly even on the countryside, from where a large part of the workforce hails, they can access the information easily. The advantage of this medium is that it is rapid and inexpensive. E-mails have a great future, and they even cut across the geographical barriers, the world over. As a feature of good public relations, one of the managing directors sends e-mail birthday greetings to employees, which generates tremendous goodwill.

Speeches by Company Officials

In the corporate world there are ample opportunities when the senior officials have to address gatherings of employees. Occasions like family day, a VIP visit, service award presentations, retirement and promotion parties, bonus announcements, or even specially created events are organized to address the employees. Such speeches enjoy a good amount of credibility as they come straight from the top, hence should be used with thoughtful planning and careful delivery. If handled haphazardly, the speeches can boomerang and damage the goodwill amongst the employees. In addition to providing information, speeches should build greater employee confidence and faith in the company's policies and practices. Speeches go a long way in inculcating a sense of belonging for the company and the resultant employee loyalty.

Communicating through Supervisors

Supervisors are the first level of management on the shop floor, who make or mar the impression of the management with employees. This is the level where the communications take place directly between the employees and the management. Obviously supervisors should be so well informed about the company's policies and practices, that they can share these with employees with confidence during their day-to-day interactions.

It is but essential that the management itself believes and practises good communications and should be willing to make the necessary investment of time and resources to train and equip supervisors' to be more proficient in communication skills. The company should be ever willing to update supervisors' skills, from time to time, so that they can obtain better performance and cooperation from the employees reporting to them. Many manufacturing organizations employ a large number of supervisors and keeping them connected is a gigantic task. However, some steps taken on a continuous basis should help (See Exhibit 14.4).

Plant Walk throughs

A walk through the plant provides one of the simplest, least time consuming and most effective means of communicating with the employees, provided they are planned with a definite purpose in mind. Through the mode of walk throughs, a plant manager and the public relations practitioner can demonstrate his interest in the employee activities. This further enhances the belief amongst the employees that the management is interested in them, their progress and well being, working conditions, and the employees' attitude towards the company.

Induction of New Employees

New employees, naturally, have several questions about the company, its management, senior managers, and the benefits they expect from their jobs. A well structured induction training programme should help. Detailed introductory sessions by PR in coordination with HR training department, about the company history, achievements, policies and practices, should make a lot of sense and sets the tone for the new hires to get immersed into the mainstream of company culture. An illustrated 'induction booklet' is recommended to be given to new

---

EXHIBIT 14.4   Communication to supervisors

The simple steps towards improving the value of supervisors as communicators with employees are the following :

- Set up meetings between management and supervisors at regular intervals, to exchange company information.
- Develop and run a regular newsletter to the supervisors, to keep them informed of the company policies, practices, and progress.
- Alert supervisors, in advance about the forthcoming major developments in the company, with sufficient background information that will help them to explain these developments to their subordinates.
- Management to continue emphasizing the need

for good communications for building harmonious relations with the employees working under their supervision.

- Hold training workshops from time to time to enhance supervisors' communication skills. A half-yearly or annual training course, conducted jointly by personnel and public relations is recommended.
- Treat supervisors as integral part of the management to circumvent the feeling of isolation amongst them, due to lack of connectivity. Supervisors represent the company to the workers and workers to the company and have a sensitive and difficult role of 'man in the middle'.

hires to familiarize them with information sensitive to their jobs. This should take out the guesswork and doubts in the mind of a new employee.

MANAGEMENT MUST LISTEN

Internal public relations or employee communications is a two-way process. It is not just enough to communicate, but is also essential for the management to listen to the employees' reactions and responses. Called feedback, it is a crucial part of the system to remain connected with the workforce.

Successful communication cannot be accomplished if the management continues to say what the employees do not want to hear, if the management uses techniques that are unappealing to the employees, and if the management has no idea of the thinking, likes and dislikes, hopes and interests, and the 'gripes' of the employees. Therefore, there is need for feedback or upward communication, that is, from employees to the management (See Chapter 8).

Today's conglomerates are complex organizations and the invasion of electronic technology has been adopted to gather efficiency and solutions to several communication problems. Feedback as an essential part of the communication process, managers, big and small, are all hard pressed to gather upward information, which can help them to take right decisions. Due to a dozen hierarchical levels and thousands of people working in an organization, it is complicated to gauge public reactions to the policies and actions of a company.

There are many techniques for discovering what employees are thinking, how they react to management decisions, and what they expect from the management. Although the process of receiving the feedback from the employees differ from company to company, depending on its size, structure, and operations, yet each technique should produce some information that could be helpful in planning and conducting sound employee communication programme.

The feedback techniques are many times invented by managers to suit their needs, yet generally known systems are: *information from supervisors, survey of employee opinions and attitudes, interviews with ex-employees/exit interviews, interviews with newcomers, interviews with veterans,* and *the grapevine.*

Information from Supervisors

Supervisors are close to the employees; they have frequent contacts with them; and their daily exposure should help them develop the facility for interpreting employees' attitudes, opinions, and statements. A supervisor, generally has his finger on the pulse of the employees' opinion, and serves as a good source of feedback for the management.

Survey of Employee Opinions and Attitudes

For maximum effectiveness, such surveys are conducted under professional supervision. Either the PR can conduct an in-house survey or if need be, contract an outside research agency to handle it. Whereas the inhouse exercises are inexpensive, the outside agency fees are expected to be high enough.

For instance, if the employee publication editor wants to establish as to how much contents of his house journal interest the employees, they can conduct a sample survey. Logically enough, a questionnaire should be drawn so as to get the requisite feedback and interview a cross section of the employees and make the desired changes in the house journals as per the findings. Similar opinion surveys could be conducted on various critical issues concerning the organization and get the necessary feedback for policy adjustments and course correction.

Interview with Ex-employees/Exit Interviews

It has often been observed that the in-service employees do not speak out their mind for fear of reprisals by their managers, but when they are retired or have resigned their jobs, they are bolder and frank enough in expressing their candid opinions. Also known as exit interviews, such interaction can reveal some startling facts which can be useful for doing some rethinking on the policies and practices of the organization.

Interviews with Newcomers

The new hires offer some very candid and fresh information as to what they have been hearing about the company, particularly from the older employees. Quite a few lessons can be learnt from such a feedback.

Interviews with Veterans

Veterans in the company, who have put in long years of service, have their own kind of secure position in the company. Because of their experience or proven loyalty to the company, their views are respected and cared for. Veterans are generally well-wishers of the organization and their opinions are valuable contribution to the feedback system. Irrespective of their position in the hierarchy, veteran's voice is expected to be sincere and sober.

The Grapevine

Grapevine is an informal system, but considered very meaningful in the feedback process. Some characteristics of the grapevine though are usually accepted by managements on their face value, yet are meaningful (Also see Chapter 8).

1. Grapevine is not controlled by management on the face of it, yet many

managers have lot of interest in the system and keep their information conduits active.

2. It is a general perception that more than the official communiqués, the news spread by grapevine enjoys higher degree of credibility amongst employees and other concerned public.

3. Grapevines are infested with self-styled leaders with vested interests of their own or their sponsor managers.

Grapevine feedback gives managers the feel of the morale of an organization, identifies the issues that the employees consider important, and helps tap into employees' anxieties. It acts, therefore, both as a filter and a feedback mechanism, picking up the issues that employees consider relevant.

Grapevine, which is also considered as rumour mill, is perhaps, difficult for any organization to demolish. It is also said that the rumour mill works overtime to produce many frivolous news detrimental to the general morale in the organization and even to malign certain persons or a management decision. One sure way seems to be, is timely scotching of the rumour by communicating the real versions of an issue or a problem. This sets the speculations at rest and normalcy prevails.

The communication system of any company can be likened to the nervous system of a body. It is vitally important to the corporation's total operation, policy establishment, management decision making, execution of decisions, corporate cohesiveness, effective training, and development of any company's 'most important asset', its people.

Summary

The success or failure of any organization depends on the responses of its employees. Managements have priorities to run their plants to the fullest capacity and maximize profits. Employees, in this context, are an important public and establishing a mutually beneficial relationship is essential.

Employees, who are humans, also have hopes, aspirations, and expectations from managements. They want better wages, bonus/incentives, safety from injury/accidents, job security, welfare for self and family, career growth, social status, and participation in the process of management. Managements today encourage employees to show interest in the company and run suggestion schemes.

Running of employee public relations or communication programme is fraught with challenges. It is essential that the management should have a well heeled HR policy. Some basic conditions for success of the communication system is mutual trust and honesty of purpose. Unfortunately, managements impose their own views on the employees, which have little or no relevance to employees' mindset. Also labour management adversary relationship is a hard reality of industrial life.

Managements also have some problems like productivity maximization, quality improvement, waste reduction, safety and housekeeping, banishing absenteeism, loyalty, indiscipline, union pressures for which the whole hearted support of the employees is needed. A good communication system's basic characteristics can have a sobering effect on the issues.

Out of a variety of communication media available, public relations practitioners with their specialization, should very skillfully and creatively use them for success. A mix of employee publication, news bulletins, management newsletters, posters, booklets, etc. can fill the gap.

Internal public relations being a two-way street, managements must collect and evaluate the feedback from employees for policy adjustments and course correction. Channels like supervisors, surveys, interviews, grapevine, etc. serve as good sources of upward communication.

Last, but not the least, communication is the life blood of an organization, which runs the company like the nervous system in a human body.

Key Terms

Badli **worker**   One who is employed on a day-to-day basis in any vacancy caused by the absence of any employee and who is paid for the number of days he works, either daily or once in a month

Captive audience   Employees are termed as captive audience as they are available at one place for communicating whenever needed

House journal   A publication produced by the company for circulation to employees

Manufacturing capacity   The capacity of the machines installed in a factory to produce a number of units per day

Quality of life   The degree of enjoyment and satisfaction experienced in everyday life as opposed to financial or material wellbeing

Concept Review Questions

1. The success or failure of an organization, to a large extent depends on the attitude and response of the employees. Explain the statement with reference to internal public relations.
2. Draw up a comparison between the expectations that the employees and the managements have from each other. Explain the scenario in details.
3. What are the characteristics of a good communication programme? What are the challenges that a management have to meet to make a success of the employee communication system? Explain.
4. What are the media used for communication? Explain the characteristics of each media. What media mix do you recommend for a plant manufacturing tractors?

Project Work

1. Draw up a employee communication programme for a car making

company, say Hyundai, to inform and inspire employees to meet a production target of 500 cars per day.

2. Create a set of 5 posters to support a waste reduction campaign in the LG plant manufacturing washing machines.

3. Draw up a questionnaire to conduct a survey amongst employees to gauge the readership response to the company's employee publication titled 'Honda Parivar'.

Case Study

Communication in Stress

The progress and success of any company depends on team work at all levels, particularly between the management and the employees. And the fostering of team spirit, to a large extent depends on the quality and quantity of communication, downward, upward, and horizontal. Well managed communication system of a company makes employees feel more secure, confident, more interested in their work, and loyal to the company.

With the rapid development of the industrial township of Faridabad, industries cropped up and hired a workforce, which hailed from surrounding rural areas. One such plant was Hyderabad Asbestos manufacturing asbestos sheets. This brought along a challenge of inducting the employees into the new life style of an industrialized society. Interestingly enough, such employees lived two lives, one in their centuries old village and the other in the industry. One was rural and the other was urbanized life style. So they found themselves maladjusted posing a serious discipline, productivity, and quality problem. The enforcement of industrial discipline posed serious problems as enforcement generated militancy. The vested political interests outside the factory played their own malicious roles to mislead the workforce.

The rural life style hung heavily on industrial production. The marriage and harvesting season took toll of production by unscheduled absenteeism mounting to 35 per cent on certain days. House keeping and vandalism, and typical careless habits of a villager heavily pushed waste figures of the material beyond tolerance. Unions took law in their hands, shouted provocative slogans inside and outside the plant, and one day a few miscreants attacked some managers. The unions slapped an illegal strike and the management had no option but to clamp down a lock-out.

Thanks to the company's faith in the communication system and the need to step up the effort before, during and after the industrial unrest, the steps taken by public relations in that direction, stood in good stead. Management held regular meetings to update the supervisors so that they could explain issues to the employees, sent frequent news bulletins to the workers to save the employees from getting misled by undesirable elements.

When after the lock-out employees went away to their villages and were not approachable, the company printed some 10,000 leaflets and distributed in the villages, in the 30 miles radius, through a mobile van, to build public opinion. In the meantime, some notorious anti-social elements incited the workforce, who indulged in vandalism and caused considerable damage to the property. The authorities had to intervene to restore order.

To explain, a jumbo sized poster was plastered on the vantage points like markets, panchayats, etc. in the middle of nights fearing hostility, and to make the message reach to the people.

The government conciliation agency brought the management and the unions to the table to resolve matters and the factory opened again after three weeks. The plant director addressed a general assembly of the employees to restore trust and confidence. Public relations played a vital role in preparing the speech and providing the logistics support. To reinforce the public opinion, the company officials visited several '*sarpanchs*' to explain their view point to get their support.

Goodwill thus earned, made an assembly of village heads to invite the plant director to hoist the national flag on Independence Day, which was round the corner. Public relations was all involved in the contact work, and the networking carried out in the past paid dividends.

Public relations, who had been in touch with the local press, provided enough information to the journalists, who wrote some favourable articles appreciating the efforts made by the company to restore industrial peace.

Discussion questions

1. Research and write a lucid note on the role of public relations in maintaining industrial peace in the house of TATA for past about 100 years.
2. Design and develop a management bulletin for the information of supervisors of a company, say Hero Honda, about steps and systems of maintaining high quality of the vehicles manufactured by them. Also briefly list, therein, the points to motivate their subordinates to adopt good quality practices.

References

Bevan, Richard and John N. Bailey (1992), *Lesly's Handbook of Public Relations and Communications*, Probus Publishing Company, USA and published in India by Jaico Publishing House, Bombay, p. 215.

Cutlip, Scott M., Allen H. Center, and Glen M. Broom (1985), *Effective Public Relations*, 6th edition, Prentice-Hall International, Inc., USA, pp. 312 and 329.

The Economic Times, 16 April 2006, p. 1.

Moore, H. Frazier and Frank B. Kalupa (2005), *Public Relations, Principles, Cases and Problems*, 9th edition, Richard D. Irwin, Inc. USA, and printed in India by Surjeet Publications, Delhi, p. 314.

O'Reilly, Maurice (1983), *The Goodyear Story*, Akron Ohio, USA, p. 35.

Sachdeva, Iqbal, *The Observer of Business and Politics*, 21 August 2000.

15

Investor Relations

INTRODUCING INVESTOR RELATIONS

There is never a dull moment at the stock market. The rise and fall of BSE benchmark, Sensex is, as if, the pulse of the nation. The bulls and bears are the heart beats of the investing public. The gainers think they are lucky and the losers miss a heart beat. A look backwards, a couple of decades, the share market has undergone a sea change, from good to bad, from responsive to indifferent, and alongwith that have changed the reflexes of the investor publics.

Government policy of economic liberalization, the opening of Indian economy, and the entry of several global organizations into India with registration at the stock exchanges have tickled the money making taste buds of several new investors with opportunities to mop up some quick gains. Investors, big and small, developed keen interest in trading at the bourses.

India, a couple of decades ago, witnessed long queues of investors at the banks to file applications for new shares. The issues got over subscribed. Some master manipulators pushed the stocks to sky rocket and then abruptly crashed. The huge losses sent many investors in a tizzy and left them heart broken.

Thereafter, for almost a decade the stock market remained sluggish and depressed when the Sensex would not cross 4000 points. With government policies allowing foreign direct investments in certain business segments, and the emergence of new entrepreneurs like Reliance, the market started booming and once even touched 20,000 points, only to bounce back. The developments in the stock market have a strong bearing on the equity dilution by some companies, economic, social, political situation, and a sea change in the investors attitude. In the recent past, the meteoric rise of the oil prices, threatened to touch $200 a barrel, ultimately receding to $40, upset the investors apple cart, who are sitting with fingers crossed.

In this historical perspective and the current scenario, a challenge that the public relations faces today is to retain the trust and credibility amongst the investors. The current investors and the prospective ones, the individuals and institutions, hold the key to a company's position. The investors, big and small, all provide the necessary capital, to make an organization viable and thrive in business. Until the investors cooperate, the corporations may not be able to contribute to the economy of the nation, may not be able to provide jobs and produce goods and services, so essential to make life enjoyable for the people.

Investors, by their buying and holding the shares, bonds, debentures, mutual fund contributions, seem to express their confidence in the corporation, an industry, or the private enterprise. Investors shying away from the purchase of stocks tend to express their lack of confidence, approval or support for the company. The mood of the investors is of crucial significance, when a privately held company wants to go public and raise capital from the stock market. The doubts and questions about the lack of professionalism in management, extravagance in overheads, over paying directors incompatible with the profits, producing shoddy goods, or indulging in some unethical practices, and some such whispers can trigger large scale reactions in terms of investors' distress selling of stocks and running down the company. The word spreads like wildfire and can ruin the chances of success for an organization. Public relations have a job here of very high consequence to foster and maintain public trust.

PUBLIC RELATIONS ROLE AND RESPONSIBILITY

Investor relations is one of the major components of maintaining a company's financial health and also the wealth, through well planned communications with shareholders and prospective investors.

Investor relations is a highly valued and specialized type of public relations; valued because of the influence it can have on a company's share price and specialized because it requires a good feel of the working of investor's mindset coupled with in-depth knowledge of laws and regulations, and also the rules that govern the dissemination of information. The discipline demands the combination of expertise in the areas of communications and finance, to project an accurate and convincing perspective to the investors, from their view point.

Being a very sensitive and specialized area of activity, the public relations practitioners with good experience and knowledge of the subject are in demand and hence highly paid. One big reason is their knowledge and experience in finance and a host of laws, like SEBI (Security Exchange Board of India) regulations concerning initial stock offerings (IPOs), mergers and acquisitions, accounting systems, contents of the financial reports, public disclosure of information, etc. which need to be observed by the companies.

In the process of handling the investor relations, the public relations practitioner and the staff have to communicate with institutional investors like banks, financial institutions like LIC, IDBI, UTI, large industrial houses, individual investors, stock brokers, financial analysts, etc., and networking with media for release of information that could be of interest to several prospective investors. The total exercise has to be backed by lot of home work comprising presentations to the management, conducting field trips for analysts and portfolio managers, analysing stock brokers' psychographics and demographics, producing corporate annual reports and prepare material for potential investors.

In America, 'A corporation's policies concerning financial relations are strictly the province of top management. Guided by law, ...by the SEC (Security Exchange Control) rules and regulations, by stock exchange requirements, and by the attitude of management toward minimal, moderate, or generous disclosure. The implementation of policies falls largely to financial officers and public relations staff or outside counsel, Legal counsel also has a significant role. In most publicly owned corporations the financial relations wing of public relations will be found closely related to the top management,' wrote Scott M. Cutlip et al. (1985).

In India, a company's relationship, dealings, policies, and practices are guided by the Government agencies such as SEBI, Bombay Stock Exchange, National Stock Exchange, etc. There have been enacted some rules and regulations for the companies to act upon in matter of raising capital from the investor market, as well, dealing with the existing shareholders. The main purpose of all the regulations is to protect the share holders from the over enthusiasm of certain companies to mop up funds by promising certain benefits which may not be there. BSE, particularly, have been in the past undertaking a public relations exercise to advise and alert the investors to take certain precautions while investing (See Exhibit 15.1).

In other words, public relations may come under pressure from the over enthusiastic top managements to develop and design certain clever communications to by-pass the law to entice investors into a honey trap. Professionals, naturally, should exercise their judgement and see the situation in the light of the professional ethics and law with courage and conviction. As a step to

Source: The Times of India, 12 December 2007.

safeguard investors' interest, the Ministry of Corporate Affairs, Government of India, floated an 'Investor Education Fund' to educate and empower investors to exert their rights against unfair pratices in corporate affairs. The fund provides an efficient investor grievance redressal mechanism.

However, public relations have certain roles and responsibilities which should be looked at with care and caution, which are:

Gauge Investor's Mood

Assessment of the investors' attitude towards the company, which generally forms the basis of investors' response to the company in terms of their decisions to buy company shares, is an important area where public relations should play a crucial role. Shareholders' opinions of the policies, practices, and progress of a corporation are of major interest to the managements as they form the basis of developing good relations with the investing public. It is relevant for any organization to be aware of the attitude of the investors towards their style of functioning, as far as the flow of communication to them is concerned. The shareholders consider themselves to be part owners of the company and expect to be consulted on some important matters that may affect their chances of earning a respectable return on their investments. For instance, Power Grid Corporation of India Ltd sent one postal ballot consent form to the stockholders to get their approval for enhacement of borrowing limits from Rs 25,000 crore to Rs 50,000 crore to finance an expansion plan of the company's power generation facilities.

To avoid certain sections of the shareholders creating some difficult scenes at the annual general meeting, it is of considerable importance to know the expectations of the share holders. Not for this reason only, but also that the shareholders do not feel isolated as part owners of the company, managements occasionally pamper them with some goodies. It serves two purposes—the company enhances sales and enlarges its customer base for its products, and also makes stakeholders feel happy that the company cares for them. For instance, Reliance Industries send discount coupons to their share holders promising up to 15 per cent discount on their Vimal brand fabrics (See Exhibit 15.2).

Feedback from Investors

As most of the companies have a large number of shareholders, survey about the shareholder's attitude is conducted by a direct mail questionnaire alongwith a self-addressed post paid envelope. The companies also resort to at random interviews with the investors to have a representative opinion. The latest annual report by Reliance Industries Limited carries a feedback form for the investors to respond with their ratings about the various aspects of the company's operation and financial systems (See Exhibit 15.3).

EXHIBIT 15.2   Reliance gesture to investors

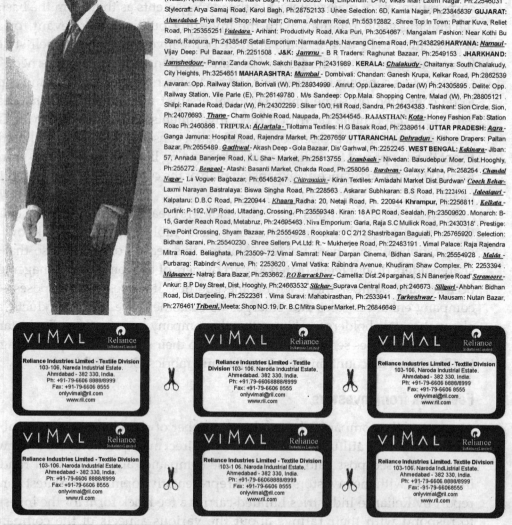

Source: A direct mailer to shareholders by Reliance Industries Limited (2008).

EXHIBIT 15.3   Feedback questionnaire

Reliance
Industries Limited

Members Feedback Form 2007-2008

Name : _____   e-mail id : _____

Address : _____

DP ID. : _____

Client ID. : _____

Folio No. : _____

(in cash of physical holding)

No. of equity shares held : _____

(the period for which held)

Please rate on a 5 point scale of 1 to 5

Signature of member

1. Excellent	2. Very Good	3. Good	4. Satisfactory	5. Unsatisfactory	1	2	3	4	5
Directors' Report and Management's Discussion and Analysis			Contents						
			Presentation						
Report on Corporate Governance			Contents						
			Presentation						
Shareholders' Referencer			Contents						
			Presentation						
Quality of Financial and non- financial information in the Annual Report									
Information on Company's Website			Contents						
			Presentation						
INVESTOR SERVICES									
Turnaround time for response to shareholder query									
Quality of response									
Timely receipt of Annual Report									
Conduct of Annual General Meeting									
Timely receipt of dividend warrants / payment through ECS									
Promptness in confirming demat / remat requests									
Overall rating									
Views/Suggestions for improvement, if any									

Members are requested to send this feedback form to the address given overleaf.

Source: Reliance Industries Annual Report (2007–08).

The collected data when collated together reveals useful information about the investors' perceptions about the company, its functioning style, dividends, information system, and other related matters, which can help the company to adjust its policy and practices in keeping with the expectations of the investors. This is one logical way to assess the acceptability of future proposals, if any, or the company may have to collect additional capital from the market.

Communications

Communicating to the investor public is a crucial role that public relations is expected to play, to keep this potential segment connected to the organization. The responsibility of preparing financial literature such as letters welcoming the new shareholders, preparation of annual financial report, letters forwarding the dividend warrants, specially designed information to brokers and financial analysts, to institutional investors and even preparation of a prospectus and application form for purchase of new shares (in coordination with finance manager), advertising and publicity, all fall in a public relations practitioner's role area.

What makes a good public relations professional and a communicator is the knowledge of the field he or she is working in. While handling the financial communications, it is but necessary to be familiar with the financial vocabulary, so that the message goes across to the target audience in the language they understand. Therefore, mastering the key terms of the financial side of the business should be helpful in a big way in making sense of the message developed and delivered. For a rough and ready list of such terms, see Exhibit 15.4.

Logistics Support

Public relations is expected to get fully involved in arranging the logistics by making physical arrangements for the annual general meeting of the share-holders, and also support the programme with the necessary informational

---

EXHIBIT 15.4   *Key financial terms*

- Balance sheet
- Profit and loss account
- Return on capital employed
- Return to shareholders — EPS (earning per share)
- Gross profit, net profit, and taxation
- Control of working capital and liquidity
- Cost concepts
- Depreciation expenses

- Investment and dividend
- Market capitalization, debt, and equity
- Profitability index
- Budgets and plans
- Key strategies and operating concepts
- Sales and distribution expenses and overheads
- Bonus shares and rights shares
- Share value — par/premium
- Bulls and bears

material. Presentations to be made by the top management to such meetings, are also developed to influence shareholders' perception about the organization. Tour to the company's factories, if needed, are also a part of the support system provided by public relations in coordination with manufacturing team.

Media Networking

Preparation of news releases about the quarterly, half yearly, and annual financial results and networking with the financial press is an important public relations function. Release of advertisements in the media about financial results and chairman's speech at the annual general meeting, etc. also fall in the purview of public relations job functions.

INVESTOR PUBLICS

There is a wide variety of investors, who are connected with the organization because they have stakes which they constantly watch. They range from small investors to large players, from individuals to institutions, brokers to financial analysts, media to legal monitoring agencies, etc.

Caroline Black (2003) wrote, '...financial and corporate public relations are frequently interrelated given a main common objective in the creation and protection of corporate reputation. A positive reputation is vital in attracting investment. ...The financial PR advisor or investor relations manager, whether in-house or consultant, is usually a member of the elite team comprising other professional advisors, including lawyers and financiers....An important feature of financial PR is the specialized group of target audience it seeks to communicate with...' (See Exhibit 15.5).

INVESTOR RELATIONS OBJECTIVES

With a view to build investors' confidence and trust in the organization, investor relations as part of the larger public relations have some very obvious objectives:

- Create understanding between the investors, financial community, and the company.
- Arouse interest of the prospective investors in the company's stocks.
- Reduce the turnover of shareholders and promote the holding of company stock as a long-term investment.
- Encourage investors to show interest in the company's products, purchase themselves, and recommend others to buy.
- Subdue shareholders' critical views on management and avoid any organized attemp to raise any anti-management lobbies.

EXHIBIT 15.5   Investor publics

Shareholders	Current shareholders and prospective investors
Institutional investors	Large fund managers of mutual funds, insurance companies, bankers, and pension funds, and key players in the money market
Financial analysts	Financial and stockbroker firms who keep a track of the companies. Their recommendations are generally trusted and acted upon by investors while making investment decisions
Consultants	Some chartered accountants who advise the investors about future prospects
Opinion leaders	Business community, industry members, politicians, customers, employees and opinion leaders
Government	Government agencies who monitor and enforce certain regulations on companies. Amendments and additions is often a topic for discussion amongst investing public
Media	The financial press like *Economic Times*, *Financial Express*, *The Mint*, economic and business journals, independent financial writers, TV channels exclusively monitoring companies and business

---

- Take steps and actions to keep the stock market quotations at an attractive level.
- Build corporate image of the organization amongst shareholders' constituencies.
- Generate timely response to assuage the feelings of the financial community.
- Float information that ensures management's full control over the company operations.
- Enlist existing shareholders' favourable support for company's plans to raise additional capital.
- Take enough credit for the reasonable dividends distributed by the company to shareholders and justifiably explain its reasonableness.
- Keep up the two-way communication between the investors and the company to keep the cordial relationship to grow and flourish.
- Garner enough favourable support for the management to carry out certain expansion programmes, borrowings from the institutional investors and also execute certain plans for the benefit of investors and the community.

COMMUNICATIONS FOR INVESTORS—PR TOOLS

Effective communication with the shareholders provides a two-way exchange; so the management may obtain the views of the shareholders as well as give them information about the corporation. Like communication with any other publics, the messages to the shareholders should also be simple and conform to the financial vocabulary generally understood by investing public. Though talking money is an interesting subject, yet the financial information is generally fraught with difficult terms, and the skill lies in making it more interesting and palatable and even romanticizing it.

A variety of communication media or tools are used for reaching the shareholders. Amongst the printed and oral media are: *annual report, annual general meeting, chairman's address, financial results advertisements, new stock announcements, media relations, films, audio/video CDs and power point presentations, Internet mail.*

Annual Report

H. Frazier Moore and Frank B. Kalupa (2005) are of the opinion, 'The corporation's annual report is the primary medium of communication in stockholder relations and a secondary medium of communication with the non-shareholder employee, community, distributors, and supplier publics. The annual report is the one opportunity a company has each year to tell shareholders and other publics what it has done, is doing, and plans to do. It reflects a corporation's image and the caliber of its management, and it may attract new investors and affect the price of its stock.'

For a public relations practitioner, designing and printing of an annual report is an annual exercise which is time bound with a deadline. As the basic document is created by the finance manager, he seems to be driving the public relations effort, although his role ends the moment the balance sheet is delivered to the public relations manager.

Publication of an annual report is once in a year opportunity for the organization to project its image and corporate philosophy to the publics. The top management is interested in this. Nowadays, annual reports are more comprehensive, dramatic, and colourful in appearance, as if showcasing the greatness of the company. The profile of its appearance depends on the quantum of profits that company made last year. If the financial results were outstanding, the annual report is also dressed up to give that massege of progress, growth, and bright future. If otherwise, it will be a low budget and low profile publication. Loss, if suffered by the company, the management makes it look depressing, and mundane.

Generally, an annual report should highlight information about financial position, production progress, marketing performance, personnel activities and some issues like litigation, taxation, impact of new laws, future outlook, growth programmes, etc. A professionally produced annual report should have some distinct characteristics to look appealing and trustworthy (See Exhibit 15.6).

- The cover should project the corporate philosophy, technology, growth, or focus on people or economy. It should be compatible with the core competence of the organization and project corporate identity in clear focus
- It is logical to devote a page to the table of contents showing page numbers and position
- Photographs, graphics, or technical charts to showcase new products and major highlights of the year
- Project the board chairman and members in clear focus, with their brief profiles to bolster investors' confidence in the professional management

- Chairman and managing directors report to the shareholders briefly giving the achievements and events like awards, rewards, and innovations of the year, to project the company's growth prospects and future
- Bare facts of balance sheet, profit and loss account, etc.
- Historical data projecting past five years performance statistics, if the company is proud of the steady progress
- Auditors' reports, which is mandatory under the law

Annual General Meeting

Many public relations practitioners consider the annual general meeting as an annual wrestling match between the management and the share holders. Yet it is a legal obligation for a company to organize an annual general meeting once a year, after closing of the books of account for the previous financial year. Some organizations would like to get away with the meeting in as short a time as possible, making it only a formality, while some companies use it as an important image building event.

To escape the usual trouble makers, who make it their business to create ugly scenes and show themselves off as saviours of the shareholders' interests, some companies would have a meeting in some distanced location from main town, while others would hold such meetings in main metros with all the fan fair. 'You will see the same set of people in AGMs of quite a few companies, who make it their business to create nuisance and gain some loaves and fishes for themselves,' said one company executive. Humorously enough, some retirees with minor share holdings make it a pastime to keep themselves occupied and would be often seen in most of the AGMs within their reach.

The agenda for most of the stereotyped annual general meetings is usual, as the purpose is to transact business as per the legal requirements. It includes chairman calling the meeting to order, chairman's speech, counting of proxies, a reading and approval of the minutes of previous year's meeting, appointment of election officers, polling, if any, on passing of certain resolutions about appointment of new directors or reappointment of existing board members, passing of resolutions concerning company's business growth and expansion and closing of the meeting. The dreaded part of the meeting by some company executives is the question–answer session, where shareholders seek clarifications or action on certain issues. To assuage investors feelings' the meetings are followed by high tea and a gift. The camaraderie and heated exchanges over the tea are usual.

As a preparation to meet the ordeal, the executives are often asked to pool up questions that are likely to be asked by the shareholders, so that answers can be prepared in advance to save embarrassment, if any, to the management. Public relations in coordination with the chairman, takes an active part in this exercise, besides providing presentations to be made at the meeting. Providing the logistics support is the usual action. It is relevant to look at the ususal questions raised by the shareholders (See Exhibit 15.7).

Chairman's Address

Chairman's address to the shareholders is a ritual at the annual general meetings. Public relations have a responsibility to write the speech by collecting inputs from other divisions of the company, get the final draft approved by the chairman and the board of directors and print sufficient number of copies, in the shape of a booklet, for distribution to the shareholders and other interested publics like media, financial community, opinion leaders, etc. As part of the image building effort, some companies show off by advertising a well designed version of the speech in the mainline daily newspapers, usually occupying an expensive space of a full page. ITC, Indian Oil Corporation, Godrej, etc. often advertise to showcase their performance and corporate philosophy.

Financial Results Advertisements

It is mandatory for the companies to make public the quarterly, half yearly, and annual financial results. After the condensed balance sheet is provided by the finance manager, public relations advertises the results in the press. As a policy, some companies do it routinely to keep a low profile, but given the choice, public relations creatively flaunts the company's outstanding results to build prestige

---

EXHIBIT 15.7   Usual questions by investors at AGM

- Directors' salaries and perks, bonuses, stock options, pensions, and special privileges
- Recruitment policy, employee wage levels, productivity levels, training and development, seniority rights and benefits, labour relations, retirement age, and benefits
- Safety, health, and environment
- Stock ownership by management, conflict of interest
- Voting rights and proxies
- Outside directors, appointment, and compensation
- Dividend — how much and why less or more
- Retained profits and their appropriation
- Product range, quality, services, discounts, prices, warranties, marketing strategies, advertising, and distributor appointment policy

in the financial community and public at large. Such attempts also support the company's efforts to keep stock quotations at an attractive level in the share market. Reliance Communications announced its unaudited consolidated financial results for the third quarter through a release as given in Exhibit 15.8.

New Stock Announcements

Floating information about a company's plans to solicit capital from the investors' market is a major exercise. Public relations, in any case, is involved in the process, and hands on the job, starts with the designing and printing of prospectus, application forms, and putting advertisements in the media inspiring investors to buy stocks. These days the stocks of any company are very rarely sold at par (face value), but the bids are invited from investing public by setting an upper limit which may be five, ten, or more times the face value, as permitted by law.

EXHIBIT 15.8   Financial results of Reliance Communications

RELIANCE Communications   Media Release
Anil Dhirubhai Ambani Group

Mumbai, January 23, 2009: Reliance Communications Limited (RCOM) today announced its unaudited consolidated financial results for the quarter ended December 31, 2008.

Highlights of the financial performance for the quarter are:

- Net Profit of Rs. 1,410 crore (US$ 290 million), higher by 2.7% compared to Net Profit of Rs 1,373 crore (US$ 348 million) in the corresponding quarter last year.

- EBITDA at Rs, 2,353 crore (US$ 484 million), growth of 11.7%, EBITDA margin at 40.2%

- Revenue growth of 20.0% at Rs 5,850 crore (US$ 1.204 million) from Rs 4,874 crore (US$ 1.237 million).

- Return on Net Worth is 33.3% reflecting improved resource utilization.

- Shareholders Equity (Net Worth) increases to Rs 29,065 crore (US$ 6 billion)

- Conservative capital structure - Net Debt to Equity Ratio maintained at a conservative level of 0.64:1, despite capex spend of Rs 4,361 crore (US$ 900 million) during the quarter.

Reliance Communications Limited, Registered Office: H. Block. 1st Floor,
Dhirubhai Ambani Knowledge City, Navi Mumbai - 400710
Tel: 022-3038 6286, Fax: 022-3037 6622

Source: Adapted from http://www.rcom.co.in/webapp/Communications/rcom/ir—pressrelease.jsp.

If the issue is over subscribed, another advertisement is put up in the media with 'Thank You Investors' for the support by reposing confidence in the company by oversubscribing the issue.

Besides, the old practice of adopting only the print media for selling stock, the organizations are extensively using TV medium to inspire investors to invest. Reliance Power, from the house of Ambani's, very creatively and aggressively used this medium, resulting in a media hype that generated investors' hysterical response.

To support the effort, smart radio jingles are broadcast at the FM radios at high frequency, to remind investors to avail of the lucrative offer.

Media Relations

In today's business world where the media plays an important role in the spreading of credible information to the publics, networking with the media is part of the public relations portfolio. The concerted networking with the media at all stages of investor relations, has paid handsome dividends to several companies. When handled well, it pays, but the mishandling can be very damaging. Public relations professionals involved in the investor relations, undertake several steps to cultivate media for obvious benefits. Some of the tools used are: press release about new issue or the annual results, declaration of dividends for shareholders, announcement of quarterly, half yearly, and annual results, circulation of copies of the annual report for review and report, evenly spread of the copies of the chairman's speech, organizing press conferences, exclusive interviews with the chairman to recount company achievements and growth plans. With 'pink press' showing focused interest in this business activity, the media relations has become a crucial element in the investor relations area (Also see Chapter 16).

Film, Audio/Video CDs, and Power Point Presentations

All the public relations tools that can effectively communicate to investor public are developed and used by the public relations professionals. With the advancement of information technology and electronics, public relations have acquired new skill sets like computer literacy. With technology at their command, professionals design and develop special presentations in the form of films, audio/video CDs and even power point presentations, converted into CDs or pen drives, which come handy at the annual general meetings or any other meeting with investors. Presentations can be made to the groups of stockholders almost at no notice with modern gadgets, which nowadays are generally available at hand.

Internet/e-mail

Most of the investors of any consequence are available for communication through Internet, irrespective of their location or time. Internet has spanned the globe and shrunk the world into a small village. Company websites are open round the clock almost anywhere, where investors can log on to get the information that they desire. Public relations now has a responsibility to keep such websites updated. The online trading facilities for investors have added all the excitement to the investors' business life. Organizations like Yahoo and Google keep flashing the stock quotations and the happenings in the world market on a 24/7 basis.

In addition, the e-mail system comes very handy for communicating to the investors frequently about the status of their stocks, right in the comfort of their homes and offices. Some of the mutual fund managers like Reliance and Tata regularly flash the status reports to the investors on their e-mail inboxes.

Summary

With the expansion and surge of the stock markets and also growing number of investors, the business organizations have a need to develop and maintain good relations with the investors. With hyper business activity in the stock exchanges and sensex scores becoming the heart beat of Indian business, public relations have a special role in promoting relations with investors based on trust, confidence, and understanding. Sensex jumping from a sluggish score of about 4,000 to 20,000 and then crashing down, has sent many investors in a tizzy. The market mood swings pose serious challenges for an organization, and the public relations has to be as sensitive to the constantly changing scenario as the top management.

Public relations with the blessings and coordination of the top brass, has a responsibility to foster confidence and trust amongst the investors in the company, so that they continue to hold on to their investments, safe and secure. As the investor relations area is fraught with a host of legal rules and regulations, those who know the discipline well, are paid very well.

The role and responsibility of public relations in handling investor relations involves good understanding of the working of institutions like stock exchanges and SEBI regulations, etc., gauging the mood of the inves-tors, gathering feedback about investor's perception of the company, communications, providing logistics support for various events like annual general meeting and media networking.

Public relations should have a clear perception of the various target audiences amongst the investor publics from individuals to institutional investors, regulatory authorities, media, and opinion leaders. Also the objectives of the programme should be spelled out for understanding.

The important public relations function of communications to the investors needs the use of public relations tools while handling the various aspects of investor relations like publication of annual report, providing back-up support to the annual general meeting, developing chairman's address, advertising financial results, new stock announcements, media relations, electronics media usage, up and updating the Internet website and effective use of the e-mailing system.

Investors are a very sensitive publics who have one priority to safeguard their investments and receive good returns on their investments. Public relations endeavours should focus on reinforcing investors' trust and imbibing their confidence in the organization on a continuous basis.

Key Terms

Bulls and bears   Term used to indicate the upward and downward swings of share prices and the share market index

Demographics   Socioeconomic factors (or population statistics) such as age, income, sex, education, occupation, or even family size that composes the population of a market niche

Historical data   Past-period's data, used usually as a basis for forecasting the future data or trends

Institutional investors   Financial institutions like LIC or banks that invest in company stocks in bulk

Proxies   Shareholders' voting forms for or against a resolution without being personally present

Psychographics   Analysis of consumer lifestyles to create a detailed customer profile

Concept Review Questions

1. Describe in your own words the share market scenario today. Also paint a historical perspective to bring out the importance of the investor relations.
2. What is the main underlying idea of developing good investor relations, amongst the host of objectives every organization has? What is the role of public relations in this endeavour? Also give an outline of the target publics that form a part of the investors community.
3. What are the PR tools that a public relations practitioner is expected to use for communicating to the investors? Define and describe the working of each of these media in the process.

Project Work

1. Draw up a public relations plan to handle an annual general meeting of shareholders of Apollo Tyres, covering all communication aspects, including providing a logistics support to the main event.
2. Hypothetically draw up a list of 15 questions that shareholders may ask at the forthcoming annual general meeting of the retail chain Big Apple. Also write a brief answer that you think should be appropriate for each question.
3. Write a chairman's address of about 700 words for the Escorts Limited. You may base it on the financial results and achievements of the company during the last year.

● ━━━━━━━━

Case Study

DLF Investor Relations Strategies

India's biggest real estate company, DLF entered the share market with a bang in July 2007 and generated feverish response amongst the investor public. Amongst the various public relations strategies that were used, was a high powered advertising campaign projecting their corporate image as premier real estate developer poised for providing style and comfort to all those aspiring for a house of their own.

Their media relations was well conducted by a professional public relations consultant with lot of success, so much so that the company became the talk of the town. The company successfully raised a whopping sum of more than Rs 9,000 crore as it became the most sought after script by the investors, who most willingly paid the IPO price of Rs 525 per share.

To further boost the morale of the investors and house hunters, the company sponsored a mega event 20:20 cricket matches amongst the privately funded cricket teams by the big wigs of this country like Shahrukh Khan, Preity Zinta, and Vijay Mallya. They even took the country by storm and greatly enhanced the value of DLF in the perception of investors in particular and public in general.

Now that the share market has nose dived and has hurt many scripts, DLF is no exception. The share value dropped from Rs 525 to Rs 459 on the Bombay Stock Exchange. According to media report, the script lost up to 57.21 per cent between 1 January–10 July 2008. This naturally has shaken the confidence of share holders in the company who seem to be asking a question as sell or retain the share in the hope of improvement. The bulk buyers particularly are nervous about the future, as the loss would be substantial.

The DLF management has now risen to the occasion and to bolster the confidence of the investors have announced that its board has approved a buy-back of shares that could cost as much as Rs 1,100 crore. The company has announced an attractive buy-back price of Rs 600 per share which is more than 14 per cent than the price of Rs 525 on which the company sold stocks in the middle of 2007.

'The intention of the offer is to send the message that equity price of the company is undervalued and if someone is thinking of selling DLF he can do so at a maximum price of Rs 600,' said Ketan Karani, Vice President research, Kotak Securities (*Hindustan Times*, 11 July 2008).

It is noteworthy that the company's IPO that was priced Rs 525 per share, soared as high as Rs 1,225 on a day in January 2008, and slided downhill since then and once hit a lifetime low of Rs 350 on 2 July 2008.

To assuage the feelings and build lost confidence, DLF on this very day made a spectacular announcement to buy back shares which cost the company a huge amount of Rs 1,100 crore. This showed instant results and the price of the script was appreciated by 15 per cent.

The media carried very favourable reports about this announcement when the vice chairman of the company said, 'We see the buy-back decision as a highly attractive opportunity for our shareholders....While we respect the market, we believe that our current share prices do not reflect the intrinsic strength and future growth potential of DLF' (*The Mint*, 11 July 2008).

Though there are some sensitive details about the proposal to buy-back, yet the very announcement can be taken as an outstanding effort to maintain good investor relations.

Discussion questions

1. Design and develop a press release on the DLF situation for distribution to the press explaining the details of buy-back proposal. Your release may be limited to 400 words.
2. Develop a power point presentation of about fifteen minutes duration for presenting to the investors at the next annual general meeting of DLF Limited.

References

Black, Caroline (2003), *The PR Practitioner's Handbook*, Hawksmere plc, printed in India by Crest Publishing House (A Jaico Enterprise), New Delhi, p. 159.

Cutlip, Scott M., Allen H. Center, and Glen M. Broom (1985), *Effective Public Relations*, 6th Edition, Prentice-Hall, Inc., USA, p. 492.

Moore, Frazier and Frank B. Kalupa (2005), *Public Relations, Principles, Cases and Problems*, 9th editon, Richard D. Irwin Inc, USA, printed in India by Surjeet Publications, Delhi.

Reliance Industries Limited, Annual Report 2007–08, pp. 189–190.

The Mint, New Delhi, 'Sebi to Finance, Nurture Activist Investor Clubs', 20 February 2009, vol. 3, no. 44, pp. 1 and 24.

The Times of India, New Delhi, 12 December 2007, p. 3.

16

Media Relations

Chapter Outline

- Public relations and media
- Media relations—a balancing act
- Networking for good media relations
- Public relations assistance to media
- Media relations norms
- Holding a press conference
- Measurement of success

PUBLIC RELATIONS AND MEDIA

With media explosion in the last quarter of the twentieth century, media relations, a major responsibility of public relations practitioners, has become rather a complex affair. Once limited to making friends of a few journalists and influencing them with supply of newsworthy information in general, it has now assumed the proportions of a specialized job. Media has become an integral part of the society, as it is a very credible source of information. People trust media and make some important decisions which influence their lives. It appears that it is difficult for anyone to survive without the supply of daily news. Since public relations has a responsibility to build bridges of understanding between publics and their organization, media is a vital link in the process. Independent media, in a democratic country like India, plays an important role in shaping public opinions, and hence media and public relations have complementary roles, but with a tinge of caution. Both disciplines have responsibilities and obligations to each other.

India, after independence, fortunately adopted a democratic form of government and a constitution which grants some liberties to the citizens as well as the press. The freedom of expression is the hallmark of a democracy. The founding fathers of India's democracy like Nehru, Gandhi, and Patel had their own ideas about this liberty of the press, that freedom brings responsibility along with it. Gandhi sounded an alert for the media to be responsible, as the negation of which can be devastating. He said, 'The newspaper press is a great power, but as an unchained torrent of water submerges the whole countryside and devastates crops, even so an uncontrolled pen serves but to destroy. If the control is from with out, it proves more poisonous than want of control. It can be profitable only when exercised from within.'

Nehru, expressing his opinion about the freedom of press, had said, 'I would rather have a completely free press with all the dangers involved in the wrong use of that freedom, than a suppressed or regulated press.'

Media in the present century is a reality of life. Media, like friendship, can be very helpful when handled with care, but can spell disasters when mishandled. Napoleon Bonaparte had said, 'Four newspapers are more to be feared than a thousand bayonets.' The American President, Lyndon B. Johnson, commenting, in his own way, on a journalist J. Edgar Hoover, had said, 'I would rather have him standing in my tent and pissing out, than standing outside and pissing in.' The statement only highlights the power of media and the importance of deftly getting along with the media, who have their own kind of priorities and obligations to bring out the facts and truth in front of their readers and viewers.

Besides the self imposed discipline, the press laws of India (see chapter 26) and the Press Council of India advocates a code for media organizations, with an aim to imbibe responsible journalism (See Exhibit 16.1).

With the onslaught of financial press with a major focus on commerce, industry, and corporations, media is on search for pegs to write news stories which affect the lives of a large number of people. Also called 'pink press', financial media's main focus is on India's changing economic scenario, which

---

EXHIBIT 16.1   The Press Council of India Code

'The press shall eschew publication of inaccurate, baseless, graceless, misleading or distorted material. All sides of the core issue or subject should be reported. Unjustified rumours or surmises should not be set forth as facts.' It adds: 'On receipt of a report or article of public interest and benefit containing amputations or comments against a citizen, the editor should check with due care and attention its factual accuracy – apart from other authentic sources with the person or the organization concerned to elicit his/her version, comments or reaction and publish the same with due amendments in the report where necessary. In the event of lack or absence of response, a footnote to that effect should be appended to the report.'

Source: Adapted from http://presscouncil.nic.in/norms.htm.

deeply influences the changes in social attitudes, habits, and life styles and even some divergent views or controversial issues. Besides, the news is no more a mere piece of information about the happenings but also a source of entertainment. Business leaders, political manipulators, and media-made celebrities make the news, which have deep ramifications in the business world, and people have their interest in their doings, for reasons of their own. With the phenomenal growth of media, press, TV, Internet, catering news, views, and entertainment to the society, the information industry is now on a fast track and is slated for high rate of growth (See Exhibit 16.2).

In the historical perspective, there existed a love–hate relationship between the journalist and the PR people, as both thought that their objectives are different from each other. The journalists always want news whereas the PR seek free publicity. So the media response to the public relations was measured and cautious. Fortunately for both, the scenario has changed in the last about three decades. Looks like no media person can function without the active support of a public relations professional, as the latter serves as a major source of information that goes to build a news.

Effective media relations has many benefits. It complements other communication efforts of an organization, commercial, social, cultural, or political. News coverage informs and educates people on some socially sensitive issues and help them to get the answers to their problems and make right choices. For PR professionals, media relations skills help them to avoid or dispel rumours,

---

EXHIBIT 16.2   Media on a growth path

A joint report by Ernst and Young and Assocham, titled 'India's Digital Revolution: Impact on Film & Television Sectors', says that the Indian media and entertainment industry will grow at twice the rate of the country's GDP over the next few years. By 2010, 28 per cent of an estimated 100 million pay TV households go for digital pay TV. termed as DTH (Direct to Home) will lead over digital cable and IPTV within the next three years.

By 2010, in digital cable, from a current share of 78 per cent for local cable operator (LCO), 5 per cent for multi system operator (MSO) and 17 per cent for the broadcaster, the share is expected to be 54 per cent for the LCO and 23 per cent for the MSO and broadcaster each.

The study says that 70–80 per cent of the broadcasters' revenue are ad-driven. TV commands

43 per cent of ad budgets. Over the next three years, the TV ad market is expected to grow at 14 per cent year-on-year and will continue to maintain its share in the total advertising pie. Home entertainment will constitute 25 per cent share of a film's revenue within three years, up from the current 5 per cent. Higher penetration of DVD players, reducing DVD prices and clampdowns on optical disc and cable piracy will help.

Growing telecom and Internet density and superior bandwidth availability will see entertainment content consumption across them grow over the next three years. Mobile VAS revenues will grow to Rs 4,600 crore by the year end. Within two years, mobile music sales are expected to account for 88 per cent (currently 56 per cent) of the total Rs 4,200 crore music market.

Source: Adapted from the *Hindustan Times*, 12 December 2007.

respond to criticism, defuse controversies, and even turn adversity to advantage. News coverage is also crucial to draw the necessary attention of the policy makers and also garner support of the opinion leaders, for or against an issue. Also the media itself takes care of the distribution of messages at its own cost. It is an advantageous and cost effective way for an organization to evenly spread information about its business amongst the intended publics, and that too in a credible way.

Media relations is of paramount importance to an organization, as the news coverage helps to confirm and reinforce the information that people receive about a corporation from other sources, such as entertainment programmes, brochures, field salesmen, family members, and friends. This is truer in a democratic set up where the media enjoys the freedom of expression and is independent of the government controls.

Media also very zealously and jealously safeguards its position as the champion of issues or public causes. Therefore, taking them for granted is perilous for any organization or a professional, yet the idea of inter-dependence cannot be rejected outright.

Frank Jefkins (2006) opines, 'The media still reflect Hearst's view, or at least they pretend to but they do have to grudgingly admit their gratitude for and sometimes their dependence on PR sources of information. Nevertheless, an adversarial situation does exist between the media and PR practitioners, mainly because neither understand the other or because their objectives are different...' But, 'The professional PR practitioner knows that unless his story is of interest and value to the reader, viewer, listeners or web browser, it will not be accepted by the editor or producer. If he deviates from this he is a menace to PR. A lot of news release writers are.'

Therefore, public relations professionals are advised to walk into a media man's moccasins to understand his mindset and respond accordingly.

MEDIA RELATIONS—A BALANCING ACT

'Media relations take up a good part of the practitioner's working day, are exacting in their demands, and are often exasperating in their consequences. Practitioners standing with media gatekeepers and reporters shapes the limits of their accomplishments. Journalists' confidence is one of the practitioner's most valuable assets. Employers and clients come and go, but the media and their gatekeepers are here forever. The bedrock of the practitioner–journalist relationship must be one of mutual trust and mutual advantage,' wrote Cutlip et al. (1985).

PR practitioners, in the area of media relations, have to walk on a tight rope and balance their act. They represent the organization to the media and media to the organization. In this role of 'man-in-the-middle' they have a need to have the trust and confidence of both the media and employers. More often than not, the media relations job comes under fire, as the journalists, due to their priority of bringing out something controversial in front of the public, for which the company blames the public relations. On the other hand, the companies have a priority to get all the favourable news published in the media for the furtherance of their interests and attainment of their business goals. So the war is on, as if, forever.

In today's scenario, when the financial press and business TV channels are exclusively concentrating on the commerce, industry, and corporations, the journalist–practitioner relationship can be termed as an 'inter-dependent relationship'. Gone are the days when journalists were very skeptical of the intentions of the public relations persons in their attempts to flood the media with 'publicity seeking' press releases, which media took precautions not to get trapped. Public relations person is an important resource for journalists. They are sitting at the fountain head from where the news flows and that in a ready-to-publish form. Some practitioners are considered as in-house journalists for the companies, who churn out stories of reader and business interest. One would be surprised that 50–60 per cent of the material published in many financial newspapers is written by public relations people, who work behind the scenes.

To cap it all, a public relations professional has to play the role of a mediator between the media and the organization, which calls for patience, knowledge, and skills to educate people on both sides of the fence.

Media relations is like a dance where two parties are involved, media and public relations. Since it takes 'two to tango', each dance partner has some opinions about the other (See Exhibit 16.3).

NETWORKING FOR GOOD MEDIA RELATIONS

For effective media relations, personal contacts with the journalists are crucial to networking effort by any public relations professional. Organizations, in the mutual interest can help journalists to identify newsworthy topics, obtain access to sources, and prepare interesting stories. These activities benefit both the journalists and the organizations themselves by generating more coverage and more accurate reporting. Networking effectively with the media is an effort to seek media understanding by supplying useful, factual, and timely information that journalists would like to use for generating stories for readers' consumption. If the information is newsworthy, interesting and is delivered to them in time before the deadline, they are more likely to make use of it.

EXHIBIT 16.3 Public relations and media—their interdependence

Public relations views	**Media views**
Media coverage priority	*News priority*
• Generate news	• Need news, real news
• Create news	• Inform and educate readers/viewers
Lobbying priorities	*Issues/causes priorities*
• Plant stories	• Need stories that make sense
• Kill stories	• Shun conscience killers
• Influence decision makers	• Be fair and impartial
Image management	*Corporate performance*
• Get credit for good performance	• Show real performance
• Handle controversies/rumours	• Show a perspective—be impartial
• Gloss and correct image	• Adopt objective approach
Marketing priorities	*Watch consumer interest*
• Announce new products	• Are products really new?
• Generate sales	• Show no direct interest in sales
• Improve brand salience	• Wanted news, only news
• Save advertising money	• No free publicity to make up for advertising

So, some media men love to hate PR men

Also, it is of great consequence to know as to which story will interest whom because there is a variety of people who work in a media outfit and specialize in some particular areas like business and commerce, politics, society and fashions, international relations, etc. Just like any other organization, the media house is also structured with layers of authority and job functions. Therefore, all news releases are not good for all the people and is judicious enough to deliver the right material to the right people. For various media functionaries, see Exhibit 16.4.

The key to good networking and developing relations with the media is that a public relations practitioner should establish credibility. It is of paramount importance to be honest and accurate in the matter of sharing news and information with the media not just once in a while, but always and ever. Once a practitioner or the organization starts enjoying this reputation for trustworthiness, the media men begin to have trust in them as reliable resource persons and would like to carry the stories supplied by him, more often than not.

Media men hate to be manipulated or deal with hostile public relations person standing in their way of news gathering. For them news—honest, real news—is a valuable commodity; therefore, the sources that come in their way, are detested.

EXHIBIT 16.4   Media functionaries

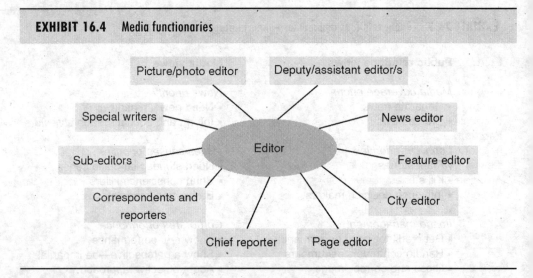

Any attempt, to 'manage' media in terms of supply of canned or manipulated or twisted information, that is, denying access to information will make a practitioner harbour more enemies than friends.

Many managements expect their public relations personnel to prevent media men from writing some negative stories about the organization or its bosses. It may not be possible because media men cannot be influenced beyond certain limits. Therefore, some adverse stories may appear no matter how skilled an organization's media relations person may be. Some managements also want to publicize events and information that have little or no new value. This practice seldom pays because a media organization, everyday receives hundreds of such press releases, which meet the ultimate destination, the trash can. Media relations job is not easy. The public relations person often comes under pressure for doing something which is unethical, unjustified, hence wrong. In such a situation, good judgment, experience, and calmness should help the practitioner to strike a balance between the organizational and media interests. The courage of conviction, open mind, and professional attitude should pay in such a situation.

The time tested thumb rule, 'Five Fs', followed by many seasoned media relations professionals should stand in good stead for a public relations practitioner (See Exhibit 16.5).

PUBLIC RELATIONS ASSISTANCE TO MEDIA

PR professionals engaged in the area of media relations would be quite successful and also in demand by the media men if they diligently and consciously assist the media persons as good resource. The sure way to get the cooperation of media men is to provide them with human interest stories and pictures that

---

EXHIBIT 16.5 The five Fs of media relations

Fast: Respect media men's deadlines. A call seeking information should be returned soonest, even beyond working hours. Responding next day would be too late as by then, the story may already have been telecast or published or even dropped.

Factual: Give actual and factual information. Press has lot of demand and favour for human interest stories. Narrate them in a manner that interests them. Also give the credible source of information. Statistics and photos are welcome too.

Frank: Be candid. The reasons for withholding information, if explained, most media men will understand and respect the source.

Fair: Organizations must be fair to media in matter of distribution of information fairly to all media outlets. Favourtism does not help and generates animosity amongst those not being served.

Friendly: Like everyone else media men appreciate courtesy. Remember their names; read what they write; listen to what they say; know their interests; thank them for their coverage and also appreciate a good story.

Source: Adapted from Population Reports (1996).

---

they should find suitable for use. Journalists are under pressure to meet deadlines and hence are short of time. The material provided to them in an almost ready-to-publish form would be most welcome and appreciated. The most important task of a media relations person is to find newsworthy information and present it to the media in a manner they can use it. Many successful practitioners have faith in certain time tested techniques, methods, and materials, which include the following:

- Provide accurate, timely, and interesting information.
- Collect and analyse information that interests the news media and meets their needs.
- Produce news releases, feature stories, opinion pieces, newsletters, backgrounders and other readily usable materials.
- Prepare press kits, fact sheets, expert lists, and aids that can be of help to media persons.
- Present story ideas to the journalists and supplement the ideas with relevant information and assistance.
- Arrange news conferences, conduct site visits and other events that may have potential for developing stories.
- Arrange exclusive interviews with organizational leaders, who have potential for media coverage.
- Keep the company website updated for facility of logging and downloading.
- Open a media query portal to receive and reply media men's queries.
- Deal with public controversies, when they arise and counter false rumours, by providing timely contradictions and clarifications to media.
- Have a crisis management plan for media relations, whenever an organization is faced with one.

Once the media relations professionals establish a rapport with the media, they come to have a reputation of reliable and credible resource persons. Media trusts such a person who provides this valuable service irrespective of the time of day and night and such a response results in a mutually beneficial relationship.

MEDIA RELATIONS NORMS

There are certain unwritten rules of the game called media relations. All PR practitioners have their own experiences in handling this sensitive and intricate part of their job in their own way, yet norms and rules are generally acceptable to all. One thumb rule that holds good in this area is that cordial and understanding relationship with editors, publishers, editorial writers, columnists, reporters, or the news telecasters is very conducing to gaining publicity for the organization. Good relations normally depend on proper understanding of the needs and aspirations of each other. Proper understanding of the job priorities and points of view of the media are basic to getting their cooperation in matter of their reporting objectively fairly, and accurately about the business of an organization.

Some of the rules that may be borne in mind by the practitioners are: *honesty accuracy, integrity, service, dignity, selectivity, candour, confidence,* and *data base.*

Honesty

Today's world is full of complexities and motivated by personal and organizational goals. Yet someone rightly said, 'Honesty is still the best policy,' at least in the media relations area. Journalists are trained to have a piercing sight to see through any game plan and an analytical mind to differentiate between real and phony. The doubting nature of the media, most often helps them to decipher if someone is trying to manipulate them. Once or twice a public relations person may be able to get away with some dishonest representations, but when caught, the word spreads very fast and he may lose face with the entire media fraternity. This may block his prospects for professional progress.

Accuracy

Professional reporters are often given sermons by their editors to be sure of what they are reporting in their stories. They insist that the information should be actual and factual and should not be contradicted by the people or the organizations mentioned in the reports or the readers at large. Obviously, it is very embarrassing for a media organization to apologize for some inaccuracies and issue corrections. A reporter may be reprimanded or even fired for no fault of his, just because of a trusted PR person, who let him down. Such bloomers and some minor inaccuracies with negative connotations may invite unwarranted criticism from those aggrieved. 'I have to check for accuracies of facts and figures, dates and time, names and places before I file a story. My news agency is very fanatic about it,' commented Dev Sagar Singh, senior India correspondent of JiJi press, a Japanese news agency.

Integrity

Hitherto fore, in India, public relations, because of lack of awareness about the profession amongst people and also because of the nefarious activities of some self styled fixers, masquerading as professionals, all those engaged in the profession were considered as dubious characters. Though in a lighter vein, a senior civil servant, once pronounced, 'A PR person is corrupt himself and a master in the art of corrupting people.' On the other hand, some PR people think that some media men also carry a price tag and can be cajoled into publishing some commercially and politically motivated material. On both sides, this is unethical and lacks integrity, which must be maintained by professionals.

Service

The fast breaking news does not have any fixed time. It is a round-the-clock phenomenon and the journalists following a story have no time limitations. Also the news becomes stale very fast. What is news today, would be history tomorrow. Due to this urgency, journalists are under pressure to meet and beat the deadlines. The practitioners who understand this make endeavours to assist the newsmen, any time of the day and night, by providing them information, stories, and photographs, if any, which is appreciated by media men. This binds the practitioner and the media men in a mutually beneficial relationship.

Dignity

Some advertising agencies, consultancies, and even PR practitioners seem to believe in the idea that they can leverage media coverage by the advertising support that their company extends to a publication or a news channel. There have been instances when the media was threatened with withholding the advertising from certain publications. In large and professional media organizations, the editorial and advertising departments work independently, and they resent interference into their areas. Exerting such pressure on media becomes counter productive and to pressurize media to carry certain stories that do not merit publication, is definitely below the dignity of public relations professionals and their organizations.

It is also very naive to beg editors to publish some news stories that may have publicity value but of no interest to readers or viewers. In fact, it is below the professional dignity of a public relations person to stoop low. This amounts to professional degradation and is sure to forfeit prospects of success.

Some professionals commit the cardinal sin of assuming that they know much more about the media than the media men themselves and hence try to usurp certain roles that do not belong to them. Indulging in patronizing editors and journalists is highly resented and they may scornfully block the way for future coverage.

Selectivity

Since media plays a vital role in influencing the thinking of the people in general and certain government functionaries in particular, there are several lobbies in a democratic set up that advocate for and against certain issues. Even the parliamentarians are more often educated and guided by the reports in media. Lobbyists, if not openly but clandestinely, persuade editors to select or reject certain stories that represent a particular interest. Hypothetically, if a multi billion rupee order for the purchase of aircrafts is going to be placed on a company, the competitor lobbyist prevails upon the media barons to plant a story about the doubtful safety record of that aircraft, thus block the order. On the other side, the selected aircraft company may pressurize the media to kill the story and bag the order. The game goes on, but, perhaps, at certain high levels of media hierarchy.

However, it is not ethical for the PR professional to ask for planting or killing a story. The choice of selection of a story lies with the media. On the professional side, PR practitioners, to facilitate objectivity in journalistic writings, should continue to update media by providing backgrounders about the history and statistics of their organizations, which the journalists often fall back upon for researching stories.

Candour

Most of the PR practitioners fall an easy prey to manufacturing press releases rather than creating them, when appropriate. This routinizing of the job takes the punch or the news value out of the releases. Such press releases, instead of appearing on the pages of a publication, land in the waste paper basket. Therefore, it becomes essential, not only to recognize publicity opportunities but also the news value. News means something new and the media men are on the look out for something which is newsy, interesting, fresh, and frank.

Thanks to the advent of electronics mail today, the flood of papers to the media offices has reduced. Many media organizations do not accept hard copies and insist on receiving press releases through e-mail, as the disposal of unwanted material is easier with the click of a button. Good old days, the editors kept large size waste paper baskets, on both sides of their desk, to dump stale and uninteresting papers. When emptied every couple of hours, the trash may be weighing a few tons every month.

. Therefore, it is only essential that every time a press release is distributed, it should have some candour which should be of media and readers' interest.

On the contrary, the protagonists and campaigners for some social issues like family planning think that the publicity must be generated, one way or the other, to make the programme a success. Michael Pertschuk (1990) holds some divergent views (See Exhibit 16.6).

Confidence

Confidence level of all those who interface with the media is of great importance. Most of the business leaders have to keep up the public appearance to influence people and decision makers in the government, as far as the policies that affect the business, are concerned. There is no room for shy and withdrawn businessmen who shun the limelight and want to do business quietly and unnoticed. Business today is under media scan and transparency is the need. Once in a while they have to be prepared to face a hostile press and answer some difficult questions, carefully and tactfully.

PR practitioners or consultancies make some focused efforts to train the chief executives to make them media savvy. Some veteran public relations professionals often lend a helping hand in the process, of course, for a fee.

A lot can be learnt from Henry Kissinger, the former US Secretary of State under Presidents Ford and Nixon, who regularly interfaced with the media. They often quoted him as 'a senior state department official'. Kissinger once

---

EXHIBIT 16.6 The divergent views

Michael Pertschuk, while advocating the increase in the family planning awareness, observed that 'the first task of the media advocate—and perhaps the first task of the health educator—is to recognize a good story and know how to market it. But the greatest art of media advocate is to recognize a non-story and transform it into a story.' As such, some mundane family planning stories have potential new value. Here are some examples:

- **New people**—'Noted physician to head health programme'
- **New Services**—'Ministry launches rural health initiative'

- **New policies**—'Programme to provide condoms for youth'
- **New contraceptives**—'Injectibles become available here'
- **New hours**—'Clinics open weekends to meet rising demand'
- **New data**—'Number of rural clinics sets record'
- **New funding or resources**—'Leading bank donates mobile vans'
- **New trends**—'More couples postponing births, survey shows'
- **New ideas**—'Community discussion groups spark interest in family planning'

Source: Adapted from Population Reports, October 1996.

remarked, 'Everybody really know that I was the senior official. The advantage of doing it in this manner was that it enabled foreign governments not to have to take a formal position about what I said, and not to force me to take a formal position. Since everybody in the negotiations was, theoretically, pledged to secrecy, but at the same time, since everybody was giving a briefing on their own version, I felt it was important that American version be also available, so we all played this complicated game.'

It is significant to note a number of media training institutes are mushrooming in India to prepare not only young aspirants but also some senior business leaders in the techniques of facing television cameras.

Data Base

Media men are highly mobile and migratory people and keeping a track of their whereabouts is an essential part of the networking exercise. It is advisable to keep the address book on the computer updated every couple of months or as soon as a change is noticed in the shift of a media person to a new location or publication. Also adding the new incumbents as any material addressed to the previous person, may earn annoyance rather than goodwill. Ensure the names are spelled right as people are quite fussy about the way their names should be written. For instance, even after leaving his public relations job, a practitioner continued to receive many mailers for a couple of years, adding to his pleasure and annoyance. 'How dumb, can't they update their mailing list even once in two years!', he would say.

Putting the above norms differently and briefly, as a ready reminder for the media relations persons, the suggested 'Ten Commandments' should be of help (See Exhibit 16.7).

EXHIBIT 16.7 Ten commandments of media relations

1. Provide news stories and materials, in an accurate, on time, and ready-to-publish form.
2. Be honest and open to build trust with media men.
3. Share information, for and against an issue to project a perspective.
4. Keep confidence of media men chasing a 'scoop' to safeguard their exclusivity.
5. Confide in media men with prior understanding that will rarely let you down.
6. It is unethical and undignified to plant a story or getting a story killed.
7. Ignore minor errors but take up for major corrections.
8. Spread information evenly without playing favourites. Leaving some out may earn media men's wrath.
9. Don't brag and boast, until facts support it. Show performance. Actions speak louder than words.
10. Don't grumble or resent if a story is not picked up. Better luck next time.

Source: Adapted from Ghosh, Subir (1994).

HOLDING A PRESS CONFERENCE

Press conference is a very convenient and comfortable way of releasing certain information to the media, all at a time. At the same time it is risky and can boomerang on the organization and the PR professional if there is not enough justification for doing so, in terms of a newsworthy announcement or event that warrants such a get together. One of the big reasons for the media person to come to the conference is their expectation of some fast breaking news about the company or some burning issues like labour situation, floating of a new issue, or a major expansion plan or even justification for a sudden layoff of couple of hundred employees.

Experienced and veteran PR professionals are of the opinion that a press conference should not be called unless the importance of the news clearly warrants so, and then it should be timed so that the news will get the widest coverage. Needless to say, a press conference is an occasion that demands the presence of the chief executive of the organization, or the authorized spokesperson, to answer certain queries that media may float to seek clarifications.

As a part of the preparation for holding a press conference, certain steps and actions have to be taken to make it a success. Some aspects of the event are: *invitees, spokesperson's skills, press release — structure, writing, and designing, media kits, venue and menu, equipment, etc.*

Invitees

Amongst the national and local press and the electronics media, there is a choice to be made according to the nature of the news that will be distributed. Certain news that is of national importance, can also be of equal interest to the local media. Therefore a decision to that effect should be taken. Sometimes the mainline daily reporters may think it below their professional status to mix with local stringers; therefore, a careful choice should be made.

Also certain events are of greater interest to the electronic media as it has greater number of picture and video possibilities. Some PR professionals prefer to hold two separate press conferences, one for print and the other for electronic media, as they think that the whirring of the cameras and TV journalists modus operandi do not gel well with print journalists. Whereas the print media men are more sober and well grounded, the electronic media reporters are more interested in sensational items.

Now it is appropriate to go by the media list or the data bank that has been created and pick and choose the invitees. Depending on the urgency or the importance of the conference, it may be appropriate to obtain telephonic confirmations of the acceptance of invitations.

Spokesperson's Skills

Now a days, most of the business leaders are media savvy and have learnt the art of facing reporters and TV cameras. Yet it is of paramount importance that the spokesperson of the company should be smart, impressive, knowledgeable, and highly communicative. The journalists like the people who talk coherently and convincingly and give some crisp and well thought out lines for their usage. The PR professional, however, is always around to assist the spokesperson, with necessary home work behind him. The practitioner, in coordination with the chief executive, have already created bank of expected questions and the right answers, to face the most difficult or provocative questions from the reporters who have mastered the art of ferreting out newsy information on some controversial issues.

However, there are certain rules of the game that the spokesperson should bear in mind, rehearse them, and emerge successful. James Hoggan (1991) enumerated the tips to face the press (See Exhibit 16.8).

Press Release—Structure, Writing, and Designing

A press release, when issued by an organization of substance, enjoys good acceptability, and serves as a credible source of information for a journalist. Also a well designed and well written press release would often give the story almost in a 'ready-to-publish' form, which most of the media men love, as it saves their precious time to rewrite. At the most a couple of commas, writing a headline, or chopping off a few lines or a paragraph, would make the material ready for publication.

PR practitioners understand that writing a press release is not like writing that stereotyped 'essay on cow' but a creative piece written in the format journalists have been trained to write. A smart press release makes it easy for readers/viewers to catch up with the news in short time. As the PR person is expected to write on behalf of the journalists, to earn publicity they are often called 'in-house journalists'.

Structure

Besides, gathering the answers to a well accepted norm of 5 Ws and 1 H (who, what, when, where, why, and how), it is important that the sequence should be arranged in the release, in order of the news value each element has. That is very basic to the writing of a good release. However, experienced media men have mentally devised a system called 'inverted pyramid' to take care of the news writing (See Exhibit 16.9).

EXHIBIT 16.8 Facing up to the press—a mini-survival guide

Keep it simple: Avoid legalese whenever possible and use everyday English during interviews. Reading a prepared statement is sometimes necessary, but speaking directly to reporters in a conversational tone and in your own words is far more effective.

Expect the worst: Talking to the news media can be an exceptionally unpleasant experience. Reporters can blindside an unprepared interview subject. Anticipate antagonistic questions and make sure you have rehearsed an adequate response.

Remain calm: When faced with hostile questions, remain calm and strive to maintain emotional control of your voice, facial expressions and gestures. Getting angry or allowing yourself to be drawn into an emotional debate with a reporter may generate headlines, but probably not the kind you want.

Record interviews: Some reporters working under tight deadlines will disregard the context of what was said during an interview in order to get their stories to air on time. Most will be less likely to do so if you politely ask to make a tape recording of the interview yourself.

Negotiate ground rules: Before you agree to talk to a reporter, find out who else will be interviewed and the amount of time or space that will be devoted to your views in the finished story. Make sure you understand the focus of the interview.

Keep it short: Talking too much during an interview can increase the chance of being quoted out of context. Television and radio news reports feed on short interview clips. Long-winded comments are ruthlessly edited. The average length of a quote in a TV news report is usually no more than 20 seconds.

Stick to your message: To avoid embarrassment, resolve beforehand what you want to say and, if possible, try to develop a series of key points to express your message clearly and succinctly. Make your points immediately and then elaborate if time allows. Never wing it.

Avoid being led: Watch hypothetical, leading, or loaded questions. A smart reporter in search of a juicy quote may try to trip you up by putting words in your mouth, boxing your answers or attempting to get you to repeat the loaded phrasing in his or her question. One way of responding to such 'trick questions' is to make note of them in your response — 'I would prefer not to answer hypothetical questions' — and then restate your key message.

Answer directly: Clever or misleading answers during an interview can often backfire. Avoid joking with reporters or indulging in sarcasm.

Watch cutaways: During a television interview, keep your expressions neutral while the camera operator does cutaways or wide shots of the reporter and yourself talking.

Avoid 'off-the-record': In theory, 'off-the-record' statements are made to reporters for the purposes of giving background information not intended for publication or broadcast. In practice, if you don't want to see something in print, don't say it. If you do decide to make an off-the-record statement, make sure the reporter agrees beforehand not to publish what you say.

Be cautious with 'not for attribution': The 'not for attribution' statement is intended for publication, but without revealing the source. If you want this, ask for statement not to be attributed before making it, not after. And always explain whether the lack of attribution applies to your company, your client, or your client's company.

Source: Adapted from *Communiqué*, September 1991.

Writing

For professional and aspirants alike, it is important to bear in mind some tips and techniques of writing a press release. When written and presented in a proper style, it improves the chances of its getting published.

Therefore, some tips are the following:

- Zero on the objective of the release.
- Target readership.

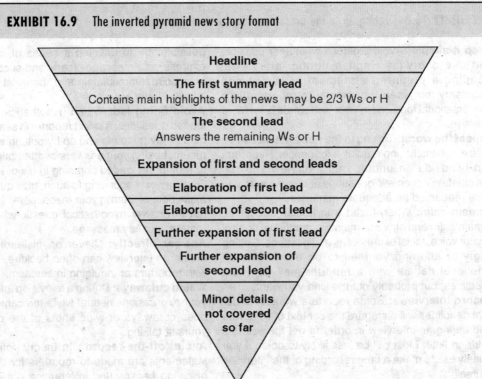

EXHIBIT 16.9 The inverted pyramid news story format

Headline

The first summary lead
Contains main highlights of the news may be 2/3 Ws or H

The second lead
Answers the remaining Ws or H

Expansion of first and second leads

Elaboration of first lead

Elaboration of second lead

Further expansion of first lead

Further expansion of second lead

Minor details not covered so far

- Give date line.
- Headline should be smart, crisp, and punchy.
- Identify the main lead and put in the first paragraph.
- Adopt news style and advertising copy writing.
- Don't lose track. Keep news in focus.
- Don't dilute the topic. Deal with the one you decided.
- Use simple and grammatically correct English and punctuate properly.
- Limit release to two pages.
- Type write neatly in double space.
- Give contact details.

Designing

The press release should be designed and dressed up judiciously and creatively, as it works as an ambassador for the company. It should be so designed that it represents the corporate identity in clear focus. Once a standard form has been designed and adopted, the company should send all releases typed on this form. Time and again, when such releases are received, media men develop a familiarity with such papers, and if the material distributed is often of good news value, it is more likely to get picked up for publication. However, the tips above may be borne in mind.

Media Kits

Media kit is an information folder containing copies of the press releases, photographs, biographies, backgrounders, special publications like annual report, house journal, a writing pad, and a pen, etc. prepared by the public relations to be distributed amongst media men on certain special events like product launch, inauguration of a new plant, a race or rally, and other important events. It is only advisable to present these kits to the media person, a little ahead of the beginning of the programme, so that they can run through the information and make up their mind about asking questions to seek additional information of their readers' interest.

Venue and Menu

The venue for holding a press conference should be conveniently located that takes least travelling time to reach. The ease and time saving is always appreciated by media community because of their time pressured jobs.

Hospitality is an important part of a press conference. Unless the company has the need to be modest about the menu, there is no harm in being liberal with high tea or dinner that precedes or follows the meeting. There is no need to give an impression of being stingy as it may trigger a negative attitude which is not conducive to good media relations. As a part of the courtesy, several companies also present the media men with their products they make or a token memento to mark the event.

Equipment

With the phenomenal spread of the TV networks and multiplicity of news channels, no press conference is meaningful without the presence of media men from the television. Naturally, they bring along their gadgets and other paraphernalia, which run on certain basic amenities like electric outlets, etc. Therefore, it is imperative for the PR to ensure availablability of such facilities and check and recheck that all connections are working fine. It is advisable to have skilled electricians around to grapple with breakdowns, if any. Keeping in view the possibility of a power outage, provision for stand-by generators should be considered.

MEASUREMENT OF SUCCESS

Evaluation of the success of any corporate activity is part of the management system, and media relations is no exception. Many PR professionals do a splendid job of conducting the media relations for their organizations and get contented with the verbal kudos from the management. The big harvest of press clippings also makes them feel elated. But it is appropriate to measure the quantum of success in terms of quantification and qualification of the exercise and take the necessary credit for career advancement.

Quantification

The usual method of evaluating the effectiveness of a media relations programme is to assess, on quarterly or yearly basis, the column centimeters of the company news published in newspapers, and magazines of all kinds, and the telecast minutes earned free from new channels, and then add up the quantum and arrive at a currency figure to demonstrate the amount of money saved, which otherwise would have to be spent on advertising. Similar exercise can also be done on the basis of each event conducted by the company and arrive at the money worth of the publicity earned, all free (See chapter 7 Exhibit 7.3). Public relations often subscribes to the clipping service agencies, who supply clippings for an annual subscription.

Qualification

It is but normal that all media reports cannot be in favour of the organization. There is always an element of negative reporting, for fault or no fault of the company. Some media men, to make their reporting juicy, indulge in running down the companies, on the pretext of objectivity, whereas others adopt a neutral path. So there can be three kinds of reports appearing in the media, positive, negative, and neutral. Smart PR professionals can keep a good track and keep plotting all the three kinds of reports on a yearly graph, to arrive at the quality of coverage they get during the year. This exercise, is not only a pointer towards professional performance but also an eye-opener for the company about their management style, policies, and practices. Lessons learnt can help in course correction.

Summary

Public relations and media are intimately related disciplines with different objectives, but one goal of reaching the readers and viewers. In a democracy, like India, media enjoys freedom of expression and functions independent of any government control. Whereas it provides checks and balances on certain issues, at the same time it has deep influence on the thinking of the people and their life styles. But freedom also brings responsibility in the form of self imposed discipline and a code of conduct as laid down by the press laws and the Press Council of India.

Media relations role is to assist media by supply of newsworthy information in the shape of press releases, back grounders, photographs, etc., with a view to earn publicity for the organization, thus influence public to generate desired responses. This relationship has assumed greater importance with the media explosion in the last quarter of the last century, and is slated for high growth. The multiplicity of newspapers, magazines, and TV channels beaming news, views and entertainment, is phenomenal. The maturing of 'pink press' mainly focusing on business, commerce, industry, and corporations, is a new stream of journalism.

Public relations has a peculiar role of a 'man-in-the-middle' to interface with media on behalf of the organization and vice versa. This poses a challenge to continue educating both sides about each side and balance it out. The expectations of media and a business organization may be somewhat conflicting, yet the inter-dependent role can hardly be ignored.

Public relations professionals have a role responsibility to understand media needs of news, and provide them with the necessary information in a readily usable form in a timely and accurate manner. Extending professional assistance to media brings the necessary rewards to the organizations.

To make a success of the media relations, certain norms need to be followed by public relations, which are honesty, accuracy of new, integrity, personal and professional, dignity, selective news, candour, mutual confidence and trust, and maintaining a database of journalists.

Holding a press conference is a crucial part of the media relations. A conference should be called only when justified, for distribution of some fast breaking news or timely views on certain issues. The spokesperson should be trained and communicative enough to make an impression. To make it a success the home work involves extending invitations to media men, developing press releases, media kits, deciding venue and menu, and providing the necessary equipment and facilities at the conference location.

The results of the media relations effort should be measured in terms of quantity of publicity generated and the quality of coverage to showcase to the management. Monitoring positive, negative, and neutral coverage, when plotted on a yearly graph, can provide a sense of direction to the organization and also enlighten the professional.

Key Terms

Deadline The time by which a story must be filed for publication or telecasting

Legalese Language that is typically used in legal documents and is generally considered by lay people to be difficult to understand

Lobbyist Somebody who is paid to lobby or advocate causes or issues with political representatives on behalf of an organization

Media fraternity People who work in the media world

Peg The main focus of a news story

Protagonist An important or influential supporter or advocate of something such as a political or social issue

Scoop An exclusive news story that is published by a newspaper, magazine, or news programme before its rivals

Concept Review Questions

1. Write a note to highlight the role relationship of public relations and media. Also match the conflicting and yet interdependent relationship.
2. What are the basic norms that a public relations professional should bear in mind for smooth and proficient handling of media relations?
3. What is the nature of homework required to be done by a media relations professional to make a success of a press conference? Discuss each element in detail.
4. What cautions and precautions a spokesperson should take while facing a press/TV interview? Discuss.
5. How would you evaluate the quality and quantity of the coverage produced by a media relations effort? Why is such assessment necessary? Explain.

Project Work

1. Write a press release on behalf of the company you work for, say Reebok, to announce its annual financial results.
2. Collect press clippings of the coverage given by media to a company in the last three months and develop a mini presentation to the management to highlight both quantity and quality of the coverage.

References

Communiqué (1991), A Canadian Public Relations Society newsletter, vol. 15, no. 3, September 1991.

Cutlip, Scott M., Allen H. Center, and Glen M. Broom (1985), *Effective Public Relations*, 6th edition, Prentice Hall Inc., USA, pp. 425 and 436.

Ghosh, Subir (1994), 'Media Relations', published by the Public Relations Society of India, Calcutta chapter, p. 21.

Hindustan Times, 'The Entertainment Media on Growth Path', New Delhi, 12 December 2007, p. 28.

Jefkins, Frank (2006), *Public Relations for Your Business*, Management Books 2000 Limited, UK, and printed in India by Jaico Publishing House, India, p. 36.

'Population Reports' (1996), published with USAID support, by Population Information Programme, The John Hopkins University, Baltimore, USA, vol. XXIII, no. 4, October 1996, p. 7.

http://presscouncil.nic.in/norms.htm.

17 Corporate Social Responsibility and Community Relations

CORPORATE SOCIAL RESPONSIBILITY AND COMMUNITY RELATIONS

Public relations professionals, today, have no two opinions about the value system that the business of the business is not just business, but the business of the business is also to make the lives of the people more enjoyable and worth living. Corporations have some definite obligations to the society. The objective of every business is not just to reap rich profits, but also to contribute to the quality of life. After all, it is the society who can make or mar the chances of success for a company.

As such, the concept of corporate social responsibility (CSR) or community relations means the obligation of a business enterprise to make such decisions and follow such lines of action, which are in line with the objectives and values of the society. Social responsibility is an obligation of corporate decision makers to adopt such policies and practices, which contribute to the welfare of the society. Such decisions and actions, actually, are in the interest of an organization itself.

An organization's relationship with its neighbours and community is crucial to the growth and prosperity of the organization because the society and particularly the neighbours of a manufacturing facility supply the necessary workforce, provide an environment that attracts or fails to attract talented personnel, provide vendors to vend materials and essential services, and even repose a trust in the company and invest its hard earned money to finance the operation. The society also provides a customer base for the goods and services manufactured and marketed by a company. And if for any reason the community is angered and anguished, it has the potential and influence enough to impose restraints and hurdles in the smooth functioning of an institution or industry.

In other words, it is the community or the society who is intimately connected with the business of any organization. The multi billion rupee manufacturing plants would not be possible to function, if the community does not provide the skilled workforce, if the community boycotts its products as not being socially responsible, if the community gets anguished that a company's plant is aggravating the pollution through discharge of industrial affluence thus risking the health of the people, if the community resents some policies and practices of the company. An organization functioning in isolation of the society, may never be able to survive for long and may face troubles and hardships.

H. Frazier Moore and Frank B. Kalupa (2005) wrote very appropriately, 'Community is a group of people who live in the same place, share the same government, and have a common cultural and historical heritage. The people who live in a community and the institutions that serve them are mutually dependent. The people cannot enjoy a good life without the institutions, and the institutions can exist only with the consent and support of the people. …. A business serves the community by providing regular employment, reasonable wages and financial benefits; by purchasing goods and services from local suppliers; by paying taxes to maintain local government; by contributing to charities and cultural projects; and by assuming in all respects the role of a good citizen.

The community, for their part, supply skilled labour, management personnel, and investment capital; and they consume the goods and services which business produces. Through local government, they provide fire and police protection, public utilities, highways, and sanitary services. The welfare of both community and business depends upon what each contributes to their mutual benefit.'

Economic Times (10 April 2000) mentioned that Henry Ford II once reasoned, 'Business is undergoing a revolutionary change where organizations are going to receive financial returns in the long run only by assuming social respon-sibilities. So is binding on the young incumbents to align social conscience with profit objectives.'

PR role though not legally or professionally defined, yet the CSR or community relations is part of the portfolio. PR practitioners definitely have role and involvement to direct and execute some definite community relations efforts for their companies. The basic bottom line of this responsibility is to generate a healthy relationship between the organization and the community based on understanding and mutual trust. The mutuality of this interdependent relationship is the key to this effort.

Fortunately for India, more and more organizations are taking on the mantle of community development that should impact the people's lives in a positive manner. It is a healthy trend that many companies are taking the cognizance of this fact. Progressive organizations are becoming proactive in their attitude as they acknowledge that

- Business must also result in the larger good of society.
- Business cannot operate in isolation from society.
- A social mission should form an essential part of an organization's business vision.
- Profitability is of paramount importance and an entrepreneurial necessity, and only when an organization makes profit, can sustain growth in its business, reward shareholders and fulfil social responsibilities.
- Organizations want to be known as good corporate citizens.

CSR—THE INDIAN TRADITION

For India, the concept of CSR is not new, but has been a tradition with the business community. For ages the businessmen have been dedicating a portion of their profits towards social causes. Known as *Dharmada*, the businessmen of yester years have been contributing to support some social welfare activities. Donating money to religious places, building night halt inns for travellers, drinking water booths, known as *Piao*, are still a common practice. However, the activity was not organized as the business was all scattered and diversified.

Some small unknown and nondescript businessmen seem to have acquired lot of good reputation for being very kind hearted as they liberally donated towards causes, mainly religious. Some old business families like Birlas, Dalmias, Modis, Tatas, etc. have been quite active in this area. Some of the beautiful temples with attached night halt and eating facilities, still remind us of this philanthropic work done by these business houses and many unknown businessmen in their own silent way.

Now with the emergence of large business houses, CSR has become the main focus of the nation's economic and social activity. Business leaders have become more conscious towards their social obligation. So the corporate social responsibility is the buzz word in the business world today.

PRIVATE SECTOR INITIATIVES

The business leaders of India have woken up to the corporate responsibility, which has spread a nationwide awareness amongst business men towards this social obligation.

According to a report in the *Economic Times* (20 October 2005), philanthropy touched a new high in India's corporate sector when the private sector companies donated Rs 400 crore cumulatively during 2005. This is the highest ever contribution made by the corporate sector in the history and compared to the previous year, there has been a quantum jump of 75 per cent.

The big private sector donors include Reliance Industries, Infosys, Hindalco, Grasim, Jaiprakash Associates, Dr Reddy's, ITC, Bajaj Auto, Gujarat Ambuja, Sterlite Industries, Hindustan Zinc, and Videocon International. While the total number of companies who made donations, even if a minuscule amount, was lower than the figure five years back, the number of companies making donations of over Rs 1 crore swelled up. A total of 70 companies donated more than Rs 1 crore during 2004.

On the other hand, some of the top public sector companies included IOC, HPCL, SCI, fell in the Rs 10 crore plus range followed by NTPC, BPCL, and GAIL. It should be interesting to look at the top ten donors who demonstrated their keen interest in the corporate social responsibility (See Exhibit 17.1).

Infosys

Speaking at the Hindustan Times Leadership Summit, the co-chairman of Infosys, Nandan Nilekani (October 2007) had said that corporate leaders must boost personal philanthropy by corporate leaders, as it has happened in the US, in order to prevent criticism from shareholders about diversion of funds for pursuits other than profits. However, he said that 'companies cannot go beyond a point

---

EXHIBIT 17.1 CSR—the top ten donors

	Rupees in crore
Reliance Industries	38.3
Indian Oil Corporation	26.5
Hindustan Petroleum	21.1
Infosys	21.1
Hindalco	13.5
Sci	12.2
Grasim	9.8
Ntpc	9.7
Jaiprakash Associates	9.0
Dr Reddy's	8.8

on philanthropy.'

Aditya Birla Group

Rajashree Birla (2007), Director, Aditya Birla Group, said that CSR could be used, as her group has done, to empower the less privileged by doing everything from housing for the poor to helping vocational education that creates jobs, while winning over the affections of the community in which a business group functioned. She urged the business community to get down to work, avoiding 'cheque book philanthropy'. 'I would urge you to subscribe to compassionate capitalism,' she advised the business leaders.

Hindustan Unilever

Defending the charity named after the controversial 'Fair and Lovely' brand, Harish Manwani (2007), president of Unilever, Asia and Africa and chairman of consumer goods giant Hindustan Unilever Limited, said that his company had built its social work around its brands. Lifebuoy soap was linked with the largest programme of its kind on the promotion of washing hands for health and hygiene, while Project Shakti empowered poor rural women by building income programmes around the selling of soap.

General Electric India

President and CEO of General Electric India, Tejpreet Singh Chopra (2007) had said at the HT Leadership Summit that 'I don't see anything sinister about it. If corporates don't do it in an ethical and transparent way, it won't work. It is quite clear that corporate social responsibility has to be included in the definition of success.'

Reader's Digest

World's leading publication, *Reader's Digest* has taken the initiative of recognizing the outstanding work done by socially conscious corporate organizations and constituted the annual Pegasus corporate social responsibility award. The award which has been sponsored by Maruti Suzuki is conferred on the corporations who have set new standards by going beyond the call of duty. The others who have associated themselves with the effort are NDTV Profit and Impact Printers. Enough public relations effort was initiated by the organizers to hold the awards evening to generate interest in the corporate community towards their obligation to the society (See Exhibit 17.2).

It appears that the corporate world, with the arrival of economic liberalization, has come alive towards their obligation to improving the lot of the people. Some

EXHIBIT 17.2 Reader's Digest CSR Awards

PEGASUS

CORPORATE SOCIAL RESPONSIBILITY

AWARDS 2007

A Reader's Digest Initiative

Reader's Digest salutes the spirit of selfless doing at the
Pegasus Corporate Social Responsibility
Awards 2007

The Pegasus CSR Awards have been constituted by Reader's Digest to recognise outstanding work done by socially conscious corporate organisations. Winners would be selected among those who have set new corporate standards by going beyond the call of duty.

The Pegasus CSR Awards are brought to you by Maruti Suzuki, India's favourite automobile company.

Venue: Taj Lands End, Bandra, Mumbai
Date: 12th December 2007
Time: 7.00 pm onwards
For details, contact Deepti Todi - 022 66522516

MARUTI SUZUKI

Presents

Exclusive Telecast on	Print Partner
NDTV PROFIT	impact

Entry by invitation only.

Source: Hindustan Times, 12 December 2007.

EXHIBIT 17.3 Computers for 60 city schools

Underprivileged children in 60 schools in Delhi will soon have an opportunity to enter the world of computers, thanks to the vision of some of the top corporate names in the country.

These schools which run on shoestring budgets, are to be equipped with computer labs and will have access to the Internet. And making all this possible is Shiksha India, a project initiated by the Global Leaders of Tomorrow, under the auspices of the World Economic Forum. The aim of the project is to 'bridge the digital divide in education'.

While speaking at the launch of the pilot project at the Indian Economic Summit 2001, J.N. Godrej, chairperson of Shiksha India, said the launch was the first step of the long journey. At the end of the journey Shiksha India intends to reach over 20 per cent higher secondary schools across the country.

Apart from Godrej, other corporate heavyweights behind the project include Infosys head N.R. Narayana Murthy, CII chief Tarun Das, NIIT's Rajinder Pawar, C.K. Birla, and Sharmila Dalmia.

Shiksha India is based on a similar project in Argentina which met with resounding success. 'It was in the September 2000, Geneva meet of the GLT that Shiksha India was conceptualized,' said Godrej. Since then the industry and the government have been cooperating to try and realize the project.

The first place where the idea was tested was in Government Boy's School, Anandvas, in Delhi. The project was a success. Education suddenly became fun for children and even teachers realized that they could learn a lot.

'Shiksha India is based on the concept of the 5 Cs. Computers, connectivity, content, coaching, and commercial sustainability,' said Godrej.

The project intends to donate 10 to 15 computers to each school, provide Internet connectivity, develop specialized content to help students enjoy the learning experience and coach teachers so that the project can be utilized to its full potential.

So far, Shiksha India has been able to identify 37 schools for its pilot project. The remaining schools are expected to be shortlisted by September.

The second pilot project launched by Shiksha India will cover 200 rural schools. Already ties have been established with government-run Navodaya Vidyalaya Samiti. The third pilot project will cover 500 urban schools across the nation. For this, Shiksha India has allied with the Kendriya Vidyalaya Sangathan.

Source: The Times of India, 3 December 2001.

may be of the opinion that industries have a vested interest in philanthropy as this is an investment in the enlargement of their consumer base and also in building a future sources of manpower supply. All said and done, this is an interdependent world and the industry and the community have to coexist and thrive on each other's support. However, some of the efforts made by an industry for the welfare of the community deserve kudos, as they will go a long way to pave way for a bright future. The plans of the Shiksha India look praiseworthy (See Exhibit 17.3).

Tata Consultancy Service

The Times of India (2003) reports that TCS has charted out a plan for revamping key engineering colleges of the country. The basic aim is to create a clutch of world class graduate schools that will churn out bright young minds ready for radical innovations in engineering processes and creative product development, and for engaging in fundamental research. TCS plant was planning to start with three state institutes VJTI (Mumbai), College of Engineering (Pune), and Guru

Gobindsinghji College of Engineering (Nanded) before extending the project to other colleges in the country. As per the plan, these colleges will be funded by industry, alumni, and international agencies.

Taj Hotels

Terrorist attacks at the Taj Mahal Palace and Tower on 26 November 2008 caused a lot of loss of life and property. The house of Tatas rose to the occasion and reopened a wing of Taj Hotel in record time. In addition to restoring the confidence of hotel staff, the Tata group set up the Taj Public Service Welfare Trust, as part of their CSR, to provide immediate relief to individuals and families affected by the attack. In an advertisement, the company appealed to the people to contribute their moral and material support to conquer despair with compassion (See Exhibit 17.4).

CII INITIATIVES

The Confederation of Indian Industry (CII) set up the Social Development and Community Affairs (SDCA), formerly known as Corporate Citizen Council, in 1995 with the primary objective of sensitizing the Indian industry towards CSR and involving the industry in major social sector initiatives. The main purpose of the SDCA is to satisfy a social 'balance sheet', to ensure that the benefits of the economic reforms and industrial growth are available to the people living in poverty and unemployment and that the image of the industry as a 'concerned' group about community development be enhanced and strengthened. The CII has formed three National Committees on community development, population and health, education and literacy to oversee the mandate of the council.

SDCA has finalized the approach to make it happen and some of the objectives that they have set forth for the council are as follows:

- Motivate CEO's and corporate personnel to adopt a policy statement vis-à-vis social development.
- Establish a strong consultative base to help industrial houses develop a long-term sustainable programme of action.
- Evolve strong interactive and networking systems.
- Adopt a proactive approach thereby building bridges between the industry and the community.
- Design and initiate major 'awareness' drives and campaigns on 'development' theses through publications.

Some of the areas where the CII along with SDCA council has been taking initiatives are

- An aids advocacy and options for action package
- A literacy package developed with the National Literacy Mission to achieve 100 per cent literacy for industrial workforce

EXHIBIT 17.4   The Taj Public Service Welfare Trust

THE TAJ PUBLIC SERVICE WELFARE TRUST

The recent events in Mumbai have left many in need. We cannot replace that which is lost, but we can help heal.

In the aftermath of the unprecedented attack, The Taj Group has witnessed an outpouring of support from well-wishers in India and across the globe. In response, the Tata Group has set up The Taj Public Service Welfare Trust to provide immediate relief to individuals and families affected by the recent terror attacks in Mumbai: the general public, police and security forces, employees of the Taj and other establishments.

The trust will henceforth, come to the aid of victims of terror, natural calamities and other tragic events that inflict damage to life and property.

Now is the time for us to conquer despair with compassion. And keep the light of humanity burning bright.

Individuals or companies wishing to donate as well as intended beneficiaries can contact us at : The Taj Public Service Welfare Trust, Mandlik House, 2nd floor, Mandlik Road, Colaba, Mumbai 400 001. Tel: +91-22-66395515. Fax: +91-22-22027442. Email: tpswtrust@tajhotels.com

TAJ
Hotels Resorts
and Palaces

A TATA Enterprise

Source: Hindustan Times (2008).

- A family health care manual to facilitate introduction of health care initiatives at the work place
- Experience sharing missions
- Interactive workshops on community development, literacy, strategies for social development
- Aids orientation programmes
- Project 'inspire' to facilitate the re-entry of the Indian students and mid-level professionals into the Indian economy
- A Fulbright – CII programme for mid-level managers
- Craft development projects

Perhaps, a progress report on the strides made by CII, since the inception of the programme, would make an interesting reading.

COMMUNITY EXPECTATIONS

The community while seeing the corporate business prospering, have an expectation to share the benefits of prosperity. The community and the neighbourhood, particularly living on the periphery of the manufacturing plants of the organizations, expect that the benefits of the business growth should percolate down to the society and help them to improve their lot. The under privileged sections of the society, particularly, have high hopes. Some of the expectations that the community have are: *employment, education, commercial prosperity, housing, health, and medical care, municipality, safety and security, cleaner environment,* and *good corporate image.*

Employment

Employment opportunities, when generated by the arrival of an industry in certain locations, are highly appreciated. The local community always have hopes that their sons and daughters will find opportunities to work for the neighbouring plants and contribute to the family incomes. In India, the communities have been demanding that companies should adopt 'sons-of-the-soil' policy in matter of awarding jobs. However, industries have to has a broader vision to hire personnel with special skills to fill up some specific jobs.

Education

Any community has a strong desire that their children should make lot of progress in their lives through acquiring good education. Unfortunately, the lack of good schools is always felt by the people who are keen to get their children educated and be successful in life. The large organizations are expected to set up schools and colleges or indirectly aid such institutions, who are doing a good job of providing education to younger generation. Birlas, for instance, set up a pioneering institute of engineering in Pilani.

Commercial Prosperity

The setting up of some industrial giants in the locations, propel a host of commercial activities in terms of opening up opportunities for starting many small businesses. Often the industrial townships have attracted several traders to open shop in the area to supply a variety of consumer goods of daily use to the people and even enter into a band of regular vendors to the organization, who supply materials of all kinds. From small parts to major components that go into the making of finished products, that are supplied to the company, promise reasonable returns. This commercial activity has a cascading effect on the community, who benefit from the residual prosperity which the society so ardently desires. Industrial towns like Faridabad, Jamshedpur, or Bokaro, etc. are examples of this phenomenon.

Housing, Health, and Medical Care

It is but desirable that the people who come to work for an organization, expect facilities like proper housing, health, and medical care for themselves and their families. It is in the interest of the company to provide medical facilities to help employees in particular, and people in general, to enjoy good health. Availability of the necessary medical assistance, in an emergency, is highly desirable. Escorts Limited, for instance, set up a hospital in Faridabad to take care of their employees and people at large.

Municipality

No town or city can function without a good municipal system. A company's presence should not be like that of a guest but as an integral part of the community. It is only desirable that the organization should contribute to strengthen the municipal system financially, over and above the municipal taxes that it is expected to pay. Municipal services like roads, street lighting, drainage, running water, scavenging and hygiene, etc. if organized well, should bring lot of comfort to people in the community, and good name for the organization.

Safety and Security

To remain safe and secure is the inborn need of all humans and the community in which they live. The presence of properly organized police system to ensure safety and security to the lives and property of the citizens, is an essential part of the urban existence. Police surveillance to keep the law and order under check is an essential part of the community life. The police is indirectly funded by the taxes paid by the corporations. Besides, the companies are expected to extend a helping hand to the police by providing logistic support in their efforts in educating citizens in areas like traffic management, and generate public awareness to deal with the menace of drug trafficking and terrorism, etc.

Cleaner Environment

Industry is often accused by the community of polluting the environment by the smoke emitted by its chimneys and the industrial affluence discharges into the nearby canals. This results in air pollution that makes breathing difficult and brings problems like asthma, TB, allergies, etc. The sources of drinking water are contaminated making it unfit for consumption. It is but a genuine expectation, and the community may force the industry to take certain steps to contain problems. Some reputed companies are now, on their own, setting up water treatment plants and increasing the heights of their chimneys to take care of the problems.

Good Corporate Image

Good reputation of an organization is a valuable asset. It is a force that generates many favourable responses from the publics. Good corporate image attracts good quality personnel, imbibes customers' and shareholders' confidence and a reasonable attitude of the government. Good reputation comes about with good deeds and professional style of functioning by the company. The community, when thinks high of an organization, extends all kinds of moral and material support to the organization. Families feel proud of their sons and daughters working for such a company. In sharp contrast, people shun association with a company of ill repute. PR, particularly, has a focused responsibility to keep up good corporate image.

OBJECTIVES OF COMMUNITY RELATIONS

The objectives of a community relations programme or the corporate responsibility endeavours of a company are guided by the overall corporate objectives, its profitability levels, the size and nature of the community and the public relations goals. Honestly enough, the obligations to social welfare are linked to the financial health of a company and its corporate philosophy. However, some of the major objectives are to:

- Share enough information with the community about the corporate operation concerning employment, education, public health, and the contributions made towards upliftment of living standards of the community.

- Involve opinion leaders amongst the employees in various activities connected with social welfare, so that they spread the information for a ripple effect.
- Collect sensitive feedback about the attitudes that various community leaders have about the corporation.
- Cultivate and maintain congenial relations with community leaders and other functionaries of the neighbouring organizations for a mutual exchange of ideas.
- Keep a tab on the pressure groups' activities and forestall attacks with actions and appropriate communication.
- Get involved in certain social welfare activities like blood donation camps, eye donation camps, family welfare programmes, free medical checkups, etc., organized by agencies like Red Cross and other NGOs.
- Float events like sports, cultural evenings, childrens' painting competitions, scholarship programmes, awards and rewards, etc. for the community.
- Hold an annual open house and invite employees, their families, friends, and neighbours to showcase the operation, achievements, and company's interest in the people.
- Project organization to the community as a good corporate citizen with genuine interest in the community.
- Project, in the employment market, that the organization is a fair employer and is a congenial place to work.
- Develop a well thought out communication programme to keep the community informed about the company' activities and get credit for the efforts.

COMMUNITY NETWORKING

PR practitioners, by virtue of their knowledge and experience, know that it is not advisable to jump into the area of community relations abruptly. Like any other management discipline, there is a need to do the necessary homework. The first and foremost action is the networking with the members of the community who matter. Until a public relations practitioner or community relations manager puts himself in the place where the action is, the success of the programme would be doubtful.

Also, it is important to identify the opinion leaders in the community and establish a relationship with them. Identifying and developing networks of influentials is a starting point in community relations. Many such networks just come about through the socializing abilities of a practitioner. Some networks have to be created with a definite objective of solving a community relations problem. The 'man-in-middle' role of a public relations person in this area is highly relevant. He may even act as the central coordinator for many a social and cultural activities organized for the community like Ram Lila, Ganesh Puja, Durga Puja, Guru Purv, etc.

The importance of opinion leaders or thought leaders in the communities, can hardly be exaggerated. The groups of such influentials often get together to exchange ideas on a variety of social issues and generate important opinions that percolate down to the lower levels of the society. In fact they are the trend setters and the solutions devised by them are generally acceptable to many.

The society, as if, has got arranged into two layers, the class and the mass. The masses often follow what the classes do. Ultimately, everyone wants to identify himself with the class. Therefore the simple rule of reaching the masses is to first reach the classes and the messages will get percolated to the masses, as everyone wants to align oneself with the class. The class is composed of professionals, doctors, journalists, public relations professionals, senior government officials, celebrity actors, poets, singers, priests, legal professionals, *Sarpanches*, teachers, etc. Any value system or message that gets accepted by the class, ultimately finds its acceptance with the masses. So the community networking has to start top down (See Exhibit 17.5).

COMMUNICATING TO THE COMMUNITY

Sharing information about certain matters that impact the community is of vital importance to good community relations. Neighbours always want to know as to what is cooking in the pot. Sharing information builds strong bonds between a company and the people living around the organization. Whereas PR can get credit for the organization for all the welfare work, the company has done or has plans to do, it may also be prepared to share some bad news. Hiding or withholding certain information does not help. Incidents like accidents, fires,

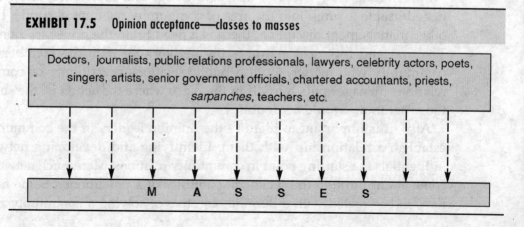

EXHIBIT 17.5 Opinion acceptance—classes to masses

Doctors, journalists, public relations professionals, lawyers, celebrity actors, poets, singers, artists, senior government officials, chartered accountants, priests, *sarpanches*, teachers, etc.

M A S S E S

gas leaks, or labour situation or technology mix up, etc. when frankly shared, may generate some critical discussions in the community, but good sense soon prevails.

THE COMMUNICATION MEDIA

Amongst the variety of media and innovations that are used for communicating to the community are newspapers, radio and television advertising, publicity through various mass media channels like press, radio, TV open house and conducted tours of the facilities, public speaking, meetings with the opinion leaders, visits to community institutions, videos and films, exhibitions and displays, house journal and institutional literature, etc.

Some of the usual ways of communicating are: *advertising, open house, conducted tours, house journal, special events, sponsorships, contributions to funds,* and *media relations.*

Advertising

With the power of the mass media and its effective reach, the organizations and communities remain connected. Occasional advertising, focusing on the institutional achievements or felicitating the community on special occasions like Independence day, Republic day, Diwali, Baisakhi, Pongal, etc. serves two good purposes—the messages connect the community to the company and help to cultivate the local media like small time newspapers, or cable operators, who provide good audience selectivity. If available in the area, using of FM radio could also be considered for this purpose. Messages thus released also help in communicating to the employees and make them feel proud of their organization amongst their own clusters. Such advertising also helps funding the local media, generally operating on shoestring budgets.

Open House

Events like an open house offer a powerful opportunity to cultivate the community. It has an advantage of bringing in large number of people to the organization to enthuse them to know and understand the company operations. Though personal interactions may not be possible, yet the occasion creates a high connectivity. Many good companies organize such events under the banner of 'Family Day' or *'Parivar Divas'* when employees, families, friends, and neighbours are invited to come to the organization. Generally, an entertainment programme is followed by a lunch or refreshments for the invitees. A stage is also set for the company management to communicate messages about policies, progress, and practices of the organization and seek community support.

Conducted Tours

A conducted plant tour for the members of the community makes a good impression about the company's operations, and is, therefore, an effective way of building understanding. Employees are also encouraged to bring along their family and friends for such a tour of the facilities on certain fixed days of the week, to show off their workplace. Going by the good reputation of a company, most employees take pride in showing their work stations. PR coordinates the effort with the help of tour guides drawn generally from the technology department. As a gesture of goodwill the visitors are treated to high tea and also presented with a memento and a tour booklet.

House Journal

The extended circulation of the internal or employees' magazine, when it contains material of community interest, serves a useful purpose in cultivating good community relations. PR practitioners, who are also the editors of such publications, increase the print order and mail such issues to the community members. For instance, such a publication, when for some weeks, stays at the local doctors' clinics, gets the necessary attention from the waiting patients and generate a ripple effect in the society. Panchayats, barber shops, public reading rooms, schools and college libraries are also appropriate places for reaching out to community for building an understanding about the organization amongst the target publics. Some useful information about health, hygiene, family life or travelling tips, etc. make an interesting reading for the people, courtesy the company house journal.

Special Events

Special events like a presentation for the visiting dignitary, spiritual lecture by a religious leader, inauguration of new building block, children's painting or dance competition, ladies tailoring training programme, etc. are the kinds of events which interest the community. Special invitations to the community leaders give them a pride of association and mileage to the organization to earn goodwill. For instance, DCM group would sponsor annual Ram Lila in Delhi, which has been a sought after event. Such a show poses some security problems, yet with little care, things become manageable.

Sponsorships

A community often looks forward to a company's patronage for certain activities. Funding a blood donation camp, free eye checkup camp or running a free kitchen at a religious congregation, etc. are highly appreciated. The industry in Faridabad have been funding a YMCA Institute of Engineering and the Country Golf Club. Donating books to a school library, or cash donation to a village school to build a drinking water system for kids, are the kind of sponsorships. For instance, a company sponsored the raising of a school brass band and funded for maintaining the kids' uniforms and instruments, etc. (See Exhibit 17.6).

Contribution to Funds

Contribution to certain funds is seen as an important initiative by the business community towards social causes and community welfare. Companies earmark certain portions of their profits for philanthropy. For instance, Faridabad Industries Association persuaded all its members to sponsor a number of seats for funding the building of Nahar Singh Cricket Stadium in Faridabad. When, unfortunately, any state is affected by natural calamities like drought, floods or earthquake, etc. the corporate sector respond to help the people by making

EXHIBIT 17.6   A school brass band in action

The Carmel Convent School, Faridabad, band is sponsored by neighbouring industry.

financial and material contributions to the relief effort. Obligation to the society in troubled times is one major item on corporate charity.

Media Relations

The nature of media relations at the local level is somewhat different. The local media comprises some small and medium newspapers, cable TV network, or a limited coverage radio station. Most of these outfits function on very small budgets and do not subscribe to expensive news services. As such the local news is more valuable to them than the national or international news. Press releases originating from the local sources are readily accepted and published by the editors. Public relations, off and on, organizes some press meets or press conferences with the company executives to boost media morale. Local advertising programme, though not directly linked to media coverage, for the company, is yet always welcome to keep them afloat. On the other hand, though the readership is very limited, yet because of the local colour, the publications enjoy good credibility.

Summary

The business of the business is not only to make profits but also to contribute to the improvement in the quality of life for the members of the society. Corporate social responsibility or community relations are vital because it is the community who provides skilled work force, customers, and investments to make the corporation a success. If aggrieved and anguished, the community can make the operation difficult. This is an interdependent relationship. Therefore, the corporate world has obligations towards the community.

India has an age old tradition of serving the community. Indian business, though not organized on that large a scale, yet have been contributing a part of their profits to social welfare. The corporate world has now woken up to their obligations towards society and have been making sizable contribution to this effort. The corporate leaders have been expressing whole hearted support to the concept of corporate social responsibility and have been taking steps to translate ideas into actions.

The Confederation of Indian Industry has taken initiative and formed a social development and community affairs body in 1995 to sensitize the Indian industry towards social obligations and have certain aims and objectives.

Public relations have a role and responsibility to get involved and draw up objectives of the community relations programme. The expectations of the community must be understood and the objectives of the programme be carved out accordingly.

People in the communities want to know the business policies and practices of a company. Therefore, public relations has a vital responsibility to keep the community informed through a well planned communication programme and use certain media of communication to generate the necessary harmonious relationship and mutual understanding.

Key Terms

Extended circulation   When a publication increases print order for circulation beyond regular readers

Good corporate citizen   Like an individual, a company should also obey the laws of the land and demonstrate its moral obligations towards society

Opinion leaders   Influential members of a community, group, or society to whom others turn for advice, opinions, and views

Social conscience   An attitude of sensitivity and sense of responsibility regarding injustice and problems in society

Socially responsible products   Products that do not damage the social fabric or individual's health

Thought leaders   Somebody who is in the vanguard of opinion or knowledge about an issue

Concept Review Questions

1. Define and describe the concept of corporate social responsibility with special reference to community relations.
2. Describe the Indian traditions, old and new, about the initiatives the Indian corporates have been taking to demonstrate their interest and actions on community welfare front.
3. What are the expectations of community from the corporate business? Describe the public relations role in developing objectives and programme of community relations with reference to communicating to the community through various media.

Project Work

1. Contact the Confederation of Indian Industry (CII) to ascertain the progress made on their efforts to sensitize the Indian industry since 1995, and write a report on the subject.
2. Develop a community relations programme for a five star hotel, say Maurya Sheraton, for which you are the public relations manager.

Case Study

Social Mission and Business Vision*

Ms Rajashree Birla spearheads the Aditya Birla group's activities in community work. She has not only maintained her late husband's image as a responsible industrialist, but also made value addition

---

*Source: Adapted from The Financial Express, New Delhi, 24 December 2000, p. 7.

to it through her wide and far-reaching activities. The group's community activities include providing the rural youth with substantial employment, making safe drinking water accessible, and undertaking healthcare, education, and training projects. Here are some extracts from an interview by Rajiv Tikoo of Financial Express.

What is it that inspires you to undertake community work?
This is an area I have been involved in for over three decades now as I worked along with my husband, Shri Adityaji. Both of us very strongly felt that we should be engaged in welfare-driven activities, which benefit the weaker sections of society. Shri Adityaji passionately believed in the spirit of giving and caring for people, in helping to restore their dignity and self-esteem. For him doling out money to the poor could never be a long-term solution. Instead, he said we should help people in a way that they are able to stand on their own feet and earn money continuously. In this way, their livelihood is never at stake. He felt making people productively employed was vital.

But why do you think business should shoulder community responsibility?
We have to reckon with the fact that millions of people living in both the rich and poor countries suffer economic poverty and social deprivation. The government cannot single-handedly tackle this issue. In today's increasingly complex environment, which has led to a changed and new social ethos, the onus of social responsibility, which rested earlier with the government, is being moved to the private sector.

Therefore, more and more organizations have to take on the mantle of community development that will impact people's lives in a positive manner. It augurs well that many companies are taking cognizance of this fact. Progressive organizations are becoming proactive in their attitude as they acknowledge that

- Business is not simply an end in itself, but that it must result also in the larger good of society.
- Business cannot operate in isolation from society.
- A social mission is as much integral to a corporation as a business vision. In fact, social mission must form a part of an organisation's business vision.
- Profitability is, of course, of paramount importance and an entrepreneurial necessity. Only when an organization makes profit can it sustain and grow its business, reward its shareholders, and fulfil social engagements too.
- Organizations want to be known as good and responsible corporate citizens.

But these don't seem to be good enough reasons. At the best, they may enlist only a cosmetic involvement from corporates.
Business houses who do social work no longer treat social responsibility as a fringe activity. Their commitment is genuine. And there are several reasons, compassion among them being the foremost. While compassion stems from the heart, there is a definite rationale behind the social work motive.

Like?
Firstly, shareholders expect the companies in which they invest to be sensitive to the needs of the society.

Secondly, professionals want increasingly to align with a company that not only enjoys a reputation for quality products and services but is also committed to social causes. There is a tremendous feel-good factor about such companies.

Customers show a definite preference for companies with a social conscience. Social projects are also a means of sharing with the community the values that an organization stands for. As a result of these factors, a large number of organizations have begun embedding a social investment strategy as part of their business strategy.

Then how come there are very few businesses that undertake community work?
The day is not far when an increasing number of industrial houses will realize the virtues of being good corporate citizens who reach out to communities far beyond the call of business.

What are the community initiatives that your group has undertaken?
For nearly fifty years now, we at the Aditya Birla Group have been and continue to be involved in meaningful, welfare driven initiatives that distinctly impact the quality of life of a marginalized people, surrounding hundreds of villages near our plants spread all over India.

Our group's activities are wide and far ranging. These include innovative projects that provide the rural youth with a chance to shape their future through economic development schemes. Similarly, the group undertakes education and training, and health-care projects. We also reach out to physically impaired people who are tremendously disadvantaged. We also espouse social causes like widow remarriages and dowry-less marriages. Women empowerment programmes are also on our agenda. Besides, we also sponsor art and cultural events.

We believe in the trusteeship concept of management. From this stems our social involvement, far and beyond business. Our projects mirror the moral conscience of our group. They reflect our values. Our community work is a way of telling the people among whom we operate that we care for them.

Please elaborate about your community activities?
For example, Tata Hindalco has adopted 162 villages in and around the plant at Renukoot in Uttar Pradesh. With the UP Jal Nigam and UNICEF, Hindalco is helping provide drinking water to over 103 villages. Hindalco's widow remarriage programme is very heart rending. Hindalco has managed to get more than 250 widows remarried in the last three years. Grasim's work with the physically impaired is also noteworthy. Grasim has provided the Jaipur Foot to more than 1000 physically impaired individuals.

Indo Gulf also fosters sustainable livelihood through its rural development and vocational training centers. Skills in different vocations such as electric, auto repair, electronic equipment maintenance and repair among others, are imparted to the locals at this center. The locals are also trained in simple skills, including tailoring. In the last 10 years, Indo Gulf has been able to provide training to over 3000 persons. Our group is involved in the healthcare as well. All our group companies run hospitals, conduct medical camps and have healthcare centers in the villages. We have a Leprosy Treatment and Care Center at Jagdishpur, off Lucknow, where more than 250 leprosy patients are treated.

Who are the beneficiaries of your initiatives—your own workers or the community at large?
The communities, of course. Slowly and silently our group is trying to change the face of villages. From abject poverty to meeting the necessities of life. From dependence to freedom. From backwardness to progress. There is a palpable difference. Tens of thousands of villagers now seem self-assured, confident, and happy at being able to move towards a sustainable livelihood. There is a new found dignity among them. For all of us in Aditya Group, every project when successfully executed brings a humble sense of happiness. It's a way of living our values. Above all, it helps us to play a leadership role as a respectable caring, cooperative citizen.

While we have done and are doing social work in our own small way, we know that there is so much more that needs to be done.

Being a woman, have you undertaken any major projects targeting women?
In this regard one of the notable projects is that of the women carpet weavers undertaken by Grasim. To empower women through helping them to become economically independent, Grasim hones their inherent learning skills through a number of training programmes. These are marginalized women and include the physically handicapped, divorcees, widows, and those from the poorest of the poor families. These women have been trained in weaving carpets. They have now mastered the art and are full-fledged carpet weavers. What is most gratifying is that besides creating a meaningful employment opportunity for women that affords them good monetary return, their products have gained recognition. Carpets made by these women are showcased in the best of the showrooms at Jaipur and Udaipur and are today exported to the United States and other countries in the West.

Similarly, in some places women had to trek miles in search of water. Very often the water would not be safe to drink. Now they find it at their door steps. So the time that they used to take in getting water is invested in other gainful activities, such as making bamboo baskets.

Convincing the womenfolk to enlist in our welfare-oriented activities was also a formidable task. Every project is unique and involvement varies from project to project. For instance, the mobile (hand pump) women mechanics were unused to leaving their villages without their men. Initially the women themselves had some reservations. Handling tools and other mechanical equipment was for them inconceivable. That was the male domain.

But we were able to persuade them to attend the hand-pump mechanics training programme. Today we have more than 50 trained women mechanics.

Any other programme you would like to mention?
We have already begun this population control approach through ten of our units such as Hindalco, Indo Gulf, Grasim, Vikram Cement, Rajashree Cement, among others. In a uniquely collaborative venture with the state Innovations in Family Planning Services Projects Agency and the State Health and Family Welfare Department, we have embarked on an initiative that aims to stem the population explosion. Our collective goal is to popularize the small family through a focused attention on the mother and the child.

The scope of our work is varied. It includes providing easy access to the entire gamut of family planning services, distribution of contraceptives, prenatal and postnatal counselling, medicare, immunization, and medical checkups. Rural clinics set up at Dakhinwara, Babupur, Gaura, Goriabad, Hagaon, and Katari in Jagdishpur provide the requisite services. Alongside we carry out an ongoing awareness campaign. Creatively worked out dance and street plays with a moral are a cultural medium we often use to reinforce the family planning message.

Those in need of specialized gynaecological/surgical services and care are treated at the Indo Gulf Jan Seva Trust Hospital. So far, more than 11,000 children in the age group of one month to five years have been immunized, and 700 new couples have opted for planned families.

But which of the projects are close to your heart?

All of our projects give me a deep sense of satisfaction. They are value adding and they make a difference to the lives of the people. They are equally close to my heart. But of all our projects, I think widow remarriages is truly path breaking.

Discussion questions

1. Prepare an outline of the philosophy Aditya Birla Group has behind their efforts in the area of corporate social responsibility. Make some value addition by giving details of some outstanding social welfare schemes and their impact on the community relations exercise.

2. Research and develop a brief but comprehensive report on the corporate social responsibility activities of Reliance Industries Limited. Highlight the public relations angle and role in the total effort.

References

Hindustan Times, New Delhi, 12 December 2007, p. 7.

Hindustan Times, New Delhi, 15 December 2008.

Hindustan Times, 'Corporate Honchos Back Social Responsibility', New Delhi, 14 October 2007.

Moore, H.Frazier and Frank B. Kalupa (2005), *Public Relations, Principles, Cases and Problems*, Richard D. Irwin, Inc., USA reprinted in India by Surjeet Publications, New Delhi, p. 386.

The Economic Times, 'Teaching the Art of Caring', New Delhi, 10 April 2000.

The Economic Times, 'Companies Loosening Purse Strings like 'ver before—India Inc donates Rs 400 crores'.

The Financial Exprees, 'Social Mission must form a Part of an Organisation's Business Vision', New Delhi, 24 December 2000, p. 7.

The Mint, 'Captive Use—Essar Oil Commissions GE for Water Desalination Project Study', New Delhi, January 2008, vol. 2, no. 9, p. 3.

The Times of India, 'TCS Inks Plan to Upgrade Engineering Colleges', New Delhi, 28 November 2003.

The Times of India, 'Computers for 60 City Schools', New Delhi, vol. CL X IV, no. 288, 3 December 2001.

18

Corporate Image

CORPORATE IMAGE DEFINED

Corporate image is probably the single most important asset of a company that must be protected, with all seriousness by the top management in coordination with public relations professionals. Maintaining, improving, and correcting the corporate image is one of the major responsibilities of PR, as the professionals, by virtue of education and experience, specialize in this area. Managing corporate image is the core competence area of PR practitioners as they understand that the image of a company should be protected and nurtured with the same serious care as other assets of the business, namely, money, manpower, materials, machinery, etc. as good image is like money in the bank.

Image, per se, has been defined by many experts, but the abrupt way of describing image is the positive perception that publics carry about an organization. The industry and business leaders have described image in their own ways, as image, to different people means different things, depending on the objectives that they carve out for their organizations. But the 'positive perception' is the key description. Going by the dictionary meanings of the word, image is the impression that a person or an organization or a product gives to the public. Also image is a mental picture of something not real or present. The society has a tendency to think of the image as something different from reality, yet it is a factor that moves many mountains.

'An image might be considered as a photographic film which is on the point of 'developing' in people's minds. It provides the receiver (an individual) with a means by which to simplify the reality of objects through concepts such as 'good-bad' and 'pleasant–unpleasant'. The image of an object develops through a set of impressions that individuals experience when they directly or indirectly, are confronted with the object,' defined Cees B.M. van Riel (1999).

Image is generally considered a high flown word, associated mainly with large corporations and global companies, who very carefully and consciously nurture their corporate images. As such, going by the relevance to the finer side of the business, many industrialists and professionals have defined image in many ways. A collection of such definitions should imbibe considerable academic and professional interest (See Exhibit 18.1).

Image is a mental perception, which is difficult to define and describe. Even when someone has a fairly good idea about the perception, it is often quite hard to describe and define it. It is almost like telling the taste of a sweet chocolate to someone who has never tasted anything sweet. The perception is made up of several bits and pieces of information, stories, events, experiences, and a flash of visuals and symbols, which contribute to the maturity of an image. By nature, human mind keeps storing information, opinions, experiences, visuals, etc. the sum total of such collections emerges, either as a well painted and spruced up

---

EXHIBIT 18.1   Definitions of image

Image is the sum of functional qualities and psychological attributes in the mind of the consumer.

–Martineau (1958)

Image is the profile of the object, meaning the sum of impressions and expectations as gathered in the memory of an individual.

–Topalian (1984)

Image is the sum of experiences that someone has with the institution.

–Ford (1987)

Image is a subjective and multi-dimensional form of representation or imprint of reality in human brain, as a consequence of which this reality is presented in a reduced, coloured and thus often transformed manner.

–Fauconnier (1988)

Image refers to a holistic and vivid impression held by a particular group towards a corporation, partly as a result of information processing (sense-making) carried out by the group's members and partly by the aggregated communication of the corporation in questions concerning its nature, i.e., the fabricated and projected picture of itself.

–Alvesson (1990)

Image is a combination of product aspects that are distinct from the physical product characteristics but are nevertheless identified with the product. Examples are the brand name, symbols used in advertising, endorsement by a well-known figure, and country of origin.

–Erickson, Johannsen, and Chao (1984)

It takes 20 years to build a reputation and five minutes to ruin it.

–Warren Buffet, *Reader's Digest*, June (1998)

building or weather-beaten and neglected ruins that need to be reclaimed and reconstructed. In other words, the positive and negative image of a company is the collection of odds and bits, majority of which are positive or otherwise, resulting in a good or poor image.

In this world of cut-throat competition, survival of the fittest is the reality of business. This world is full of conflicts of interest, diverse opinions and ideologies and each company has some philosophy of its own and makes great efforts to advocate and communicate that philosophy to all the concerned publics. But the propagating of such corporate philosophies is not a one-day wonder, but takes years together to come to be known and result in a particular image. The process of image has to be nurtured over a long period of time. Once established, good corporate image stands in good stead for the companies in turbulent times. Good corporate image is something that a company can fall back upon in times when going gets rough and tough.

CORPORATE IMAGE—THE INDIAN SCENARIO

In the historical perspective, although the Indian businessmen have a fairly good idea about the importance of maintaining a good reputation of their business, yet it has been a misnomer. They have been and are even today adopting good business practices to keep up their reputations and image in their business circles in particular and the community in general. Certain fair trade practices like charging the right price for the right product, treating customers well, observing financial discipline strictly, and donating certain portion of the profits to charity, are some of the aspects of old style Indian business. There are many moralizing stories afloat about the ethical standards adhered to by businessmen of today and yesteryears, to protect their image and credibility in the business world. See one such story in Exhibit 18.2.

With the arrival of several multinationals in India, the PR practice and the art of managing the corporate image has assumed greater importance. With the changing business scenario, the word 'image' has acquired richer connotations. The challenge of corporate image is to make public perceive a company, as a company wants to be perceived. Enlightened businessmen think that good corporate image is the transmission of focused communication to dust off the cobwebs of confusion in people's mind about the company.

STOCK MARKET AND THE IMAGE

Under the changed economic scenario, business has become the focus of public attention. The business organizations are no more the private domain of a few business families. Business and industry are a public trust which the publics are

EXHIBIT 18.2   The Gujarati nose

THE WEEKEND OBSERVER

INCORPORATING THE OBSERVER OF BUSINESS AND POLITICS

SATURDAY MAY 27 2000 VOL IX NO 20

MID-VIEW / Iqbal Sachdeva

The Gujarati nose

THE nose, perhaps, is the most vital part of the body, as humans live by breathing through the nose. But to a Gujarati businessman, nose (*naak* as they call it), is the symbol of his public image and credibility. Early in life, he is taught to do everything to keep his nose high, even if it means losing money at times. Honouring cheques and other business commitments are part of the Gujarati business ethics.

While I was working in Ahmedabad as a business manager for a multinational company, to my utter shock, Kantibhai's cheque for Rs 1,50,000 returned unpaid. 'Impossible', was my spontaneous response. After all, Kantibhai, who did a flourishing oil, grain and transport business in Amreli, 300 miles from Ahmedabad, was a name to reckon with. 'This looks like some accounting gobble-up,' I said, and called up Kantibhai.

'Gud morning, sir,' was the usual response in his typical Gujarati accent, when Kantibhai came on the line. But he went mute for half-a-minute when I broke the bad news to him. 'I will call you back in five minutes,' he said, adding, 'let me check shoo locho che (what the problem is).

I had often visited Kantibhai's Ambreli business house, where he sat on a spotless white rug in his sparkling white kurta, dhoti and boat like white cap. On his left squatted

three third generation accountants (Mehtajis) writing long red cloth bound account books. I would take my pump shoes off and would always be invited to sit next to Kantibhai on the white rug.

'Gud morning, sir' came back Kantibhai on the phone. 'We have found the mistake,' he said and added to my utter relief, 'we recently

opened our account with a new bank. Mehtaji, by mistake used this cheque on our earlier bank. I 'll come to your office tomorrow by 11 am and pay you cash. Don't worry, Sir, there is no money problem. But one request, Sir, please hold the cheque with you and don't tell anyone that Kantibhai's cheque had bounced. It is a question of my *naak*.' I readily agreed.

Next day, as the clock struck eleven,

Kantibhai in his usual sparkling while kurta, dhoti and boat cap, meekly entered my office.

'Gud morning, sir,' he said, and placed a brown large envelop on the table in front of me. Hands folded apologetically, he said: 'Please, sir, ask someone to count the cash and give me the receipt.' While my accountant took his time to prepare and bring the receipt, we sat sipping tea and discussing the mix up.

'Thank you, sir,' he said putting the receipt in his pocket. 'But one more request, sir.'

He wanted the bounced cheque returned to him, as he did not want to leave any blemishes on his clean financial record with our company. My accountant resisted, quoting company policy. But I overruled him, saying that we had got the cash, and I gave the cheque back to Kantibhai. He looked happy and grateful.

When asked to stay for lunch, Kantibhai excused himself and again requested that this incident should never ever be told to anybody.

'*Naak* is very important in business, sir. No one should ever talk about Kantibhai's bounced cheque. It is a question of my self and business image and nose, sir. In business, if you lose *naak*, you lose everything.'

'It is a Gujarati nose, after all,' I said to myself.

Source: The Observer, 27 May 2000.

watching with keen interest. Publics have stakes and for many their future is linked to the organizations. Going by the image perception, publics extend their matching responses to an organization, in terms of investments and stock trading. With the emergence of the Indian stock market and a new breed of stock market players, the Indian organizations have become very sensitive to the ups and downs of the market. The swings in the market index have become a benchmark of the image of a corporation. The market quotations of a company's stock speak high or low of the company, and generate matching responses.

The prospects of raising capital from the public are sensitively influenced by the image of a company. Surprisingly enough, there is hardly any company worth its salt, who does not float its shares on a premium. The sale of a share as per value is, as if, a thing of the past. But the important question is, as to how much premium a company can claim on its stock and yet get its shares fully subscribed. The key factor is the corporate image. The response of the investing public is generally not based on some hocus pocus notions, but on certain factors that are seriously considered by the investors, which are the following:

- How professional is the management of the company?
- Is the company financially stable and has good reserves to take care of its growth plans?
- What products it markets and what are its marketing strengths?
- What is the status of the top brass of the company?
- What is the public perception and the top of the mind awareness level?
- How good is the corporate image?

More often, the investors may not go thoroughly through the financial results of the company, but just take investment decisions on the image perception they have in their mind. Therefore, as the bulls and bears dominate the market position, many a company takes such steps that keep the market quotations high to retain the investor confidence. The case in focus is the announcement by DLF universal to buy back its stocks to restore investors dwindling confidence in the company.

THE IMAGE MAKERS

The corporate image of an organization emerges bright as a consequence of certain strategies and actions contemplated and executed meticulously. As image management is mainly a PR activity, obviously it is related to the target publics who should perceive the company in a manner the organization wants it to be perceived. The underlying idea is to come up to the expectations of the publics, so that a minimum gap is maintained between the promises and performance of a company.

Contrary to the belief of some that the image of an organization emerges out automatically, the effort has to be planned and managed by well thought out action plan in several areas of corporate activity. The process is slow and the cup of reputation gets filled drop by drop. Once the PR, in consultation with the top management, defines the identity of the organization and develops a plan of action, all steps and actions that follow should be in line with the plan. Image management activity is not those typical emotional outbursts of an organization or a bubble burst, but a long-term and continuous communication programme.

Some of the crucial areas in which the company should follow a programme of action are the following: *customer delight, industry goodwill, employee loyalty, media response, legislator's perception, government understanding, shareholders' trust, dealer's loyalty, vendors' dedication, community goodwill,* and *institutional advertising.*

Customer Delight

In today's market scenario, when companies are vying with each other to please the customers, customer satisfaction has become an old fashioned expression. Marketing organizations are consciously making efforts not only to satisfy customers but to delight them. They want that the customers should be delighted to use their products and stay loyal to the company for good and never go to the competitors. For certain lifestyle brands, the customers feel pride in flaunting their possessions. Riding a Mercedes car, owning a Parker pen, wearing a Beneton T-shirt or enjoying a coffee at Barista, all give a feeling of delight to the customers.

Several customer-driven organizations look for opportunities to flaunt their association with some prominent customers to boost their corporate image. Like individuals, the orgnizations are also known by the company they keep. This not only provides an impetus to their corporate reputation, but also inculcates a sense of credibility in the minds of customers vis-á-vis positive image perception. For example, Delhi's well known hospital, Moolchand, in an effort to enhance their corporate image, ran a series of advertisements in the media. The one that appeared in the 'Brunch' of the *Hindustan Times*, explains the point (See Exhibit 18.3).

Industry Goodwill

In every industry, say cement and steel, etc. there are companies which take on themselves a leadership role. Such leader companies enjoy a great reputation amongst followers as they set the trends and some corporate practices which others emulate. In such a situation, the leader company should enjoy the goodwill of the fellow members who all look to that company for inspiration. Such organizations enjoy a distinct image in the business fraternity, with a ripple effect in the business world. Companies often showcase their strengths to demonstrate their leadership roles and take credit for it. Leadership in technology,

EXHIBIT 18.3   Customer delight—Moolchand Hospital

RELIANCE INFOCOMMUB GROUP
MARUTIMcDONALDS
AIR INDIABENNETT & COLEMANBHEL
TATANESTLEONGCOBEROI GROUP
HULHERO HONDA MOTORS
ITCJINDAL STEELJUBILANT ORGANOSYS
KOTAK MAHINDRANIIT
FIDELITYMOTHER DAIRYUNITECH
WHIRLPOOL EMBASSY OF USA
IFFCOIRCONNEROLAC
AIR FRANCEVOLVO
WHOAIR CANADABLUE DART
ICICI PRUDENTIAL LIFE INSURANCE
HONDA SIEL CARS INDIAN OIL CORPORATION
LG LIFE SCIENCES LTDITDC
UNITED NATIONSWIPRO TECHNOLOGIESSUZLON ENERGY
RENAULTTHE BROOKE INDIA
SBIBAJAJ ALLIANZBLUE STARSAILGAILTISCO
MAHINDRA & MAHINDRA

When it comes to healthcare, the companies you trust, trust Moolchand.

MOOLCHAND
health • happiness • life

Lajpat Nagar III, New Delhi 110 024, India, T + 91 11 4200 0000, F + 90 11 4200 0300, W www.moolchandhealthcare.com

Source: Hindustan Times, 30 December 2007.

outstanding financial results or a century of existence, are some of the popular themes. For instance, an advertisement of Tata Steel showcased its 100 years of leadership role in the steel industry (See Exhibit 18.4).

Also the Tata Group, according to a report in *The Times of India*, 6 June 2008, has been adjudged as world's 6th most reputed company. The report says, 'Diversified Indian conglomerate Tata group has emerged as the world's sixth most reputed company…Tata group leapfrogged over 100 positions from last year's 124th rank in the annual "Global 200: The World's Best Corporate Reputations" list, compiled by US-based Reputation Institute.'

Employee Loyalty

Like charity, good corporate image begins from home. Image management efforts are equally relevant, as far as building a harmonious relationship with the employees is concerned. 'Employees are our best asset', says the century old tyre company, Goodyear. Most important are the employees, whose expressions of satisfaction and loyalty towards the company, speaks volumes about the genuineness of the policies and practices of an organization. Good human relations and deft handling of labour relations becomes a symbol of good image. Perhaps, the only company in India is Tata, which can take pride in the fact that there has never been a labour strike in their Jamshedpur manufacturing facilities, in the last one hundred years.

Media Response

The transparency practised by an organization in the matter of sharing information, appropriately with the media, goes a long way to spread the good word about the company. Also the responsiveness of an organization in dissemination of information and news with media, helps in positive coverage in the print as well as electronic media. Public relations as a part of the job responsibility, interface with the media and serve as a vital link for transmission of news and views, about the company. The spread of information to publics, through the credible media channels, help the process of maintaining, enhancing and correcting the corporate image (also see chapter 16).

Dealers' Loyalty

Dealers are an authentic and credible source of information for the consumers and public in general. Dealers with their responsible utterances can contribute tremendously to the building of good corporate image and if aggrieved can spread all the bad blood in the market. It pays a company considerably, to keep dealers in good humour through fair dealings and professional marketing management. Good corporate image generates a healthy climate in the market

EXHIBIT 18.4   *100 years of Tata Steel*

Today we celebrate a hundred years...

of steel as enduring

as our values

This day in 1907, our company, The Tata Iron & Steel Company Umited, now Tata Steel, was registered–marking the birth of the Indian Steel Industry. Since then, never losing sight of the values propounded by our Founder Jamset ji Nusserwan ji Tata, we continue to create wealth and well-being for the communities and the nations where we operate. Making business a tool to improve the quality of life, we follow the highest standard of corporate governance, delighting customers, reinforcing the trust all stakeholders repose on us, filling every member of the Tata Steel Family with pride.

As we turn hundred, we continue to enhance India's stature on the global stage and look forward to enriching more lives across more communities for another hundred years and more.

The first prospectus of the company

TATA STEEL

1907–2007

and enhances the brand value for a company's products, so essential for corporate success (also see chapter 12).

Vendors' Dedication

The pride of association amongst vendors of a company carries an aura of good corporate image. Vendor's pride is reflected in the professional and fair dealings of the company in areas of payment terms, regular supply schedules and percolation of company's growth prospects to vendors' business. Vendor outfits are also known as ancillary units surrounding a large manufacturing organization. Obviously, vendors are independent, small but important enterprises, that serve like satellites of a large organization. All actions that contribute to the positive attitude of the vendors towards the company, speak well of the corporate image of the principals (also see chapter 13).

Shareholder's Trust

The trust and confidence reposed by the shareholders in a company's professional management, sound financial discipline, good returns on their investments, attractive market value of the shares, speak loud enough in the world. Conscious efforts made by an organization to imbibe investors' trust improves not only corporate reputation but also prospects of collecting additional capital, if required, from the market (also see chapter 15).

Community Goodwill

Citizens, who live around the plants of the organization and people at large, are an important public, whose opinions count and should be cared for. Called community, it supplies skilled manpower to the company and a large base of customers. Therefore, the organization has to demonstrate its keen interest in the social welfare as a part of its corporate social responsibility. Such corporate endeavours help to carve out a positive perception in the minds of the community members. Handling of corporate social responsibility in terms of organizing social welfare programmes and also making socially responsible products, speak volumes about the humanitarian and ethical side of the business and hence a mark of good image (also see chapter 17).

Legislator's Perception

Business cannot prosper in isolation of the people and their elected representatives, the legislators. Naturally, legislators are interested in knowing if the business is contributing to the economic progress, the benefits of which should percolate to the people, who are their vote bank. The parliament and the state legislative assemblies most often discuss business and related matters to formulate government policies, which directly affect the organizations and indirectly the people at large. The positive perception about an industry, like steel and oil, etc. and the member organizations of that industry, deeply influence the thinking of legislators, in the process of supporting or opposing certain laws like taxation and expansions, etc. A good corporate image perception goes a long way to make the economic climate more conducive to corporate growth.

Government Understanding

Fortunately for industry, the business, to a large extent, has moved out of the bureaucratic controls, yet it is not possible for any organization to function and grow without the positive understanding of the government, whose regulatory authorities exert lot of control in the name of public interest, fair competition, and profiteering. An ethical and professional business house needs to project itself with the government agencies to earn their understanding, so that business can function smoothly. All said and done, the concept of free enterprise will continue to be a pipe dream. Thanks to the changing economic environment in India, the quota permit *raj* is gradually disappearing paving way for business to function competitively. Yet every business needs a degree of government understanding to make a success of the enterprise. A good corporate image enlarges the area of influence with government agencies (also see chapter 22).

Institutional Advertising

If an organization achieves some outstanding results, develops some path breaking innovations, signs a collaboration with a global company, produces a millionth unit or touches some such landmark in its history, the company must take credit for the job done well. PR is always alive to such publicity possibilities and should use such opportunities to boost up the image perception of the company. A full page advertisement in a national daily, should impact a large public base and produce a positive perception of the organization. This, in turn, may generate many magical responses in public minds. For instance, Hero Honda, when the company rolled out the millionth motorcycle from their plants, used a public relations programme that provided a great boost to the company's corporate image. Public relations can use such opportunities to make the organization ride the high current of popularity with resultant benefits including good corporate image (also see chapter 24).

PUBLIC RELATIONS ROLE

A PR professional, in an organization, usually occupies a strategic position to serve as a source for generation of resources and also coordinate corporate image building activities, which should reflect in the policies, practices, and the decision-making process of the company. All this has to be done not in a haphazard manner but in a pre-meditated and planned style.

As such the corporate image management programme needs to be developed and executed with a company's corporate priorities kept in mind, as related to the economic environment. A reference to the PR objectives of the company should serve as a guide while developing such a plan and then keeping it on track.

Also should be taken into consideration, the needs of the organization. Amongst the objectives are building the image from a scratch, maintaining the present level of image perception, polishing the image to rise and shine or the most sensitive situation of correcting the image. As image management is one of the major responsibilities of PR, it has to be handled skillfully with fullest involvement of the top management. Perhaps, no other person, than the chairman and the managing director himself, along with the public relations practitioner, has a need to get deeply and seriously involved in the image management endeavours.

The quality of actions and demonstration of professionalism in several areas of activities of an organization, speak loud enough, and may result in building a positive perception in the minds of the publics. As already mentioned, the publics extend their response to the company based on the impressions that they carry. Depending on the size of the organizations, management objectives, public relations goals and resources, the focus of action may be contemplated in some of the key areas (See Exhibit 18.5).

IMAGE MANAGEMENT PROCESS

Like any management system, image management has to adopt a process to go through the exercise. The system, which may be called 'scan-plan-act-check-evaluate' or SPACE should serve as a guideline, to keep the process on track.

EXHIBIT 18.5 Focus of public relations action

- Professionalism in advertising and promotions
- Deft handling of employee relations situations
- Attract the best personnel to work for the company
- Educate publics on certain view points and product usage
- Implement corporate policies and practices sincerely
- Discover and dispel public misunderstandings and prejudices, if any, in a timely manner

- Scotch rumours that may harm corporate image
- Anticipate takeover bids and forestall attacks
- Have a crisis management plan ready and updated regularly
- Conduct periodic research to determine the level and nature of image perception
- Take corrective actions appropriately but in a planned manner

---

EXHIBIT 18.6   The process—SPACE

- Define corporate identity and communication forum
- Scan the environment and determine the target publics
- Develop a corporate mission statement
- Prepare a communication plan
- Plan and determine campaign milestones and events, etc.
- Develop a media plan backed by research on reach and OTC, etc.

- Prepare a public relations budget and get management approval
- Implement the plan seriously
- Actively collect constant feedback during and after the communication programme is over
- Make quantitative and qualitative evaluation to determine success
- Repeat programme, if necessary, and take advantage of the residual impact.

In other words, image management process, instead of depending on some dreamy ideas, should go through a well structured plan or through a five step system: 1. Scan 2. Plan 3. Act 4. Check 5. Evaluate.

This is just another version of the system as outlined in chapters 4 to 7, in this very book, which is scan the environment, create a communication plan, implement the plan, and evaluate the results. However, for readily reckoning the system, see Exhibit 18.6.

Points to Ponder

The points to ponder in this context are, that the image building process is a very slow moving system which calls for patience and persistence for the ongoing effort by an organization and the public relations practitioners. There is no quick fix for this job. The programme may have to be sustained over a long period of time. The cup of good corporate image gets filled drop by drop. There is no one day wonder. For instance, the Tata Steel sustaining public relations effort for a century, is a case in point (See Exhibit 18.4).

The good corporate image may not emerge through sheer glorification of the organization without something substantial to back it up. PR practitioners cannot afford to forget the basics of 90:10 story, i.e., the organization must do a good job with their performance in several areas of activity, which represents 90 per cent and then 10 per cent is the drum beating or communicating about it to get credit for the job done well. Image building is not a vain glorious hullabaloo but a well-directed effort backed by serious homework.

Summary

The corporate image is the single most important asset of an organization and one of the major responsibilities of public relations in coordination with the top management. The image, therefore, should be as much cared for, as the other assets of the business.

Image has been defined as a 'positive perception' of a company in the minds of the publics composed of experiences, imp-ressions, information, corporate stories, visuals, etc.

In a cut-throat competitive situation and globalization of business, the corporate image stands in good stead in times, good and bad, for an organization.

Indian business has been aware of the concept of image and had adopted several fair business practices to keep up their reputations.

The surge of stock markets has demonstrated that a good corporate image means higher script (share) value and share-holders' greater trust in the company.

Some image making actions that help boost the image are: customer delight, industry goodwill, employees' loyalty, media response, legislature's perception, government understanding, shareholders' trust, dealers' loyalty, vendors' dedication, community goodwill and institutional advertising.

Public relations has a major role in maintaining, polishing, and correcting the corporate image and should go through a planned programme to make this happen. Certain actions, when taken in a well meditated manner, go a long way to help. The process called SPACE—scan, plan, action, check, and evaluate—should serve as a guide to keep the effort on track.

Corporate image is not a one day wonder and takes long long time to rise and shine.

Key Terms

Ancillary unit   A vendor's outfit manufacturing components for a manufacturing unit

Benchmark   Standard, or a set of standards, used as a point of reference for evaluating performance or level of quality

Corporate philosophy   The value system of a corporation

Public trust   Trust created for the promotion of public welfare and not for the benefit of one or more individuals

TOM awareness   Top of the mind awareness

Top brass   The people with the highest rank in an organization

Concept Review Questions

1. Define and describe corporate image. Also establish your understanding of the concept with examples.
2. Draw up the Indian scenario related to business practices, traditional and modern. Also express your opinion on the subject.
3. How is the stock market influenced by the corporate image of a company? What image related parameters investors apply for making investment into a company's stock?
4. What are the areas in which the actions and activities of a company contribute to the emergence of a good corporate image? Develop a detailed reply.

5. What is the system that public relations professionals should use to execute an image management programme for a company? Explain the process, step by step.

Project Work

1. Develop a programme of action for a tobacco company, say ITC, for building its corporate image with special reference to a general disapproval against smoking being highly injurious to human health.
2. Develop a newspaper advertisement for a tractor manufacturing company, say Mahindra and Mahindra, on winning a gold medal for quality from the Indian Farmer's Forum. The advertisement should specially help in furbishing the present corporate image of the company.

Case Study

LG Electronics—A Success Story

Background

LG Electronics was established in 1958 under the name Goldstar Company, under the flagship company known as LG Group which was founded way back in 1947, initially known as Lucky Chemical Industrial Company. Within a year of its inception, LG (then Goldstar) manufactured Korea's first radio—A 501, followed by the first telephone, refrigerator, and a black and white television. Inspired by domestic growth, LG Electronics stepped out to foreign lands and established its first overseas operation in New York in 1968. In the same year, the company made Korea's first air conditioner.

Image management strategy

As a customer-driven company, the organization believes in innovating new products to meet customer needs. On entry into India, the company thoroughly researched to ensure that the products meet needs and imagination of the Indian consumer. Inspired by the zeal to capture the Indian market, LG Electronics extended its reach from metropolitan cities to semi-urban markets. To enhance top of the mind awareness for their brand, the company pushed publicity vans across the country, covering a distance of 5,000 kms every month.

Initially, due to import, their products were priced high, at par with Japanese brands. They used this stance to demonstrate to Indian consumers that Korean products are in no way inferior to those of the Japanese. Soon the company started their manufacturing in India in 1998. To increase their market penetration they launched 'Sampoorna', a low price TV. LG mainly targeted at the rural customers.

Adopting a strategy akin to marketing of FMCG products, which depends heavily on advertising, they stepped up their advertising budget to 5 per cent of their sales turnover. The strategy has paid and the company can claim to be the market leader in electronics goods selling colour TVs, air conditioners, microwave ovens, washing machines, and frost free refrigerators.

The aggressive strategies have helped the company to position itself as leader of the electronics goods market of India, with a positive image perception in the minds of the consumers.

Future plans

To further boost their corporate image they have now moved from the previous 'value-for-money' communication plank to 'differentiated' products rather than the 'me-too' approach. To project their corporate image, the advertising now showcases quality, unique features, and strong after-sales customer service supplemented with expansion of product range from mobile phones and IT products. To demonstrate their technology leadership they also launched Pearl Black LCD TVs and new range of 'Shine' handsets. They also have plans to launch their Blu-ray (an optical disc technology) players in India shortly.

Advertising and sales promotion

LG Electronics banks on heavy advertising and believes that communication creates a mind space amongst consumers which they have occupied fairly well. In 2007, their ad spend touched Rs 600 crore and the company strategically spreads advertising year round rather than on seasonal basis.

Public relations strategies

To give a boost to their corporate image, LG Electronics announced the release of 22 ad films featuring world-class cricket to associate itself with cricket which has the highest awareness base in cricket crazy India. Their public relations campaign 'Cricket First' featured captains of the 14 teams of World Cup 2003 with tagline, 'Captains of Cricket World, for the Captain of Consumer Electronics and Home Appliances'. This provided the expected boost to their corporate image and market leadership position.

All these strategies have paid the Korean electronics conglomerate to occupy a positive image perception in the minds of Indian consumers.

Discussion questions

1. Draw up a questionnaire, containing at least ten questions and interview a customer to determine his perception about the corporate image of LG Electronics. Interview 25 customers and draw up a report of your findings.
2. Prepare a report to justify your purchase of a LG mobile phone compared to the world famous Nokia, when both handsets are priced almost the same.

References

Riel, Cees B.M. van (1999), *Principles of Corporate Communication*, Prentice Hall, Hampstead, Hertfordshire, p. 73.

The Times of India, 'Tata Group World's 6th Most Reputed Company', New Delhi, 6 June 2008, p. 25.

The Observer, 'The Gujarati Nose', New Delhi, 27 May 2000.

Hindustan Times, 30 December 2007.

19 Corporate Identity Management

CORPORATE IDENTITY DEFINED

One of the most important issues in the life of a corporation is the question, as to what its identity is and how the organization is recognized and reckoned amongst several publics. Perhaps, nothing in an organization is more important than the issue of identity, simply because identity affects everyone and because it goes to the core of what an organization is and what it does.

With several global organizations entering the Indian market and also the Indian companies emerging from their cocoons, the corporate noise has increased tremendously. The question, as to how to get noticed and retain public attention with a distinct identity, has gripped the attention of managements and particularly the public relations professionals representing such organizations. Every corporation has a style of functioning and its policies, practices, and systems by which it runs its business. One way, perhaps, would be to work by the gut feeling and take certain actions, right or wrong; the other professional way would be to perform all organizational functions in line with the set corporate philosophy, culture, and code of conduct. In today's competitive and tumultuous scenario, a company must address its identity in all its actions in order to inculcate a strong sense of belongingness amongst the target publics.

Every organization carries out thousands of operations every day. A corporation sells its products, promotes the products through advertising and sales promotion; it purchases raw material and components to support its manufacturing operation; it hires personnel and also, if need be, fires them; it manufactures and manages the manpower; etc. In all such operations, the management adopts a style of transacting such business that vividly reflects in its identity, which publics carry in their minds. All those who come in contact with the organization, perceive the organization in a manner the company deals with them, in keeping with the style of its operation.

Therefore, the sum total of the way an organization presents itself is called identity. 'Originally, corporate identity was synonymous with logos, company house style, and other forms of symbolism used by an organization. The concept has gradually been broadened and more comprehensive, and is now taken to indicate the way in which a company presents itself by the use of symbols, communication, and behaviour. These three elements constitute the so-called corporate identity (CI) mix. All elements in the CI mix can be used both internally and externally to present the personality of an enterprise, according to an agreed company philosophy,' wrote Cees B.M. van Riel (1999). See some more definitions in Exhibit 19.1.

According to van Riel (1999), 'The word identity is derived from the Latin word *idem* (meaning 'same'). There is probably also a connection with the Latin *itentidem*, meaning 'repeatedly' or 'the same each time'. The interpretation of identity is derived from the dictionary definitions, for example, 'the characteristic or condition of complete agreement, absolute or essential similarity, unity of being', provided design specialists with a strong argument to press for consistent use of symbols by companies'.

Further on, Frank Jefkins (2006) wrote that, 'The corporate philosophy derives from the PR philosophy of creating understanding, but obviously it lends itself to every form of physical representation whether it be print, packaging, premises, websites, vehicles, dress, or advertising. It is essential that a corporate identity is distinctive, easily recognized and remembered and, if possible, characteristic. Moreover, it can be an extensive operation, involving everything by which a company be identified.'

CORPORATE IDENTITY—A VITAL ELEMENT

In today's business environment, a company must define its identity in very clear terms, as to what it should be known as. A particular identity generates a particular response from various segments of the business as well as publics.

EXHIBIT 19.1   Corporate identity definitions

Corporate identity is the strategically planned and operationally applied internal and external self-presentation and behaviour of a company. It is based on an agreed company philosophy, long-term company goals, and a particular desired image, combined with the will to utilize all instruments of the company as one unit, both internally and externally.
— Birkigt and Stadler (1986)

Corporate identity is the sum of all methods of portrayal which the company uses to present itself to employees, customers, providers of capital, and the public. According to organizational units, CI is the sum of all the typical and harmonized methods of portrayal of design, culture, and communication.
— Antonoff (1985)

Corporate identity reflects the distinctive capability and the recognizable individual characteristics of the company. Identity in this sense also includes the distinction and recognition of parts of the whole company, and the attribution of those parts to the whole.
— Tanneberger (1987)

Corporate identity is the total of visual and non-visual means applied by a company to present itself to all its relevant target groups on the basis of a corporate identity plan.
— Blauw (1994)

Corporate identity is the tangible manifestation of the personality of a company. It is the identity which reflects and projects the real personality of the company.
— Olins (1989)

Corporate identity is the expression of the personality of a company, which can be experienced by anyone. It is manifested in the behaviour and communication of the company, and in its aesthetic, formal expression; it can also be measured as the perceptual result amongst internal and external target groups.
— Lux (1986)

Corporate identity embodies, besides all visual expressions, also all non-visual expressions and behaviour in the social, economic and political field.
— Henrion (1980)

The corporate identity is the firm's visual statement to the world of who and what the company is — of how the company views itself — and therefore has a great deal to do with how the world views the company.
— Selame and Selame (1975)

Corporate identity is the strategy which helps to increase the economic performance and the efficiency of a company. It coordinates achievements, values and information, and leads to integration in the sense of cooperation.
— Hannebohn and Blocker (1983)

Source: Riel, Cees B.M. van (1999).

Identity of an organization is the most vital element, because identity represents its core competence and reflects in all its activities.

Corporate identity should not represent only the core competence of the organization but also its inner truth. It should focus on the key strengths, business purpose philosophy, value system it stands for, and the policies, the organization believes in strongly.

Identity is an instrument of inspiring confidence amongst customers, a launch pad for new products, a means of attracting and motivating workforce, and a symbol of confidence to shareholders.

Corporate identity, when in clear focus and perceived well by various target publics, can induce many positive reactions and responses. The identity helps them to align themselves with the name, culture, or philosophy of the organization and respond in a very positive and constructive manner. A look at a few representative areas where corporate identity becomes a driving force behind the actions and acts of some of the publics will be helpful.

Employee Motivation

Clearly recognizable identity to the employees become a source of confidence and pride in the organization they work for. It inculcates a sense of loyalty among them and hence motivates them to deliver at their optimum level. The name helps to promote team building and a cooperative attitude, which every public relations practitioner tries to induce as a part of the internal public relations programme. For the human resource person, the identity leads to improved utilization of manpower resources. That is why may often hear an employee proudly pronouncing that 'I am an IBMer' or 'I work for Sony.' Don't be surprised when an employees brags, 'You must have heard of "Reliance", I work there only.'

Customer's Confidence

A well defined corporate identity becomes a source of inspiring customer confidence, which provides the very basis for the existence of a company. The name induces a sense of association and a long-term relationship between the company and customers, a trend that all PR and marketing people crave for. Customer's confidence ensures the future of a company and the corporate identity plays a vital role. In the maze of sign boards in the shopping arcades, a customer intending to buy a pair of shoes, looks for that red and white Bata sign, walks into the store, and buys with confidence. They even take pride in flaunting their new 'Hush Puppy' pairs to their friends, colleagues, and peers.

Dealers' Pride

What authenticates the pride of association of the dealers with a company, are the identity signages upfront on their business premises. A powerful corporate identity when exhibited at the dealers' premises, makes the dealers proud of the association. Dealers are known by the company they represent in their community and enjoy a status and respect amongst their people and customers, as a credible representative of the company. One must have heard a Ford Tractors dealer in the market talking to an irate customer, 'Talk sense, you should know that you are talking to a respectable dealer of an international company!'

Shareholders' Trust

Next to the customers, shareholders are perhaps the second most important public for an organization. They are the source of precious capital which they invest in large sums and take business risks because they trust the company, which is inspired by the corporate identity, when kept in clear focus. Perhaps, these are not the impressive financial results that are reflected in the annual report, but the identity, which goes a long way to enthuse and inspire investors' trust in the company. Even the share market quotations, as seen and perceived by the investors' community, are influenced by the identity of an organization.

Confidence of Other External Publics

Likewise, other external publics like vendors, media, government, parliamentarians, and the community develop a sense of confidence in the organization, as being very professional and sincere in their business policies and actions. The powerful corporate identity helps people to evolve a very clear picture in their minds about the genuineness of the company, as forthright and professional. Keeping the company in clear focus pays. When the multiplicity of several messages transmitted by the organization convey the underlying corporation philosophy and consistent visual representation, they imbibe confidence, compared to the relaying of unrelated and erratic messages that create a confusion in the minds of the target publics. Therefore, a well planned corporate identity programme pays rich dividends.

The corporate identity, therefore, when projected in a planned and thoughtful way by the PR practitioners, cements strong relationship between an organization and the target publics on a long-term basis.

CORPORATE IDENTITY MIX

Depending on the needs and strengths of a company, the corporate identity of an organization generally reflects itself in four major areas of activities, actions, policies, and practices, either singly or in a mix. The four areas are as follows:

1. Products/services—what an organization manufactures and sells
2. Environment—the environment or location where the company manufactures and markets its products/services
3. Communication—how a company communicates, advertises, promotes, and sells its products/services—the promotional style and business philosophy
4. Behaviour—the behaviour pattern of the company employees amongst themselves and their dealings with the outside publics

Products/services

A product oriented company considers its products as the most significant aspect of its strength and identity amongst various publics. Their products are an important element in the identity mix. It may so happen that the brand name of their product may be more known than the company which manufactures such a product. Perhaps, publics know 'Dettol' more than the company, which manufactures and markets this product.

The organization takes a lot of pride in its products it makes and markets, so much so that the product name becomes an umbrella brand and takes in its fold several other products and the corporate activities and actions get mentions by the product name. Names like TATA, which has a strong identity as a steel manufacturer, promotes, projects, and markets several products like trucks, cars, oils, soaps, etc. under one name TATA.

A company's staunch faith in the quality of its products and resultant customer satisfaction makes a legend and get established as the corporate identity. The vivid examples are Rolex, Rolls Royce, Honda, Coca Cola, etc.

On their re-entry into India, Coca Cola, in an attempt to Indianize their identity, carried out a series of advertisements to generate and reinforce the new Indian identity for the company, as Coca-Cola India (See Exhibit 19.2).

Environment

Several local and global organizations take a lot of pride in their work environment and the ambiance that they fanatically maintain in their establishments. Organizations, like malls, retail stores, hotels, and restaurants keenly concentrate on keeping up the environment in their outfits and are well known for that 'customer friendly' environment to their target publics.

Superb house keeping and art heritage oriented offices, lobby, and reception areas, resembling an art gallery or a museum, reflect the history, corporate culture, and work ethics of some organizations. This impeccable environment generates a positive and favourable perception and a particular identity of a tastefully and professionally managed company.

For instance, Hero Honda motor cycle manufacturing plant takes lot of pride in the environment they maintain and consider it a good part of their corporate identity. Maruti, of late, refurbished their customer outlets to showcase their interest and focus on this part of their corporate identity. A visit to the Escorts corporate office, with paintings of some famous artists on display, give the look of an art gallery. Also the offices, canteens, and manufacturing facilities and other work places, so well kept, have a powerful influence on the way the employees and the external publics perceive the organization. The environment, as such, powerfully communicates to the publics some connotations like quality mindedness, customer service, and professionalism, as significant part of their corporate identity.

Communication

An organization's well thought out, planned, and highly creative strategy to communicate is used as a crucial element of the corporate identity mix. A company devises various strategies to communicate to its target publics about

EXHIBIT 19.2 Coca Cola India—new corporate identity

Source: The Times of India (2008).

its activities and actions, products and innovations, contributions and cultural ethos, thus always keeping the basic elements of its identity in sharp focus. A corporate uses a distinct style of communication on every opportunity to boost its identity powerfully, in its advertising and sales promotion efforts.

The companies that think that their communication style is the main element in their identity mix, very meticulously maintain that stance. For instance, Rooh Afza, the oldest brand of India backed by Hamdard Dwakhana, has maintained the constant and consistent style of promotion for little over a century. The identity powerfully communicates the strength of the company as a highly knowledgeable institution in the area of *Unani* medicine and naturopathy and Rooh Afza as a part of that centuries old tradition.

Koutons, the famous clothing company, with their romantic lifestyle advertising, has gained fame to emerge as one of the leading garment brands of India. Through its communications, along with their products and environment, it makes the target audience aware about the unique positioning of their company's corporate identity. Pepsi, Amul butter, *Kachua chap* mosquito coils are similar examples, whose peculiar way of communicating imprints their identities on the mind screen of their publics.

Behaviour

Besides identity elements like product, environment, and communication, what is very closely cherished by some companies, is the iconic behaviour of their employees amongst themselves and the external publics. To some organizations, polished parlance, distinct behaviour patterns of their personnel with outside publics, unique selling styles form a major part of their corporate identity.

Perhaps, one of the most difficult acts of any management is to control and guide the people in an organization. People inside the company are a crucial element, because a company is a formation of people and it has to do business with people. Harnessing and training this force to behave in a particular style is a challenge. When once moulded in a behaviour pattern, company personnel serve as a powerful symbol of corporate identity.

Global companies particularly face this challenge, where people come from various nationalities, ethnic groups, religions and faiths and a variety of skin colours and physical features, bring along their distinct behaviour patterns, personality traits, and life styles. Global companies have acquired professional strategies and training programmes to harness this diversity of behaviours and canalize them into one unified single behaviour pattern, which reflect in the distinct corporate identity of an organization. The typical behaviour patterns of policemen, army officers, airlines staff, five-star hotel employees, and some corporate executives are examples, as to how they conduct themselves in their respective areas of operation. All represent the identity of the organization that they belong to. World over, Singapore Airlines air hostesses are known for the demeandor and dress, that serves as a symbol of the airlines identity. Many Singaporean girls proudly flaunt the airlines dress to show their polish and poise.

Balancing the Mix

A combination of product/service, environment, communication, and behaviour, when they come together in various quantities, a mix of these elements projects the organization as a whole. A well thought out, creatively developed, and balanced mix of these elements should guide the PR practitioners and the managements to determine the corporate identity. Once a decision to this effect is taken, then all PR efforts may be directed towards making the publics perceive the company, the way the company wants to be perceived.

DEVELOPING A CORPORATE IDENTITY

Besides the philosophical side of the corporate identity, it is essential to communicate this identity to the publics through visuals. Most companies grow up with an identity which has emerged naturally, as if, itself in line with the business that a company is involved in. Whatever has emerged is, perhaps, the result of some random visuals conceived by many managers and owners, without much coherence of one visual with the other. That is some companies suffer from a kind of confusion, as to which visuals stand for an organization as a whole.

Also besides the involvement of the PR, it is the responsibility of the top management to evolve and implement the corporate identity programme. Once finalized, the responsibility percolates down to all levels of management to protect it and comply with the identity norms. To nurture the corporate identity, it is almost mandatory that the top management should almost fanatically and enthusiastically protect it. It must be ensured that the middle management levels are sensitized about it from the introduction stage to that of implementation so that the levels down below also take it seriously. PR takes it as a job responsibility to communicate continually to keep the identity alive and in clear focus amongst all levels of people in the organization. Exhibit 19.3 should explain the point.

Frank Jefkins (2006) said, 'Your company could look like a woman who makes frequent changes of hair-style, make up, and dress. She lives in a perpetual disguise.' Jefkins further wrote, 'Why not take a closer look? Collect examples of everything that is printed in your company's name, business cards, letter heads, invoices, sales literature, catalogues, house journals, advertisements, and annual reports. Collect them from every branch and plant. Then collect pictures of premises, vehicles, and any other form of transportation. And what about other items like giveaway ashtrays, pens, calendars, diaries? Then there is dress, caps, overalls, uniforms, dresses, and other apparel with which staff are supplied. A study of this could be a shock. They all exist. They are all necessary. Yet at various times different people have introduced their own ideas. Colours and

EXHIBIT 19.3 Corporate Identity works top down

typography or sign writing may vary, and there may be a logo, or variations on something produced years ago. It is a creative mess. It needs the discipline of a corporate identity scheme.'

So to cut through the confusion, the PR professionals take on themselves the job of streamlining the corporate identity system from the development of a logo, letter heads, business cards, dresses, and trucks, all carrying a uniform identity sign for publics to get a focused picture of a company. At this point, we should know that the corporate identity is of two kinds, non-visual and visual.

Non-visual Identity

Obviously the non-visual identity is not something graphically presented, but an identity that forcefully reflects in the total functioning style of the organization and its employees, in particular. Non-visual identity has two aspects, personal and impersonal.

Personal

This non-visual identity means the personal behaviour of the employees, as to how they conduct themselves and their business activities, how they carry themselves in the market place. Some of the major elements are the following:

Sales style   Many professional companies take a lot of pride in the unique sales style of their sales personnel. They are trained and briefed on techniques of good human behaviour, personal grooming, etiquettes, product knowledge, and structured presentations to customers, that exude the uniqueness of the

---

EXHIBIT 19.4 The ten commandments for a sales executive

1. Tell and sell. Art of telling is the art of selling. Listen and respond when right.

2. Get customers' friendly attention and appeal to logic and emotions.

3. Sell products' value and benefits. Sell satisfaction.

4. Size up prospects early and drop if not responsive. Be patient. Try again.

5. Be a professional. Solve customers' problems. Handle objections and close sale.

6. Sell with prestige. Don't stoop low to get order.

7. Time is money. Be punctual. Honour commitments.

8. Dress neatly and care for personal grooming, hands, nails, collars, cuffs, shoes, and body odour. Avoid chewing pans, smoking, and over drinking.

9. Maintain friendly customer relation, neither too familiar, nor too official.

10. Count calls at sun down and make that extra last call.

---

professional and polished selling style, that the company projects through their sales executives, as a mark of the corporate identity (See Exhibit 19.4).

Customer service policy   Several customer driven companies are devoted to the art of 'customer relations management'. They have adopted certain policies which aim at satisfying the customers, not only in the ultimate situation, but through a distinct culture of sparing with the customers to keep up their comfort level in situations when a customer is aggrieved. Personnel are trained to spar with the irate customers so as to conclude such situations into more sales and profits to the company. Experts think that customer complaints are opportunities for more sales. A customer friendly policy speaks volumes about a company's culture and identity.

Telephonic response   Telemarketing is the order of the day. Companies take special care to train employees who are conversing upfront with the customers on the telephone. Lifting phone, before the third ring goes, identifying your company and yourself and then interacting with the customer sweetly and politely and empathizing with the customers, speaks high of the company. Selling on the telephone or helping customers with solutions to their problems, the tele-marketer exudes a distinct corporate culture and identity.

Correspondence   To avoid reinventing the wheel by their executives and also to keep the corporate identity in focus, many companies have devised standard formats for responding to customers' queries or complaints. This not only saves valuable company time, avoids hassles of dictating letters to the secretaries, but also maintains a premeditated style, distinct to the organization, in matters of corresponding with customers and other publics. It may not be unusual to come across a kind of manual, in a company, showing a collection of model letters to be used in certain familiar and usual situations.

Impersonal

The corporate identity also reflects in some of the impersonal communication aspects of an organization. The company or representatives are not physically present in such actions, yet there is strong impersonal presence which speaks loud enough to show up. Some areas of impersonal contact are the following:

Advertising   To leave an imprint on the minds of the publics about its corporate identity, the organization adopts a distinct style of advertising. Sloganeering, visuals, copy, and the tagline, all represent a peculiar way in all marketing communications to keep the corporate identity in clear focus. Amul's 'Utterly Butterly Delicious' and 'The Taste of India' or Hero Honda's *'Desh ki Dhadkan'* are typical examples.

Publicity   An organization's distinct way of generating publicity in the media, reflects its corporate identity. Adopting certain themes like 'technology leadership', 'environment protection', 'aids control', 'road safety', etc. are some of the planks an organization chooses to identify itself with and become known for that. Also certain public relations events that help build media hype and resultant publicity are the distinctly adopted forums by the companies. Such associations become a identity mark for a company. Organizing 20:20 cricket championship by DLF, beauty contest by Lakme cosmetics, or the ITC *Sangeet Sammelan*, are the publicity styles which speak loud enough to communicate a corporate identity of such organizations.

Visual Identity

Public relations has a crucial role to showcase the visual identity of a corporation through designing, developing, and projecting the corporate identity through all available means and methods. Needless to say, this calls for creativity in correlating the visuals to the corporate business philosophy, core competence, and the inner truth that a company holds close to itself. However, some of the elements that need to be appropriately incorporated in the visual identity are: *corporate logo, house colours, typeface family, mnemonic device,* and *tagline.*

Corporate logo

A logo is a powerful graphic or a visual that represents the corporate philosophy, culture, or identity. It is the first step towards developing the identity of an organization. Although there is no single way of deciding the logo and different companies work out different options to invent their logo. A logo can be based on many aspects of the organization—the initials of the founder like Birla or Tata, the abbreviation of the large name of a company like ICICI, SAIL, or ONGC, numbers TV18, or technology plus Panasonic, the name of a town like Bhilwara and many other options. But whatever the theme, when transformed into a visual, comes to stay as a symbol of corporate identity.

House colours

To improve prospects of high recall for the identity, corporations associate themselves with particular colours, so much so, that some colours have already come to be known as a particular house colour of a company like Bata red, Goodyear blue, JCB yellow, etc. Once selected, the house colour is strictly followed to project the identity of the organization. PR practitioners, who monitor the execution of the identity programme, strictly follow the implementation of the house colours from advertising to merchandising, from staff uniforms to delivery trucks, from dealer identification to product packaging, etc. Goodyear, to implement its store identification programme, specially prevailed upon the acrylic sheet manufacturer to produce sheets of a particular colour. The PR got it codified and spread the code across the branches to conform to the house colours. Kingfisher Airlines' red house colour is visible across the country in its operations, from airhostesses' uniforms to the painting of aircraft tail fins.

Typeface family

Different type families and font sizes represent different connotations. Some faces stand for polish and sophistication, some for romance, some for affluence and power, while some others for traditions of joy and gloom. From Times New Roman to Aerial and Gothic, etc. each type face has its own flavour. The black and light, fat and thin, straight and script type faces convey different feelings to the minds of the publics. PR professionals understand the sensitivities of various typefaces and direct the logo writing of the company in the typeface that gels well with the name, corporate philosophy and the nature of the business. A collage of logos should clearly demonstrate the idea (See Exhibit 19.5).

Mnemonic device

A mnemonic device is a graphic or a caricature of an object, which is used to stir some feelings like joy, thrill, love, sympathy, romance, etc. in human mind to perceive the company in a particular manner. Pictures of birds, animals, and even humans are used as devised to stir feelings with which each object is associated. For instance, a picture of Bagpiper on a liquor bottle represents musical brave heart, eagle represents high spirits like the one on the bottle of Golden Eagle beer, a lady for fashion and finer side of life, the founders' picture for KFC, a demon representing Onida, etc. There are endless ways of selecting a device to suit the organizational business philosophy and identity.

EXHIBIT 19.5 Corporate logos

Source: Metro Now, 25 August 2008.

Tagline

Tagline or punchline, generally appended below the company logo, represents the core competence of the organization and in the briefest possible way to communicate the philosophy that the company stands for. Perhaps, it is the smartest way of telling the corporate story to the publics. The punch line is generally conceptualized on some major strength of the company and stands for the corporate identity. Punchlines such as 'Sense and Simplicity' represents Philips; 'The Ultimate Driving Machine' for BMW; 'Owners' Pride, Neighbours Envy' stands for Onida, etc.

To recap the above information about the visual identity, it may be relevant to look at Exhibit 19.6, which gives a rough and ready list of the items that constitute the visual identity of an organization.

IDENTITY AND IMAGE RELATIONSHIP

Once the corporate identity mix, that is a premeditated combination of all the four elements, product, environment, communication, and behaviour has been decided, an organization's identity should emerge in clear focus. With concerted communication programme and actions that reflect in the policies and practices of the company, publics may start perceiving the company, as such. Although, this may not happen overnight, as it is a slow process that sometimes may take some decades, the perception thus born leads to a company enjoying corporate image. In other words, image is the reflection of the corporate identity. Sharper the identity, more attractive and positive will emerge the image of a corporation. A graphic representation of the concept explains (See Exhibit 19.7).

CORPORATE IDENTITY — LEGAL ASPECTS

PR practitioners have to be mindful and careful while evolving a corporate identity, particularly, the visual identity, so as not to flout certain laws through sheer ignorance. The intellectual property rights in India must be adhered to so as to avoid unnecessary legal situations which are generally expensive and also

---

EXHIBIT 19.6 Visual identity elements

- Corporate logo/symbol
- Corporate philosophy punchline
- Mnemonic devices
- Well defined product and packaging appearance
- Uniforms/badges/flags
- Stationery/forms/memos

- Displays/exhibits
- Point of purchase display
- Audio/video/tunes/films
- Dealer identification signs
- Company buildings
- Delivery vehicles and publicity vans
- House colours

EXHIBIT 19.7   Image as reflection of corporate identity

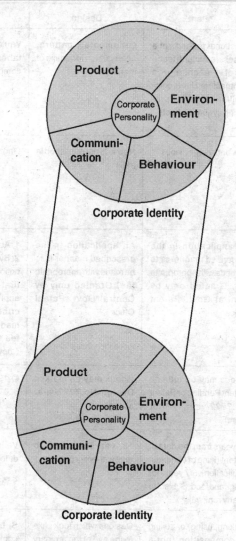

Source: Adapted from Riel, Cees B.M. van (1999).

embarrassing to the managements. Therefore, it has to be ensured that the new logo or graphics or mnemonic visuals do not infringe on any visual which have already been adopted and registered with the appropriate authorities. Such violations, though unintentional, are liable to invite litigation and even claiming of sizable damages by the original owners. There are already a few such cases in the courts, challenging the violation of such visuals. Therefore, with sufficient knowledge of the legal aspects of certain logos or trade marks and patents already registered or copyrighted, should help to avoid problems. For a ready recknoner of the intellectual property rights in India, see Exhibit 19.8.

| EXHIBIT 19.8 | Intellectual property rights in India at a glance | | | |

Type of right	Patent	Design	Copyright	Trademark
What is protected	Functional features of a process, structural features of a machine or a manufactured item, composition of matter producing synergic effects	Ornamental pattern, outer design for article of manufacture	Writings, photos, music, labels, works of art, computer programmes	Words, names, symbols, and devices combination
Criteria for protection	New and 'non-obvious'	New and not published in India	Originality	Should be capable of identifying and distinguishing the goods. Should not conflict with pre-registered pattern, mark
How rights are obtained	An application in the prescribed manner is to be made with appropriate fee. Granted only by Central Govt. Patent Office	An application in the prescribed manner is to be made with appropriate fee. Granted only by Central Govt. Patent Office	1. Automatic on creation 2. By applying Copyright notice @ 1991 (year of the first publication). An application in the prescribed manner to be made with appropriate fee to the Registrar of Copyrights	1. By Common Law: Adoption and Use. 2. An application in the pres-cribed manner is to be made with appropriate fee to the Registrar of Trade Marks
Marking	Goods may be marked Patent Pending or Patent No.????/year (After grant)	Goods may be marked Design No.????/year after grant)	© 1991	Use ® for Registered Trade Mark and (T) for unregistered.
Life	14 years from the date of Patent (filing of complete application). 5/7 years for drugs and food. Subject to yearly renewal	15 years subject to renewal every 5 years	Valid for 50 years from date of death of author	Common Law: As long as properly used as a mark. Registration is perpetual subject to renewal every 7 years
Test of infringement	Making, using, or selling or composition (not a drug) or carrying on a process embodying the claimed invention	Designs which look alike to the eye of the ordinary observer	Substantial portion copied. Similarity. Public performance without licence	Likelihood of confusion, mistake, or deception. Deliberate copying
International protection	Indian patents are not valid for any other country, just as foreign patents are not valid in India unless granted in India	Indian designs are not valid in any other country just as foreign designs are not valid in India, unless registered in India	Indian copyrights are valid in countries which are members of the Bern Convention	Indian trademarks are not valid in any other country just as foreign trademarks are not valid in India unless used or applied for and granted in India

Source: D.P. Ahuja & Co., Patent & Trademark Attorneys, Kolkata and Bangalore, India.

CORPORATE IDENTITY CHANGES—WHEN AND WHY?

Most companies may grow up with an identity which emerged naturally as part of what they are. However, there may come a time in the life of an organization, when their identity may look out of touch with reality and necessitate a change. Certain situations that can bring about this development can be the following:

- The company may find that the nature of its business activities is rapidly changing or growing, but its name and reputation still remains associated with its original business, which is now dwindling or altogether eroding.

- The company either acquires new business or merges with a major corporation which has similar business. Such a merger may also call for a merger of identities and to project a new unified identity. The identity may warrant the merger of common cultures and traditions, to come out with a new cultural ethos.

- A company may adopt a diversification plan by moving from commodity trading to manufacturing, from traditional to high technology areas, but their old reputation does not fall in line with the new change. Hence a change becomes necessary.

- The organization finds that its weaker brands are being pushed out of the market by some new and powerful brands. This may call for a powerful projection of the company name to support and strengthen its brands.

- The present line of business, though well known, suffers from low profitability. The low returns may adversely affect the morale inside and outside the organization, and there may be felt the need to rejuvenate the company and project its inner strengths.

- A company, despite its inner strengths, may be under a takeover threat and may need to hammer out its intrinsic power to stall such attempts.

- A company eyes to takeover some business and flexes its muscles to make the offer attractive and credible to the takeover candidates.

- A company may need to re-integrate its operations. Its various divisions may be doing a good business in terms of selling to the same customers or buying raw materials from the same suppliers, who have some faint perception about the size and strength of the company. Hence the company may feel the need to project a new and unified corporate identity.

- Due to lack of internal coordination, a company's various divisions may be duplicating research and development efforts, thus forfeiting its chances of introducing some new products. The resources may be frittering away due to lack of cooperation and poor team work. This may call for re-engineering the organization and projecting it as a powerful and well coordinated institution.

EXHIBIT 19.9   The changing Indian corporate identities

The Times of India and the PTI (18 February 2008) reported that at least 50 Indian companies have decided to change their names at the beginning of the year 2008, and the reason for this change is either mergers or acquisitions and some other reasons for projecting their names more forcefully in the market.

The list of such companies included some who's who of the corporate India ranging from Tatas, Ambanis, and Mallya to some state-run entities. It has been reported that about 1,100 Indian companies have changed their names at least once during the past.

The 50 companies who have opted name change include Tata group owned VSNL rechristening itself as Tata Communications and the budget airline Deccan Aviation deciding to call itself Kingfisher Airlines, both reflect the new ownership structures. Other major changes due to mergers and acquisitions deals include Motor Industries Company to Bosch Limited, while there have also been cases where the names have been changed to reflect changes in the business line-up of the companies.

Other companies with new names this year include National Mineral Development Corporation Ltd which became NMDC Ltd, while Timex Watches Limited was renamed as Timex Group India Limited.

The publication also reported that the words like 'infra', 'engineering', and 'industries' look attractive to the companies. Goldstone Teleservices has become Goldstone Infratech, AMD Metplast is now AMD Industries, Era Construction (India) is now Era Infra Engineering, and Suvarna Cements has rechristened itself Keerti Industries. In addition, Acknit Knitting has become Acknit Industries, MP Oil and Fats changed to Exelon Infrastructure, and Vas Animations and Entertainment is now Vas Infrastructure.

According to the newspaper and the news agency, the word 'technology' is also attractive to some of the companies. Proto Infosys has changed to Proto Developers and Technologies, while Birla Kennametal has become Birla Precision Technologies.

Other changes of 2008 include Continental Credit and Investments which changed to Contil India, Tatia Intimate Exports to Tatia Global Venture, Shringar Cinemas to Fame India, Mittal Securities Finance to Clarus Finance and Securities, IOL Broadband to IOL Netcom, Transworld Infotech to Sterling International Enterprises, Solid Granites to Solid Stone Company, Salora Finance to Artheon Finance, and Forbes Gokak to Forbes and Company, the publication reported.

Source: Adapted from *The Times of India* (2008) and Press Trust of India (2008).

The mentioned factors and circumstances that prompt a company to put on a new identity, is very visible in the current Indian corporate scenario. So much so that at the beginning of the year 2008, some fifty companies have changed their identities for one or the other reason given here (See Exhibit 19.9).

Summary

Corporate identity is one of the most important issues in the life of a corporation, as a company is recognized and reckoned by its identity. Every company has a functioning style and a corporate philosophy, which should reflect in all walks of a company's business activities, may it be selling, promotion, or human resource management.

Corporate identity has been defined by many experts as a mix of symbols, environment, communication, and behaviour patterns by company personnel to generate desirable responses from amongst the publics.

Corporate identity should represent the core competence and the inner truth of an organization and should focus on the key strengths, business purpose philosophy, and its value system to inspire a sense of confidence and trust in the minds of various publics. Some focus areas are employee motivation, customer confidence, dealers' pride, shareholder's trust, and a sense of faith in the company by other external publics.

The expert opinions say that the corporate identity emerges out of a mix of four elements, products/services, environment, communications, and behaviour.

Developing a corporate identity is the responsibility of top management in coordination with public relations, and should percolate top down to all levels of the organization. It is an aspect that should be seriously and even fanatically protected. Once decided, the identity should reflect in all its business activities from company to dealer signages to business cards, with uniformity and unity of logo, colours, and designs.

Corporate identity has two aspects, non-visual and visual.

The non-visual identity can be broken down into two parts, personal and imper-sonal. The personal aspects cover the selling styles, customer service policies, telephonic response, correspondence, etc. The imper-sonal deals with advertising and publicity styles.

Visual identity covers certain visual aspects like corporate logo, house colours, typefaces, mnemonic designs, tagline, etc.

Corporate identity and corporate image are inter-related aspects of an organization. Whereas the corporate identity is real, the corporate image is the reflection of identity.

Public relations practitioners, while developing the corporate visual identity should take due care of the intellectual property rights to avoid any legal compli-cation.

Corporate identities do change, though not frequently, yet certain changes in the nature or growth of business necessitate adjust-ments.

Key Terms

Corporate culture   Pervasive, deep, largely subconscious, and tacit code that gives the 'feel' of an organization and determines what is considered right or wrong, important or unimportant, workable or unworkable in it, and how it responds to the unexpected crises, jolts, and sudden change

Corporate identity   Combination of colour schemes, designs, words, etc., that a firm employs to make a visual statement about itself and to communicate its business philosophy. It is an enduring symbol of how a firm views itself, how it wishes to be viewed by others, and how others recognize and remember it

Corporate logo   Distinctive design, mark, or symbol that uniquely identifies a firm. A corporate logo is a powerful corporate identity tool and, as the symbol by which public recognizes a firm, is in some cases more valuable than the physical assets of the firm

Corporate philosophy   The business principles and ideology of a company

House style   All the characteristics, conventions and use of colour and language of a company, institution, website, etc. that serves to make it distinct from others

Plank   A stance that a company adopts to position itself amongst the target publics

Concept Review Questions

1. Define and describe the concept of corporate identity. What is the significance of an identity for an organization to succeed in the business world?
2. What is the system and basis of developing an identity? What are the elements and the mix of these elements, which contribute to the developing and projecting corporate identity for a company?
3. Describe the kinds of identity—personal, impersonal, non-visual, and visual. What are the characteristics of each kind? Give a detailed answer.
4. What is the relationship between corporate identity and corporate image? Please illustrate your answer with graphics and examples.
5. Write a lucid note on the Intellectual Property Rights in India. How relevant is the law to corporate identity? Explain.

Project Work

1. Develop a plan of corporate identity programme for an upcoming super deluxe seven star hotel in your town, with a special reference to establishing its corporate reputation amongst the relevant target publics.
2. A large distributor of medicines in India has diversified into manufacturing of life saving drugs. He has a lucrative trading business for which the distributor is known for. What corporate identity change would you plan for the new corporate, so that the new company is not plagued by the reputation of a mere trader?

Case Study

Godrej—The New Identity Programme*

The 110 years old Godrej group decided to transform itself into a company with a new identity. This Rs 7,500 crore company has adopted a new logo and a marketing slogan in its first brand makeover ever since it was founded in 1897. This is the company's well thought out endeavour to state its marketing position and a new corporate identity.

The group's current logo, founder Ardeshir Godrej's signature in a running hand, is red in colour. The company planned to replace it with a bright rainbow coloured cursive signature of the founder. Now the new slogan of the group is 'Brighter Living'.

According to a report published in *The Mint*, New Delhi (14 April 2008), Adi Godrej, the group's chairman said, 'The new slogan 'Brighter Living' implies a modern approach and feel. It is completely based on consumer insights.' The group has also planned to launch an advertising campaign with its new logo and slogan, which as a consumer products group, will reflect the life style of its consumers. According to an estimate of their advertsing agency, the group has budgeted Rs 40 – 50 crore to implement the programme.

Source: Adapted from *The Mint*, New Delhi, 14 April 2008.

'Legacy brands such as Godrej have to constantly reinvent themselves to be relevant to their consumers. They have to position themselves in a way that they are equally aspirational to the next three generations as they are to those (generations) that grew up using the brand,' commented the group consultant agency director, Sanjeev Malhotra, of Alia Creative Consultants Private Limited.

Having started their business as a security equipment and soaps manufacturer, more than a century ago, the Godrej group has today diversified into a variety of consumer goods and services sector. Its entry into the new businesses has been backed by the sturdy and trusted Godrej brand.

Commenting on the decision, the chief executive of the Nobby Brand Architects and Strategic Marketing Consultants said, 'It was about time that Godrej undertook this exercise as the brand was getting too dissected. Corporate image is very important for mega heritage brand such as Godrej because all the values can be carried across new lines as well without losing ethos of heritage, transparency, and trust.'

Notably quite a few group companies have been eyeing expansions. For instance, Godrej Consumer Products Ltd (GCPL) completely revamped brands as Cinthol soap and Renew hair colour. The company also acquired four other companies and programmed to raise Rs 400 crore from the capital market.

Another group company, Godrej Properties Limited planned to raise some Rs 600 crore from the market as a part of the makeover plans.

The new corporate identity of Godrej group seem to have ambitions to rise above the status of local name to a global corporate of repute.

Discussion questions

1. What, according to you, are the reasons that a 110 year old company like Godrej wants to transform itself into a new and modern organization? What are the elements, that the Godrej are using to reposition its corporate identity? Give a detailed reply.
2. Draw up a questionnaire to target Godrej dealers to acertain their perception and response to the new identity that the company is making efforts to project itself as a progressive organization. Interview about 20 dealers and prepare a report for the information of the management.

References

Jefkins, Frank (2006), *Public Relations for Your Business*, Management Books 2000 Ltd, Forge House, UK, published in India by Jaico Publishing House, India, pp. 32 and 34.

Metro Now, New Delhi, 25 August 2008.

Press Trust of India, 17 February 2008, New Delhi.

Riel, Cees B.M. van (1999), *Principles of Corporate Communication*, Prentice-Hall, pp. 28, 30, 31, and 33.

The Mint, 'Brand Revamp—Godrej Set for Makeover, with a Slogan, New Logo', 14 April 2008, New Delhi, vol II, no. 89, p. 6.

The Observer of Business and Politics, 'Resolving the Corporate Identity', New Delhi, 7 June 1996.

The Times of India, 'Companies Sport New Identities', 18 February 2008, New Delhi.

20

Event Management

EVENTS—A POWERFUL COMMUNICATION

Event management as a subject has attracted considerable attention of several public relations professionals, due to its being a powerful tool for communicating to the target publics. Undoubtedly, events offer a direct and quick exposure to the intended audiences. Today, special events are an important PR activity as the events reach out to several people and peculiarly satisfy the desire of most of the people to participate in the event, who have quite a few objectives to obtain like the special benefits offered to the visitors, to enjoy some entertainment, to gather some stimulation, to socialize, and also to become more knowledgeable on subjects, etc. To organizers also it is a specially created forum to share information, showcase achievements and products, and even to express gratitude to the publics for their support.

PR practitioners, knowing fully well the power of this media of communication, understand that such events should reflect an organization's qualities as a professional, reliable, and innovative corporation, and more importantly should make a dent in the minds of the publics with a favourable image. Obviously, the events have the necessity to be of a very high quality, creative, well planned, and executed professionally.

Organizing events has come to stay as an integral part of the PR responsibility for obvious benefits to the business organizations. Needless to say that events are not a mere show business, but an objective based activity in which the companies invest sizable amounts of money for obvious benefits and returns. Therefore, before an event is put up, it is important to determine the objectives of such an event, so that the event pays back in terms of good returns on investment. Particularly, in the market area, the measurement of the effectiveness of such events would become immediately possible in terms of the sales an event was able to generate. Therefore, the objectives of an event must be spelled out, right before starting the ground work.

OBJECTIVES OF SPECIAL EVENTS

According to The Standard Oil Company of America, there has to be a policy for organizing special events, which is as follows:

It is company policy to hold open house, conduct tours, and participate in special events that give us an opportunity to show our goodwill toward the community, as well as gain new friends and customers. Such public relations activities give our neighbours a chance to meet us and see how we live. When properly conducted, they offer visible proof that we keep our house in order, that we spend our funds wisely, and that we are a desirable neighbour, a good citizen, and a steady, considerate employer.

As such, 'In planning a special event, a comprehensive statement of objectives is essential in determining the theme, emphasis, scope, and progamme. The objectives should consider the particular interests, background, and knowledge of the persons to be invited.

Some of the objectives of special events in community programmes are to maintain or enhance community approval, correct possible misconceptions about the sponsor's organization, present the company as a good employer, and inform the community of the volume and value of the company' local purchases,' wrote H. Frazier Moore and Frank B. Kalupa (2005).

There can be a wide variety of objectives for organizing events. Various companies, depending on their size and nature of business, may have different objectives behind holding such events. Amongst the several reasons, some of the objectives generally are: *generate market excitement, win public support for a company/cause, generate publicity/media hype, enhance, polish, or correct corporate image, launch a new product, alert customers to sales/clearance, provide after-sale-service reinforcement, win customers and their confidence, mould public opinion, take credit for good performance, celebrate company milestones like silver jubilee, fund raising, hire personnel, celebrate mergers and acquisitions,* and *win elections.*

Generate Market Excitement

As a part of the MPR, the marketing department of organizations have a need to generate excitement in the market about the products and the company, so that the customer gets motivated enough to purchase the products. Also, one of the objectives is to increase share of the voice in the market for better brand salience and the awareness levels about the company. Certain events like 'operation concentration' are held by some companies in various towns and cities to promote sales and product acceptance.

Win Public Support for a Company/Cause

Sometimes in life, the company is faced with a controversial issue and needs to clear misunderstanding from the minds of the publics. Besides all the communications floated in the media for the information of the public, a personal contact becomes essential to muster support for the company. In such a situation, an organization may hold a conference or a get together of its supporters like customers, dealers, shareholders, etc. to clarify its stand and also showcase its strength.

Generate Publicity/Media Hype

With a purpose to bolster their corporate image, companies arrange some exhibitions, displays or cultural evenings, races and rallies to kick up some publicity or build a media hype. The spin doctors are generally behind such efforts who float newsworthy stories for media usage, which eventually help to increase its market presence and also to adjust its positioning in the public minds.

Enhance, Polish, or Correct the Corporate Image

To enhance, polish, and particularly to correct image perception, a company would showcase its profile as a good corporate citizen. Various themes, like 'helping the green revolution', 'pain killer of the nation', 'helping good causes', etc. are used to showcase the contributions that the organization is making to the growth of the nation, improving quality of life, or lending a helping hand in the eradication of certain diseases like, aids, malaria, etc. Invention of a life saving drug may be a good reason for holding an event to demonstrates to the medical community the new breakthrough. Doing all this, the company may get the mileage of projecting itself as a socially responsible organization, which hitherto, was not its reputation. Thus the objective would be image correction.

Launch a New Product

Launching a new product, is perhaps, the biggest challenge for the marketing professionals and the PR gets the share of the challenge. In fact, as a support system to the marketing efforts, the MPR is most often assigned the responsibility to plan and execute a major launch event. Customers, dealers, and opinion leaders, when invited to the launch event, public relations has to play roles at various stages, pre-launch publicity, launch programme execution and the post-launch efforts.

Alert Customers to Sale/Clearance

'Sale-Sale-Sale' or 'Sale clearance' are familiar signs one sees in the shopping areas announcing special discounts, etc. Such events are mainly aimed at botching up the sales and also clearing slow moving inventories by the company. Such events attract hordes of customers, who walk away with bulk purchases due to reduction in prices. The event is both ways good, good for the company and good for the customer. Bata sale or 'sweater mela' in winter months are familiar events.

Provide After-sale Service Reinforcement

To assure and reassure customers that the company stands firmly behind its products and is eager to fulfil its warranty commitments, the manufacturers of white goods like refrigerators, washings machines, etc. often organize events. Vehicle manufacturers, particularly who market cars and motorcycles organize events like 'service camps' to invite customers to get a free check for their vehicles. Strategically, this is a step towards relationship marketing and also an opportunity to service the customers. Generally, the companies would service the vehicles free but charge for the defective parts and components, if any, which need replacement. Maruti, Hero Honda, etc. often hold such camps.

Win Customers and their Confidence

In these days of aggressive and competitive marketing, the companies vie with each other to attract favourable attention of the customers. Events that encourage the customers to walk in, is an opportunity to explain the features and benefits of the products and allay fear, if any, in their mind about the technology or quality of the product. The exercise is aimed at wining over the customers and even sell products to them. Such events inspire customer confidence and makes them comfortable with price, quality, etc. The Godrej group, Airtel, and ICICI bank putting up booths at vantage points in the market place, are some such events, to make it happen.

Mould Public Opinion

Moulding public opinion for or against an issue is one of the most challenging jobs faced by all those engaged in the area of PR and communication. Several social issues like family planning, vasectomy, blood donation, etc. are still detested by large segments of population. People need education to change their opinions in favour of an issue. As part of the government PR, some NGOs, organizing events like 'health mela' or a 'free vasectomy camp' are examples. A voluntary organization like Red Cross setting up a 'blood donation camp' on roadside, or in some educational institutions and commercial organizations, is one such event.

Take Credit for Good Performance

When a company achieves an outstanding target or accomplishes a project, it is an occasion to celebrate. Events like employees' picnics, dealers' cocktails and dinner, or a special address by the managing director to the opinion leaders, are all aimed at taking the credit for the job well done. It is also an occasion to thank all involved in the process for the support and goodwill. For instance, a company clocking an annual turnover of Rs 1,000 crore has a reason for celebrations.

Celebrate Company Milestones such as Silver Jubilee

Occasions like golden jubilee in the life of an organization is the time for celebrations. It is time to showcase the milestones in the glorious history of an organization and also an opportunity to take credit. It is also appropriate for the company to thank all the publics for the valuable support to make it possible for the company to survive and grow. Several events such as a musical evening, donation to a big cause, or honouring the oldest employee or similar features mark the celebrations. The idea is to invigorate the workforce, build confidence amongst customers, dealers, share holders, in the professional management, and also to refurbish the corporate image.

Fund Raising

Voluntary organizations like temples, churches, and gurudwaras involved in the service of the society, often organize events to raise money to fund certain projects like building a hospital, a school or an old home. Special celebrations of anniversaries and festivals, are the occasions to hold congregations to raise money. A high powered motivator inspires people to donate liberally towards the cause and solicite the blessings of the Almighty. Organizations like rotary clubs, lion clubs, etc. also organize special events like social evenings where seats next to the dignitaries are auctioned or sold to some well-to-do fame seeking persons. All such events are meant to raise funds to support some causes like public health, family welfare, building a school, or drinking water projects, etc.

Hire Personnel

To cut through the bureaucratic delays, the business companies, particularly IT companies these days hold events to recruit suitable personnel on the spot. Nowadays some of the foreign universities also hold such events like educational melas to attract students to take admission in their universities. Some English and Australian universities and the University of New Zealand have been organizing such events regularly for obvious benefits.

Celebrate Mergers and Acquisitions

The mergers and acquisitions in the corporate world are great occasions to observe as an event. The new partnerships or the takeover of a company necessitate a need to spread the word about this development. Many times, such a development call for change in the name or giving a new name to the corporate marriage. Besides the communications floated in the form of advertisements and the press releases, an event may be organized to showcase the new identity and the newly acquired strengths of the company. The merger of Glaxo and Smithkline Beecham has been one such situation.

Win Elections

The bouts of political rallies and marathon speeches delivered at the mass gatherings by the political leaders are a familiar event. The blaring of mikes, fluttering flags, banners and posters, drum beatings and dance are all part of the political electioneering, which is a major national event in the life of every democratic country.

Besides certain elections to professional bodies like CII, FICCI, and PHD chambers of Commerce and Industry or All India Management Association, etc. are the electioneering events, though on a small scale, but with the same spirit to influence the voter and win the elections.

EVENT MANAGEMENT INDUSTRY—A HISTORICAL PERSPECTIVE

India, over the past couple of decades has witnessed a phenomenal growth of the event management industry. Events have always been a part of the Indian culture and have been organized by one and all, in their amateurish way, but with the marketing pressures growing and challenges becoming tougher, the live entertainment industry or the sales promotion techniques called events, have gripped the attention of all marketing and public relations professionals. So far the function of organizing these special events was undertaken by some advertising and PR agencies who would consider it as an offshoot of the major advertising or PR plan. But realizing the complexity of this art, there have mushroomed several event management companies who specialize in this PR function.

A look at the historical perspective reveals that the event management companies are nothing new to the Indian scene. Since time immemorial, we have witnessed mega events organized for different reasons and occasions. From the gorgeous wedding of Lord Rama and Sita organized by King Janak to today's events like Miss World contests and Filmfare awards evening, all are the old and new versions of the event management effort.

However, managing an event, from start to finish, has come to stay as a specialist job. The event management outfits now function on the lines of a company, with plenty of professionalism in conceptualizing, planning, and executing an event and even managing the aftermath of the event for corporate publicity advantage. The job not being a stereotyped effort, there is a need for every event to be distinctly different than the other.

A look backwards reveals that a decade ago, the term 'event management', which has become an integral part of the PR vocabulary, was not heard of. Having witnessed the growth prospects and attractive returns in terms of high billings, profits, glamour and excitement, the event management art has matured enough to be a profession. So much so that event management has become an area of specialization in the management education field and some new generation professionals take lot of pride in flaunting their specialist skills in the profession.

According to the FICCI and E&Y Entertainment report for the year 2004, the event management industry has grown from Rs 50 crore during 2002 to Rs 350 crore in 2003, which is very outstanding. As this segment, which some consider still in its adolescence stage, becomes an increasingly important part of the media pie, it is expected to demonstrate a growth of 30 per cent per annum over the next five years, in fact, more than doubling its size, approximately to Rs 1,443 crore by 2008 end.

By this time the estimates may have changed considerably. There are 10–15 players in the field with revenues above Rs 20 crore each and many small players, who are still considered to be in the unorganized segment.

Factors that Help Growth

The factors that have favourably helped the growth of the event management industry are attributed to the stability in the economy and the economic growth in the country. The economic surge of India, through policies of liberalization and globalization, also reflect in the event management industry scenario, which has now grown into a multi-crore enterprise.

Some major factors, however, which provide impetus to this industry are: *population growth, opening of the Indian economy, liberalization, increase in disposable incomes,* and *the new rich class.*

Population growth

Whereas the population growth in India is the root cause of several economic and social problems, there is some silver lining in the dark cloud. In the face of acute employment problems, the event management industry has opened a new area for the new kinds of jobs. The young population aspiring for gainful employment, find this area interesting and rewarding. Some enterprising young men and women have floated their own event management outfits or found for themselves some suitable jobs. Whereas this activity propels some direct and indirect employment opportunities, the events organizing jobs carry a romantic flavour which fascinate the young people and suit their tempers with attractive rewards.

Opening of the Indian economy

With the change in the economic policies of the government of India and opening doors for foreign direct investment, several multinational and global companies have entered the Indian market. Obviously, this development has increased the need for such companies to make their presence felt in the market. To achieve that objective, companies are increasingly participating in the corporate events, trade fairs, conferences, and exhibitions, thereby creating enough opportunities for the event management organizations.

Liberalization

The liberalization of economy, alongwith opening the doors for international companies, has, as if, also created opportunities for the cross fertilization of cultures. There seems to have taken place a silent marriage of traditional culture with that of the West. Indian youth, today, has become conscious of the brands and styles of the dress they wear, are addicted to mobile telephony and are also conscious about the new fashion trends. The prominent global brands have targeted the youth population below 30 years of age with disposal incomes. Along with this comes the popularity of fashion shows, carnivals, gala nites, dinner and cocktails, and some theme parties. All these developments, naturally, have generated ample opportunities and challenges for the young population for some lucrative jobs in the event management field.

Increase in disposable incomes

India's youth, which constitute almost 50 per cent of the population, due to several new employment opportunities in industry and business, have experienced an increase in their disposable incomes. Also the surging middle class of India with great buying power, has brought in its wake a desire to impress and enjoy life. Mundane events, like celebrating the birthday of your loved ones, now can be outsourced to make it a memorable occasion for the guests and host alike. The event management companies have, nowadays, designed certain packages to suit several pockets.

The new rich class

Gone are the days when you could count the rich and famous in a town on your finger tips. With the surge of new business and industrialization, India has experienced the emergence of a new rich class. This creamy layer of the society has a great desire to make style statements in the society about their newly acquired wealth. Socializing in the form of promotional parties, celebrating milestones in their business success or even their personal success, has become the order of the day. Rather than leaving it to the in house resources, they prefer contracting an event management company to handle everything on a turn key basis. All this has provided all the impetus to the event management industry.

EVENTS—CLASSIFICATIONS

The event industry segment can be divided into several key sub segments that include corporate events, competitions and decorations, cultural events, sports events, festivals and celebrations, personal and social events. It is quite interesting to look at Exhibit 20.1 as a perspective.

EVENTS—TYPES

It is perhaps very difficult to list the types of events organized by the PR practitioners, as the area is wide open where the creativity can run riot. However, for academic reasons, listing them would contribute to the understanding of the system. Some of the types are anniversary celebrations, awards functions, open houses, conferences, exhibitions and shows, parades and pageants, community meetings, inaugurations, product launches, election rallies, protest marches, contests and competitions, reality shows, talent hunt, annual dinners, memorial lectures, dignitary decoration functions, etc.

Most of the special events can probably be classified into some broad categories, such as: *anniversaries, awards and rewards, exhibitions and trade fair, conventions and conferences, open houses and family day, contests and competitions, pageants and fashion shows, celebrity shows,* and *special weeks and fortnights.*

Anniversaries

Anniversaries of business and non-profit organizations are good opportunities to communicate with the target publics highlighting the progress, accomplishments and the contributions of the organization in order to build public confidence and prestige. Also opening ceremonies, inauguration ceremonies, ground breaking and corner stone laying ceremonies, are events

EXHIBIT 20.1   Event management industry—classification

Sub segment	Types	Examples
Corporate events	• Product launches • Promotions • Training meets • Annual parties • Trade fairs • Celebrity management	• Nano car • Hero Honda show • Maruti servicemen training • Employees' Family Day • Auto Expo • *Economic Times* top businessmen awards
Competitions and decorations	• Awards • Contests/talent search • Reality show • Beauty pageant	• Khel Ratna award • Voice of India • Quiz championship • Fashion parade
Cultural events	• Films • Theatre • Music • Dance	• Premier show • Khalid ki Khala • Rabbi Shergill night
Sports events	• Sporting events	• Olympic Games • Cricket World Cup • Durand football • Asian hockey
Festivals and celebrations	• Government sponsored • Corporate sponsored • Society sponsored	• Children's day • Hero Honda 'Sa Re Ga Ma Pa' • Ram Leela
Personal and social events	• Wedding anniversary • Birthdays • House warming	

which symbolize the progress for the organization, its employees, customers, or the users of their products, industry members, local community, and the country as a whole.

Awards and Rewards

Some special awards to employees, stockholders, dealers, or consumers provide public relations opportunities. Trophies, certificates, medals, holiday trips, banquets, and promotions, which are given to employees for suggestions, record attendance, length of service, safety record, sales and other accomplishments are publicized both in the employee publications and in the community news media. Goodyear spirit award, for instance, is one such event that is held every year at the country, regional and international level.

Dealers are honoured for efficient management, merchandizing cooperation, or record sales and are presented awards at conventions. The events are covered in trade magazines and dealers' periodicals. News of consumers who win contests is released to local newspapers and announced in corporate advertising.

Certain professional groups also organize special events to showcase the outstanding achievements by the members of such organizations. Medical associations, management associations, chartered accountants, publishers' association organize special events to honour their members for their outstanding achievements. For instance, the Lalit Kala Akademi, Sangeet Natak Akademi, or Sahitya Akademi all organize awards events to honour outstanding artists, painters, and writers. Public relations society of America also organized some awards and rewards programmes (See Exhibit 20.2).

Exhibitions and Trade Fairs

Exhibitions and trade fairs to showcase and promote products and services are a regular feature in the industrial and commercial life of the country. Perhaps, it is the most powerful opportunity to communicate to a variety of publics, who flock to such exhibitions, either on business or just for human interest. Besides, exhibitions afford a potential outlet for prospecting and networking with the prospective customers and some serious minded businessmen. Besides putting up exhibitions individually, the companies, countries, and states participate in such exhibitions and trade fairs to promote their business. The annual industrial trade fair held in New Delhi in November every year has become a regular feature in India in which several interested organizations participate. As an offshoot of this effort, certain exhibitions on special themes are also set up to cater to the people involved in a particular industry. SmartCards Expo 2008 is one such example (See Exhibit 20.3).

EXHIBIT 20.2 Public Relations Society of America Awards

The Silver Anvil for outstanding achievement in public relations is a coveted recognition awarded annually by the Public Relations Society of America. It now has 31 separate classifications for entries, which are judged by a panel of 45 business and communication experts. The competition is open to members of PRSA and to non-members. Award-winning programmes are on file in the research information center at PRSA headquarters. The society also sponsors a Gold Anvil Award for a public relations professional who has made a significant contribution to the profession, an award for distinguished service in public relations teaching, and the Paul M. Lund Award for a member of the society who has made significant contribution to the common good through personal participation in important public service activities.

Source: Adapted from www.prsa.org

EXHIBIT 20.3   SmartCards Expo 2008

Source: *The Times of India*, 28 August 2008.

Conventions and Conferences

Professional get togethers called conferences and conventions are organized by the professional bodies to create occasions for members to be together and discuss issues concerning the profession. Conferences are also created to float a consensus for or against an issue concerning the nation on economic, political, and social front. Business companies also organize such conferences at various intervals for various external publics to communicate some information and also solicit their support for the company's growth programmes. Annual general meeting with the shareholders, annual sales conference with the total sales force, etc. are such examples. Annual dealers' or vendors' conference are some more events which a company will hold to honour dealers for their outstanding performance and know their problems and suggestions to supplement the marketing strategies of the company. A vendors' conference is often set up to integrate the manufacturing effort, with their support. An exhibition of parts and components on the sidelines is put up to make the vendors interested in developing much needed parts.

Open Houses and Family Day

With the entry of several global corporations into India, have come along the popular tradition of holding open houses, as a part of their corporate relations programme. Various publics like employees' families, community leaders, and government officials are invited and such events which include features like a plant tour, a film show, and some presentations by company executives. A small memento may also be given to the departing guests. Such events when carefully handled, help to produce better understanding of company business amongst the publics. Annual family day and a sports day at the factory grounds by some companies is an example of such events.

Contests and Competitions

Programmes like scholarship programme for employees' children, an on the spot painting competition for children and essay writing competition or a slogan contest on themes like quality and customer service may be an important event for some of the organizations. Contests amongst consumers, a sales race amongst dealers, etc. may be used by some of the marketing companies, with public relations support, to finally organize a show to recognize and reward such winners of the contest. TV shows such as 'Hero Honda Sa Re Ga Ma Pa' and the 'Voice of India' are very popular with a large number of audience, hence a great tool for sales promotion and image building by the corporate world. Competitions and contests naturally foster healthy competitive spirit amongst the publics that an organization can mould in its favour for its growth and progress.

Pageants and Fashion Shows

Pageant or procession is a favourite event of several religious and cultural organizations. The famous Indian Ram Lila, Krishna Leela, Diwali, or Baisakhi *melas*, Chrismas Carnival, are the events which are an annual ritual and great events in the Indian life.

Fashion shows and sponsored glamorous events are a major communication tool for influencing consumers of clothings, cosmetics, and household goods. Several companies use this medium to their marketing advantage.

Celebrity Shows

Celebrities make news. A visiting dignitary like the international boss, a film star, a famous singer, or a spiritual leader are often occasions for organizing a special event to be attended by a cross section of the publics. Events like 'An evening with Amitabh Bachchan', or a discourse by a famous religious teacher are some of the events, which are sometimes sponsored by some companies.

Special Weeks and Fortnights

Several organizations celebrate a week or fortnight or even a month or a year to spread awareness about a problem or an issue amongst the publics. The government and social service organizations plan such events on an annual basis for fixed week or a fortnight, which includes many smaller events as a part of the larger event.

Delhi police celebrates a 'safety week' every year, government's social welfare wings organize a fortnight dedicated to the concept of motherhood, etc. 'Year of the girl child' has been celebrated to counteract some social evils like foeticide amongst Indians who crave for a male child.

Several pharmaceutical marketing companies observe a particular week of the year as public service effort through organizing or sponsoring 'free health check week' or 'eye care fortnight' or 'diabetes prevention fortnight'. The events are used by them to spread awareness about the ailments and thereby promote their drugs.

As a part of the marketing strategy, companies organize special festivals to promote their products. For instance, Himachal Tourism organizes 'The apple festival' to attract tourists to the state and also promote their produce of apples (See Exhibit 20.4).

ORGANIZING AN EVENT

Organizing an event mostly is the focused responsibility of PR, though it is never possible for any one person to make it happen. In the marketing area of a company, the responsibility is assigned to the personnel incharge of the regional operations, with the head office PR providing the concept, plan, and other support to carry out the exercise. The personnel at the regional level hold sufficient infrastructure and means to execute the plan, thereby carry out the promotional work. It is naturally logical for an organization to keep the spotlight on the region. However, PR remains an important functionary in the process.

EXHIBIT 20.4 The apple festival of Himachal

Source: Hindustan Times, 25 August 2008.

When the events like family day or community sports, etc. is to be organized at the plant level, then the plant PR in coordination with the corporate public relations, undertake the job. However, generally an organizing committee is formed with public relations as chief co-ordinator to carry out the function. Sub-committees are formed with responsibilities like reception, parking, entertainment, hospitality, and safety and first aid, etc.

The effort to organize the event can be divided into three phases: *the ground work, preparations and execution,* and *the post event review.*

Phase I—The Ground Work

Events are never an impromptu effort. PR professionals put in a lot of thoughts and deliberations into the exercise before deciding to hold an event. The major question arises, as to why an event should be organized? The events are not to be organized for the sake of organizing an event or make it yearly ritual for the company to squander the hard earned money. No sensible business spends money until they feel some mileage will accrue out of the event. Therefore, it is of utmost importance that the necessary groundwork should be done, with lot of thought put into it to conceptualize the event with a definite purpose or objective.

A rough and ready action list should be good to look at to streamline the thought process of a public relations practitioner (See Exhibit 20.5).

Define the problem/objective of the event

Undertaking to organize an event without determining the problem, would be an exercise in futility. Quite a few events are directed at the building of public opinion for or against an issue or a problem, which could be social or even product acceptance. Defining the problem helps to have a sense of direction.

Therefore, the objective behind holding an event should be amply clear and well defined so that all aspects and features of the event are directed only towards that objective. For instance, if the object is to launch a new product, all activities and messages should have product as the main focus of the event.

Conduct the situational analysis

Before a public relations practitioner sets out to take action, it is important that a good study of the present situation should be undertaken. An environment scan should lead to the conclusion, about the situation as is today. In other words,

---

EXHIBIT 20.5 The groundwork

- Define the problem/objective of the event
- Conduct the situational analysis
- Focus the event on the heart of problem/objective
- Define the target public and compose a data of important people
- Plan your plan and work your plan
- Be honest about the purpose of the event
- Dedicate to the event with professional sincerity
- Develop media networks, right news for right media
- Keep management in the picture, right from start
- Prepare budget and obtain management approval in advance

where does the company stand as far as the problem or the objective to be achieved through the event. Also determining the goal to be reached should give a clear vision.

Focus the event on the heart of problem/objective

To achieve the necessary communication impact, the total theme of the event should have one single focus. The theme should address the heart of the problem or objective, and it is necessary to ensure that the focus is not allowed to be diluted. All the activities or features of the event should have the same theme. With one single focus, the event is most likely to have a powerful impact on the publics at whom the event is targeted.

Define the target public and compose a data of important people

As a system of mass communication, an idea or a value system gets the acceptance of masses, only if the opinion leaders accept it. So to target the opinion leaders or important people, a database of such people should be composed to be used for their involvement in terms of invitations to them and also to get their endorsements or support to the values advocated in the event. Perhaps one of the reasons that India's family planning programme flopped is that the opinion leaders paid only lip service to the small family norm.

Plan your plan and work your plan

Invariably the successful event programme has to be backed by sound planning and also adhering to the plan. Therefore, it is of utmost importance that a well thought out plan should be put together. Not only that, the plan should be followed thoroughly, systematically, and sincerely, to make the event a success.

Be honest about the purpose of the event

Unlike some self-styled professionals, who would like to create some events to merely contribute to their own popularity, the event is a serious communication effort by the organization to influence their target public, at a considerable expense. Honesty pays and in this case more obviously. Therefore, the honesty of purpose is of prime importance.

Dedicate to the event with professional sincerity

PR practitioners, who are very clear about the professional ethics, would not do anything, that is below the professional standards. They would not compromise on the quality or creativity standards of all the communications, which are required to be designed and developed for the success of an event. The professional sincerity is an idea that travels far and wide to build the reputation of the professionals as well as the organizations that they work for.

Develop media networks, right news for right media

Networking with the media for generating the necessary publicity for the event is not a one day wonder. It takes time and a planned effort. All practitioners maintain an updated media list of the journalists from the print and electronic media. This is a long-term effort that pays dividends to the PR practitioners on a continuous basis. The right news when delivered to the right people in the media, results in coverage, so necessary to generate publicity for the event and the eventual benefits to the organization.

Keep management in the picture, right from start

From the concept stage till after the end of the event, it is only advisable to keep the management well informed about the ongoing developments and progress being made. It is actually the top management on whose behalf the public relations functions; therefore, it is only appropriate that the management is always in the picture. Problems or hurdles, if any, in the way of execution of the plan, can be removed by the management by its authority to do so.

Prepare budget and obtain management approval in advance

Budgeting for the event is a crucial part of the plan. Once a budget based on almost actual expenditure is finalized, it is utmost essential to present it to the management for the necessary approval. This exercise improves the comfort level of the managers from other departments, involved in the event. For instance, it is the finance managers, who by virtue of their job responsibility, may raise some technical objections. But if the budget is already approved and advised to all concerned, it will put the public relations practitioner in a commanding position to run the show without much problem.

Phase II—Preparations and Execution

Once the plan and budgets are approved by the organization, it is now time for action. Certain preparations for finally executing the event programme are essential. It is like planning a strategy before the attack. A look at Exhibit 20.6 should make sense.

Designate an overall coordinator

The public relations practitioner, whatever his job title, is in a vantage position

---

EXHIBIT 20.6   *Preparations and execution*

- Designate an overall coordinator
- Nominate sub-committees
- Give a thematic name to the event
- Fix a date and timings

- Finalize the chief guest and speakers, if needed
- Update guests list
- Set up an event secretariat
- Publicity arrangements and media relations

to act as the chief coordinator for the event. However, to get the necessary support from a variety of people from managers to down the line supervisors, it is advisable to form an organizing committee. Either the top boss or one of the directors has to be the chairman of the event organizing committee. This helps to steer clear the way for smooth functioning.

Nominate sub-committees

To delegate authority, the committee may be broken down into half a dozen or more sub-committees with responsibilities in some specific areas of the event. For instance, these committees may be described as programme and stage management committee, entertainment and hospitality committee, reception committee, parking arrangements committee, safety and security committee, water and hygiene committee, souvenir committee, etc. At the periodic meetings of the sub-committee heads, the progress can be reviewed for corrective actions, if required. A rough structure of the system is represented in Exhibit 20.7.

Give a thematic name to the event

Depending on the objective for which the event is being organized, a thematic name should be given to the event. The theme could also be the most focal part of the message that the organization wants to communicate to the publics. The theme name should be direct, catchy, crisp, and even colloquial and should

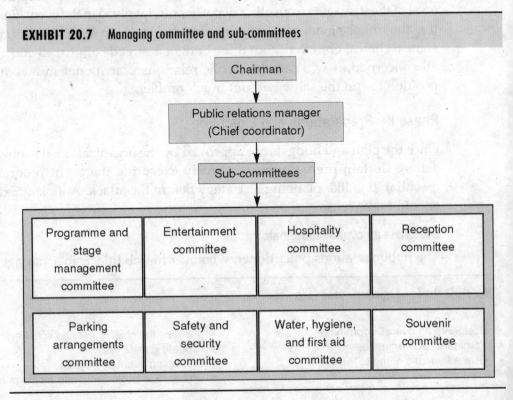

EXHIBIT 20.7   Managing committee and sub-committees

capture the very spirit of the event. The theme should be easy to pronounce and easy to remember. Some of the names, for instance, that are generally used are 'the family day', 'annual sports day', 'golden jubilee celebrations', 'talent search', 'Voice of India', 'awards night', etc.

Fix a date and timings

Time fixing is important. The date and time of the event should be fixed well ahead of time in the interest of advanced planning and preparation for execution of the event. Also, when circulated to all concerned, it ensures participation and support, so essential for the success of the event.

Finalize the chief guest and speakers, if needed

If the nature of the event so demands, it is only advisable to fix the chief guest well ahead of time. Prominent persons in the society like ministers or actors generally have tight schedules planned ahead, many months in advance. Similarly, the suitable speakers are not available at a short notice. Therefore, it is only advisable to make appointments with such important persons well ahead of time, to avoid last minute crisis. However, it is a good idea to have an alternative arrangement at hand, just in case a VIP cancels the engagement at the last minute, due to some unforeseen and pressing engagements.

Update guests' list

The success of an event, to a large extent, depends on the right kind of guests from the target publics attending the event. Therefore, scanning through the guest list is important so that the right public is available for communication. It is not a question of pulling crowds to the event and showing off the numbers. It is not the quantity but the quality of the guests who come that matters. Therefore, a careful scanning and updating the guest list is of considerable consequence.

Set up an event secretariat

Certain kinds of events need lot of communications to be floated and received from time to time. Therefore, it is only advisable to have a secretariat set up in the anteroom of the venue to facilitate flow of messages. In addition, such a set up also takes care of facilities like travel arrangements and hotel bookings, etc. for the guests. Gadgets like computers and Internet connections, duplicators and telephones, are all but necessary. Certain events need some press rooms fitted with Internet connections to make it possible for the reporters to file their news stories to their parent publications, right from the venue of an important conference or convention.

Publicity arrangements and media relations

Experienced PR professionals understand the needs of the media men and make all arrangements to facilitate the operation to generate publicity for the event. See Exhibit 20.8 for taking care of the media relations and publicity needs (also see chapter 16).

Phase III—The Post Event Review

The PR professionals, by virtue of their training and experience, understand that there is always some scope for improvement. The organizing of an event, in this regard, is no exception. Every PR activity, when reviewed after it is over, will tell that there are always certain areas, where certain steps could be taken towards excellence. So, every event leaves behind some lessons to be learnt. To assess the quantitative and qualitative success certain steps that could be taken are the following:

- Float a feedback questionnaire to be filled up by the people who attended the event, to have their candid opinions to determine, if the objectives have been met.
- Hold a review meeting of the organizing committee and record the problems, difficulties faced and the suggestions for future similar events.
- Hand out a letter of appreciation for the committee members signed by the chairman and the coordinator, for their cooperation and excellent work to make the event a success. A token gift is also recommended.
- Collect the harvest of press clippings about the coverage and assess, if enough publicity has been generated. Figure out what more could be done to enhance the effort.
- Run an 'expense to budget performance' review to learn if the money budgeted was sufficient or would need stepping up for the next similar event, due to change in prices or organizing strategies.
- An informal exchange with seniors and peers should help to know their impressions, suggestions, and criticism. The information can be objectively sifted through and taken advantage of.

EXHIBIT 20.8 Publicity and media relations

- Initiate pre-event publicity by spreading the news to the appropriate media well ahead of time.
- Communications to the media could be through press releases, photographs, or video clips, etc.
- Send invitations to the print and TV news channels to cover the event.
- If appropriate, hold a press conference on the eve of the event.
- A press kit containing copies of speeches, if any, biographical sketches and photos of the chief guest and the organization's top leader/s, and other informational literature, etc. may be circulated to the media, in advance.
- If an opportunity exists, organize some special interviews with the 'people who matter', to boost publicity.
- Produce posters, handouts, booklets, etc. to enhance visibility of the event.
- Collect all the press clippings of the coverage and present them to the management.

Summary

Events have come to be known as a powerful tool for communication to the target publics and as such are now considered the focused responsibility of all public relations practitioners.

Some of the objectives of organizing events include generating market excitement, winning public support for a cause/issue, generating publicity, polishing or correcting corporate image, launching new products, alerting customers to sale clearance, providing after-sale-service reinforcement, winning customers and their confidence, moulding public opinion, taking credit for a good performance, celebrating mergers and acquisitions, and winning elections.

Organizing events is an old Indian tradition. The tradition has transformed itself from Lord Rama's wedding to modern day fashion shows to Miss India beauty contests and awards nights.

As a consequence of the effectiveness of this communication media, several media management organizations have sprung up with an estimated billing to touch more than Rs 1400 crore at the end of 2008.

Some of the factors that have helped the event management business to grow are the population growth, opening of the Indian economy, liberalization, increase in the disposable incomes, and the new rich class of people seeking glamour and affluent life styles.

For academic understanding, the events' categories fall in areas such as corporate sector, competitive sector, art and culture, sports and festivals, and some personal events.

Amongst the kinds of events organized are anniversaries, awards and rewards, exhibitions and trade fairs, conventions and conferences, open houses, contest and competitions, pageants and fashion shows, celebrity shows, and special weeks and fortnights.

For organizing an event, a public relations practitioner needs to go through three phases, one, the ground work; two, preparation and execution; and three, the post event review. Phase one calls for situational analysis, determining the objective and budgeting; phase two is action time; and the third is to review performance and learn lessons for future guidance.

Key Terms

Acquisition   Taking control of a firm by purchasing 51 per cent (or more) of its voting shares

Disposable income   The amount of personal income an individual has after deduction of taxes and government fees, which can be spent on necessities, or non-essentials, or be saved

Event management   The application of the management practice of project management to the creation and development of festivals and events. It involves studying the intricacies of the brand, identifying the target audience, devising the event concept, planning the logistics, and coordinating the technical aspects before actually executing the modalities of the proposed event

Merchandizing   The methods, practices, and operations conducted to promote and sustain certain categories of commercial activity

Merger   The joining together of two or more companies or organizations

White goods   Large household appliances typically finished with white enamel, e.g., refrigerators, stoves, and dishwashers

Concept Review Questions

1. An event is a powerful tool of communication that a public relations professional can use to impact the target publics. Explain the statement.
2. Paint a scene in words and graphics to depict the growth of event management business in India in the past decade. What is the future of this business? Explain.
3. What are the kinds of events that are organized by various organizations for various reasons? Give a detailed answer.
4. What are the phases through which the process of organizing an event should go through to make it a success? Explain in detail.

Project Work

1. Develop a plan for the launch event of a new detergent, branded as 'Chamko' for a fairly new company entering business. What justification you will give to get management acceptance of the concept and the necessary expense budget for this event?
2. A company wants to recruit 300 middle level IT professionals on urgent basis. Suggest a programme of action to the company to attract such personnel and make them join the company.

References

Hindustan Times, New Delhi, 25 August 2008, p. 17.

Moore, H. Frazier and Frank B. Kalupa (2005), *Public Relations, Principles, Cases and Problems*, 9th edition, Richard D. Irwin, Inc, USA, printed in India by Surjeet Publications, New Delhi, pp. 289, 292, and 295.

The Times of India, New Delhi, 28 August 2008, p. 9.

www.prsa.org

21 PR and Crisis Management

DEFINING A CRISIS SITUATION

Perhaps there is no organization in the world that would not have faced a crisis situation at one time or the other. The description of a crisis may differ from a storm in a cup of tea to a tempest in the Pacific Ocean, but crises do come. They are not always like mild changes in the weather conditions but some of the crises leave behind lot of destruction and devastation in terms of financial reputation and the well earned corporate image of a company. Of all the streams of management, what comes under direct firing in a crisis situation is the public relations department. A crisis pushes the PR up front to face it and come alive out of the situation. That is why, a crisis situation could be called an 'acid test' of PR.

According to an expert opinion, a crisis can be defined as a moment of danger, or suspense, which can do serious harm, if not resolved in time. This moment of danger could have taken some time to develop, perhaps, as a series of problems, which in itself were not big enough, and which reached crisis point almost unnoticed; or it could be a sudden catastrophe, which took everyone unaware with harmful consequences. Further, to be considered as a crisis, the possible harm should be enough to do damage to financial standing of an organization, or its business performance, reputation, or its major stakeholders. In extreme cases, all of these can be at risk. Of course, the worst case of all is when human life is lost or hangs in balance.

Defining the crisis, Frank Jefkins (2006) wrote, 'Nothing is certain in this modern world where we are so often at the mercy of events, people, and technologies over which we have absolutely no control.'

Predicting the unforeseen is, perhaps, never possible. We may expect the unexpected anytime of the day and night without any warning signal. We, today, live in the world infested with chemical, nuclear, electronic, and terrorist threats. Therefore, it is only advisable for a public relations professional to be prepared for the eventualities with a crisis management plan.

One of the significant characteristics of any crisis situation is the breakdown of communication. Also a crisis creates considerable confusion and misunderstanding amongst the publics, who start perceiving the organization in a bad light. Known as 'noise', it brings along severe challenges for the PR to grapple with the situation and set the record straight by timely management of the communication system. Evidently, the people affected and involved in the crisis and also the public at large look for an authentic version of the crisis and then wait for a clarification and action plan that it is expected to silence all the noise. It becomes very necessary because most often the rumour mill engineered by the interested parties works over time to compound the situation and turn the ugly events in their favour. So the PR have to rise to the occasion.

The nature of the business and operations of a company has lot of relevance to the crisis that a company may face. There are certain crisis-prone companies like airlines, railways, and manufacturing plants and there are some others who do not generally expect crisis except the vagaries of weather or acts of God, like earthquakes, floods, etc. The negligence of men and laxity in observing the safety norms, at times can create some serious crisis, like fires and lethal gas leaks, etc. The company may face a crisis in the market place due to product failure or the sinister designs of the competitors. All said and done, crises do come. As quoted by Skinner et al. (2007), the British Prime Minister Benjamin Disraeli had said, 'What we anticipate seldom occurs. What we least expect generally happens.'

The gravity of a crisis is generally measured on two counts, first and the most important is, the loss of human life, and the second, the financial loss. In India, the obvious question in a crisis situation is: How much is loss of *jaan* (human life) and *maal* (financial loss)? Both these measurements determine the gravity of a crisis, and rightly so.

KINDS OF CRISIS

Perhaps, it is quite difficult to put the crisis situations in some categories, yet going by the nature of a crisis that the corporate world is faced with, the situations may have some similarities. A rough and ready list of the situations should make sense and tickle our thought process, as to how public relations can play its own kind of role in each situation. They are the following:

- Product failures
- Image loss
- Top management changes
- Financial crisis—cash crunch
- Industrial unrest
- Hostile takeover
- Global economic and political changes
- Natural calamities
- Man-made disasters

Product Failures

Product failure can be one of the major disasters that a company can face. Since the present and the future of a company entirely depends on the acceptability and reputation of the product and its brand name, any failure, either caused by company's own mishandling or the sinister designs of the competition, can wreck untold damage to the market position of a company. Fast moving consumer goods (FMCG) products are more susceptible to such situations. A complaint from a customer about contamination and resultant reactions on human health or a discovery by some consumer activists, can be the reason for such a crisis. The government and its regulatory authorities soon swing into action and ban the product, spelling a gigantic marketing crisis. The problems that the global brands like Cadbury and Cola faced about a decade ago are well known.

Even some of the high tech products can sometimes push the companies into a crisis. Firestone's infamous radial tyre Eagle AT was shunned by major vehicle manufacturers in America due to fatalities caused by the product. Firestone had no option but to sell off the company and its subsidiaries all over the world, to pay for legal compensations.

Image Loss

One of the most serious crisis that any organization may face is the loss of image, due to some act of omission or commission. With all the good intentions with public welfare in mind, a company may take a decision to revise its policies and practices, but the action may boomerang. Unfortunately the negative messages spread very fast than the positive communications. The actions may result in distortion of positive perception that the publics may be carrying in their mind about the company for a long time, but get destroyed in a few hours or days. According to Warren Buffet, the largest investor of the world, 'It takes twenty years to build an image and only five minutes to destroy it'. When a crisis of this nature strikes a company, it is often expensive and time taking to repair and restore the lost image. For instance, the Cadbury, when perceived in bad light by the publics, over the product contamination, had to designate a high profile celebrity like Amitabh Bachchan as their brand ambassador, at a very high cost, to help restore the lost reputation.

Top Management Changes

Unlike the Indian family owned companies, where the management control often is passed on from father to the sons and onwards, the global corporations are large industrial democracies where the presidents and the board members keep changing. Any time or every time a chairman and managing director is changed, he naturally rearranges the management chess board. The development many times upsets the apple cart sending many related publics in a tizzy. The changes the new head makes in the policy decisions may spell disaster for many associates and businesses related to the company. Some of the world famous business leaders known for reviving sick organizations, when join such a company, ruthlessly shed few thousand jobs, creating crisis not only for the organization to face the public wrath but also hardships to these rendered jobless. For instance, in the recent past, when one of India's leading airlines, Jet Airways, announced retrenchment of their staff, the employees created a furore by taking it to the streets. The crisis drew national attention and pressure from press, public, and government, forcing Jet Airways to shelve their downsizing plan.

Financial Crisis—Cash Crunch

The situations like economic melt down, demand recession, technological backwardness, or changing trends and fashions, or an unforeseen cancellation of a bulk order, may lead to a sudden precarious financial situation, called financial crisis. Changing market conditions, product failures, and high rate of returns may generate financial losses, resulting in serious squeeze on cash. Such situations have adverse effects and may result in creditors all at one time overcrowding the organizations to demand payments due to them. Also when a company is running into losses, it suffers from a constant long-term crisis and needs help either from financial institutions or the government. This situation may lead to distress selling of the organization at a compromising price. Air India, for instance, having accumulated losses over the years, have been asking for government help to tide over the financial losses. Recently, the company represented to the government for a grant of Rs 2,000 crore to grapple with such problems. Now that the two national carriers, Air India and Indian Airlines, have marged, it is one indication of the two public sector corporations together taking care of the crisis.

Industrial Unrest

Strikes and lockouts in an organization can send a company into a crisis situation. Militant workers' unions and violent labour strikes result in work stoppages and suspension of the manufacturing operations causing a tremendous loss, to the organizations. Besides, dealing with agitating labour unions and their hot headed and hard bargaining leaders becomes a tough nut to crack. The government attitude and the media responses all compound the situation. The crisis not only plunges a company into dire straights but sends several employees into severe hardships bordering on erosion of subsistence levels (See Exhibit 21.1).

To muster the necessary public support, organizations make conscious efforts to keep the employees and the public at large, informed and educated. Also to comply with the legal aspects of the labour situation, the organization sends out advertisements in the media to persuade employees to shun illegal strike as otherwise they may invite stern actions under the law. For instance, the Delhi Government published an appeal to the striking paramedical staff of Delhi hospitals (See Exhibit 21.2).

Hostile Takeover

Companies are often threatened with guerilla attacks in a takeover bid by some interested parties. A hostile takeover starts when someone starts quietly buying a company's stocks and when that party holds the majority shares of the company, may legally slap a takeover on the existing management. Obviously, by virtue of losing the majority ownership, it loses the right to govern the company. On the other hand, the peaceful takeover is the direct settlement between the companies for a price. This often happens. The first situation poses a crisis for the company when the challenge is to rise to the occasion and muster enough strength in terms of shareholders' support, to retain the control of the company.

Global Economic and Political Changes

With the communication revolution becoming a reality, the world has shrunk into a global village. Whatever happens, economic and political, in any part of the world, directly or indirectly affects people in general and business in particular. Situations like changes in rupee–dollar parity, emergence of United Europe, Iraq–US war, or developments in Pakistan affect the Indian economy and business. For instance, when the American dollar dipped in comparison to the rupee, several Indian businesses were threatened with a crisis, as the export business became unremunerative. To come to the rescue of the business commu-

---

EXHIBIT 21.1 Anatomy of a labour situation

Scene I
A large multinational company plans to celebrate the 'family day' at their manufacturing plant. The Rs 500 crore plant employs some 3,000 employees. The employees, families, and members of the community, numbering about ten thousand assembled to have a day out, to be entertained with music and lunch for each family, etc.

Scene II
Unions threaten management to meet two demands or face a boycott of the show. Demands are, one, let suspended employees join celebrations, and two, announce 20% profit bonus for workers. Management not willing to succumb to pressure tactics.

Scene III
Unions start demonstration shouting anti-management slogans, which many workers join in. Management persuades unions to remain calm and not to spoil the show. Employees get more agitated.

Scene IV
Employees led by some miscreants uproot tents, destroy eating stalls, and loot the lunch stock to destruction, with people running for safety. They manhandle the cameramen and take out their exposed films to avoid evidence of vandalism. Show devastated beyond repair. Management keeps calm.

Scene V
Next day, union toughs assault some managers with a couple of bloody noses. Police shows up. Instigated by unions, the workers walk out and a wildcat strike takes place. The public relations distribute a single sheet handout advising employees to maintain self control and discipline. Management left with no choice but to declare a lockout, in the face of an illegal strike.

Scene VI
Instigated by local politicians and union leaders, the employees indulge in mass demonstration and smash company property by stoning and also rough up the security staff. Police controls mob by *lathi* charge. A midnight attempt to set the factory on fire foiled by alert police vigil.

Scene VII
After fifteen days' stalemate, management and the union leaders brought to the negotiating table by the government conciliation officials. Sensing trouble the public relations stepped up communications through a newsletter to the employees explaining the necessity of discipline and issues like bonus, etc. Also sufficient communications sent to the concerned government officials to keep them informed of the situation. A supervisor's newsletter sent to this level of employees. A meeting held with floor supervisors to explain the situation. To get public support, posters pasted, during midnight, on the walls of the surrounding areas, explaining management stand.

Scene VIII
Tough negotiations between management and unions lasting some twenty hours resulted in an agreement. The day for opening of the plant fixed.

Scene IX
Public relations swings into action to inform the public in general and employees in particular, about the time table for the resumption of operations. The following communications were floated.

- Posters announcing the plant opening, put up on the city walls and in the villages, covering a 30 mile radius, from where the employees hailed
- PA system fitted on to a mobile van went around announcing the plant opening and other related information
- Press conference and a press note distributed to the media
- Organized a special press visit to the plant
- General house meeting with employees explaining the situation and need for normalcy and good work. Public relations provided speeches to the plant manager
- Visit to community leaders by senior management personnel to explain and solicit community understanding and goodwill
- Plant director invited as the guest of honour, to hoist the national flag on Independence Day, by the local community, to show their appreciation for the company. Plant director makes a special contribution to the local school building funds, as a gesture of gratitude to the community.

EXHIBIT 21.2 An appeal by Delhi Government

GOVT. OF N.C.T. OF DELHI
DEPARTMENT OF HEALTH & FAMILY WELFARE
9th Level, A-Wing, Delhi Secretriat, New Delhi

APPEAL

All Group-C & D Paramedical Staff who are on unwarranted indefinite strike since 23rd February 2009 are requested to resume their duties as patient care is badly affected in Hospitals of GNCTD.

Representatives of the Sanyukt Sangharsh Samiti have already been called for discussions and have been assured that the government of NCT of Delhi is taking up sympathetically all those demands which can be resolved at its level. Their other demands are being taken up with the union health ministry. The Sanyukt Sangharsh Samiti has agreed that they have no grievance against Govt. of NCT of Delhi.

Therefore, there is no need or justification for continuance of this strike. The staff involved in the strike is directed to immediately resume their duties. In case the Group-C & D Paramedical Staff does not resume duties, stern action even extending to imprisonment would be taken against them, under the provisions of the Essential Services Maintenance Act (ESMA).

(PROF. KIRAN WALIA)
MINISTER OF HEALTH
27.02.2009

DIPI2257108-01

Source: Hindustan Times, 27 February 2009.

nity, the Finance Minister of India announced a subsidy of Rs 5,000 crore to take care of the crisis situation.

Natural Calamities

More than any other reason, the acts of God create many a crisis situation. Earthquakes, floods, tornados, typhoons, tsunami, etc. bring in the gravest kind of crisis situations resulting in mass destruction and tremendous loss of human life. Most often the people are not expecting such things to happen and the unexpected happens bringing in untold misery. The aftermath of such disasters is more ghastly and difficult to manage. The challenge of saving the precious human lives, providing timely medical relief and life saving assistance, and rebuilding the destroyed infrastructure on emergency basis, poses gigantic challenges and a huge strain on the economy. For instance, the unexpected tsunami and the floods in Bihar are some of the glaring examples of such crisis situations.

Man-made Disasters

Until otherwise careful and conscious, the humans themselves are responsible for causing disasters, which spell grave misery for the people and even the loss of human life. Terrorism, hijacking planes, carelessness in maintaining hygiene in the surroundings bring crisis-like situations, which often become a challenge for the administration. The 9/11 attack on the World Trade Tower, the terrorist attack on Indian parliament, series of bomb explosions in Jaipur, Mumbai, and Ahmedabad, and the 26/11 terrorist attacks on Mumbai hotels are well known national crisis.

PR AND CRISIS MANAGEMENT—THE PLAN

Since the crisis situations or disasters never give notice, and managements are most likely to be caught napping, the professional PR persons should have a crisis management plan kept ready and constantly updated from time to time, to cope up with the eventuality. Importantly, the planning for crisis is not a one time activity, but something to be reviewed and revised periodically. It is most important to maintain a good level of crisis response capability. Some of the notorious corporate crisis like Bhopal Union Carbide tragedy, can perhaps be attributed to the response system getting neglected. The plan may have existed but its capability to appropriately respond to the situation did not exist. Therefore, the crisis management plan should be reviewed, revised, and a mock exercise put into action occasionally.

Some of the aspects and parameters that should encompass the plan are: *the message, the crisis management committee, the target publics, the responsibility, the media relations,* and *the aftermath.*

The Message

When a crisis strikes an organization, many outside forces hinder its ability to effectively communicate. Some of the factors like confidential nature of the information, certain time bound limitations, the pressure and stress caused by crisis, and the human emotions become a stumbling block in the way of transmission of messages to the target publics. Particularly in a crisis situation, it is the most vital necessity of an organization to effectively convey the key corporate messages and monitor them. The fact remains that the management and for that matter the PR professional, who has a communication plan, has already taken the necessary steps towards meeting the challenge of a crisis situation. For instance, amongst the steps that should be taken to provide relief to flood affected people in Bihar, the *Hindustan Times* (11 September 2008) suggested, '…marooned villagers do not listen to songs, or health programmes—all they hear is the regional news bulletins of All India Radio. The local news should improvise—it should become the vehicle for snippets of crucial information that will save lives—like boiling water before drinking, how to avoid malaria and precautions with food.'

Developing a well thought out crisis management plan with a major focus on the process of communication, pays dividends to the PR practitioner. Since the occurrence of a crisis does not allow anyone to go through the detailed plan, it is only appropriate that the plan should be reduced to a single page ready reckoner. Such a single page checklist helps to take all the guesswork out for all those involved in the process of fire fighting.

The Crisis Management Committee

Formation of a crisis management committee is an important step in the right direction. This committee is a coordinated structure created to pool up the talents and skills to handle various aspects of the crisis. Typically, such a team includes the PR, legal affairs, manufacturing operations, security, and the top management representatives and other personnel with appropriate skills and resources. Generally, the PR manager works as the coordinator and the company spokesperson during the crisis situation.

The crisis management committee should meet off and on to review and update the plan, replicate the responses, and also do some loud thinking about the changing scenario and possible threats. Such meetings also help in emotionally integrating the team to be ready for the eventuality. Generally headed by the CMD, the structure of the committee may look as seen in Exhibit 21.3.

EXHIBIT 21.3   The crisis management committee

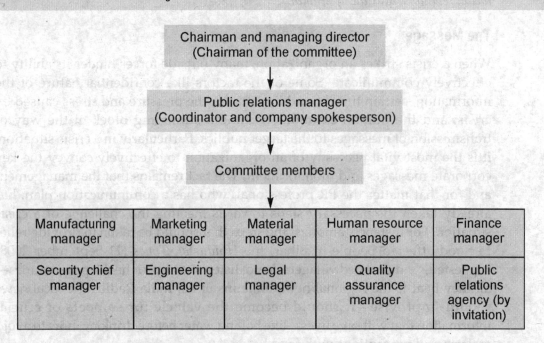

The Target Publics

If any organization, by any reason or standard, have arranged the target public in some order or priority, the same may not hold good in crisis times. The importance of various publics changes in accordance with the nature of a crisis. For instance, if it is a train accident, the most important public is the next of kin of the passengers, who should be communicated with, the soonest. The other publics come next. It may be appropriate to classify the publics into primary, secondary, and marginal. Besides, the list of publics may include the officials in the national and local level regulatory and emergency agencies like police, medical authorities, and the important government officials. Depending on the nature of the crisis, publics like customers, dealers, and media, and even union leaders and retirees of the company, etc. may also be kept in the loop.

The Responsibility

Fixing specific responsibilities for each member of the committee and other personnel involved in the crisis management system is of utmost importance. Ambiguity or overlapping responsibilities can lead to confusion and ego problems amongst the individuals. Specificity of roles ensures proper performance of duties assigned to each individual. This should be done in peacetime and not at the nick of the time, as in difficult times, people tend to avoid responsibilities. Perhaps, the crisis situation is the time for sharing the blame, rather than the credit. Therefore, the people avoid getting involved.

The Media Relations

The bad news is good news for media. Therefore, the interface with the media, which most often is the responsibility of public relations, have to be taken care of with skill and far sight. Since PR works as the spokesperson of the organization, the media statements should be specifically cleared with the top management and also the crisis management committee. Due to the knowledge and the skills professionals have, it has to be ensured that the media interface is handled by PR only and no other person should be authorised to interact with the media.

However, it is relevant in this context that certain strategic decisions be made about the techniques to be used. The choice can be made from the menu consisting of media relations and publicity, printed material in the form of publications, etc., video and audio method, personal contacts with the media, or the paid for advertising, to communicate facts and views about the crisis. All these elements can be used either singly or in a combination in an integrated manner.

The press releases to the media, particularly, have to be pre-prepared explaining whatever the company knows about the crisis. This is also an opportunity to bolster media and public confidence in the company by releasing material that may have bearing on the crisis. For instance, the outstanding safety record of a company in the event of a major fire, may fortify the public faith in the organization. The considered responses to the media are more likely to receive constructive appreciation of the crisis rather than the media indulging in usual blame game.

It may also be appropriate for the CMD of the company, to go through a training session on media relations with special emphasis on handling hostile press during a crisis situation.

The dire and unusual situation calls for public relations persons to be mindful of certain dos and don'ts while interacting with the press. For such precautions, see Exhibit 21.4.

The Aftermath

Once the immediate crisis is over, it is time to sit back and assess the success of the project campaign. Once the main crisis is over it leaves a residual impact on the organization and the mindset of various publics connected with the organization. Experienced crisis managers suggest certain strategies till the time the situation normalizes. Naturally it takes time to erase the bad memories of the crisis from the minds of the publics, who often start perceiving the

---

EXHIBIT 21.4 Media relations—dos and don'ts

Dos
- Gather full facts and transmit them from one focal point
- A credible and expressive person to be spokesperson
- Get media training for CMD to face hostile press
- Be accessible to the media persons
- Report your own bad news
- Tell your story quickly, openly, and honestly
- Listen carefully to respond
- Scotch rumours soonest
- Provide enough evidence to authenticate facts

Don'ts
- Avoid the answer 'no comments'
- Don't indulge in arguments with media persons
- Don't try to fix the blame
- Don't overreact to provocative questions
- Don't exaggerate
- Don't deviate from the corporate policy
- Don't make 'off the record' comments

---

organization negatively and adjust their responses accordingly. So some strategies are the following:

1. A crisis stricken organization should use a single spokesperson; provide open, prompt, and accurate information to the publics. In the post crisis situation, although it takes time for the company to recover from the trauma, the publics, particularly the media, demand immediate and honest response from the company.

2. Rather than indulge in hair splitting over the cause and effect of the crisis, the organization may chose 'apologizing' as one of the options to pacify the agitated public sentiment.

3. For the restoration of lost image, an organization may resort to highlighting the past laurels like outstanding and creditable performance, and try to bolster the image that may have got wholly or partially damaged by the crisis.

4. Blaming certain individuals to be relieved of responsibility or some outside vested interests, but not without sufficient evidence, may also be one of the options, though not a very smart option. Firing or transferring some individuals might salvage the lost position.

5. Publicly airing certain corrective actions taken to restore the state of affairs, that existed hitherto, and committing to prevent such ugly situations to happen again, may be another option before the organization. This may pay, if the company in the past have been perceived by the publics, as an honest, upright and genuine one.

6. Counteracting and adopting the posture of a victim, rather than a defendant, can be another strategy. Giving your own bad news yourself and projecting that the company has been victim of circumstances and some outside force, can help to receive sympathy and a clean chit from the publics.

EXHIBIT 21.5   The ten commandments of crisis management

1. Develop a 'crisis management plan' in anticipation.
2. When the crisis strikes, be prompt and honest in communicating it to the concerned publics.
3. Maintain a proactive response to face agitated emotions. Keep cool.
4. Be flexible to adjust and cope with levels of uncertainty and confusion.
5. Closely monitor media reports and reactions.
6. Keep doors open to receive feedback from publics concerned.
7. Maintain consistency of messages and relay through designated spokesperson, public relations, or CMD.
8. Coordinate with the members of the crisis management committee.
9. Maintain constant public relations with corporate image restoration in mind.
10. Have the aftermath strategies worked out to bolster public confidence.

---

7. Compensating the parties who suffered losses due to the unforeseen and unfortunate incident, is one of the common strategies to assuage public feelings. Although no amount of compensation can restore the lost lives or injured feelings, yet such an announcement should have a sobering effect on the victims in particular and publics in general.

8. To ensure serious involvement of company personnel, so that they extend the wholehearted support in the crisis situation, it may be in order to make such a role as part of the annual employee appraisal system, allowing special weightage while viewing their loyalty to the company and career growth prospects.

THE TEN COMMANDMENTS

The unforeseen crisis leaves no time for anyone to ponder over the things. It is time for action. The actions that are prompt and timely make all the difference in not only diffusing the crisis, but also managing it in all its hues and colours. The ten commandments can serve as a ready reference guideline for the crisis management (See Exhibit 21.5).

Summary

A crisis, big or small, does strike every organization one time or the other. A crisis situation is a moment of danger when an unforeseen and unexpected event happens and leaves behind lot of harmful consequences. One significant aspect of the crisis is the breakdown of communications. Certain companies, such as railways, airlines, or some chemical plants, the virtue of the nature of their operation are more crisis-prone. Public relations comes under stress and strain in a crisis situation and such a time is often considered at the acid test of the professional competence of a practitioner.

Though difficult to categorize the crisis situations, yet generally the kinds of crisis can be product failure, image loss, top management changes, hiring and firing, financial crisis, cash crunch, industrial unrest, hostile takeovers, global economic and political changes, natural calamities and, man-made crisis.

PR comes under tremendous stress in a crisis situation. Developing a 'crisis management plan' in anticipation is essential and most appropriate. Some of the important elements of such a plan are the message, the crisis committee, the target publics, the responsibility, media relations, and the aftermath. Developing a single sheet action list should cut down the time consuming effort of going through the detailed plan.

Remaining in tune with the ten commandments for managing a crisis can stand in good stead for public relations professionals.

Key Terms

Cash crunch The shortage of cash related to slow collections of bills from the market

Crisis Critical event or point of decision which, if not handled in an appropriate and timely manner (or if not handled at all), may turn into a disaster or catastrophe

Crisis management Set of procedures applied in handling, containment, and resolution of an emergency in planned and coordinated steps

Hostile takeover A takeover of a corporation that is viewed as undesirable by existing stockholders, owners, or management

Rumour mill The process by which rumours are started and spread

Concept Review Questions

1. Define and describe a crisis. What are the kinds of crisis that can generally be experienced by the corporate world? Illustrate your answer with examples of real life situations.
2. A 'crisis management plan' developed in anticipation by a public relations professional can work as a road map to meet the challenge faced in a crisis situation. Explain the statement with special reference to the elements of a plan.
3. What postures do you suggest to an organization, to take in the aftermath of a crisis, to emerge successful and restore normalcy? Explain in detail.

Project Work

1. Study the crisis situation faced by Cadbury chocolates thoroughly and prepare a crisis management plan incorporating the strategies used by the company.
2. Develop a series of four advertisements by Tata Motors Limited for educat-

ing the public about the company stand on crisis faced by them on the manufacturing site of Nano car in Singur.

3. Prepare a list of twenty probable questions that media persons may ask the Tata Motors CMD about the Nano crisis.

Case Study

Sir Ganga Ram Hospital—Disaster Management Plan

Introduction

In the event of a natural or man made calamity, that is, earthquake, floods, fire, mass transportation accidents, industrial explosions, civil disturbances, riots, terrorist violence, etc., there may be a sudden influx of mass casualities in the hospital for which the emergency medical care services in the hospital have to be in a state of ever readiness. Accordingly, as per instruction from Directorate of Health Services, Govt. of National Capital Territory (NCT) of Delhi, a contingency plan called 'Disaster Management Plan' for our hospital has been evolved which will be activated as soon as information of such disaster is received from the Directorate of Health Services, Govt. of NCT of Delhi. The duties and responsibilities assigned to various personnel and departments of this hospital are given in the following paragraphs.

Communication

As soon as the information about disaster and the likely mass influx of casualities in the hospital is received, the hospital telephone exchange will immediately inform the following:

(a) Medical superintendent
(b) Joint medical superintendent – I and II
(c) Deputy medical superintendent on duty
(d) Operation theatre
(e) Chairman, Department of General Surgery
(f) Chairman, Department of Anesthesia
(g) Chairman, Department of Orthopaedics
(h) Chairman, Department of Neurosurgery
(i) Co-coordinator, Department of Plastic Surgery
(j) Admission desk
(k) Medical stores
(l) X-ray department
(m) Pathology department
(n) Blood bank
(o) Security office
(p) Ambulance

Hospital telephone exchange will keep a few lines available for incoming calls regarding the casualities.

Code word
The code word allotted to the 'disaster management plan' is 'hospital red alert', which will be activated on orders of the medical superintendent.

Control room
A central control room will be immediately set up adjacent to the casuality. It will be manned by the public relations officer, one clerk, and one ward boy. The control room will be provided with a telephone and have a list of all casualties along with their addresses and telephone numbers, if available. The task of the control room will be to provide information of the casualities to the relatives/attendants/police, etc. All enquiries from outside pertaining to the casualty will be promptly and courteously attended to by the control room staff.

Medical superintendent
Medical superintendent will be the chief coordinator of the plan. He will at once inform the chairman, board of management, and in consultation with the chairman, departments of general surgery and orthopaedics, take steps to constitute the following teams:

1.	Orthopaedic surgeons	02
2.	General surgeons	02
3.	Cardiovascular surgeon	01
4.	Neuro surgeon	01
5.	Plastic surgeon	01

The chief coordinator will direct the personnel of the above mentioned teams to proceed to operation theatre and be available for emergency.

The chief coordinator will further instruct all resident staff in the departments of general surgery, orthopaedics, and neurosurgery to proceed to the casualty and be available there to attend to the casualties.

In case of instructions coming from the Directorate of Health Services, the chief coordinator will make immediate arrangements to send a special team of one orthopaedic surgeon, one general surgeon, one physician, two staff nurses, and two ward boys to the site of the disaster in an ambulance. The team will carry sufficient quantities of life saving drugs, dressings, splints, and I.V. fluids. Such essential emergency stores will always be kept in separate boxes and bags in the casualty ready for immediate use.

He will organize opening up of a special ward with 15 beds in the verandah of male general ward.

Joint medical superintendent – I
(a) Will arrange that medical stores and pharmacies are kept open.
(b) Will supervise adequate supplies of life saving, dressings, splints, I.V. fluids, linen, etc. in casualty, O.T., and ward.
(c) Will organize proper blood bank services, to be made available round the clock in consultation with consultant-in-charge, blood bank.

Joint medical superintendent – II
(a) Will supervise the arrangements for receiving casualties in the casualty department.
(b) Along with the senior most surgeon available in the casualty, will arrange, allotment of priorities to casualties as per the principles of 'triage' to ensure that cases who stand maximum chance of survival following immediate surgical care are given top most priority.
(c) Will instruct the security staff to control any unwanted crowd assembled around the casualty and to keep any undesirable elements away.
(d) Will organize for the relieving staff medical/non-medical.
(e) Will arrange that adequate number of trolleys and wheel chairs with staff are available in the casualty.
(f) Will organize proper arrangements for quick documentation of all casualities.
(g) Will keep the mortuary open with one attendant.
(h) Will make arrangements for tea/coffee/food, if necessary for staff.

Nursing superintendent
(a) Will immediately proceed to the casualty and arrange availability of adequate number of nursing staff in the casualty, operation theatre, and other critical areas.
(b) Will supervise the nursing care being given to the casualties by the nursing staff in the wards.

Casualty department
(a) Will be ready to receive the sudden influx of casualities.
(b) Check the essential life saving drugs, bandages, dressings, resuscitative fluids, splints, etc. are readily available.
(c) Ensure that trolleys, wheel chairs, etc. are available outside the casualty department.
(d) Adequate staff is available that is, nursing staff, ward boys, messengers, safai karamcharis.

Operation theatre, anesthesia, and surgery departments
(a) Arrange to make available at least two operation theatres within 30 minutes of receipt of information.
(b) Check availability of essential drugs and other equipment for at least 20 casualties.
(c) Arrange adequate number of I.V. fluids for at least 30 casualties.
(d) Organize O.T. teams by name comprising of anaesthetist, O.T. technicians, nursing staff, bearers, safai karamcharis, etc. and allot duties to them.
(e) Arrange for organizing resuscitation in the preoperative area and ensure that adequate supply of resuscitative stores is available.

Medical stores
(a) Will take immediate steps to replenish all vital drugs, stores to casualty, O.T. and various other wards.
(b) Ensure that the hospital pharmacies are kept open 24 hours.

X-ray department
(a) Will remain open for 24 hours.
(b) Duty roster of staff of radiology department will be especially prepared for ensuring availability of continuous radiology service both in department and in O.T.
(c) Ensure that adequate films and chemicals are available.

Pathology department
(a) Prepare duty roster for continuous service by laboratory staff in the department.
(b) Arrange to position laboratory staff at the casualty department for collection of specimens for examination.

Blood transfusion department
(a) Will remain open 24 hours.
(b) Will liaise with O.T. and casualty to collect demand for blood for casualties.
(c) Arrange to position staff in casualty and O.T. for blood grouping and matching.

Maintenance department
(a) Will ensure availability of maintenance staff continuously.
(b) Will ensure continuous supply of water and electricity.
(c) Will ensure that standby generator is in working condition and is switched on immediately, when required.

Security staff
(a) Be in a state of alert.
(b) Clear the hospital of all unwanted elements roaming about in the hospital.
(c) Clear the casualty area of onlookers and people not connected with the casualties.
(d) Assist the casualty staff in unloading of casualties from ambulance vans/other vehicles.
(e) Direct visitors/attendants making enquiries about casualties to the control room/casualty.
(f) Control sudden rush of traffic.
(g) Ensure that security staff is available for help at:
   • reception / control room
   • casualty
   • O.T.
   • X-ray department
   • each floor

Public relations
(a) Coordinate in activating the existing modern communication equipment installed at the hospital as per the advice of the centralized accident and trauma services.
(b) Co-ordinate with CATS control room phone No.1099 for proper communications.
(c) Coordinate with police/deputy commissioner/sub-divisional magistrate to sound alert.
(d) Help in communicating, to all concerned, the nature of disaster, place of disaster, number of casualties, and steps being taken for shifting victims to the nearby hospitals.

(e) Remain in touch with media—press and TV—to share news in the public interest.

(f) Work as the spokesperson on behalf of the hospital, in coordination with medical superintendent.

(g) Interface and empathize with traumatized relatives of the victims.

Discussion questions

1. Review and revise the public relations role in the crisis management plan of Sir Ganga Ram Hospital. Do you think that public relations should be assigned a greater role in the process? If so, develop the format for the revised and enhanced role.

2. Develop a crisis management plan for a five star hotel in the case of an unforeseen eventuality like fire. Spell out the public relations role in the process with full details of the actions and strategies to be used.

References

Hindustan Times, 'Disaster Prescription', New Delhi, 11 September 2008, p. 13.

Hindustan Times, New Delhi, 27 February 2009, p. 6.

Jefkins, Frank (2006), *Public Relations for Your Business*, Management Books 2000 Limited, UK, printed in India by Jaico Publishing House, Mumbai.

Skinner, Chris, Llew von Essen, Gary Mersham, and Sejamothopo Motau (2007), *Handbook of Public Relations*, 8th edition, Oxford University Press, South Africa, p. 288.

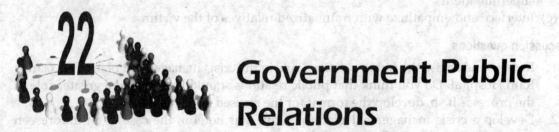

Government Public Relations

Chapter Outline
- Government public relations
- Elections and public relations
- Objectives of government PR
- Government PR agencies
- Government PR problems
- PR—public and private sectors

GOVERNMENT PUBLIC RELATIONS

India is the largest democracy of the world. The problems and solutions of a democracy everywhere should be the same as people everywhere crave for their participation in the process of governing themselves. But unfortunately, the historic statement by Abraham Lincoln, 'Government of the people, by the people and for the people', brings along several challenges for the direction to become a reality.

Perhaps one of the major problems of a democracy is the isolation of people from their government. Despite tremendous advancement in the information technology and other means of communicating the information to them, the citizens are increasingly disenchanted with the governments because they know so little as to how the government functions and what it is doing about certain burning issues. The lack of information fosters distrust and a major mistrust in their elected representatives.

'Government today, federal, state and local, is so complex and often so remote that citizens tend to become apathetic and bewildered. Who can determine the exact number of billions of dollars and kinds of weapons required to provide adequate military security? Who can assess with confidence the solution for difficult problems in foreign relations? Who can devise a solution to the welfare problem, or come up with a plan for an effective health care delivery system? It is hard for the busy, self-centred citizen to become interested in things he or she cannot easily understand. Relentlessly the problems and pressures of society are putting increasing strains on the machinery of government' (Cutlip et al. 1985).

All the experienced and knowledgeable public relations professionals understand the sensitive relationship of business with the government. No business or for that matter corporation, can function in isolation of the government. All the laws, policies, and taxes imposed by the government can make a tremendous difference to the success or growth of a company.

In the opinion of Moore and Kalupa (2005), 'The federal government acts in numerous ways that have a tremendous effect on business. For example, when the government borrows from individuals through the sale of government bonds or when it raises or lowers taxes, these actions have a significant effect on purchasing power and hence on business. The federal government invests tax receipts in education; contributes to state-highway construction; supports social security and medicare; provides funds for urban redevelopment, air and water pollution control, and mass urban-transportation systems. In these and many other ways government affects the cost and freedom of doing business.'

Further, 'Nearly everything business does is influenced by government, which provides and enforces the rules by which business is conducted and determines the climate in which business must function. To protect its interests and serve the public interest, business representatives must help write the rules and have a part in determining the political climate. They must have a voice in what legislation is enacted and play a part in determining government fiscal policies and taxation, directly and cooperatively, through constructive programmes of government relations.'

The American Scene

In a mature democracy like the US, which is more than two centuries old, the bewilderment of the people from the government can be gauged by the voting patterns in elections there. Though the global media channels show people's great involvement and excitement in the presidential elections in that country, the voting patterns do not seem to support the scenes. 'Public apathy, well termed the "loss of citizenship" is sharply etched in each election by the millions of Americans who do not vote. In the last three presidential elections, according to the US census bureau, between 45 to 46 per cent of the nation's eligible voters did not vote' (Cutlip et al. 1985).

Being alive to the need of open communication between the people and the government, several efforts have been made to bridge the gap, yet to many the government is perceived as a complex mechanism controlled by some elements who have some interests and priorities of their own. Some American presidents tried to set up a system to bring the government and the people closer to each other. For instance, former US President Jimmy Carter tried to open the channels of communication to bridge the gap, but lost his election for reasons that need to be looked at more carefully. However, in the American history, President Franklin D. Roosevelt started the telephone call-in system to the White House and was flooded with calls and questions which were tough to answer. However, it gave the ordinary citizen a feeling that it is possible to communicate with the president and other officials in his office and seek some answers. He is also said to have started some techniques like town hall meetings, accountability sessions, walk along the city streets, toll free call-in lines, TV shows, frequent news conferences, etc. to get closer to the American people.

Thanks to the communication explosion everywhere, the Americans are more exposed to elections, TV talk shows, TV debates, and the media playing a mediating role to bring much sought out answers to certain questions. Viewers and readers are encouraged to send in their most caustic comments and opinions on certain issues facing the nation. All this calls for the great role that the PR professionals are expected to play on behalf of the government, to keep the government connected with the nation.

The Indian Scene

In India, until the proceedings of the parliament were not being directly telecast, the Indian democracy was faced with people's greater bewilderment with the system. People, even the educated lot, would wonder what their elected representatives were doing in that grand hall. The former Lok Sabha speaker, P. A. Sangma had commented in the *Hindustan Times*, 'The idea is to bring the parliament closer to the people. There are lots of misconceptions about the functioning of Parliament and the conduct of the members. A whole lot of serious business also takes place and the people should know about it.' According to him, there is more to Parliament than the scenes of 'pandemonium' and 'turmoil' when once the house sat round the clock to finalize the important railway budget. The state legislative assemblies are no exception. It is difficult to erase the ugly scenes that took place in the UP assembly when the legislators indulged in violence and vandalism, a few years ago.

With almost 30 lakh people employed in civil and military services, the Government of India is a web of confusion and chaos to the ordinary citizens. To them government is a gigantic dinosaur, whose dimensions are difficult to comprehend. The leaders and bureaucrats often advocating the cause of transparency sound incredible and doubtful. The latest RTI (Right to Information) Act passed by the parliament seems to be a distant dream to the ordinary citizen to whom the government is a big jigsaw puzzle, difficult to solve. There are numerous laws in India aimed at assuring and reassuring the citizens of the good intentions of the government to protect their rights, which create more confusion than order. So the Indian citizen, like any other in any other country, lives in a state of bewilderment.

The teeming millions of India with high population growth rate and about 26 per cent people living below the poverty line and low literacy rate in several parts of this vast country, the problem of distance between the government and the people further gets compounded. Typically, the Indian politicians, who are often blamed for all the ills, seem to thrive on the confusion caused by multiplicity of religions and languages.

Despite the good intentions of some in the government to improve the lot of the people, blaming and criticizing the government is a big pastime for an average Indian. Despite the reach of information through channels like TV and radio, to the remote corners of India, there exists a wide gap between the government and the population. Many development programmes, day in and day out, aired by the government, sail over the heads of the people, as perhaps, nothing or very little trickles down to the masses, who have expectations from the government. The list of problems can be longer than we see in Exhibit 22.1.

So the challenge with the government is not only to devise ways and means to eliminate or reduce the intensity of the problems but also to inform the public about the actions taken. So doing whatever is possible is one thing and keeping people informed about the actions is another. The challenge of government PR

EXHIBIT 22.1 India's many problems

- Family planning
- Women empowerment
- Alcoholism and drugs
- Road safety
- Environment protection
- Dowry deaths
- Unemployment
- Terrorism
- Communalism
- Crime against women
- Red tapism
- Cultural changes
- Prostitution
- Religious conflicts
- Regionalism
- Female foeticide
- Child labour
- Polio
- Public health
- Illiteracy
- Bride burning
- Corruption
- Poverty alleviation
- Eve teasing
- Child marriage
- Erosion of family structure
- Homo rights
- Minority rights
- Language problems
- Nepotism

lies in connecting the masses with the government through dissemination of information to them.

ELECTIONS AND PUBLIC RELATIONS

Compared to corporate PR, the government PR is somewhat different. Whereas all the corporate objectives are linked to the bottom line of making profits, the government has a priority to keep the people informed about the efficient functioning of the government elected by them. As in a democracy, the elected representatives have to seek the public mandate for their re-election, they have no option but to continuously try and win the confidence of their people. The political careerists have to demonstrate to the electorate that the promises made by them at the time of the election are being fulfilled by them, so that people trust them and re-elect them.

Elections and Public Behaviour

The faceless democracy of India is something that no political party can take for granted. The voters' behaviour and attitude towards elections and candidates is quite unpredictable. However, there are three features of the Indian electorate, which are important for a PR practitioner in the government, to bear in mind. They are the following :

1. The voter turnout at the elections does not follow the worldwide trends of decline, but the pattern has remained almost steady between 50 to 60 per cent.
2. The voter turnout does not go down through the other tiers of democracy; the voting percentages clock higher in the assembly and *panchayat* elections than at the national level.
3. The poor, downtrodden, Dalits, and minority citizens are more likely to vote than the urban rich or high caste Hindus, etc.

Two other factors that possibly influence the voter behaviour are; first that mere populism, earlier a strong element in the voting pattern, is changing. The voter has acquired more maturity and looks for good parties and candidates who can keep promises. The new Indian voter cannot be taken for granted. They are less susceptible to emotive appeals and demand performance. The emotional issues like *mandal*, *mandir*, and *masjid* seem to have been replaced by demand for *sadak*, *bijli*, *pani*, and employment for all.

The second factor that influences the voter behaviour is the vital role of media in shaping up their thinking. The powerful penetration of TV media to the remotest parts of India, has the capacity to cover each constituency and highlight the local issues, which become a decisive factor for electors to decide the course of action.

EXHIBIT 22.2 Voting patterns	Voter turnout
1971	58 per cent
1977	61 per cent
1983	57 per cent
1984	62 per cent
1989	61 per cent
1991	59 per cent
1996	58 per cent
1998	61 per cent
1999	60 per cent
2004	59 per cent

Source: Adapted from http://eci.nic.in/Statistical Reports/Election Statistics.asp

Besides, the public apathy towards elections is reflected in the voting patterns at each election. The percentage of voters has remained 50 per cent to 60 per cent. The first two elections 1951 and 1957 recorded only 45 per cent. With the spread of education, media reach, and consciousness of rights, the pattern has since improved (See Exhibit 22.2).

Malpractices and Control

After every election, one often hears stories of malpractices indulged in by some unscrupulous politicians. Problems like rigging, booth capturing, violence, and fake voting are common occurrences. Rarely has the election commissioner declared re-election or cancellation of the candidature. The democracy comes under fire and tends to make people think that the elections are only a farce. This loss of faith has made the election machinery to devise ways and means to make the elections fair.

Amongst the steps taken are the introduction of electronic voting machines (EVMs) and the issue of voter's identity cards. In a city like Delhi, the Chief Electoral Officer has undertaken a PR campaign to restrict the printing of election pamphlets, posters, etc. (See Exhibit 22.3).

OBJECTIVES OF GOVERNMENT PR

The government PR, by and large, depends on a couple of factors. The first and the foremost in a democratic set up is the people's constitutional right to transparency in the functioning of the government. People have a right to information and rightly so the Parliament of India has passed the RTI Act to grant to the citizens the right to demand information and the government's duty to provide it.

EXHIBIT 22.3 Public relations campaign for printing of pamphlets and posters

OFFICE OF THE CHIEF ELECTORAL OFFICER, DELHI
Old St. Stephen's College Building, Kashmere Gate, Delhi

PUBLIC NOTICE

Sub:- General Election to Lok Sabha, 2009-Restrictions on the printing of Election Pamphlets, Posters, etc.

The Public are informed that Section 127A of the Representation of the People Act, 1951 enforces certain restrictions on the printing of election pamphlets, posters, etc. The relevant provisions of the Act are given below:

RESTRICTIONS ON THE PRINTING OF PAMPHLETS, POSTERS, ETC.

(1) No person shall print or publish, or cause to be printed or published, any election pamphlet or poster, which does not bear on its face the names and addresses of the printer and the publisher thereof.

(2) No person shall print or cause to be printed any election pamphlet or poster-

   (a) unless a declaration as to the identity of the publisher thereof. signed by him and attested by two persons to whom he is personally known, is delivered by him to the printer in duplicate; and

   (b) unless, within a reasonable time after the printing of the document, one copy of the declaration is sent by the printer, together with one copy of the document;

    (i) where it is printed in the capital of the State, to the Chief Electoral Officer; and

    (ii) in any other case, to the District Magistrate of the District in which it is printed.

(3) For the purpose or this Section:-

   (a) any process for multiplying copies of a document, other than copying it by hand, shall be deemed to be printing and the expression "printer" shall be construed accordingly; and

   (b) "election pamphlet or poster" means any printed pamphlet, hand-bill or other document distributed for the purpose of promoting or prejudicing the election of a candidate or group of candidates or any placard or poster having reference to an election, but does not include any hand-bill, placard or poster merely announcing the date, time, place and other particulars of an election meeting or routine instructions to election agents or workers.

(4) Any person who contravenes any of the provisions of sub-section (1) or sub-section (2) **shall be punishable with imprisonment for a term which may extend to six months, or with fine which m ay extend to two thousand rupees, or with both.**

As per the orders issued by the Election Commission of India, **a copy of each of the document mentioned above alongwith three extra copies has to be submitted to the Chief Electoral Officer, Delhi in respect of all such material printed in Delhi within three days of the printing, in the prescribed proforma. Similarly, the Printer must obtain a declaration from the publisher in duplicate in the prescribed proforma and submit a copy to the Chief Electoral Officer Delhi within three days of the printing**. The proforma are available at office of the Chief Electoral Officer, Delhi.

Any person who violates the above provisions of the Law shall be severely dealt with.

DIP/2374/08-09   **CHIEF ELECTORAL OFFICER: DELHI**

Source: Hindustan Times, 24 March 2009.

Since PR is basically a discipline of two-way communication, it is but natural that the government and its officials should be interested in knowing the public views on the issues facing the nation. Gone are the days when governments were run on the basis of *raja* and *praja* (the government and the governed). In today's democratic set up, the people are entitled to full participation in the process and to express their desires the way they want to be governed.

Keeping this in view, the objectives of the government PR may be to:

1. Minimize public apathy and bewilderment and ensure a positive understanding of the system of functioning of the government.
2. Solicit public support for government policies, laws, and programmes in the context of changing social, economic, and political scenario.
3. Inform and educate the citizens about the merits of the policies pursued by the elected government so that they can make wise and appropriate decisions at the election time.
4. Strive through honest public relations efforts to maintain a sense of confidence and trust amongst public in their elected government.
5. Share information, in a transparent manner about the government's plans, policies, and future prospects for the benefit of citizens.
6. Assure the public about the fair and effective use of public funds and solicit public support and cooperation in the process of the implementation of development plans.
7. Report to the public on the progress of development plans, government achievements, and benefits to the public, promptly and correctly.
8. Undertake educational, informational, and entertainment activities, particularly in the under-privileged segments, to improve the quality of life, through the usage of modern electronic systems of mass communication.
9. Facilitate the non-coercive compliance by public of the laws and rules by highlighting the merits and demerits of the system.
10. Plan publicity and information exchange programmes to bridge social, cultural, and economic gaps to inculcate a feeling of oneness of the nation.
11. Maintain high level of public confidence and trust in the government's role towards social, economic, political, and international issues. Provide enough avenues for public to communicate their feelings and emotions to the government to facilitate adjustments in policies and practices.
12. Provide to the citizens a simple, efficient, and comfortable process for the redressal of their grievances.

Government Agenda

Fortunately, the Government of India makes all efforts to communicate its policies and programmes to the people with a view to assure and reassure the masses that their government is taking all the necessary steps to come up to their expectations. The policy of Bharat Nirman declared by Prime Minister Dr Manmohan Singh is the testimony of this basic principle of sharing information with the people and learning about their responses and reactions (See Exhibit 22.4).

Government and Publics

The post independence scenario has drastically changed. From a conservative and traditional society, the new social order brings new insights worth taking note of by PR practitioners, not only involved in the private marketing companies, but also by those engaged in the government public relations. Called generation Y, India is a youthful country with 65 per cent of the population below age of 35 and 50 per cent people below the age of 25 years. With voting age lowered to 18, the aspirations of the younger generation to participate in the process of government, have been answered.

EXHIBIT 22.4   Bharat Nirman plan

"Bharat Nirman will be a time-bound business plan for action in rural infra structure for the next four years. Under Bharat Nirman, action is proposed in the areas of irrigation, road, rural housing, rural water supply, rural electrification and rural telecommunication connectivity. We have set specific targets to be achieved under each of these goals so that there is accountability in the progress of this initiative."

—Dr Manmohan Singh
Prime Minister

Bharat Nirman Agenda
- Every village to be provided electricity: remaining 1,25,000 villages to be covered by 2009 as well as connect 2.3 crore households.
- Every habitation over 1,000 population and above (500 in hilly and tribal areas) to be provided an all-weather road: remaining 66,802 habitations to be covered by 2009.
- Every habitation to have a safe source of drinking water: 55,067 uncovered habitations to be covered by 2009. In addition all habitations, which have slipped back from full coverage to partial coverage due to failure of source and habitations, which have water quality problems to be addressed.
- Every village to be connected by telephone: remaining 66,822 villages to be covered by November 2007.
- 10 million hectares (100 lakhs) of additional irrigation capacity to be created by 2009.
- 60 lakh houses to be constructed for the rural poor by 2009.

While the agenda is not new, the effort here is to impart a sense of urgency to these goals, make the programme time-bound, transparent, and accountable. These investments in rural infrastructure will unlock the growth potential of rural India.

Source: Hindustan Times, 14 August 2008.

EXHIBIT 22.5   The public profile

- 65 per cent of India's population is below 35 years, comprising of 70 crore people.
- 50 per cent of India's population is below the age of 25 years, comprising of 55 crore people.
- The people involved in earning the livelihood has gone down by 10 years.
- Several new job opportunities have cropped up in the country.
- More and more women are employed in gainful jobs.
- More than 50 per cent youth earn while they learn.
- Gadgets like mobile phones, computers, digital cameras, I-pods, and MP3 players are popular with people.
- Most young people are involved in blogging, cyber chatting, and playing games online.

- Youth, today, is media savvy and is hooked on to networking on Orkut, Myspace and, Face book, etc. They would often log on to YouTube, IPTV, etc.
- The voting age in India is 18 years.
- The population of India has surged from 36 crore to 112 crore since 1950.
- Adult literacy has jumped from 18 to 65 per cent.
- The per capita income of an Indian is computed at Rs 22,553.
- More Indians are working in many overseas jobs as specialists and on prime positions.
- India has the fourth largest billionaire population in the world, according to Forbes list of world billionaires.

Source: Adapted from the *Mint*, 4 February 2008, the *Hindustan Times*, 15 August 2008, and Mind Share Insights.

As is desirable for a PR practitioner to know the public profile, Exhibit 22.5 makes an interesting reading and should serve as a guideline for the professionals in the process of planning the communication programmes.

Government Report Card

In keeping with the tradition of effective public relations of keeping the public informed about the progress made on certain public welfare programmes, the Indian Prime Minister addresses the nation, every year, from the ramparts of the Red Fort in Delhi. His speech is but a report card in front of the nation about the performance of the government. The ten point public welfare programme of UPA government and the progress made against each (Exhibit 22.6) is in keeping with its PR objectives.

To bolster the nation's morale and inspire patriotic feelings amongst the public, the government PR as seen by the Ministry of Information and Broadcasting released a powerful advertising campaign (See Exhibit 22.7).

GOVERNMENT PR AGENCIES

Though not named as such, the Ministry of Information and Broadcasting is entrusted with the responsibility of taking care of this government PR function. Headed by a minister, the organization is a countrywide network to inform and educate the public about the functioning of the government. The ministry has a

EXHIBIT 22.6 The government report card

The programme	Action taken
1. Implementation of national rural employment guarantee scheme across the country.	Scheme extended to all rural districts with effect from 1 April 2008.
2. Rs 25,000 crore farm plan to increase food production, farmers' livelihood.	Rashtriya Krishi Vikas Yojana launched soon after.
3. National policy for rehabilitation and resettlement of people displaced by projects.	Policy with enabling bill and land acquisition (amendment) bill, 2007 introduced in winter session; referred to parliamentary standing committeee.
4. 6,000 new model schools, one in every block of the country; plan for universalizing secondary education.	Model schools and Rashtriya Madhyamik Shiksha Abhiyan approved by Expenditure Finance Committee; HRD ministry circulating cabinet note.
5. 370 new degree colleges in districts with low gross enrolment ratio at higher educational level.	HRD ministry consulting states over mode of fund flow from centre.
6. Thirty new central universities.	Bill enabling establishment of 16 central universities waiting to be put before parliament; committee under UGC working out modalities of 14 world-class universities.
7. Eight new IITs, seven IIMs, twenty IIITs, five IISERs.	IIM-Shillong and six new IITs in place and two IISERs starting activities; consultations on IIITs still on.
8. National vocational education mission for skill development for one crore youth.	Proposal sent to plan panel for setting up 1,500 new industrial training institutes and 50,000 new skill development centres.
9. Social welfare for unorganized workers.	Unorganized sector workers social security bill, 2007 awaiting parliament nod.
10. Pension for BPL citizens above 65; life and disability plan and health insurance for poor.	Indira Gandhi pension plan launched in November; Aam Aadmi Bima Yojana announced; Rashtriya Swasthya Bima Yojana implemented from April.

Source: Adapted from the *Hindustan Times*, 14 August 2008.

dozen of outfits to take care of the responsibilities in their own streams. They are the following:

- Akashvani (All India Radio)
- Doordarshan (The Indian TV network)
- Press Information Bureau
- Publications Division
- Research, Reference, and Training Division
- Directorate of Advertising and Visual Publicity
- Photo Division
- Song and Drama Division
- Directorate of Film Festivals
- Films Division
- National Archives of India
- Indian Institute of Mass Communication

This Independence Day

let us celebrate

THE EMERGING NEW INDIA

Join the Massive National Efforts for Economic and Social Development

Ministry of Information and Broadcasting, Government of India

davp 22202/13/0068/0809

Source: The Times of India, 15 August 2008.

GOVERNMENT PR PROBLEMS

Unlike the business world, where the PR is allowed and expected to play a vital role in the smooth and profitable functioning of the corporate, the government PR has certain limitations and typical problems that the profession faces. Some of the glaring and well known problems, according to some experts, are the following:

Lack of Transparency

Confidentiality is the buzzword in the government. Until declared public the information is generally not expected to be shared with public. Though the government often claims to be a transparent operation, yet it may not be true and the people at large are not willing to accept these claims. Perhaps, the tendency prevails due to legacy of the British *raj*.

Public Apathy

Howsoever hard the government and its agencies may try to relate its policies and practices to the public, the people generally reject such stances. Rightly so, it is very rare to hear a citizen appreciating what the government does or communicates. Criticism of the government, is perhaps, a major pastime of the Indians.

Bewilderment

Public often throws their hands up in an expression that the functioning of the government is beyond their comprehension. This is, perhaps, the biggest challenge of government public relations. The dichotomy between the rulers and the ruled exists and many times the dividing furrows become deeper. The public relations may try to fill these gaps and blur the lines, yet the bewilderment of the people with their government seems almost impossible to erode. The low voting turnout at the general elections may be one indicator of this tendency.

Bureaucracy Stranglehold

Amongst the other functions of the government, the bureaucracy seems to have a strong grip on the policies and programmes of the government. The bureaucrats who are the policy planners and the custodians of the government interests, seem to have their stronghold on the system. Though the democratic principles advocate people's participation, the high ranking officials rule the roost.

Politicians' Interference

Politics and corruption are, as if, two inseparable aspects of political game plane.

The scams and scandals, often attributed to the career politicians, is familiar subject in most of the social circles, high or low, in India. Though, going by the ethics, PR should not be a part of the unfair game, yet cannot remain aloof. Corruption comes in the way of smooth and ethical way of functioning by PR practitioners who may have no option but to toe the line.

Vote Bank Pressures

Playing to the gallery, it appears, is unavoidable by those who seek public mandate. The number game compels many to advocate certain policies which are irrational and unethical. But what can a poor politician, howsoever strong he may be, can do to counteract the majority who wants it their way? One of the glaring examples is the weak or no implementation of the population control programme, which can be considered a major PR failure of the last century.

Low Literacy Levels

Although it is officially claimed that India's literacy rate has touched 65 per cent level, yet the appalling lack of education amongst masses is a major threat for the government PR. Literacy, some think, is sheer knowledge of Rs 3, but it should mean some level of comprehension of the facts and figures. Going by that criteria, the percentage rate may not be realistic. The lack of literacy is a stumbling block in the way of effective public relations. Many times it is difficult to answer a question for the traffic top cop, 'How to educate the illiterate truck drivers the value of road safety?'

Media Habits—A Riddle

Despite media explosion and communication revolution visible today in India, it is still quite mind boggling to understand the media habits of the people at large. The multiplication of TV channels, soaring number of radio stations, manifold increase in the number of publications, the wider coverage by Internet and mobile telephony, has made the situation more complex. In other words, understanding the media habits of the people poses a considerable threat to the public relations, both in the government and private sectors.

Government's Poor Image

Apart from the political colour, the governments of all hues and colours suffer from the problem of poor image. The task of governing being massive, particularly in India, the government is often the butt of criticism by the people resulting in a poor image perception of the government. The political turbulence, as characterized in a democracy, keeps the public relations occupied in fire fighting rather than long-term efforts to correct and polish the government image.

EXHIBIT 22.8 Public relations—public and private sectors

Public	Private
Policies, only policies	Customer driven
Myopic vision	Global vision
Employment and welfare	Profit motive
Large bureaucracies	Industrial democracies
Political intervention	Lobbying in government
Thrive on govt. support	Live by corporate image
Top and bottom heavy	Lean and mean company
Systems ridden	Flexible and adjustable
Tow government line	Follow business rules
Yes sir! Yes sir!	Beg your pardon! no!
Job security	Hire and fire
Employee servants	Employee associates
Reward and punishment	Generate motivation
Commodity czars	Innovate new products

PR—PUBLIC AND PRIVATE SECTORS

Though it may not be very rational and logical to divide the profession of public relations into two streams, yet it is an interesting study to look at the two areas of operation characterized by certain tendencies and norms. With no intention to show one stream better than the other, a comparative study should give an insight into the practices, both to the students and the professionals (See Exhibit 22.8).

Summary

The biggest challenge of a democracy is to relate government to the people and reduce their bewilderment. Despite many modern means of communication, people are disenchanted with their governments. India and America, as two major democracies of the world, face similar problems. The voting patterns in each general election in India, depict the situation, when on an average not more than 60 per cent people vote. By that measure, bringing people closer to the government is a challenge of government public relations.

It so appears that the functioning of the government is beyond the comprehension of an ordinary citizen. The unruly scenes in the parliament, now shown on the television, makes an average Indian think that the parliament is a place for rowdies to show their muscle and lung power and the members of parliament seem to have no concern for the several issues facing the country.

Going by the trends at the general elections, besides voting being low, more people from the lower strata of the society vote than the educated and enlightened lot, which, in a way, speaks for the quality of the government India elects. The election process is still plagued by some malpractices and the Election Commission of India has introduced electronic voting machines (EVMs) and voter identity cards to prevent such unfair practices.

Public relations function in the government has certain objectives. The major objective being the communication to the people about the various policies and actions of the government and collect the necessary public reactions, to facilitate adjustments in the policies and practices.

To assure and reassure the people that the government is actively working for the development of the country and for improving people's lot, the prime minister has given out a Bharat Nirman plan to the nation. So that the government knows the mindset of the people, government and the private agencies have profiled the Indian population for public relations advantage.

As the Independence Day every year is the time for the government to showcase the government performance to the people, Prime Minister Dr Manmohan Singh exposed his ten-point agenda and the performance against each point to the nation.

Government has several agencies, working under the aegis of the Ministry of Information and Broadcasting to undertake the public relations effort on behalf of the government. Yet the government public relations suffer from certain problems typical to the government like lack of transparency, interference by the politicians, the stranglehold of bureaucracy, low literacy levels, etc.

The sharp contrast in the functioning styles of the public relations in the public and private sectors, is a matter of academic and professional interest.

Key Terms

Bureaucracy   An administrative system, especially in a government, that divides work into specific categories carried out by special departments of non-elected officials

Bureaucracy stranglehold   Concentration of executive powers in the hands of bureaucrats

Democracy   The free and equal right of every person to participate in a system of government, often practised by electing representatives of the people by the majority of the people

Government   A group of people who have the political authority or power to make and enforce laws for a country or area

Government public relations   Public relations efforts to keep the people informed about the efficient functioning of the government elected by them

Government report card   A government's period performance report showcased to the public to bolster vote bank confidence

Vote bank   A group of voters whose votes can be won by offering policies that meet their special interests related to religion or cast

Concept Review Questions

1. Write an explanatory note on the challenges a democracy faces with special reference to public relations practice.
2. If the low turnout of voters at each general election in India is an indicator of the low or no interest of the people in the government, then what roles

and goals would you like to assign to the government public relations, to make the democracy a meaningful system? Support your answer with explanations and historical data.

3. What are the various objectives of government public relations? Explain.
4. What are the various problems that government public relations suffers in its smooth functioning with a special reference to the public relations practices in the private sector?

Project Work

1. Write a report on the views of the cross-section of the society about their understanding of the system by which the government functions. Interview people at various levels of the society to bring out the representative opinions.
2. Develop a questionnaire and conduct a survey of the state of public relations profession in the public and private sectors. Prepare a comparative study to bring out the contrast.
3. Collect maximum number of advertisements put out by a metropolitan police, say Delhi Police, and run a critique.

Case Study

Public Relations in Action–Focus: 2004 Elections

Introduction

General elections 2004 were held in India, the world's largest democracy, in four phases between 20 April and 10 May 2004. Over 670 million people were eligible to vote for electing 543 members of the 14th Lok Sabha. On 13 May 2004, the ruling Bhartiya Janata Party conceded defeat after the Indian National Congress was able to put together a majority with the help of its allies under the direction of Gandhi family matriarch Mrs Sonia Gandhi. The post-poll alliance was called the United Progressive Alliance.

The former Finance Minister Dr Manmohan Singh, a well respected economist, took control of the new government as the prime minister. Singh had previously served under Congress prime ministers in early 1990s, and is seen as the architect of India's first economic liberalization plan that staved off an impending national monetary crisis.

The parties that got elected in the election are:

National parties	Seats contested	Seats won
BJP	364	138
INC	417	147
BSP	435	19
CPM	69	43

NCP	32	9
Total	**1351**	**364**
State parties	801	159
Registered parties	898	15
Independents	2385	5
Grand Total	**5435**	**543**

Main features of the 2004 General Election

Voters
- 675,000,000 eligible voters
- Voting on 4 days spread over 2 months

Candidates
- 542 seats in the Lok Sabha
- 5,398 candidates including 2,369 independents

Infrastructure
- 1,025,000 electronic voting machines used
- 700,000 polling stations

Turnout
- 387,453,223 votes cast
- 57.4 per cent turnout

Public relations campaign by Bhartiya Janata Party

'India Shining' campaign was popularized by the then ruling Bhartiya Janata Party (BJP) for the 2004 General Elections. The slogan was initially a part of the Indian government campaign to promote India internationally. Advertising firm Grey Worldwide won the campaign account in 2003; the slogan and the associated campaign was developed by national creative director Prathap Suthan, in consultation with Finance Minister Jaswant Singh.

The BJP-led government spent an estimated US$20 million of the government funds on national television and newspaper advertisements featuring the 'India Shining' or 'Bharat Uday' slogan. The same slogan was then used as the central theme in the BJP's campaign for the 2004 national elections.

The Rs 65 crore multi-media 'India Shining' campaign was launched by the Ministry of Finance, which was very high on visibility. According to TAM India, for the month of January alone, the campaign generated gross rating points (GRPs) of 2400, making it the most visible brand on television, second only to the brand Wheel detergent with just 730 GRPs.

In the print media too, it was a trail blazing campaign. For the first fortnight of January 2004, the campaign was ranked fourth amongst the top brands in terms of insertions in newspapers for this period, had commented AdEx India, an agency engaged in tracking the ads in the print media.

Due to the large sized advertisements that were placed by the BJP, the 'India Shining' or '*Bharat Uday*' brand ranked second amongst the top brands for the period in terms of advertising volume when measured in column centimeters.

According to TAM India, India Shining campaign was aimed at a very broad target group. It was clearly targeted at anybody and everybody across all states and all strata. Airtime was bought not only on Doordarshan and its regional kendras but advertisements on mass private enter-tainment channels and specialist channels such as Discovery and National Geographic were also aired. 'India Shining' advertisement was the second most frequently telecasted brand on television during the time December 2003 with the advertisement being aired 9472 times.

As per the analysis, there were as many as 392 'India Shining' insertions in over 450 newspapers, monitored by AdEx India. In terms of the nature of the advertisement, about 93 per cent of the advertisements were in colour. Besides, around 39 per cent of the India Shining ads were placed on back pages and full page advertisements account for about 18 per cent of the total advertisements placed.

The tremendous positive response generated by this campaign prompted the BJP to ride on its success and carry the theme forward. Therefore, the then Deputy Prime Minister, L. K. Advani's '*Rath Yatra*' was also named as '*Bharat Uday Rath Yatra.*'

Amongst the political parties, the BJP left its rivals way behind in terms of techno-savvy media management. The BJP's e-campaign stormed into millions of Indian homes using the country's vast telecom network, e-mail, mobile phones, and even spots on popular TV channels. BJP call centres were set up and details were collected of the 72 million phone connections in the country (46 million fixed lines and 26 million mobile phones). The party used the Reliance and BPL subscriber base to play a message by the PM seeking votes over the phone. The e-campaign allowed voters with mobile phones to download ring tones of BJP's anthem and photographs of Vajpayee. E-mail and SMS included anti-Sonia and Congress baiting jokes. Party had database of 25 lakh e-mails and 15,000 mobile numbers. Atal Behari Vajpayee had to record 340 personalized messages for BJP candidates contesting from different constituencies.

The famous SMS was '*Yahi hai feel good. Laksh Atal, vote kamal*. Believe in a new India. For a powerful India, vote BJP powerful. Vajpayee, the world admires.'

Another gimmick used was — Dial 3030 to listen to the PM. The recorded voice of PM said, 'This is Atal Behari Vajpayee speaking. Let us build a confident nation.'

The print campaign emphasized the work to be done — '*Hum ab rukenge nahin*'. The TV campaign said, 'Atal = Stability'.

BJP refashioned its India Shining slogan by making the feel-good factor more felt. Stung by the overkill of India Shining, the new campaign insisted that BJP had delivered a lot in every sector (roads, telecom, water, power) but it needed 5 more years and a '*Mazboot janadesh*' (a stronger public mandate) in Lok Sabha to fulfil all its promises. The catch line accompanying the slogan to vote for BJP was '*Sau crore challenge, mahashakti banenge*' (If a billion march, a super power will emerge).

The BJP lined up a host of stars and starlets from Bollywood and the television world. Besides dream girl Hema Malini and the country's most popular bahu Smriti 'Tulsi' Malhotra, it had others such as Poonam Dhillon, Yukta Mookhey, and Nagma urging voters to cast their ballot in favour of the lotus. Sculpted icons of prime minister were among the hottest selling merchandise in MP in the final stage of the poll campaign.

Public relations campaign by Indian National Congress

The Congress, on the other hand, was trying very hard to get its act together. While it appointed Leo Burnett's second agency, Orchard Advertising, to handle the account, the estimated Rs 60 lakh public relations budget was being handled by Perfect Relations.

Congress challenged the India Shining campaign with its 'Aam admi ko kya mila' (What has the ordinary man got). The first set of print advertisements talk about the issue of employment. '5 crore jobs were promised. *Am admi ko kya mila?*', read the ad. Taking on the BJP-led National Democratic Alliance (NDA), the ad said that in the last five years, employment in the organized sector has shrunk by 1.5 crore. 'This time elect the party that is with the youth …*Congress ke haath, aam admi ke saath*', conveys the advertisement.

The language of the common man was used to counter Sonia Gandhi's foreign origin issue. —'*Jan jan ki yehi pukar, Sonia Gandhi bahu hamar*' (Voice of the common man, Sonia Gandhi is our daughter-in-law). The strategy had two parts to it. While the metro audiences get macro messages, for rural audiences micro messages were customized, along with the big picture, to hammer the points.

Congress party was affected by the ban on usage of the electronic media. However, with the Election Commission (EC) not permitting political parties to advertise on the electronic media and the Information and Broadcasting (I & B) Ministry citing the law and monitoring problems, the party election campaign was a hit. It was deprived of using a very important communication medium, which the BJP could do when it was part of the government with the India Shining series.

The Congress was banking on the star power of siblings Priyanka and Rahul Gandhi and managed to rope in Shakti Kapoor and Moushmi Chatterjee, apart from a host of others, to campaign for the party. Besides these, SMS recorded phone messages and e-mails were also being used to woo the voter.

The Internet was used to spearhead the campaign by Congress. It set up warroom.com. At 119, the grand old party finally became IT savvy. It set up website plank with 600 districts. An event management firm was retained to send inspirational text messages (SMS).

SMS by Congress—'Some only feel good, some have good feelings for you. Vote for Congress.'

Sonia Gandhi travelled 64,000 kilometers and addressed 64 candidates. The campaign was low key, traditional, and conventional. The party also focused on the positive agenda with slogans like '*Mera bharat meri shaan, yehi hai Congress ka armaan*' (My India is my pride, this is the Congres desire). A series called '*Nahi chalega*' (It won't work) was released focusing on the NDA government's policies.

The broad communication and media strategy of the Congress was to correct the incorrect hype around the feel-good factor and follow the ground-up model to convey to the populace the real picture. Apart from Congress president Sonia Gandhi's *Jan sampark* rallies, the junior team, comprising the youth brigade of the party, was used to spread the message of '*Disha 2004: Shiksha aur rozgar*' (a theme revolving around education and employment), something that was identified as the 'weakest link in the BJP armour'.

Not only the Congress teams were prepared well, but modern technology was liberally used to update them on issues related to the youth of the country as they toured the length and breadth of the country. The states, where PR focus was less, were the ones where the party was strong.

The party also identified at 48 media centers, both urban and rural, from where viewpoints on radio, television, print, Internet, and other media were disseminated. Regional media channels were given importance. Dainik Bhaskar in the Hindi belt, *Eenadu* down south, and other regional language print media publications were used.

The outcome

The scene that emerged after 2004 general elections is clear. Congress came to power and BJP lost with its India Shining campaign and feel-good factor. What affected the masses was Congress party's low profile campaign against the BJP's high-tech mega show. As compared to the Congress campaign, BJP's India Shining and feel-good factor campaign was perceived as arrogant and over-confident.

Firstly, BJP started its election campaign very early. It started from the day Lok Sabha was dissolved on 4 February 2004. Secondly, BJP could not keep up the tempo for three months long election campaign. As the campaign progressed, the idea of Atal became more visible than the man himself and the slogan was fast losing its sheen. Thirdly, when exit poll results began to frighten the BJP leaders, BJP didn't have another plan, another slogan. Suddenly, all leaders looked nervously defensive and with low political morale.

As compared to BJP's unrealistic techno-savvy campaign, Sonia Gandhi's grass root '*Jan sampark*' rallies were welcomed by the masses, rural as well as urban.

Discussion questions

1. Run a comparative critique on the election campaigns of both the parties—BJP and Congress. Which communication campaign do you rate better within the professional parameters?
2. Collect all the public relations and communication material released by the government in preparing the nation for the successful execution of Commonwealth Games 2010, and write your observations and recommendations, for effectiveness of the programme.

References

Cutlip, Scott M., Allen H. Center, and Glen M. Broom (1985), *Effective Public Relations*, 6th edition, Prentice-Hall International, Inc., USA, p. 559.

Hindustan Times, New Delhi, 14 August 2008.

Hindustan Times, New Delhi, 15 August 2008, p. 15.

Hindustan Times, New Delhi, 24 March 2009.

Mint, 'Campaign', New Delhi, 4 February 2008, vol 2, no. 5, p. 1.

Moore, H. Frazier and Frank B. Kalupa (2005), Richard D. Iwin, Inc, USA, published in India by Surjeet Publications, New Delhi, pp. 426 and 427.

The Times of India, New Delhi, 15 August 2008, p. 14.

23

PR and Lobbying

LOBBYING AND LOBBYISTS

Amongst the four columns of a democracy, judiciary, executive, media, and legislature, parliament is the play field of several conflicting opinions. This is one area, which is open to pedalling ideas by several interested parties for or against issues facing a nation and its business and industry. This process of advocating ideas to the legislatures is known as lobbying. Known as the influence industry in American democracy, lobbying, more often handled by the public relations professionals, over the years, has become a sophisticated job, and despite the occasional scandals, it is a respectable profession. The term 'lobbyist' acquired recognition and some popularity in the United States during the 1800s to describe the persons who hung around the lobbies of the US Congress and state legislatures. Their main job was to influence the lawmakers to support the interests they represented.

In India, the term got mentions in the 60s, as the parliament and the parliamentary systems started maturing up. Although there is no organized activity visible in this area, yet a large number of people, with dubious reputation of fixers masquerading as liaison managers or even PR professionals, go about the business of lobbying. However, certain organizations, public and private, themselves undertake the job of advocating their own interests. Sugar, rubber, cigarette, IT, and car manufacturers are some such industries, which make efforts to defend their businesses.

Lobbying Defined

'The term lobbyist has several meanings. In its broadest sense, it is often used interchangeably with the term pressure group to mean any organization or person that carries on activities, which have as their ultimate aim to influence the decisions of Congress, of the state and local legislatures, or of government administrative agencies. In a narrower sense, it means any person who, on behalf of some other person or group, and usually for pay, attempts to influence legislation through direct contact with legislators', wrote Moore and Kalupa (2005).

Under the Lobbying Disclosure Act of 1955 in the United States, a lobbyist is defined as any person who:

1. spends more than 20 per cent of his or her time for a particular client on lobbying activities,
2. has multiple contacts with legislative staff, members of Congress or high-level executive branch officials, and
3. works for a client that pays more than $5,000 over six months for that service. Additionally, an organization employing in-house lobbyists does not need to register unless expenses exceed a $20,500 for a semiannual period. Since all criteria must be met to be considered a lobbyist, some people who secure income for lobbying can avoid registering.

'Because lobbying deals with relations with government, however, it is conceptually part of the public relations function of an organization. In practice, lobbying is closely coordinated with other public relations efforts directed to non-governmental publics whose voices are also heard by lawmakers and officials in government. And in its primary role, serving as a credible advocate and reliable source of information, lobbying is similar to other public relations efforts,' wrote Cutlip et al. (1985).

THE AMERICAN SCENE

In the democratic America, lobbying has become a big business. Having started as a very unorganized activity, the lobbying profession has acquired professional recognition. Despite dubious reputation of 'fixers', the American lobbyists tend to be experienced lawyers, many of whom have served in government or worked in campaigns, sometimes repeatedly walking through the revolving door between making of public policy and influencing it.

In his book *The Years of Lyndon Johnson: The Path to Power*, Robert A. Caro recollects that the tools of the lobbying trade were hardly subtle in the wild old days. At the turn of the century, for example, lobbyists freely roamed the floor of the Texas Legislature and freely dispensed what came to be known as the 'Three Bs: beefsteak, bourbon, and blondes' to grateful legislators. Now in place of the proverbial 'Three Bs', today's lobbyists dole out political action committee (PAC) money, raise funds for candidates and parties, organize extensive 'grassroots' and public relations campaigns, and brandish the findings of customized public opinion poll.

A report in *The Times of India*, a couple of years ago, said, 'Lobbyists provide access to decision-makers, monitor and influence important legislation, provide knowledge, expertise and analysis, and generally lubricate the wheels of government to the advantage of their clients. Of course, lobbyists are neither saints nor scientists. But the fact that they are part of a recognized profession (there is even an American League of Lobbyists or ALL), which lobbies on behalf of the lobbyists, gives it some respect and legitimacy.'

Lobbying, which until 1955 was a sort of hush hush activity, has become a big business. Nobody quite knew how big this business was, until Lobbying Disclosure Act of 1995 was passed when the lights shone brighter on the profession. Now under the law, the lobbyists are required to file documents disclosing more information about their craft. These reports, filed semiannually, list the organizations that hire lobbyists, the lobbying firms that are retained, the dollar amounts spent on lobbying, the names of the individual lobbyists, legislative areas of interest, and whether the lobbyist was a 'covered' employee, who had worked in a specified legislative or executive branch position within the previous two years.

The lobbying reports filed by the organization are required to be publicly available, but only at two locations: the office of the public records in the senate and the legislative resource centre in the house of representatives. Searching the reports to analyse data about an industry or a company, have been a difficult and time consuming job and the wealth of information was rarely brought to public notice.

The onerous task of compiling the information contained in the reports filed by the lobbyists and the lobbying firms, and making it available to the people has been done by the Centre for Responsive Politics. They even created a website for public to access the information and explore the world of lobbying and lobbyists in Washington.

Revolving Door

Although the influential powerhouses that line Washington's K. Street are just a few miles from the US Capitol building, the most direct path between the two doesn't necessarily involve public transportation. Instead, it's through a door, a revolving door that shuffles former federal employees into jobs as lobbyists, consultants, and strategists just as the door pulls former hired guns into government careers. While members of the executive branch, congress, and senior congressional staffers spin in and out of the private and public sectors, so too does privilege, power, access, and, of course, money.

Whether they are a presidential appointee plucked from an elite position in corporate America to run a government commission or an outgoing member of congress looking for a more lucrative job in the influence industry, Open Secrets.org' revolving door database tracks anyone whose résumé includes positions of influence in both the private and public sectors. Government employees may have had the president's ear or may have simply been the doorkeeper of the congressional cloakrooms. Influence-peddlers merely have to be in a position to influence government policy on someone else's behalf, commonly as a 'hired gun' at a K. Street firm, an executive of a professional trade association or as a vice president of government relations for a large company.

In addition to campaign contributions to elected officials and candidates, companies, labour unions, and other organizations spend billions of dollars each year to lobby congress and federal agencies. Some special interests retain lobbying firms, many of them located along Washington's legendary K. Street; others have lobbyists working in-house. The lobbying methodology as outlined by Center for Responsive Politics, USA, should be of interest to public relations students (See Exhibit 23.1).

Genuinely well-connected, the lobbyists are amongst Washington's movers and shakers. Typically, lobbyists are engaged by various interest groups representing business, a profession, and even labour unions, and foreign countries and organizations. Although there are a couple of hundred organizations that spend millions of dollars on lobbying, the top twenty spenders during 2007 amply state the enormity of the lobbying business in America (See Exhibit 23.2).

It should be also relevant for the students of PR to look at the multi-million dollar business done by some twenty registered lobbyist firms in the US (See Exhibit 23.3).

THE LOBBYING MAJORS OF AMERICA

The observers and the agencies concerned with environmental protection and

EXHIBIT 23.1   The lobbying methodology

The lobbying data has been compiled using the semi-annual lobbying disclosure reports filed with the Secretary of the Senate's Office of Public Records (SOPR) and posted to their Website.

Lobbying firms are required to provide a good-faith estimate rounded to the nearest $20,000 of all lobbying-related income in each six-month period. (Lobbying firms sometimes double as law, accounting, or public relations firms, the income for non-lobbying activity is supposed to be excluded from the lobbying reports). Likewise, organizations that hire lobbyists must provide good-faith estimates rounded to the nearest $20,000 of all lobbying-related expenditures in a six-month period. An organization that spends less than $10,000 in any six-month period does not have to state its expenditures.

There are three different filing methods. Two options are largely identical (one for profit groups, the other for non-profits) and use a definition of lobbying provided by the Internal Revenue Code (IRC). The third follows the definition of lobbying contained in the Lobbying Disclosure Act of 1995 (LDA). Filers using the IRC methods must report state and grassroots lobbying costs, which are not included in LDA reports. However, the list of covered public officials under the IRC is much narrower than the set covered by the LDA. Thus, lobbying expenditures may not be strictly comparable among organizations.

Where an organization 'self-files' (reports spending by in-house lobbyists), the center generally uses that figure to represent their total lobbying expenditure for the period. Where an organization does not 'self-file,' the sum of its contracts with outside lobbying firms is used to represent their total lobbying expenditure for the period.

Annual lobbying expenditure and income totals are calculated by adding mid-year totals and year-end totals. Whenever a lobbying report is amended, income/expense figures from the amendment are generally used instead of those from the original filing.

Similarly, where a termination report is filed, generally figures from that report replace those of the original filing.

Occasionally, income that an outside lobbying firm reports receiving from a client is greater than the client's reported lobbying expenditures. Many such discrepancies can be explained by the fact that the client and the outside firm use different filing methods. When both organizations use the same method, discrepancies are generally due to filer error. In cases not already resolved in previous reports and where the discrepancy exceeds the $20,000 that can be attributed to rounding, the client's expenditures, the smaller amount, rather than the lobbying firm's reported income are used. The only exception is when a client reports no lobbying expenditures, while the outside lobbying firm lists an actual payment. In such cases, the figure reported by the lobbying firm is used.

In cases where the data appear to contain errors, official senate records are consulted and, when necessary, the center contacts SOPR or the lobbying organizations for clarification. The center standardizes variations in names of individuals and organizations to clearly identify them and more accurately represent their total lobbying expenditures.

However, to calculate lobbying expenditures by sector and industry, each subsidiary is counted within its own sector and industry, not those of its parent. The Center makes this distinction when it has the information necessary to distinguish some or all of the subsidiary's lobbying expenditures from either the subsidiary's own filing or from the receipts reported by outside lobbying firms.

When companies merge within any two-year election cycle, their lobbying expenditures are combined and attributed to the new entity. This is done in order to correlate lobbying data to campaign contribution data for each particular organization and industry.

Source: Adapted from Center for Responsive Politics, USA, http://www.crp.org.

---

safety for human life think that there are four major lobbies operating in America, who are so powerful that they mould the US congress decisions and the laws, as they want them to be. A poster put up by some unknown campaigner, a few years ago, highlighted that the major lobbies in America are: *the roads lobby, the tobacco lobby, the guns lobby,* and *the chemical cartel lobby.*

EXHIBIT 23.2 Top 20 spenders on lobbying (2007)	
Lobbying client	**Total**
US Chamber of Commerce	$ 398,224,680
American Medical Association	$ 190,662,500
General Electric	$ 173,052,000
American Hospital Association	$ 152,947,280
AARP	$ 140,492,064
Pharmaceutical Research & Manufacturers of America	$ 135,663,400
Edison Electric Institute	$ 120,195,999
Northrop Grumman	$ 118,315,253
Business Roundtable	$ 112,280,000
National Association of Realtors	$ 107,960,380
Blue Cross/Blue Shield	$ 104,256,172
Lockheed Martin	$ 102,800,721
Freddie Mac	$ 94,854,048
Boeing Co	$ 93,138,310
General Motors	$ 93,001,483
Exxon Mobil	$ 90,166,942
Verizon Communications	$ 87,048,610
Southern Company	$ 86,290,694
SBC Communications	$ 79,851,656
Fannie Mae	$ 79,497,000

Source: Adapted from Center for Responsive Politics, USA, www.crp.org.

The Roads Lobby

They are an alliance of all oil companies, car manufacturers, construction firms, and road-user organizations pushing for continual construction and widening of roads and highways, however damaging it may be, to the environment. The lobby is often blamed for causing serious damage to human life and environment. The poster alleged that the cartel: (1) cause fatal road accidents, pushing the per car fatality rate to highest in the world, (2) cause brain damage due to lead gasoline additives in the urban atmosphere, (3) emit poisonous benzene and greenhouse gases like carbon dioxide, which contribute to respiratory ailments and climate deterioration, and (4) encourage high-speed stress and sedentary isolation of car culture, contributing to road rage, heart disease, and the destruction of communities.

The Tobacco Lobby

The members of the tobacco lobby, who are manufacturers of cigarettes and tobacco products, are blamed for causing serious health hazards to human life. The allegations against the lobby are the following:

1. They sell a highly addictive drug that has killed millions of people over a

EXHIBIT 23.3   The top 20 lobbyist firms (2007)

Lobbying firm	Billings
Patton Boggs LLP	$ 42,220,000
Akin, Gump et al	$ 31,720,000
Van Scoyoc Association	$ 25,250,000
Cassidy & Association	$ 24,410,000
BGR Holding	$ 22,220,000
Ogilvy Government Relations	$ 22,200,000
Dutko Worldwide	$ 22,192,500
Hogan & Hartson	$ 18,810,000
Quinn, Gillespie & Associates	$ 17,800,000
PMA Group	$ 16,370,132
Williams & Jensen	$ 16,120,000
Holland & Knight	$ 15,890,000
Ernst & Young	$ 13,969,480
K&L Gates	$ 13,800,000
Brownstein, Hyatt et al	$ 12,980,000
Carmen Group	$ 12,740,000
DLA Piper	$ 12,600,000
Covington & Burling	$ 12,489,512
Podesta Group	$ 11,020,000
Ferguson Group	$ 10,801,000

Source: Adapted from Center for Responsive Politics, USA, www.crp.org.

period of decades. The World Health Organization (WHO) predicts that this number will be ten million by the year 2020.

2. They are responsible for an explosive rise in the cost of healthcare due to the increase in smoking-related ailments such as a range of cancers, heart disease, and emphysema.

3. They deliberately promote addictive products to people least aware of their health impact. Most smokers are hooked as gullible teenagers.

The Guns Lobby

The weapon manufacturers who represent on this lobbying effort are often blamed, the poster alleged, for many social woes in the American society and also creating deaths through political upheavals in the rest of the world. The allegations against the guns lobby are the following:

1. They flood the world with small weapons, from pistols and assault rifles to machine guns and gross ten billion dollars every year from this deadly business. Specially culpable are the countries of Europe and North America.

2. They fuel a spiral of violence that has killed millions in the civil conflicts of the 1990 from Congo to East Timor to the former Yugoslavia. They are

implicated in 30,000 gun-related deaths each year in the US and high rates of gun homicide elsewhere in the world.

3. They indirectly aid the drug traffickers, rogue police, criminal gangs, out-of-control militaries and right-wing and ethnic militias in pursuit of other activities.

The Chemical Cartel Lobby

According to an anonymous poster, the cartel of chemical industry is responsible for creating serious health hazards and environmental disturbances. The charges levelled against the lobby are quite a few:

1. They put dangerous chemicals such as PCBs, dioxins, and various other persistent organic pollutants (POPs) into the environment on a worldwide scale. Build-ups of chemical residues are now in everything, from the fat of Arctic polar bears to your local drinking water.
2. They are responsible for the fact that today there are 500 measurable chemicals in our bodies that were not there before the 1920s.
3. They are implicated in cumulative health damage leading to various cancers (including skin cancer from ozone depletion), reproductive disorders, and a generalized weakening of the human immune system.
4. They are responsible for some of the worst industrial accidents in the world—Bhopal in India, Serveso in Italy, and Love Canal in the US, showed in dramatic form how vulnerable people are to chemical poisons.

THE INDIAN SCENE

Chidanand Rajghatta (2003), in one of his reports in *The Times of India*, wrote, 'In New Delhi they are called fixers. Washington has a much more respectable term for them, lobbyists. But quite unlike the safari-clad sleeze bags in India, mouthing off and making out in front of the hidden cameras, America's lobbyists are an impressive lot.'

Unlike in United States, the profession of lobbyist in India is not legally recognized but suffers from the dubious reputation of fixers and con men. Until the proverbial permit and quota *raj* was prevalent, such persons who were called liaison managers and also masqueraded as PR professionals, as they went around expediting matters in the lower ranks of the government and given the resources and clout would go around influening policy makers for or against a law, which would serve the commercial interest of their employers. Such persons, even today carry around a stigma of a 'corruptor'.

However, with the adoption of a policy of liberalization and globalization the scenes have changed. Lobbying, though not named as such, can be divided into two categories, international and domestic.

International Lobbying

Like Japan, Saudi Arabia, Pakistan, etc., India also got involved in its efforts to influence the American congressmen so that they form some pro-Indian stance in matters of world affairs and economic cooperation. India has been relatively new to the lobbying game in the United States. When the economy was declared open, the need for influence peddling became greater. India and Indians started having the taste of the lobbying game. For instance, late Dewang Mehta, the President of NASSCOM (National Association of Software and Service Companies) had said that when he first came to Washington, he did not even know how important lobbying was, but when a top info-tech lobbyist offered his services for $36,000 a year to represent India's then fledgling software industry, he considered it too expensive an assignment.

The Times of India reported, 'For the longest time in the Nehru era, India's main lobbyist in Washington was a Nehru–Gandhi family friend from Kashmir named Janaki Ganju, who, for a princely sum of $95,000 a year, huffed around the capital trying to drum up support for New Delhi. It was only in 1993 that the Indian Embassy in Washington first hired a professional lobbying firm, Springer, Rafaelli, Spees and Smith for a tidy sum of half a million dollars per year.'

According to *Economic Times* of 24 October 1994, 'The bulk of the expenses, $96,000, went to a PR company, Daniel Fedelman, Inc, with the balance going towards lunches, taxis, airfares and hotel accommodation in India, and to ethnic newspaper and magazine subscriptions, according to the firm.' Since then India has grown quite adept at the game, and signed up Verner Liipfert, one of the top firms in the city amongst whose advisers are Bob Dole and former senate leader George Mitchell.

The growing population of Indians in America and their active participation in the local politics and political affairs, the Indian American community has come to carve a position for itself in the American life. The group now acts as a pressure group to influence several congressmen most with pro-India stance.

Meanwhile, something even more remarkable has happened on the other side of lobbying, reports *The Times of India*. The 1990s saw an increasing number of first and second generation Indian–Americans become politically active. Dozens of Indian–Americans now work in the administration and the legislatures, in positions ranging from key staff members (such as Kris Kolluri, a chief aide to house minority leader Richard Gephart) to interns doing drudgework like sorting mail and answering phone calls. One such staffer with nearly a decade of experience on the Hill took the plunge into the high-powered world of lobbying, starting a modest little firm called the KS Group.

Kapil Sharma, an England born law graduate from Rutgers University (his parents are from Jalandhar), or Kap, as he is popularly known, began hanging out on the political bandwagon even before finishing school. Each summer, he would head out to help Frank Pallone, a New Jersey lawmaker whose district holds a significant Indian–American vote. Twice in the early 1990s, he worked on the Pallone campaign, and in between in 1994, he also hopped on to the Clinton–Gore bandwagon. In 1996, Pallone took him on as fulltime staffer, in which capacity Kap worked closely with the Indian–American Caucus that was his boss' brainchild.

In 1998, Kap made his first move in the lobbying world, joining Verner Liipfert just as it bagged the India account. After two years at the elite firm, he joined the staff of senator Robert Torricelli, once a caustic Indian-baiter. After a little more than a year with the Senator, he started out on his own as KS Group.

As reported in *The Times of India*, New Delhi, 'Twenty two years ago, Swadesh Chatterjee, an electronics engineer went to the US with his physician wife. He had just $35 in his pocket. Today he is a known campaigner and fund raiser for the cause of Indians of American origin and a lobbyist with the US administration, congressmen, and senators. Recognizing Chatterjee's contribution towards public affairs in the US, the Indian government conferred the Padma Bhushan to him.'

Chatterjee came to limelight while accompanying Bill Clinton during his India visit. While Chatterjee runs a small instrumentation firm with 40 employees and heads the TiE chapter in the North Carolina district, he is better known as president of the Indian American Forum for Political Education. He is considered the pointsman for Indian lobbying efforts and is said to have direct contacts with over 126 congressmen in the senate. Over the years, Chatterjee and his team brought Indian–Americans doctors, motel owners, professors, IT professionals, student community, under one banner. The Indian-Americans have excelled in their job, so much so that one Sikh gentleman worked as fund manager for the present president, Barack Obama, in the 2008 elections.

Domestic Lobbying

The political scientists and thinkers opine that Indian democracy is still in its infancy, which has a long way to attain maturity. Unlike America, where business is the life line of economy, the Indian legislators are mostly not favourably inclined to business and businessmen. Their perception of business suffers from lot of distortions and misunderstandings. Generally perceived as an institution for profit mongering, hoarding, back marketing, and manipulations for making fast buck somehow, the business does not fall in their list of favourites. Since the Indian political system has so far been predominantly dominated by communists and socialists, and the policy of liberalization has arrived rather late, changing the mindset of the legislators is rather a difficult job. Most of them are hard nuts to crack and still cling to their concept of welfare state and not profit.

One of the major bottlenecks in the way is the low education and limited exposures due to their emergence from small and backward constituencies and many of them being the first time members of parliament. The need for a change in the mindset of the members of parliament brings a big challenge for the public relations and the persons involved in the lobbying for one interest or the other. There is a need to break into the pre-conceived ideas and notions to support or oppose certain issues, causes, ventures, etc. in the new business environment.

It is very relevant to look at the state of affairs of the Indian democracy which often hits several road blocks in its smooth functioning. Several constitutional crises that the history of modern India has witnessed, leads one to think as to what ails the Indian democracy (See Exhibit 23.4).

Despite rampant scams and scandals in their own areas, the legislatures have all the expectations from the corporate world. They would like companies to adopt honest business practices and undertake social welfare activities in the name of strengthening and developing their constituencies by setting up industries, etc. and generate employment opportunities for their voters so that the legislators can continue to cling to power. They also want that the corporations should pay their taxes honestly, observe certain morality in the matter of producing socially responsible products and take care of the corporate social responsibility.

As an offshoot of a democracy, the subject that often comes up for discussion amongst politicians and the industry leaders, is the funding of the political parties. Donations to political parties by industrial houses, once considered unethical and illegal, has come some way to be recognized as legitimate and fair. The practice of donating money to the parties, has gone through several trials and tribulations to attain maturity in the democratic set up. Once considered bribe in exchange for a favour, is now an acceptable fair practice. However, under-the-table contributions are still much larger than the legitimate ones, observed one parliamentarian. A chronology of the political donations by the companies (Exhibit 23.5) should be of considerable interest to the students and the public relations practitioners alike.

EXHIBIT 23.4 *What ails the Indian democracy*

- Money and muscle power in politics
- Mis-use of official position
- Communalism and provincialism
- Majority myth: vote bank, the number game
- Centre–state conflicts
- Floor crossing—*Aya Ram, Gaya Ram*

- Multi-party system
- Poor quality of legislators
- Economic disparities
- Low level of literacy
- Mass's ignorance
- Corporate corruption

The Election Commission of India limits the total candidate expenditure on each Lok Sabha election to Rs 25 lakh and that for each assembly seat Rs 10 lakh.

1969 The private sector company donations to the political parties is banned by Indira Gandhi.

1975 The parliament of India amends the Representation of the People's Act or the RPA, makes the party and supporter's expenditure for a candidate's election not to be counted towards candidate's own expenditure for the purpose of ceiling on election expenses.

1979 Morarji Desai exempted the political parties from the income and wealth taxes. He, however, still kept it compulsory for the parties to file their tax returns.

1985 Rajiv Gandhi re-legalized the company donations.

1993 The Confederation of Indian Industry (CII) sets up a task force, which recommends corporate contributions be made tax deductible and state funding for elections.

1996 (February) The Supreme Court orders parties to file IT returns on response to a PIL (no party had filed returns for all the years from 1979 till January 1996).

1996 (April) The Supreme Court upholds the validity of Explanation 1 of Section 77(1) of the RPA, subject to filling audited accounts by all political parties

1998 (April) With I K Gujral as Prime Minister, the Indrajit Gupta committee on state funding of elections recommends partial state funding, mainly in kind, and says parties failing to maintain and submit audited accounts and IT returns should not qualify for such funding. The committee also recommends that all subscriptions and donations received by a party above Rs 10,000 should be by cheque or draft and should be mentioned in party accounts.

2001 Under the Prime Ministership of Atal Behari Vajpayee, the Finance Ministry takes internal position against state funding for budgetary reasons.

2002 A draft bill called Elections and Other Related Laws (amendment) Bill scrutinized by a parliamentary committee, which includes recommendations like making donations to parties tax-deductible for both companies and individuals.

2003 Lok Sabha approves the bill amending three laws. These include allowing contributions by private companies to political parties with a maximum limit of 5 per cent of their profits, making contributions by cheques mandatory apart from providing that parties audit their annual accounts while maintaining a list of donors who give more than Rs 20,000 (to be submitted to the EC).

Source: Adapted from the *Mint*, 4 October 2008.

THE PRESSURE GROUPS OF INDIA

Unlike the organized and legal lobbying practices in the US, the avocation, in India, is known as advocacy by pressure groups or special interest groups. With the growth of political freedom as well as spurt in business and commerce, the activity has gained momentum though not that high a pitch, yet the Indian lobbyists, better known as pressure groups, have a notable presence in the democratic system of peddling influences.

Some political thinkers feel that the pressure groups have been slow to develop and the existing ones have not made much progress. Parliament and bureaucracy, on the pretext of nationalism, poverty alleviation, national integration, or threats on borders, have often turned a deaf ear to the demands of such interest groups, to amend certain laws. However, depending on the support they can muster at each general election, the special interest groups, represented by political parties have been having their ways.

Some of the characteristics of such pressure groups should be of interest to public relations professionals who may be assigned specific jobs in their respective organizations, either to run the show themselves or to indirectly lend support to such activities managed by another department like legal cell. The characteristics are: *universality, political fence sitters, self-centred groups,* and *proxy groups.*

Universality

The nature and operation of such groups is universal. Such groups are found everywhere in the world. Groups like trade unions, business associations like FICCI, CII, farmers' cooperatives, and professionals' associations like the Chartered Accountants Association, Public Relations Societies, Indian Advertisers Association, Indian Union of Journalists, etc. are found everywhere in the world with certain similarities, who advocate their causes and issues that serve their interest.

Political Fence Sitters

In a democratic set up umpteen number of associations and societies claiming non-profit and non-political status pursue certain causes and value systems. They claim to have no political colour, yet tacitly support one political party or the other. Some such associations are even covertly funded by political parties and their colour is evident, yet they would put up a façade of non-alignment. Several religious, cultural, and social organizations also sometimes known as NGOs (non-government organizations) operate in the country. Generally headed by a political personality, the interest group works behind the scenes to garner public support for a party, particularly when the election fever grips the country. More often than not, such associations would change their alignments with the change in the government, and sit on the fence to wait which way to turn.

Self-centred Groups

Certain special interest groups have been formed with the philosophy that 'Self interest is the best interest'. Many such groups have certain objectives and interests to pursue. Such interests can be commercial, social, and political. For instance, the Communist Party of India have their own agenda to push; corporations like Tatas or Ambanis have their own commercial interests to influence the government in forming such policies that serve their objectives. Almost all the states of India pursue their own interests of gaining a better share of the union financial budget in the interest of development of their states or to have a better clout with the government at the center. Many parties with a religious flavour like Akali Dal, Bajrang Dal, DMK, Muslim League, etc. are the groups who have their own agendas to pursue.

Proxy Groups

A democracy is a cobweb of complexities. A careful look at the scenario reveals that there are groups operating in the country who work like satellites of one political party or the other. They seem to be a part of the proxy war between the political parties. In politics, many media-made and party sponsored religious leaders, who claim to reform the society and bring solace to the disturbed minds, work as influential vote banks for a party. It is no surprise that they function as pockets of great influence due to the clout that they have with the political bosses. The con men, with influence in high places, work as consultants for large business houses to watch their client's interest. Many work as conduit for siphoning money for the party funds in exchange for favours. Many such influence peddlers seem to be master minding the government through proxy.

LOBBYING—INDIA'S HISTORIAL PERSPECTIVE

Now that the country has adopted the policy of liberalization and have been inviting foreign direct investment and the picture looks rosy, the historical perspective does not support it. India went through turbulent times on the economic front in the past. Some observers think that it has been the socialist and communist lobbies who with their political clouts dictated the ouster of several global organizations from India and advocated social control on industry. Some of the historical events in the country tell the story and these are the following:

- bank nationalization
- enormous growth of public sector
- banishing of the multi-national companies like IBM, Coca Cola, Pepsi, Burmah Shell, Caltex, Mercedes, Ford, etc.

The re-entry of the several global corporations has once again opened the field for the interested lobbies to campaign for putting several restrictions on several areas of business activity. Bringing pressure on the government for restricting equity participation in areas like insurance, banking, media, etc. have been a bone of contention amongst various partners of the ruling UPA. The poetic slogan painted on the walls of a favourite coffee house walls of Delhi University, by the student campaigners for restricting role of multinationals, should interest the public relations professionals. The slogan was:

Coca Cola, Pepsi Cola, Jahan dekho cola hi cola,
Peene tak ko, boond nahin, jab bhi nal khola.

(Coca Cola, Pepsi Cola, it is cola and cola everywhere, but whenever you open the tap, there is not a drop to drink)

The campaign smacks of the resistance put up by some advocates of social control on everything in India.

The Early Starter

In the sixties, the one who started lobbying in India in the right earnest was one Mr Vinayak, who set up an institution called the Public Relations Council of India. His style of functioning was perhaps not liked by the parliamentarians and he was one day reprimanded by the speaker for entering the private domain of the legislatures. He would first send some relevant parliament questions to the concerned company and then offer his services to that company to investigate the sources of those question, for a fee. This act at that time was, perhaps, not known to the system, so he had to shut shop. However, the activity continues in many other ways.

SOME MAJOR LOBBIES OF INDIA

Though not organized as a profession on the lines of the US business, yet some of the lobbies, in their own manner, have been advocating certain causes mainly to further their own interests. Leave alone some conglomerates like Tatas, Ambanis, Birlas, etc., who themselves take care of their interests, some of the industries that lobby conspicuously for themselves are: *rubber, automobiles, cigarette, farmers, IT, sugar,* and *cement*.

Rubber

The rubber growers, mostly concentrated in Kerala, is known to be a strong lobby who have a good number of parliamentarians to represent them and safeguard the interest of the rubber growers. Some allege that there exists a rubber cartel in India, which dictates prices and regulates supplies to the rubber manufacturers. They also influence the government to keep the import duties high to maintain their unenviable position. Besides, occasionally, they demonstrate in New Delhi to show their strength. Exhibit 23.6 shows the rubber farmers' protest in front of a 'Rubber Mountain'.

Automobiles

SIAM (Society of Indian Automobile Manufacturers) seems to have emerged as a powerful lobby. All the automobile manufacturers, under its banners, do all what they can to influence the government and the parliamentarians to adopt certain taxation and pricing policies that can help the industry to grow and prosper. The explosion in the car population in India, and the presence of all kinds of world class cars zooming on Indian roads, is one indication of the success

EXHIBIT 23.6	Rubber lobby—show of strength

Rubber farmers protest in front of a 'Rubber Mountain', a heap of natural rubber sheets, during a demonstration in New Delhi on Friday. They were demanding a raise in import duties on natural rubber.

Source: The Times of India, 22 December 2001.

the lobby has attained. Incidentally Delhi's vehicle population exceeds the vehicle population of Mumbai, Chennai, and Kolkata, put together. One more mark of this lobby having their way, is the unrestricted sale of cars in Delhi, when the roads are bursting with vehicles.

Cigarette

Though most taxed industry of India and with lot of voluntary and legal restrictions on smoking cigarettes and tobacco, the cigarette lobby has a heyday. According to a report in *Business Standard* (8 December 2000), 'Cashing in on the high excise collections from cigarettes, tobacco lobbyists have asked centre not to increase taxes on the product in the short term saying the tobacco sector has a potential of contributing around Rs 542 crore (it should be four figure now) to the coffers in the coming five years.' Thanks to the lobby, that despite opposition to smoking, the industry is on a growth path. It is good to see the government advertisement banning smoking in public places (See Exhibit 23.7), but the responses are obviously otherwise.

Farmers

With a majority of population of India, directly or indirectly, engaged in agriculture, the farm lobby is one of the strongest. The farmers community holds the key to the formation of a government, as they are the largest vote bank of India. Besides, the BKU (Bharatiya Kisan Union) and several other farmers groups are always demanding more subsidies and better procurement prices for their produce. The UPA government, in 2008, dishing out Rs 70,000 crore to the farmers, and declaration of free electricity and diesel for the farmers by Parkash Singh Badal, the chief minister of Punjab, are all indicators of the influence the farm lobby carries in India.

Information Technology

Influential groups like NASSCOM and computer peripheral manufacturers association, and host of others, have emerged as a new lobby to represent the information technology industry. These associations have been lobbying, with lot of success, to carve a position of priority in the developing economy of India.

Sugar

Indian Sugar Mills Association, which represents the powerful sugar lobby in India, has always been advocating causes like fixation of statutory minimum price (SMP) payable to the farmers and the recovery rate of sugar from each quintal of sugar cane. As reported in *The Economic Times*, New Delhi (29 December 2003), 'In the run-up to the government's declaration of an SMP for sugar cane, the sugar industry has started lobbying against the CACP recommendation of Rs 73 per quintal at 8.5 per cent recovery. The industry is now pitching for cane to be treated on par with other crops. The government should only announce a minimum support price and not make it statutory, for mills to pay that amount to the cane farmers, as is the case for sugar cane now. It is being said, the government would end up saving a lot of money and headaches in unpaid arrears to cane farmers, if it took a deviant route.'

Cement

The alleged cartel of the cement industry invited the wrath of the government, which threatened to control the spiralling cement prices. The cement lobby, under

EXHIBIT 23.7   BANNED—cigarette smoking in public places

PUBLIC NOTICE

Starting 2- October Smoking in 'Public Places'

BANNED

As per the notification GSR 417(E) dated 30- May 2008, the Central Government has revised the rules relating to 'Smoking in Public Places' w.e.f. 2- October, 2008. The salient features of these rules include

* Smoking is strictly prohibited in all public places. "Public Place" includes auditorium, hospital buildings, health institutions, amusement centres, restaurants, public offices, court buildings, educational institutions, libraries, public conveyances, stadium, railway stations, bus stops, workplaces, shopping malls, cinema halls, refreshment rooms, discotheques, coffee house, pubs, bars, airport lounge etc.

* Any violation of this act is a punishable offence with fine upto <u>Rs. 200.</u>

* However, a Hotel having thirty or more rooms or restaurant having seating capacity of thirty persons or more & airports may provide / have a separate smoking area or space, as required by the rules.

* The owner, proprietor, manager, supervisor or in charge of the affairs of a public place shall ensure that:

  a) No person smokes in the public place (under his jurisdiction/ implied)
  b) The board as specified in schedule –II of the rules; is displayed prominently at the entrance(s) of the Public place and conspicuous place(s) inside.
  c) No ashtrays, matches, lighters or other things designed to facilitate smoking are provided in the public place.

* The owner, proprietor, manager, supervisor or in charge of the affairs of a public place shall notify and display prominently the name of the person to whom a complaint of any violation may be made.

* If the owner, proprietor, manager, supervisor or the authorized officer of a public place fails to act on report of such violation, the owner, proprietor, manager, supervisor or the authorized officer shall be liable to pay fine equivalent to the number of individual offences.

Issued in Public Interest by
Ministry of Health & Family Welfare, Govt of India.

The details of the specifications are available are www.mohfw.nic.in

davp 17102/13/0171/0809

Source: Hindustan Times, 1 October 2008.

the banner of Cement Manufacturers Association, have been lobbying hard to maintain the balance. The case in focus is the asbestos cement industry, which have been threatened with the stigma of a health hazard. To save the industry from extinction and to allay fears amongst the people at large and the environmentalists in particular, they ran full page supplement in *The Times of India* on 7 November 2003 and followed by a series of advertisements (See Exhibit 23.8).

PR ROLE IN LOBBYING

A major commodity that the legislators, executives, and for that matter the lobbyists deal with is the information. The democratically elected people's representatives have no choice but to fall back upon information that becomes available to them from various sources including PR practitioners handling the advocacy on behalf of their organizations. A parliamentarian's intelligence concerning the social, political, economic developments and the happenings in

EXHIBIT 23.8   Asbestos cement industry's advertising campaign

Since we are responsible for providing drinking water to millions...
we are responsible

Asbestos Cement Products
| it shelters | it provides | it protects |

"...the general consensus is that imbibed asbestos via drinking water supplies poses no assessable risk to the health of the consumer" WHO (World Health Organisation) White Asbestos cement Products play a vital role in the life of India, 1400 Million units of electricity are saved every year, which otherwise would be spent in producing metallic alternatives. Alternatives that consume almost 36 times more energy adding its share of toxins into the atmosphere. 400,000 MT of flyash, a thermal power waste, is used as raw material by the AC industry every year, saving valuable national resources on one hand and freeing the environment of pollution hazards on the other. **It's time you opened your eyes to the truth.**

Chrysotlle Asbestos Cement Products
Manufacturers' Association

807 Ashok Bavan | 83 Nahru Place | New Delhi 110 019 | Tel 2642-2823 | Fax 011 2646 1729 | E-mail acpma@satyam.net.in

(Contd.)

Exhibit 23.8 (Contd.)

Since we are responsible for generating employment across India...
We are responsible

"Mortality studies on work in asbestos cement plants give little or no suggestion of raised mortality associated with the use of chrysotile asbestos only in this industry."

M.J. Gardner and C.A. Powell
MRC Environmental Epidemiology Unit
University of Southampton

White Asbestos Cement Products play a vital role in the life of India. 1400 Million units of electricity are saved every year, which otherwise would be spent in producing metallic alternatives. Alternatives that consume almost 36 times more energy adding its share of toxins into the atmosphere. 400,000MT of flyash, a thermal power waste, is used as raw material by the AC industry every year, saving valuable national resources on one hand and freeing the environment of pollution hazards on the other. It's time you opened your eyes to the truth.

Asbestos Cement Products
| it shelters | it provides | it protects |

Chrysotile Asbestos Cement Products
Manufacturers' Association

807 Ashok Bavan | 83 Nehru Place | New Delhi 110 019 | Tel 2642-2823 | Fax 011 2646 1729 | E-mail acpma@satyam.net.in

---

❝ Exclusive use of Chrysotile (White) fibre in the manufacture of asbestos cement products is not associated with any excess of lung cancer ❞

– **Thomas H.F. Etal** *(UK) 1982**
– **Ohison & Hogstdet** *(Sweden) 1985**
– **Gardner M.J. Etal** *(UK) 1986**
– **HSE** *(UK) publication "Review of Fibre Toxicology" - 1986**
– **Environmental Health Criteria 2003** *"Chrysotile Asbestos". **WHO** publication 1998; 8*
– *Source: J.Soc. Occup Med (1986) Vol. 36P.124 & 126. Great Britain*

White (Chrysotile) Asbestos Cement Products play a vital role in the life of India. The health issues being debated in the Western World relate to the extensive and uncontrolled usage of Blue (Corcidolite) & Brown (Amosite) variety of Asbestos Fibre, which is neither produced nor allowed to be imported into India. Moreover, application of Asbestos in the West has been mostly in friable form for insulation purposes in buildings. Whereas in India, Asbestos Cement Products represent 95% of Asbestos usage in which the Asbestos content is only about 8-9%, the rest being cement and other binding material. As such, Asbestos Cement Products do not pose any health hazards.

It's time you opened your eyes to the truth

Asbestos Cement Products | it shelters | it provides | it protects |

Chrysotile Asbestos Cement Products
Manufacturers' Association

807 Ashok Bavan | 83 Nehru Place | New Delhi 110 019 | Tel 2642-2823 | Fax 011 2646 1729 | E-mail acpma@satyam.net.in

Source: Hindustan Times, 28 August 2003; 4 September 2003; and 10 September 2003.

their particular constituency, should serve as a source of strength for the legislator.

In fact, the two-way communication is as much important to them, as it is to a public relations professional. Therefore, the vital support that a PR practitioner handling advocacy, can extend to a parliamentarian is keeping him updated with information, both for and against an issue. This logically should help the legislator to decide to support or oppose an interest.

As a part of the lobbying game, the information can be communicated to the parliamentarians or executives by two ways, *personal* and *non-personal*.

Personal

The personal way envisages personal meetings and discussions.

Education

The PR practitioners may take the education route to influence the legislatures through personal meetings with them, individually or in groups. A personal meeting can be equated to a sales call where the idea, instead of a product, is required to be sold. Strategically enough, the area sales managers working in the home constituencies, may establish a personal contact for an information exchange, but with a pre-planned brief. A personal call often generates an open exchange of ideas and the legislator may accept or reject the proposal to advocate the issue.

Alternatively, presentations can be made to parliamentary committees to push an issue. Sometimes, the organizations may arrange a special workshop programme for the select MPs to enlighten them. This kind of activity may be rare but many companies in England and their PR professionals have some such plans.

Socials

Inviting members of parliament to social gatherings like an evening dinner, or some informal lunches or breakfasts, serve as a good opportunity to have a heart-to-heart exchange and lead to some conclusive consensus. Occasions, as such, created by holding a seminar or a commemorative lecture by an important legislator, joined by some of the friends in arms, followed by a lunch or dinner, may serve the purpose. Such social get-togethers provide ample opportunities for PR people to circulate socially for a good networking exercise.

Representations

The technique involves the visit by a delegation sponsored by a corporation, industry or an association to a legislator's office to represent the problem in the form of a petition, for his consideration. More often, such an exercise may lead to an impromptu discussion on the subject and may result in some positive support for the issue. For instance, years ago, a delegation of farmers, lead by the farm equipment manufacturers' association, met the late prime minister Lal Bahadur Shastri that resulted in the reduction of excuse duty on tractors.

Conducted tours

Seeing is believing. When despite sufficient information provided to the legislators does not cut ice, it may be advisable to sponsor a site tour for a group of parliamentarians to see for themselves, the ground realities. Such trips, particularly, to some manufacturing plants, can be a calculated risk. Enough care has to be taken to conduct the tour by a well informed and authorized spokesperson of the company, to avoid any slip ups or ambiguity.

Non-personal

The non-personal information sharing exercise may be done through printed or electronic medium.

Backgrounders

Assuming that the legislators are absolutely ignorant about the issue, PR practitioners develop a backgrounder, which gives all the information, specific and peripheral, on the subject. Due care is taken that it is readable with a reasonable length of the text and simplicity of vocabulary, as some of the legislators are hard pressed for time and also come from dismal backgrounds. In the face of the opposition by the then prime minister Morarji Desai, to relocation of Rajneesh Ashram from Pune to Kutch, the Rajneesh Foundation sent out a detailed backgrounder to garner legislators' and media support for the proposal.

Advertising

Many companies and associations choose to take the battle to the media to influence the policy makers for or against an issue. Cement asbestos sheet industry is a case in focus. Once the Vanaspati Producers Associations of Jharkhand and Bihar sent an SOS to the then finance minister Yashwant Sinha to save the industry (See Exhibit 23.9). During a tiff between the Government of India and Maruti takeover by Suzuki Motors of Japan, both parties flashed their views in some full page advertisements in the national media.

Media relation

Media in a democracy is one channel that takes the messages far and wide. Perhaps more than any other public, the legislators and the executives monitor the media coverage very carefully to arrive at certain decisions in the larger public interest. Public relations practitioners know the value of media and ways

EXHIBIT 23.9   An SOS to the finance minister

> ## SHRI YASHWANT SINHAJI
> ## FINANCE MINISTER OF INDIA
>
> # SOS
>
> Protect Vanaspati Industry in Jharkhand and Bihar from the onslaught of cheap duty free Vanaspati from Nepal.
>
> Import Duty on Crude Palm Oil (Raw material) for Vanaspati Industry at 75% or even 55% makes it impossible to manufacture and sell Vanaspati by Indian manufacturers in comparison to the 'DUTY FREE' Vanaspati from Nepal allowed under Indo-Nepal Trade Treaty.
>
> Sinhaji, we request your personal intervention to save Jharkhand, and Bihar Vanaspati Units by either reducing Import Duty on Crude Palm Oil to 25% as applicable earlier or otherwise by imposing similar Import Duties on Vanaspati imported from Nepal.
>
> In case immediate and urgent measures are not taken, Vanaspati Industry in Bihar and Jharkhand will face closure.
>
> Jointly issued by,:
>
> **JHARKHAND VANASPATI**   **BIHAR VANASPATI**
> **PRODUCERS ASSCIATION**   **PRODUCERS ASSOCIATION**

Source: The Economic Times, March 2001.

and means to handle media relations (see chapter 16). Some of the strategies like calling a press conference, distribution of press releases, press briefings, press visits are some of the steps. One step ahead, some vested interests play the media game by hitting below the belt. Planting and killing the stories is one of the favourite game plan of many peddlers of influence. This tantamounts to unscrupulous and unethical practice but then everything is fair in love and war and also lobbying.

Build public opinion

Building pressure on the legislators through public opinion is another way of influencing the decision makers. Certain hot topics, which no one likes to touch in fear of burning their fingers, are often brought to the forefront for public debate and consensus gathered through opinion, polls, either through open debates on the TV channels or through a survey by a research agency. Programmes like 'Big Fight', 'Devil's Advocate', or 'The Nation Speaks' are some of the examples. Voting for and against through mobile phones has assumed serious proportions, to mould public opinion. The famous controversies like Cola and Cadbury, stirred considerable public response, to influence certain decisions by the government.

Parliament questions

PR professionals assigned with the lobbying work by their organizations, are familiar with the technique of getting some pleasant and unpleasant questions asked in the parliament and state assemblies, to influence certain impending laws. The starred and un-starred questions, often upset the apple cart, in favour or against a policy decision.

Summary

Amongst the four pillars of democracy, judiciary, executive, media, and parliament, the parliament is the play field of conflicting opinions. It is an open forum for advocating opinions for and against issues and to form policies and laws to run a government. Lobbying is one art of influencing the elected representatives of the people to advocate ideas on behalf of certain interests. Business and politics being well connected, the system has lot of relevance to the functioning of a democracy. Lobbying and lobbyists is a recognized and organized profession in the US but not legally sanctioned in India.

In the US, it is a well organized activity and called the 'influence industry' by some, so much so that there exists an Ameri-can League of Lobbyists (ALL). To make the profession more transparent, the US government passed a Lobbying Disclosure Act in 1955 wherein an organization is required to disclose the amounts of money spent on lobbying. The Center for Responsive Politics took the initiative to collect all the relevant information, which is now accessible on their website.

Organizations spend billions of dollars every year to safeguard and advocate their interests.

The major lobbies operating in the US are the roads lobby, the tobacco lobby, the guns lobby, and the chemical cartel lobby, who all have often been blamed for several woes in the lives of the people of America and elsewhere in the world.

In India, lobbyists, who are not known as such, do not enjoy any professional recognition and reputation, but suffer from the ill repute of being 'corruptors'. The Indian scene has two area of activity, international and domestic. Internationally, the main focus is US Congress where the Indian Embassy pays huge sums to some lobbying firms to influence senators to adopt pro-India stance. Now some Indian–Americans have got into the lobbying business with some success, so much so that there is one Sikh gentleman who is the fund manager of the presidential candidate Barack Obama.

On the domestic front, India has some major lobbies who indulge in lot of influencing efforts. Often termed as bribery, the activity has not been legalized. However, the donations to the political parties by the companies and the individuals have now been legalized.

The well known lobbies working in India are pressure groups from industries like rubber, automobiles, cigarettes, farmers, IT, sugar, and cement. In historical perspective, the ousting and re-entry of foreign companies reflect the success or failure of certain lobbies working for and against the system.

Lobbying is considered to be the direct or indirect responsibility of public relations. PR practitioners, when assigned the lobbying job, may go through personal and impersonal ways to influence the legislators and the executive. The personal efforts cover the education of MPs, socials, representations, and conducted tours of the facilities and the non-personal efforts call for information dissemination through backgrounders, advertising, media relations, public opinion building, and moving the parliament questions.

Key Terms

Campaigner One who is campaigning, especially a politician running for elective office, or one of the supporters

Influence peddler A person who uses one's influence with persons in authority to obtain favours or preferential treatment for another, usually in return for payment

Lobbying To try to influence legislators or other public officials in favour of a specific cause

Lobbyist Somebody who is paid to lobby political representatives on an issue

Pressure group A number of people who work together to make their concerns known to those in government and to influence the passage of legislation

Political fence sitter Groups who remain non-aligned with any political party or ideology

Proxy war A war where two powers use third parties as a supplement to or a substitute for fighting each other directly

Concept Review Questions

1. Define and explain the system of lobbying in a democratic system of government.
2. Paint an exhaustive picture of the practice of lobbying in US with a special reference to the laws that make lobbying a legal and transparent profession.
3. What are the few reasons that India spends considerable sums of money on lobbying efforts on influencing the American congressmen? Are these efforts justified? What role the Indian–Americans are playing now? Are they successful? Explain.
4. Describe the Indian scene as far as the lobbying by several pressure groups is conducted here? Express your opinion on the legitimacy of such a practice.
5. What actions and strategies the public relations practitioners can use to make a lobbying effort successful for an organization?

Project Work

1. Gutka and Pan Masala, though not socially responsible products, is a multi-crore industry of India. As the public relations manager of an NGO fighting for social causes, what lobbying plans will you devise to prevail upon the members of parliament to ban these products, which pose a major health hazard for several Indians? Draw up a detailed plan.
2. Study the American lobbying law and develop an objective project report for convincing the government of India to legalize lobbying practice. Count the number of advantages that such an action will bring in favour of the public relations profession.

Case Study

Lobbying—a Pervasive, Flourishing Racket in Washington*

Lobbying in Washington is like corruption in India. It is so very pervasive in the corridors of power, that says Jeffrey H. Birnbaum, of *The Wall Street Journal*, 'You have to pay to play, is the rule number 1 in today's Washington.'

'A thousand dollars get you through the door,' Mr Birnbaum said in his book *The Lobbyists: How Influence Peddlers Get Their Way in Washington*, 'Six thousand dollars lets you mingle with the House of Democratic Caucus.'

Almost every interest group and corporation in the US, from the Truck Drivers Association to Coca Cola and Westinghouse, employ the services of influential lobbyists. Since the 1980s, foreign governments have entered the scene, adding a new dimension to what many see as a flourishing racket in the US capital.

Highest paying

If Japan, Saudi Arabia, and Kuwait (which paid a whopping $10 million to Hill and Knowlton) are among the highest-paying clients of lobbyists, here poor, debt-ridden third world countries are also getting increasingly drawn into the system, paying annual fees ranging from $100,000 to $1 million.

Many knowledgeable commentators, however, are extremely skeptical and out rightly critical of the high-flying lifestyles of lobbyists, their lofty promises, and doubtful results.

According to Mr Birnbaum, for a lobbyist, 'the best issue is an insoluble problem'—an issue, 'that will yield fee generating work as far into the future as the eye can see.'

Flaunting connections

Typically, the 'Blatchford approach' would flaunt connections and promises: connections to key congressmen—congressional committees, and even to the White House.

---

*Source: Adapted from Vaidya, Abhay, *The Times of India*, 'Lobbying—a Persuasive, Flourishing Racket in Washington', New Delhi, 4 September 1993.

The Indian government's eagerness to employ a lobbyist in Washington relates not just to such promotional campaigns by lobbyist firms, but largely to the changing situation here. Over the past three years particularly, the human rights situation in India has drawn considerable attention in the US congress, with significant anti-Indian lobbying by the Khalistan council and anti-Indian Kashmiris.

With barely a congressman or two by their side, the pro-Khalistan lobbyists have been successful in repeatedly raising issues in the congress some way or the other. In addition to this, the Indian government perhaps feels compelled, given the post-Cold War competition between India and Pakistan in seeking to draw US influence in their favour.

Having realistically assessed the limitations and potentials of lobbyists, the names of 10 firms have been forwarded to New Delhi and a short-term appointment of up to six months may be expected in the next five weeks.

'Mr Solarz is no longer there in the congress and others are not as well-briefed on South Asian's issues,' a senior embassy official said.

Sell ideas

According to senior diplomats, appointed lobbyists will serve as an additional instrument to reach congressmen.

Typically, their responsibility would include using their contacts within the administration and the congress and alerting Indian embassy to resolutions that are likely to be tabled; to target attention towards specific, influential congressmen, and organizing briefing sessions with key congressmen at short notice.

On a highly sarcastic note, Mr Birnbaum says, 'The lobbyists' day begins with a fund-raising breakfast for a member of the congress …and ends with fund raising cocktail parties that tax the lobbyists' stamina and bladder control.'

Undeniably, money plays a big part and accounts for much of the success or failure of lobbying: If you have the money, you have the attention, seems to be the rule.

Operating phase

In their book *How to win in Washington*, Earnest and Eliabeth Wittenberg noted, 'Be careful how you approach your target.' Mentioning "money" is crude. The operative phrase is—I'll like to do something in the next election.'

At least in this area the parallels with India are astounding.

Following the retirement as associate chief counsel for medical devices at the Food and Drug Administration, Mr Mark Heller, landed himself a $385,000 job as a lobbyist with a leading law firm. His new role was to assist 'a breast implant manufacturer with legal requirements that he had helped impose during his government days.'

With lobbying having become a booming business in the recent years thanks to the interest shown by foreign governments, the number of registered lobbyists last year escalated to 7,500 from 3,000 in 1976.

Anti-lobbyists point out that the influence of lobbying firms is insignificant on major issues as differences on key policy matters do not change through lobbying.

While senior embassy officials concede that Indian insistence on retaining its nuclear and missile options, its differences with the US on trade and commercial issues are bound to instigate anti-India policies; through lobbying, officials hope to counter the US-based anti-India propagandists.

According to observers, since no amount of lobbying can counter credible and damaging reports in prestigious American newspapers or television stations the solution lies elsewhere. The US-based Khalistanis, for example, seem to have lost their voice, not because of any pro-India lobbying but because the situation in Punjab has changed significantly.

Thus say observers, the solution to India's woes in Washington, lie not in patronizing a lobbying firm but in concentrating on key human rights issues back home.

Discussion questions

1. Develop a questionnaire and interview about fifteen members of parliament or the state assembly to get their opinions, for or against, making lobbying profession legal and transparent. Develop a report by collating all the information thus collected.
2. Assuming that you are appointed the public relations manager at the Indian embassy at Washington, please submit a public relations plan of action to project India as an emerging power, amongst the US congressmen.

References

Business Standard, 'Cigarette Lobbyists Press for No Raise in Taxes in Budget', Kolkata, 8 December 2000, www.crp.org.

Cutlip, Scott M., Allen H. Center, and Glen M. Broom (1985), *Effective Public Relations*, 6th edition, Prentice-Hall International, Inc., USA, p. 14.

Hindustan Times, New Delhi, 28 August 2003; 4 September 2003; and 10 September 2003.

Hindustan Times, New Delhi, 1 October 2008, p. 15.

Mint, 'Tax Filings Point to Lack of Transparency', New Delhi, 4 October 2008, vol. II, no. 236, p. 3.

Moore, H. Frazier and Frank B. Kalupa (2005), Richard D. Irwin, Inc, USA, published in India by Surjeet Publications, New Delhi, pp. 432 and 433.

The Times of India , New Delhi, 4 September 1993.

The Times of India, 'Asbestos Cement—Bubble of Myths Burst by Facts', New Delhi, 7 November 2003.

The Times of India, New Delhi, 22 December 2001.

The Economic Times, New Delhi, March 2001.

The Economic Times, 'Sugar Industry Lobbies Hard to Get SMP out, MSN in', New Delhi, 29 December 2003.

Corporate Advertising

ADVERTISING AND PUBLIC RELATIONS

Advertising serves as a powerful tool of public relations as a means of communication. Advertising is a tool of PR but PR is not a tool of advertising. Rather than impacting the market with high powered advertising campaigns to sell company products, PR uses advertising to project the company's profile to build image and foster the confidence of the publics in the organization.

Moore and Kalupa (1987) wrote, 'Advertising is a major public relations tool used to communicate with both internal and external publics. When so used, it is often referred to as "institutional" or "corporate" advertising in contrast with product advertising. It has as its primary purpose the projection of the company as a public service institution so as to create a favourable public image.'

Conceptualizing the corporate advertising, Belch and Belch (1995) remarked, 'One of the more controversial forms of advertising is corporate advertising. Actually an extension of the public relations function, corporate advertising does not promote any one specific product or service. Rather, it is designed to promote the firm overall, by enhancing its image, assuming a position on a social issue or cause, or seeking direct involvement in something.'

Corporate advertising has also been used by PR practitioners for lobbying for certain issues and also for safeguarding the organizational interests. Cutlip et al. (1985) opined, 'The use of advertising as a public relations tool for business advocacy has practical advantages. It fits the need to speak up and out to vast audiences beyond those who already support business. Advertising enables its sponsors to control the messages into an environment of public opinion harbouring various shades of approval, suspicion, hostility, and apathy. Business people feel more comfortable with advertising than with publicity. In a climate of adversity, advocacy advertising can be justified as one of the business activities necessary to portray motives and performance accurately. And this, in turn, can be rationalized as a significant contribution in preserving the profit system.' Hence, corporate advertising has a significant role to play in continuation and strengthening of a business organization.

In India, with the adoption of free market policies, the competition is fast becoming global and it is no more possible for some of the traditional companies to thrive on their old reputations, but to gear up to acquire a stature to match their profile with several multinationals who have arrived in India. To attain such an envious position, several companies have been resorting to corporate advertising. For instance, the electronics giant, Videocon resorted to such advertising to project the company as the 'first Indian multinational'. The Indian Posts and Telegraphs Department undertook a high profile advertising campaign to project their 150 years of service to the Indian public and now a new, modern, and transformed organization to match the expectations of the new generation business community, in particular and public in general.

The traditional belief that if you make the products of good quality and price them right, there is hardly any need for advertising, is no more valid. To several businessmen today, it is not just enough to make high quality products, follow marketing norms, distribute products strategically, price them right, promote them very creatively and sell them to the customers. What gives a powerful push to the products is the positive profile and a good understanding of the fair policies and practices of the organization. Publics will not come to know until they are told through projection of the company through advertising, termed as institutional advertising. Rather than advertising to sell products, the company advertises to sell the corporate personality.

Since no organization can grow and prosper in isolation of the society, which provides a customer base and much needed human resource, it is only appropriate, not only to produce socially responsible and consumer friendly products but also to showcase its activities to the society to imbibe trust. This would make the society continue to extend their much needed support to the company.

In the opinion of Alvie Smith, a public relations executive of General Motors, 'The large corporations, whether government or private often become vague, faceless symbols in the mind of the public.' That is why, 'a major object of public affairs advertising at the General Motors is to show the human side of the corporation — that it is highly concerned about people inside and outside the company, and that is made up of thousands of individuals'.

Besides resorting to advertising as a part of the strategic marketing, one or some of the reasons given above, a company would venture into corporate advertising.

ADVERTISING CREDIBILITY

The concept of advertising has been described as—'Advertising is paid, non-personal communication through various media by business firms, non-profit organizations and individuals who are in some way identified in the advertising message in the hope to inform or persuade members of a particular audience' (See chapter 10).

Going by the objectives, corporate advertising is also known by some more nomenclatures like public service advertising, public affairs advertising, advocacy advertising, prestige advertising, and institutional advertising.

Since the ultimate purpose of corporate advertising is to impact the publics, it should bring certain inner strengths of the company to the fore, for the publics to perceive them in the right perspective and form some positive opinions, based on facts communicated by the company. The core competencies of the organization when highlighted appropriately through advertising, should help publics to form their opinions and generate responses desired by the company. As such corporate advertising has some characteristics, which should be of interest to the PR practitioners.

A Question of Credibility

Advertising has always been accused of exaggerations and making extravagant claims, merely to sell products. Experts have an opinion that, all what appears in an advertisement, is taken by the readers or viewers with a pinch of salt. According to one advertising professional, there is hardly any advertisement anywhere in the world which is 100 per cent true. Therefore, all advertising suffers from a universal question—'Is this true?' Readers' trust varies from ad to ad, depending on the company behind it or the way it has been presented.

Corporate advertising, likewise, also suffers from the same lacuna of credibility. The company undertaking such prestigious advertising has all the liberty to play with the space it has bought in the print media or the telecast time that it purchased in the electronics media. The advertiser company can develop the headlines, copy, and illustration of its own choice, to tell the story most convincingly, but the menace of credibility looks unavoidable. The target audiences do understand that it is all paid- for communication, where the advertisers can say what is appropriate from their point of view. Uppal's is a real estate builder of India, advertised in the November 2008 issues of *Business Outlook* to harp upon the credibility, which is the basis of any good business practice. To Uppal's, 'Credibility is like a city, it is not built in a day' (See Exhibit 24.1).

Conspicuously, most of the advertisements work hard to substantiate their claims by providing facts, figures, and statistics to make the public believe the message. Incidentally, when the same material or information is presented by media professionals in their editorial columns or channels, as news and views, the handicap of credibility generally disappears.

A CRITICAL VIEW

From the point of view of quite a few professionals, corporate advertising is not worth the money spent by many corporations. Rather than generating some positive images in the minds of the publics, the advertisements give birth to some ideas, which could be harmful to the interests of a company. Rather than perceiving the organization in good light, the firms may be accused of indulging in reckless advertising either to satisfy the egos of top management bosses or for legitimizing their way of indirectly influencing or even corrupting the media, through the money spent on such advertising programmes.

Some of the accusations that are generally made against such advertising are: *dismal public response, mere show off, wrong perceptions*, and *money squandering*.

Dismal Public Response

Though not measured and researched, certain advertising professionals are of the opinion that all corporate advertising suffers from a serious credibility problem. Rather than creating a positive impression, publics often have a feeling of skepticism in their minds. They seem to be asking a question, as to how much of the message thus advertised should be believed? As such many viewers and readers of such advertisements seem to take them on the face value and think that the company has put on a façade of something, which actually it is not.

Mere Show off

Most of the corporate advertisements smack of particular slant in favour of the management, which is generally the viewpoint of the top management of the

EXHIBIT 24.1 Uppal's credibility advertising

Source: Outlook Business, November 2008.

company, rather than a reflection of the facts. According to one PR executive, the best copy done by the agency is often set aside and replaced by the one that the top management wants to put forth. The professionals seem to have no choice but to succumb to the pressure because it is the management fiat, which is more important than all the creativity and research put in by a PR agency. As such all corporate advertising may not be the reflection of corporate culture or reality but something that the top management wants to show off.

Wrong Perceptions

Though the motives behind such advertising are best known to the company, how the publics perceive the advertising is an important question. Some experts think that many corporate advertisements are a camouflage to hide the real problem, which may have some ramifications in certain crucial areas of management like finance, personnel, labour relations, or a takeover threat or even to enhance the value of the organization, if the management is getting ready for a sell out. The corporate advertising to jack up the public image may be aimed at enhancing the market value of the organization by highlighting the corporate strengths to induce better bids by the prospective buyers. Publics, at large, may perceive that the company is putting up a brave front in the face of a threat that the company is facing due to some environmental changes or competitive aggression.

Money Squandering

Many business organizations are infested with career managers, who, to enhance their market value in the corporate world, may indulge in corporate advertising to show off the role that they have played to make a company vibrant or pulling it out of dire straits. The games that the top managements play are often perceived by the gullible publics, in the way they are intended to be perceived. The corporate advertising may be aimed at self-glorification, by some careerist managers at the helms of affairs, and hence sheer money squandering for ulterior motives. The sole aim, perhaps, is to kick up personal publicity in the interest of advancement of their careers in the corporate world and eventually emerge as great business leaders and even bag some prestigious awards like 'Entrepreneur of the Year', etc.

OBJECTIVES OF CORPORATE ADVERTISING

Public relations plan corporate advertising for a variety of objectives, which may include the following: *enlarge awareness base for corporate identity, enhance public understanding of company business, sober up public attitudes, highlight corporate policies and philosophy, take credit for corporate achievements, polish or correct company image, bolster investors' confidence, improve government relations, build employee morale and labour relations, showcase corporate social responsibility role, earn dealers' understanding and goodwill, showcase anniversaries* and *founder's day, sign new collaborations and mergers,* and *organize ground breaking ceremonies.*

Enlarge Awareness Base for Corporate Identity

A large awareness base of a company paves the way for success in many areas of business activity. More known a company is, better is the response from various publics in the process of meeting organizational objectives. Higher the awareness base, lower is the need for frequency of advertising, hence boosting cost savings and resultant profit improvement. Bata and Colgate, for instance, would advertise mostly during selling seasons or to combat the competitive aggressiveness. Corporate advertising is one way to enhance the awareness base, so essential for business to grow and succeed. In Exhibit 24.2, we see how Punj Lloyd brings out its corporate identity through advertising.

Enhance Public Understanding of Company Business

Business for a company may be running efficiently enough to make reasonable profits to keep the firm on the growth path, but if the publics do not understand the nature of the business, or its policies and practices, then the organization

EXHIBIT 24.2   Punj Lloyd's corporate identity

Source: *The Economic Times,* 17 March 2009.

may be surviving on weak foundations. Floating enough information for public consumption and understanding helps to reinforce its base. Thanks to the continuous outflow of information, well known IT companies like Infosys and TCS (Tata Consultancy Service) have thrived on public understanding.

Sober up Public Attitudes

Positive public attitude towards a company generates positives response. Public animosity towards a company is a dangerous phenomenon. Compared to the positive perceptions, the negativity spreads faster and may have a dangerous ripple effect in several areas of corporate activity. Crisis, big and small, always comes in the life of a company but the positive public attitude helps to tide over such situations. A labour situation in a manufacturing company can upset the apple cart, but if the community, for instance, carries a positive attitude, the labour trouble may take shorter time to fizzle out due to lack of public support for the unions. Companies resort to corporate advertising to allay fears and doubts, if any, in the minds of the publics, and build a bank of public support when a management pre-empts a crisis. For instance, in the face of the rumours about its future, the ICICI Bank advertised on the front pages of mainline national newspapers to sober the depositor's attitude and earn public confidence (See Exhibit 24.3).

Highlight Corporate Policies and Philosophy

Corporate advertising is used by the PR practitioners to highlight the company policies and its corporate philosophy. The advertising message, as such, seeks to show to the publics a value system and the business purpose philosophy of the company. The benefits naturally result in confidence building amongst various publics so that they can extend a matching response to the organization. 'A statement of purpose' advertisement put up by Procter and Gamble India is self explanatory (See Exhibit 24.4).

Take Credit for Corporate Achievements

Some milestones in the history of a company are so outstanding that they deserve to be showcased to the publics. A breakthrough by a pharmaceutical company in inventing a drug that can cure Aids, an engineering company touching a sales turnover of one thousand crore, and automobile manufacturers rolling out a millionth vehicle from their plants, inauguration of a company sponsored hospital for the benefit of the community, celebration of a company's golden jubilee, are some of the examples of the achievements that a company can very deservingly take credit for. For instance, a few years ago, India's leading motor cycle manufacturing company, Hero Honda, very proudly put out full page

EXHIBIT 24.3   ICICI Bank sobering public attitude

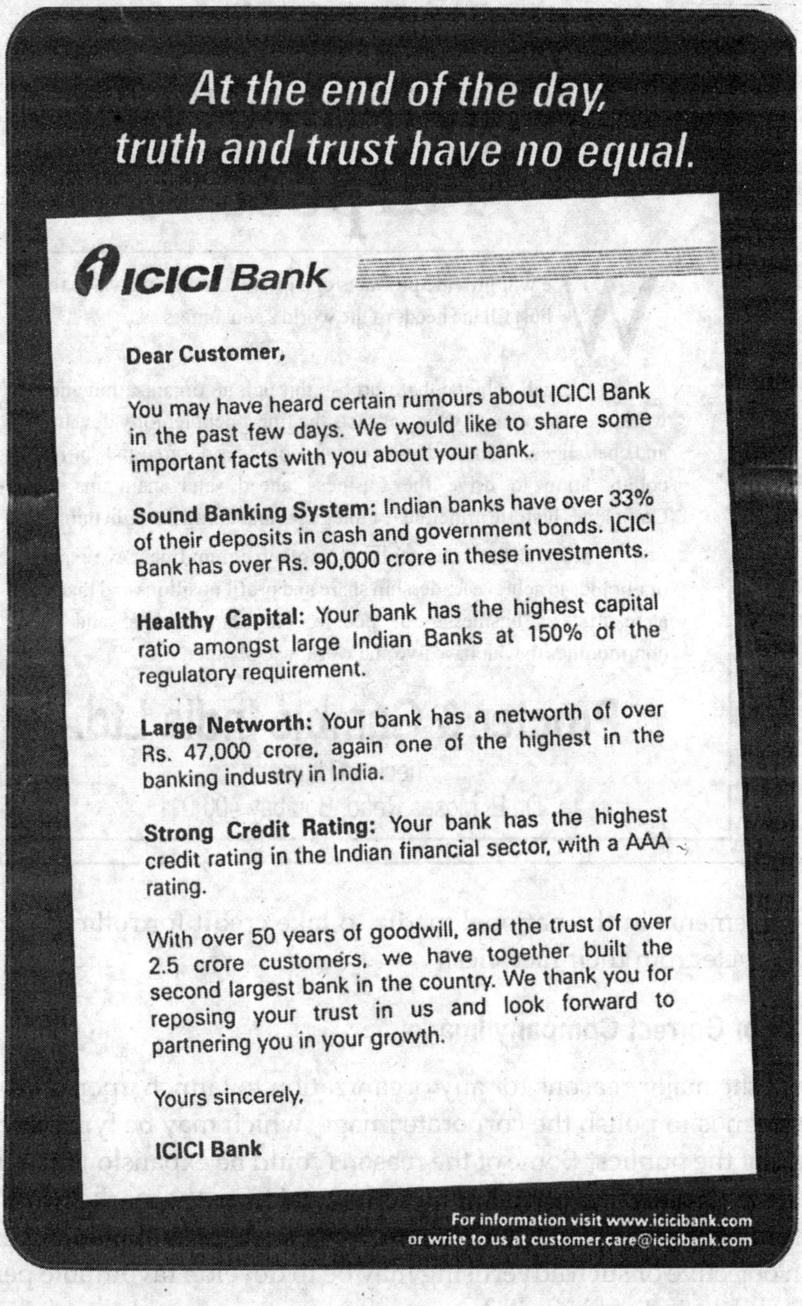

At the end of the day, truth and trust have no equal.

ICICI Bank

Dear Customer,

You may have heard certain rumours about ICICI Bank in the past few days. We would like to share some important facts with you about your bank.

Sound Banking System: Indian banks have over 33% of their deposits in cash and government bonds. ICICI Bank has over Rs. 90,000 crore in these investments.

Healthy Capital: Your bank has the highest capital ratio amongst large Indian Banks at 150% of the regulatory requirement.

Large Networth: Your bank has a networth of over Rs. 47,000 crore, again one of the highest in the banking industry in India.

Strong Credit Rating: Your bank has the highest credit rating in the Indian financial sector, with a AAA rating.

With over 50 years of goodwill, and the trust of over 2.5 crore customers, we have together built the second largest bank in the country. We thank you for reposing your trust in us and look forward to partnering you in your growth.

Yours sincerely,

ICICI Bank

For information visit www.icicibank.com
or write to us at customer.care@icicibank.com

Source: Hindustan Times, 15 October 2008.

EXHIBIT 24.4   Procter & Gamble's 'A statement of purpose' advertisement

---

Procter & Gamble

A Statement of Purpose

W e will provide products of superior quality and value that best fill the needs of the world's consumers.

We will achieve that purpose through an organization and a working environment which attracts the finest people; fully develops and challenges our individual talents; encourages our free and spirited collaboration to drive the business ahead; and maintains the Company's historic principles of integrity, and doing the right thing.

Through the successful pursuit of our commitment, we expect our brands to achieve leadership share and profit positions and that, as a result, our business, our people, our shareholders, and the communities in which we live and work, will prosper.

Procter & Gamble India Ltd.
Tiecicon House
Dr. E. Moses Road, Bombay 400 011.

---

advertisements in the national media to take credit for rolling out a millionth motor cycle from their factories.

Polish or Correct Company Image

One of the major reasons for any organization to launch upon a PR advertising campaign is to polish the corporate image, which may be lying dormant in the minds of the publics. Some of the reasons could be expansion of manufacturing facilities or to mop up some additional capital from the market. Public relations practitioners understand the benefits from such institutional advertising. The main objective of such advertising may be to develop favourable perceptions in the public minds, which in turn may generate more sales and profits, attract some talents and specialist employees, reduce personnel turnover, generate sufficient community support and even develop mutually beneficial relationship with dealers and suppliers. A good image perception helps shareholders to have trust and confidence in the company management. A company with good corporate image, more often receive government officials' favourable and understanding response. The Royal Bank of Scotland Group, on their entry into India, resorted to image building campaign with the involvement of Indian cricket icon Sachin Tendulkar (See Exhibit 24.5).

Institutional advertising or prestige advertising is also resorted to by several companies suffering from a negative image perception. Some incident or event, in the functioning of the organization, rightly or wrongly, damages a well earned image and needs correction. The reason for such problems could be company policies or practices or the product getting into trouble due to contamination or outmoded technology. The problems of Pepsi, Coca Cola, and Cadbury are a case in focus, which forced the companies to mount high powered image correction campaigns with the involvement of some expensive brand ambassadors like Amitabh Bachchan and Aamir Khan (See chapter 18).

Bolster Investors' Confidence

To boost and bolster investor's confidence, several companies from time to time, undertake well planned and thought out advertising in some specific media, which enjoy the reach to the investors' community. The high morale messages favourably reflect on the market, enthuse the investors to put their trust and confidence in the professional management. Such advertising campaigns boost investors' confidence in terms of their investments being in the safe hands.

Improve Government Relations

Corporate advertising is often used by certain companies to clarify their stands on certain issues concerning an impending law, municipal matters, taxes or issues concerning the community health. Such advertising is more directed towards lobbying efforts conducted by the PR persons on behalf of their respective organizations. Also see chapter 23 on lobbying.

Build Employee Morale and Labour Relations

Prestige advertisements put in the local media like community newspapers or the TV channels run by local cable operators, are used to inculcate feelings of association amongst employees' families and friends in particular and community at large. Such advertisements project the firm as a good employer. Also in difficult times such as a labour situation, the companies explain their stand on the issues concerning labour relations to garner community support in sobering down the agitations.

EXHIBIT 24.5 The Royal Bank of Scotland image building advertisement

Every now and again a player appears on the scene who will change the way the game is played.

Like RBS Global Ambassador Sachin Tendulkar, we believe that actions speak louder than words. That's why we've become one of the largest bank in the world with a reputation for helping customers get things done. To find out how we are changing the face of banking in India visit www.rbs.in or call 1800 209 2345.

Make it happen

Source: Outlook Business, November 2008.

Showcase Corporate Social Responsibility Role

To take credit for community service and showcase the efforts made by the company towards their corporate social responsibility role, advertisements make lot of sense to the target publics. Such corporate advertising generates positive perceptions in the minds of the people that the organization is alive to its obligation to improve the quality of life in the society (See chapter 17 on corporate social responsibility).

Earn dealers' understanding and goodwill

The marketing organizations advertise to invite enterprising businessmen to enlist franchisees and some active partners in their business. Taking due advantages of the strengths of the firm, some advisory advertisements are also put in the trade journals and retail management publications to inform, educate, and train dealers in the areas of inventory control, merchandising, store decorations, and upkeep of the identification signs to build customer traffic.

Showcase Anniversaries and Founder's Day

Company anniversaries and founder's day, etc. are occasions for a firm to take credit for outstanding performance record and rededicating the organization in the service of the customers and the nation. Reliance group of companies paying homage to their founder Shri Dhirubhai Ambani through full page advertisements in the newspapers in the country is one example. 'Goodyear goes golden' or 'Half century in the service of nation' are some of the kinds of advertisements that are flashed out by corporations for obvious corporate benefits.

Sign New Collaborations and Mergers

Signing of technological or financial collaboration with national or international companies or a merger of two companies, are important landmarks to be advertised to project a new corporate identity amongst publics. Such occasions signify the emergence of a new enterprise slated to rise and shine on the corporate sky and hence need to be triggered into prominence. Corporate advertising is one sure way of projecting the new identity.

Organize Ground Breaking Ceremonies

Events like ground breaking ceremonies or laying the foundation stone by a celebrity to mark the beginning of a new manufacturing plant or a research center, are appropriate occasions to apprise publics with the long strides being taken by a company towards growth and prosperity.

Although in the matter of choosing a subject, the PR practitioners can run riot, yet for academic reasons, the above reasons may be usual. Cutlip et al.

(1985) reported in their book *Effective Public Relations* some uses of advertising as catalogued by George Hammond, former chairman of the Carl Byoir public relations firm (See Exhibit 24.6).

MEDIA FOR CORPORATE ADVERTISING

A departure from the media selection for marketing advertising, the media mix for the corporate advertising seems to have different considerations. However, the main consideration remains the same, that is, reaching the right target publics. The mainline national newspapers, business and professional magazines, certain radio stations, direct mail, Internet, outdoor, and cinema are amongst the main media channels selected for the purpose of corporate or institutional advertising.

PR professionals understand their preferences for the media that can reach the desired publics, who may be employees, shareholders, customers, suppliers, opinion leaders, business leaders, or the journalists, etc.

Some companies may budget separately for corporate advertising so as not to mingle it with the ongoing marketing advertising, while others may create a special emergency budget when the eventuality arises. While selecting the media, the budget considerations do prevail, and the media mix has to be planned to obtain the maximum benefits out of the resources provided for the purpose.

In this context, it is relevant for the PR practitioners to know the strengths and weaknesses of each media while deciding the media mix to make the budgeted resources work harder. For strengths and weaknesses of each media, see Exhibit 24.7.

EXHIBIT 24.6   Reasons for corporate advertising

Corporate advertising reasons*
(George Hammond, former Chairman, Carl Byoir Agency)

1. Community relations—plant openings, expansions, open houses, anniversaries, annual statements, promotion of community activities such as cleanup weeks, safety, community chest campaigns, and so forth
2. Employee relations, including the employer's side of labour disputes
3. Recruitment
4. Promotion of art contests, essay contests, scholarship awards, and so forth
5. Statements of policy
6. Proxy fights for control
7. Consolidation of competitive position
8. Records of accomplishment
9. Public misunderstandings that must be cleared up immediately
10. Position on pending legislation
11. Consolidation of editorial opinion
12. Supplier or member relations
13. Celebration of local institutions, such as the press during National Newspaper Week
14. Presentation of employer's point of view on matters of public concern

*As per George Hammond, 'These 14 suggestions only scratch the surface of possible uses.'

EXHIBIT 24.7 Media—strengths and weakness

Television strengths
- Intrusiveness
- Wide reach
- High frequency possible
- Demonstrative
- Immediacy
- Prestige in advertising
- Emotive involvement

Weaknesses
- Indiscriminate demographics
- Short message life
- Program suitability problems
- Simple messages needed
- Easy distractions
- Expensive soft and hardware
- Long production lead time

Newspapers
- Editorial section selectivity
- News value and immediacy
- Wide market coverage
- Long messages possible
- Advertisement design choice
- Budget flexibility

- Part issue readership
- High cost of broad coverage
- Low demographic selectivity
- Short message life
- Seasonal clutter
- Small ads lost

Magazines
- Pass along readers
- Long shelf life
- Ad message durability
- Ad size flexibility
- Quality reproductions
- Demographic selectivity
- Special interest groups
- Editorial compatibility
- More affluent readership
- Merchandizing possible
- Full colour reproductions

- Long deadlines
- Small reach
- Slow exposure build-up
- Less intrusive than TV
- Lack of urgency
- Clutter problems

Radio
- Low production cost
- Large 'pool' possible
- High frequency possible
- Audience segmentation
- Intimacy
- Timings flexibility
- Mobility

- No visual information
- No visual impact
- Recall ratings low
- Short message life
- Small audience per station
- Reception clarity troubles
- Low attention value
- Low prestige

Cinema
- Captive audience
- Highly intrusive
- Product demo possible
- Emotively involving
- Some audience selectivity
- Long production lead time

- Short message life
- Lack of urgency
- Small reach
- Slow exposure buildup
- High production cost

Internet
- Economical medium
- Worldwide coverage
- Target audience reach
- Multi-media presentations
- Interactive reach possible
- Faster feedback
- Brand salience support
- E-commerce possibilities

- Irritating interruptions—pop ups
- Limited reach in India
- Impact measurement difficult
- Lack credibility/reliability
- Cyber crimes

TYPES OF CORPORATE ADVERTISING

Advertising, in India, has come a long way. The advertising professionals are every day inventing new and more powerful ways of advertising to take the corporate stories and profiles to the farthest point. A look at the daily newspapers and the television channels reveals the high voltage creativity in the area. It may be difficult to categorize the corporate advertisements into types. However, the basics remaining the same, the corporate advertising, for academic reasons, can be classified into some categories like: *straightforward advertisements*, *advertorials*, *editorial features*, and *special supplements*.

Straightforward Advertisements

Whatever be the objectives, the organizations develop straightforward advertisements in the well known horizontal or vertical formats for the print media or usual thirty seconds slots for the television, to project corporate stories. The necessity of conceptualizing and creatively developing the messages, however, remains essential. Generally speaking such media advertisements are so familiar that sometimes, it may become difficult for the publics to differentiate one company advertisement from the other. However, the PR practitioners juggle with the mechanical data in shapes, sizes, type fonts, illustration, copy, etc. to make their advertisements look distinctive and hence acquire the power to attract public attention. However, the usual challenge to use advertising as an effective tool of public relations remains ever alive.

Advertorials

Knowing fully well the credibility contrast between advertising and editorials, PR invented a new form of corporate advertising by combining advertising with editorialization, called advertorials. Whereas the all media coverage is free and not paid for because of the news value of the press releases, the advertorials, a look alike form of an editorial material, are paid for insertions in the newspapers.

Most often, the press releases distributed by the PR are changed, chopped, and edited to suit the newspaper policy and reader interest and most of the time the company's managements express exasperation about what finally comes in the media. Many times the very objective of distributing the press release may be defeated, as the editors are not dumb enough to print them as it is. The media relations exercise, in this case, becomes counter productive.

Therefore, the advertorials are developed in a manner to gel with the style book of the newspaper and it so appears that it is a news item rather than the paid for advertisement. However, the newspapers make it necessary for such advertorials to be identified by inserting 'advt' at the bottom right hand corner of such items. Conspicuously, the word 'advt' is kept so small as not to get noticed by the gullible reader. As such, the advertorials start enjoying the credibility at par with their counterparts in the publications contributed by the editors or reporters.

Typically enough, advertorials grant liberty to the advertisers to tell their story the way they want to tell, without any interference by the editorial department of the publications, who have their own norms and ethics of editing media reports. The logic behind advertorials is simple—'You pay and play' (See Exhibit 24.8).

EXHIBIT 24.8   An advertorial

South Indian Bank MD & CEO Dr. V.A. Joseph receives the award for the best bank in asset quality among all private sector banks in India from Mr. James E Thompson, GBS, Chairman & Chief Executive, Crown Group of companies. Accompanied by Dr. Manoj Vaish, President & CEO, Dun & Bradstreet, India.

SOUTH INDIAN BANK
GETS BEST BANK AWARD

Mumbai: South Indian Bank on the occasion of eightieth anniversary secured yet another award for the best bank in asset quality among all private sector banks in India from Dun & Bradstreet.

The award was presented in "Banking Awards & India's Top Banks 2009" function organized at Hotel J.W. Marriott, Juhu, Mumbai. The award comes at a time when the banking industry faces challenges on account of global downturn and industry is looking for maintaining quality of assets in its books.

South Indian Bank could bring down its gross non-performing assets from 4.99% in March 2006 to 1.85 % as at Dec 08. The net non-performing asset was brought down from 1.86% to 0.39% for the same period through effective recovery measures.

SIB also topped the Business Today's list of Indian Small Size Banks ranked on the basis of quality of assets. It was acknowledged as the best performer in asset quality by the Analyst 2008 Survey. The bank also was the Top NPA Manager in the ASSOCHAM ECO PULSE Survey. Apart from these, it has also shown a notable increase in the business reach and the net profits.

Dr. V.A. Joseph, who has been decorating the position of the MD and CEO of the bank, is extremely glad about these achievements. His team has been formulating many more innovative ways to develop the customer reach and satisfaction.

During the beginning of the year the bank targeted for an additional 560000 new clients. The Bank has already exceeded the target. The year 2008-09 is celebrated as year of youth and the bank has been targeting the younger clientele. The bank plans to celebrate the ensuing year 2009-10 as a year of Non Resident Indians. The bank has also extended management support to M/S. Hadi Express Exchange both at Dubai and Sharjah. One more office of the said exchange company will be opened shortly at Ras al-Khaimah.

Bank which has got 522 branches has received permission for opening 40 more branches from Reserve Bank of India during the current year. Out of these 11 branches are going to be in its Delhi Region. Bank which has its presence in 23 state and union territories is planning to open branches in the state of Himachal Pradesh, Meghalaya and Tripura during the current year. By 2011 bank plans to cover remaining states also.

Advt.

Source: The Times of India, 23 February 2009.

Editorial Features

An editorial feature is generally a full page feature in a daily newspaper, fully paid for by the advertiser. Also called a pull out, it may also be designed as a four pager and the total space carries the corporate story in full form according to the desired objectives of the advertising organization. The corporate and marketing advertisements can also be a part of such features. Depending on the priorities, the editorial feature may even be limited to a half page.

Besides the objective of projecting the organization in a powerful manner amongst the publics, the companies resort to editorial features to combat the public misconceptions. When the organizational interests are adversely affected by some public misunderstandings or false rumours, it becomes necessary for the company to present the facts quickly and in full media light, to clear the mess from public minds.

Despite the best efforts of the PR practitioners to feed all the information and news to the media, the response expected from the media in terms of coverage and presenting the management view points, is never that satisfactory, and a firm resorts to buying advertising space and publish the corporate story in a manner the company wants to.

Contrary to the general belief that the advertising and editorials departments of a newspaper or periodical, work independently, in complete isolation from each other is, perhaps, never possible. Many business leaders feel that many publications do not give publicity to non-advertising companies. Therefore, buying your own space and telling your own story is the right approach to corporate advertising, hence through editorial features.

Editorial features are also taken out by the industry groups to present a united front for reasons of advocacy, when all members of industry are invited to pool resources and jointly advertise the products and corporations.

Also sometime, the corporate story finds itself too thinly spread over the media outlets and there is felt a need for presenting a consolidated picture to the publics and solicit their support and response. The complete information when given on a full page editorial feature, makes the job easier for readers to look at all the facts and figures in one shot and extend the desirable response. For instance, the State Bank of India (SBI) had several advertisements strewn in the media and felt the need of presenting a consolidated story to the prospective depositors and, therefore, resorted to a full page editorial feature in the *Mint* (See Exhibit 24.9).

Special Supplements

Several business and economic newspapers and periodicals occasionally take out special supplements on some particular industries like cement, tobacco,

EXHIBIT 24.9   State Bank of India editorial feature

Fixed Deposit : No Volatility, All Safety

MINT Media Marketing Initiative

The fine print...

What are the features which make an FD a win-win for investors? Shilpa Pandya goes through the fine print

A Fixed Deposit (FD) is not just a term deposit, in today's scenario which is responsive to investors, banks have started providing various options. "If you are planning to open a fixed deposit account, you have a variety of choices," says investment advisor Priyadarshan Kulkarni. "There are fixed deposit accounts that offer you safe and secured high returns and, there are fixed deposit accounts that also offer you flexibility linked to a savings account or the ability to break a part, of the deposit without impacting the interest earned on the remaining amount," he says.

Market-responsive schemes allow excess balance in a savings account get transferred to a FD and earn a higher rate of interest. Alternately, a FD product can also have the flexibility of allowing partial withdrawals in an emergency, without going through a long-drawn procedure, explains Kulkarni.

Flexibility in an FD also comes from two main choices it offers that of tenure and Interest payments, says Kulkarni. "You can open an account of any maturity period that suits you: from 15 days to 5 years and even more - at monthly intervals. Receive your interest quarterly or request the bank to reinvest your interest every 3 months and maximise your returns," he adds.

In a scenario where internet banking is the buzz word, Kulkarni says FDs as an investment product have kept pace. Now, opening a fixed deposit is just a click away. "FD accounts with flexibility mean that you get a cheque book and a Debit card on a 'linked savings account'. Should you need to draw funds from your fixed deposit, you don't need to make an application or fill in a bunch of forms. All you need to do is simply write a cheque or use your Debit card to draw cash," he points out.

Some banks, says Kulkarni, allow a FD holder to break a part of the FD at any time without affecting the interest on the rest. This gives the FD holder the flexibility to respond to cash emergencies, as also to sit back and let his/ her money earn interest.

Not just a term deposit, smiles Kulkarni. "FDs are a win-win option because of the other investor-friendly features it offers," he concludes.

Safe & Secure: SBI Term Deposits

For an investor, earning a higher income on surplus funds is easy when the option is SBI's Term Deposits, which provide security, trust and a competitive rate of interest. It has a flexible period of term deposit' (from 15 days to 10 years).

SBI's Term Deposits also have affordable low minimum deposit requirement, and an investor can open a term deposit with SBI for a nominal amount of just Rs 1000. One also has flexibility in choosing the amount to invest, as also the maturity period.

SBI understands the value of investors' hard earned money and continues to deliver on a promise of safety and security since over 200 years. The investor can avail a loan/overdraft against the term deposit. SBI provides a loan / overdraft upto 90% of the deposit amount at a nominal cost, so the investor continues to earn interest in the deposit and still meet urgent financial requirements.

Interest to be charged on premature withdrawal of term deposits will be calculated at 1.00% below the rate applicable for the period deposit has remained with SBI.

Transfer of Term Deposits between "SBI's wide network of branches is done without any charge. Tax is deductible at source, as per the Income Tax Act.

With the advantage of nomination facility, Term Deposits are available at all SBI Branches.

Fixed Deposits earn you higher interest than a saving account

Among various investment options, a fixed deposit is a financial instrument for those who want to deposit their money for a fixed duration. Former banker Ramesh Khakharia says there are two main categories: deposits with banks and deposits with corporates. "Each has its plus points, but the banks score simply on the fact that Indians have the perception that banks are safer as they have a government backing," explains Khakharia. Tenures range from 15 days to a year and above, and FDs earn a higher rate of interest as compared to a conventional savings account, explains tax consultant Tarun Ghia. "On maturity of the fixed deposit, an investor gets a return which is equal to the principal plus the interest earned on this principal over the entire duration of fixed deposit," he explains.

Over the years, says consult

> Fixed Deposits help secure hard earned money for long durations wile giving higher risk-free returns as compared to a regular savings account, says Kamlesh Pandya

ant Rajesh Bijlani, fixed deposits have been very popular among investors and keeping this fact in mind, banks have come up with a wide variety of fixed deposit schemes to suit almost every need. "Senior citizens, who opt for fixed deposit schemes, are eligible for an additional 0.5 percent increase, which makes it a win-win scenario for them," he adds.

He adds that while Fixed Deposits are invested for a certain time period, they can be a source of money and funds and withdrawn partly, in times of need. "Depending on the bank's policies, this withdrawal may or may not attract penalty," he explains.

Ramesh Khakharia explains that the interest rates on regular fixed deposits are time based, which is why fixed deposits for a longer duration attract better interest rates. "If you have surplus funds, instead of keeping them in your savings account and thereby earning a paltry interest rate, you can add them to your fixed deposit. This way the funds will earn a much higher rate of interest," he says.

The earning potential of a fixed deposit is increased by something called 'compounding', explains Khakharia. "If the fixed deposit has the potential to earn compound interest by reinvesting the principal amount along with the interest earned during the period, it can dramatically increase the amount one gets at maturity of the fixed deposit. But, to get the maximum returns, a prudent investor should compare fixed deposit schemes from various banks before Settling for what he/ she feels is the

best one," he adds.

Opening a FD

The process of opening a fixed deposit, says Tarun Ghia, is simple and this is an investment product accessible to almost all section of the Indian population. Banks in India have a certain minimum initial deposit limit (which may be Rs 1,000 or the like) to open a fixed deposit and the value of fixed deposit can be increased in multiples of a minimum amount (like Rs 100). "These limits can vary, and also depend upon rural, urban or semi-urban nature of the population. The limits are very low for rural areas so that even those with low incomes can open a fixed deposit, "he adds.

The actual calculation

The actual manner of calculating the interest rate on your fixed deposit varies from bank to bank. "For a fixed deposit of six months or above, the banks may calculate the interest on a quarterly basis," says Rajesh Bijlani. "In case the tenure of the FD is less than six months, the interest may be calculated at maturity as simple interest. The compounding factor or interest for re-investment is calculated on a quarterly basis," he adds.

Taxation

Every fixed deposit is subject to the Indian income tax regulations, as prevalent from time to time. "Keeping these regulations in mind, banks deduct tax at source from your fixed deposits and issue you a TDS certificate for the same," says Tarun Ghia. "Regular, fixed deposits bring increased returns on your funds as compared to a regular savings account. This is what makes them a great instrument for investing money. They can be used as guarantee for loans and financial transactions, which makes them even more valuable," he concludes.

State Bank of India — Pure Banking Nothing else. With you - all the way

Festival offer on Term Deposit for 1000 dayys.

10.50% P.A.

11.00% P.A.

For senior citizens

FDs gain in investor perception

Returns on investments are pivotal to any investment decision and FDs are fast gaining on this parameter, says Ami Pandya

F or investors, equities are no longer the 'hot and happening' option, given the downward movement in the SENSEX and the NIFTY. As stock markets indices dropped, interest rates have consistently risen and, Fixed Deposits (FDs) have become the flavour of the month," says research and analysis agency Llases Foras' CEO Pankaj Kapoor. "Till a few weeks back, the stock markets had an edge over fixed deposits, because of the booming stock indices," he says.

Till recently, the situation was one where the government's saving schemes,

especially the post office saving schemes, would have seemed to have an edge over FDs. "But, the recent changes have again brought investment in FDs in the limelight," says tax consultant Tarun Ghia. "The contributing factors include the decision to give tax breaks in terms of coverage under Section 80C of the Income Tax Act. Another important factor has been the gradual increase in the interest rates on FDs," he adds.

Investors will go in for FDs if the perceived returns are high enough, says Kapoor. "FDs will compete with other investment avenues available to investors, who ideally should take into consideration interest rates, returns, lock-in periods, liquidity and security, before taking an investment decision," he concludes.

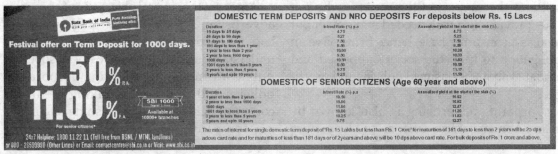

State Bank of India — Pure Banking Nothing else. With you - all the way

Festival offer on Term Deposit for 1000 days.

10.50% P.A.

11.00% P.A.

For senior citizens*

SBI 1000 — Available at 10000+ branches

24x7 Helpline: 1800 11 22 11 (Toll free from BSNL / MTNL landlines) or 080 - 26599990 (Other Lines) or Email: contactcentre@sbi.co.in or Visit: www.sbi.co.in

DOMESTIC TERM DEPOSITS AND NRO DEPOSITS For deposits below Rs. 15 Lacs

Duration	Interest Rate (%) p.a	Annualised yield at the start of the slab (%)
15 days to 45 days	4.75	4.75
46 days to 90 days	5.27	5.25
91 days to 180 days	7.50	7.50
181 days to less than 1 year	8.50	8.50
1 year to less than 2 year	10.00	10.38
2 year to less than 1000 days	9.90	10.33
1000 days	10.50	11.63
1001 days to less than 3 years	9.50	10.38
3 years to less than 4 years	9.75	11.17
5 years and upto 10 years	9.25	11.50

DOMESTIC OF SENIOR CITIZENS (Age 60 year and above)

Duration	Interest Rate (%) p.a	Annualised yield at the start of the slab (%)
1 year of less than 2 years	10.50	10.92
2 years to less than 1000 days	10.50	10.92
1000 days	11.00	12.27
1001 days to less than 3 years	10.00	11.20
2 years to less than 5 years	10.25	11.03
5 years and upto 10 years	9.75	12.27

The rates of interest for single domestic term deposit of 'Rs. 15 Lakhs but less than Rs. 1 Crore' for maturities of 181 days to less than 2 years will be 25 dps above card rate and for maturities of less than 181 days or of 2 years and above will be 10 dps above card rate. For bulk deposits of Rs. 1 crore and above,

Source: Mint, 21 October 2008.

rubbers, and steel industry, etc. They then invite the leading manufacturing and marketing companies to advertise and also give 'free' write ups in lieu thereof.

Taking out special supplements on some of the foreign countries is a favourite method of some of the print media publications to mop up additional advertising revenue. From the readers' view point, it is a mere show off but to some, it is a meaningful exercise to cultivate business relations with some of the countries abroad. Also it is a meaningful exercise for some of the local embassies to project their respective countries as good investment centres and tourist destinations. Supplements on France or Indo–Soviet trade, etc. seen occasionally are some of the examples.

Some PR practitioners often prompt the publications to plan such supplements for mutual advantage; the organization represented by the PR professional gets publicity and the publication gets a handsome slice of the advertising cake from the corporate world. All that the independent media will not willingly publish could be seen in such supplements. However, such supplements have high commercial value and serve as a good source of information and reference for business to business activities and marketing networking.

Summary

Advertising is a tool of PR, but PR is not a tool of advertising. Companies resort to advertising not only for promoting their products and services but the institution itself, to enhance its corporate image as one of the major objectives.

Corporations use advertising for advocacy purposes to justify the company's business activities and the motives of making profits for which there is always a need for moulding favourable public opinion.

Since all the business emanates from society, corporate advertising needs to relate itself to the society. No company can succeed without the support of the society, who not only provide the much needed manpower but also as a consumer base, hence firms have an obligation to keep the society apprised and updated about its business policies and practices.

Corporate advertising is also known by many nomenclatures such as public service advertising, public affairs advertising, advocacy advertising, prestige advertising, and institutional advertising.

As all advertising suffers from credibility problems, corporate advertising is no exception. Therefore, the companies need to substantiate the claims that they make in advertising with facts and figures. Some managers do not think very high of corporate advertising and term it as an exercise in futility. Some of the accusations made against advertising are dismal public response, mere show off, wrong perceptions and money squandering.

Amongst the several objectives of corporate advertising, some are: enlarging awareness base for corporate identity, enhancing public understanding of company business, sobering public attitudes, highlighting corporation policies and philosophy, taking credit for corporate achievements, polishing or correcting company image, bolstering investors' confidence, improve government relations, building employee morale and labour relations, showcasing corporate social responsibility role, earning dealers' understanding and goodwill, showcasing anniversaries and founder's day, signing new collaborations and mergers, organizing ground breaking ceremonies.

The question of media selection and media mix, in principle are almost the same as marketing advertising, but the mix would change according to the weaknesses and strengths of each media, in co-relation to the objectives of corporate advertising.

Some of the well known types of corporate advertising are straightforward advertising, advertorials, editorial features, and special supplements.

Key Terms

Advertising   The activity of attracting public attention to a product or business, as by paid announcements in the print, broadcast, or electronic media

Advertorial   Large advertisement deliberately styled to look like the editorial matter of a newspaper or magazine in which it appears

Collaborations   A partnership agreement between two business companies

Corporate advertising   Advertising whose objective is to build a firm's corporate image, reputation, and name awareness among the general public or within an industry

Credibility   The quality, capability, or power to elicit belief

Mergers   Two companies merge into one with a new identity

Money squandering   The money allegedly wasted on advertising with no or negligible benefits

Concept Review Questions

1. Establish your understanding about the difference between marketing advertising and corporate advertising.
2. What are the reasons for all advertising suffering from credibility problems? Is corporate advertising an exception? Explain the concept in detail.
3. What are the various objectives for a company to resort to corporate advertising? Explain in detail.
4. What are the various types of advertising resorted to by the companies to meet organizational goals? Write a lucid note.

Project Work

1. Develop a series of three ads for insertion in daily newspapers to project the corporate personality of the company you work for, say Escorts Limited.
2. AIIMS doctors have gone on a strike for a pay hike. Design and develop a series of four advertisements to muster public support in favour of the management stand that it has taken to deal with the labour situation.

References

Belch, George E. and Michael A. Belch (1995), Richard D. Irwin, Inc, a division of the McGraw-Hill Companies, United States of America, p. 536.

Cutlip, Scott M., Allen H. Center, and Glen M. Broom (1985), *Effective Public Relations*, 6th edition, Prentice-Hall International Editions, Prentice-Hall of India Private limited, New Delhi, pp. 386 and 485–87.

Hindustan Times, New Delhi, 15 October 2008, p. 1.

Mint, New Delhi, 21 October 2008, vol II, no. 250, p. 7.

Moore, H. Frazier and Frank B. Kalupa (1987), Richard D. Irwin,Inc, USA, and published in India by Surjeet Publications, Delhi, p. 229.

Outlook Business, New Delhi, 19 October 2008.

The Times of India, New Delhi, 23 February 2009, p. 5.

The Economic Times, 17 March 2009, p. 4.

25

Anatomy of a House Journal

A HOUSE JOURNAL DEFINED

The beginning of the 21st century has witnessed an information explosion and a booming growth of newspapers and publications. What adds more to the overcrowded media scene is the mushroom growth of TV channels, resulting in an information overload for the publics. Therefore, a question arises that when the publics are already overburdened with excessive information and are faced with a problem of plenty, where is the need for one more publication, called house journal?

In this very context, a look at the scenario reveals that there are also hundreds of publications and magazines published in India, which are specialist magazines or are aimed at catering to the information needs of specific groups, to keep them updated in their knowledge and skills and also keep them connected. Therefore, the publication of house journal by a corporation has all the relevance because of its role of communicating with both internal and external publics.

'The public relations periodical, also called company magazine, house organ, or industrial publication, is a major medium of communication used by business and nonprofit organizations in communicating with employees, shareholders, suppliers, dealers, customers, and the general public,' wrote Moore and Kalupa (1987).

In other words, a house journal has come to stay as a well recognized part of the management's communication process. The benefits may look invisible and intangible but the public relations professionals have come to a conclusion that having a house journal for a company is not just a fashion, but a necessity to weld the bonds between the organization and the publics.

In the words of Rita Bhimani (1994), 'As an integral part of an organization's communication structure, a house journal, far from being relegated to the status of being the past-up smile of a company for its employees and other publics, is still today, the surest means of establishing a two-way traffic that is not propaganda, nor persuasion, but good, planned in-house prattle. … A successful house journal today is one, which remains homely enough to be an intra-company publication, but is slick enough to evoke favourable comment from an outsider. It is somewhat like an office play, which apart from the standing ovation at the annual social, gets column inches of praise by a drama critic in a national daily'.

As defined by the Indian Association of Industrial Editors (IAIE) (1968), 'A house journal is a medium of communication, which projects the image of a company or an organization to one or more sections of the public, within the organization or outside, with the purpose of (a) improving employee morale, (b) creating or fostering a favourable climate for the working of the company or the organization, and (c) promoting goodwill.' The association is now known as Association of Business Communicators of India (ABCI).

An organization wants to tell their own story in their own manner and express own opinions forcefully to the target publics, where a house journal fits the bill. When a company publishes its own journal to carry its own versions to their own readers, for building goodwill amongst customers or reinforcing the employee loyalty, the house journal serves as a means of achieving such aims and objectives. In other words, a house journal is a newspaper or a magazine published by an organization, mostly without any cover price, and is distributed to selected target publics.

Also, most of the organizations are never satisfied with the way media covers their stories and one such communication tool, known as house journal, provides a strong platform for a company to advocate its own view points and goal oriented messages that media would generally resist to carry, due to commercial bias or certain editorial ethics of their own.

As such, the publication of a house magazine is a well accepted activity by all the enlightened managements to maintain a two-way communication with various publics. Not only that the journal, when planned that way, may serve as an ambassador or a mouthpiece of the organization, but also as a means of keeping the corporate identity in focus. PR practitioners endowed with the journalistic skills and assigned the important responsibility of running the communication programme of a company, most often have to don the hat of an editor of such publications.

A HISTORICAL PERSPECTIVE

Today, in the face of the surge of electronic media, the relevance of a house journal seems a misnomer. The chances of survival of house journals, when the organizations are aiming at paperless offices, look bleak. Some organizations have now transformed this activity into e-papers, wholly or partially doing away with the paper publications. Yet in the opinion of many PR professionals, the house journals are here to stay and rather get stronger. They think that house publications have certain peculiar characteristics that the electronic media cannot match or replace. Comparing the two, the life span of a television coverage is only a few seconds, whereas the life of printed house journal can be a week, a month, or even a quarter of a year, or even a year or more. The house journals even serve as an archive for an organization to rediscover itself, many years later.

The publication of house journals started at a time, when the electronic media was virtually non-existent. The famous 'Lloyds' of London brought out the world's first company publication 'Lloyds News' in 1696. It is published even today as 'Lloyd's List'. The first industrial periodical, in the modern sense, was published by Lowell Cotton Mills of Massachusetts, USA, in 1840 under the title of 'The Lowell Offering'.

The population of house journals have flourished over the years and there is no way to know, as to how many journals are published in USA. According to the rough estimate of International Association of Business Communicators (IABC), the number of house journals should be about 30,000, with audience running to more than 300 million.

In India, the first employee publication was taken out by the United Planters' Association of Southern India in 1905 titled as 'Planter's Chronicle'. It was followed by house journals of Delhi Cloth Mills, Bombay Port Trust, Indian Railways, and the House of Tatas. Several house journals have sustained long existence and currently there are estimated to be more than 2,000 house magazines published in India. The circulation of such journals range from 500 to 2,00,000. SBI's 'Colleague' is said to have the highest record circulation with a reported print order of nearly three lakh copies per issue.

OBJECTIVES OF A HOUSE JOURNAL

Depending on the management priorities and the target publics, there can be a variety of objectives that the public relations publications seek. Generally speaking, the objectives may be the following:

- Showcase the company philosophy and value system as reflected in the various activities.
- Inculcate the corporate culture amongst employees and other publics directly associated with the organization.
- Explain the appropriateness of the company's policies and practices as related to various organizational objectives and activities.
- Further the PR role of ushering in a change amongst publics for mutual benefit.
- Inform, advise, entertain, and guide publics about the optimum usage of capacity, right usage of products and services for public benefit including employees.
- Foster a feeling of harmony and mutual trust between management and employees and serve as a common platform to voice out ideas.
- Build the confidence of dealers, suppliers, and shareholders in the professional management of the company for the success of the enterprise.
- Dispel rumours and provide clarifications about misunderstandings, if any, in the minds of various publics about actions of the organization and maintain tranquility and harmony.

TYPES OF HOUSE JOURNALS

Though it is difficult to classify the kinds of house journals published by various business houses and even non-profit organizations, the house journals have been categorized as: *internal house journal, external house journals, internal–external house journals*, and *market-oriented house journals*.

Internal House Journal

An internal house journal, with employees as the main target publics, is often brought out by a company to foster a sense of loyalty amongst the employees towards the company and build a work culture that can help the organization to grow and prosper. Such employee publication is designed to build *esprit de corps* amongst the employees with the objective of welding the employees together as a team, so essential for operational success.

As a part of the management responsibility to keep the flow of downward communication to the employees, a company uses an employees' journal as a tool of informing, educating, motivating, and even entertaining the employees through the human interest stories born out of the employees' lives. Even the disciplining function of the management is taken care of, sometimes, through the internal house journal. For instance, a company would publish a 'Grievance Procedure' to educate and direct the employees to seek redressal of their gripes through proper procedure and not resort to any undesirable mean to assuage their feelings.

What should be the content of a house journal, is often debated amongst the public relations practitioners. Perhaps, there is no difference of opinion that the employee journal should serve as a two-way communication bridge between the employees and management. If the main focus of an internal house journal is employees, then anything that interests the employees is worth while to heighten their interest in the publication. Some PR persons, who also work as *ex-officio* editors of such journals, commit a cardinal mistake of filling pages with the photographs of the managing director and his wife doing some insignificant things. This way the publication becomes a one-way traffic from management to the employees, who may have no interest, whatsoever, in what the top management is doing. Decidedly, they would like to read about themselves, their friends and colleagues, and their families, rather than the top bosses.

Keeping this in view, the National Thermal Power Corporation (NTPC) Communication Department has laid down some guidelines as to what a house journal should contain. These include major highlights of the organization or the unit, brief news of the corporation, human interest stories, poems, short stories, cartoons, or caricatures from employees and their wards, quiz for children and housewives, social matters, interviews with award winners, and other success stories of employees and their family members.

TISCO News is worth emulating. It provides lot of food for thought and action, thereby enriching the reader's knowledge. In one of the issues it carried articles like 'managing hypertension' and other health related matters like prevention of burns, eye donation, and more. The journal also addresses topics like team building, human relations, etc.

However, if the story and pictures have relevance to the role played by the top bosses, as it touches employees' lives, then it does make sense to show their pictures as such. For instance, a few years ago, ACC News of the ACC Cement Company published the news pictures of the wife of their managing director launching an ambulance service for the employees in need. Such stories that touch employees' lives are important to them and generate tremendous employee readership of an internal house journal.

However, it is very relevant for the PR practitioners to know the objectives of an employee journal (See Exhibit 25.1).

External House Journal

An external house journal is brought out by an organization with a view to reach out to the external publics—customers, dealers, vendors, investors,

---

EXHIBIT 25.1   Internal house journal objectives

- To build bridges of understanding between the management and the employees
- To inform, educate, motivate, discipline, and even entertain the employees
- To inculcate company loyalty amongst the employees
- To knit the employees together in the interest of team building
- To encourage family feeling amongst the employees

- To address issues like productivity, safety, quality, absenteeism, and employee health
- To communicate to the employees the ways and means of improving quality of life
- To allow employees to voice out their emotions and suggestions through house journal
- To promote understanding amongst employees about management–union adversary relationship.

---

government agencies, opinion leaders, and even media. The main objective for publishing such journals is to project the corporate personality in front of such audiences. Explaining policies and practices of the organization is another good reason. An external house journal when tastefully published goes a long way in building the company image amongst a cross section of the readers.

More often than not, such publications devote lot of space to market development with customers and dealers, as main focus. There is a wide variety of articles, photos, and news features that are included to interest a wide base of readers spread over the length and breadth of the market. Dealer profiles, customer satisfaction stories, outstanding product performance, marketing manager's messages and activities, a sales person's outstanding victory in a sales race, rewards and awards, sales conference coverage, or a dealer winning a sales contest are familiar stories.

With businesses acquiring larger dimensions and diversifications, the nature and number of such publications has also multiplied. In the pharmaceutical industry, the fashion garments industry, the IT industry, and the tourism industry, etc. there is seen publications galore. Every organization worth its salt, today, thinks of publishing an external house journal, with one specific or more objectives in mind. For instance, the mushrooming of security companies has led many such companies to come out with publications of their own to educate and sell the merits of contracting the security agency who can look after the safety and security of the organizations' property and personnel. Particularly the terrorism threats have given a shot in the arm to the industry vis-à-vis communications sent out to target publics in the form of external house journals.

The opening of the aviation sector and the cut-throat competition amongst private airlines have made the companies to think of ways and means to assuage the feelings of the travellers. To make the flights more enjoyable and meaningful, the publication of in flight publications has also boomed. The airlines like Jet Airways, Kingfisher, SpiceJet, etc. have their own in flight publications, besides the old Indian Airlines, who for long have been publishing their external house journal named 'Namaskar'.

The mushrooming of external house journals, naturally, makes a public relations practitioner's job more meaningful to work as editor of such publications and help the organizations to meet their corporate objectives. Obviously, in business, no one spends money for nothing until the returns are visible and ensured. Therefore, the external house journals are playing a meaningful role in the process of making the companies vibrant. It should be of interest to the public relations practitioners to acquaint themselves with the aims and objectives of publishing an external house journal (See Exhibit 25.2).

Internal–External Combined House Journal

Depending on its size, resources, and target publics, a company decides to publish a combined house journal, rather than one for employees and the other for external publics. Some managers and PR practitioners may think that publishing such a house journal is a fad to satisfy the management ego or to show to the corporate world a 'me too' attitude, but it so appears that no company would spend the hard earned money on some wasteful activities. Hence, a combined house journal has an objective of seeking employee support from within the organization and the cooperation of several external publics, in a bid to integrate the total operation for obvious business benefits.

A combined internal–external house journal seeks to meet the combined objectives of both types of journals and also ensure the advantages of both kinds of journals to the organization.

Important enough, the combined journal bridges the so-called dichotomy between the internal and external publics and represents the organization to all publics in a unified manner. It helps the employees to realize that their future and welfare is hinged on to the understanding of the external publics and it is

EXHIBIT 25.2 *Objectives of an external house journal*

- To win confidence and trust of various publics, particularly the customers
- To disseminate information about the companies' policies and practices
- To showcase success stories and get credit for the organization's achievements.
- To promote products and services of the company and induce a favourable marketing environment
- To educate customers for the proper use and maintenance of the products, for maximum satisfaction

- To build sales force and dealers' morale to sell with confidence
- To imbibe shareholders' confidence and faith in the professional management of the company
- To bolster vendors' interest in the company to ensure regular supply of components, etc. and invite them to participate in the product development work
- To provide a common platform for interaction between various target publics and the management, to facilitate a mutually beneficial relationship

their obligation to keep the external publics happy, particularly customers, by making high quality products, reduce manufacturing waste, and extend the necessary cooperation to the management in their efforts to pursue the public focused policy for the benefit of all.

Market-oriented House Journals

Certain large marketing companies with a large customer base or a well identified band of institutional buyers consider that a market oriented house journal goes a long way in imbibing the customer confidence. Particularly for a business firm, who manufactures and markets high technology products, mother machines or handles turn key projects like setting up power plants with a long-term maintenance contract, a market oriented house journal plays the useful role of keeping the customers updated with new technological breakthroughs. Such pertinent and useful information helps the customers to keep their operations moving smoothly.

Such market oriented house journals carry special articles and photo features about the inauguration of new installations, success and satisfaction stories about key customers, introduction of new design machines, or an invention in the offing that may bring a spectacular change in the total system. For instance, the merits of solar energy or wind power, when highlighted in such specialist publications, would interest the institutional customers tremendously, as such an information would promise substantial cost savings and profit enhancements.

A pharmaceutical company, whose main focus is doctors, would bring out a special publication to inform and educate doctors about the new drug introductions, the features and benefit stories about such drugs, and induce them to prescribe these medicines to their patients for results.

Addressing the homemaker ladies, a market oriented house journal from a white goods manufacturing and marketing company, would project the introduction of a new machine, like a dish-washer that would cut out the drudgery of kitchen chores and make their lives more comfortable and enjoyable.

LAUNCHING A HOUSE JOURNAL

Launching a house journal calls for considerable advance preparation and planning. It may be likened to drawing up of a blueprint before starting the construction of a building. Besides seeking the management approval for an appropriate budget, the editor has to put in some serious thoughts into the process through which a journal finally emerges and reaches the readers' hands.

However, the experienced professionals know that certain prerequisites must be met by the management of a company to put the editors in the right position to do their job appropriately. The spirit of understanding, delegation of authority, and the mutual trust between the editor and the management is of utmost importance for the publication to succeed and meet the objectives for which it is taken out. 'The commandments for publication of journals' as suggested by Norman Woodhouse on behalf of the British Association of Industrial Editors, should set the system and make it work (See Exhibit 25.3).

Some of the aspects that need to be addressed, as a part of the preparation, are the following: *objectives, target publics, periodicity, content,* and *style.*

Objectives

Depending on the nature of the journal, internal, external, or combined, the objectives of the publication should be kept in clear focus by the editor. If it is an internal house journal solely directed at the employees, then all those aspects of the organization, which influence the employee morale and efficiency, have to be the main objective of taking out such a publication. Similarly, an exclusive external publication should be focusing in all its intent and content on the external publics. Such publics can also be prioritized like customers, dealers, shareholders, or vendors, etc.

In the light of the above, it is most appropriate for an editor to clearly understand the management objectives, policies, and programmes behind their willingness to start the publication. This should lead to the logical conclusion of adopting a communication forum from which the target publics should be addressed. Some of the usual priorities a management have are building the corporate image, projecting the corporate identity and personality, expressing organizational view points on certain issues, or even connecting publics to the

---

EXHIBIT 25.3   Ten commandments for journal publication

1. The policies of the board must be fully understood by all management staff and by the unions.
2. These policies must be clearly explained to the people employed in the enterprise. Here the internal publication has an important place among the many skills and techniques of effective communication.
3. The editor must be at the heart of the communication network. They must be kept informed of management problems and decisions, and have access to the entire management team.
4. The editor's task must be clearly defined and they must be directly responsible to top management, preferably to the chairman or managing director.
5. The editor, their staff, and their publication need to be professional and as well equipped as any other part of the enterprise.
6. The publication must be regular and on time.
7. The publication must be credible to its readers.
8. It should cover the full range of their interests, as employees, as trade union members, as family men and women, and as citizens.
9. It should promote two-way communication.
10. The overriding aim must be to inform, educate, and interest readers in an entertaining way.

Source: Skinner et al. (2007).

organization for earning their understanding in the process of meeting corporate goals.

Target Publics

Once the type of the publication is decided, the target public becomes very obvious. The editors can always get to know the hopes and desires of such audiences and cater to their tastes and needs. Since no reader of any publication can be forced to read what the editor wants them to read, it is always advisable to cater to the tastes of the readers. The editor may be an expert writer on political affairs, but this ability in that area may be of no relevance, if the readers have no interest in politics. Needless to say, all target publics have their own priorities and need for certain kinds of information that directly or indirectly influence their lives. The information that can bring some benefits to them and the lack of which can cause some financial loss or loss of respect in their societies, will always be read with interest. Therefore, doing a proper homework on the needs and tastes of the targeted audiences is of prime importance for any house journal editor.

Specifically, even in the area of employee publication, it is essential to determine the category of employee like shop floor workers, office clerks, floor supervisors, middle level managers, or the management members themselves. For this very reason, many professionally managed companies bring out a couple of such publications which specifically cater to a category of employees. For instance, a company publishes a house journal which covers almost everyone in the organization, and there may be another publication named 'Management Newsletter', which is strictly circulated to the managers of all levels.

Even in the area of market oriented publications, a company may publish exclusive journals for dealers and for customers separately. For instance, Escorts Limited would bring an exclusive dealer publication, titled 'Profitably Yours' besides some other periodic stories indirectly targeted at the end use customers, about the upkeep and maintenance of their tractors and farming techniques.

Periodicity

It is a familiar sight to see a large variety of house journals taken out by the companies in the business world—weeklies, fortnightlies, monthlies, bi-monthlies, half yearlies or annuals. The periodicity or frequency of publication is a matter of management choice, need, objectives, and the budgets earmarked for such effort. There is no single rule that would serve as a guideline for the periodicity of the publication. The frequency decisions may also not be linked to the size or the sales turnover of an organization, but the volume of information and communications that a company needs to float, may form the basis of frequency. Achieving certain organizational objectives may also be a good reason for deciding the frequency.

Content

The content denotes the writeups and photographs about the company stores which cover management achievements, milestones, and even human interest stories about employees and their families. As there is no definite policy about contents, the house editors can use one standard, that is, 'What is good for the company is good enough for the house journal coverage.'

Style

Ask any publisher of a newspaper, about the style book, that is like a master guide to take care of several aspects of publication, namely the *title, masthead/design, language, format, grid, type face, justification,* and *frequency.* Most of these aspects are connected with the production side of a journal, from the manuscript stage to its distribution to the readers.

Title

The title of a publication represents the personality of the house journal. Naming a publication often becomes a debatable point in the organization as many people have many names to suggest for the new baby to be born. Inviting participation in the process of christening the publication is a good beginning to ensure its acceptability and popularity. However, the title should have some characteristics for success, which are the following:

- It should be unique, so as to stand out.
- It should be crisp, punchy, relevant and easy to pronounce and remember.
- It should be born out of the organization's identity or culture.
- It should sound like the name of a publication.
- It should have distinct spellings transformed into a logo.
- It should have adoptability for different Indian languages.

Though it may not be possible to have a title acceptable to all and sundry, yet the PR practitioners should be guided by some of the above mentioned considerations.

Title design/masthead

Once the PR practitioner has been able to name the publication through consensus, it is now essential to dress it up in a particular design. Known as the masthead or a particular writing style of the title, it may be appropriate to take the services of a graphic designer or the PR agency to design it. Once the title design has been chosen, then there is a need for the editor to stick to such a design, issue after issue. This helps to establish a recognition or identity of the publication with the target publics, so essential to strike a familiarity with the readers. A look at several house journals reveals that many publications have stuck to one single design and even a colour for a number of years, for the same reason of attaining a reader association, on a long-term basis.

If the journal is planned in a magazine size, such as *India Today* or *Onlooker*, the title page design stays on a long-term basis, with a window cut out to take in photographs, cartoons, or caricatures to heighten the reader interest, in each new issue of the journal.

Journal format

The final appearance and personality of the publication depends on the format that has to be decided in co-relation with the objectives, budget, readership, and mailing convenience of the journal. The generally adopted formats are A4 or A3 sizes. Some companies may adopt even A5 size, that is, *Reader's Digest* size for reasons of reading convenience, storage reference, etc.

A4 size, which is *India Today* size, is mostly popular for house journals. It is convenient; can be folded while reading and mailing; serves as a good travelling companion; and also fits into the standard folders for record keeping. This format has been adopted by a majority of organizations for obvious advantages of full treatment to text and photographs, etc.

A3, which is double the size of A4, is the tabloid size like that of the *Metro Now*. Like a tabloid, which has a short life and is just thrown away after flipping through the pages, the house journal may also meet the same fate. It is difficult to handle, has to be folded in the horizontal middle for fitting into the standard envelopes for mailing, and hence not a very popular format. Of late, quite a few companies switched over from the A3 to A4 format, for obvious reasons.

A5 has its limitations and narrows down the scope of printing pictures in full form and hence, perhaps, good for more of written material than illustrations.

Grid design

After a decision on the overall format is taken, the editor in consultation with the agency and the graphic designer, gets down to deciding the making of the page designs, which includes the number of columns on each page, and some box items to heighten the reader interest. There is no standard rule about the number of columns in a page and the choice can be very flexible to make each page attractive enough to look at and interesting enough to read. Some editors think that it is advisable to follow the arrangement of columns per page from cover to cover, but today, the variety and balancing of the spaces on each page is the trend. The desktop publishing provides editors some imaginative and creative layouts, to design and decorate the pages, as priorities of the material demand. Even the colour combinations provide a wide choice of playing with the facilities available. However, it is very advisable for the editors to acquire enough computer literacy, to make house journal publication more rewarding an experience.

Typefaces and fonts

Different typefaces convey different feelings. In fact, it appears that the designers and printers have developed different typefaces to be used for different subjects and purposes. Some faces denote serious and pensive moods, whereas others convey happy feelings. There are typefaces for conveying greetings and some to convey some sad messages. For the publication purposes, generally there are two type fonts used, the Times Roman or Arial, in their bold, italic, and normal versions. These are two businesslike type fonts, and decision has to be made to adopt one typeface. But once one is adopted, it is advisable to stick to that type family for several forthcoming issues. Switching types may disturb the personality of the papers and public perception. Certain editors do not advise mixing up type faces, while others believe in making a cocktail of them to achieve variety and creativity in presentation of the material. Whatever the case, a decision has to be taken to continue the style for several issues of the publication.

Language

Depending on the language known to the target publics, either the publication should use the language known to a majority of the readers, such as English or Hindi or make it a bi-lingual to cater to all readers. Many Indian house journals have adopted a bilingual pattern for reaching the readers of both the languages. Some organizations also bring out two editions of the same house journal, one in English and other in the language read and understood by a section of the audience.

Another issue is the level of the language used in such journals. There is definitely a need to stick to a language, which reaches the level of a particular audience and raise the language profile to meet another level. For instance, the level of language used in an employee publication, where shop floor employee readers are generally semi-literate, has to be adjusted to their level. On the other hand, writing for a senior management newsletter, the level of the language should match the professional and intellectual level of the managers.

In both the cases, however, the clarity and readability is the main question and editors have to be careful to avoid fog in their writings. There is no place for a show off, of the great flair for writing, which the editor may have very stillfully he should adjust his vocabulary and expression to the readers' level. The matter of fact saying—'Express, do not impress'—holds good.

Printing

Once the in-house task of preparing the material and collecting the necessary photographs and illustrations is over, it is the time to move over to the printers. Most of the house journals are today printed on off-set process, particularly, if the print run is larger, ideally, more than 10,000 copies. Now it is the time for the printer and the editor to work together to publish the house journal. There is a need for active coordination between the printer and the publisher to meet the printing schedule, which may be mutually decided by putting dates to the various stages of production. A flow chart through which the process has to go through should be of interest to public relations students and house journal editors (See Exhibit 25.4).

So that there is proper coordination and understanding between the printers and the editors, it is naturally very important that they should understand each other and the terminology used in the process of publishing. They would then work in harmony and ensure meeting the schedules set by them on mutual basis. A collection of these technical terms used should be of interest to public relations professionals assigned with the responsibility of working as the editors (See Exhibit 25.5).

As most of the people engaged in the print shops are semi-literate, they may not understand the corrections marked on the proofs. Therefore, the printing industry has developed a collection of proof reading signs, which when put on the left and right margins of press proofs with an oblique in the middle of the text, is readily understood by the print shop workers and corrections carried out promptly.

This problem, however, has been mitigated to a large extent with a built-in spell check system in all the computers, yet the proof reading signs have not been done away with.

EXHIBIT 25.4   A house journal process flow chart

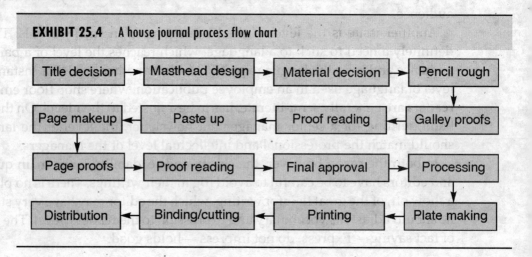

EXHIBIT 25.5	Layout and printing terminology

Artwork	Final stage of the layout before going in for processing and printing	**Impose**	Mark pages on forme to show them in correct sequence
Paste up	One stage before the final layout showing position of the matter and pictures	**Insert**	A loose sheet inserted in the publication
Dummy	A mock layout, also known as pencil rough	**Layout**	The basic design of the way publication will appear
Bleed	When photos are extended to the edge of the page in final printing leaving no space for trimming	**Letterpress**	Oldest printing process using lead typeset by hand
Block	Used in letterpress printing. Images are etched in reverse on metal plate and fixed on wooden board	**Offset printing**	The modern and faster printing process
By-line	A line attributing article to the writer's name	**Machine proof**	Press printout, one before the final
		Manuscript	Also know as MS, first draft before going to press
Caption	The lines that describe a picture	**Masthead**	Name of the publication shown on title page
Centre spread	Two page facing each other in the centre of a publication	**Page proofs**	Press proofs shown page wise for corrections
Circulation	The print order for a number of copies	**Point system**	Printer's denote typeface size in points, i.e., 1/72 inch
Composition	Setting the matter in a font size for printing	**Progressive proofs**	Proofs of the colour positives in offset printing
Copy	Editorial material meant for printing	**Ream**	A pack of 500 sheets of paper of various sizes
Cut-out	Blocking portions of a picture to bring out the most important personality or illustration	**Grammage**	The weight of one sheet in grams to show paper thickness
Drop letter	A big or ornamental type face alphabet that sinks into three or four lines, at the beginning of an article	**Screen**	Dots or lines per square centimeter to print photos
		House style	Format to follow a set style in design and fonts
Flush	Printing up to the edge of the page like bleed	**Tabloid**	Publication of half the size of a newspaper page
Gatefold	A page opens or folds out to create reader impact	**Trim size**	The final size of publication after trimming
Galley proof	First proof from press for corrections and paste up	**Wall newspaper**	A single sheet news-sheet for plastering walls
Headline	Selected words on top of the text to denote subject	**White space**	Space left in between the photos and text for reading-comfort by readers

THE LEGAL SIDE OF PUBLISHING

The public relations practitioners and editors are aware of the laws that govern the bringing out of a newspaper, magazine, or a journal. Under the Press and Registration Act 1867 (25 of 1867) certain provisions have been laid down for the preservation of copies of newspapers printed in India and for the registration of such newspapers.

The definition of 'Newspapers', as given in Section 1 of the Act, is quite wide and also covers house journals. Most of the house journals in India are already registered under the provisions of the Act. However, while starting a house journal, it is obligatory on the part of the editor, printer, and the publisher to get the publication registered. No newspaper shall be published in India unless the printer and publisher makes a declaration before the district or sub-divisional magistrate or with the press branch of the local commissioner of police, within whose jurisdiction such newspaper (house journal) is printed or published.

To file such a declaration, it is necessary for the public relations personnels to obtain a written letter from the management, appointing them as the editors of such publications. Also it is mandatory for the editors to seek advance clearance from the registrar of newspapers and periodicals, New Delhi, so that there should not, at any time, be two publications appearing under the same title.

It is also necessary to make a fresh declaration in Form I, whenever, the place of publication or printer is changed, or when the publication is temporarily suspended and later revived.

Under the Act, the publisher has to submit every year a statement in Form II, giving details about the publication, its circulation, ownership, etc. Also in the first issue of the newspaper, published after the last day of February every year, the publisher must publish a statement in the publication in Form IV.

Summary

Despite the multiplicity of newspapers and magazines now published in India, a house journal has a position of its own in the corporate world. It continues to be a major medium of communication to the internal and external publics to keep them informed and connected to the organization.

A house journal serves an organization as a two-way communication tool of inspiring the employee morale, creating a favourable working environment in the company, and also promoting goodwill amongst various publics.

Amongst the various objectives of publishing a house journal are to showcase corporate philosophy and culture, clarify company policies and practices, inform publics about the products and services, and also to foster a feeling of trust amongst various target publics.

House journals can be categorized into various kinds like internal house journal, external house journal, internal–external combined, and the market-oriented house journal.

Whereas an internal house journal helps to generate understanding between the employees and the management, inculcate employee loyalty, build team spirit, it also serves as a form to address issues like productivity, safety, quality, etc. All these aspects of management are essential for the success of a company.

An external house journal serves the company as a communication system to build trust amongst the customers, dealers, vendors, investors, etc. and help the company to take credit for the organizational achievements.

A combined company publication helps to weld relationship and understanding between the employees and various external publics and develop a healthy business relationship, so vital for the success of a venture.

A market oriented publication exclusively targets the customers and dealers and addresses all the market related issues like customer care and strengthening the dealer network.

Launching upon a house journal calls upon the managements and the public relations personnel, who generally work as editors, to bear in mind certain guidelines for success, objectives, target publics, periodicity, style, etc. As the styling involves the printing process, editors need to be familiar with printing terminology and technicalities.

Since a house journal is considered as a newspaper, enough care needs to be taken to abide by the legal requirements as stipulated in the press laws of India, such as registration of title, etc.

Key Terms

esprit de corps Feeling of pride in belonging to a group and a sense of identification with it

House journal A medium of communication which projects the image of a company or an organization to one or more sections of the public, within the organization or outside

Human interest story A news story that discusses a person or persons in an interactive and/or emotional way; presents people and their problems, concerns, or achievements in a way that brings about interest or sympathy in the reader or viewer

Journal format The size, colours, typography, etc., which are adopted as standards, issue after issue

Turnkey project A type of project that is constructed by a developer and sold or turned over to a buyer in a ready to use condition

Concept Review Questions

1. Write a note to highlight the importance of a house journal in the corporate world. Also list and explain the various objectives that a company has in publishing a house journal.
2. What are the various kinds of house journals published by the companies? Explain the characteristics and objectives of each kind.
3. What are the various aspects that must be taken care of while planning to publish a house journal? Establish your understanding of each aspect.

Project Work

1. Develop a plan to publish an employee house journal to cater to 1,000 employees working in a sugar mill, say Mawana Sugar Mills. Also show the proper flow chart to educate the management about the system.

2. Make a pencil rough layout for a eight page A4 size magazine for a pharmaceutical company, say Ranbaxy, for communicating mainly to the doctors' community about various drugs and their use in the treatment of cancer.

References

A Directory of House Journals in India (1968), published by the Indian Association of Industrial Editors, now known as Association of Business Communicators of India, p. 7.

Bhimani, Rita (1994), Monograph published by the Public Relations Society of India, Calcutta chapter, Calcutta, p. 1.

Moore, H. Frazier and Frank B. Kalupa (1987), *Public Relations, Principles, Cases and Problems*, Richard D. Irwin, Inc, USA, printed in India by Surjeet Publications, Delhi, p. 255.

Sardana, C.K. (2001), *Public Relations—An Agenda for the Next Millennium*, Public Sector Public Relations Forum, New Delhi, pp. 93–96.

Skinner, Chris, Llew von Essen, Gary Mersham, and Sejamothopo Motau (2007), *Handbook of Public Relations*, 8th edition, Oxford University Press Southern Africa (Pty) Limited, Republic of South Africa, p. 204.

26

Ethics and Public Relations

Chapter Outline
- Public relations and ethics
- Some legal aspects
- Ethical codes
- IPR code for public relations
- IPRA code of ethics
- ASCI code

PUBLIC RELATIONS AND ETHICS

No profession can succeed until backed by a code of ethics, and the public relations profession is no exception. The word 'ethics' means a system of moral principles governing the appropriate conduct of a person or a group. It includes many components, one of which is behaviour. It implies behaviour, personal or organizational, which must comply with certain standards. There are hardly two opinions about behaviour being ethical, but the subject becomes debatable as to, which behaviour is ethical and, which is not. Disagreement sets in when we begin to specify those ethical standards. Different people set different standards. These standards depend on the values and norms held by the people concerned. Since they differ from one person to the next, standards of behaviour also differ.

In the corporate and industrial world, it is generally agreed that the minimum standard for behaviour is that the laws of the country or state should be observed. Laws, however, are a reflection of the norms, values, beliefs, as well as the political system of a country. These vary from country to country. Among such values, truth and justice are of prime importance. Besides, both these values represent universally acceptable principle, which have a special relevance to the field of PR. Unfortunately, in India, the profession of PR is still perceived by many, as something that deals with wheeling dealing and juggling with rules, hence, unethical.

SOME LEGAL ASPECTS

Most of the ethical standards are not mandatory in nature and are expected to be accepted on a voluntary basis by members of a society. Despite several social controls that the society imposes on its members to follow, there is never a situation when people follow the ethical code put forth by a society. The situation calls for the formation of certain laws, which have the sanction of the government and made mandatory to be obeyed by all citizens, and flouting of which warrants certain punishments. It is, therefore, important that PR professionals have a thorough understanding of the country's laws, especially those laws which apply to the information area. The laws that govern the information dissemination, which is the prime responsibility of PR practitioners are: *libel, slander, defamation, copy right act, intellectual property rights*, and *privacy rights*.

Libel

It tantamounts to libel when an untruthful statement about a person, published in writing or through broadcast media, injures the person's reputation or standing in the community. As libel is a tort (a civil wrong), the injured person can bring a lawsuit against the person who made the false statement. Libel is a form of defamation, as is slander (an untruthful statement that is spoken, but not published in writing or broadcast through the media).

The law recognizes in every man a right to have the estimation in which they stand in the opinion of others, unaffected by false statements, to their credit. Any discouragement of a person's good name is a wrongful act, and in India, the remedy is available to the aggrieved person in a civil action under the common law or criminal proceedings for defamation. In a civil action, the claim is one essentially for damages by monetary compensation for the wrong done namely injury to character. In criminal proceedings, vindication of the grievance of the complainant is punishment with fine and/or imprisonment.

Slander

A slander is a type of defamation. Slander is an untruthful oral (spoken) statement about a person that harms the person's reputation or standing in the community. As slander is a tort (a civil wrong), the injured person can bring a lawsuit against the person, who made such a false statement. If the statement is made via broadcast media, for example, over the radio or on TV, it is considered libel, rather than slander, because the statement has the potential to reach a very wide audience and damage the reputation of a person on a larger scale.

Defamation

There emerges a case of defamation when a false statement injures someone's reputation and exposes him to public contempt, hatred, ridicule, or condemnation. If the false statement is published in print or through broadcast media, such as radio or TV, it is called libel. If it is only spoken, it is called slander.

The Indian Penal Code defines defamation as, 'Whoever by words either spoken or intended to be read or by signs or by visible representations makes or publishes any imputation concerning any person, intending to harm or knowing or having reason to believe that such imputation will harm the reputation of such person is said to defame that person.'

The press, for that matter anyone engaged in publication of information, such as the PR practitioners, do not in any way enjoy privileges or are not exempt from the purview of the law. The law treats public and the press at par, however, the journalists have to be extra careful and conscientious in this matter.

The main defences to an action for defamation are justification, privilege, fair comment, and innocent dissemination. However, there are exceptions and it may not be construed as defamation in certain situations, which like journalists, the PR practitioners may also bear in mind (See Exhibit 26.1).

Copyright Act

Copyrights are exclusive legal rights that protect works of authorship, composition, or artistry. A copyright protects the publication, production, or sale of the rights to a literary, dramatic, musical, or artistic work or computer program or to the use of a commercial print or label.

The law of copyright in India is embodied in the Copyright Act, 1957. The copyright is a right accruing to people in respect of a work produced by them as a result of exercise of skill, judgement, and labour. The law does not permit them to make profit and appropriate it to themselves what has been produced by the labour and skill of others. The noticeable feature of this enactment is that registration of any work in which copyright exists is entirely voluntary. Registration merely establishes the originality of the work. In the absence of registration, redress for infringement would be under the common law. It is open to a person to file an action for infringement and carefully apply for registration as a copyright in which case the matter would be proceeded with under the Copyright Act.

It is only desirable that PR practitioners should take due care while reproducing any matter that it be fair and for a legitimate purpose. Copyright may be infringed by using the whole or substantial part of the work in which the copyright exists, if the consent of the owner of the copyright has not been obtained.

A copyright is a form of protection provided by US law to anyone who creates 'original works of authorship'. Essentially, a copyright protects literary, musical, dramatic, artistic, and other qualifying creative works. The Copyright Act of 1976 further clarified copyright protection: A copyright owner now has the exclusive right to reproduce the work; prepare spin-off works based on the copyrighted work; and to sell, perform and/or display the copyrighted work in public.

One of the nice things about copyrights is that securing such protection is fairly straightforward. Copyright protection is created the moment one's work is fixed in a 'tangible form of expression' (paper copy, CD, disk, videotaped performance, etc.) for the first time. In other words, once one's story is put in writing, their song is transcribed as sheet music or recorded, or the creative work is given some fixed form, the copyright is automatically secured. From that moment on (assuming creation occurred after 1 January 1978), the work has copyright protection for the creator's lifetime, plus 50 years after death.

If the work was commissioned or created as part of the creator's job, the

---

EXHIBIT 26.1 Exceptions to defamation law

When the information is publicized in good faith, certain exceptions that do not attract the defamation law, can be to:

1. Impute the truth about a person for public good
2. Express in good faith any opinion respecting the conduct of a public servant in the discharge of his public functions or respecting his character so far as his character appears in that conduct
3. Express in good faith an opinion respecting the conduct of any person touching any public question
4. Publish a substantially true report of the proceedings of a court of justice and the result of such proceedings
5. Express in good faith any opinion on the merits of a civil or criminal case decided by the court or regarding the conduct of the parties or witnesses to such a case
6. Express in good faith any opinion on the merits of a performance which the author has submitted to the judgment of the public or respecting the character of the author so far as his character appears in the performance
7. Ensure in good faith the conduct of a person over whom one has authority in so far as such authority relates
8. Prefer in good faith an accusation against a person to any person having authority over that person
9. Make an imputation on the character of another in good faith if it is for the protection of the person making it or of any other or for the public good
10. Convey a caution in good faith to one person against another if such caution is for the good of the person to whom it is conveyed or for another person or for the good of the public

Source: Adapted from http://www.helplinelaw.com/docs/criminallaw/defamation.php.

employer is considered to be the author. After all, the author was paid for the work with wages. In this case, the term of copyright is calculated differently. If copies of the work are distributed to the public for sale, that first date of sale is called the publication date. The term of copyright protection is calculated as 75 years from the publication date or 100 years from the creation date; whichever is shorter.

When you see the letter 'C' enclosed in a circle — ©, you are being informed the work is declaring copyright privileges. This symbol used to be required under US law but is not required today.

Intellectual Property Rights

Intellectual Property Rights (IPR) are temporary grants of monopoly intended to give economic incentives for innovative activity. IPR exist in the form of patents, copyrights, and trademarks.
Intellectual property refers to creations of the mind: inventions, literary and artistic works, and symbols, names, images, and designs used in commerce.

Intellectual property is divided into two categories: industrial property, which includes inventions (patents), trademarks, industrial designs, and geographic indications of source; and copyright, which includes literary and artistic works, such as novels, poems, plays, films, musical works, artistic works such as drawings, paintings, photographs and sculptures, and architectural designs. Rights related to copyright include those of performing artists in their performances, producers of phonograms in their recordings, and those of broadcasters in their radio and TV programmes (Refer chapter 19).

The Central Board of Excise and Customs, New Delhi, has taken some initiatives to spread the awareness amongst people in general and businessmen in particular about the IPR and various other related statutes (See Exhibit 26.2).

Privacy Rights

In general, violation of the rights of privacy can be claimed on three grounds. First, when there has been an invasion or intrusion of a person's private affairs, seclusion, or solitude. Second, when disclosure of private facts has proved to be embarrassing. Such publicity as was given had resulted in embarrassment and had placed the person concerned in a false or bad public light. Third, intrusion can also occur as a result of mistakes, as when, without prior permission one person's photograph is used to represent someone else, especially when the latter is represented in an uncomplimentary manner.

In general, items that are considered to be newsworthy are safe from such charges. Defenders against invasion of privacy charges must show that the statement was 'of public interest'. Another line of defence is to show that the

EXHIBIT 26.2 Intellectual property rights

Imports violating Intellectual Property Rights are under watch

Imports infringing intellectual property rights of the right holders under the Copy Right Act 1957, the Trade Marks Act 1999, the Patents Act 1970, the Designs Act 2000 and the Geographical Indications of Goods (Registration and Protection) Act 1999 are prohibited by law.* The Intellectual Property Rights (Imported Goods) Enforcement Rules 2007** lay down detailed procedures to be followed by the right holders as well as Customs Authority for suspension of clearance of such goods and other related matters. The right holders under Copy Right Act 1957,

Trade Marks Act 1999, Patents Act 1970, Designs Act 2000, and Geographical Indications of Goods (Registration and Protection) Act 1999, who desire to have clearance of infringing goods suspended, shall be required to give notice to the jurisdictional Commissioner of Customs or an officer authorised by him in the manner as specified in the said Rules, and shall also be required to follow the procedures and conditions specified therein.

Visit our website:
http://www.cbec.gov.in
http://www.icegate.gov.in
for further details.

* Notification No. 49/2007-Customs (NT) dated 8-5-2007
** Issued under notification No. 47/2007-Customs (NT) dated 8-5-2007

As a trade facilitation measure enabling right holders to file the notice electronically, a user friendly web-enabled application form has been made available at http://www.icegate.gov.in

CENTRAL BOARD OF EXCISE AND CUSTOMS
North Block, New Delhi

Source: *Hindustan Times*, 9 March 2008.

complainant is a 'public figure'. The line of defence would also be clear if the reported matter were already a matter of public record. In addition the reported matter could be shown to have some 'social value'.

ETHICAL CODES

Ethical behaviour goes beyond just observance of the law. Observing the law, in letter and spirit, warrants the minimum required behaviour. Therefore, a voluntary discipline called a 'code of conduct' has been devised by PR practitioners and other professionals for themselves. Such codes, because they are based on actual practice and are devised by people professionally operating in that area, become relevant and acceptable.

Some common principles can be found in most codes of professional conduct and they apply to most professions. One general principle applicable to all professions is that there should be no conflict of interests. This means no client, who is in an adversary or competitive role to another, should be contracted.

Also the PR practitioners should not have any vested interest in the activity that they undertake. This principle also states that one's own interests should be disclosed fully to stay clear of any complication. If the practitioners stand to gain commercially from a certain course of action that they recommend, then they should disclose their interests fully. Transparency is the bottom line of professional ethics.

As many provisions of the codes deal with information, it is advisable not to knowingly or recklessly disseminate false or misleading information, and even avoid doing so inadvertently. Information should not be used or divulged without express consent of the client or employer. Any form of action, which would tend to corrupt the integrity of the media communication, must be avoided.

Codes are also formulated by several specialized groups amongst members. More attention is paid to the requirements of its own members. Despite attempts to be as comprehensive as possible, codes can never be complete. Also there is no compulsion in observing them. Yet, the moral force behind these principles make the members believe in the codes and also find it advantageous to follow. Non-observance of these codes may attract penalty, though not legal, yet by peer censure, which may hamper or lower the reputation of a professional amongst his colleagues, friends, and competitors in the same vocation.

No other mechanism of enforcement may be necessary, if the code is respected and adhered to by all. The observance of ethics goes to enhance the professional reputation of its members. By fostering spirit of ethics, there emerges an ethical relationship amongst the members of the association and the publics.

A code of ethics, when accepted voluntarily, serves as a professional benchmark by which one's colleagues can be measured. It provides strength and justification to those who insist on doing only what the code of conduct advocates. Contrary to the general comment that 'Everything is fair in business and love', the observance of moral code leads to emergence of an image which is invaluable in business. PR practitioners are particularly mindful of this professional fact of life. Several global companies fanatically guarding their policies and practices world over, testify this value system.

IPR CODE FOR PUBLIC RELATIONS

Though the associations of PR professionals in India have not so far paid much attention to developing a code of conduct for themselves, yet they are all conscious of the standards advocated by some international professional bodies like Institute of Public Relations (IPR) and International Public Relations Association (IPRA).

The Institute of Public Relations, UK, has developed for its members a code for professional PR practice, which provides PR practitioners with guidelines for ethics in their working and operations. The code has been revised from time to time to be compatible with the prevailing business and economic environment. The IPR code of professional conduct should interest the students and professionals alike (See Exhibit 26.3).

EXHIBIT 26.3 The IPR code of professional conduct

The conduct concerning the profession of public relations

1. A member shall:

1.1. Have a positive duty to uphold the highest standards in the practice of public relations and to deal fairly and honestly with employers and clients (past and present), fellow members and professionals, the public relations profession, other professions, suppliers, intermediaries, the media of communication, employees, and the public.

1.2. Be aware of, understand, and agree to abide by this code, any amendments to it, and any other codes, which shall be incorporated into it; remain up-to-date with the content and recommendations of any guidance or practice papers issued by the IPR; and have a duty to conform to good practice as expressed in such guidance or practice papers.

1.3. Observe this code and cooperate with fellow members to enforce decisions on any matter arising from its application. A member without knowingly causes or allows his or her staff to act in a manner inconsistent with this code is party to such an action and shall be deemed to be in breach of this code. Staff employed by a member who act in a manner inconsistent with this code should be disciplined by the member.

A member shall not:

1.4. Professionally engage in any practice, or be seen to conduct him or herself in any manner detrimental to the reputation of the Institute or the reputation and interests of the public relations profession.

Conduct concerning the public, the media, and other professionals

2. A member shall:

2.1. Conduct his or her professional activities with proper regard to the public interest.

2.2. Have a positive duty at all times to respect the truth and shall not disseminate false and misleading information knowingly or recklessly, and take proper care to check all information prior to its dissemination.

2.3. Have a duty to ensure that the actual interest, or likely conflict of interest, of any organization with which he or she may be professionally concerned is adequately declared.

2.4. When working in association with other professionals or institutions, identify and respect the codes of those professional or institutions.

2.5. Respect any statutory or regulatory codes laid down by any other authorities or institutions, which are relevant to the actions of his or her employer or client, or taken on behalf of an employer or client.

2.6. Ensure that the names and pecuniary interests of individual members, all directors, executives and retained advisors of his or her employers or company who hold public office are disclosed and recorded in the IPR register of interests. This includes members of either of the Houses of Parliament of the United Kingdom or the European Parliament, a local authority or any statutory body.

2.7. Honour confidences received or given in the course of professional activity.

2.8. Neither propose or undertake, nor cause any employer, employee, or client to propose or undertake any action, which would be an improper influence on government, legislation, holders of public office or members of any statutory body or organization, or the means of communication.

2.9. Take all reasonable care to ensure that professional duties are conducted without giving cause for complaints of discrimination on grounds of age, disability, gender, race, religion or other unacceptable references.

(contd.)

Exhibit 26.3 (contd.)

Conduct concerning employers and clients

3. A member shall:

3.1. Safeguard the confidences of both present and former employers of clients: shall not disclose or use these confidences to the disadvantage or prejudice or such employers or clients or to the financial advantage of the member (unless the employer or client has released such information for public use or has given specific permission for the disclosure), except on the order of the court of law.

3.2. Inform an employer or client of any shareholding or financial interest held by that member or any staff employer by that member in any company or person whose services he or she recommends.

3.3. Be free to accept fees, commissions or other valuable considerations from persons other than the employer or client, if such considerations are disclosed to the employer or client.

3.4. Be free to negotiate and renegotiate with an employer or client terms that are a fair reflection on demands of the work involved and take into account factors other than hours worked and the experience involved. These special factors, which are applied also by other professional advisors, shall have regard to all the circumstances the specific situation and in particular to:
   (a) the complexity of the issue, case, problem, or assignment and the difficulties associated with its completion
   (b) the professional and specialized skills required and the degree of responsibility involved
   (c) the amount of documentation necessary to be perused or prepared, and its importance
   (d) the place and circumstances where the work was carried out, in whole or in part
   (e) the scope, scale, and value of the task and its importance as an activity, issue or project to the employer or client.

A member shall not:

3.5. Misuse information regarding his or her employer's client's business for financial or other gain.

3.6. Use inside information for gain. Not may a member of staff managed or employed by a member directly trade in his or her employer's or client's securities without prior written permission of the employer or client and the member's chief executive or chief financial officer or compliance officer.

3.7. Serve an employer and client under terms or conditions, which might impair his or her independence, objectivity, or integrity.

3.8. Represent conflicting interests but may represent conflicting interests with the express consent of the parties concerned.

3.9. Guarantee the achievement of results, which are beyond the member's direct capacity to achieve or prevent.

Conduct concerning colleagues

4. A member shall:

4.1. Adhere to the highest standards of accuracy and truth, avoiding extravagant claims and unfair comparisons and giving credit for ideas and words borrowed from others.

4.2. Be free to represent his or her capabilities and service to any potential employer or client, either on his or her own initiative or at the behest of any client, provided in doing so he or she does not seek to break any existing contract or detract from the reputation or capabilities of any member already serving that employer or client.

4.3. Injure the professional reputation or practice of another member.

In the interpretation of this code, the Laws of the Land shall apply.

Source: Adapted from Institute of Public Relations, UK, www.ipr.org.uk.

EXHIBIT 26.4　The Code of Brussels

Adopted in 2006, the Code of Brussels, building on the Codes of Venice and Athens, specifies the conditions for the ethical practice of public affairs.

RECALLING that the Code of Venice 1961 and the Code of Athens 1965, of the International Public Relations Association, which together specify an undertaking of ethical conduct by public relations practitioners worldwide;

RECALLING that the Code of Athens binds public relations practitioners to respect the Charter of the United Nations which reaffirms 'its faith in fundamental human rights, in the dignity and worth of the human person';

RECALLING that the Code of Athens binds public relations practitioners to observe the moral principles and rules of the 'Universal Declaration of Human Rights';

RECALLING that public affairs is one discipline undertaken by public relations practitioners;

RECALLING that the conduct of public affairs provides essential democratic representation to public authorities;

This Code of Brussels is a code of ethical conduct applying to public relations practitioners worldwide as they conduct public affairs and interact with public authorities including staff and public representatives. In the conduct of public affairs, practitioners shall:

1. Integrity
Act with honesty and integrity at all times so as to secure the confidence of those with whom the practitioner comes into contact;

2. Transparency
Be open and transparent in declaring their name, organization, and the interest they represent;

3. Dialogue
Establish the moral, psychological, and intellectual conditions for dialogue, and recognise the rights of all parties involved to state their case and express their views;

4. Accuracy
Take all reasonable steps to ensure the truth and accuracy of all information provided to public authorities;

5. Falsehood
Not intentionally disseminate false or misleading information, and shall exercise proper care to avoid doing so unintentionally and correct any such act promptly;

6. Deception
Not obtain information from public authorities by deceptive or dishonest means;

7. Confidentiality
Honour confidential information provided to them;

8. Influence
Neither propose nor undertake any action which would constitute an improper influence on public authorities;

9. Inducement
Neither directly nor indirectly offer nor give any financial or other inducement to members of public authorities or public representatives;

10. Conflict
Avoid any professional conflicts of interest and to disclose such conflicts to affected parties when they occur;

11. Profit
Not sell for profit to third parties copies of documents obtained from public authorities;

12. Employment
Only employ personnel from public authorities subject to the rules and confidentiality requirements of those authorities.

Sanctions
Practitioners shall co-operate with fellow members in upholding this Code and agree to abide by and help enforce the disciplinary procedures of the International Public Relations Association in regard to any breaching of this Code.

Source: Adapted from International Public Relations Association, www.ipra.org/detail. asp? articleid = 25.

IPRA CODE OF ETHICS

In absence of a code of ethics of their own, the PR professionals in India more often make a reference to international codes like the one developed by the International Public Relations Association (IPRA) in Athens in 1965. This code was developed to get international agreement and acceptance of certain PR practices. Most of its clauses are, therefore, expressed in general terms to make the code applicable to different countries and situations. IPRA being a very vibrant public relations association in the world, keeps revising and updating the code of ethics, at the various international conferences held at intervals.

The Athens Code of 1965 was further modified and improved by the IPRA in 1968, and updated in 2006, and is now known as Code of Brussels, which is expected to serve as a beacon light for the professionals worldwide (See Exhibit 26.4).

ASCI CODE

In the much related field of advertising, that often overlaps with public relations, the Indian advertising industry has formed an Advertising Standards Council of India (ASCI) with a code that seeks to ensure that the advertising profession conforms to its code of self-regulation, which requires the advertisements to be truthful and fair to the consumers and competitors. Although the decisions of the council have no legal bearing, yet it has been reported that most of the agencies and professionals have, by and large followed the code. Some of the salient features of the code should be of interest to the PR practitioners (See Exhibit 26.5).

EXHIBIT 26.5   Advertising Standards Council of India Code

Salient features of ASCI Code

1. Advertising messages should be so designed as to conform not only to the laws but also to the moral, aesthetic, and religious sentiments of the country in which it is published.
2. Advertisements that are likely to bring contempt or disrepute to the profession should not be allowed.
3. Advertising should be truthful, avoid distorting facts, and misleading the public by means of implications and omissions.
4. Advertising should not be permitted to contain exaggerated claims that inevitably disappoint the public.
5. Direct comparison with competing brands or firms and disparaging references are in no circumstances permitted.
6. Indecent, vulgar, suggestive, repulsive, or offensive themes or treatment should be avoided.
7. No advertisement should offer to refund the money paid.
8. Advertisements must not carry claim of drugs to prevent or cure any diseases or ailments specified in Schedule J.

Source: Adapted from Jethwaney, Jaishri and Shruti Jain (2006).

Summary

No profession can succeed without a code of ethics and PR is no exception. Ethics are beyond the scope of law and deal with norms, values, beliefs, and reflect in the functional system of an organization or the political structure of a country.

PR professionals, whereas they are expected to follow certain ethics, have also to be mindful of the laws governing the information area, which is the focal part of public relations function.

Laws such as libel, slander, defamation, copyright act, intellectual property rights, and privacy rights are the legal aspects governing the area of information dissemination.

The law of defamation is an important element and does not distinguish between the general public, press, and the public relations practitioners. However, the information when published in good faith and public interest or concerning the discharge of public duties by an official, does not attract the provisions of the defamation law.

The copyright act protects the exclusive rights over the writings and works of art born out of the skill and experience of an individual and unauthorized copying of the same tantamount to infringement and hence illegal.

The intellectual property rights grant monopoly over patents, copyrighted material, and trademarks, etc.

Privacy rights grant an individual the right to privacy and safeguards against intrusion into their private affairs.

Although the associations of public relations practitioners in India have not developed a voluntary code of conduct of their own, yet often references are made to IPR Code and IPRA Code of Brussels.

In the much related field of advertising, ASCI exercises a moral authority on the ethics of communication, as far as advertising is concerned. The code equally relates to the profession of public relations, to a considerable extent.

Key Terms

Code of conduct A set of unwritten rules according to which people in a particular group, class, or situation are supposed to behave

Copyright The legal right of creative artists or publishers to control the use and reproduction of their original works

Copyright act The law does not permit somebody to make profit and appropriate it to oneself what has been produced by the labour and skill of another

Defamation To attack somebody or somebody's reputation, character, or good name by making slanderous or libelous statements

Ethics A system of moral principles governing the appropriate conduct for a person or group

Intellectual property Original creative work manifested in a tangible form that can be legally protected, e.g., by a patent, trademark, or copyright

Invasion of privacy Offensive or unjustifiable access obtained to someone's personality or personal affairs without their permission and/or knowledge

Libel   Negligent or intentional publication or broadcast of a defamatory statement that exposes a person to contempt, disrespect, hatred, or ridicule

Patent   The exclusive right to use documented intellectual property in producing or selling a particular product or using a process for a designated period of time

Privacy   The right to be free from secret surveillance and to determine whether, when, how, and to whom, one's personal or organizational information is to be revealed

Privacy rights The right against unsanctioned invasion of privacy by the government, corporations, or individuals

Slander   The act or offense of saying something false or malicious that damages somebody's reputation

Trademark   A distinctive name or symbol used to identify a product or company and build recognition

Concept Review Questions

1. Write a lucid note on the various laws, which have a bearing on public relations function of dissemination of information.
2. What is the law of defamation? What are the various situations and actions that do not attract the provisions of defamation law?
3. Compare the ethical codes developed by the Institute of Public Relations (IPR) and the International Public Relations Association (IPRA) and bring out the commonalities.
4. How is the ethical code of Advertising Standards Council of India (ASCI) relevant to the profession of public relations? Discuss.

Project Work

1. Develop a communication in the form of an advertisement, for publishing in daily newspapers, to clarify and educate the public about the efficacy of a drug 'AIDGO' manufactured by your company, say ABC Pharmaceuticals, about which a rumour has spread that it causes cancer as a side effect. Also send an alert to the public about some parties manufacturing and marketing fake drugs under your company's brand name.
2. Develop a ten point ethical code for the Indian public relations professionals which, in your best estimation, should be followed voluntarily to establish and enhance the reputation and credibility of the public relations profession in India.

References

Hindustan Times, New Delhi, 9 March 2008, p. 17.

Jefkins, Frank (2006), *Public Relations for Your Business*, Management Books 2000 Limited, UK, published in India by Jaico Publishing House, Mumbai, pp. 199–202.

Jethwaney, Jaishri and Shruti Jain (2006), *Advertising Management*, Oxford University Press, YMCA, New Delhi, pp. 481–482.

Mint, New Delhi, 17 September 2008, vol II, no. 221, p. 3.

Mint, New Delhi, 24 September 2008.

Mint, New Delhi, 10 October 2008, vol 2, no. 241, p. 1.

24 and 17 September 2008, vol. II no. 221, p. 3.

Bahl, Sushil (ed) (1991), Public Relations Manual, Advertising Agencies Association of India, Bombay, pp. 59–65.

www.ipra.org/detail.asp? articleid = 25

www. ipr.org.uk

PART V

SUPPORT SERVICE

Chapter 27: Public Relations Agency

27 Public Relations Agency

PUBLIC RELATIONS AGENCY DEFINED

A public relations agency is a professional outfit, which functions independently for a fee or on a retainership basis for one or more client companies, to advise and counsel them on virtually all aspects of public relations—employee public relations, media relations, marketing aspects, and even public affairs. It counsels and assists the company in several aspects of business like dealer and shareholder relations and even lobbying on behalf of the company. Since PR is a top management responsibility, an agency functions in consultation with senior management levels rather than working with lower ranks of the organization.

In stricter sense of the profession, persons engaged in press agentry, lobbying, liaison work, publicity experts, union management conciliators, motivation specialists, or even ghost writers, who may claim themselves to be running such outfits, does not deserve to be called as such. PR agency is a very demure and professionally sound organization, which gets associated with another business company to serve as a public arm to the company in all matters related to a company's business activities. This is not a 'kiss and go' relationship, but a marriage of the two professional outfits based on understanding and trust.

However, as generally perceived or expected, a PR agency is not a miracle maker but an ethical and professionally sound business organization, which takes care of the client's needs and eventualities, dispassionately, for a fee.

Delving on the PR counsel role, Philip Lesly (1992) wrote, 'The public relations counsel is often the face of an organization put before its most important publics: the press and broadcasters, important organizations, schools, communities, all of whom the counsel deals with on behalf of the client. For this reason, the counsel an organization chooses is important to its own "image". The organization frequently can rise no higher in the esteem than the caliber of counsel it retains, no matter how good a programme may be conceived and executed. For this reason, the caliber of a counsel's stature and clientele is one of the most important measures to be applied by a prospective client. A client concerned about its esteem and prestige is more likely to advance it with a counsel who is esteemed than with one known for lesser characteristics.... In a real sense, clients and counsel tend to find each other on the basis of characteristics they have in common.'

The foregoing leads to some conclusions that a PR agency and its personnel should have some unique abilities to strike a business-like chord with the clients. The mismatch can be disastrous as it is of great importance that the agency personnel should come up to the intellectual level and business expectations of the clients.

An agency is often endowed with the skills, imagination, and creativity to devise certain ideas and programmes, which the in-house public relations often are unable to perceive. Notably, the internal PR personnel are more conditioned to the corporate cultures and policies and may suffer from the lack of boldness of a professional. The agency often enjoys the benefit of free thinking without any hangover of clients of policies, likes or dislikes, and as such, offers some breezy ideas to the client, which are mutually beneficial.

As such, an agency should have some unique characteristics to generate and create programmes, activities, and events that can help the clients to meet their corporate PR objectives. Some of these may be the following:

- The agency should have the courage and guts to think creatively and logically but with sharp focus on the problems of the client.
- The agency should have a good judgement of the environment in which the client is conducting its business.
- The agency personnel should be competent in their ability to speak and write with sharpness and clarity.
- The agency should have a far sight to visualize the present and future through a deep study beyond usual dimensions.
- The agency and its personnel should have the necessary management skills

to direct, guide, and control the elements of the programmes when floated for implementation.

- The agency should never lose objectivity and honesty of purpose and compromise their own view points, as outsiders, and not get conditioned in their thinking.
- The agency should be flexible in its attitude and have an open mind to think that 'there must be a better way'.
- The agency should have the ability to sell ideas and causes to the client like a skilled sales person.
- The agency should have the courage of its conviction and stick to the guns, even if it means risking business.
- The agency should have an eye for details and be able to pick some finer points from the larger plans.
- The agency should have an inclination to take interest in people and their behaviour and should be able to relate behaviour patterns to the problems and solutions.
- The agency and its personnel should have the humility, polish, and sharp sense of humour to enliven the relations with clients in carrying out the campaign programmes.

Highlighting a public relations agency's role as an outsider counsellor and yet connected with the inner core of the client's business, Cutlip et al. (1985) wrote, 'Counsellors rank *variety of talents and skills* as their greatest advantage, compared with internal staffing. The *objectivity*, as relatively free agents untrammeled by the politics within an organization, ranks second. The *range of prior experience* is third, the *geographical scope* of their operations fourth, and the *ability to reinforce and upgrade a client's internal staff* fifth.'

FUNCTIONS OF A PR AGENCY

From one man outfits, the PR agencies have come to establish themselves as full service agencies to assist the clients in various aspects of the management of their companies. The agency services extend from the internal public relations to almost all functional areas of a company and fill in a useful and vital role in making the companies function congenially and profitably.

According to the Public Relations Society of America, a PR counselling firm is expected to assist their clients in a wide range of activities which cover the following:

- Establishment and definition of short- and long-range public relations goals
- Counsel and guidance to management on actions or policies, which affect public relations goals

- Support of the marketing programmes, including product or process publicity, news releases, feature articles, case studies, audio visual aids, press, radio, and TV coverage
- Stockholder and financial relations, annual, quarterly, or interim reports to shareholders, special releases to financial news media, assistance with the annual meeting, liaison with security analysis, investment dealers, and the professional investment community
- Employee and internal communications, company publications, information programme for employees on profits, the economics of industry, quality control, and over-all company operations
- Community relations, counsel of public relations policies at the local plant or branch office level, liaison with local news media, assistance in establishing policies of corporate giving, staging special events such as open houses and plant tours
- Government relations, international, federal, state, and local, PR counselling and liaison with agencies of government officials whose policies influence the operations of the client
- Evaluation and measurement, analysis of the effectiveness of public relations programmes, application and use of budget, and attainment of objectives
- Industry—education cooperation—helping preparing teaching aids in cooperation with teachers; creating programmes for the recruitment of scientific personnel from colleges; conducting seminars in which industry executives meet and discuss with educators industry problems; arranging educators to carry out research projects; developing plans for financial assistance to educational institutions; and providing programmes of instructional assistance and in-service development of teachers.

A HISTORICAL PERSPECTIVE

The American Scene

With the American democracy attaining maturity and the media becoming more and more a complex mechanism, a new kind of professionals called press agents came into existence. This vocation further transformed itself a new brand of public relations counsellors some time during the 1930s. The main task that they undertook for certain corporations was to restore public confidence in their business, so far lost due to bringing in of a new value system by the labour insurgency fostered by the New Deal movement in the American history.

To start with most of the PR counsellors were one-man shops and they continued their business operations till the end of the Second World War in 1944. When the business recovered from the pangs of war psychosis, certain enterprising men set up some counsellor firms or for that matter PR agencies, some of which are still in business. In this context some of the pioneers like Ivy Lee, Edward L. Barneys, Albert Lasker, etc., who made notable contributions to the profession, spearheaded the agency business and strengthened their organizations by nurturing teams of professionals and made them a part of their counselling firms.

Today, it is estimated that there are at least 750 public relations agencies or counselling firms which are members of the Public Relations Society of America. The Yellow Pages reported some time in the past that there are more than 4,000 public relations firms operating in USA. The number of persons engaged in the PR work are estimated to be more than 1,20,000. Today, most of the corporations worth their salt have contracted the counsellor or public relations firms in addition to their internal public relations departments. However, some other companies occasionally contract the PR agencies on assignment-related consultancies.

The Indian Scenario

In India, till the early eighties, for all PR activities and issues, the companies mainly depended on the advertising agencies, as the PR was only a misnomer. Then a spate of public issues by the companies to raise capital from the market, brought in an opportunity for the PR practitioners to showcase the prowess of the profession. One universal reason for the surge of the PR agency business was that in addition to the paid for advertising by the fund raisers, which usually suffered from the credibility problems, the media coverage by journalists, often prompted by agency personnel, carried far greater credibility for the investors.

Then started the corporate wars, which have been a blessing in disguise for the public relations profession vis-à-vis the agency business. With Reliance defending their corporate image and the Escorts Limited and DCM group fighting the hostile takeover threats by Lord Swaraj Paul, the PR saw for itself a role cut out in the process. The daily reporting about the developments in the media columns, relegated the advertising to a secondary role.

Murad Ali Baig, who, as the PR manager, was deeply involved in the Escorts takeover episode at that time, wrote in an article in *The Observer of Business and Politics* (7 June 1996) that the 'rising media costs also played a role. To be heard over the cacophonic din of advertisers hawking their products, services and image needed huge sums of advertising money. PR, however, was not money intensive but very activity intensive because what a client did or was being perceived to be doing determined media interest. Small clients who could not afford big advertisement spends found that they could generate highly significant PR awareness if they could find ways to make their corporate story interesting to the journalistic world.'

The government of India's policy of liberalization and globalization after 1985 opened the floodgates for many multinational corporations to enter India to do business. Right on their heels followed some of the PR consultancy firms to take advantage of the new opportunities emanating in India. World famous agencies entered into partnership deal with their Indian counterparts, giving a push to the PR agency business. For instance, Burston Maarsteller tied a knot with Roger Pariera, Hill and Knowlton tied up with IPAN. Several PR outfits with links to foreign advertising agencies tied up loosely with branches of the foreign agencies in India. At the same time, several Indian entrepreneurs engaged in the communication business floated their own public relations agencies, specially to take care of the PR needs of the companies vying to take good slice of the capital market.

The scene, since then, has taken a turn in favour of the PR agency business. Like in the US, where some leading advertising agencies added public relations as an additional service to the clients, some well known Indian agencies also floated subsidiary companies under the same banner. IPAN, affiliated to the J. Walter Thompson (then known as Hindustan Thompson Associates) was perhaps, the first one. PR agencies like Enterprise, FSA, Sistas, Mudra, O&M, LinPR, etc. became active to take advantage of the developments taking place in the market.

Over a period of three or more decades, the PR agency business, with its ups and downs linked to the business climate of India, has survived. Now with the business scenario looking up, the agency business is here to stay and prosper. According to some rough estimate, there are more than 200 agencies functioning and some of them are well known. It is quite relevant to know the leading public relations agencies of India and their clients (See Chapter 3 Exhibit 3.5).

SELECTION OF A PR AGENCY

There are two schools of thought about the appointment of a public relations agency. One school thinks that it is rather risky to contract an outside agency, as it means sharing of lot of sensitive information with the outsiders, who may leak it out to competition and thus, bring loss of business and reputation.

On the contrary, several professionals are of the view that agencies, which are professional and committed to a code of conduct and ethics, would not indulge into practices that would let their clients down. The agency business to a very large extent depends on the reputation of an outfit and once that asset of reputation is lost in the market, the door for more business is closed. Agency even runs the risk of losing some valuable clients, and may have to close shop.

The Public Relations Society of America (PRSA), in article 5 of the Code of

Ethics have spelled it out in clear terms and all responsible public relations agencies everywhere vouch to adhere to this ethic (See Exhibit 27.1).

Taking a cue from the world of advertising agency business, which is intimately related to PR, maintaining confidentiality of client's information is a vital question. According to a report on the subject in the *Mint* (5 November 2008), a media specialist such as Chandradeep Mitra, President, Mudra Max, Mudra Communications Private Limited, says, 'Sharing of category knowledge is fine as long as no client-specific information slips out.' He, however, points out that agencies, in their enthusiasm to handle diverse clients where there could be a conflict of interest, do not have the right controls in place. Agencies handling rival accounts can find themselves in a tight spot when dubious clients demand competitive information. Mitra recalls an incident when a client demanded something similar from him and he had resisted. 'Top bosses must not break the rules, however much the pressure,' he maintains, advising that 'it's prudent to limit access to confidential brand information.'

For obvious reasons, while selecting a PR agency, a company management has to take into consideration many factors and aspects. Since the agency, thenceforth, will work in tandem with the company, almost like an integral part of the organization, it is only appropriate to go through all the pros and cons of the proposal and the professional profile of the agency. Due care also needs to be taken if the agency size and resources are compatible with the stature, nature, and size of the business, the company is involved in.

The counsellor section of PRSA suggests that there is a need for getting answers to the following questions, before a final decision is taken on the selection and retaining of the agency. The questions are the following:

EXHIBIT 27.1   PRSA ethics—Article 5

A member shall safeguard the confidences of present and former clients, as well as of those persons or entities who have disclosed confidences to a member in the context of communications relating to an anticipated professional relationship with such member, and shall not accept retainers or employment that may involve disclosing, using, or offering to use such confidences to the disadvantage or prejudice of such present, former, or potential clients or employers. Interpretation of the article:

1. This article does not prohibit a member who has knowledge of client or employer activities which are illegal from making such disclosures to the proper authorities as he or she believes are legally required.

2. Communications between practitioner and client/employer are deemed to be confidential under Article 5 of the Code of Professional Standards. However, although practitioner–client/employer communications are considered confidential between the parties, such communications are not privileged against disclosure in a court of law.

3. In the absence of contractual arrangement, the client or employer legally owns the right to papers or material created for him.

Source: Extract from the Code of Professional Standards adapted by the Public Relations Society of America, as adapted, approved, and revised by the PRSA Assembly in 1963, 1977, and 1983.

- What is the professional competence and background of the principals of the counselling firm?
- How much of this experience has been in areas of particular importance to the organization seeking counsel?
- What is the general reputation of the counselling firm; does it adhere to the PRSA code of ethics, and are the counsel's integrity and professional standing above reproach?
- Who are the present clients of the counsel; how long have these organizations been served; and what is the rate of client turnover?
- Who among the principals and staff of the counselling firm will be working on the account; and what are their qualifications, special training, and background as related to the needs of the organization?
- Does the counsellor make speculative presentations?

Although it may not sound practicable to apply the American ethics of agency business to the Indian situation, yet the ethics seem universal in nature and hence, good to follow. However, a client can always draw up the terms and conditions of the contract to wrap up the ethics into it to make the arrangement practical and workable.

Some of the practices of advertising industry seem good enough for the PR agency business. For instance, it may be considered illogical and unethical for an agency to represent two conflicting and competitive accounts, until both such clients give their express consent to do so. But as a rule, it is not done.

Keeping the sensitive information confidential for both the former and the present clients is considered a sacrosanct norm, which the clients would insist and the agency should observe. It appears absolutely unethical for an agency to siphon such information to the present client for some commercial or business benefits. Some clients are quite touchy about this aspect. According to a report in the *Mint* (5 November 2008) '…clients like Proctor and Gamble Co. have been known to make surprise visits to agencies to make sure that fool proof systems exist….'

Although much as the clients would like to extract an assurance from an agency about the guaranteed achievement of certain results, yet it is neither professional nor logical for an agency to give such an undertaking to the client. Since the total business environment is constantly exposed to changes, such assurances may boomerang on the agency, hence not advisable.

Advantages of Retaining a PR Agency

Some PR professionals are of the opinion that retaining the services of a public relations agency has several advantages for a company. They think that the in-house PR personnel may soon get cast into a rigid company mould and suffer from mental blocks to experiment with the new ideas, so essential for the public relations effort to be creative and interesting. On the other hand, the outside agency enjoys the freedom to think with an open mind and try out several creative public relations solutions to several issues related to the clients. However, contracting a public relations agency also has certain disadvantages and limitations. Motivated by the priority to generate revenue, an agency may resort to suggesting solutions that would be good enough for collecting agency fee and commissions. A look at the comparison of advantages and disadvantages of retaining an agency should be relevant for the students and professionals alike (See Exhibit 27.2).

THE AGENCY STRUCTURE

A comparison of the organizational charts of the various PR agencies would reveal that there is no set pattern as far as the management hierarchy is concerned.

EXHIBIT 27.2   PR agency retainership—a comparison

Advantages

- Agency specialists give expert advice to the clients on diversified aspects of company affairs and issues.
- Generally an agency carries more credibility with top management than the in-house public relations department.
- A public relations agency is more economical to retain, for a medium size company than maintaining an in-house public relations department.
- A PR agency brings in a diversity of specialization to deal with complex management problems.
- A vibrant and established agency can express independent opinions and ideas without fear of losing a client.
- PR agency has a wider public perspective to offer than the 'myopic' perceptions of in-house public relations.
- A PR agency which is a flexible outfit, can adjust its services to a client's needs, which differ from company to company.
- Public relations agencies, due to the exigencies of business, maintain a data base of target publics so as to reach them, when needed.

Disadvantages

- A public relations agency is handicapped in its grasp over the internal problems and policies of the company in comparison with the in-house public relations department.
- Most public relations agencies have a major focus on the marketing activities of a company like product publicity, but may not be competent to advise the management on matters ranging from employee relations to community activities.
- A public relations agency may have superficial involvement in a company's policies and practices and hence may remain a cosmetic attachment to the organization.
- A public relations agency may face an under current of resentment to their presence by the in-house public relations personnel who may perceive themselves incapable of handling the job to the entire confidence and satisfaction of the management.
- The in-house public relations manager may get overwhelmed by the presence of the public relations agency personnel, who snobbishly masquerade the contacts with the top bosses.
- The agency fee, generally high, may make the company management feel as an additional drain on the expense account.

EXHIBIT 27.3 A public relations agency structure

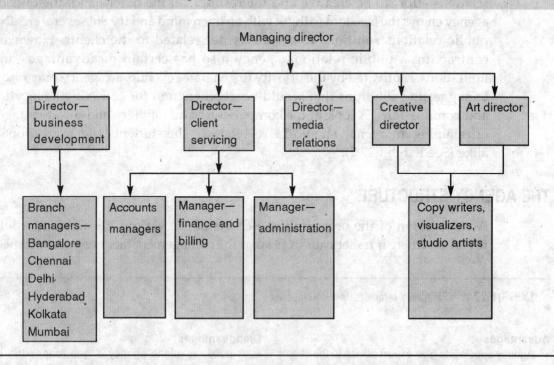

The agencies are structured according to the exigencies and the size of the operation that may change with the growth and expansion of the business. Each agency may have its own structure and the designated positions of its personnel. There is no hard and fast rule that governs the structuring of the agency personnel (See Exhibit 27.3).

AGENCY EVALUATION OR AUDIT

The relationship between the PR agency and the client is purely based on a businesslike association. All clients invariably expect their agency to be effective and assist them in accomplishing the corporate PR goals. Although an agency is retained by a client as an independent professional consultancy service with trust, yet the relationship is rather sensitive and fragile. Many professionals think that this relationship is like an arranged Indian marriage but is always on the rocks. In other words, the client is always watching the agency the way it performs and the results it delivers, as per its expectations.

This sensitive relationship leads to the need for a periodic evaluation of the agency performance by the client. According to some PR practitioners, certain parameters which may be applied to the agency audit, can be: *knowledge of clients' business, understanding of clients' PR objectives, responsiveness to clients' brief, ability to understand clients' problems, ability to plan creative events, ability to devise effective communications, competence to handle company publications, influential media network, agency–client congenial relationship,* and *cost consciousness.* For a ready reckoner audit system, see Exhibit 27.4.

Knowledge of Clients' Business

The client–agency relationship can only grow and flourish if the agency thoroughly understands the nature of the business the client is in. It should not be very difficult for an agency to know the clients' business from several sources, including media and Internet, yet the professional clients willingly sharing enough information with the agencies facilitates their effective agency functioning in the mutual interest. Whereas the agencies take lot of interest and pains to keep the clients updated about the environmental and economic changes and how these changes would affect the clients' business, the clients also share enough information in their own interest. The level of such knowledge serves as a basis for agency evaluation.

Understanding of Clients' PR Objectives

Most professional companies have their corporate PR objectives and annually

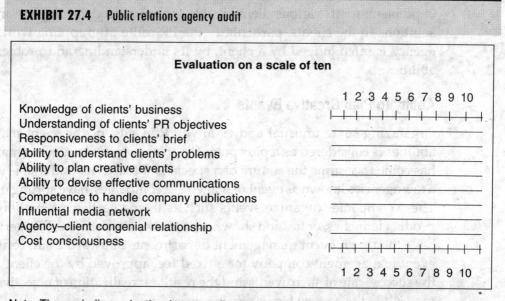

EXHIBIT 27.4   Public relations agency audit

Evaluation on a scale of ten

1 2 3 4 5 6 7 8 9 10

Knowledge of clients' business
Understanding of clients' PR objectives
Responsiveness to clients' brief
Ability to understand clients' problems
Ability to plan creative events
Ability to devise effective communications
Competence to handle company publications
Influential media network
Agency–client congenial relationship
Cost consciousness

1 2 3 4 5 6 7 8 9 10

Note: The periodic evaluation is generally done on an annual basis but it may be done at intervals, as the clients deem fit. Obviously, if the rating in majority of the parameters is less than five, it is obvious that it is time for the client either to change the agency or to counsel the agency to improve performance.

review and rewrite them with an invitation to the agency to participate in the exercise. The PR agency, as an independent outfit with wider exposures, is in an advantageous position to advise the client in the process. This means the fuller involvement of the agency in the finalization and realization of public relations objectives. However, it is of prime importance for both the client and the agency to fully understand the intent and content of objectives to facilitate certain actions and steps to achieve. This basis of assessment of agency effectiveness is vital.

Responsiveness to Clients' Brief

Experienced PR professionals understand that the client brief giving details about the platform, etc. from which a corporation wishes to address the publics, provides a sense of direction not only to the PR personnel themselves but also to the PR agency. When understood properly in intent and content, the agency finds itself on track to think strategies and actions that keep the PR programmes and campaigns on track. The brief helps the agency personnel to remain focused in their endeavours to serve the client.

Ability to Understand Clients' Problems

There is no organization, big or small, which does not have some problems, but the nature and enormity of problems differ from company to company. An experienced and pro-active agency, because of its experience in handling a variety of problems for its various clients, is able to comprehend the problem and suggest solutions to the clients, particularly the PR route of grappling with them. An agency is often judged by a client, by its understanding and problem solving abilities.

Ability to Plan Creative Events

Organizing some unusual and creative PR events, or the event management abilities is considered as a plus point for an agency. Of late, event management has come to assume the stature of a specialist PR activity and that is why, quite a few agencies known as event management companies, have sprung up in India. These companies organize events such as theme parties, promotional events, product launches, or fashion shows, on a turnkey basis. Some PR agencies either have their own event management departments or award a sub contract to an event management company for a fixed fee, approved by the client. Going by the success rate of such events and the resultant realization of objectives, a client may judge the agency for its effectiveness.

Ability to Devise Effective Communications

A company is constantly in need of running its communication system, internal and external, as a part of the larger PR programme. The in-house PR personnel are quite competent in handling their communication responsi-bilities, yet the agency serves as an important resource to supplement and complement the effort. Due to wider exposures in the business world, an agency is quite often in a position to devise creative communication solutions in several corporate areas. Therefore, the agency may be perceived as effective or otherwise on the basis of the inputs and advice that it renders to the client.

Competence to Handle Company Publications

Every organization, as a part of its communication system, publishes several kinds of publications—a house journal, newsletters, dealer magazine, annual report, and press releases at various intervals. A client who decides to outsource the editing and printing of such publications would expect the agency to be well equipped with skills and means to handle the assignment. If the agency has the means and skills to produce brilliant publications, which add to the corporate image of the client, it would be perceived as a professional outfit and enjoy high respect with the client.

Influential Media Network

Media relations is, perhaps, the most challenging area of public relations. The PR practitioners working in the companies, most often enjoy a wider reach to the media men through constant networking, yet they have their own limitations. A PR agency, due to a wider involvement on behalf of several of their clients, enjoys a greater clout with the media and journalists. Many agencies take a lot of pride in presenting their clients a good harvest of press clippings on a month-to-month basis. For them this is one measure to demonstrate the effectiveness of the agency by showing clients the volume of publicity they generate every now and then. The clients also feel happy and tacitly calculate the agency performance by the volume of column centimeters of space or the telecast time earned for them, which when converted into advertising space, would mean a sizable cost savings on advertising expenditure.

Agency–Client Congenial Relationship

Mutual trust is the basis of any relationship and the agency–client relationship is no exception. Practically though, each one is trying to get the best of each other, yet there is a need for congeniality and compatibility of this relationship. A mis-match does not work for long. The association amongst equals is always congenial and none of the parties should have any kink in their mind or consider the relationship as a marriage of convenience. For long-lasting relationship, compatibility is important. When this congeniality falls out of balance, it is often evident that either the client sacks the agency or the agency opts to resign.

Cost Consciousness

Cost factor, to any business, is a single factor that influences many decisions. PR practitioners know fully well that cost saving is contribution to the profit. Some short-sighted PR agencies eye the client budgets to be hogged fast enough to make a fast buck. Once a client gets an impression that the agency, rather than making a long-term relation, is interested in making the buck in the shortest possible time, the days of such agency–client relationship should be numbered. Naturally, the clients are looking for value for money and maximum public relations advantage. Once a client perceives the agency as artificially expensive, the ratings should go down and the downfall of the agency is evident.

Summary

A PR agency is an independent professional outfit that works for a client for a fee or on retainership basis. The agency counsels and assists the client company on various aspects of PR such as marketing public relations, employee relations, image management, etc. An agency is an external arm of a company, which undertakes the assignment connected with the public relations aspect of the organization.

A PR agency is a combination of personnel, who are endowed with skills, imagination, and creativity to devise certain programmes and activities to keep a company in the limelight. Naturally, such an agency has to be a competent outfit and should be compa-tible with the client in stature, size, and intellect.

According to the Public Relations Society of America, an agency should be expected to assist the client company in several ways, ranging from counselling to meeting the short-term and long-term public relations goals as far their relevance to the various publics is concerned.

The agency business started in the US in the 1930s during the labour insurgency and the New Deal movement. Subsequently, pioneers like IvyLee, Edward L. Barneys, and Edward Lasker, opened agencies, some of which are still thriving. It is estimated that there are at least 750 PR agencies in America today.

In India, till the eighties, companies depen-ded on their advertising agencies for their PR needs. With threats of hostile takeovers by some foreign interests, some exclusive agencies cropped up to cope up with the situation. India's policy of liberalization and globalization in 1985, which encouraged the entry of multinationals, also opened the door for some overseas agencies to start busi-ness in India.

The question—whether it is safe enough for a company to retain a PR agency and share all sensitive information with it—is answered by the PRSA code of ethics. How-ever, some advertising professionals, con-cerned with this aspect, have expressed divergent views about total confidence in an agency. They have advised due care to be taken in the matter.

A business organization, while signing up an agency, needs to check on the competence level of the agency and also the compatibility with client's stature and business. The mis-match may soon result in break away of relationship.

Whereas there are enough advantages of retaining a PR agency, the proposition is not altogether devoid of dis-advantages.

Agency structures and organizational chart depicting management hierarchies differ depending on the size of the operation and the nature of their clients' business.

In all appropriateness, the client companies periodically, generally and annually, evaluate their agency on certain parameters which either determine the continuation of the association or otherwise.

Key Terms

Account   A customer company for an agency

Agency evaluation   A performance audit of the agency by a client

Client   A business company who contracts a public relations agency

Competitive accounts   Companies who are the competitors of an agency's clients

Event management company   An agency which specializes in conceptualizing an event and executing it

In-house PR department   A company's own PR department

Liaison man   A link man between a company and government departments to expedite matters

Outsourcing   An agency subcontracts another agency to handle an assignment on turnkey basis

Press agentry   An agent who gets paid on the press coverage on column centimeters basis

Retainership   A fixed consultancy fee irrespective of the assignments taken up by the agency

Concept Review Questions

1. Define and describe a public relations agency. What are the basic characteristics of an agency that serve as a useful purpose for their clients? Explain.

2. Should a business organization contract a public relations agency? If yes, why? What are the various advantages and disadvantages of retaining an agency for counselling an organization on various issues concerning a company?

3. What are the various parameters of evaluating the performance of a public relations agency? Describe each parameter to establish your understanding of the system.

4. Paint a perspective of the development and growth of public relations agency business in America and India. What do you think is the scope for growth of this business activity in India, particularly in the light of the policies of liberalization and globalization? Describe in detail.

Project Work

1. As a business development manager of a leading public relations agency, say Primage India, develop a presentation of your agency for presentation to a prospective client to sign up a retainership contract.

2. Develop a public relations strategic plan to assist your client for the successful launch of a new product, say a new car model, in the market. If you want to outsource this job from an event management company, then list and explain the merits of doing so for the knowledge and comfort of your client.

Case Study

Concept PR — An Agency Profile*

Concept PR Ltd–PR agency of the year 2007

Come to the Experts   *Sea water turns sweet! Though irrational, this news about sweet water in the sea spread faster than forest fire and engulfed the entire city of Mumbai.*

'Lord Ganesha is drinking milk!' went the frenzied rumour. In less than a couple of hours, long queues materialized at milk shops and temples across the country. It took a whole day of scientific explanation to convince spell-bound devotees that there was nothing even remotely 'divine' about this phenomenon. Yet, they stubbornly refused to see the truth.

A rumour suddenly erupts in a small town in Gujarat that ICICI Bank is in trouble. The rumour mill works overtime. And, the inevitable happens. Overnight, the country's leading private bank has customers across the country thronging its ATMs to withdraw their money. It was only the next day that ICICI Bank's strong denial of the rumour could be seen in print.

As can be seen from the above examples, word of mouth sometimes spreads faster than forest fire! Rumours tend to have disastrous effects. However, information that has been correctly positioned in the minds of people could have a positive impact. This is where a well thought out and sustained public relations exercise comes into play.

Public relations have expertise at relationship building and, therefore, it can influence good image building for a company, individual, or organization.

The emergence of PR as a branding tool is getting more respect and is a boon to the industry.

Brand is a perception; we, at Concept PR Ltd, take the challenge to motivate a significant

---

Source: www.conceptpr.com.

majority of the audience being targeted to perceive a brand in a positive, desired manner. We play a major role in establishing and shaping those perceptions.

With over 30 years of experience in the business of communication and clients, which include some of India's top corporate houses, we are well-positioned to help you strategize, plan, execute a sustained communication programme and to boost brands in creative new ways.

We take pride in our commitment to understanding your communication needs. For us your own image is a trust for which we will, often, go beyond your brief.

All our strategic inputs are preceded with, and accompanied by continuous research. From media relations and investor relations to content management and marketing communication, we offer a gamut of solutions to help you project your business better in the minds of your stakeholders.

When crisis comes calling

Crisis is like an uninvited guest. It comes calling when you least expect it and is usually the source of a major headache. For a company, the first reaction on encountering a crisis is panic. If not dealt with appropriately, a crisis can seriously damage a company's image in the eyes of the public, an image usually nurtured over several years. However, a well thought out crisis communication plan can help reduce the effects of a negative situation.

The first and most basic step in creating a sound crisis communication plan, is to take into account every possible scenario, which could lead to a problem, internally or externally. Can any of your products be contaminated or adulterated? Could any of your employees have an issue with the company? Can a shop floor worker have a potentially life threatening accident during the manufacturing process?

Every scenario, no matter how small, can explode into a potentially damaging situation for the company. It is important to share these probable situations with your communication advisors to enable them to adequately plan for the same. It is also important to identify and train a spokesperson to speak to the media in case of a crisis. Confidence must be reflected in all that the company says and does. Crisis or no crisis, it's business as usual.

Try and plan ahead. To cite an example, when Reliance was building its refinery at Jamnagar, the company ensured that the facility could withstand an earthquake of the intensity of 9 on the Richter Scale. The foresight paid off, as the refinery survived a quake measuring 7 on the Richter Scale.

Another way of looking at a crisis is to view it as an opportunity to learn and do better in future. After the worm contamination incident, Cadbury changed the packaging of its chocolate slabs to incorporate stronger, insect proof foil. This proactive method of handling a crisis paid off and the company emerged stronger from the situation. After all, the Chinese character for both crisis and opportunity is one and the same.

Creating value on the ticker

Every time the bulls start their thunderous run, the stage is the Bombay Stock Exchange (BSE). This is far from surprising, as the BSE has one of the highest per hour rates of trading in the world with approximately 70,000 deals taking place every day. Moreover, the market capitalization of the BSE is around Rs 5 trillion.

No wonder companies are lining up to join the over 4500 already listed on the BSE. However, life after you list is suddenly different. There are certain regulatory compliances you have to adhere to, especially when it comes to public communication. Every thing you say or do is under the scanner. In fact, your very heartbeat is linked to the movement of the BSE sensex. And to keep it beating regularly and strongly, you need a strategic investor relations (IR) programme in place.

A successful IR programe should consist of proactive, two way communication from the company to the investor universe and should result in a fair market valuation for the company, a reasonable level of liquidity of its shares, a strong group of supporters, easier access to capital, and favourable ratings.

In a nutshell, it means that an investor knows you, respects your company, believes in your future and is willing to put his money where his mouth is, with a little help from us.

Services

Regular updates to shareholders: Performance reviews, every quarter with analysis and fund managers:

- Design and development of annual reports, Chairman's speech and other communication
- Corporate presentations and institutional investors, influencers, etc.
- Road shows
- Equity research reports
- Financial and corporate PR, across all sectors
- IPO led PR
- Brand and product PR
- Advocacy and lobbying PR
- Events management

The team

'A consultancy is a sum total of its people.'
Our team has an intuitive grasp of effective communications particularly in ensuring alignment of messages streamlined across internal and external stakeholders.

We are equipped and prepared to handle any situation in a timely, professional and cost effective manner. No matter how large or small the job may be, we have ready solutions for all the individual needs. The team is structured with the expectation that members will contribute to the success of the organization.

Mumbai

Vivek Suchanti - Managing Director
With more than 13 years of experience in the business, Vivek exemplifies the new breed of communication professionals in India. He brings to the table an aggressive dynamism, a passion for innovation, and perseverance for results.

Ashish Jalan – Director
Ashish is a Chartered Accountant with ten years' experience in senior management in the media sector. He brings with him strong project handling skills backed by exceptional strategic thinking, management, and leadership capabilities.

B.N. Kumar – President
Associated with the media for close to three decades with rich experience in mass media, B.N. Kumar has worked with UNI, *Business India*, *The Week*, and *Indian Express*. He was also instrumental in setting up O&M PR and his last assignment was with the corporate communication division of Reliance Infocomm.

David Franklin - President - Investor Relations
David is the President of Concept Investor Services Ltd. He has over 17 years of experience in the communication industry. A BSc Zoology graduate and a management professional, he has extensive experience in the financial industry, excellent communication skills and a flair for creativity. David has a strong desire to excel and constantly strives to meet the high standards he has set for himself.

Ahmedabad

Ankit Shah – Vice President
Ankit has seven years of PR experience; he has exceptional leadership quality, excellent media relations, and good rapport with the clients.

Kolkata

Dilip Ranjan Ray - Regional Director
A communications professional with over 29 years of experience in account management, Dilip has worked with Hindustan Thompson Communications and React Advertising.

New Delhi

Ravi Aurora - Director
An all-rounder, Ravi brings over 37 years of hard-core experience to his role at Concept. He has been involved in sales, marketing, product and brand management, research—consumer and social, advertising, promotions and events. He also draws on a deep and rich insight in the world of rural communication and marketing.

Indroneel Roy- President
He brings over 15 years of hard core PR experience to Concept's table. Amongst his many strengths are advocacy campaigns for various corporates across India.

Hyderabad

R. Neelamegham – CEO
In charge of all southern operations, R. Neelamegham is one of the most respected professionals in the field of advertising and PR. Exceptional leadership qualities and requisite expertise to handle every area of advertising and PR is his forte. 'Neelu' as he is fondly known, is the vice chairman of the governing council of the PR council of India.

Geeta Phadnavis – Vice President
Geeta is an Arts graduate from Nagpur University with English and Political Science. Geeta has worked across sectors such as health, infrastructure, aviation, and technology. An expert

in media liaison, Geeta is in her element when hosting press conferences and targeted interviews with select journalists with whom she has developed an excellent rapport during the past 10 years.

Bangalore

C. Vinod Kumar - Vice President

With more than 10 years of experience in the public relations industry, C. Vinod Kumar has been associated with O&M Direct, Prism PR, etc., and worked on brands such as Pepsi, Airtel, TTK Prestige, ANZ Grindlay's Bank, and Birla AT&T.

Chennai

D. Ram Raj - Vice President

Has a Master's in English and post graduate diploma in journalism. He has 27 years of hard core media experience (print and online). He has worked with *The Economic Times*, *The Asian Age*, and *Bangalore Mirror*. He meticulously grew up the journalistic ladder taking up challenging assignments in the desk and reporting. He launched the erstwhile *The Times* (now *The Times of India*), *The Asian Age*, and *The Bangalore Mirror*.

Dubai

Syed Izzathullah – CEO

Syed is the man behind advertising strategies and PR exercises, a huge knowledge bank of product and capital market. He has 23 years of hard core experience in advertising (financial, product, and corporate). Syed has mastered the art of winning clients and maintaining excellent rapport with them, a lethal combination of creativity and management skills blended with the new age capabilities.

Our clients

Corporate Clients

Aditya Birla Group	Cbay Systems
Allen Solly	Core Projects & Technologies
Asian Star Company	DLF
Anu's Labs	East India Cotton Association
Atherstone Capital	Easun Reyrolle
Ashapura Minechem	GEI Industrial Systems Ltd
Ashika Stock Broking ltd	Gokaldas Exports
Accel Frontline	Goldstone Technologies Grasim
Aqua Logistics	Gremach Infra Equipments
Birla Sunlife Insurance	HOV Services
Bombay Rayon Fashion	HDIL
BSEL Infrastructure Realty	ICSA India
BPTP Infrastructure	India Bulls Real Estate
Blend Finance	IDBI Fortis
Cathay Pacific Airways	J K Cement
Crest Animation	

Jetking

JK Tyre

KSL & Industries

Lok Housing and Constructions

LKP Shares

MAAC

Modern India

Murugappa Group

Omnitech Infosolutions

Orbit Constructions

Prithivi Information Solutions

Pioneer Embroideries

Parekh Aluminex

Pidilite

Puravankara Project

Ramsarup Industries

Royal Classic

Sunil Hitech Engineers

Sumeet Industries

SE Investments

Unity Infraprojects

Van Heusen

Ventura Securities

Vivimed Labs

Wanbury

Welspun Retail

West Coast Paper

Win Medicare

 IPO Clients

ACME Telepower

Apollo Health Street

Brahmaputra Consortium

BGR Energy

Deccan Aviation

Empee Distilleries

Educomp

Gitanjali Gems

GMR Infrastructure

GVK Power & Infra

IRB Infrastructure

IVRCL

Koutons

KSK Energy

Lodha Builders

Mandhana Industries

Maruti Udyog

Microsec

Motilal Oswal

NHP

CNTPC

ONGC

Pipavav Ltd

Power Finance Corporation

Rural Electrification Corporation

Reliance Power

Sun TV

Tech Mahindra

Vishal Retail

Contact us

Ashish Jalan, Director

Concept PR India Limited

1st floor, Queens Mansion

Prescot Road

Near Cathedral School

Fort, Mumbai – 400 001

Tel: 91 22 4055 8900

Fax: 91 22 4055 8901

e-mail: ashish@conceptindia.com

Discussion questions

1. What factors do you think have helped make Concept PR the agency of the year 2007? Discuss.

2. Hypothetically, you have decided to float a public relations agency. Write an agency profile for presentation to the prospective clients. In view of the several agencies already in business, what are the unique features of your new agency, which should serve as a cutting edge in the corporate world?

3. Develop a power point presentation for projecting your public relations agency to the

prospective clients, which should give enough confidence to such clients to sign up the contract. As a comprehensive projection is important for securing business, the presentation should justify your proposal.

● ————

References

Cutlip Scott M., Allen H. Center, and Glen M. Broom (1985), *Effective Public Relations*, 6th edition, Prentice-Hall International, Inc. USA, pp. 95 and 96.

Lesly, Philip (1992), *Lesley's Handbook of Public Relations and Communications*, 4th edition, Probis Publishing Company, USA, published in India by Jaico Publishing House, Mumbai, p. 739.

Mint, 'Client Confidentiality: Agency Controls Come Under Lens', New Delhi, vol. II, no. 262, 5 November 2008, p. 8.

Public Relations Society of America, New York, USA, www.prsa.org., accessed on 4 December 2008.

The Observer of Business and Politics, 'PR Scenario Looking up', New Delhi, 7 June 1996.

Index